THE ENCYCLOPAEDIA OF SPORTS

THE

ENCYCLOPAEDIA

OF

SPORTS

(in 4 vols.)

Edited By
HEDLEY PEEK
AND
F.G. AFLALO

Vol IV

SAND-Z

GYAN PUBLISHING HOUSE

NEW DELHI-110 002

THE ENCYCLOPAEDIA OF SPORTS
(Sports, Physical Education)

ISBN: 81-212-0276-0 (Set)
ISBN : 81-212-0280-9

Published in 1997 in India
by Gyan Publishing House
5, Ansari Road
New Delhi-110002

Printed at Goyal Offset Printers, Delhi-110035

SANDPIPER—A general term applied to such of the smaller wading birds (*Limicolæ*) as frequent the sandy shores, sea ooze, and mud flats of tidal rivers, in search of the small mollusca, crustacea and sand worms upon which they feed.

Classification—In a restricted sense the "sandpiper" would exclude the ringed plovers (locally known as "sand-plovers" and "sand-larks") the turnstones and oyster-catchers, as well as the curlews, godwits, and snipes, whose divergent structure correlated with habits has caused them to be placed in different sub-families.

Roughly speaking, and to facilitate recognition, the sandpipers proper may be divided into two typical groups: one (*Tringa*) comprising species characterised by possessing a short sensitive bill, short legs with toes cleft to the base (as in the plovers) and with the tail feathers plain, *i.e.*, not barred; the other (*Totanus*) including such as have a harder or more horny bill, the toes either wholly or partially connected by a web at the base, and tail feathers more or less barred. Within and around these two groups we find several species showing modifications of structure, or seasonal peculiarities of plumage, which have induced ornithologists to place them in distinct genera under such names, *Actitis*, *Actodromas*, *Ancylochilus*, *Arquatella*, *Bartramia*, *Calidris*, *Ereunetes*, *Limonites*, *Pelidna*, *Symphemia*, *Tringoides*, *Tringites*, &c. The points of difference, however, on which some of these genera have been separated from the above-mentioned types are slight in character and of doubtful importance, the multiplicity of names serving only to create confusion and obscure relationships. These names, however, having found their way into the literature of the subject, cannot be wholly disregarded.

Geographical Distribution—Sandpipers are amongst the most cosmopolitan of birds, many of them being found in almost every quarter of the globe. Thus the dunlin (*Tringa alpina*), locally known as stint and ox-bird, the commonest sandpiper which is found in this country, ranges from Iceland and the Faroe Islands throughout Europe far into Africa, where it spends the winter; from Siberia in Asia to India and China (where also it is a winter visitor); and in North America from California to the West Indies; it sojourns also in Greenland.

The curlew sandpiper (*Tringa subarquata*) which visits us in spring and autumn, often in considerable flocks at the latter season, is even a greater wanderer than the dunlin; for although it has not yet been met with quite so far north, that is, in Iceland, Greenland, or Spitzbergen, it is found from Archangel throughout Europe and Africa down to Cape Colony; throughout the Indian region, Ceylon, the Andamans, Java, Australia, and Tasmania, and on the American continent has been found as far to the south as East Patagonia.

Species Breeding in Great Britain—The sandpipers which breed in the British Islands are comparatively few in number. They are the greenshank, redshank, ruff and reeve (formerly; see **Ruff**), common sandpiper, purple sandpiper (probably), dunlin, and red-necked phalarope.

REDSHANK.

Distinguishing Characters. Greenshank (*Totanus glottis*)—Entire length, 12 inches; bill, somewhat recurved, 2; wing, 7; tarsus, 2·25. General colour, in summer, grey mottled with black; rump, white; wings, black; the shaft of the first primary, white; chin, throat, and breast, white, longitudinally streaked with black; belly, pure white; bill, slate-colour; legs and toes, pale green. In winter all trace of black disappears from the upper portion of the plumage, and the whole of the under parts, from chin to vent, are pure white.

Redshank (*Totanus calidris*)—Entire length, 11 inches; bill, 1·6; wing, 6·5; tarsus, 1·75; bare part of tibia, ·9. General colour, in summer, above, hair-brown, transversely barred with a darker shade; below, white, streaked longitudinally with dark brown; tail, white, barred with dark brown; bill, horn-colour, orange at base; legs and toes, orange. In winter the plumage is more or less of a uniform grey above, throat dusky, under parts pure white; legs and toes paler than in summer. The birds of the year are intermediate in colour between the summer and winter plumages of their parents.

Ruff and Reeve (*Machetes pugnax*)—Entire length, male, 12 inches; female, 9; bill, 1·25; wing, male, 7·25; female, 6; tarsus, 1·5. The colour of this species varies so much in individuals that it is impossible to describe it in a few words. In summer the males have the dorsal plumage of all shades of brown, buff, chestnut, and purple; on the neck a large frill or ruff (hence the bird's name), of a different colour to the back. Sometimes this frill is of a uniform colour, as chestnut, purplish-black, or white; sometimes it is variegated. It is assumed only during the breeding season, and has entirely disappeared before the shooting season has commenced. In the autumn and winter the plumage resembles that of the godwits at the same season; but its smaller size, short and straight bill, and dark rump will always distinguish it. The female, or reeve, never assumes the frill, but retains much the same colours throughout the year, except that they are much more intense in summer. The colour of the legs and toes varies very much. As a rule they are lemon colour or orange. But occasionally one sees a bird with pale green or grey legs.

Common Sandpiper (*Totanus hypoleucus*)—Entire length, 7·5 inches; bill, 1; wing, 4·25; tarsus, ·9. General colour, above, bronze; throat, longitudinally streaked with hair-brown; breast and belly, pure white; bill, horn-colour, the base flesh-colour; legs and toes, greyish-green.

Purple Sandpiper (*Tringa maritima*)—Entire length, 8·50 inches; bill, 1·4; wing, 5·3; tarsus, 1 inch. The dorsal plumage is purple only in winter. In summer it is variegated with black, brown and buff, the breast at the same season being spotted. The legs and toes at all seasons are of a yellowish-clay colour. The colour of the legs (which are very short) will distinguish this bird at all times from any of its congeners.

Dunlin (*Tringa alpina*)—Entire length, 8 inches; bill, male, 1·3; female, 1·5; wing, 4·5; tarsus, 1. General colour, in summer, head, back and wing-coverts mottled with various shades of brown, black and rufous; on the belly a patch of black. In winter the dorsal plumage is, more or less, light brown or grey; the whole of the underparts pure white. Young birds, in autumn, have the breast and flanks spotted with black. Bill, legs and toes, at all seasons, black.

Red-necked Phalarope (*Phalaropus hyperboreus*)—Entire length, 7 inches; bill, ·8; wing, 4·5; tarsus, ·8. General colour, in summer, black and grey above; on the throat and neck a patch of bright chestnut; under parts pure white. In winter the rufous colour on the neck disappears, the dorsal plumage becomes much lighter, and the whole of the under parts, from chin to vent, are pure white. The bill is much more slender and pointed than in the grey phalarope. The feet are lobed. This little bird nests regularly in Scotland and the Hebrides, and visits England in autumn on its way southwards for the winter.

Periodical Migrants—In addition to the above-named species, we have as passing visitors in spring and autumn, on their way to and from their breeding haunts, the dusky redshank, green sandpiper, wood sandpiper, knot, curlew sandpiper, little stint, Temminck's stint, sanderling and grey phalarope.

Distinguishing Characters. Dusky Redshank (*Totanus fuscus*)—Entire length, 12·5 inches; bill, 2·3; wing, 6·75; tarsus, 2·25; bare part of tibia, 1·5. General colour, in summer, sooty black, with a few of the feathers margined and spotted with white; belly and rump, more or less white; tail, closely barred; bill, horn-colour, the base orange; legs and toes, vinous. In winter the plumage above is more or less uniformly grey, the throat faintly spotted, and the breast and belly pure white. Legs and toes, lemon-colour. Birds of the year have the upper portion of the plumage sooty brown, minutely freckled with white; the whole of the under parts, from chin to vent, white, closely freckled with light ash. The tarsus and tibia are much longer than in the common redshank, and the bill is not only much longer, but also more attenuated towards the extremity, and the upper mandible curves downwards at the tip.

SANDPIPER.

Green Sandpiper (*Totanus ochropus*)—Entire length, 9·5 inches; bill, 1·2; wing, 5·5; tarsus, 1·25; bare part of tibia, ·7 inches. General colour, above, greenish-brown, in summer minutely freckled with white, in winter almost uniform; below, throat white, longitudinally streaked with dark brown; breast and belly, white; rump, white; tail, with outer feathers, white, centre feathers broadly barred with black; bill, slate colour; legs and toes, greyish-green. This bird has a very peculiar musky odour, akin to that of the petrels.

Wood Sandpiper (*Totanus glareola*)—Entire length, 9 inches; bill, 1 inch; wing, 5 inches; tarsus, 1·4; bare part of tibia, ·8. General colour, similar to the last-named, from which it differs in having a shorter bill and longer legs; all the feathers in the tail barred, and the shaft of the first primary white. In the green sandpiper all the quills are black.

Knot (*Tringa canutus*)—Entire length, 10 inches; bill, 1·2; wing, 6·5; tarsus, 1·1. General colour, chestnut in summer and grey and white in winter, like the curlew sandpiper and godwits at the same seasons, except that the rump is variegated, and not white. In summer the legs and toes are olive, the soles of the feet yellow; in winter they are entirely black.

Curlew Sandpiper (*Tringa subarquata*)—Entire length, 8·25 inches; bill, 1·5; wing, 5; tarsus, 1·2. General colour, in summer, chestnut, variegated above with black, below with white; bill, black, slightly curved downwards like that of a curlew; legs and toes, black. In winter the general colour above is grey and buff; the rump, white; under parts, pure white. Young birds, in autumn, have a tinge of buff on the breast, as remarked in the case of the godwits.

DUNLIN.

Little Stint (*Tringa minuta*)—Entire length, 6 inches; bill, ·8; wing, 3·75; tarsus, ·9. Resembles a miniature dunlin, except that there is never any black on the under parts. In summer the neck and breast are spotted with rufous, and the dorsal plumage has a large admixture of the same colour. In winter the spots on the neck and breast disappear, and the dorsal plumage becomes considerably lighter in colour. Bill, legs, and toes at all seasons black.

Temminck's Stint (*Tringa temminckii*)—Entire length, 5·75 inches; bill, ·6; wing, 3·75; tarsus, ·6. Resembles a miniature common sandpiper, and may be distinguished from the little stint by its shorter and more slender bill, shorter legs (which are greyish-green instead of black), by its white outer tail feathers, and by having the shaft of only the first primary white, whereas in the little stint all the shafts are white.

Sanderling (*Calidris arenaria*)—Entire length, 8 inches; bill, ·9; wing, 5 inches; tarsus, 1 inch. General colour, in summer, reddish-brown, black, and grey above; chin and breast, ditto; from breast downwards, pure white. In winter, grey and white above; from chin to vent, pure white; bill, legs, and toes, black. Bill as in the sandpipers. Toes, three, as in the plovers.

Grey Phalarope (*Phalaropus fulicarius*)—Entire length, 8 inches; bill, 1; wing, 5; tarsus, ·8. General colour, in summer, brown, white, and rufous above; from chin to vent, chestnut. In winter, grey and white above; the under parts pure white. Bill very flat. Feet lobed like a coot. This bird is seldom met with in the British Islands in its summer dress. It visits us regularly in autumn (September and October), by which time it has acquired its winter plumage, and in some years is very numerous.

Occasional Visitors—The sandpipers which remain to be considered are those which make their appearance as rare and accidental visitors, usually during the period of the autumnal migration. Of these may be mentioned the Broadbilled sandpiper (*Tringa platyrhyncha*), which breeds in Lapland, Finland, Norway, and the tundras of European Russia, and the following American species: Yellowshank, Solitary sandpiper, Bartram's sandpiper, Buff-breasted sandpiper, Spotted sandpiper, Pectoral sandpiper, Bonaparte's sandpiper, and Wilson's American Stint, *Tringa pusilla* of Wilson (1812), *Tringa minutilla* of Vieillot (1819).

It is to be observed that in this article attention is of necessity confined to those sandpipers which are known as residents or visitors to the British Islands. The species to be met with in other parts of the world are far too numerous to be dealt with here, however briefly.

J. E. HARTING.

SCOTTISH SCHOOL CHAMPIONSHIPS—The interest in games, and indeed in school life generally, has been greatly promoted by what are called the Football and Cricket Championships. These are not formal institutions, and there are no written rules as to how they are decided. But, with the exception perhaps of one occasion, it has always been quite clear which school has been the top of the tree for any particular season, or sometimes two have been equal.

Briefly the matter stands as follows:—There are seven schools which can play each other on something like equal terms; four of these are purely boarding-schools—Glenalmond, Fettes, Loretto and Blair Lodge; one, Merchiston, is partly a boarding and partly a day-school, while the Edinburgh Academy and George Watson's College are purely day-schools. Of the boarding-schools Fettes is the largest, with about 220 boys, and Loretto the smallest, with about 120. Watson's has about 1,200 boys, and the Academy about 400. But the day-schools, though they have a greater pick, do not as a rule keep their boys so long as the boarding-schools. All these schools do not, however, play each other; but the exceptions have not hitherto affected the Championship. Merchiston has been most successful in the Football Championship, and Loretto in Cricket; Fettes having run close up in both.

The Cricket Championship may be said to have become a recognised institution from the first two-day match between Loretto and Fettes in 1875, and in the majority of years the issue of the Cricket Championship has depended on this match, which is played on the same days as Eton and Harrow. The Football Championship, again, may be said to have begun in 1881, when Fettes, Merchiston and Loretto first began to play each other regularly. It is the custom for all these schools, except Glenalmond, whose distance sometimes makes it impossible, to have football matches every Saturday from the end of October to the middle of March, and cricket matches for every Saturday of the summer term. Some of the day-schools sometimes turn out as many as ten teams, and the boarding-schools never less than three.

This rivalry between the schools naturally produces great attention to physical education generally. Particulars of the system of Merchiston are subjoined, as for its size and numbers it is probably the best football school in the world.

Boys are called at 7, when they turn out in flannels, and have a run or smart walk of about three-quarters of a mile, then a cold bath and rub down. Breakfast at 8; school from 9 to 12.

Monday, 12.30 to 1.30—Big side (as often as possible a team of masters and old boys play the Fifteen on Monday).

Tuesday, 12.30 to 1—The Fifteen look after the lower teams and make them play up. From 1 to 1.30 they practise drop and place kicking, and the halves and quarters practise passing.

Wednesday, 2.30 to 5—Football match, or, if before a school match, a cross-country run of from seven to ten miles, usually over the Pentland Hills.

Thursday, 12.30 to 1.30—Big side.

Friday, 12 to 1—Cadet corps drill; 1 to 1.30—kicking in field, as on Tuesday.

From 3 to 6—There are four periods, three of work and one of gymnastics; so that every boy gets about forty minutes' gymnastics every day. On Friday night they have in addition fencing and boxing. The Fifteen have also half an hour of this every night after preparation.

The tuck shop is not an institution among the schools, which stand high in the Football Championship.

Every boy in the school must play football, unless exempted by the school medical officer.

All boys are accurately weighed and measured twice a term.

The physical system of the other boarding-schools does not differ widely from this.

H. H. ALMOND.

SEA-FISHING—In spite of much that has of late years been done to popularise this branch of angling, which, it is recognised, offers great benefits both to fishermen who cannot afford the outlay nowadays incidental to good sport inland, and to the rivers and lakes which a temporary defection of anglers to the sea must relieve from the threatening ills of over-fishing, the general idea of sea-fishing as a sport continues as erroneous as it was when Mr. Wilcocks endeavoured, many years ago, to acquaint amateurs with the then new field for their operations. It is regarded by the many as a clumsy and unpicturesque pursuit, and the sea-angler is but too often looked upon as a successful, or unsuccessful, pot-hunter who has tried to make great hauls, by fair means or foul, and failed only by the lack of knowledge of the craft. Thus, however great his catch, he is condemned. The few, however, know that sea-fishing is, in its way and with necessary reservations, as truly a sport as any other kind of fishing, and that the same distinction may be drawn, as on river and lake, between those who try to catch for the market as many fish as possible with the least outlay and trouble, and those who, on the other hand, try to catch for amusement every fish, no matter what the aggregate, in sporting fashion. The increase in the ranks of sea-anglers, which has not escaped attention during the last ten years, may be regarded as in great measure due to the disgust aroused by the modern monopoly, either on the part of angling clubs and syndicates or of private owners, in inland fisheries, as well as to the general variety and healthfulness of the sport. No one, or not at any rate the present writer, would attempt to place for those with opportunities for both, sea-fishing on a level with the more gentle and artistic pursuit of trout or salmon; but it would not be difficult to demonstrate that, to men of limited means and leisure, to say nothing of the recreation it may furnish to becalmed yachtsmen, it offers attractions to be found in few other branches of angling nowadays available.

Sea-fishing is a somewhat wide subject for treatment in a restricted article, and perhaps the most convenient course will be to consider in alphabetic order the principal fish encountered by the amateur, together with the tackle and baits recommended for their capture. A few topographical notes are offered under the head of each fish, and the concluding portion of the article contains general hints. It is, however, necessary to grasp the fact that sea-fishing is not, like pond-fishing or (in India) tank-fishing, a comparatively circumscribed branch of the art, but an aggregate of at least as many (considerably more, if we add the semi-professional methods sometimes followed) styles as those practised in fresh water.

I. Fish.

Bass (*Labrax lupus*)—This is a sea-perch, distinguished by Mr. Boulenger from the true perches, with which it formerly was classed. It is encountered on both rocky and sandy ground, chiefly on the latter, and often feeding in the surf in less than six feet of water. Almost any bait, if sufficiently large, is accepted by this fish, nor is freshness a matter of great moment. Thus, live sand-eels, pilchards (*minus* head, tail and backbone), soft green crab, ray's liver and the entrails of chickens are all accounted in their way deadly; and, besides these, it takes a salmon-fly and various spinning-baits. It is therefore taken by fly-fishing, spinning, whiffing, and drift-lining; also in ground-fishing with leger or paternoster (*see* below).

Among the favourite spots on our coasts for bass may be mentioned the east breakwater at Hastings, where they are caught on throw-out lines baited with fresh herring or soft crab; the harbour at Shoreham, where live sand-eels seem the best bait; the river Arun *above* Arundel, where they take a live roach or dace on snap-tackle; the Passage Bridge at Weymouth, where a strip of mackerel is most appreciated; the Cornish sand "splats," where the angler uses an unleaded line with a single large hook embedded in a decapitated pilchard; and parts of the Welsh coast, where ray's liver is a favourite bait.

Bream (*Pagrus vulgaris*)—The sea-breams, of which the common species may be taken as typical, are caught among the rocks at a moderate depth. They are mostly taken on ground-lines, though occasionally on drift-tackle, and the chopstick is as good as any other arrangement (*see* below). For bait, mussel, green crab, and pieces of herring, pilchard, or mackerel are all good. Small sea-bream, known as chad, are a great nuisance when the angler is anchored for pollack, though they form a fairly good bait for the latter fish. The Black Bream (*Chrysophrys*) of Australian inlets is the favourite fish of colonial anglers, who catch it on the finest of gut tackle, and with shrimps for bait, a ground-bait compounded of tinned salmon and cheese, and known as "berley," playing no unimportant part in the success of the day.

Cod (*Morrhua vulgaris*)—This is another ground fish, which is, however, caught on both rock and sand, the best season on our coasts being the late autumn. Amateurs use the paternoster more than any other tackle from a boat, or the throw-out tackle from the shore; and for bait, lugworm, sprat and whelk are perhaps equally good. Deal is one of the cod-fisher's favourite spots on our south coast, and the catches made there by amateurs in the months of October and November are certainly tempting. A few good fish are even landed by anglers on the pier, but the greater part are taken in boats. Bexhill is another spot, within easy reach of London, where I have seen good cod.

Conger (*Conger vulgaris*)—The great sea-eel is caught, chiefly at night, among the rocks. Only the smaller congers are caught by day, and these are never far from the rocks. It is of interest to note that every conger above 4 or 5 lbs. in weight is a female, the males not exceeding that weight. Large females, however, up to 50 lbs., or even more, may be hooked at night on inshore reefs within a mile of the beach, especially down in Cornwall, or in the west of Ireland. Very strong ground-lines are used, each carrying two hooks, and the bait is a piece of fresh squid, well hammered to make it soft, or a pilchard with the bones removed. Congers object to any but a soft, fresh bait.

Dab—*See* Plaice.

Dory (*Zeus faber*)—This ungainly but sweet-flavoured fish is caught in the neighbourhood of rocks or piers, but not as a rule in numbers, though there is occasionally a fair sprinkling of large dory with the bream and pollack on the deep-water rocks off Falmouth and Mevagissey. Otherwise, the drift-line, baited with a small pout or large sand-eel, would be the most likely way to catch these fish.

Flathead (*Platycephalus*)—An Australian fish, allied to our gurnards, which is caught on the sand, both at sea and in the estuaries. Colonials distinguish grass-flatheads and rock-flatheads, but these may probably be regarded as races rather than as valid species. The flathead, which is excellent eating, takes shrimp freely, the tackle being used without lead. It is a powerful fish for the light tackle used in its capture.

Grouper, or **Groper** (*Cossyphus*)—An Australian fish, allied, though not closely, to our wrasses, which is taken on the rocks. The ledges from which gropers, often scaling up to 50 lbs., are taken would be inaccessible to the visitor, save under the guidance of a colonial angler. The line is used without lead, and the bait is soft crab, similar to that used at home for bass.

Gurnards (*Trigla lyra*, &c.)—The gurnards, of which our seas contain several, do not give great sport, but are admired by all for the beauty of their colouring, and by some esteemed for their table qualities, which, in the writer's opinion, are not high. He prefers, in fact, regarding them in the light of accidental catches; but those who desire to hook them in number can generally do so throughout the summer by anchoring their boat on the sand at the edge of the rocks and leaving their hooks on the bottom, any bait a shade too large for pout being suitable.

Mackerel (*Scomber scomber*)—The mackerel may be regarded as one of the amateur's best fish, for it gives, for its size, first-rate sport; it is generally present, if at all, in numbers, and, when quite fresh and properly cooked, is excellent for the table, though too rich for some digestions. It is captured at all depths, within a foot of the surface in warm summer weather, and within a foot of the bottom later in the year. Almost any baits, natural or artificial, will attract when mackerel are in the humour; and, according to the depth at which they are feeding at the time, they are taken on whiffing-lines, drift-lines, or chopstick-tackle; on the first when feeding near the top, on the second at any depth up to half a dozen fathoms, on the last when near the bottom. The most agreeable and artistic method, when practicable, is with a light drift-line and single hook baited with a couple of large mussels or a strip of mackerel or pilchard.

Mullet, Grey (*Mugil chelo*)—If, as it is fair to presume, the sporting value of a fish increases in direct ratio to the difficulty of catching it, then may the grey mullet be allowed to stand first among the English amateur's sea-fish. In Italy, these mullet are less fastidious; and the present writer has more than once filled a larger creel in the Mediterranean in a couple of hours before breakfast than he would undertake to fill in a week anywhere in the Channel. The grey mullets are partial to estuaries, in the mud of which they doubtless find the soft food on which they subsist. Light tackle used with a stout rod is best for their capture, a paternoster with three or four small hooks baited with ragworms being the accepted style at Littlehampton, in Sussex, the headquarters of south coast mullet-fishers. These use a rod of 7 feet, No. 5 (Redditch) hooks, and a pear-shaped lead weighing ½ lb. The favourite spot during the season (June to September inclusive) is the Beacon, at the end of the east works; but a few good fish are caught early in the season from boats moored to a tree two-thirds of the way down the works, as well as from the various quays on the left bank as far up as the railway wharf. A landing-net is always used, as mullet are tender-mouthed, and the hook easily breaks away.

Mullet, Red (*Mullus barbatus*)—The present writer had always regarded the red mullet as a somewhat unusual catch for the amateur on our coasts, but his attention was recently drawn by Mr. Wilcocks to its almost frequent capture both at Shoreham and in Guernsey; and other anglers have sent him accounts of similar cases from Cornwall and the coast of Brittany. (Another still rarer hook-fish is the Shad (*Clupea alosa*), of which, however, since the publication of *Sea Fish*, in the Anglers' Library, the writer has had note of several taken on Deal pier, one by Mr. Burgess, on Easter Monday, 1897, weighing 2½ lbs., another, more recently, by Mr. Litchfield of the B.S.A.S.) The red mullet, essentially a ground-feeder, has a preference for soft baits, and lugworm and mussel appear to be equally deadly. A small hook, 8 or 9 (Redditch), would answer the purpose. One red mullet has been reported as taken on a whiffing line, a most unusual event. The baits must have been close to the bottom.

Plaice and **Dab** (*Pleuronectes platessa* and *P. limanda*)—The plaice and dab, indeed most of the flat fish, may fairly be bracketed from the angler's standpoint, for all are ground-feeders, all comparatively small-mouthed and therefore requiring a small hook, and all with a fancy for soft baits, such as lugworm and mussel. Soles are taken in the mud, and mostly at night. Flounders are taken in estuaries, and far above the tidal waters in rivers.

Pollack and **Coal Fish** (*Gadus pollachius* and *G. virens*)—In these, again, we have two fish that, while valid species like the plaice and dab, may fairly be considered together, so similar are their habits and consequently the methods employed in their capture. With the bass and mackerel, they constitute the sea-angler's "game-fish," and they are taken at all depths, accepting the live sand-eel or artificial baits on whiffing-lines, or mussel and pilchard on drift-tackle. Of artificial baits, the various rubber eels, with or without a tin spinner at the head, are the most deadly. Neither fish can be accounted of high merit for the table.

Pout, or Whiting-pout (*Gadus luscus*)—Like the last two, this is a member of the cod family, and is also one of the commonest fish in the Channel, being taken on probably every reef of rocks within even a hundred yards of the beach. The pout taken on these inshore grounds are mostly very small, but further out in the offing there are pout up to 5 lbs., which, coming up two at a time, give good sport in the autumn. For bait, pieces of almost any fish or mollusc may be used, the pout being among the least discriminating of fish. The chop-stick tackle is the best. The boat must be anchored well over the rocks, and the hooks may be kept a couple of feet from the bottom. Pout are found to bite best with a little tide running.

Scad, or Horse-mackerel (*Caranx trachurus*)—Somewhat resembling the mackerel, in the company of which it is usually taken, the scad may be distinguished by its duller colouring, as well as by the presence of a row of bony processes along the lateral line. The name of this fish must be kept distinct from that of the aforementioned shad and chad, with both of which it is not seldom confused. It is caught accidentally with the mackerel, and takes the same baits.

Schnapper (*Pagrus unicolor*)—In this great red bream we have the most sporting sea-fish of the Australian colonies. It is caught on the reefs of rocks that skirt that inhospitable coast, and it is usual to undertake schnapper-fishing expeditions in small steam-tugs chartered for the purpose. Handlines of great strength, and at least a hundred yards long, are used; the hook is large, and is baited with pieces of fish or squid, and the fish are hauled aboard, often running the gauntlet of innumerable sharks, as quickly as possible. In addition to its sport-giving qualities and large size, the schnapper is a most delicate table-fish.

Smelt (*Osmerus*)—The true (salmonoid) smelt is hooked mostly in East coast estuaries. [The so-called "smelt" (*Atherina*) of the South coast is really the Atherine, a distinct fish.]

Turbot (*Rhombus maximus*).—Like the garfish, red mullet, dory and some others, the turbot is not a fish to the capture of which the amateur expressly applies himself, as he would, for instance, in the case of bass, conger, or mackerel. It is not improbable that, with increased information relating to the habits and whereabouts of our sea-fish, a future generation of amateurs may find themselves in a position to follow turbot-fishing by design. There is no reason indeed why, given the requisite knowledge, they should not do so; there is every reason why they should. The turbot is a powerful fish, giving great sport, and it makes, properly cooked (*not* in portions) a desirable dish. At present, however, it ranks among the "accidents"; and, beyond suggesting a small hook, lying on the sand, and baited with a two-inch strip of sand-smelt or the half of a large sand-eel, the writer prefers offering no hints for its capture.

Whiting (*Gadus merlangus*).—The whiting, on the other hand, is among the amateur's favourite and most familiar fish. There are, of course, different qualities of whiting-fishing, and the usual handling of small ½ lb. fish close inshore is a far less inspiring performance than really brisk handlining, ten miles out, with the fish running a couple of pounds each and coming up two at a time. The sid-strap tackle, which can be recommended for whiting in deep water, is figured below; and sprat, herring, mussel and squid are all good baits. [The so-called Whiting (*Sillago*) of Australian estuaries is related to our weevers, and is caught with rod and fine tackle, baiting with shrimps.]

The fish with which the amateur may expect to meet, even in our coast waters, are by no means exhausted by the foregoing; for the writer once took, during a few weeks in Cornwall, no fewer than thirty-two species, and these included neither bass nor mullet. The principal kinds omitted in the above lists are the sharks (blue and porbeagle), dogfish and skates, all of which cartilaginous fish may be regarded as "vermin." It may be borne in mind, however, that the sharks, though unsought, give good sport, while the rays and skates are, according to some fancies, agreeable eating.

II. Tackle.

Handlining.—It is not necessary to open once again the vexed question of the relative merits of rod and handline. The writer has endeavoured to show, whenever occasion offered, that both have, in his opinion, their proper place, the rod in shallow water and fine weather, the line in deep water and wind. He is enabled, however, by the kindness of Mr. Walter Shaw, of Salcombe, one of the most accomplished anglers on the south coast, to give one or two hitherto unpublished improvements in the making and use of the hand-line.

In reference more particularly to pollack-fishing, Mr. Shaw says that he uses single gut at the end of the line, and allows the fish to run, as holding on to it generally means a break. His line is as follows:—

6 ft. single gut next the hook, then 7 ft. or 8 ft. twisted gut, the two traces being divided by a swivel; next come 30 ft. of very fine snooding, also separated by a swivel from the twisted gut, and lastly a large swivel to which is attached the main line, of which there are 10 fathoms, with a single pipe-lead strung on it. The lead is thus over 40 ft. from the hook, a great advantage in fine water. The main line of 10 fathoms is comparatively fine, and to this Mr. Shaw makes fast 40 yards of stouter line wound on a large pike-reel, which is fixed in a thole. By standing in the stern and sculling with a long oar out through the chock, holding the line in the free hand, he is able to go out single-handed, and he insists strongly on the advantage of the gentle way on the boat and absence of fuss in shipping oars; for the paddle, being made fast to the boat

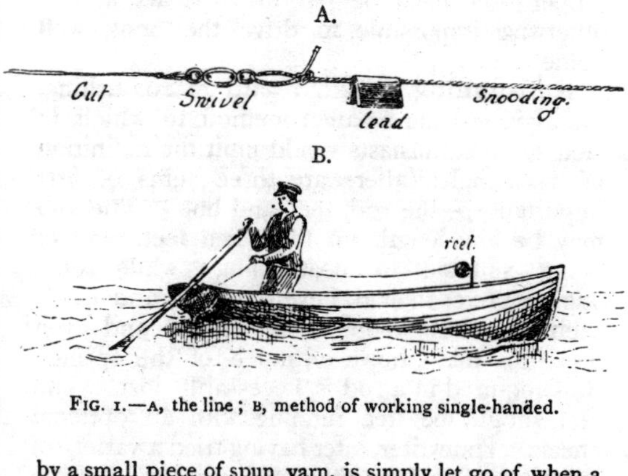

FIG. 1.—A, the line; B, method of working single-handed.

by a small piece of spun yarn, is simply let go of when a fish is fast. Sometimes Mr. Shaw uses a very small (under ¼ oz.) piece of sheet lead to straighten out the snooding quickly, as he found that in slack water chads would too often remove the bait before the line tightened.

Leads are an important consideration in hand-lining, for it is only in fine drift-lining that they play so light a part as in this tackle of Mr. Shaw. For "plummeting," as the Cornish fishermen call mackerel-whiffing (see Glossary),

FIG. 2.—PLUMMET.

a plummet, specially cast by them for the purpose, is used, in which two arms of waxed cord are let. To one of these is attached the main line; to the other, the finer snooding carrying the gut and hook.

For bottom-fishing, few leads are better than the Cornish shearing lead, also with arms of

FIG. 3.—SHEARING LEAD.

waxed cord, to which, in like manner, are attached respectively the main line and hook-race. The method of throwing this lead so as o avoid a foul is peculiar: the hooks are first hrown overboard and allowed to go off with he tide, and then, and not till then, the lead is hrown *against* the tide. The writer has always ;een the hands kept *inside* the boat in hand-ining, the brunt being allowed to fall on the gunwale; but Mr. Shaw objects, and with much reason, that the hands should be kept outside, so as to produce in a measure the give and take of a rod. One more hint in respect of hand-lining in deep water, and that is, that in striking proper force must be put into the act, as it is otherwise impossible to drive the hook well home.

Rod-fishing.—With regard to rod-fishing, the more popular amateur method, to which, in fact, some enthusiasts would limit the definition of "sea-angler," there are three items of first importance,—the rod, reel and line. The rod may be any length up to fifteen feet, ten feet being suitable to boat fishing; while some anglers prefer their rod even shorter, and catch their fish on weapons of seven feet and even less. In these, however, much of the springiness required in a rod is necessarily lost. The reel should be free running with an optional check. The writer, after having tried a variety of substances, prefers either the somewhat costly vulcanite, or the cheaper and almost equally efficient Nottingham wood reels, bound with brass or gunmetal. The reel should, in any case, be not less than 4½ in. diameter, and the barrel should be capable of carrying 100 yards of line. The line itself may be of dressed cotton, or tanned hemp, and should be free of kinks. A deal depends, however, on its treatment, and, unless frequently washed in fresh water and carefully dried before winding back on the reel, these lines soon rot from the effects of salt water.

FIG. 4. PATERNOSTER.

Various tackles.—Three tackles, the paternoster, leger and chopstick, have been mentioned in the foregoing notes, and it is now desirable to explain their nature. Briefly, the paternoster is a length of gut, gimp, or other material, having at the lower end a pear-shaped lead of various weight, and hooks, usually three in number, attached at short intervals above the lead. The upper end is looped, either with or without the intervention of a brass swivel, to the main line. This tackle may be used either with rod or hand-line, the former being necessary when using it from piers in order to keep it clear of the ironwork below. The leger is merely a line running freely through a pierced lead. It runs freely, at least, in one direction, viz. away from the angler, its passage in the opposite direction being checked by a shot nipped on to it and too large to pass through the lead.

The chopstick, of which there are various forms, consists of two arms, or spreaders of wire, from the end of which depend the hooks,

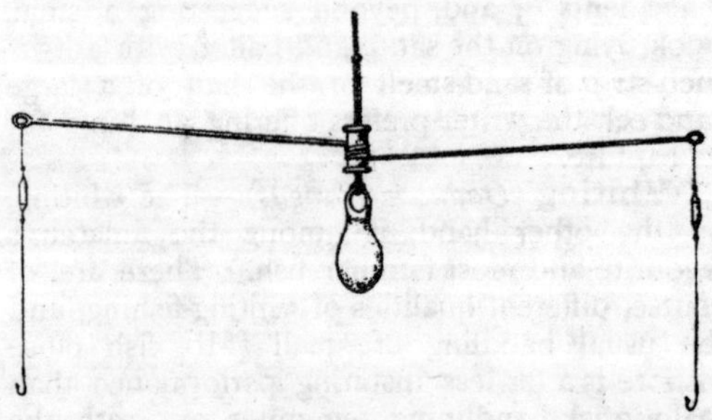

FIG. 5.—CHOPSTICK.

the lead being usually fixed at the centre point of the spreader, though, in some forms, hanging below it.

On the subject of float-fishing in salt water, one of the most promising methods under the lee of pier heads, it is not proposed to offer any remarks, as the practice does not materially differ from the use of the slider-float (see vol. i., p. 23) in fresh water. A rod is, as in the latter case, indispensable, and the float should be heavier and larger in proportion to the greater disturbance of water usual in the sea. It may be used either in conjunction with a light paternoster, or with a single hook at the end of a long-shotted gut trace, more after the fashion known to river-anglers. A modification of float-fishing is sometimes used by pot-hunters when pollack are biting furiously, two or three additional lines being thrown over the side, and each carrying a large cork bung which indicates a rush. The sportsman will, however, prefer to confine himself to his own rod or line.

One more tackle, the sid-strap, was mentioned above in connection with the capture of whiting in deep water, and it remains

FIG. 6.—SID-STRAP.

to show its construction in the adjoining figure. The material used is generally gimp, and the lead, as will be seen, is boat-shaped.

Opinions vary much as to the best size of hooks, it being, and with reason, urged on the one hand that it is best to use the smallest hook compatible with safety, as many fish are easily frightened by a large hook and bait, while it is objected, also with truth, that the small hooks are often a great trouble to get out of the fish, and consequently entail much needless delay. As in most matters, a moderate course may safely be counselled. The sizes subjoined are those much used by the writer in the capture of the fish specified, but it would be dogmatic to insist

FIG. 7.—SIZES OF HOOKS.

1. Smelt. 2. Flat Fish and Pout. 3. Whiting and Mackerel. 4. Pollack and Bream.

on them as necessarily the best size for the purpose. The fact is that the best size of hook varies greatly according to the average run of the fish at any particular spot and also according to the state of the water, a factor that mus regulate the consideration of light or heavy gear, or even of baits, on each particular outing.

Sundries—Under the comprehensive head of sundries come a number of articles that are the indirect means of improving the angler's chances. Such are the basket, or creel, the landing-net, and the gaff. The landing-net and gaff have already been defined (*see* ANGLING) in the present work; and it remains only to add an alternative, for which the writer is indebted to Mr. James Railton, of Teignmouth, and which is very serviceable on rocks or pier,

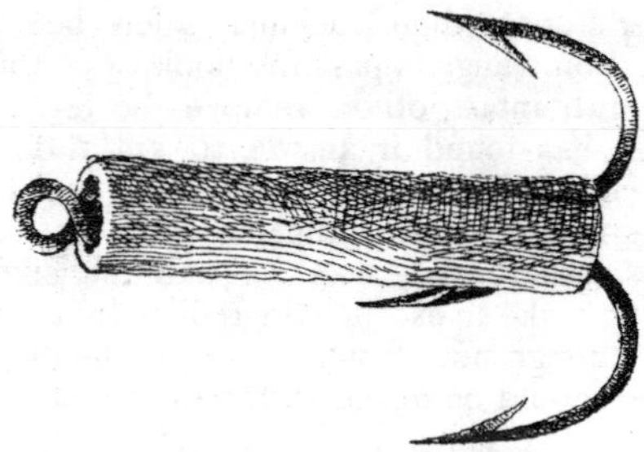

FIG. 8.—LANDING-HOOK.

where neither net nor gaff could be used, the angler being at too great a height above the water. The figure explains itself, the apparatus consisting merely of a wide brass tube filled with lead, having a strong brass ring at the one end, to which is attached a stout cord, and three large galvanised hooks at the other. Its use consists practically in getting it under the fish hooked and foul-hooking it. The objection is that, if missed, the fish might be badly wounded, and, in any case, this means of landing the fish should not be used unless the more usual and legitimate gaff or net are absolutely *hors de combat*, and the fish thoroughly played out. It would, in fact, be the very thing for Australian rock-fishing.

Yet another article of great use in keeping sand-eels and other bait alive is the "courge," a torpedo-shaped basket into which the baits

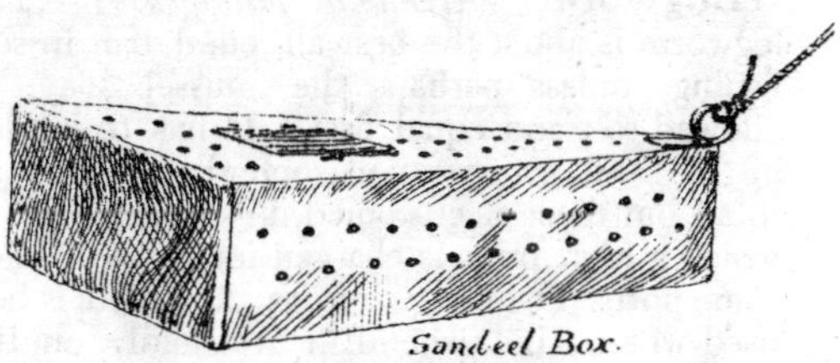

FIG. 9.—BAIT-BOX.

are introduced by an aperture that is closed with a bung, the whole being towed astern of the boat. The writer is likewise indebted to Mr. Railton for the suggested alternative of a triangular box of white deal, perforated by numerous small holes. It is said to keep the sand-eels in better condition and alive longer than the courge. The lid is secured by a peg and eye. The measurements of a convenient size are given at 18 inches long by 6 inches deep.

III. Baits.

A very few notes on the chief baits mentioned in the foregoing remarks must here suffice; and they may, for convenient reference, be considered in alphabetic order.

Crab (*Carcinus mœnas*)—Like birds, crabs moult, and are so sensitive of intrusion at this period of their helplessness that they hide away under stones, where they may safely be looked for. Some anglers pass the hook twice through the crab intact, others remove the legs. The writer has found it answer to kill and bruise the crab before using it for bait, and this is certainly the more humane plan. Crushed crabs, where they can be had in sufficient plenty, make an excellent ingredient in a ground-bait, though not of sufficient consistency alone. They should be mixed with pounded shells and sand. The tail-end of a hermit-crab (*Pagurus bernhardus*), quite distinct from the soft crab, is found to be a good bait for most flat fish.

Herring (*Clupea harengus*)—Fresh herring is one of the best all-round sea-baits, and the writer has even taken good bass with bloater when the fresh herring was unobtainable. Large strips may be used for bass and conger, or small squares for flat fish and whiting. A killing combination may be made with a small strip of herring and another of mackerel, both being placed on the hook with the bright skin outwards. For conger, herring should be fresh, and all bones should be removed. It is even an advantage to hammer the bait with a stick before using. Unless herring is perfectly fresh, few fish but a bass will touch it, and it also comes away from the hook very easily, which is a great disadvantage when there are small fish round the hooks. On the south-west coast, the pilchard (*C. pilchardus*) takes the place of the allied herring, and is similarly used.

Lugworm (*Arenicola piscatorum*) — The lugworm is about the best all-round bait in sea-fishing, unless perhaps the mussel may be allowed to stand equal first. It has to be dug in the sand, an operation somewhat distressing to all but those accustomed, in consequence of which a high price is charged for these baits at some ports. The lug, as it is usually called, is best used whole; but when fish are madly on the feed, sport may be had with the smallest fragments, barely sufficient to cover the hook. There are various processes of preserving, or drying, these worms, but the best of these can be regarded only as a *pis aller* for the fresh-dug worm. Of other worms in common use by the sea-fisherman, mention may be made of the delicate and deadly nereid worm (*Nereis*) that hides in the shell tenanted by the hermit-crab, to obtain which it is necessary to break the shell with a stone. This may, after a little practice, be accomplished so neatly as to destroy neither the crab nor the worm for bait. Yet another favourite worm above-mentioned is the ragworm (*Glycera*), which is found in the soft mud of harbours and estuaries. It is exceedingly delicate, and can only be kept alive for a comparatively short time in some dark, cool place. The same remark applies to the crab-worm, which should not be taken from the shell until required.

Mackerel—The remarks which were made above in connection with herring apply to the mackerel. The "last" or "snade" of mackerel used in whiffing for these cannibal fish is cut from just above the tail, a very sharp knife being necessary for the purpose. A Cornish fisherman will sharpen his knife every hour or so for this purpose. The hook is inserted in the pointed end of the bait, which is triangular in form, and pushed home with the thumb and forefinger, or sometimes with a loop of the line, so that the "last" hangs from the bend.

Mussel (*Mytilus edulis*)—The mussel is one of the most easily procured, and also one of the most deadly baits on our coasts. Opening mussels is not a very easy matter, but, with a little practice, and by watching an expert (it is one of those matters almost impossible of explanation on paper), the novice soon acquires the knack of inserting the blunt knife in the aperture beneath the byssus, and rapidly working the blade round either shell until the whole mollusc comes away from the gaping shells. Nor is it without practice and instruction, that the angler may hope so to fix the mussel, even when thus extracted, on the hook that it shall not immediately come away in the water. The point of the hook is to be inserted in the round white substance observed at one end, and resembling gristle, then passed twice through the middle of the creature, and finally buried in the stringy material at the edges. Small portions of mussel are used for sand-smelts, but as a rule it is necessary to use them intact.

Sand-Eel (*Ammodytes lanceolatus*)—This very attractive bait has, somewhat like the lug-worm, to be scraped in the sand, or, better still, since it easily perishes and is of little use when dead, caught in a small-meshed seine. Mention has already been made, and a diagram given, of a special box for towing live sand-eels to the fishing-grounds, a device that is considered by those who have tried both an improvement on the orthodox Channel Islands "courge." There are many methods of putting live sand-eels on the hook, but the writer invariably hooks them through the upper lip in a strong tide, in the lower lip in slack water.

Shrimp (*Crangon vulgaris*)—Shrimps are

extremely effective baits used alive, the hook being passed through the tail. They are also used, though with less success, dead; and pout are even taken with peeled boiled shrimp. Prawns (*Leander*) are also used alive, especially for pollack. At Selsea, they are the only successful bait.

Mention has been made of ground-bait, and it must be borne in mind that its successful use in the sea is regulated by proper attention to the altered conditions. Thus, it would be useless to throw in balls of ground-bait after the fashion of the Thames fisherman, for the tides and currents would quickly carry these far from the angler, and would in all probability thus draw the fish away from him instead of having the desired result. Ground-bait must therefore be lowered by the sea-angler in some form of receptacle. There are special "diving-bells" sold for the purpose, and if these were less fearsome, they could not be improved upon easily. The writer has had good results with a small piece of fine meshed net at the end of a cord, the latter being occasionally shaken to liberate some of the contents. It is important to place the baited hooks in respect of the ground-bait so that the tide flows to them past the latter, so that fish travelling along the streak of oil and particles of bait that emanate from the bait-net must first pass the larger and more attractive morsels on the hook before coming to the net itself. Crushed mussels and crabs, shell and all, make an excellent ground-bait for use in the sea.

Concluding Hints.

It is impossible to give in greater detail the elements of the sport under notice, but a few general remarks may be offered in conclusion, which the beginner will do well to note.

First, sea-fishing—boat-fishing more particularly—is not suited to every temperament, and the aspiring sea angler will be wise in ascertaining, ere he invest his money in tackle, whether he can stand the movement of a boat, or even the exposure to wind, sun, or cold, the glare of the reflected light, and the general roughing it. This caution may seem almost superfluous in a work addressed to sportsmen who are presumably prepared for some exposure; but the writer has come across many cases of men who would think nothing of the temporary exertion of a football match finding the long exposure, often night as well as day, too much, if not for their constitution, certainly for their ideas of enjoyment.

Again, some acquaintance with the handling of boats, rowing at any rate, is absolutely essential, and no one should go afloat who cannot swim. Upsets are, it is true, not frequent, but the first might for a non-swimmer also be the last. Much has been said in this connection of the necessity of the sea-angler acquainting himself with the "rule of the road" at sea, the cases in which responsibility lies with him, and those in which it lies with some other craft that threatens collision with his own. *Theoretically*, if his anchor is down, the entire responsibility would rest with any steamer that should run him down: in practice, however, it will be found better to ignore the rights of the case and get out of the way of the larger craft with as little delay as possible.

Dress is also an important consideration, not in the matter of appearance, but of health. Proper protection against the sun in summer and against cold in winter should be taken into account, and it is also desirable that all garments, boots and all, should be easily removable in case of an upset. It is not intended in the present remarks, which must now conclude, to offer any suggestions as to places where sport may be obtained. A few notes were given above in this connection. For the rest, the angler may be advised to seek his sport, if possible, on a rocky coast, like that of Cornwall, as the fish generally run larger, and are always in greater variety, than on sandy shores.

When in doubt on strange waters, and without the advantage of local guidance, the fisherman should always look after the gulls and other birds. The gannets, in particular, know where the fish are.

Those anglers to whom expense is no object should not on that account hugely overpay the fishermen and boatmen at the different ports they visit. They merely accustom them to wages which subsequent visitors will be either unable or disinclined to afford, and spoil them for future employment. There are parts of our coasts, on which unthinking visitors from town have spoilt these once unsophisticated men, in the same way as some African travellers have spoilt the native servants.

Sea-anglers cannot be too strongly urged to take note of all matters, however insignificant they may appear at the time, pertaining to the local fishing. The sport is yet in its infancy, and more information is wanted on all sides. They may elect to publish the information thus gained, or they may, and with perfect reason, prefer keeping it for their own use. Let them in either case not trust to memory, but jot down the facts. The time may come when they might desire to impart these in exchange for corresponding information about an unknown country.

Bibliography—Brookes, *Art of Angling: Rock and Sea-Fishing*, 1801; Lord, *Sea-Fish, and How to Catch them*, 1863; Young, *Sea-Fishing as a Sport*, 1872; *The Angler: How, Where, and When to Fish in River and Sea*, 1871; "Wildfowler," *Sea-Fishing Trips*, 1879; Wilcocks, *The Sea-Fisherman* (4th ed.), 1884; "John Bickerdyke," *Angling in Salt Water*, 1887; Hudson, *Sea-Fishing for Amateurs*, 1887; Aflalo, *Sea-Fishing on the English Coast*, 1891; Paske and Aflalo, *The Sea and the Rod*, 1892; "Ichthyosaurus," *Hints and Wrinkles on*

Sea-Fishing, 1894; "John Bickerdyke," *Sea-Fishing* (Badminton Library), 1895; Aflalo, *Sea-Fish* (Angler's Library), 1897.

GLOSSARY OF TERMS NOT EXPLAINED ABOVE.

Bend—A simple method of joining two ropes, or lines, without any actual splice.

Booms—Cane outriggers projecting over the gunwale with the object of keeping the mackerel-lines clear of the boat.

Briming—The fisherman's expression for phosphorescence of the sea at night.

Disgorger—A notched implement of iron or wood, used in twisting the hook free when the fish has gorged it. For large fish with sharp teeth, it should be 18 ins. long, so as to enable its manipulation without endangering the hands of the operator.

Drift-Lines—Those which, bearing little or no lead, are allowed to drift with the tide.

Grapnel—An attachment of claws used in very strong tides, in conjunction with the lead, or sinker, to keep the hooks near the bottom.

Guffin—The Cornish name for ground-bait.

Hitch—The jam-hitch and timber-hitch are two simple fastenings, the former used for looping the mainline on to a gut trace, the latter for tying up the killick.

Killick—A large stone used in place of an anchor on rocky grounds.

Marks—Taking marks is the method of re-discovering known fishing-grounds at sea, the plan being to get two sets of objects ashore, imaginary lines through which converge, when produced, almost at right angles, at a point immediately over the fishing-ground. As an example, one set of bearings may consist of a chimney covering a more distant church steeple, the other of a particular tree coinciding with the flagstaff of a coastguard station. Care should be taken to choose marks of a more or less enduring nature, churches and lighthouses being preferable to more ephemeral buildings.

Pipe-Leads—Cylindrical leads, usually tapering from the centre, and pierced to admit the line.

Railing—The name given to trailing lines, with either natural or artificial bait, behind a boat under sail, as distinguished from whiffing, a similar style of fishing, only with the boat propelled by sculls.

Rig—The various patterns of chopsticks in use on different parts of the coast are known as Kentish rig, Dartmouth rig, &c. ("Rig" is also the Kentish name for the common tope, one of the dog-fish.)

Seine—A bag-net, which is shot from a boat, and hauled in a semi-circle towards the shore.

Snood, or **Snooding**—The finer material to which the hook is directly attached.

Splice—A method of joining two twisted snoods, or lines, by untwisting a short length of each and interlocking the strands.

Trot—A long line, with sometimes several hundred hooks at intervals, kept on the bottom by heavy stones, or an anchor, at either end. Also known as a boulter, or spiller.

Whiffing—[*See* RAILING.]

F. G. AFLALO.

SHARK FISHING—Sharks are of many kinds and cosmopolitan distribution. They are usually captured with a hook and line, except the largest of all, the Basking Shark, which is taken with the harpoon. The Pacific Basking Shark is the largest of the sub-class. The record of the capture of two of these fish will be found in *Fisheries of the United States*, Goode, vol. ii. page 58. However, the real home of the northern "Basking Shark" is off the west coast of Ireland. Brabazon (*Deep Sea and Coast Fisheries*) says, if the weather is warm at the end of April, these fish appear on the Sun Fish Bank, situated about a hundred miles west of Clew Bay, and remain until the middle of May. The writer has made many inquiries of old fishermen as to the exact position of this bank, but without success. In the months of May and June they are also found off Boffin Island and at the entrance to Blacksod Bay, and they are said to run from 18 feet to 40 feet in length.

The following methods appear to have been used at different times to effect the capture of sharks:—

1. Harpoon, either hand or fired from a gun, line and lance.

2. Bait, hook, line and lance. Or, in lieu of a lance, a noose is slipped over the tail, and the fish is hauled bodily on board the ship, where a blow from a hatchet renders the tail powerless.

3. A bait, such as a dead horse or bullock, is placed where these fish abound, and they are shot with a rifle.

4. In some of the islands of the Pacific, the natives attack the ground-sharks with nothing but a knife, and come off victorious.

5. A bait containing a charge of some explosive, such as dynamite, and fired by electricity.

The most sporting of these fish is the aforementioned Basking Shark, or "Sun Fish," as the Irish fishermen call it; and the writer proposes to give briefly the method of harpooning which in his experience is most suitable for Irish waters. Of course, the best class of boat for this fishing would be an ordinary whale-boat, either Scotch or American, such as is used in the Arctic fisheries, or in pursuit of the sperm whale; but it is totally unnecessary to go to the expense of such a boat, for the shark has not the power of a whale. A yacht's whale-boat, or a good powerful gig, could be easily fitted for this fishing, and, if neatly done, no injury would be done to the boat, and the fittings could be removed when no longer required.

On the bow of the boat a piece of hard wood is fitted, in which is cut a score, or notch. This score ought to be from 3 to 3½ inches deep, and from 2 to 2½ inches wide, according to the size of the line used.

It is better to have it too deep than too shallow, as, if the line were to slip out of the score, the consequences might be serious. On the first or second seat from the bow fit a step and iron similar to that used for shipping the boat's mast. In this is shipped the "bollard head," a piece of hard wood about 3 to 3½ inches in diameter at the top, left sufficiently high above the gunwale to enable one to take one or two turns of the line round it, so as to bring a steady strain on the fish.

A 2½ inch whale-line is what the writer used; but a good 2 inch soft laid tarred rope should be strong enough. The only guide as to length is the depth of the water fished; probably 120 fathoms would be far more than would ever be required, provided the harpooner keeps a good steady strain on the line as the fish sounds. A similar line, of from 50 to 60 fathoms, will be required for the second harpoon.

In case of the line running short, this second line can be bent on to the eye or loop spliced into the end of the first line for this purpose. Half a paraffin barrel, with rope handles to lift it in and out of the boat, will take the first line nicely, and a smaller tub will hold the other.

Bore a few holes in the bottom of the tubs to allow the water to drain off. One of the most important points is to see that all turns are taken out of the lines before coiling them down.

Splice an eye on the end of the line, and, leaving out about a fathom, commence to coil round the outside edge of the bottom of the tub from left to right (with the sun) until you have worked into the centre of the tub, then carry the line out to the side, and proceed as before. Each time you bring the line out from the centre of the tub preserve the formation of the spokes of a wheel, following the course of the sun.

Great care should be taken in coiling lines, for many accidents in whaling have occurred from carelessness in this respect.

Two or three ordinary hand-harpoons, with half a dozen ash handles about 5 to 6 feet long, such as are used by the Scotch whalers, three or four handy lances with handles of ash, and a light hatchet to cut the line in an emergency, complete the necessary equipment. Mr. J. C. King, of Peterhead, could supply the harpoons and lances.

If whale-harpoons are not procurable, any fairly good smith could make an ordinary arrow-head harpoon; but care must be taken that they are made of the best soft Swedish iron, so that they will bend into any shape and not break. If badly twisted, which they are sure to be if you obtain any sport, they can be heated slightly, and beaten into shape with a lead hammer or a wooden mallet.

If the sportsman decides to fit a harpoon gun to his boat, he must be careful to ascertain if her bows are strong enough to resist the recoil of the gun when fired. Probably an intelligent carpenter could strengthen the boat sufficiently for the purpose. In a fairly strong boat, all that is required is to carry a slight salvage deck from the stem-head aft for about 3 feet. The gunwale must be raised about 3 inches over the salvage deck, and, as it comes aft, narrow to nothing.

In the stem-head is cut a score, or notch, about 3 inches deep and 2½ inches wide, to admit the line.

About 1 foot 3 inches, or thereabouts, from the stem-head, and slightly on the port side (to give room for the line to run), is placed the bollard head, to carry the gun. This bollard head can be made of a tough bit of oak, round at the head, and about 5 inches diameter, for a whale-gun. A smaller head would probably do for a porpoise-gun.

A hole is bored in the head, to take the crutch which carries the gun, and on this a light iron ring is slipped, to prevent the wood splitting. If the ring be warmed in the fire, it will contract as it cools, and remain in its proper position.

The best way to fix the bollard head is to slip it through the salvage deck, behind one of the little deck-beams, into a light step fixed to the boat's keel.

Although it must be heavy enough to carry the gun-crutch above the deck, it does not require the same strength below, and can be carried down square and crooked, to adapt itself to the shape of the boat.

On the port side of the stem a small eye-bolt is screwed, from which a preventer-stay is carried to the neck of the gun-crutch to bear some of the recoil of the gun.

A line attached to the bend of the crutch is carried down through the deck and made firmly fast below. This is necessary, as crutches are liable to break, and, without these precautions, the gun would be lost overboard.

On the port-side, far enough aft not to interfere with the movements of the gun, a small tub (about 1 foot diameter and 6 to 8 inches high) is fitted on the deck and held there by a bolt which passes through the deck, the nut being screwed on below. This tub holds the part of the line that is fired, viz., from ten to twelve fathoms of beautifully made Manilla line, slightly thinner than the other lines, and called the "foregore." One end of the foregore is either spliced to the end of the line just outside the score, or an eye is spliced in the end of the foregore, and the line is hitched on.

The latter plan is most convenient for sharks. The other end of the foregore is spliced to the shackle of the harpoon, and the bight coiled carefully down in the tub, in the same manner as the lines.

About 1 foot 4 inches from the gun, and in the centre of the boat, ship the line bollard head, which, if it was for whaling, would require to be of hard wood from 3 to 3½ inches diameter, but for sharks any wood will do. This bollard head can be made and fitted in the same manner as the one that carries the gun. The gun most in favour is a muzzle-loader by Greener, and, with crutch and harpoon, weighs about 75 lbs.

The harpoons, weighing from 8 to 12 lbs., are propelled by from 5 to 6 drachms of coarse-grained powder.

The writer's harpoons weigh about 12 lbs., and he found a charge of from 5¼ to 5½ drachms made the best practice.

Harpoon-guns shoot very wild at times. This

is most probably caused by the check the harpoon receives from the line when just clear of the gun, so that perhaps the slower the harpoon is to leave the gun, the less check it receives, and what is lost in velocity and trajectory is more than gained by increased accuracy.

For loading and cleaning the gun, two rammers are required; the one of iron, with a screw at the end, and the other of wood, with a brass cup at the end.

Directions for Loading—To clean the gun of oil, squib off a small quantity of powder with a light wad of tow.

Measure the charge of powder, and, placing it in the brass cup, lower the muzzle of the gun as far as possible.

Insert the cup of the rammer as far as it will go, and, retaining it there, raise the muzzle of the gun.

This insures all the powder reaching the breech of the gun. On the powder ram firmly a wad of oakum or old tarred rope, 2 or 3 inches thick, just sufficient for the harpoon to rest against.

Like all muzzle-loaders, these guns are liable to miss-fires, and it is necessary to carry a flask of very fine-grained powder, a small funnel to fit over the nipple, and a pin to work the powder down through the nipple, as well as a wrench to remove the latter. The best chance of avoiding miss-fires is to keep the barrel very clean and not leave it long loaded.

Some harpooners place a piece of cork between the bars of the harpoon at the end that is inserted into the gun, with a view to lessen the shock to the harpoon shackle when the gun is fired.

Run the harpoon into the gun, first seeing that the shackle runs easily down the harpoon (a tight shackle will probably cause a miss); put on a cap, insert the pin that acts as a bolt to prevent the gun going off, and everything is ready for a fish.

After the shot, the handle of the gun is swung round to port and rested on the side of the boat, to be clear of the line.

A painted canvas cover, which slips down over the muzzle and laces round the crutch and the handle, will be required to keep the gun dry.

The Norwegians have a workmanlike-looking breech-loading gun with lighter harpoons. The moveable single barb of these harpoons is made like two spoons joined together by the handles. One end of the barb is lightly secured to the harpoon with spun yarn. When the strain comes on the barb the spun yarn breaks, and the barb opens, exploding a shell in front of the harpoon. The only objection the writer ever heard made to these guns was that there was no proof-house in Norway to test guns, and therefore they might burst.

A small locker, open towards the stern, is placed generally on the foremost seat to protect the points of the harpoons and lances, which are covered with strong grease, and wrapped round with old canvas.

The handles are kept in their places aft by a light lashing to the side of the boat.

A porpoise gun would do well; but get Mr. King, or some other well-known harpoon maker, to supply the harpoons. Be careful to have your harpoons and lances as sharp as a razor.

Now suppose a fish in sight. Lower your boat; place the line you are going to run as far aft as it will conveniently stand, and, bringing the end of it over the seats out through the score, attach it to the harpoon.

See that the hatchet is placed in the bow in readiness to cut if anything goes wrong. The harpooner stands in the bow of the boat, and the fish is approached on the starboard, or right hand side, and, when opportunity serves, a dash is made for the big fin, when the harpooner must endeavour to drive his harpoon well home alongside the fin.

In approaching, do not let the boat get too far ahead; for the fish, if it were to see her, would disappear. The moment the fish is fastened, the harpooner should take a turn round the bollard head and keep as much strain on the line as the boat will safely bear. The crew ship their oars, and the steerer, or nearest hand, should watch the line running out, and, as it is taken in again, coil it back neatly in the tub.

The fish will tire, and be gradually brought to the surface.

Now the danger of these fish lies in the tail; and it is therefore necessary to let two of the crew get out their oars, and, facing the bow, endeavour to keep the boat away from the tail.

The harpooner now takes his second harpoon, being relieved of the first line by a careful man, who must be ready to let the fish take a little line on the receipt of the second harpoon.

The harpooner, watching his opportunity, places this second harpoon as far forward as he can, if possible, through the gills.

Slack the first line, and hang up the fish on the second, when a few thrusts of the lance through the gills will bring the matter to a satisfactory conclusion; but do not in the excitement forget the tail, for it is powerful enough to stave in a boat's side. The best way to do this is to keep backing the boat away from the fish.

All true sportsmen like to make use of anything they kill. Up to the present, the liver, which is converted into oil by boiling down, appears to be the only part that has been utilised; but there seems to be no reason why some use should not be made of the skin.

[Should any sportsman wish to try this fishing, he could not do better than get the assistance of Michael Halloran, of the Sound of Shark Cleggan, Galway, who has been in at the death of over a score of these fish.]

H. W. GORE BOOTH.

SHARK—MEASUREMENTS, &c.—This shark is largest in circumference about the situation of the pectoral fins, diminishing in size towards each extremity. Head conical. The snout (especially in the young) appears like a beaked projection, being of much less circumference than the anterior end of the jaws; it is also covered with small pores. *Eye*—small, situated over the anterior end of the mouth: nostrils situated at the edge of the upper lip. Spiracle small, and situated midway between the eye and the first gill-opening. *Teeth*—small and conical, with smooth edges, and in from four to six rows. *Gill-openings*—very long, extending down the entire side of the neck. *Fins*—the first dorsal is of medium size: it commences on a line just posterior to the insertion of the pectoral, is highest in front and concave along its upper border. The second dorsal, which is about one-third the size of the first, is inserted just anterior to the anal, than which it is larger. Pectoral placed low down, rather small and nearly triangular. Caudal, with the lower lobe the longer and the upper notched, a pit at the root of the fin. Skin rough, especially when the hand is passed from behind forwards; a keel along the side of the tail. *Colours*—dusky black, brown, or blue along the back, becoming lighter on the sides and beneath. Snout of a dull reddish, becoming dull white beneath. (Day's *Fishes of Great Britain and Ireland*.)

SEROW (*Nemorhœdus bubalinus*)—*Serow*, *Serrow*, or *Surrow* in the central Himalayan ranges generally; *Thar* in the more eastern ones and those of Nepal; *Ramoo* in Kashmir, and divers other names in different localities extending as far eastward as, if not farther, than the Malay Peninsula.

Description—This somewhat nondescript animal, by naturalists considered to be a link between the antelope and goat tribes, might, from its general appearance, be supposed to have a strain of the ass as well. It stands over 3 feet at the shoulder, slightly lower at the croup, neck thick, short, and surmounted with a bristling mane of coarse black hair extending back over the withers, which, with its almost black face, large mule-like ears and dark fiery eyes, gives this animal a fierce expression which its character does not belie. General colour of its roughish and rather scanty-haired coat dark roan grey, intermixed with black; black dorsal stripe and tail, the latter very short; flanks and forequarters reddish brown. Sturdy limbs, creamy white from above the knees and hocks. Muzzle and chin whitish. The black, round horns rise almost in a line with forehead, curving slightly backwards, closely annulated, and creased longitudinally for nearly half their length, which, in good specimens, average 10 inches, with base circumference of about 5½ inches and 3 or 4 inches between their sharp tips. The sexes much resemble each other, but the female's horns are less distinctly annulated.

The serow, like the musk deer, has the noteworthy peculiarity of ordinarily depositing its droppings together in largish heaps. These, when found fresh, afford a sure sign of serow harbouring near by. Its alarm cry resembles a single sharp kind of shriek emitted at short intervals, but is comparatively seldom heard.

Habitat—In India the serow confines itself to the Himalayan Mountains, where it may be found at any altitude between about 4,000 and 10,000 feet, usually in deep, craggy wooded gorges, as a rule solitary, or accompanied by its mate and sometimes their young offspring. It is, however, about the most scarce of all Himalayan horned game.

Hunting—Although of very shy habit, its disposition is so bold that, if closely approached when wounded, it is always ready to show fight. The writer knows an authentic instance of a man, whilst handling a serow just shot, being charged by its unwounded mate from out the thick cover hard by. In some respects it may be termed almost a stupid animal. The writer

SEROW.

Av. ht. at shoulder, 38 in. Av. horn meas. 10 in. Max. horn meas. 12 in.

has known it stand and gaze when suddenly surprised out feeding, even after having been shot at and missed: but when thoroughly alarmed it almost invariably dashes off down hill, however steep and broken the ground may be, until lost to view in the nearest dense cover below.

In the more Eastern Himalayas a reddish-coloured serow is met with, and is sparsely found as far east as the Malay Peninsula and Sumatra. Two smaller sized varieties are said to exist in China and Japan.

When serow are known to affect a certain thickly-wooded gorge or hill-side, driving quietly is often successful when stalking would be impossible.

Weapon—A double ·450 bore express rifle

with hollow-pointed bullet of unhardened lead, plugged with copper-tube or bit of wood, will be found as good as any weapon for shooting serow.

DONALD MACINTYRE.

SHOOTING — Carrying the Gun—If "the nice conduct of a clouded cane" was an essential part of a gentleman's education in the

WILL EITHER REACH HIS DESTINATION ALIVE?

eighteenth century, surely the careful manipulation of firearms should be a far more important branch of knowledge in these days, when most people affect to be sportsmen, and nearly everybody in the country carries a lethal weapon of some sort, with the ostensible purpose of destroying fur or feather, and to the greater or less danger of his fellow creatures.

Although it is hardly possible that anybody who did not begin as a boy, or as a very young man, can ever acquire that subtle facility of handling a gun which shows familiarity without contempt, there is no sort of reason why a person of any age, in full command of his faculties, should not learn how to carry rifle or fowling piece in such a manner, and with such precautions, as to place an accident almost beyond the range of possibility.

It is obvious to the meanest capacity that a gun which is not pointed at anybody can do no harm even if it does "go off of itself," and surely it is possible with a little care always to keep the barrels directed earthwards or skywards, so that the only evil result of a chance discharge shall be a slight shock to the nerves of the bystanders. I remember once being present when an old sportsman, standing in the midst of a crowd of beaters, keepers, &c., just at the luncheon gathering, suddenly fired in the air. We all turned round in amazement, but he calmly, gazing upward, remarked, "Curse that wood-pigeon," withdrew the remaining cartridge, handed his gun to his loader, and walked on. Every one was satisfied, and only he was for some time aware that in half cocking he had pulled the wrong trigger.

He told some of us afterwards, adding that he thought it better to say nothing at the moment, as it might have made us nervous to know that he could possibly do such a thing. He was right.

In Mr. A. Grimble's excellent book on shooting are numerous illustrations of the various ways most in vogue of carrying the gun, and the author adds his comments thereon. He is, if anything, hypercritical, for there is surely no danger, though he avers there is much, in the very common practice of tucking the gun under the arm with the front of the trigger-guard resting above the wrist, but if he errs it is on the side of safety, always a good error, safety being the one thing absolutely indispensable, to which readiness and elegance must be mere secondary considerations.

"But it's so unsportsmanlike," reasoned Mr. Winkle.

"I don't care whether its unsportsmanlike or not," replied Mr. Pickwick. "I'm not going to be shot in a wheelbarrow for the sake of appearances, to please anybody."

And that wise man insisting, it will be remembered that Mr. Winkle and Mr. Tupman marched with reversed arms, like a couple of privates at a royal funeral.

At any rate Mr. Grimble would admit that all requirements of safety will be satisfied by "breaking," *i.e.*, opening the gun and letting it

PERFECTLY SAFE: GUN BROKEN.　　GUN ON SHOULDER: CORRECT POSITION.

hang thus on the forearm, when it can be closed and used in an instant if occasion requires.

Never carry a gun at the trail; if carried on

the shoulder let it always rest with the trigger-guard uppermost; by the reverse method the barrels are apt to come on a level with the faces of those walking in the rear.

Always draw cartridges before crossing a fence, and as a rule when walking from covert to covert. Half cock or put the locks at "safety" the moment a beat is finished.

Never shoot in the direction of anybody, however great the distance, some guns being apt to perform prodigies in the way of carrying when it is least desired.

By attention to these few simple rules a shooter may reasonably expect to pass his life without incurring the guilt of manslaughter.

Though the practice of walking in line has become unfashionable, it is still in vogue in counties which do not easily lend themselves to driving. Let the young sportsman, therefore, when thus engaged, keep his dressing. It is unfair to get ahead of the others, it is unwise to drop behind.

The safest position is obviously on the right, the best sport is usually obtained in the centre; the host will do well to occupy the former place, and to put the best shot in the middle. The most dangerous man of the party should invariably have the left flank, though in this style of shooting, where everybody is, or ought to be, in full view, there is no possible excuse for hurting anybody; when harm is done it is generally to one of the keepers or beaters who have stayed back to search for a wounded bird, and is quite unpardonable. A man with his wits about him can see the instant he turns round if the coast is clear, and if it is not, and he lacks the self-restraint to refrain from firing, he should never be allowed to shoot in company.

The worst accidents happen at driving, perhaps most of all at grouse driving. By some inexplicable infatuation some people seem impelled to pull the trigger just when their barrels cover the next box or station, and loss of eyesight has resulted only too often. It seems idle to warn a man not to shoot point-blank at his neighbour, for he would only wax wroth at being supposed capable of such recklessness, yet the thing happens over and over again, so that the only advice worth giving on the subject is, to watch your adversaries, for as such you must consider them till they have proved themselves friends, and, if they show an inclination to shoot in your line, throw yourself on the ground and save your eyes at the sacrifice of some of your sport.

Learning to Shoot—After all, it is on the first handling of a gun that the future career of a sportsman may depend, and the best way to avoid bad and careless habits is to begin as a boy under a strict instructor, but, man or boy, the first step for the beginner is to suit his shape and make with a gun; single-barrelled, say great authorities, especially for a boy, but herein I beg to differ. Nobody intends to go on shooting with a single barrel, and the best weapon for a start seems therefore to be a double barrel with one lock fixed or removed. It answers every purpose of the single, such as preventing a careless first shot because of reliance on a second chance, and, when the time arrives of graduating to the "double," the other lock has only to be opened or restored, and lo! there is the required article already proven, to which hand and eye have become accustomed.

That well-worn joke of our forefathers about sending a boy to be measured for a gun, is turned into real earnest nowadays. The process is simple enough. Let the boy hold the gun at the ready, with the stock about an inch from the chest and three inches below the shoulder, the neck (of the gun) being lightly grasped with the right hand, forefinger close to trigger; the left arm should be extended along the barrel with a slight bend of the elbow, the left hand grasping the barrel firmly.

From this position, if the gun is a fit, an upward motion of both hands will not only bring the stock into proper position, but will also bring the barrel into a direct line between the boy's eye and that of his instructor standing some four yards away, in fact, where the eye is fixed, the hand acting in unison will mechanically point the gun.

Great care should also be given to the position of the legs. They cannot be too steady, the left foot straight in front, its fellow at right angles to it, so as to facilitate shooting to the right without moving either foot. For good shooting, the habit of perfect balance is necessary, which, once acquired, is never lost save from injured limbs, or impaired health. No trick can be more uncomely than the not uncommon one of standing on the left and kicking up behind with the right leg, accuracy of aim being, of course, out of the question with such vagaries. At the same time it is only fair to remark that many a good shot stands with his legs rather widely apart, and shifts his feet according to the direction in which he wishes to fire. This cannot be right, since it disturbs the balance, and in shooting, as at billiards, firmness and equilibrium are of the first importance. To the well taught it becomes a matter of second nature to come to the proper position at the moment of firing, whether walking in line, standing in a grouse box, or at the corner of a covert.

The next step with a boy is to show him on a target the effect of his lessons in manual and platoon exercise. Do not allow him to poke his gun about and *seek* for his aim, or he will acquire the "following" trick, a most pernicious and constant cause of mischance in the field. On the contrary, make him put up his gun and fire with full confidence that it must be levelled right, and when confidence and knack have been obtained at the inanimate object, let him try his 'prentice hand at sitting bird or squatting rabbit. One of the great joys of life is a boy's first success in this line, and how easily and often such shots are missed the *emeriti* only know.

The first series of lessons once completed, he will make rapid progress and soon get fairly proficient at game going straight away from him. After this stage come the difficulties and complexities of shooting, such as allowing for the movement of the proposed victim, whether it be flying or running, straight or obliquely across, or in calculating with what deflection from the straight line it may be approaching or retreating, at what distance and at what rate of speed, problems which have to be mechanically seized and solved within the space of a fraction of a second. Of all these, the judging of distance is perhaps the most difficult, nor is it possible to lay down rules for the guidance of the beginner. It seems that practice alone can bring the necessary instinct, but let him do his best to note, whenever practicable, where it is that his shot does strike, and he will find in nine cases out of ten that he is behind his mark from having fired point-blank at it. Two ways there are, however, of taking the angle, *i.e.*, of finding the spot, be it on earth or in air, where gun-

A WELL KILLED BIRD.

charge and game shall arrive simultaneously. Both are in common use and both satisfy their various exponents, though one seems rather quicker than the other. The first is called "chucking" the gun, which means that you cover the object and then give a slight swing or movement ahead, pulling the trigger at the same instant, thus effecting the desired collision between ammunition and fugitive, which latter will have traversed the two—three—ten yards, or whatever it may be, of given margin, whilst the charge is going up. Indeed, birds flying down wind with a sixty mile an hour gale behind them will often have covered a much larger space than that. The other and quicker method is to pitch up the gun and fire slap at the spot which you consider ought to be the point of contact, but it must be repeated that anything approaching to certainty in either mode can only be attained by much practice.

By way of emphasising this point, take the speed of the homing pigeon. During the sixteen hours of a summer daylight he can cover more than 500 miles, and at shorter distance has an even better record. One of these birds was timed from Orleans to Brussels on a south-westerly gale at the rate of 2,175 yards per minute, or about 36 yards 9 inches in a second. If that bird had crossed a crack-shot at 40 yards, where would he have "chucked" or "pitched" his gun? Could he, with all his practice, decide the rate of flight?

Sharp rabbits in furze, fern or underwood are the best tutors for a beginner. There is no time for aiming. Whatever the rabbit's point may be, the shot, to hit him in the head, must be there almost before him, and as it is more or less easy to track a miss, the principle of the thing is soon picked up. Quite another matter is it to carry the principle, however well studied, into effect on fast flying birds, without ride or run to guide the eye, which is partly the reason why there are so few perfect all-round shots.

What to Shoot at—Justly enough, sportsmen have been classified as—1st, perfect; 2nd, first class; 3rd, good and moderate second class; 4th, bad. It is doubtful if more than a dozen men deserve to be placed in the first category, there are hundreds who belong to No. 2, thousands in No. 3, and millions, say many authorities, in No. 4, though from these I beg respectfully to differ: at any rate, it is far rarer to meet with a rank bad shot than was formerly the case. Thirty or forty years ago, out of a covert shooting party of six or seven, two or three were almost certain to be duffers of the first water, men who seldom hit anything but a beater, whereas nowadays even one such tailor would be a rarity. It is safe to add that, with very few exceptions, only those who have begun in early youth ever attain a higher standard than that of moderate second class.

Though the "pot" may be a gross and material consideration, it is, nevertheless, good for the beginner to be constantly reminded that game has a destiny beyond the larder, and that birds, at any rate, should be allowed to reach cooking distance before the fatal trigger is pulled; but above all things let him eschew a random style of taking long shots; the tip-top performer may and often does achieve absolute feats by apparent disregard of distance; the lesser fry of sportsmen ought never to be betrayed into such experiments. First, from a humanitarian point of view, they will often wound, and hardly ever accomplish a direct kill; next, for their own sakes, for depend upon it no host likes seeing his birds maimed.

It is astonishing that men are not ashamed of shouting, as they exultantly do, "I hit him hard; he's sure to die." Delinquents in this respect may feel pretty sure that their sins are duly noted by their entertainer.

A WINGED BIRD.

I remember Lord Coventry (who, by the way, was about the best game shot I ever saw) once saying to me, *apropos* of a notorious offender :—

"I really believe H—— fancies I have asked him down for the sole purpose of *exterminating* my game."

With sorrow and shame, be it confessed that gunners of the exterminating class are just now far too abundant. The number is increasing of men who go shooting without idea or conception of the *sport* of pursuing game, but with the sole desire of firing off as many cartridges as possible in the shortest space of time, and with the minimum of exertion. Soon we may expect to see them discarding the double-barrelled breech-loader in favour of repeating weapons. Indiscriminate slaughter is the one object of these bloodthirsty individuals, and, as they are in constant practice, there are plenty of them who are tolerably unerring at birds flying high or low. The more blame theirs for taking them as they do, with cheerful complacency, within 5 or 10 yards of the gun, so that the unfortunate host, whose guests they are, finds at the end of the day that at least half his bag is unfit for table or market. Quickness is the test of merit with these murderers; the "plasterer" is their ideal; the man who kills his game at "kitchen range" they call a slow, bad shot. Picking birds off beater's heads is not only unsportsmanlike but dangerous; the most perfect trigger may clog and go hard, down drops the muzzle, and unless the beater is quick enough to drop himself he has every chance of going home in the cart.

What a tough uncomplaining lot too, are these beaters! Many a man receives, without a word, wounds which would cause the inflictor to yell with pain and apprehension.

"'Tis over now, Bill, we can get out," said one of the smock frocks to another at the end of a hot rabbit corner. "And I be main glad of it," replied Bill. "That there gent in the brown jacket have been a powring the shot into I turr'ble."

At any rate, when the injury does become known, the compensation should be ample, instead of, as is too often the case, of the most meagre description. I have seen half a crown given where a couple of sovereigns would have been hardly adequate.

Selling Game—Having inveighed against the sporting "tailors" who smash up game and render it unfit for market, it may be *apropos* to add that nothing can be more unwise or unfair than to deride and decry those who thus dispose of their superfluous fur and feather. The public means to have game to eat; if it cannot be bought from the legitimate owner, then the poacher will become the purveyor. There will be the old story of excessive custom duties regularly accompanied by smuggling.

A TOWERED BIRD.

It is true that, perhaps, forty or fifty years ago there were many gentlemen who thought it derogatory to their position to sell game. What was the consequence? Poaching was a profitable profession and flourished, and, however openhanded the owner might be, as he seldom had the means of packing and distributing his game in small quantities before it became bad, the wretched result followed that a large proportion had sometimes to be buried as unfit for human food.

Surely the more sensible system is that which now prevails; when nearly everybody sells of their abundance, the market is fully supplied on reasonable terms from the right quarters and the trade of the poacher becomes more and more discredited.

STRUCK BEHIND.

Loaders—To return to the actual details of the sport, the loader plays by no means the least important part in the rapid shooting of our modern days, more especially as in most cases he is the man who has charge of the guns, and his duty it is to clean and overhaul them, so that no speck of rust may invade any part of our weapons. Not that there is any great difficulty about the business, though, like everything else, it involves a certain amount of tuition, of which the first part relates to the gun itself. One can hardly expect the average loader to be a skilled mechanic, and to understand the mysteries of locks, bolts, &c., for which reason it is best absolutely to forbid interference with those vital parts, since there is always the maker to fall back upon when anything goes really wrong. He will also willingly instruct the loader in the rudiments of his craft, will give all necessary information as to probable contingencies and how to deal with them, and having been able during the process to form a very fair estimate of his pupil's aptitude and intelligence, will furnish thereon a useful report to the employer.

An untaught, even an inexperienced, loader is worse than none; setting aside the danger to the whole party, a man will shoot far more comfortably and quickly loading for himself, than when he has to supervise the clumsy struggles of a numb-fisted attendant. Yet loading is one of the things which anybody will undertake even if he has never seen a gun before.

"Am I to load for you to-day, sir?" said a new servant to me, on the morning of what was sure to be a very heavy shoot.

"Why, have you ever done such a thing in your life?"

"No, sir, but no doubt I could if I tried."

He was rather hurt when refused the trial. As already laid down, the rule should be that the man must never tamper with the mechanism—removing screws in order to look inside may easily prove as fatal as a child's curiosity to inspect the interior of a drum. Still, accidents will happen, such as a roll in a snowdrift, or a tumble in a bog, where locks may get clogged, and then it is that the lessons learnt in the gun-shop come into use and everything may be set right in a few minutes. Then, too, it may well be that a third gun in the ammunition wagon comes handy. But of that more anon.

The loading pure and simple, the mere act of charging the guns, must also be a matter where practice alone can make perfect. But the sportsman who aspires to eminence as a shot should be in continual harmony and accord with his loader. There is even a particular angle at which the latter should stand with his principal, who, if he is an experienced hand, may quickly teach the art with dummy cartridges in a room. The first thing to be considered is the exchange of guns. The moment the shot is fired, the barrel should be thrown up, the shooter grasping the gun by the neck and slightly turning, so that the loader may easily seize the empty and replace it with the loaded

CHANGING GUNS.

piece. If this manœuvre is properly executed, the guns will never touch each other, and many an indentation will be thus avoided.

The exact position of the loader cannot be laid down by rule, one man liking his servant on the right, another preferring the left side. Variety of game also affects the situation—*e.g.* when rocketing pheasants are the sole object, the loader may stand right half forward without in the least interfering with his master, who, indeed, will be rather helped than hindered; but if hares and rabbits are also coming out of covert, the man must be well half back. In grouse driving, a position on the immediate right is obviously to be recommended, for, thus placed, the loader will only interfere with a shot which would pepper the occupant of the adjoining box on that side. For partridge driving over high fences or belts, the rule is the same as with tall pheasants. The great essential for rapid firing is that the man should never be looking at the game—a most difficult principle to instil—since many loaders are as keen as if shooting themselves, and it is a sore trial to them not to watch the performance, though a second's inattention to their work may throw away the chance of a shot. Brass cartridges, which are the most waterproof and least likely to stick in the gun, with a wide opening cartridge bag, will also facilitate business. The best shooting waterproof is the Aquascutum—with this both master and man should be provided, and the loader should always carry in his pocket a little bag containing spare tumblers, a cleaning brush and lead. The latter used during a pause in heavy shooting will save a lot of recoil.

Rules for carrying the gun have already been given and apply equally to all parties concerned. It is almost needless to add that a spirit of loyalty should prevent the loader from pointing the weapon into his principal's legs or back.

Guns.—To the manifest advantage of trade, the life of a gun is now reckoned by years, and very few of them, instead of by generations, as once was the case; no doubt they are as good and durable as ever, better they could hardly be, but we may take it for granted that all self-respecting sportsmen order new guns twice or so in a decade. While they are about it they had better have three than two in the case, which is not materially larger than the old double, and they should always take the third gun out in the cart. Accidents will happen, and, apart from the inconvenience and humiliation of finishing a day with one gun, it must be remembered that a gun-maker should never be bustled over his repairs. If given proper time, he will do the work effectively and well, if hurried, he has no choice but to return a hastily patched-up article, which will soon have to return to the shop, and mending may in the long run become almost as expensive as making. Moreover, if a man can afford to devote his autumn and winter to shooting, he can surely manage this slight additional outlay for the immense convenience of a spare gun.

Ammunition.—On the matter of ammunition, it is imprudent as well as difficult to dogmatise. The maker knows from experiment what charge best suits guns of his own manufacture, and therefore it is wise to be guided by his dictum; but whose advice should we seek in the matter of powder, about which the only certainty seems to be that none is perfect? The old black powder, on the whole, gives the best result to the bag, but it has the undesirable disadvantage of filling a ride with smoke, and, on a damp close day, with ground game abundant, the smother is as bad as a London fog. Schulze & E. C. are perhaps the next best for strength, but they both have the great fault that when one is shooting up wind they fill the eyes with grit. There are many nitro-powders which make good practice enough up to thirty yards, but what we want is the penetration at long range of the "old black" without any of its defects. Still, an ounce of No. 5 or 6 shot propelled by a proper charge—say 42 to 44 grains of Schulze or E. C.—will make a very pretty pattern at 40 yards, either horizontally or vertically, and for the present we must rest satisfied at that. Nevertheless, there is a fortune in store for the inventor of a smokeless, gritless, and really powerful powder.

SUFFOLK AND BERKSHIRE.
W. G. CRAVEN.

HOW TO BUY A RIFLE—"What game do you propose to shoot with it?" is the natural question which arises. If you want to shoot a rhinoceros or an elephant, a small cannon will be best, *i.e.* anything from a ·500 express with expanding bullets to an eight or ten bore. If, on the other hand, your game consists of small deer such as gazelles, antelopes, or roe, a good rook rifle will be sufficient. But for almost all purposes the two best rifles at present in use are the ·450 express and the ·303 Lee-Metford, the latter used with the black bullet and cordite or rifleite powder. I say the black bullet, because it makes a more killing wound than the nickel-covered army bullet, which goes clean through any stag and does not stop him at once unless it strikes a vital part. I used to prefer the ·303 to the express, owing to the noiseless and smokeless ammunition and to the absence of recoil; for, in stalking, noise and smoke are naturally prejudicial to a second chance.

But of late many experiments have been made with the ·450 express with ·400 chamber and smokeless powders; and, if the proper powder is used, I have but little doubt that this will supersede all other weapons. The size of the bullet and the wound it makes give it a great advantage over the ·303. Besides, the lead of the black bullet is less likely to remain in the groove of the express than in that of the ·303. Some experiments with tubeite have succeeded well, fired from the ·450, and this gives all the advantages of the ·303—*i.e.* no noise and no smoke, plus a lighter and less delicate weapon and a larger bullet.

In buying a rifle, soundness and shooting are the points to be ascertained first, and then the pull of the triggers, which latter entirely depends upon the purchaser's taste. I prefer the pull to be very light, and in hammerless rifles the half cock or safety bolt should have a guard so as to prevent its slipping when carried. The bend of a rifle is not so important as that of a gun, as it is very rare that one requires to put it up quick to the shoulder and snap off as one does with a gun. But the sighting is quite a study; and though the sight of a rifle may make admirable practice in one good shot's hands, it may not do so in the hands of another equally good shot, for the reason that the two men's eyesights may be quite different. A man may shoot well with an army ·303 rifle if he has young sight or even if he wears spectacles to assist short-sightedness. But a man with old eyesight, that is, who can see any distance within reason, but cannot read without glasses, will be apt to find the back-sight of his rifle totally useless. Such a man will generally be able to read the leader type of the *Times* newspaper, for a very short while, by holding it well away from him, say 26 inches or so, though it will make his eyes ache. If the back-sight, therefore, is put at the usual distance from the eye (said to be 14 inches) the old sighted man will not see it clearly, though he sees the bead at the end of the barrel. If he puts on his "clearers" he will see the back-sight, but not the bead or the bull's eye. This very common form of eyesight is rarely properly attended to on sighting rifles, and yet the remedy seems simple enough, viz.: to put the back-sight forward until it is clearly seen. It will of course involve the altering of the V, but it will not hurt the shooter's eye for the few seconds he takes in aiming, as it would if he tried to read for any length of time at the same distance. But before using this extreme measure, *i.e.*, of placing the back-sight so forward, I would recommend a trial of the bar-sight, which was so strongly advocated in the Deerstalking article in this *Encyclopædia* by Mr. Grimble. It suits some people with old sight, and its outline is very distinct, being white platinum on a black ground, but even this requires adjusting to the purchaser's sight. Hundreds of rifles are bought on the strength of a target pattern which is shown to the customer. They have been sighted to the proper eyesight of a man of thirty; but no offer is ever made by the seller to adjust the sight to the eyes of the actual purchaser. This the latter should see to himself. The most conscientious gun-makers fall into this error, an error which eventually does them as much harm as any other shortcoming in the rifle they sell, for their customer shoots badly and the maker gets a certain amount of the blame. We know that a rifle is rather disfigured by having its back-sight forward on the barrels, but the outward appearance is only a secondary consideration. I prefer the double-barrelled Lee-Metford to the single barrel and magazine. The former is a nice handy weapon, and to my mind two barrels should be sufficient, unless the *sportsman* (?) is of that blood-thirsty tribe who go out with the intention of killing all they can, not by fair stalking, but by penning deer into gorges and slaughtering them. Let them use magazines if they like, I shall not even be surprised if I hear some day of their adopting the Maxim!

As to the care necessary for preserving both guns and rifles during the non-shooting season, it is best to take the advice of a gun-maker. But the essential point is never to keep them in a damp place; and to examine them thoroughly not less than once a month, wiping every part each time and oiling where necessary. The browning of the barrels should also be attended to at the end of a season, as a small rub may give a shiny barrel.

W. G. CRAVEN.

THE SEWIN.

ENGINES AND ACCESSORIES—**Sewin**—The sewin, as applied to sport, is not a modern invention, although its original form has been much modified and improved in recent years.[*] Moreover, owing to the difficulty experienced in many districts in obtaining the

SEWIN ON FRAME, READY TO BE RUN OUT.

requisite number of boys as stops, the practical use of the sewin is likely to extend.

four days successively. Under these circumstances the sewin, if properly worked, offers an effective and economical substitute. The sewin itself consists simply of a white cord, in 300 or 600 yards lengths, to which is attached, at intervals of 12 inches, white feathers and scarlet tape. Brass ferret bells, or "ruggles," are also fastened at intervals of 5 yards. The cord thus prepared is wound round a large reel, which is secured on the shoulders of the bearer by a light iron frame. Prior to the placing of the sewin in position, hazel or ash sticks, 2½ feet high and split at the top, should be inserted in the ground at suitable intervals to carry the sewin. Directly the sewin is set up a boy is left at the reel end, whose duty it is to keep jerking the cord. The sewin is used not only inside the covers, but also at varying distances outside. In the latter case, it is generally supplemented by red and white flags, which are placed in position first thing in the morning. The appearance of the sewin when wound round the reel, and when stretched, is illustrated in the three illustrations. The reel, iron frame, and sewin show the apparatus as modified by Mr. Jarvis Reckless, The Paddock, Ross, Herefordshire, who supplies the various parts at the following prices:—

Reel for sewin	5*s.* 6*d.*
Iron frame for winding reel .	5*s.* 6*d.*
Sewin, per 100 yards . . .	13*s.*

The accompanying plan represents the actual mode of working. This plan shows the position of the sewin and of the guns during the first beat. In subsequent beats the sewin is indicated by a dotted line drawn between the letters A B, &c., and the position of the guns described in the text is not shown. The cover represented is somewhat irregular in

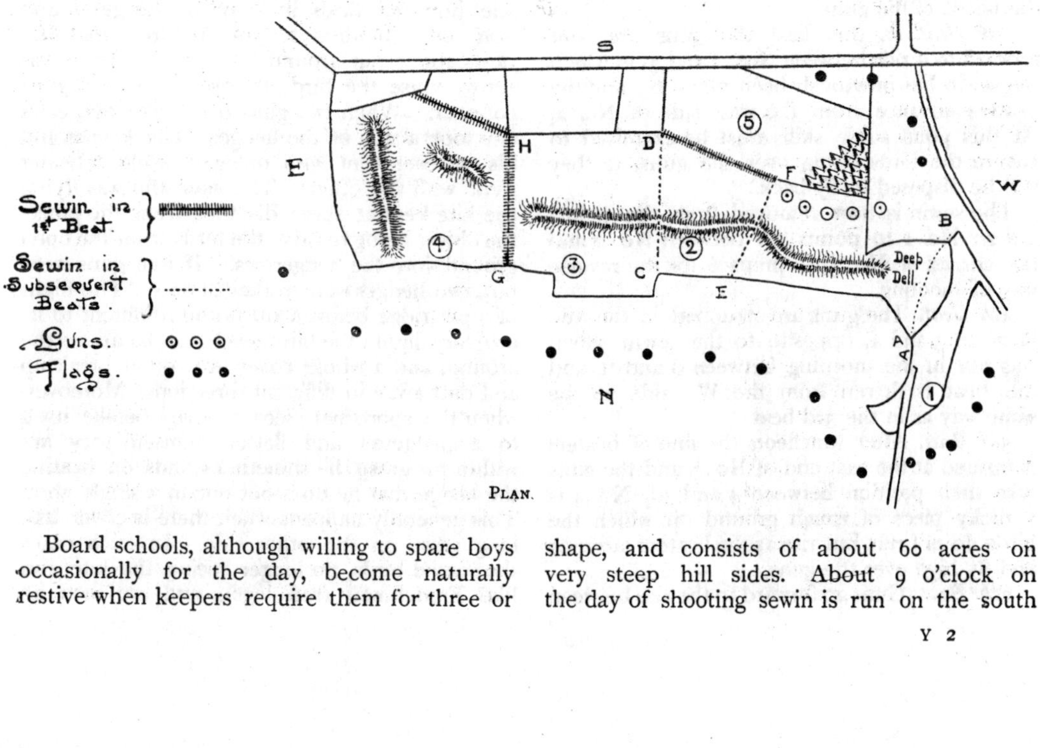

PLAN.

Board schools, although willing to spare boys occasionally for the day, become naturally restive when keepers require them for three or

shape, and consists of about 60 acres on very steep hill sides. About 9 o'clock on the day of shooting sewin is run on the south side of No. 4 plot in the plan and continued between Nos. 4 and 3.

1st Beat. Half an hour before the guns arrive the line of beaters form at the north end of No. 1, and, keeping the right shoulder forward, sweep the birds into No. 2; they then re-form at the north end of No. 2 and drive into No. 5. The sewin is now run between Nos. 2 and 5 to prevent the birds running back. The corner of No. 5 is thick underwood, and affords good cover for the birds. The guns are then placed across the deep dell, and the birds are driven towards them as the beaters advance from the south-east side of the plot. From the corner the birds fly back to Nos. 1 and 2.

2nd Beat. The sewin is now removed from between Nos. 2 and 5, and is run out across No. 1 between the points A and B, the guns are placed on the opposite side of the deep dell,

SEWIN IN POSITION.

facing the sewin. The beaters then advance from the further corner and drive the birds over the heads of the guns.

3rd Beat. In this beat the guns are sent forward to a ride between Nos. 2 and 3, in which the sewin has previously been run, C D; and the beaters advance from the west side of No. 2. At this point some skill must be exercised to ensure the birds rising over the guns, as they will be disposed to fly back.

The sewin is now removed from the points A B on No. 1 to points E F between No. 2 and the corner of No. 5, to prepare for the reverse way of shooting.

4th Beat. The guns are stationed in the ride between 3 and 4, opposite to the sewin which was run in the morning between G and H, and the beat is driven from the W. side in the same way as in the 3rd beat.

5th Beat. After luncheon the line of beaters is formed at the east end of No. 4, and the guns take their position between 4 and 3. No. 4 is a rocky piece of rough ground on which the birds do not run, but rise as the beaters advance and fly high over the guns.

6th Beat. Guns go forward to the rise between 2 and 3, and beaters advance from the E. side as in the 5th beat.

7th Beat. Guns now make a *détour* to the right for the corner of No. 5, while the beaters form line at the north end of No. 2 and drive it into No. 5. While the birds are being driven across rides the sewin is removed, and is replaced after they have passed if necessary. The rest of the day may be made out in another cover.

It is scarcely necessary to add that the plan of beating ground backwards and forwards in the manner we have described can only be adopted where game is unusually abundant.

Kite (*artificial*)—Partridge shooting with the kite, which, twenty or thirty years ago, was not uncommonly practised by sportsmen, is now largely a thing of the past. It was chiefly used in dry seasons, when roots and cover in the open were scarce, or when the season was advanced and the birds refused to lie. In both these cases it has since to a great extent been superseded by driving. The artificial kite was made of brown calico, stretched on a wire frame; and although when closely viewed the likeness was very rough, yet in mid air the appearance of a hovering hawk was strikingly realised. In flying the kite, the object was to keep it as steady as possible, and to facilitate this, a cord was fastened to the tail, on which three or more caps of silk, or very light metal, were threaded at intervals: in rough winds more of these caps were needed. Owing to the calico being stretched somewhat loosely over the frame, its outer edges, when the kite was steady, were kept in continual agitation by the air, thus producing the almost perfect illusion of a hovering hawk. The mode of procedure was as follows:—The kite was always worked down wind, about one hundred yards in front of the guns, and from one hundred to one hundred and fifty yards above the ground: if flown lower it was apt to cause the birds to rise before the guns got near. When two guns only were out, each one took a side of the hedge. The keeper and his retriever went with one gun, while a beater went with the other. The man who was flying the kite kept at some distance from the guns: the object being to drive the birds from the open ground into the hedgerows. If four guns were out, two hedges were worked at once. The flight of a partridge before a kite is quite different to its ordinary flight; the bird never rises far above the ground, and a whole covey will often break up and dart away in different directions. Moreover, when the sportsman sees a covey betake itself to a hedgerow and flatters himself they are within his grasp, he sometimes finds on beating the hedge that he does not obtain a single shot. This generally happens when there is cover like long grass on the other side. In such cases the scared birds, no longer seeing the kite, run like Frenchmen (red legs), and are seen no

Shooting under a Kite.

more. The kite is better adapted to large manors than to small ones; but it may be used without detriment on the latter, provided there are plenty of hedgerows, or young plantations, for the birds to fly into. It is worse than useless to attempt kite flying in a wide, open country without hedgerows, gorse, or cover of some sort; for at the very first sight of the kite the birds will scatter in all directions, skimming or shooting in a long-sustained low flight, which will possibly carry them right away for the day.

A kite should never be used after the birds have paired, which in average seasons may be taken as January 10th. To use a kite after that date would be to run the risk of driving your birds on to an adjoining manor. Where partridges are found pairing, there or thereabouts they generally make their nests. So to drive them from such spots is not only impolitic, but somewhat cruel.

On the whole we cannot regard it as altogether unfortunate for sport that the art of kite-flying has practically been allowed to lapse. For whatever may be said in its favour, one thing is certain, that unless the practice is very sparingly resorted to, it must tend to frighten the birds away.

We have heard of recent experiments to prevent pheasants from straying, by flying kites on the outside of an estate. But what degree of success has attended these efforts we are not prepared to state.

Game Carts—The description of game cart required will depend on the nature of the bag. For partridge shooting, or for small days, a light, two-wheeled vehicle is all that will be necessary; but in covert shooting, where hares and rabbits, besides a large head of pheasants, are killed, a heavier cart is needed. A good light cart on two wheels is constructed as follows:—The cart consists of a moveable tilt fixed on a panelled body, 18 ins. high. The back of the cart is entirely closed in, so that all game must be put in from the front. The tilt is made of stiff waterproof canvas, stretched over a wooden framework. The body, which rests on iron springs, must be strong, as also the frame of the tilt, otherwise they will not bear the weight when loaded. About 18 ins. from the top of the tilt a moveable shelf, of the same width as the cart and about 3 ft. long, is fitted at the back end of the cart. This takes coats, waterproofs, &c. The front of the tilt should be hood-shaped, projecting well over the seat; and good stiff canvas curtains, suspended from the roof and made to draw across the front, will be found very useful in wet weather. A circular opening at the back of the tilt should be left for ventilation. The driver's seat should have a slight incline outwards, so as to throw off water, and the space underneath is appropriated to cartridge bags, magazines, &c. Six bars of wood fitting into slots run transversely from side to side of the tilt. These carry screw hooks, upon which the birds are suspended. Ground game is usually put in the bed of the cart. About 180 pheasants and 200 rabbits can be carried in a cart of this description.

We are indebted to a neighbour, an experienced sportsman, for the following details of his game wagon. It was built at Bristol on the lines of a light parcel van; weight, 8½ cwt. Its dimensions are as follows: length, 9 ft. 6 ins., width, 4 ft. 6 ins., height of tilt, 5 ft. The tilt is made of white canvas on a strong frame. The colour makes it conspicuous in cover. The frame must be much stronger than usual, or the weight of game will soon break it down. The game is carried on hooks, which are hung on iron rods made from ⅝ in. gas piping. The hooks can be cut out of sheet iron and bent up at the ends. The shorter the centre hook is the better. The rods are kept in the bottom of the cart and put up as required. They are supported in the frame of the cover by a hole at one side and a slot at the other. Neither slot nor hole must go through the wood, or the rod will work through the canvas and thereby let in the rain. By hanging game in this way, a van of the dimensions stated will easily hold 1,000 pheasants, and still leave the bottom free for cartridges, magazines, &c. In the front of the van there are some strong hooks to take macintoshes and cartridge bags. The tilt is enclosed both back and front by curtains, fastened with straps and buckles. Above the ordinary tailboard there is a light board about 18 ins. wide, which is fastened on from the inside, and prevents any one from taking out the game on a dark night. The van is large enough to seat eight persons at luncheon, and a table is formed by placing the supplementary tailboard across two or more of the rods. The table runs lengthways down the centre of the van; three people sit on either side and one at each end. The side seats, which are permanently fixed, are formed by a narrow ledge placed just at the set off of the tilt. In very rough weather this arrangement affords considerable convenience in the absence of a tent or other shelter. The game removed from the inside may be placed under the van.

We may add that although in both the above instances coats, cartridges, &c., have places planned for them in the cart, yet in our opinion it is much better to carry them in a separate vehicle. We know of no better conveyance for these articles in the case of a large party than one of her Majesty's discarded mail carts, which has been fitted up for the purpose.

Clothing—We know of no greater practical discomfort attending sport than that which arises from wet clothes. In our variable climate sport often has to be pursued, day after day, under heavy rain, and the necessity of drying the garments of six or eight guns frequently is found to overtax the resources of a large establishment. Under these circumstances the sportsman may consider himself lucky who finds in the morning his boots, coat, overcoat, &c., even in a half-dried condition. Cartridge bags and gun covers often have no attention at all. Yet it is by no means difficult to make arrangements by which perfect efficiency in drying any reasonable amount of clothes may be secured in a very simple manner and at a small outlay. The task of drying clothes should not be thrown on the kitchen, servants'-hall, or pantry fire. If, however, it cannot be avoided, one of two evils must follow: either a man must be kept up nearly all night to maintain the fire and turn the clothes, or else the wearers must be content with imperfectly dried clothes. We have known the difficulty satisfactorily met by appropriating a spare room in the basement, or an outhouse, for the purposes of a drying-room. All that is actually required is that the room should be kept perfectly clean and free from all furniture, except one slow-combustion stove placed in the centre. The size of the stove must of course be adapted to the size of the room. The room must be also well ventilated, or the steam will not escape. The chimney pipe, which should be of iron to radiate the heat, should be carried across the room and up one of the walls inside, passing thence into the outer air. Cords or wires should be stretched tight across the room, upon which the clothes may be hung with pegs, as in a laundry. We have seen in a drying-room tailors' wire dummies, which not only facilitated the drying of the clothes, but kept them in form. With a contrivance of this sort it is quite possible thoroughly to dry the clothes of a large party, between six and nine in the evening, if a proper temperature be maintained.

Boots—To young sportsmen the question of dry boots may appear of little moment, but few who have attained the age of forty will despise any expedient which promises to secure to them the comfort of dry socks after walking through wet turnips or other marshy ground. Most of the old-fashioned receipts for waterproofing boots can be relied upon as effectual, but they generally include beeswax in their composition, the use of which renders the leather hard and uncomfortable to the wearer. Modern receipts are not always so trustworthy, and some of them produce a compound which is not only nasty to handle, but ineffectual to keep out water. For some years we have adopted with complete success the method of treatment advocated below, and have experienced the comfort of dry feet even when the conditions were most adverse. New shooting boots must on no account be blacked, as, if once blacked, it is more difficult to render them waterproof. The laces should first be removed, and a coat of dubbing (Prout's, we use) be applied all over with a brush. The boots should then be placed in a warm cupboard to dry; the process should be repeated three or four times till the leather is well saturated. If they are not required for some time, the boots should be brushed once again with dubbing before they are worn. After a muddy walk they must be washed thoroughly clean, treed, dried, and dubbed. Boots that have been thoroughly wetted should be dressed with bootmaker's dye, as the leather may be bleached. In every case, remove the laces before applying the dubbing. When boots are very wet they dry quicker if only skeleton trees are put in overnight; they can be treed up with block trees in the morning. On no account let them stand too near the fire. Treated in this manner, boots made with good leather become practically waterproof.

CHARLES C. TUDWAY,
JOHN FREDERICK HALL.

TRAINING SETTERS AND POINTERS FOR GROUSE SHOOTING—Setters and pointers are at the present day almost exclusively used for grouse shooting. The object aimed at in training these dogs is to teach them to gallop or range in any direction the trainer wishes, and to stand the moment they wind birds, so that the shooter may get within shot of the birds before they rise.

The keeper or feeder in whose charge the dogs continually are, and who is best known to them, has naturally the best opportunities of training them; but it is quite possible for the owner, if he can spare two or three hours daily for six weeks prior to the commencement of grouse shooting, to train two or three young dogs each year, and subsequently to work and shoot over them himself.

Dogs will always work better for the trainer than for any one else, but well-trained dogs can be trusted after their second season to work for any competent person who has had charge of them for at least a month before shooting begins.

It is a mistake to suppose that pointers and setters find their game by instinct and require little regular training. The only permanent quality on which a dog's education can be based is habit. Setters and pointers have a primary and a secondary habit. Their primary, and by far their stronger habit, inherited from their wild ancestors, is to chase their game; their secondary and very much weaker habit is to pause an instant before seizing their quarry.

In order to make a young dog of any use for grouse shooting, the trainer must entirely repress the strong primary habit and greatly develop the weaker secondary one.

From six to twelve months is the best age, and spring or summer the best time at which to begin a young dog's education. That is to say, assuming that a puppy is littered in April or May, in October or November it may be taken into the kennel and taught Lessons 1 and 2 specified below. Lesson 3 cannot be satisfactorily taught in winter, when the ground is wet and cold, and it is advisable to wait to teach that and the remaining lessons till the dog is ten or twelve months old. If the first four lessons can be perfectly learnt by the dog before the nesting season for grouse begins, it may be taken on to the moor in early spring to be taught Lesson 5, but probably July will be found soon enough for this purpose: there are then far more birds for the dog to find, and as they fly shorter distances there is less risk of disturbing the moor.

In training a young dog, a "masterly inactivity" is the

best policy: the art lies, not in doing, but in abstaining from doing, much.

The system of training may be divided into five lessons, viz. to teach a young dog

1. To keep to heel till told to go.
2. To come to heel when called by whistle.
3. To lie down when the trainer holds up his hand.
4. To gallop in the direction which the trainer indicates.
5. To stand the moment it winds birds, and to remain standing till the signal to advance is given, or failing that for at least five minutes.

These lessons should be taught in the order named, and no new lesson should be begun until the preceding one has been mastered, so as to avoid confusing the dog. The first three lessons are the most important, and the most frequently neglected. They should be taught entirely on a road, fenced if possible, or in a field free from game, the fourth lesson in a field free from game, and the fifth on the moor. A young dog should never see game until it is perfectly under control, or it may be spoiled.

SETTER AFTER PARTRIDGES. No. 1.

In about a month, at two or three hours' work daily, the first three lessons should be taught perfectly, and about a week is required for each of the two remaining lessons, or about six weeks in all.

If a young dog is properly taught the above mentioned five lessons, the shooter can walk in a leisurely manner up to his dog when it stands at birds, instead of having to tear and tumble over peat hags or rocks for fear the brute should put up the birds.

First Lesson—As soon as a puppy has been taught its name, and is old enough (say six months) to be put into the kennel with the other dogs, it should be taken out to exercise with them on the road, coupled to an old and steady dog, and should be walked about for not less than an hour early in the morning, and an hour in the evening before feeding. In a few days, the couples may be taken off the young dog a short time after leaving the kennel, and put on again before returning home. It is assumed, of course, that the old dogs are all under control, and are not exercised in couples; nothing is more injurious to the health of a dog than coupling it constantly to another dog.

As soon as the young dog follows him well without the couples, the trainer should take some biscuit in his pocket and throw some occasionally to his dogs at exercise, at the same time giving a shrill whistle; he should also make a good deal of fuss about his young dog and call it by name; dogs are just as fond of admiration as men.

Second Lesson—Viz.—to teach a dog to come to heel when called by whistle. When No. 1 lesson has been perfectly learned, the trainer may, when going away from home, with a wave of his arm sign to the dogs that they may gallop in front; he should at the same time give a low whistle. The object of this is that the dogs may be worked on the moor without a word being spoken, as nothing makes grouse wilder than the sound of the human voice. When the dogs have galloped about for a short time (always on an inclosed road, be it remembered, so that they cannot get away), the trainer should give a shrill whistle, as a signal to the dogs to return to him; at the same time he should turn round and walk away from the dogs. Dogs are not such fools as to come to a man when they see that he is coming to them. Then let him give each dog as it arrives a bit of biscuit, the last equally with the first, and let him whistle shrilly as he does so; but let the same note be always used in whistling. Dogs have a very good ear for music and take very little notice of a whistle on a strange note. It is better at first to let the dogs gallop when going away from home, otherwise a young one might be inclined, if shy or wild, to go straight off to the kennel.

The trainer may carry a whip to help to keep his dogs in to heel, but he must never do more than crack it, and must positively never beat a young dog, for any fault whatever. It is not the fault of the dog if it does wrong, but the fault of the trainer, because he has taught it so badly. It is the trainer, not the dog, who should be beaten. Who ever heard of a huntsman beating his hounds? And yet it is not uncommon for a man to whistle to his shooting dog, which comes not until it thinks proper, that is to say, after a considerable interval. When it arrives the dog is beaten, a small inducement to it to come the next time, surely! How ludicrously, how brutally absurd! Dogs should be trained by kindness and force of will alone, like children.

Third Lesson—To teach the young dog to lie down when the trainer holds up his hand. He should continue to take all his dogs out every day together for an hour and go through the first two lessons, always remembering that no dog must ever leave his heel without permission. Then let him put his dogs back into kennel, and take out one young and one steady old dog; let him make the old dog lie down and force the young dog to lie down also, holding it down with one hand and holding up the other hand; then let him reward the dogs with a bit of biscuit, and continue his walk, repeating the performance at intervals, but not often enough to bore the dog. In a day or two the young dog will lie down when the trainer holds up his hand. Let the trainer then begin retreating a few steps from the young dog, holding up his hand and cracking his whip if the dog moves, and, if necessary, let him take the dog back to its original place. Let the trainer always go back to the dog before he lets it get up, otherwise it can never be got to lie perfectly steady, and then let him reward it with biscuit as before. Every day the trainer should retreat farther and farther from the dog, and in time it can be taught to lie down at any distance at which the trainer is visible to it; then let the trainer walk out of the dog's sight while it is lying down, and teach it to remain down until he returns to it. As soon as the young dog is fairly proficient in this lesson the trainer should take it out alone. This lesson is the most difficult to teach thoroughly; it is the most important, as, if perfectly learned, the dog's steadiness is ensured. It would be advisable during this period to have three or four shots fired, say every other evening, close to the kennels, after the dogs have been fed; not before, in case those that are nervous might refuse their food. If the trainer is an amateur, he may, if he likes, assist at the feeding of his dogs, but it is not necessary. Dogs will always go with the trainer in preference to the feeder. They prefer their sport to their food.

Fourth Lesson—Is to teach a dog to gallop in the direction which the trainer indicates. This must be taught in a large grass field, absolutely free from game. Let the trainer take out one young dog and one old one and start them off with a wave of his hand in the direction in which he is walking, at the same time giving his low whistle. When the dogs have nearly reached the other side of the field, let the trainer turn at right angles to his original course; the dogs, if he has been kind to them, will be on the look-out, and will turn too. When they do so, but not before, let him wave his hand in the new direction, at the same time whistling his low note: let the trainer turn again at right angles to his second course, and so on, making a zigzag right down the field. The effect of this will be as in the diagram. Let A B C D be the field, let the straight lines E to F represent the trainer's course, and the curved line G to H the dog's course. If the trainer finds that the young dog ranges too far in front and misses ground, he has only to turn at an acute, instead of at a right angle, or, if it does not range far enough, to turn at an obtuse angle. The dog will always lean to him. By these means the trainer will make the young dog think that it is coming in the direction towards which he waves his hand, whereas it is in effect just the reverse; but if he keeps up the delusion, in time the dog will from force of habit really work in the direction which he indicates. After a few days the young dog should go through this lesson by itself. After the dogs have galloped about a bit, the trainer may then go through lessons 1, 2 and 3. It is to be observed that dogs are much more easily taught when they are a little tired than when fresh out of the kennel; it is never advisable to give a dog an order just at first, when his spirits are high.

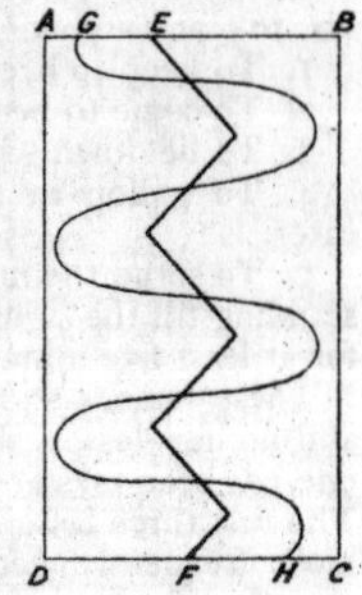

No. 2.

After a few days of this work, let a man accompany the trainer and dog into the field with a gun, and let him fire two or three shots every day, at first some distance from the dog and afterwards near it; when he fires, the trainer should make the dog lie down, and from habit the young dog will in time do so at the sound of the gun—a very necessary practice, and one which prevents a dog from moving about and putting up birds while the shooter is loading.

It is advisable for the amateur trainer to tell his kennel-man never to take the dogs anywhere except on the road for exercise, and to keep them always in to heel; the kennel-man should on no account try to do any training, or the dogs will be ruined; more than one cook will be sure to spoil this kind of broth.

Fifth Lesson—After the first four lessons of the young setter's education have been satisfactorily accomplished, the trainer can then proceed to the fifth lesson, and take the young dog with one old one out on the hill in search of grouse, but he must not carry a gun. In the south and east of Scotland, probably, July 20 will be early enough for this purpose, and August 1 in the north and west; before these dates young grouse lie so close that a young dog is apt to snap them up.

The trainer may work one young dog and one old one together for an hour or two on the hill every day: a gillie can follow the trainer at 300 or 400 yards distance, keeping as much out of sight as possible, and leading those dogs not being actually worked.

In August, the time of day when dogs most easily find grouse is before 11 A.M. or after 4 P.M.; in the middle of the day, birds are very apt to lie perfectly still and to give out little or no scent. If there is a steady breeze in the morning, it is better to work the young dogs then, as the wind is apt to drop in the evening. In any case, a young dog should not be taken out when there is no breeze; if so it will probably put up birds through no fault of its own, and this will make it unsteady. The best dogs will put up birds when there is no scent, when they are going down wind, or when their noses are not sensitive, owing to bad kennel management.

The non-attention of the trainer to this is one of the principal causes of unsteadiness in dogs. No one should allow his dogs, old or young, to draw on the scent of birds when the latter are running, unless the trainer is close by and gives the dog orders to go on. A dog should stand instantly on winding game, and never move until the trainer gets up to it. The trainer may, after the young dog has been kept lying down for five minutes, allow the old dog to draw on until the birds get up, the trainer leading the young dog on behind: immediately the birds rise the dogs should lie down, and not get up till told to do so.

Some people use a check cord on a young dog, but it is not of much use, and is apt to make a dog shy, and tires it. If the dog wears a collar, it can be easily led with the whip when going up to birds. If all goes well, and the young dog does not try to chase, in a couple of days, when there are plenty of birds, it may be taken out alone and allowed to find birds for itself; all that the trainer need do in addition to the above rules is to hold up his hand to make the dog lie down the moment it winds birds. As soon as the dog stands steadily when it winds birds and does not offer to draw on, the trainer need not make it lie down, but should do so directly the dog moves without orders. All does not, however, by any means, always go well! Very probably the moment the old dog stands, the young one will dash past him, run right into the birds, and chase them frantically all over the place. Here is the dog's primary habit asserting itself.

No. 3.

It is better not to take a young dog on a very windy day out on the moor when scent is catchy and birds are wild. Let the trainer be very particular to keep his dogs in to heel until he gives them the signal to go. Let him choose as flat ground as possible, so that the dogs may not get out of his sight, and work up wind to give the dogs the best possible chance of winding birds, making a zigzag course (as in Lesson 4) and across the line of direction of the wind.

When the young dog turns, but not before, the trainer should wave his arm and also walk in the fresh direction in which he wishes the dog to go, and it will then get into the habit of working in the direction which he indicates, and (another delusion of the dog's) it will imagine that it has changed its course in consequence of an order to that effect.

When the old dog stands at birds, the trainer should hold up his hand and try to get the young dog (which is probably galloping about after the old one) to lie down; if successful he may then move the young dog, so that it may get the wind of the birds, and keep it lying down for five minutes. This is very important, as the whole satisfaction of shooting over dogs is to be perfectly sure that the dog will remain steady to birds till the shooter gets up to it.

In this case the trainer wants to get the young dog back to him as soon as possible. Now is the time for him to pursue a masterly inactivity. He must not whistle on any account. The young dog's primary habit of chasing has asserted itself vigorously, and will quite overmaster its acquired habit of coming to heel when it hears the whistle. If the trainer whistles the dog will not come to heel, the spell will be broken, the delusion will be dispelled, the dog will discover that it is not obliged to come when it hears the whistle, and in future will do as it pleases and not as the trainer likes. Some people seem to believe that they can compel a dog to come by whistling, whereas all they can do is to delude it into thinking that it must come. Whistling will not *make* a dog come any more than pulling at a horse's bridle will *make* him stop. The animal can only be deluded into thinking so. "There's nothing is, but thinking makes it so."

In this connection it should be observed that an order should never be given to a dog, or, in fact, to a man, woman, or child, unless there is a reasonable probability that it can be enforced. No, when the dog bolts let the trainer lock up his patience and sit down. Nothing excites a dog's curiosity so much as to see its master sitting down.

The young dog may be allowed to rampage to its heart's content; it will soon get tired of doing what it is not forbidden to do, like the new shopboy at the pastry cook's, and will begin to return to the trainer. Then is the trainer's opportunity, up he gets and begins to whistle, walking away from the dog; dog comes and thinks that it does so because man whistles, whereas it is *vice versâ*, man whistles because dog comes; but the delusion is kept up.

When the dog arrives what must be done to him? Is he to be beaten? Most emphatically, no. The trainer's object is to get the dog to come quicker next time; he therefore rewards it with biscuit. Then he

described when the dog chases grouse. If no hares are killed over the young dog, it will soon give up standing at or chasing them—just as a well-trained retriever is taught to take no notice of ground game. It is worth remarking that, unless dogs are encouraged to stand at any particular kind of game, they will take no notice of it. When a dog is trained to stand at grouse it will very likely take no notice of partridges and *vice versâ*, for a day or two.

Young dogs should not be encouraged to stand at snipe, or they may begin standing at larks, the scent of which seems to resemble that of snipe

If a young dog is slow and potters, it is best to work it for the first season with another dog to excite it, and for the trainer to walk faster over his ground, and encourage the dog with his voice. There is no use in the puzzle peg or any mechanical contrivance. If a dog potters, it is probably because it has a bad nose, and possibly also because its make and shape are not good, or it has bad shoulders, or its head and neck are not put on right. The best medicine for a confirmed potterer is an ounce of lead. Usually those turn out the best dogs

No. 4.

proceeds as before. If the dog is very wild, it will be necessary to let it gallop till it is tired; then it will be only too glad to do what it is told. Occasionally dogs develop a habit, when they find birds out of sight of the trainer, of coming back to tell him so. This is not to be encouraged, but it cannot be prevented.

If a young dog puts up birds, the trainer should, by holding up his hand, make it lie down if possible—that is, when it is under control and not excited—and this practice should be kept up in old dogs; it makes them careful, and besides, even if one bird gets up, more may be left, and if the dog moves about it may put these up also before the shooter can arrive. If a young dog is wild, the sooner it is taken out by itself the better—that is, as soon as it has shown any disposition to find birds for itself; the presence of another dog is sure to make it wilder.

Probably some hares will be seen when grouse shooting. It is better to educate dogs to take no notice of ground game, which is all very well in its proper place, but is a nuisance on the moor; therefore if a young dog stands at a hare, the best plan is to take the dog away and to work it in another direction. If the dog chases a hare, the trainer should behave in precisely the same way as before

which begin by being the wildest; exuberance of spirits can easily be repressed, but it is difficult to inspire enthusiasm into a sluggard.

A young dog may be taken in hand by its trainer as late as July 1, and, if the above lessons are well learned, it may be shot over on August 12. When he takes his young dog out grouse shooting, the trainer must judge for himself whether to work it singly or with another dog, according to the temperament of the animal, and according to whether he will require the dog to work singly or as one of a brace. Only one gun should go out, and that a man who cares more for the dog's future than for the size of the bag, in other words the owner or trainer. At first two or three brace of grouse only should be killed over the dog, for fear of making it gun shy, when it should be given back to the gillie and another dog taken on. Each time the dog stands at birds, the whole performance of keeping the dog standing for five minutes, &c., should be gone through, and after a time gradually relaxed, according to the steadiness of the dog. It is not advisable to work a dog down wind its first season, its second year is time enough for that, but all dogs should do so after their first season; it is most useful. To learn this, the second season dog may be taken out once or twice with an old one that knows the business. If the dog is fond of its master, he will have no difficulty in making it work where he wishes, as the dog will lean to the direction in which it sees him going.

If the trainer wishes to make a practice of working two dogs at the same time, all that he need do, in addition to the foregoing, is first to make one dog lie down directly the other stands at birds, and they will soon learn to "back" each other without orders. Secondly, the trainer must get the two dogs to work in opposite directions, and to cross and recross each other. It is very pretty to see two dogs working in this way, but it is doubtful if more birds are killed over two dogs than over one, and the dogs are apt to get nearer their birds than if worked singly. The kennel expenses are also doubled.

To sum up, let the trainer teach the lessons above set out, one at a time. Let him make the dog fond of him. Let him give no order unless he thinks he can get it executed; having given it, let him enforce it; and, finally, let him religiously observe the great law, that corporal punishment, "is, and remains, abolished."

W. E. Lawson.

(The Editors have to express their sincere thanks to Mr. H. J. C. Anderson, of Great Crosby, for the photographs illustrating this article.)

After Curlew.

SHORE SHOOTING—By this term is intended the pursuit of the various species of plovers and sandpipers which frequent the mouths of rivers, seashores, tidal harbours and marshes by the sea, and which, by reason of their exposed haunts, extreme wariness and rapid flight, test the crafty powers of the fowler, his judgment and strength in stalking or punting, and his skill in shooting.

Many who delight in a long day's partridge shooting, grouse driving, or a big day at pheasants, are apt to refer contemptuously to what they term "shore-popping." They "do not see the fun," as they express it, "of going about up to one's knees in mud, or lying in a wet punt all day; getting aground, perhaps, on a sandbank, and having to wait an hour or two for the tide in order to be floated off."

Perhaps they have never tried it, or have never been very successful in their attempts. The style of shooting is so different from that to which they have been accustomed that there are more "misses" than "hits," or, if they lack no skill in shooting, they are unable to exercise it for want of a knowledge of the habits of the birds, and the requisite skill to approach them.

To be a successful shore shooter, one must take that real delight in the sport which will incur the necessity of early rising, with energy and indefatigable exertion, and must be sufficiently observant of tides and wind to judge where birds are most likely to be found at any given hour in any given weather.

There are several ways of getting to birds. You may punt down the harbour at low water, and shoot them on the "muds," you may stalk them at high tide under cover of a sea-wall or bank of shingle, or you may "lie up" in their line of flight just before high water, and shoot them as they leave the harbour for the beach or marshes.

The last-named plan answers admirably if you happen to select the right spot, and as soon as the last "mud" is nearly covered, and the birds begin to move, some good shooting may be the result if the gun be only held straight.

As good a plan as any is to walk round a tidal harbour, starting about an hour before high tide, keeping, when necessary, under cover of the sea wall. The advancing tide will bring the birds nearer to the shooter every minute; whereas if he goes forth on an ebb tide, every minute will see the birds farther away from him.

As the tide advances, and the area of the feeding ground becomes gradually narrowed, the highest mud flats are broken up into little islands, on which the birds congregate and remain until the water reaches them and becomes too deep for them to stand in. They then betake themselves to the sea-beach or the adjacent marshes; the dunlins and ringed plovers going to the former, and the redshanks and curlews to the latter resort; while the golden plovers and peewits congregate on the fallows or wide open pastures, where they usually contrive to keep as far as possible from fences which might serve to screen the approach of a gunner.

At high tide a few hours may be enjoyably spent in tramping about the salt marshes and visiting the sides of the great drains or "rifes" which, intersecting the marsh, mark the boundaries of the different holdings, and serve instead of fences to restrain the cattle which graze there.

In these drains at such times one may count upon finding the common sandpiper, redshank, greenshank, green and wood sandpipers, to say nothing of snipe, and occasionally Temmincks' stint, and the grey phalarope. These birds are often solitary, and though occasionally two or three may be found together, they are never so gregarious as, for example, are plovers, knots, curlews, whimbrel, or godwits, which must be looked for in very different situations.

It is a good plan, when visiting these drains, not to walk close alongside and parallel with the water; in a straight piece, should there be a bird ahead, it will instantly perceive your approach and rise out of shot. It should then be marked down and stalked in the open, by walking directly on to it, and looking quickly right and left for it to rise. It should be noted that a sandpiper of any kind, which has been flushed and marked down, is not to be sought for exactly at the point where it disappeared below the level of the drain, but some yards further on; and, should the bank be steep there, with little or no margin by the water's edge to offer foothold, the bird may go a long way under cover of the bank beyond the point where sight was lost of it before alighting. In the same way, therefore, that a huntsman has sometimes to recover the line of a fox where hounds are at fault, the shore shooter must be prepared to make a "cast" amongst the marsh drains ere he will get within shot of his fleet-winged quarry.

Dog for Shore Shooting—For this kind of sport a dog is indispensable so long as the shooter is ashore; not so much to find the birds, as to fetch them when shot, for they will frequently fall in deep water, or among reeds, or on the opposite side of a wide drain, and without a dog much time will be wasted in making a long *détour*, or in fruitless efforts to reach them.

As to the best kind of dog for the purpose, opinions no doubt will differ. So long, however, as he can retrieve, the chief points to be attended to are size and colour. Unless he can be trusted to lie down and keep quiet while his owner is stalking, and to come to him only at a whistle, he should be neither large nor light-coloured, otherwise the birds will see him at a great distance and never suffer an approach. For choice, there is nothing better than a liver-coloured Sussex spaniel, or an Irish water spaniel. The writer has used both, as also a retrieving Irish setter, but the last, though invaluable in a snipe bog, was, from his size and colour, too conspicuous for shore shooting. In a punt, a dog is not only unnecessary, but, if allowed to jump out and retrieve birds from a mud-bank (to save his master the trouble of putting on mud-pattens), he may become a positive nuisance by making the punt and everything in it as dirty as possible on his return, drenching his owner with vigorous shakes of his coat, and either whining with cold while moving restlessly about in his endeavours to get dry, or lying down generally where he is not wanted. From a purely selfish point of view, a wet dog in a punt is a most uncomfortable companion, while, on the score of humanity, no man who is fond of his dog should keep him shivering with cold and wet in a position where he has no chance of getting dry.

Shooting from Blinds and Pits—Should the shore gunner be in the habit of making repeated visits to the same shooting quarters and finding birds sufficiently numerous to warrant a prolonged stay in the neighbourhood, he will, if sufficiently observant, sooner or later discover their favourite haunts, notice where they go at high water, and mark the spots which are first laid bare at ebb tide—for to these they will regularly resort.

A judiciously placed hurdle, or ambush constructed of seaweed and big stones, within shot of such points, will sometimes enable the gunner to screen his approach until near enough to get a shot or two. Some professional fowlers are in the habit of digging pits in the line of flight when they have discovered it, and remaining therein

Shore Birds

for an hour or two, on the chance of intercepting the passing birds. This plan is sometimes pretty successful, but the necessity for remaining so long in a cramped position renders it distasteful to those who prefer a more active campaign.

Some experts indeed regard such devices as unsportsmanlike. Folkard, for example, in his excellent book, *The Wild Fowler*, remarks:—

"There are various other tricks and means resorted to for getting within range of the wary curlew, some of which are beneath the dignity of a sportsman, such as digging holes in open marshes, burying casks on the beach, and lying in ambush in those unenviable positions, thus taking the birds by surprise. Such proceedings," he adds, "may answer once or twice, but curlews soon forsake a place of resort when so assailed."

The plan recommended by Colonel Hawker as to making an artificial island by means of a few boatloads of rubbish is far better. Curlews always remain on the highest ground, nor do they leave it until the tide reaches their legs, so that by proceeding in a punt and using great caution, a good shot may sometimes be made. A variation of this plan is to lie in ambush on the island and shoot the birds as they approach it, recovering those dropped in the water by means of the punt.

Punters have usually a great antipathy to shore gunners, who often spoil their best sport, for just as they are approaching fowl, and almost within range, the report of a shoulder gun on the shore puts up the birds and spoils the shot. Shore shooters, on the other hand, have a similar dislike to the sound of a punt gun, although if they happen to be to leeward of the fowl shot at, they may sometimes profit by the occasion and get several shots at birds which, alarmed at the report, come scurrying down wind in their direction.

The fact is that in this pursuit, as in every other kind of sport, there must be a certain amount of toleration. No sportsman worthy of the name would intentionally spoil another's sport, and a shore shooter, on perceiving a puntsman "setting" or "sculling" to fowl which he himself cannot possibly reach, should be chivalrous enough not to fire until the other has had his shot. His virtue will not unlikely be rewarded; for by watching through his glasses the movements of the punter, and noting the direction taken by the shore birds which he disturbs and does not fire at, when after duck or wigeon, the long-shore gunner may get many a chance at birds which would otherwise go away unnoticed by him.

Grey Plovers and Peewits.

Calling Birds—One of the most useful accomplishments of a shore shooter is to be able to imitate the notes of such birds as plover, curlew, whimbrel, knot and redshank, so as to entice them within shot, and to acquire this needs some practice. The plan is for the shooter to listen to one of these birds calling, and "to tune his merry note unto the wild bird's throat." If he has an ear for music he will at once get the right pitch, and a little practice will enable him to deceive even the wary curlew. Young birds are more easily decoyed in this way than old, and single birds which have wandered from their companions will come to a whistle, when a flock will pass on unheeding it.

Should the flock, however, be composed of a lot of young birds, as is frequently the case in August and September, particularly with knots and godwits, which are more gregarious than redshanks and greenshanks, an imitation of the call note will bring them within shot; and, should several be dropped at the first discharge, if they are left for a time on the ground, or in the water, the remainder of the flock will wheel round and pass close to them, giving another chance to the expectant gunner.

Guns—The choice of a gun for shore shooting, on any given occasion, will depend upon whether the shooter is going to walk about all day in the salt marsh or along shore, whether he is going to lie behind a sea-wall, or spend half his time in a punt. In the former case, he will find a good stout 12-bore, weighing about 7¼ lbs., sufficiently useful for his purpose, and not too heavy to carry all day; in the latter case, if he is accustomed to the use of a heavy shoulder gun, he may have an 8-bore or a 10-bore behind the sea-wall, or a 4-bore in the punt as well as a 12-bore, using the heavier weapon for a big shot at curlews, godwits or plover, and the lighter one for single shots at birds passing within moderate range. Nothing is more disappointing at first use of a heavy shoulder gun than the frequent misses which occur from slowness of swing. For want of practice the heavy gun is not brought up quickly enough, aligned quickly enough, nor swung sufficiently ahead of the passing bird; the result is that the bulk of the charge passes behind it, and unless a pellet or two should happen to strike it in the right place, the bird gets away and is soon lost to sight.

Many persons seem to be under the impression that for shore shooting a heavy gun is indispensable, but this is really not the case. With an ordinary 12-bore, weighing 7¼ lbs., the present writer has killed curlew, whimbrel, godwits, redshanks, greenshanks, golden and grey plover, peewits, knots, and all the smaller sandpipers which are commonly to be found about

KNOTS.

the mouths of rivers and tidal harbours at low water, or in the salt marshes adjacent to the sea, besides ducks of various kinds at flight time, once a brent goose (one of three that came in shore), and on another occasion two wild swans. The fact is that with ordinary care in stalking, or with luck in getting near the birds (for one sometimes drops upon them unexpectedly within range) there is no reason why a properly loaded 12-bore should not effectually stop any shore bird that one is likely to come across.

Loads—There is perhaps no question upon which opinions differ so much as upon the proper charges for guns. Experience has proved that most guns will shoot better with one size of shot than with another, and the best load for a particular gun should be carefully ascertained by experiment. When once discovered, it should never be varied if sport be the only object. But when the shore shooter is also a collector, and is desirous of securing good specimens of particular species, the charge used must be accommodated to circumstances. No one would think of shooting a little stint with No. 5, or of firing at a strong flying curlew with snipe shot. The use of breech-loaders nowadays, amongst all but professional fowlers in remote fishing villages, makes it so easy to substitute one cartridge for another in case of need, that it is unnecessary to dilate upon this subject further. (See the article GUNS, section "Wild-fowl Guns," vol. i., p. 499.)

Care of Guns—To keep rust from guns used on or near the sea, there is nothing so good as vaseline applied with a soft toothbrush. If caught in the rain or drenched with spray from a boat, the wet should not be wiped off unless it is thoroughly done, and more vaseline applied when the barrels are dry. On getting home, the barrels should be taken off and every drop of wet should be wiped off; stock, barrels, and fore-end should all be well rubbed with a vaseline rag, and not put together again until wanted. The inside of the barrels, after being cleaned out, should be dressed with a mixture of paraffin and spirits of turpentine, half and half, and the next morning well polished with a strip of flannel rolled round the cleaning rod. If the gun is to be used again that day, superfluous vaseline may be wiped off lightly and the remaining film will protect the metal from the day's exposure.

Another recipe to keep rust from guns is to get a bottle of "Newark's Preparation for Guns," which costs a shilling for a 4-oz. bottle, and which, if used with care, will last some time, not only keeping the gun free of rust but also removing any leading that might be inside the barrels and keeping them bright and clean. A wild-fowler who has used this preparation for more than eight years asserts that he has found nothing to equal it for keeping guns in good order and free of rust.

For the stock of a gun a soft rag dipped in a little linseed is the best of all applications.

Shooting Boots—The foot-gear of a shore shooter must depend every day upon the nature of the ground to be visited. For wet, marshy ground there is nothing like a pair of long boots; not such as are made in London, for they are seldom waterproof and very expensive, but such as are made at a seaport like Great Yarmouth by a bootmaker who works for the fishermen, and who knows that if he cannot make his boots water-tight they are of no use and will not sell. They cost from thirty to thirty-five shillings.

After use they should be thoroughly washed in warm water with a brush, then dried with a rough cloth, and, while the leather is still warm from the contact with hot water, they should be well rubbed with vaseline; not lightly smeared over, but thoroughly rubbed in with the hand, the leather being well kneaded and so rendered pliable. The result of such treatment is that the next time they are worn, instead of being hard and galling to the feet, they draw on like a glove, and the shooter, wearing thick woollen stockings, feels comfortable all day. Boots thus treated (whether long boots or lace boots) will last for years, and it is advisable to have two pairs of each in use, so as not to have to wear the same pair two days running. There will then always be time to get them thoroughly dried. A good plan for drying boots is not to put them near the fire, which makes them hard, but to fill them with oats made hot in the oven. By giving the boots a thump or two and manipulating them a little, the oats will settle down and act as a boot-tree, with the additional advantage of absorbing any moisture there may be inside.

If the day is to be spent along the sands or on a shingle beach, long boots obviously would be a mistake, and would be very fatiguing. Over such ground lace boots answer best, with canvas anklets to keep out the shingle.

In a punt, shoes are more convenient, as being easier to put off and on, when one has to slip out on a mud flat or sand bank to pick up shot birds that have fallen beyond reach of the punt, or to shove the punt over land from one creek to another, to save time when birds have shifted their quarters.

Mud-pattens are always useful things to have in a punt in case one has to get out on soft ooze which will not bear one's weight without them. They may be simply made of two pieces of flat board on which the boot is placed, holes being bored on either side of toe and heel to allow of a cord passing through and tying across instep and ankle. Or they may be constructed more elaborately of ½-in. board as in the annexed figure, the centre and cross pieces being 2¼-in. broad, the side pieces somewhat narrower, the patten being adjusted to the boot with cord as in the other plan. The middle cross piece should be cut somewhat shorter on the inside to prevent its striking the ankle of the other foot. In either case a little care is needed to prevent mishap, for unless each foot is put down flat, the mud will at once work over the edge and cause the wearer to trip and perhaps fall, an event too unpleasant in its consequences to be risked.

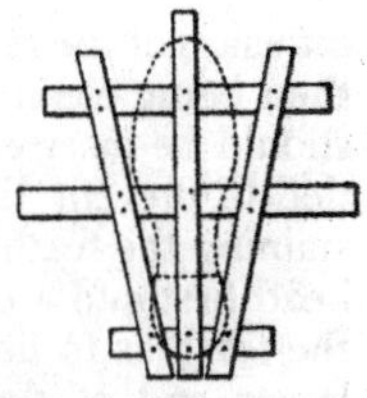

MUD-PATTEN.

Should the shooter hire a punt from a professional fowler, he may be able to borrow a pair of mud-pattens at the same time, and so save himself the trouble of making and carrying his own.

Cleaning Birds and Care of Specimens—If the sportsman be also a collector, or is desirous of taking home specimens with him in as clean a condition as possible for preservation, it is as well to know how to proceed. Too often the birds are thrown together in a heap at the bottom of a punt, or are carried about all day in a capacious pocket, or game bag, or tied by the necks and thrown down anywhere when the next chance of a shot presents itself, no one of which plans is to be commended.

If a bird, when shot, has fallen in the water, or on dry sand or shingle, well and good; but it will often happen with shore birds that they drop on soft ooze, where, if only winged, they will run and flutter and get considerably soiled with mud. This must be washed off sooner or later if the specimen be intended for preservation, and it is as well to do it as soon as possible before the mud or the blood has time to dry and stain.

When obliged to wash a bird, the collector will find it an advantage to use salt and water, instead of plain water, for the salt prevents the solution of the blood globules, and consequent

BAR-TAILED GODWIT.

diffusion of the red hæmaglobin. The specimen then being clean and dry, a plug of cotton wool should be inserted in the mouth, and the beak tied to prevent the saliva from oozing out and staining the feathers. The bird is then dropped head first into a cone of paper, which causes all the feathers to lie in the right direction, and the larger end of the cone being turned over, the specimen is kept clean and in good order until the time comes for skinning it.

This method of treatment gives very little trouble, and will make all the difference in the appearance of a bird if it is intended to be preserved and mounted.

J. E. HARTING.

RIFLES FOR FOREIGN SHOOTING—The modern rifle is still in process of evolution, and the task of writing upon rifles and rifle shooting is, therefore, in the very nature of things, always a difficult one. Within the last five years immense changes and improvements have been wrought by the introduction into general sporting use of the ·303 Lee-Metford and the ·256 Mannlicher rifles, weapons which may be said to have effected a revolution in game shooting, and especially in the stalking of deer and antelopes and the destruction of other soft-skinned game. Yet, year by year, month by month, fresh improvements are being made, and even the Mannlicher and the Lee-Metford may, no great while hence, be themselves ousted from the field by still more perfect and effective weapons.

For a good many years it was a safe axiom—laid down by big-game shooters of great and varied experience—that the sportsman hunting in India, Africa, or any other part of the world where great game existed, could not go far wrong if he took with him two classes of rifle, viz., for thin-skinned game a ·450 or ·500 Express, sighted up to 300 yards, and for heavy, dangerous, and thick-skinned game like elephants, rhinoceros, and buffalo a ponderous large-bore rifle—4-bore or 8-bore—shooting 12 drams of powder and a spherical or conical bullet. With these weapons the sportsman was sufficiently well equipped. With the Express he could account for all kinds of deer and antelope, as well as lion, tiger, and bear. With the heavy 4- and 8-bore he could rely upon stopping almost certainly, even at very close quarters, the charge of elephant, rhinoceros, and buffalo. Add to these weapons a Martini-Henry sporting rifle, for all kinds of shooting up to elephant and rhinoceros—the Martini-Henry bullet is quite good enough to master even these gigantic game—and a 12-bore shot gun, and the sportsman was perfectly well provided for any part of the world. But the 4 and 8-bore are weapons of such tremendous weight and punishing powers that only the most robust sportsmen can, or are fitted to, undertake their use. A bullet weighing four to the pound—or even eight to the pound—propelled by a charge of 12 drams of black powder, not only gives a tremendous shock to the animal fired at, but inflicts considerable punishment upon the sportsman wielding it. Only a man of strong nerves and great physical strength can long stand the use of such a weapon. The weight alone of these heavy rifles is an immense handicap in a hot climate. A single 4-bore weighs about 21 lbs., a double 8-bore about 15 lbs. Many sportsmen therefore turned their attention to other weapons. The ·577 double rifle, shooting long, solid bullets, was found to be an efficient weapon even against elephants and rhinoceros. Other gunners favoured the now well-known ball and shot guns, which can be used as shot guns, and yet carrying, as they do, short, heavy bullets, are excellent weapons, even for dangerous game, in jungle and forest, where animals are usually encountered at close quarters.

Mr. F. C. Selous was one of the first sportsmen to demonstrate that heavy rifles and heavy charges are not vital essentials for the destruction even of the biggest and most formidable game. Some years ago, when hunting elephants in South Africa, Mr. Selous found himself, after an attack of fever, too weak to use a heavy rifle. He therefore attacked a troop of elephants with no more formidable weapon than a ·450 Metford-Gibbs, using long, solid, toughened bullets and a powder charge of 75 grains. With this rifle he killed in a single day no less than six elephants—if he had been in his usual health and better mounted he would have killed probably twice the number, as he had with the same weapon and charge killed previously buffalo, giraffe, hippopotami, and even rhinoceros. It became clear that to a cool and seasoned sportsman the ·450 was practically as useful a weapon as a 4- or 8-bore. But, in addition to Mr. Selous, many other sportsmen have demonstrated the fact that the cumbrous, heavy, and punishing large bore weapons are not absolute essentials for the bagging of elephant and rhinoceros, provided the sportsman is a fair rifle shot and has confidence in his own powers. Large numbers of elephants, buffaloes, rhinoceros, giraffe, and other heavy game have been killed in South Africa—especially by Boer and native hunters—with no heavier weapon and missile than the Martini-Henry, using the ordinary government military ·450—·577 ammunition. On the other hand, it has to be said that with a single 4-bore or double 8-bore a charging elephant or buffalo can be stopped or turned at close quarters, when no lighter weapon and charge would have effected that object. If, then, the sportsman is likely to be hunting elephant, rhinoceros, or buffalo in bushy or dense jungle country, where dangerous game would, if wounded, be probably encountered at very close quarters, he would be well advised, even at the present time, to take with him a double 8-bore, or a weapon of the Paradox type (ball and shot gun); few men nowadays care to tackle the cannon-like 4-bore rifle.

Quite recently Mr. A. H. Neumann, a hunter of great experience and success, has been shooting elephants in East Africa with the ·303 Lee-Metford service rifle, having a native hunter close at hand with a Martini-Henry as "cripple stopper." As Mr. Neumann bagged in 1895–6 a good many rhinoceros and elephants with this rifle and its slender missile, it must be conceded that the ·303, even when one is hunting such immense game as elephant, has a good deal to be said in its favour. On the other hand, thanks to a hitch or fault in the mechanism, Mr. Neumann, while using this rifle, was charged, knocked over, and all but killed by a cow-elephant, which crushed in his ribs, drove her tusk through his arm, and disabled him for months. If at that moment he had had in his hand an 8-bore, the elephant would have been pretty certainly stopped, or turned from her charge. It should be mentioned that all kinds of game, even up to rhinoceros, have been killed within recent years by other sportsmen, in Africa and other parts of the world, while using the ·303 Lee-Metford sporting rifle.

For stalking antelope upon open plains, wild sheep and goats in mountain country, for deer, wapiti, moose, and reindeer, and for lions, tigers, leopards, and other carnivora, the ·303 Lee-Metford and the ·256 Mannlicher, using smokeless powder and hollow-fronted bullets, have proved themselves almost perfect weapons, and are likely, for some years to come, to be held in increasing favour by sportsmen in all parts of the world. For stalking, especially, their astonishing accuracy, immense striking energy, and flat trajectory, combined with their lightness and absence of recoil, render them almost ideal weapons.

Smokeless rifle powders are an invention which add greatly to the comfort of the gunner. At the present time Rifleite seems to be the best and most reliable of these powders, and may be recommended to all sportsmen as a thoroughly sound powder, giving splendid penetration, together with great absence of recoil and little of the troublesome smoke known of old to users of black powder. It is, however, still contended by experienced sportsmen that, notwithstanding the wonderful powers of the new small bore rifles, a much heavier and stronger weapon and charge are necessary in following dangerous and especially wounded game in thick bush, or in tackling them at close quarters. There is much truth in this contention, and the smashing and shocking power of a 4-bore, 8-bore, or even 10-bore bullet, delivered at close quarters, is undoubtedly much more likely to be effective in turning, stunning, or killing outright so dangerous a beast as a wounded buffalo, elephant, rhinoceros, or lion, than a light missile such as the ·303 bullet. For great game shooting at the present day in South Africa, India, or any part of the world, a serviceable battery would be as follows:—

1. A single ·256 Mannlicher or ·303 Lee-Metford,[1] useful for almost all kinds of sport.

2. A double 8 bore, or double ·577, or Paradox, if elephant, buffalo, or other heavy game are to be encountered.

3. A single Martini-Henry sporting rifle, shooting solid bullets. This is a useful weapon for native servants, and is always a good, cheap, and most reliable spare rifle. For hunting giraffe or eland on horseback, where shots are often fired from the saddle, it is especially useful, the solid bullet giving just the requisite shock and penetration.

[1] It should be mentioned that gun-makers are now introducing the ·303 with improved breech action, thus obviating the cumbrous and unsightly bolt which has hitherto been the chief objection to the Lee-Metford ·303 for sporting purposes.

4. A double 12 bore shot gun—left barrel partial choke—for bird shooting.

With such a battery the sportsman can safely take the field in any country where big game is likely to be found. If he is inclined to be extravagant, he can add to it, if he pleases—

5. A double ·450 express, shooting both hollow pointed and long, solid, toughened bullets, or one of the new double ·256, ·303, or ·400 rifles which are now being introduced.

If the gunner is going to a country where neither elephant, rhinoceros, nor buffalo are to be encountered, he need take with him, unless he has plenty of money to spend in equipment, no more than a single or double ·303 or ·256, a spare Martini-Henry sporting rifle (for which ammunition can almost always be readily obtained), and a shot gun. With these weapons he can obtain all the shooting he requires. The rifle should be well tried before leaving England, the sighting most carefully tested, and the trigger pull adjusted to the shooter's liking.

For antelope or gazelle shooting on the plains or in open country, sighting should be adjusted up to 400 or 500 yards. There are many and divers opinions as to the safety bolt for rifles. On the whole the balance of opinion among practical sportsmen is rather against than for this convenience.

Spare sights, strikers, cleaning apparatus, nipple wrench, and screw should be taken. If the sportsman is going for a prolonged stay, loading and recapping implements and materials may be thought necessary, but it should be remembered that, for heavy or dangerous game, new, and not reloaded, cartridges are infinitely safer and more preferable. The rifles should have eyes and a leather sling, although not every mounted man cares, like the South African Boer, to carry his rifle slung at his back. Native carriers are, more often than not, to be met with, and in the South African interior the post of rifle carrier for the English sportsman is looked upon by Bushmen and other native hunters as one of great honour and credit.

Most English sportsmen prefer for South African shooting, where horses can be freely employed, to carry the rifle in the hand, in preference to having it slung across the back, or in a bucket. For the first day or two the arm becomes tired and stiff from the unaccustomed weight; that, however, soon passes off, and the sportsman will quickly become habituated to carrying a double rifle in his right hand, day after day, during long hot rides in search of game, without noticing the encumbrance at all. In the game country, native carriers are, however, as I have said, pretty constantly to be procured. These men usually insist as a point of etiquette upon carrying the rifle until game is sighted or known to be near. Strong leather bandoliers for carrying cartridges should not be forgotten. Ammunition should be taken out in strong tin-lined cases. A sight protector for the foresight, and a waterproof gun cover for wet weather, are items that ought not to be omitted. No sportsman should be without a good but light pair of field-glasses, nor should he leave camp without having in his belt-pouch a box of matches, a pocket compass, and (unless water is plentiful) a water bottle, containing tea or any other pet beverage, slung to his saddle, or carried by his native attendant.

In stalking small antelopes or gazelles, such as spring-buck, black-buck, &c., upon open plains, the shooting can as a rule be undertaken with some deliberation, and the sportsman can, more often than not, get a steady shot in a recumbent or sitting position. Where, however, as often happens with the larger antelopes, such as wildebeest, hartebeest and the like, the quarry sets off, so soon as alarmed, at a fast gallop, the gunner has little time for judging distances and must hastily put up what he thinks is the proper sight and fire from the knee or standing. Successful shooting of this sort can only be acquired by practice and experience. Mountain stalking, again, is a complete art in itself, and success can only be attained after a severe and often trying apprenticeship, not only in the actual shooting itself, but in studying wind, changes of temperature, the habits of the animal pursued, the difficult business of calculating distances amid mountains and valleys, in various kinds of weather and at different periods of the day, and a host of other details.

Before reaching the game country, the novice may be advised to practise shooting wherever possible, to habituate himself to the changes of light and atmosphere at different periods of the day, and to practise repeatedly the art of judging distances in a hot climate, by guessing and pacing out imaginary distances in the *terrain* through which he is passing.

In forest and bush country, where the shot is often a mere snap at close quarters, incessant vigilance, cool nerves, and great quickness are absolute essentials to success. For such shooting, the handy shot and ball weapons of the Paradox description, with which aim can be rapidly taken, as with a shot gun, are extremely useful. Dangerous and heavy game, such as lions, elephants, rhinoceros, and buffalo, are more often than not shot within 50 yards, and the gunner should be very sure of his nerves and proficiency with the rifle before attempting to tackle them. It is here that the advantage of a rifle of heavy calibre comes in. Armed with a 4 bore or 8 bore, a man, even if not a first-class rifle shot at longer ranges, can, with courage and determination, await the approach of an elephant or rhinoceros to within 20 yards, confident that, if he holds reasonably straight, the tremendous impact of the heavy charge and bullet will almost certainly turn or disable his antagonist. The novice, before taking the field abroad in search of big game, will be well advised not only to read the works of reliable travellers and hunters who have exploited those regions he intends to visit, but to digest carefully the contents of some good work on rifle shooting. Mr. Augustus Grimble's *Deer Stalking* (Chapman and Hall), and that excellent little book, *The Sportsman's Vade-Mecum for the Himalayas*, by K. C. A. J. (Horace Cox), will teach him many wrinkles, which, in addition to his own practice with the rifle, will be of invaluable use to him. But, after all, even such good and practical works as these are but temporary aids to the would-be game shooter. Only an apprenticeship in the veldt, upon the mountain, or in the jungle itself, can teach a man the real art of hunting and shooting wild game. The reader will find much useful information on bullets, charges, trajectories, striking force, &c., in the article on "Ammunition" in Vol. I. of this Encyclopædia. He may be also referred to "Deerstalking" and "Big Game" in the same volume.

H. A. BRYDEN.

TARGET SHOOTING—Few outdoor forms of sport of a quiet character have attained such a degree of popularity as target shooting with the rifle. This is in some measure due to the wonderful results obtained with modern arms of precision, and the interest which the many problems connected with them have aroused. The chief cause, however, has undoubtedly been the enthusiastic manner in which the national Volunteer movement was received and the success which has attended it, causing an immense number of our citizen fellow-countrymen to become not only familiar with the rifle but expert in its use.

No industry has received a greater amount of attention from inventors than the manufacture of guns and ammunition, and improvement has followed improvement in such rapid succession that the history of the rifle is one of a continuous series of changes.

Consequent upon the recent adoption of the ·303 magazine rifle as the British service arm, in place of the ·450 Martini-Henry, the conditions of target shooting have in the last couple of years undergone a change so complete as to be almost revolutionary.

The Martini-Henry could always be relied upon to make good shooting at 200 and 500 yards, and, under favourable circumstances, at 600; but as a reliable target weapon the last distance was its limit. Under no circumstances had it the slightest chance against the old ·450 match rifle, which monopolised the shooting at the long ranges; but, as the cost of a match rifle and the necessary outfit seldom came to less than £25, the number of riflemen using it was limited. In experienced hands, however, the results obtained with this match rifle were little short of marvellous. The following are the highest scores made with it in public competitions in this country:—

Competition.	Date.	Competitor.	Yards. 800	900	1000	Total.
Competition for the Scotch Eight	1885	T. Caldwell	74	75	72	221
Regular and Volunteer Officers	1889	Capt. T. Lamb..	75	73	72	220
Elcho Shield Match	1892	Capt. T. Lamb..	75	71	73	219
,, ,, ,,	1894	Capt. G. Gibbs.	74	72	72	218
,, ,, ,,	1891	Capt. Foulkes...	74	73	71	218

The highest possible score is 225.

Black powder was almost universally used in the ·450 match rifle and Martini-Henry; but

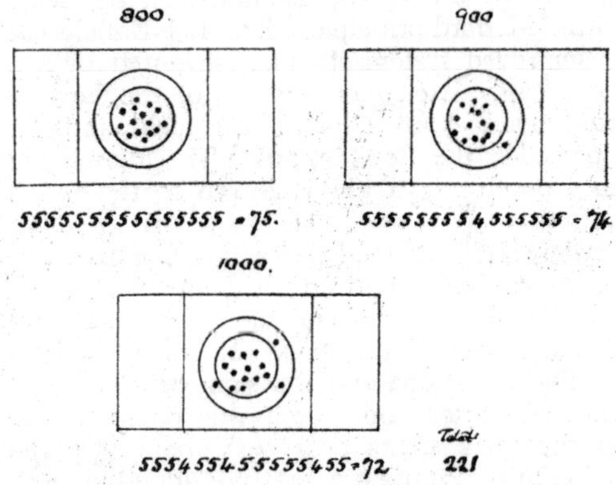

DIAGRAMS OF T. CALDWELL'S SCORE OF 221 MADE AT IRVINE, N.B., 28th June, 1885. Rigby Rifle. Strong 11 o'clock wind.

on the introduction of the magazine ·303, with its small based and long bullet, the use of a much stronger explosive was necessary, and it soon became apparent that if the match rifle were to be retained as a useful weapon and not merely as a toy, the limit of its bore should be so reduced as to bring it into touch with the new Service weapon.

Match Rifle—The *raison d'être* of the match rifle is to ascertain the degree of accuracy obtainable at the long ranges with a rifle conforming in general conditions to the Service rifle, but equipped with the finest sights and using the best ammunition.

Fortunately for target shooting, the National Rifle Association of Great Britain is admittedly the supreme authority in all matters relating to this form of sport; and its regulations with regard to ranges, targets, positions and classes of rifles are universally adopted by the various rifle associations and clubs throughout the Kingdom. Recognising the necessity of the change, the National Rifle Association, early in 1897, issued the following definition of the Match Rifle, which has governed all competitions held since.

Match Rifles—Any breech-loading rifle complying with the following conditions:—

1. When of British make, to bear proof marks both on barrel and breech.

2. *Weight*—Maximum, 10 lbs. In magazine rifles the magazine, whether detachable or not, to be included.
3. *Length*—Maximum, 52 inches.
4. *Calibre*—Maximum, ·315.
5. *Stock*—Full stocked, and sufficiently strong, in the opinion of the Bisley Committee, for service purposes, and fitted with swivels for a sling. No pad or shoe for the heel-plate of the butt allowed.
6. *Pull of trigger*—Minimum, 6 lbs.
7. *Sights*—Of any description, except telescopic or magnifying.

Nearly all the match rifle shooting under the above conditions has been made with ·303 magazine rifles of the Lee-Metford or Lee-Enfield patterns, or with Mannlichers.

(The Lee-Metford is the pattern originally adopted by the Government, the rifling being on the Metford principle. The Lee-Enfield has an improved system of rifling, invented by Mr. John Rigby, late superintendent of the Government Small Arms Factory at Enfield, and has superseded the Lee-Metford. The Mannlicher has a bore of ·256, and is known as the Dutch pattern.)

Many shooting men possessing Lee-Metfords or Lee-Enfields converted them into match rifles by having aperture sights, removable at pleasure, fitted on them. It thus became possible to use one and the same rifle throughout the service and match rifle competitions. As the extra sights only cost about £5, the saving to the competitor was considerable, both in expense and in trouble, by having only one rifle instead of two to bring about with him. It is further worthy of note that some of the most valuable match rifle prizes at Bisley were carried off by competitors using converted service rifles and Government (cordite) ammunition.

The usual *distances* for match rifle competitions are 800, 900 and 1,000 yards. A few are held at 1,100 yards, notably the Wimbledon Cup at Bisley and the last range of the Cambridge Cup.

As between the merits of the ·303 and the Mannlicher ·256 as match rifles, opinions appear evenly divided. The latter works well in wet weather, and the ammunition (Troisdorf powder) suits it. The very small hole made in canvas targets is at times difficult for the markers to find, and the bullet, being lighter, is slightly more sensitive to wind variations. John Rigby won the Wimbledon Cup at Bisley in 1897, using a Mannlicher rifle, with the magnificent score of 71 out of a possible 75 at 1,100 yards. Special match rifles of ·303 bore are now to be had from all the leading rifle firms, and particular loads which suit them are recommended by the makers. Many of these rifles are not of the service pattern, and can only be used in match rifle competitions. For those to whom expense is a matter of little importance, a special rifle for match shooting is on the whole preferable; but there are plenty of service pattern rifles to be had which shoot well with the open sights, and form equally good match rifles with the addition of the aperture ones. A few do not, owing, in most cases, to some weakness or defect in the stock.

Next only in importance to the choice of a rifle is the choice of the *ammunition* to be used with it. What a target shot most desires is an explosive giving uniformity of result, a quality possessed in a very high degree by black powder. There appears little to choose between Ballistite, Cannonite, Cordite, Rifleite and Troisdorf; but a beginner cannot do better than adopt the load recommended by the party from whom the rifle is purchased, until he is fortunate enough to discover a charge better suited to his particular weapon. To those who have time and patience, the carrying out of experiments forms one of the pleasantest phases of rifle shooting; and the discovery of a reliable load will well repay many an afternoon spent on the ranges. Having found a charge giving consistently good results, the wise shot will be slow to change it.

Owing to the strong corrosive action of the nitro-compounds, great attention must be paid to cleaning the rifle as soon as the shooting is finished. If the barrel be wiped out before it has had time to cool and the fouling to harden, considerable trouble will be saved.

In competitions cleaning out is forbidden except between ranges.

The *back position* is universally used in shooting with the match rifle. It is much steadier in a wind, and does not require the same physique or nerve to get through a long competition or a close finish.

The back position generally adopted is that illustrated in No. 1, with the rifle resting between

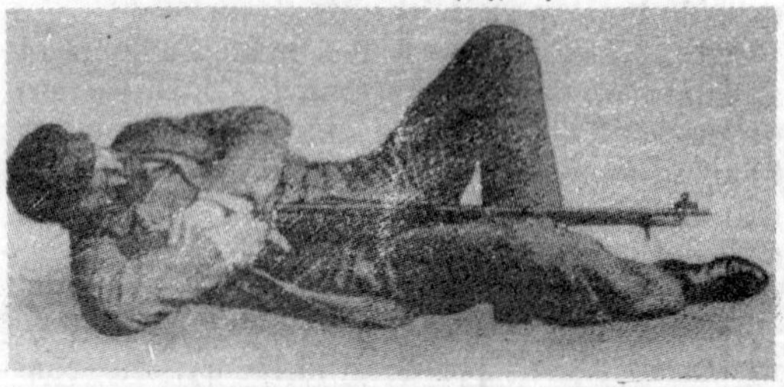

POSITION No. 1.

the legs. The left foot should be placed flat upon the ground, the knee almost upright, and the left instep gripped firmly by the inside of the right knee. The head may be supported by catching the left sleeve, or a small band attached to it, in the teeth. No. 2 is known as the toe position. As the shooter's knees somewhat interfere with his observing the wind changes whilst aiming, it is of importance that the shot should be fired as quickly as possible, consistently with a steady aim being taken, after the sights have been adjusted. A little practice will enable a beginner, by closing his hand on the grip, to release the trigger almost instantly, yet without the slightest jerk. Shooting over the thigh (No. 3) has the advantage of giving a clear view of the targets;

Position No. 2.

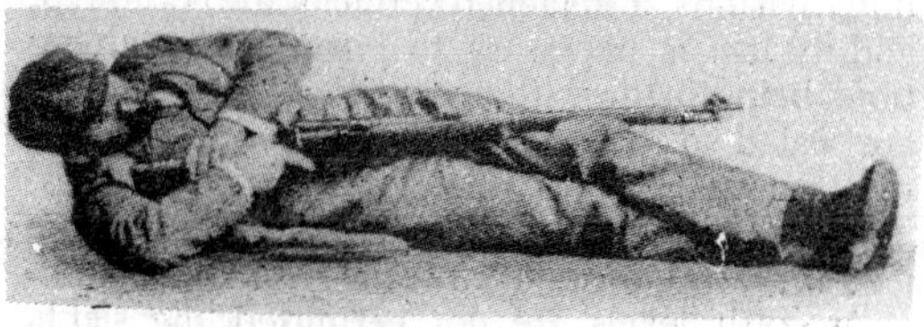

Position No. 3.

but, owing to the rifle merely resting on, and not being caught by, the legs, it is scarcely as steady as either 1 or 2.

Aperture back and front sights, adjustable by screws and scaled, are, together with the greater distances between the sights, the chief advantages of the match over the service rifle. The scales are drawn so that a movement of one division means a change of one inch on the target for every 100 yards, or eight inches at 800, &c.

With aperture sights, aim is always taken at the same spot on the target, generally at the bull's-eye, although the rifle may be pointed to throw many feet away from it.

Spirit levels are permitted, and always used, with the match rifle for the purpose of keeping the sights upright—a necessary precaution, for the line of aim is high over the centre of the barrel. Should the sights lean over to the right, the bullet will be thrown to that side, and if the lean is at all considerable, low shots will also result.

The front sights generally used are (1) the hollow bead or ring; (2) the solid bead; (3) the calipers, and (4) the earwig. The ring stands on a stem in the centre of a strong circular guard. The bull's-eye is seen in the centre of

Foresights.

Hollow bead or ring. Solid bead or pin head. Calipers. Earwig.

the ring, and this again in the centre of the back-sight, the three circles of the bull's-eye, ring and back aperture being concentric. This form of sight is excellent in good light, but is apt to strain the sight in dull weather.

The solid bead, or pinhead is either centred on the bull's-eye so as exactly to coincide in size with it when looked at through the back-sight, or is placed on the white of the target to the right or left, almost touching the bull, and forming a figure of ●●. A different sized bead is necessary at each distance. This sight is used by the majority of match rifle shots, and is undoubtedly the best for all classes of weather.

The hollow bead, calipers or earwig should be sufficiently large to permit a clear ring of white to be seen round the bull's-eye.

Long-Range Clubs find the difficulty of obtaining suitable range almost insuperable, and this accounts for their number being so small. The long-range clubs in the Kingdom are:—

The English Eight Club.
The Cambridge University L.R.R.C.
The Oxford University L.R.R.C.
The Hounslow L.R.R.C.
The Dublin Rifle Club.
The Irish Rifle Association.
The Ulster Rifle Association.
The National Rifle Club of Scotland.

The English Eight Club, the Irish Rifle Association and the National Rifle Association of Scotland hold annual prize meetings for the purpose of aiding the captains of the teams for the Elcho Challenge Shield, to choose their representatives. The Irish Rifle Association holds an open prize meeting in June, at which £200 is offered in prizes for the match rifle.

The Service Rifle—Whatever difference of opinion may exist as to the merits of the ·303 service rifle in actual warfare, there is no denying its superiority in accuracy and effective range over its predecessor, the Martini-Henry. At Bisley, 1897, the Volunteers for the first time used the ·303 in all the service rifle competitions. Such was the improvement in the shooting, and so numerous were the full scores made, that an alteration in the S.R. Ranges from 200, 500, and 600, to 300, 600 and 700 yards, or a change in the dimensions of the targets, appears by no means improbable.

The following are the winning scores made for the Queen's Prize at Bisley in the last three years:—

	First Stage.			Second Stage.		Third Stage.		Total
	200	500	600	500	600	800	900	
Highest possible score.	35	35	35	50	75	50	50	330
M.H. 1895 Private Hayhurst	30	33	32	46	55	45	38	279
M.H. 1896 Lieutenant Thompson...	32	33	30	45	55	38	40	273
L.M. 1897 Private Ward...	32	34	32	50	70	41	45	304

The shooting in the final stage of this competition clearly demonstrated the capabilities of the ·303 service rifle at the long ranges. Only one miss was recorded in the scores of the first thirty-five prize-winners, and Lieut. Ross, of Canada, who was fourth, succeeded in making 46 at 800, and 46 at 900 yards, a really fine performance with open sights.

The National Rifle Association definition of service rifle is:—

S.R. *Service Rifle.*

·303 magazine rifles as issued by the Government or of private manufacture, of *bonâ fide* Government pattern, and bearing the Government viewer's mark.

All service rifles must comply with the following conditions:—

1. *Weight*—Including cleaning-rod, oil-bottle, pull through and magazine, not to exceed the greatest weight of the regulation rifle of the corresponding pattern and mark.

2. *Length*—Maximum, measured from the muzzle to the butt when placed vertically on the ground, 49½ inches.

3. *Stocks*—Must not be checkered. No pad or shoe for the heel-plate of the butt allowed, nor may the butt-plate be checkered.

A metal fitting for the sole purpose of the attachment of a match backsight is permitted.

4. *Pull of trigger*—Minimum, 6 lbs.

5. *Sights*—Strictly in accordance with those on any pattern of Government service rifle.

As the sights are immovable laterally, allowance for wind must be made either by aiming off the bull's-eye, or seeing the fore-sight to the right or left of the centre of the back-sight. The result is the same as putting on the allowance the other way on the fore-sight of a match rifle; it brings the muzzle into wind.

With open sights great attention must be paid to changes of light, especially when a fine fore-sight is taken. As a general rule a bright light requires a higher elevation than a dull one or than shade. Some individuals are affected by these changes to a greater extent than others, and the alterations to be made must be found out by personal experience; but the effects are minimized by painting the fore-sight, so that the same amount of it will be regularly seen. (See Figures *a* and *b*.)

The back-sight consists of a sliding bar with a **V** in the centre. This bar may be reversed, or a plain bar substituted (known as a match bar), so as to have a straight edge to aim over. The sights should always be kept a dead black, to prevent the light glancing on them, and also to give good definition. Black and white paints may be used. When shooting through the **V** it is useful to paint a small white dot on the back of the barleycorn: this dot should be just visible resting in the angle of the **V**, and is a great aid in keeping good elevation. (See Fig. *a*.) In shooting over the bar, instead of taking a fine front-sight, many competitors prefer to see the whole of the barleycorn, bringing the top of the block level with or visible over the bar. In this case a small white line is painted on the barleycorn for the purpose of keeping its centre accurately over the windage line on the back-sight. (Fig. *b*.) When the wind is blowing from the

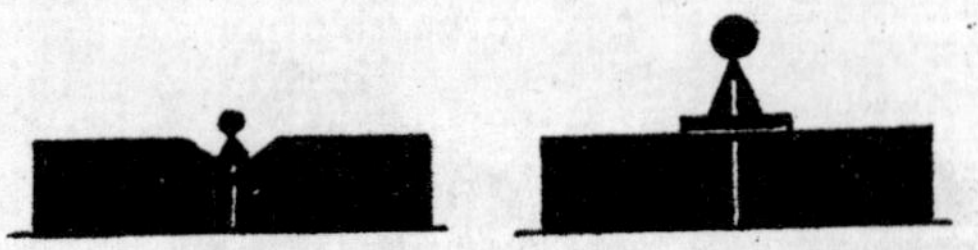

(*a*) Aid in keeping elevation when using the V. (*b*) Aid in keeping elevation when shooting over the bar.

right, the latter line will be to the right of the centre of the back-sight and *vice versa*.

Owing to the back-sight not being marked in fine divisions, a detached vernier scale is allowed, and its use is necessary to ensure sight alterations being made with accuracy. These verniers are scaled so that an alteration of one division means a change of 1 inch for every 100 yards. They are also useful for making the white line give the wind allowance on the back-sight.

As spirit levels are not permitted, the sights must be kept horizontally by aligning the top of the bar with the top or bottom of the target, or one of the uprights of the back-sight with a flag-post or other suitable object.

Position—In service rifle competitions open to all comers any position is usually permitted at all distances, but special matches are also held at 200 yards standing, and kneeling. The Volunteer positions are, at 200 yards kneeling, at 500 prone, and at all distances over 500 yards, any.

It is difficult to describe briefly the correct position for standing and kneeling shooting; and as most competitors who enter for competitions under these conditions are Volunteers, and therefore already acquainted with them, lengthened directions are scarcely worth the space required. It is well, however, to remember that the great secret is to get the body and rifle thoroughly braced together, and for this purpose the use of the sling is an advantage. In standing, the feet should be at right angles to each other, as also the arms, the left elbow being directly under the rifle, and the right elbow on a level with the shoulder.

In the prone position the shooter's body should point well to the right of the target aimed at. His legs may either be stretched widely apart, or crossed, whichever he finds

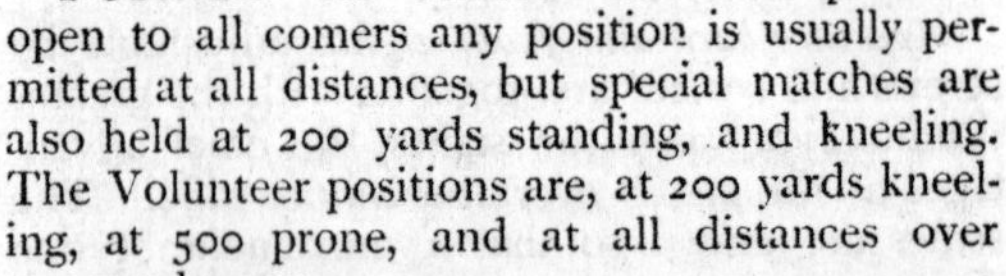

Third Class. Second Class. First Class.

TARGETS.

most conducive to steadiness. Good trigger-pulling is of much greater importance in these positions than in the back, as the slightest jerk will throw the rifle out of position.

The Dimensions of the Targets used at the different distances are as follows :—

Divisions.	Third Class. 200 yards.	Second Class. 500 & 600 yds.	First Class. 800 to 1,000 yds.	Marking Values.
Bull's-eye	8 in. diameter	2 ft. diameter	3 ft. diameter	5 marks
Inner......	20 ,, ,,	3 ,, ,,	4½ ,, ,,	4 ,,
Magpie...	32 ,, ,,	4 ,, ,,	6 ,, ,,	3 ,,
Outer......	Remainder of a target 4 ft. square.	Remainder of a target 6 ft. square.	Remainder of a target 12 ft. × 6 ft.	2 ,,

Elevation—In addition to the force of gravity, the elevation of the bullet is influenced by the direction of the wind, except when it is blowing at right angles to the range. A twelve o'clock wind depresses, and a six o'clock wind lifts it in its flight. A moderate wind will require nearly one, a stiff breeze two or even three points over or under the normal elevation at 800 yards, according as it is from the front or rear. (See diagram.)

Normal Elevation means the elevation a rifle requires in a calm. When ascertained, the normal elevations for the different ranges should be marked on the back-sight, and all calculations made from them as starting points.

The direction of the wind, or the situation of a shot on the target, is referred to by the position of the figures on the face of a watch. Thus a twelve o'clock wind is a head, a six o'clock a rear wind; a three o'clock shot is on the centre line of the target out to the right. Wind allowance, and the difference in elevation above or below the normal, are calculated in feet and inches, and the sights are adjusted to read off the required amounts.

The density of the atmosphere through which the bullet cleaves its way has also to be reckoned with. A high barometer means a heavy atmosphere, and consequently a high elevation. A low barometer and moist weather in general a low elevation.

Wind Allowances—Roughly speaking, the bullet takes about one second to travel up to the 600 yards, and two up to the 1,000 yards target. The distance it is carried out of its true course by the wind in this time has to be calculated by the shooter, and, by shifting the fore-sight to one side to the other, the rifle is pointed sufficiently into the wind, so that the bullet may strike the centre of the target. As the wind changes in direction, its effects on the bullet vary laterally and vertically in an inverse ratio. A head, or twelve o'clock wind, requires the maximum elevation, with the minimum allowance for wind. As it changes round to III, the elevation sinks to normal, whilst the wind allowance increases to its maximum, and so through each quarter, as a reference to the diagram will show. Wind allowance must be learned by experience. It is in gauging its effects on the flight of the bullet that the skill of the rifleman is chiefly displayed in target shooting at known distances. The changes in the strength of III and IX o'clock winds are the easiest to appreciate. Head and rear winds, especially those known as fish-tails, in which the direction is constantly shifting from XI to I, or from V to VII, are the most difficult to follow and judge correctly. A stiff breeze often holds its strength steadily; a soft wind, especially in hot weather, rarely.

A cloud bringing up a shower always affects both the direction and strength of the wind. A thunderstorm usually causes it to shift round suddenly to the opposite quarter, an equally

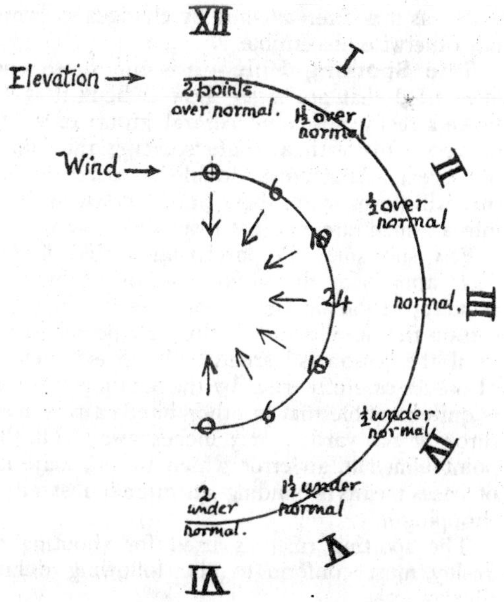

Diagram of the Alterations in Elevation and Wind Allowance, necessary upon a strong but steady Wind changing in Direction from XII to VI o'clock.

quick return to the original direction taking place when the storm is past.

Mirage is the name given by riflemen to the heated air rising from the earth. In hot weather it interferes with the aim, more especially when one is using open sights, the target appearing to rise and fall on the vapour clouds. When the mirage is strong and bubbling, a slightly higher elevation is necessary.

It is only waste of entry fees, ammunition, and temper to enter for competitions except with a good rifle in which the competitor has confidence, and until his last shot is registered he should never relax his efforts to make every possible point. Once started, the sooner a competitor has finished a competition the better; the less time occupied, the fewer changes of wind will be encountered. The unexpected happens in rifle shooting as often as, if not oftener than, in any other form of sport; and delay has often lost and but seldom won a match.

Before commencing each range, both elevation and wind allowance should be checked, and care taken that the latter is on the right way. Carelessness in these matters has ruined many a good score. Extreme and, during the continuance of a match, undivided attention must be given to the atmospheric changes. Particular note should be made in the memory of the strength and direction of the wind, on each shot being fired, for reference prior to altering for the next one.

A good field-glass is essential, to spot the patch indicating the bullet hole, and to keep a sharp look-out for changes of wind in the vicinity of the targets. Special attention should be given to the movements of the mirage when any exists, as it is often affected by changes of wind not otherwise discernible.

The Sporting Rifle—It is only those who have tried that are aware how difficult it is to make a really close and central group of shots at 100 yards with a single sporting rifle; and how great a treasure a double-barrelled one is, that will throw six or eight bullets consecutively into a 4-inch circle at that distance.

Few sportsmen in purchasing a rifle of this class appreciate the importance of testing the accuracy of the sighting themselves, and making certain that it suits their individual peculiarities, until the lesson is learned by bitter experience. However carefully tried by the manufacturer, it is quite possible that in other hands a rifle may throw at 100 yards 2 or 3 inches away from the point aimed at, an error which in the majority of cases means wounding an animal instead of dropping it.

The sporting rifle, as used for shooting at Bisley, must conform to the following definitions:—

Sporting Rifles—*Calibre*—Maximum, ·360.
Pull of trigger—Minimum, 3 lbs.
Sights—Open sights, or such as have received the sanction of the Council or of the Committee. The Lyman back-sight and the Beach combination fore-sight have been sanctioned.
No lateral adjustment of fore- or back-sight will be permitted. The centres of both sights must be fixed over the centre of the barrel. If a platinum or other line is used on the back-sight, only one such line will be permitted.
Spirit levels are permitted.
N.B. Any single, double or repeating rifle (whether of Government pattern or not) coming within the above conditions may be used in sporting rifle competitions.

The target used is a 12-inch disc, divided into inch rings. The bull's-eye is 3 inches in diameter (counting 6), with a central carton (counting 7). The highest scores recorded in the stationary target competitions at Bisley, distance 100 yards, are:—

Single Rifle—48 out of a possible 49 by Edward Ross, 1889; W. R. Joynt, 1895; Lieutenant Ranken and Mr. Littledale, 1896.
Double Rifle—54 out of a possible 56 by Edward Ross, 1889.

The competitions held at the Running Deer Ranges at Bisley are amongst the most popular on the Common, and afford sportsmen excellent practice for the migration to the North later in the season. A small target with a 6-inch bull's-eye, coinciding with the position of the heart, is marked on the deer, which is painted throughout its natural colour. To place six or eight consecutive shots within the inner ring as the deer runs first from one side and then from the other is no mean performance. At Wimbledon Earl de Grey was *facile princeps* in these competitions, and, at the present time, Earl Cairns occupies the premier position.

DAN. FRASER COMPETITION 1895. RUNNING DEER.
Distance 110 yards. Double Rifle. Four runs—both barrels fired at each run.
Earl Cairns, 3.4—3.3—4.4—3.3 = 27.

In single-rifle competitions the Mannlicher has, since its introduction, completely swept the board. The high velocity of the bullet makes only a small allowance in front necessary; and the closer it is possible to aim at the object, the better and more consistent will the results be.

Many deerstalkers now use the Mannlicher in preference to the Express, and speak highly of its performances in the field. The low trajectory, high velocity, greater accuracy and range, and small recoil amply compensate for any disadvantage in the weight and shock of the bullet. [*See* DEERSTALKING.]

The National Rifle Association and the Bisley Meeting—No account of target shooting would be complete without some reference to the National Rifle Association of Great Britain and its great annual Prize Meeting. This Association was founded in 1860 for the purpose, as its charter declares, of giving permanence to Volunteer corps, and encouraging rifle shooting throughout the Queen's dominions. Its list of members numbers about 3,000, and its annual Prize Meeting, held until 1889 at Wimbledon, and since that date at Bisley, is the most important of its kind in the world. Commencing on the second Monday in July, it lasts a fortnight, and regularly attracts not only well-known shots from all parts of the kingdom, but contingents from several of the Colonies. Upwards of 2,000 competitors stay in camp under canvas for the meeting, whilst the train service brings large additions every morning from London and Aldershot.

As will be seen from the following summary, a very large number of the individual competitions are open to all comers.

LIST OF COMPETITIONS HELD AT THE BISLEY MEETING.

Rifle used.	Total No. of Competitions.	Ditto open to All-comers.	Team Matches.	Ditto, open to All comers.
Match R.....	17	17	3	1
Service R....	42	30	25	—
Sporting R..	6	6	—	—
Revolver.....	15	15	2	1

The prizes annually offered in these competitions amount to over £10,000 in cash, the value of the Challenge Cups and Plate being at least as much again, and upwards of £3,000 additional is distributed as the results of pool shooting.

The principal team competitions are:—

With the *Match Rifle*: The *Elcho Challenge Shield* between teams representing England, Ireland, and Scotland; the *Regular* v. *Volunteer Officers' Match*, the *Humphry Cup*, Oxford *v.* Cambridge.

With the *Service Rifle* (limited to Volunteers): The *Belgian Challenge Cup* for volley firing; the *Loyd Lindsay* mounted competition; the *Mullins*, firing at moving figures; the *Chancellor's Plate*, Oxford and Cambridge Universities; the *Rajah of Kolapore's Cup*, Mother Country and Colonies; the *Ashburton Shield*, Public Schools, and the *China Cup*, inter-county match; open to all the service, *United Service Challenge Cup*.

THE INDIVIDUAL COMPETITIONS OPEN TO ALL-COMERS INCLUDE—

	Distances.	No. of Prizes.	Amount of Prizes.
M.R. The Albert	800, 900 & 1000	5	£86 and Cup.
,, The Halford. ..			
S.R. The Alexandra..	500 & 600	325	£1000
,, The Graphic ...	500	126	£340 and Cup.
,, The Daily Graphic......	200	126	£340 Sketches and Cup.
,, The Daily Telegraph......	600	112	£300 and Cup.
Open to members of all the Services—			
S.R. The Imperial	200, 500, 600 & 800	120	£250 and Challenge Cup.
And for Volunteers only—			
S.R. The Queen's	200, 500, 600 800, 900	600	£2420, Medals and Badges.
,, The St. George's..	500, 600, 900,	325	£900 and Cups and Badges.

Full information of the foregoing competitions and the regulations governing them will be found in the Bisley Programme published every June by the National Rifle Association, 10, Pall Mall East, London. (Price 1*s.*) The latest books on rifle shooting are *The Theory and Practice of Rifle Shooting*, A. G. Foulkes. (Horace Cox, 10*s.* 6*d.*) *Notes on the Rifle*, the Hon. F. F. Freemantle. (Vincent, 5*s.*)

W. R. JOYNT.

THE REVOLVER—The revolver, in its present form, is not the result of the invention of any one man, although Col. Colt was the first to make it a practical weapon; but rather the result of a long series of evolutions from the old single barrel pistol.

When the pistol was first made it was soon found that there was need of a way to fire several shots in rapid succession, long before such a pressing need was felt in the rifle.

The pistol is only used, as a rule, at close quarters; so if the first shot is a miss there is no time to re-load to take another shot.

Double barrelled pistols and then three, four or more barrelled ones were in consequence made, but in the early stages these barrels were all made of the full length of the pistol, and each barrel loaded as a separate pistol.

The double barrelled ones had a lock for each barrel, the three barrelled ones were often made with the barrels one below the other (the double barrels being either horizontal, or more rarely vertical to each other).

When more than three barrels were used, they were generally grouped in a cluster round a solid core, never, or hardly ever, with a centre barrel surrounded by others, as this would present a mechanical difficulty in firing the centre one.

I remember, some years ago, seeing a French pin fire revolver which fired twelve shots. The chambers in the cylinder seemed in a double tier, with two barrels, one for the inner circle and the other for the outer circle, but I did not have a chance to examine it closely as to the construction.

In order to fire the various barrels of the pistol, one of the earliest forms had a firing pin, which was put opposite the cap of each barrel in succession (this was not possible in the wheel and flint lock days). Another form was to have the hammer come opposite each barrel in turn, first moved by hand, and later by mechanism, automatically; this form was used in flint locks, and is retained in some modern pistols and multibarrelled rifles.

The first actual *revolver* had the barrels revolve so as to come opposite the hammer in turn. This was found mechanically weak, so the revolving cylinder with chambers coming opposite a barrel common to all in turn was evolved, and this, with modifications, is the form of all modern revolvers.

The reason the original idea of a set of barrels was abandoned for a cylinder with chambers opening on to a barrel common to all is the following:—

At the first glance it would be thought that

the former plan is the best. A barrel complete in itself shoots not only harder (owing to there being no escape of gas, such as unavoidably takes place between the barrel and cylinder of the later plan), but more accurately (as there is no joint between the cylinder and barrel). Nevertheless the cylinder revolver is not only lighter, owing to there being only one barrel instead of several, each the whole length of the pistol, but it can shoot much more accurately. At the same time, each barrel of the "pepper box," as the old revolving barrel pistol was called, shot *individually, better and more accurately.*

If this difficulty is found in double barrels, it is infinitely increased as the number of barrels is increased. In fact I do not think any amount of regulating can make four or more barrels shoot together.

For this reason the revolving cylinder has been almost universally adopted, in spite of the varying escape of gas inevitable, and of the fact that the chamber occasionally does not come opposite the barrel, owing to fouling or dirt getting into the action. If there is an extra escape of gas at a shot, it makes that shot weaker, and consequently low, and, if the chamber does not quite come round far enough, a shaving is taken off a side of the bullet, causing irregular flight and an inaccurate shot. In my opinion the revolver of the future will have an arrangement for making the connection between the chamber and barrel gas tight during each shot, so as to make it as accurate as a single barrel pistol. The cocking arrangement also needs improvement. It has either to be cocked by hand, causing loss of time, and, what is more important, loss of aim; or it is cocked by the trigger, which latter plan, though more rapid, gains rapidity by loss of accuracy, as it is impossible to "hold" on to the object, and at the same time lift the hammer by the trigger. There ought to be some

REVOLVER SHOOTING.

The reason of this seeming paradox is as follows:—

Any one who has shot, or regulated, a double barrelled rifle knows how difficult it is to get the two barrels to shoot parallel, both horizontally and vertically, to each other; each barrel may shoot perfectly in itself, but, when joined together, one barrel will be found to shoot higher than the other, or they will shoot across or away from each other. Fixing the two barrels mechanically parallel to each other is no use, as, there being more resistance to the recoil where the barrels touch each other, they shoot away from each other (or apart), and they can only be regulated by hand at great expense and trouble.

way of the revolver cocking itself by the discharge; this cocking only to take place when wanted.

A revolver with these two improvements would be, in my opinion, superior to any repeating pistol, as it would balance properly, which no repeating pistol I have seen does, and would be of much more compact shape. Also the stock should be more in line with the barrel (like the duelling pistol), instead of below it, as so many revolvers are made, especially those of the "Bull Dog" pattern.

The way revolver-shooting is practised in the Western States of America is the only real way to learn to shoot a revolver. In this country revolver-shooting is practised as a sort of game, like croquet, tennis, or golf.

Subjoined are diagrams of the best on record scores to date at various forms of revolver shooting, but I personally do not think the deliberate sort of shooting of much use. The only useful practice is rapid shooting and a

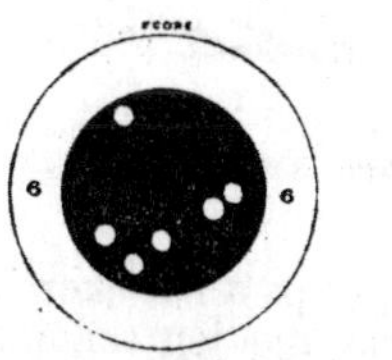

BEST ON RECORD, TARGET ADVANCING RAPIDLY FROM 50 TO 15 YARDS. BISLEY, 1896.

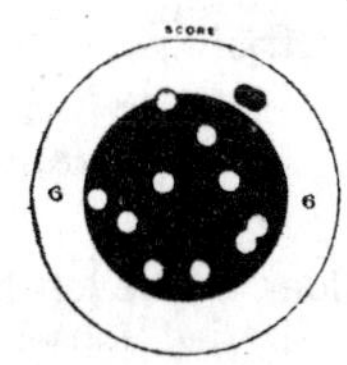

BEST ON RECORD, 50 YARDS, 12 SHOTS. BISLEY, 1894.

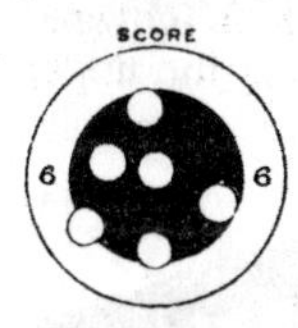

BEST ON RECORD, TARGET APPEARING AT INTERVALS OF 3 SECONDS AT 20 YARDS.

BEST ON RECORD, MOVING TARGET ACROSS LINE OF FIRE AT 20 YARDS.

moving series of competitions, as a revolver is only used for war or self-defence at extremely short range and in very rapid firing.

There are many enthusiasts who make good scores at small stationary bull's eyes, and are constantly improving at that sort of skill, who could not hit even the outer edge of the target if called on to take a snap-shot from either on foot or horse-back.

In all shooting competitions, as in fact in all competitions which were originally intended to be practised for some useful purpose, there is a constant and seemingly inevitable tendency to drift into unpractical lines, and a development in just that direction which is useless for all practical purposes.

In racing it gets into breeding racing "machines" which cannot carry a child's weight; in pigeon-shooting, clay bird shooting, and rifle-shooting, it only teaches a knack for those particular sports which is of no use in the field. In the same way revolver shooting at stationary targets spoils a man's handling of a revolver.

If I had to train a man to shoot a revolver for practical use, I would rather take one with good eyesight and a steady hand, who had never fired a revolver before, than some of our crack revolver prize winners. The former may learn to shoot properly; the latter never. I consider the Series 3 (Rapid firing, six shots in 12 seconds), which the National Rifle Association have adopted at my suggestion, a very practical revolver competition, but unfortunately very few men enter for it, preferring the stationary targets.

As revolver shooting clubs have to study the likes and dislikes of their patrons, it seems inevitable that revolver shooting will have to continue on the same old unpractical lines of deliberate shooting at stationary targets.

WALTER WINANS.

SINGLESTICK—This weapon, as we know it nowadays, is nothing more than a somewhat poor substitute for the light fencing sabre, and there are some among us who are inclined to clamour for its entire abolition; they are not, however, likely to be gratified, as its very cheapness serves as its recommendation to members of many of the minor schools of arms. Singlestick, or cudgel-play, is moreover an honest, manly old English sport, which should rather be encouraged than allowed to sink into oblivion; we can trace its progress through the ages of fence side by side with that of its more lordly relative the broadsword; we find it all over civilised Europe in the fifteenth century, and even much earlier used, in conjunction generally with a shield of some sort, as the medium of deciding in the lists a difference between two common fellows, who, being persons of low degree, were not permitted to wear swords. A few notable examples have been handed down to us; one being in England in the time of Edward III. between Walter Blowberne and Hamon le Stare, who were nothing better than a pair of thieves who had fallen out about their booty; while Olivier de la Marche gives us a most accurately detailed account of a similar combat between two tailors named Mahuot and Jacotin Plouvier, which took place at Valenciennes in the presence of Duke Philippe le Bon in the year 1447. These judicial fights were conducted with considerable ceremony, and it was the common belief in those days that the Deity himself interposed to protect the innocent. The lists were carefully prepared, and the two men also, they being clothed in a special costume of dressed leather so tight that it had to be sewn on to their bodies; their hands and feet were bare; their hair was cut close, and the nails of both fingers and toes carefully pared, while a stout gallows at the entrance to the lists was ready for the reception of the vanquished man. When the quarrel was between a man and a woman, the latter had an advantage given to her, she being at large within the "Champ Clos" and armed with a large stone tied up in a cloth, while the man, provided with a club or cudgel, was placed up to his waist in a circular pit.

In the second part of *King Henry VI.* Shakespeare gives a similar encounter between Horner, an armourer, and Peter, his apprentice, in which the King himself acts as umpire.

The judicial combat died out; but we find our cudgel in Elizabethan times in the form of the "wafter" of the London 'prentices, sometimes mounted in a handle like that of a sword, and always accompanied by the hand-buckler as a means of defence. The sport, for such it had now become, was called "playing at bucklers."

In the seventeenth century we find but little mention of the cudgel, owing to the paucity of books on such matters, because, although prize-fights were many in those days, and the practical side of the art was sedulously cultivated, the men professionally engaged in it were anything but erudite, and the few fencing books in the English language were the work of enthusiastic amateurs who naturally paid more attention to their own proper weapon, the sword. But when we come to the eighteenth century we see it in the hands of the "gladiating" prize-fighters, such as Figg, Delforce and others (about whom Captain Godfrey tells us much that is interesting), in company with the backsword, just as much as we see the fencing foil and the small-sword in the hands of the gentlemen. The prize-fights with swords died out about the middle of the last century, but "cudgelling" remained popular, in the west of England, at any rate, until the middle of this present one. The fair at Purton, in North Wilts, was famous for encounters of this kind; and somewhere about 1820 a butcher named Blackford is recorded as having broken no less than fourteen heads in one day. The "Hungerford Revel" was another festive occasion in which cudgel-play, or "backswording," as it was sometimes called, formed a prominent part; and here one Morris Pope, a blacksmith, whose skill was such that he was regarded as Blackford's "successor," scored many a victory, and as many as twenty men on each side, representing the counties of Wilts and Somerset, made their appearance. The combatants stripped to their shirts, and their play, which was something analagous to that of the German students, was directed principally at the head, on which part alone a hit counted, and not even then unless an inch of blood made its appearance. Donald Walker, in his *Defensive Exercises* (1840), gives a very clear description of the "backswording" method: the men stood very near together, and the lunge and recover, as we have them, were not in any way recognised. In the position of *guard*, "the body is held upright; the head *backward*; the leg straight; the right arm advanced and nearly straight; the hand opposite the left

THE GUARD.
(From Walker's *Defensive Exercises.*)

shoulder. The left hand grasps a handkerchief, which is tied loosely round the left thigh, and the left elbow is elevated and thrown forward so as to protect the head." Masks, it is clear, were not in general use; but occasionally a sort of demi-mask was employed, which covered the face up to the eyebrows, leaving the upper part of the head exposed.

DEMI-MASK.

This old style of "cudgelling" is now quite extinct, and the "singlestick" of to-day is mainly a medium for learning the management of the light sabre as it appears in our modern fencing rooms. When "on guard," the weapon should be held in such a position as is at once the most secure for defence and the most handy for attack, being also the least fatiguing to the sword arm; and it is clear that this position is either the "medium" or the "resting medium," in which latter the hand is lowered a little to allow the pummel to rest on the thigh.

MEDIUM GUARD.
From *The Swordsman*.)

The cuts are six in number—two diagonally downwards at the head or shoulders, two diagonally upwards at the legs, and two horizontals at the belly and ribs; but in all well-regulated schools of arms the blow at the inside of the leg is strictly forbidden, on account of its serious consequences; the thrusts are usually delivered with the hand in "pronation." In defence, recourse should be had to the parries of foil play, in which the pupil ought to be well trained before he is allowed to take a stick in his hand at all; thus "Quarte," with its high and low variations, covers everything on the inside, from the top of

QUARTE.

SEPTIME.

(From *The Swordsman*.)

the head to the hip, and the lower line is protected by "Septime," while all the outside is covered similarly by "Tierce" and "Seconde."

TIERCE.

SECONDE.

(From *The Swordsman*.)

Care should be taken to train the pupil in reposting smartly the instant he has stopped the attack with his parry; from *quarte* the best repostes are over the stick at the right cheek or shoulder, or under it at the right side or leg; and last, but not least, the point, in this case with the hand in "supination." From septime point in "supination," or give a drawing cut at the outside of the leg by reversing the hand, which, if quickly done, is almost impossible to avoid; the repostes from tierce are a cut over the stick at the left cheek, under it at the left side or belly, and the point in pronation, while from seconde the cut should be given at the right cheek, or the point should be delivered over the enemy's stick with the hand in pronation.

The above five illustrations have been reproduced from *The Swordsman*, by permission of Messrs. Grevel and Co.

ALFRED HUTTON.

SKATING—Figure-Skating is an art, in the practice of which British experts differ from all others. There are, in fact, but two schools of figure-skating, the British and the non-British. Austrians, Canadians, Frenchmen and Swedes all skate in much the same way, but British figure-skaters adhere rigidly to their own peculiar style.

Skates—The best kind of skate is one that can be attached immovably to the sole of the boot. Adjustable skates, which always work loose or shift their position, should, if possible, be avoided. The foot plates, or mounts, one for the sole and one for the heel, are best made of light metal (aluminium answers admirably), and should be attached firmly to the boot with ordinary screws, four for the sole and four for the heel. It is best not to countersink the screw holes, as round-headed screws hold more securely than those with bevelled heads. These screws, $\frac{3}{8}$-inch long (exclusive of the head) for the sole plates, and $\frac{1}{2}$-inch long for the heel plates, should be blued to prevent rusting. The skate-blade should fit closely into the jaws of the mounts, and be secured by bolts having hexagonal nuts. Rivets work loose, and should not be used.

The blade which I have always recommended as most suitable for English ice and the British style of figure-skating is one which bears my name. It is $\frac{3}{16}$-inch wide on the face, *i.e.* between the two cutting edges, and is throughout its entire length (except the extreme toe and heel, which are rounded off) ground to a curve which forms an arc of a circle whose radius is 7 feet. It projects about $\frac{1}{2}$-inch behind the heel of the boot, and $\frac{1}{4}$-inch in front of the toe, and its sides are straight, and ground to an angle of about 95° with the face, so that the edges are obtuse-angled. If this blade is intended to be used on very hard ice, such as is met with in Switzerland or Sweden, the edges should be ground to a right-angle. There are two other blades used by expert figure-skaters which need mention. One, termed "the Dowler," from its inventor, Captain Dowler, has concave sides ground to a radius of 16 feet, so that the face of the blade varies in width from toe to heel. It is narrowest 4 inches from the heel, and widest at the toe. When travelling on large curves, an increased length of edge is said to be in contact with the ice, so that friction is diminished. The other blade is the one recommended by Mr. W. F. Adams, and is similar to that used by Swedish experts. Its sides are convex, the exact opposite to those of the Dowler. The widest portion of the blade is 4 inches distant from the heel, and measures ¼-inch. At the toe and heel the width is ⅛-inch. This blade is generally ground to a radius of 6 feet, as it is chiefly used by those who practise the small curved continuous figures of the non-British school of figure-skating.

The skate, with blade fitted, should be about 1¾-inch high, measured at that portion of the skate which lies under the ball of the foot. A skater equipped with a pair of skates such as I have described, needs to keep a pair of boots on purpose for skating. For those who do not care to do this, and for children and beginners, a good pair of "Acme" or of "Barney and Berry" skates, not too highly curved, will serve.

Boots and Costume—The upper leathers of skating boots should be moderately thick, and not extend higher up the leg than those of other boots. They should not quite meet when tightly laced up, so as to allow for stretching. Eyelet holes should be nearer together than usual. Under the tongue of the boot should be placed a strip of spongiopiline to prevent galling of the instep. Heels should have straight sides, and be about 1⅛-inch high, the corresponding thickness of sole being ⅜-inch.

Members of the "Skating Club" wear tall hats, black coats and trousers when skating in London, and no costume looks better for good skaters. In the country, knickerbockers, loose tweed coats (Norfolk jackets are very popular), and caps, or soft hats, are generally worn. Personally I think trousers always look better than knickerbockers. For ladies a well-fitting tailor-made dress looks best.

Ice and its Care—I am often asked, "How did you ever learn to skate in England? There is never any ice!" but the record of the Wimbledon Skating Club shows that during the past 18 years there have been 356 skating days, giving a yearly average of 20 days. During these eighteen years there have only been three winters without any skating.

Ice of the best quality is free from snow, and frozen upon deep water at a moderately low temperature. A thickness of 1⅛-inch of such ice will just bear an adult skater, but large numbers of people should not be allowed upon less than 2½ inches. Snow ice of the latter thickness will sometimes not bear even one skater, and during a thaw a much greater thickness of the same ice is quite unsafe. Ice may be kept in excellent order for figure-skating by the use of only one tool—the "Wimbledon Scow" (Fig. 1). This (to quote Mr. Dryden in *Figure-Skating Simple and Combined*, by

FIG. 1. THE "WIMBLEDON SCOW."

Monier-Williams, Pidgeon, and Dryden; London: Horace Cox) "consists of a plain sheet of No. 18 gauge galvanized iron, measuring 4 feet 6 inches in length and 2 feet in breadth. On to the back of the sheet of metal are bolted two wooden handles which run out parallel to each other for about 2 feet 6 inches beyond one of the longer sides, so that the person using the scow can hold one handle in each hand and push the scow in front of him along the ice, with the sheet of metal at such an angle to the face of the ice as he may at the moment find convenient." The scow will remove snow better than any other tool. It gets rid of dry skate cuttings, and the soft wet cuttings of thawing ice more efficiently than the commonly used broom, and answers all the purposes of the heavy ice scraper, or plane, in removing dangerous irregularities of ice surface. For depositing the snow heaped up by the scows on the nearest bank, snow boxes and shovels are of course essential.

Artificially-frozen Real Ice Rinks—There are now many of these rinks in different parts of the world, and figure-skating can be practised upon any one of them during the winter months when they are open. London possesses three rinks (Niagara Hall, National Skating Palace, and Prince's Skating Club, the last being only available for members); Paris has two (Pôle Nord and Palais de glace), and each of the following cities has one—Brighton, Brussels, Glasgow, Munich and New York. The method of construction is much the same in all. The rink floor consists of a network of pipes laid on a solid foundation. The water to be frozen—a shallow layer only—lies between and above these pipes, through which is constantly kept circulating a liquid termed the "brine" (solution of calcium chloride or some other saline). The brine is not liable to freeze, but can be brought to a very low temperature—below zero (Fahrenheit) even—by means of a suitable refrigerating apparatus, such as one depending upon the compression and condensation of ammonia gas.

Skating Clubs—The leading figure-skating club is "the Skating Club" of London, founded in 1830. Its members skate in the grounds of the Royal Toxophilite Society in Regent's Park, and wear a small silver skate as a badge of membership. Combined figures were originated in this club. The Edinburgh Skating Club, founded in 1642, is the oldest club, and the Wimbledon Skating Club is a very important organisation. Other clubs in Great Britain are the following:—Arctic, Birmingham, Cambridge University, Chiswick, Clifton, Crystal Palace, Glasgow, Hampstead, Ipswich, Leamington, Manchester, Norwich, Oxford University, Southampton, Thames Valley and Tonbridge: for entrance into almost any of the foregoing clubs a test of ability in figure-skating is demanded. The National Skating Association was founded in 1879, and is a member of the International Skating Union. One of its objects is to promote figure-skating by means of the establishment of standards of proficiency. These standards are represented by the four tests printed at the end of this article. A distinctive badge for each test is awarded to successful candidates. There are at present some 600 badge holders.

The N.S.A. has recently instituted a competition in combined figure-skating. It is open to teams of four skaters, either (1) representing branches of the N.S.A., or (2) representing properly constituted skating clubs, or (3) composed of full members of the N.S.A. The Davos Platz Skating Club has twice been successful in winning the Challenge Shield presented to the best team.

The Amateur Championship of the World in figure-skating was held in London in February, 1898, under the auspices of the N.S.A. Herr Grenander, of the Stockholm Skating Club, was the winner. Previous champions have been, in 1896 Herr Fuchs, of the Munich Skating Club, and in 1897 Herr Hügel, of the Vienna Skating Club. No serious British competitor has yet entered in these competitions, as the British style of figure-skating is not recognised by the International Skating Union.

Form—There is a singular unanimity of opinion amongst British experts as to what constitutes good style in figure-skating. Certain rules governing the attitude of the body and intended to assist the skater to preserve stability of balance with least effort to himself, have been termed the rules of "form." These have long been accepted as embodying the best British ideas on the subject, and a skater must adhere to them if he wishes to be considered an exponent of the British style. The essentials of these rules of form may be summarised as follows:—

I. Body to be held strictly upright, moderate flexion only being permitted at the moment of taking a stroke.

II. Employed leg to be kept straight, the knee being fully extended whenever possible, flexion only being permitted at the moment of taking a stroke.

III. Unemployed leg to be carried behind the employed whenever possible, the heels being approximated.

IV. Head to be turned in direction of progress, and carried horizontally, any tendency to look down upon the ice being particularly avoided.

V. Arms to hang loosely by the sides of the body as far as possible.

When progressing upon an edge, it is usual for the skater to hold his body not facing full

PLATE I. BRITISH STYLE OF FIGURE-SKATING.

front, but with a sideways inclination, so that if he is moving forwards on the right foot, the right shoulder leads and looks together with the head in the direction of progress, while the left shoulder, together with the unemployed leg, is held back. If, on the other hand, he is moving backwards on the right foot, the position of the body remains as before, the left shoulder and the unemployed leg now leading and looking together with the head in the direction of progress. The unemployed leg is generally carried not only to the rear of its fellow, but with the knee slightly bent, and the foot turned so as to make something more than a right angle with the employed foot. In any event, the unemployed leg should be carried in an easy unconstrained attitude, and should be kept quiet and not swung about. Plate I., reproduced from a photograph taken and kindly sent to me by Mr. W. Leaf, represents Mr. Edward Pollock on a curve of outside edge backwards. It is a good illustration of the best style of figure-skating according to British ideas.

Most skaters allow themselves a certain amount of latitude in their interpretation of these rules of form, just so much, in fact, as to prevent stiffness and want of elasticity of movement. Those trained at St. Moritz and Davos, however, not only allow themselves no such latitude, but have expanded the rules of form somewhat in the direction of fostering rigidity of action. A straight unemployed, as well as employed leg is insisted upon, the former being held close against the latter. The toe, also, of the unemployed foot generally points in much the same direction as its fellow. The best exponents of this ultra-British or Anglo-Swiss style of skating are probably the strongest and most accurate figure-skaters of the day. Plates II. and III., reproduced from photographs kindly taken at St. Moritz by Mr. E. Cohen, represent Dr. Holland on curves of outside edge forwards, and outside edge backwards respectively. The reader will note how the style of this very fine skater differs from that shown in Plate I.

PLATE III. ULTRA-BRITISH, OR ANGLO-SWISS STYLE OF FIGURE-SKATING.

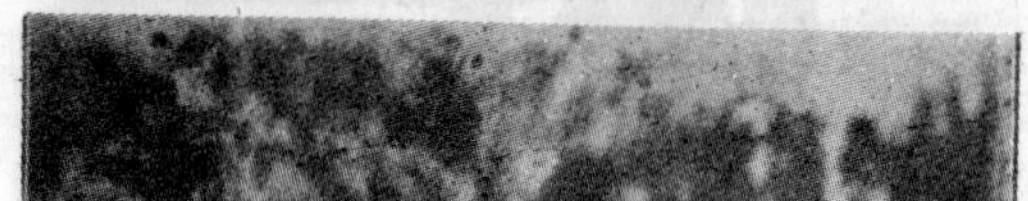

PLATE II. ULTRA-BRITISH OR ANGLO-SWISS STYLE OF FIGURE-SKATING.

With regard to the non-British style of figure-skating, no very definite rules of form have yet been laid down by its exponents, who, indeed, are not entirely agreed amongst themselves as to what is the correct way of skating the very difficult and complicated figures performed by them. There is, however, a unanimity of opinion with regard to the employed leg, the bending of the knee of which is not only permitted, but enjoined. The leg, too, which British skaters term unemployed is as much employed as its fellow, being constantly swung forwards or backwards; indeed, it appears to contribute more than anything else to the skater's balance. Somewhat extensive excursions of the arms, also, are not discouraged (*see* Plate IV.) The small circles and narrow curves which predominate in the figures peculiar to this style of skating are best performed in the way just described, while the British figure skater's rules of form are best adapted to the large curves and bold turns which constitute his ideal.

If the skater observes British rules of form, he will find that he travels approximately upon that portion of the skate-blade termed in Fig. 2 the **Travelling Area**. This is the case whether he is simply travelling forwards or backwards upon a curve of outside or inside edge, or executing one of the many turns enumerated later on. The portion of skate-blade in front of the travelling area, termed in Fig. 2 the **Striking Area**, is used almost entirely for making a stroke from one foot to the other. The table accompanying Fig. 2 explains in detail the exact portion of skate-blade used in the various edges, turns, and changes. It will be noted that the changes and some few of the turns are made a little in front of, or a little behind, the travelling area; but nevertheless the majority of the work of figure-skating is done on that area of the skate, if the skater holds himself in accordance with the rules of form. Should he not observe those rules, he will probably rock to and fro beyond the limits of the travelling area, and his balance will become proportionately unstable. The illustration, Fig. 2, and the table following it, are taken from the *Figure-Skating* volume of the Isthmian Library, now in the press, written by the author of this article, and published by A. D. Innes and Co.

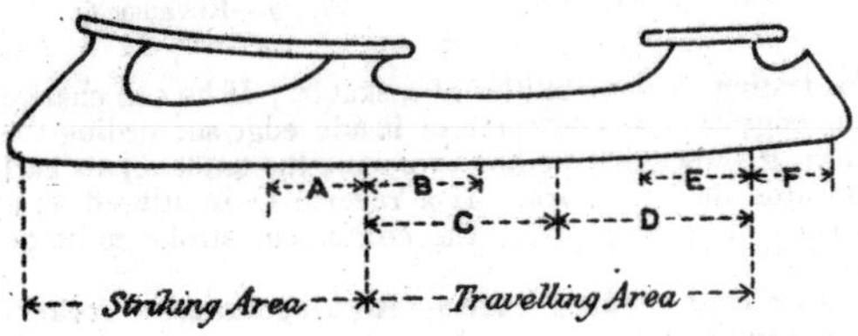

FIG. 2.

A. Inside back change made with the continuous stroke.
   Outside back change made with the continuous stroke.
   Outside forward bracket.
B. All the forward turns, except outside forward bracket.
C. Inside and outside edges backwards.
D. Inside and outside edges forwards.
E. All the back turns, except inside back three, inside back bracket, and outside back bracket.
F. Inside forward change made with the continuous stroke.
   Outside forward change made with the continuous stroke.
   Inside back three.
   Inside back bracket.
   Outside back bracket.

The four edges—Figure-skaters do not travel much upon the flat of the skate, but almost entirely upon one or other edge. The inside edge corresponds to the inner side of the foot, and the outside to the outer side, and as progression may be forwards or backwards upon either edge, four edges are spoken of.

Inside edge forwards—To make the stroke, say, from the left to the right foot, the body and right knee must be bent, and the left foot turned toe outwards at an angle of 45° with the line of motion. A vigorous thrust is then made against the ice with the left foot, the striking area (Fig. 2) of the skate-blade being chiefly used, although the whole length of blade may be employed for a powerful stroke. As soon as he is launched on the edge, the skater must straighten the body and right knee, and hold himself in accordance with the rules of form, and travel upon the portion of skate-blade marked D in Fig. 2. The next stroke on to the left foot is taken in a similar way. The main difficulty in skating on this edge is to hold large sustained curves, there being a tendency to curl inwards and make small scratchy strokes. The antidote is to hold the body perfectly upright and keep the unemployed leg well to the rear, with the toe turned outwards.

Outside edge forwards is best learnt by taking short steps as if walking, but crossing one foot over the other, and placing the skate down on the edge at each step. When confidence is established, strokes may be taken from one foot to the other without any crossing of the feet. As on the inside edge forwards, the skater travels upon D (Fig. 2).

Inside edge backwards is by far the most difficult of the four edges. The best way to learn it is to practise the forward "three" turn described later on. The stroke from one foot to the other is exceedingly difficult. Just before the stroke is taken, say, from left to right foot, the skater must forsake the proper attitude on the left inside edge and turn his head to look over the left shoulder. The left heel must then be turned sharply inwards till the foot is almost at right angles with the line of motion, and at the same moment the right foot must be placed down on the edge close to and parallel with the left foot, a push off being obtained from the latter. The skater will now be in correct attitude for the inside edge backwards on the right foot, and must travel on C (Fig. 2).

Outside edge backwards is best learnt by a gentle walking movement backwards, one foot being placed exactly behind the other at each step. If the head is turned on to the right shoulder as the left foot is put down and *vice versâ*, the skater soon gets on to the edge and makes curves of gradually increasing length. He must remember (1) not to cross the feet, but to place the rear foot down as though about to follow in the same curve as its predecessor; (2) directly the skate touches the ice to travel upon C (Fig. 2); and (3) to skate very slowly and without any hurry at the stroke.

The four simple eights consist each of two plain circles on one of the four edges, skated so that the marks on the ice resemble the numeral 8. The two forward eights are very easy, and the two backward eights very difficult, especially the inside back eight, which involves the difficult stroke from inside back to inside back. In practising these figures it is usual to commence each stroke at a fixed point or "centre," as shown in Fig. 3. An orange is generally placed on the ice for the purpose. The symbol R.O.F. means right foot outside edge forwards. Other similar symbols on the diagrams in this article need no explanation.

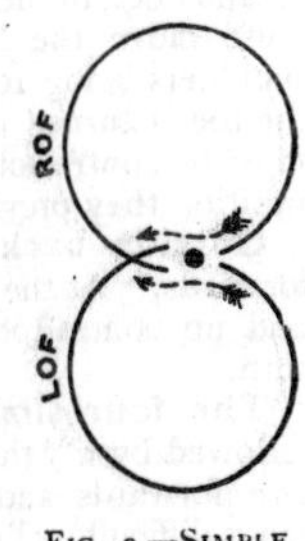

FIG. 3—SIMPLE EIGHT.

The four changes—A change of edge or "serpentine line" is made when a skater progressing, say, on the inside edge forwards, passes across the flat of the skate on to the outside edge forwards (Fig. 4). A similar change can of course be made from any of the other three edges. There is no difficulty in these movements if the skater holds himself in correct attitude on each edge.

The four "three" turns—By a "turn" is meant a turning or revolving of the body upon one foot, so that forward progression is converted into backward progression, or *vice versâ*. Three turns and bracket turns are accomplished upon two edges, rocking and counter-rocking turns upon one edge only. In corresponding threes and rockers, the body is revolved in the same direction. Similarly with brackets and counters.

Inside forward three (Fig. 5)—This is a turn from inside forwards to outside backwards. On the right foot the body revolves from right to left. In the corresponding bracket turn the revolution is from left to right. The skater travels upon D (Fig. 2) before the turn, and upon C after the turn. To make the turn the skater shifts his balance forwards on to B, and starts the revolution of the body by pressing back the rear shoulder, so that the front shoulder comes still more to the front. At the same moment the heel is turned outwards away from the unemployed foot, and the head is turned to look over the shoulder which is to lead after the turn.

Outside forward three—from outside forwards to inside backwards. The same portion of the skate is used as in the preceding figure. To commence the

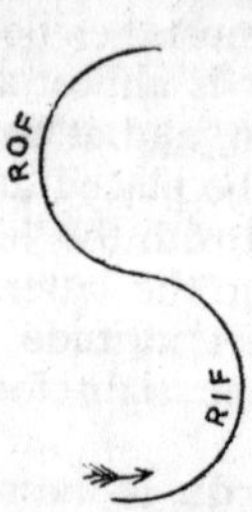

FIG. 4.—CHANGE.

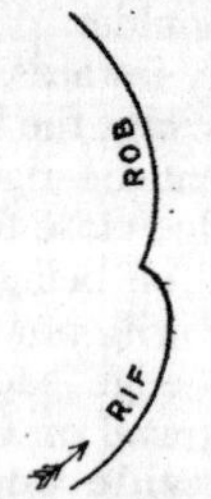

FIG. 5.—THREE.

necessary revolution of the body on the right foot from left to right, the left shoulder is brought forwards. At the turn, the heel is turned inwards and the head moved to look over the left shoulder. After the turn the left shoulder must be strongly rotated back again. The difficulty which exists of holding a bold curve after the turn, without curling inwards, depends upon this necessity for contra-rotation of the body. The turn must not be hurried, and the unemployed leg must be kept well behind its fellow after the turn, with the knee and toe turned in the direction of progress.

Inside back three—from inside back to outside forwards. This is the most difficult of all the threes. The skater travels upon C (Fig. 2) before the turn, and D after the turn, the actual revolution taking place as far back on the skate as possible—*i.e.* upon F. Some seconds before the turn, the skater, if upon the right foot, must move the head on to the right shoulder, the shoulders being rotated from left to right. At the turn the toe is turned outwards, and after the turn the body must be contra-rotated, so that the shoulders regain the position they previously occupied.

Outside back three—from outside back to inside forwards. At the turn the skater pivots upon E (Fig. 2), and no contra-rotation of the body is needed after the turn.

The four simple Q's—A Q (Fig. 6) is a change followed by a "three" turn. Hence there are four Q's, two forwards and two backwards, the latter being the most difficult. The outside back Q, which contains the difficult inside back three, is the hardest of the series. The Q's can be skated strictly in accordance with the rules of form, if commenced at a good speed; but if used as a means of gaining pace, as they often are, they must be skated with the "continuous stroke," which is described under the heading of continuous figures.

The four simple reverse Q's—A reverse Q is a "three" turn followed by a change, so that there are four reverse Q's, two forwards and two backwards. The outside forward reverse Q (Fig. 7) is an excellent figure

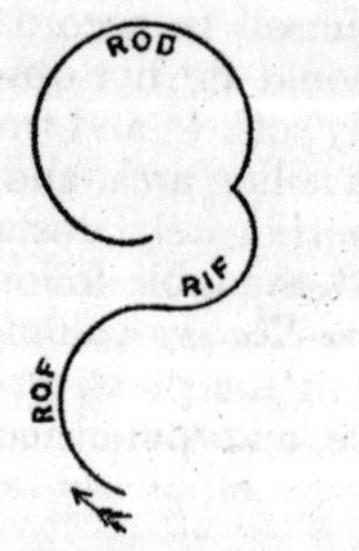

FIG. 6.—Q.

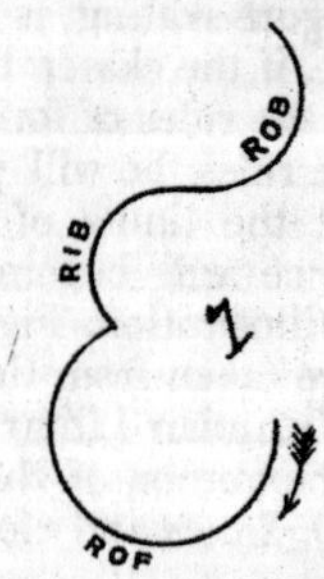

FIG. 7.—REVERSE Q.

for testing the capabilities of a skater. If he can change the edge after a bold curve of inside edge succeeding the turn, it shows that he has overcome the tendency to curl inwards after the turn. If a reverse Q is utilised as a means of gaining pace, the continuous stroke must be used.

The four rocking turns—Rocking turns or rockers are turns in which one edge of the skate only is used, the body being revolved in the same direction as in the corresponding "three" turns. Hence the outside forward rocker (Fig. 8) is a turn from outside forward to outside back, and on the right foot the body revolves from left to right. There are three other rockers, the inside forward, the inside back, and the outside back, and the last named is the easiest. The foot has to be turned through a greater angle in rockers than in threes, hence more confidence is needed. The difficulty in all is to hold the edge after the turn.

The four counter-rocking turns—Counter-rocking turns or counters (Fig. 9) are turns in which one edge of the skate only is used, the body being revolved in an opposite or counter direction to that in which it is revolved in the corresponding "three" turns. Just as there are four rockers, so there are four counters, and the

FIG. 8.—ROCKER.

FIG. 9.—COUNTER.

FIG. 10.—BRACKET.

back outside counter is far the most difficult. The use of the continuous stroke facilitates the execution of these turns.

The four bracket turns—A bracket is similar to a three, but the body is turned in the opposite direction, and the skate marks resemble a bracket in shape (Fig. 10). Brackets, like threes, can be skated from all four edges. They are all very difficult, but especially the back outside bracket. The turn of the outside forward bracket is made at A (Fig. 2), and that of the inside and outside back brackets at F. Suitable movements of the arms are essential for executing these figures—movements of the shoulders and head being unimportant.

The four mohawks—A mohawk is a drop from either of the forward edges of one foot, to a similar, but back edge of the other foot, or *vice versâ*, the direction in which the skater moves remaining the same throughout.

Outside forward mohawk (Fig. 11)—The skater, when on the outside forwards of the right foot, rotates his body from right to left and looks over the left shoulder. At the same moment he crosses the left foot, toe outwards, behind the right foot, and places it down on the outside backwards.

Inside forward mohawk—is skated in a similar manner. The two **back mohawks** are simple strokes from the back edges to the corresponding forward edges.

Choctaws—are similar figures to mohawks, except that if the skater starts, say on the outside forwards, he drops on to the inside backwards (Fig. 12).

Cross-mohawks and cross-choctaws—In these figures, which are curiosities and not serious movements, the skater crosses the second foot in front of the first, and turns his body almost completely round in a direction

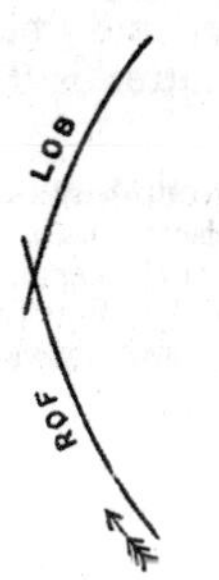

FIG. 11.—MOHAWK.

FIG. 12.—CHOCTAW.

opposite to that in which it is turned in corresponding mohawks and choctaws.

Besides the simple eights, many others are skated in which the different turns or other figures are incorporated in each circle of the eight. A **rocker-Q** is a change followed by a rocker. Similarly we have **counter-Q's** and **bracket-Q's**, and the reverse varieties of each. Two, three, four or more "three" turns can be skated in sequence. So also can rockers, counters, and brackets. The expression "two turns" always means two "three" turns in sequence. In correspondence with this practice, the term "turn" in combined figure-skating always means a "three" turn. It is usual, too, in combined figures to replace the term Q by the call "Change, turn." Similarly, a reverse Q is "Turn, change."

Combined Figure-Skating is the art of skating in combination with one or more skaters the figures already enumerated. Suppose, say, six skaters (A, B, C, D, E, and F) standing at the corners of an imaginary hexagon, in the order shown in Fig. 13. A and B, who are partners, skate towards the centre of the hexagon, and crossing one another at that point, skate away from one another to the circumference of an imaginary circle, whose centre is the centre of the hexagon. The other pairs, C and D, and E and F, take a corresponding course; but C and D start directly after A and B, and just before E and F.

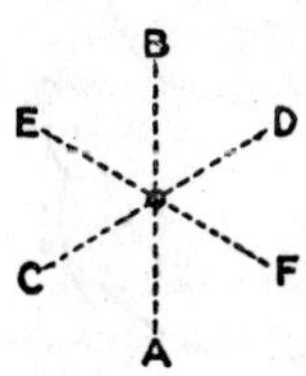

FIG. 13.

If the figure is one of the circling variety, all six skaters now skate in the same direction round the centre, at equal distances from it and from one another, each skating opposite to and in time with his partner. Towards the termination of the figure, the skaters approach the centre again in the same order as before, and partners pass one another at the centre, shoulder to shoulder, and commence a fresh figure.

Explanation of terms used in Combined Figure-Skating—(Taken from *Figure-Skating: Simple and Combined*, and founded on the "Explanation of Terms" authorised by the Conference of Skating Clubs, July, 1891)—

1. A "movement" is a figure or a part of a figure skated on one foot only—*e.g.* Q, three.
2. A "figure" is a movement or a series of movements, having a recognised name—*e.g.* Q, twice back, mohawk
3. A "call" is a figure or a series of figures beginning and ending at the centre, such figures being determined by the word of command of the caller.
4. The term "centre" applied to any figure means that it is to be executed close to the centre.
5. The terms "meet" and "pass" are used to express two methods in which the centre may be passed in the middle of a call.

When the word "meet" is called, a fresh stroke is taken up at the centre.

When the word "pass" is called, a fresh stroke, if demanded by the call, is taken up beyond the centre.

6. The term "about" applied to any figure means a change in the direction of revolution round the centre in the course of that figure.
7. The terms "out" and "in" are used in any call or part of a call in which the skaters do not circle round the centre.
8. The term "entire" may be applied at the option of the caller to any single figure in the course of which the skaters both leave and return to the centre. Should the skaters leave and return to the centre more than once in the course of such a figure, the caller must repeat the word "entire" each time he passes the centre.

Rules of Combined Figure-Skating—(Taken from *Figure-Skating: Simple and Combined*, and founded on the "Rules" authorised by the Conference of Skating Clubs, July, 1891)—

1. The caller sets the time, speed, and mode of skating all calls, and must be accurately followed by the other skaters.
2. Every figure must be commenced on the outside edge, unless the inside edge be specified in the call.
3. Whenever the foot is changed at the commencement of a new figure the word "and" must be used in the call to denote that change.
4. The centre must always be kept outside the curve on which it is approached, unless the word "off" is called, when it must be kept inside the curve.
5. When starting from rest to skate a new call or set of calls, the skater must keep the centre inside the curve on which he leaves it, and must commence the first figure on the right foot, unless it is otherwise specified.
6. Whenever the centre is passed in the middle of a call one of the words "centre," "meet" or "pass" must be inserted in the call.

Combined figures may be divided into three groups—

(1) The ordinary circling figures, in which the skater circles round the centre in the same direction throughout the call.

(2) The "about" circling figures, in which the skater, after circling in one direction, turns about, somewhat like a ship tacking, and circles back again in the opposite direction.

(3) The "out and in" figures, in which the skater does not circle round the centre at all,

but skates directly away from the centre, and directly back again

Group (1) is further subdivided into (*a*) figures in which the centre is not passed in the middle of the call, and (*b*) figures in which it is so passed.

As there are many hundreds of commonly-practised combined figures, it is impossible within the limits of this article to do more than enumerate one or two belonging to each group. The *centre* is a fixed point on the ice (an orange is generally used) from which the skaters start each call and to which they finally return to commence the same or a new call. The *caller* is one of the first pair of skaters. He decides what figures are to be skated in each call, and calls them out in a loud voice. A good caller's qualifications are as follows:—(1) He must have a facility for arranging groups of calls so that each call is skated on both feet, but with one or more different calls intervening. (2) He should as a general rule deliver a new call before the skaters reach the centre, not after they have commenced to leave it. (3) He must know every variety of combined figure, and give each call its correct name in accordance with the above Rules and Explanations, and not call figures which are too difficult for his team. (4) He should be a good, steady and accurate skater.

Twice back and forward (Fig. 14) is the commonest call belonging to Group I, sub-division *a*. The skaters, two, four, six or more, stand each about three yards from the centre, and if there are six, in the order shown in Fig. 13. The different pairs skate towards the centre to commence the call in rotation in the manner already described. Each skater starts on the right foot, and makes the first stroke to the left of the centre (*see* Rule 5). The figure "twice back" consists, as Fig. 14 shows, of a forward three followed by a drop on to the outside edge backwards of the other foot and the same two movements repeated. When all the skaters are circling round

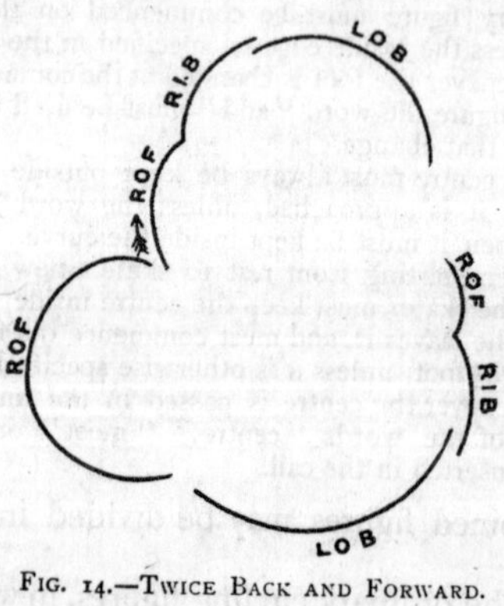

FIG. 14.—TWICE BACK AND FORWARD.

the centre they should again occupy the same relative positions adopted at the start (Fig. 13). This is called keeping the figure "square." They return to the centre on a bold curve of outside edge forwards, and, remembering to keep the centre outside the curve on which it is approached, unless the word "off" is called (*see* Rule 4), commence the same call, or any other that may be called, on the left foot. The average diameter of the circle round which the skaters move in this and other circling figures is 80 feet.

The following points must be borne in mind by the first pair of skaters in a combined figure. The caller leads the figure and sets the time, speed and mode of skating all calls (see Rule 1). The diagram represents the mode in which the average caller skates the figure. His partner's duties are (1) to watch the caller, skate as he does and keep time with him, (2) to keep the centre in a straight line between himself and the caller, (3) to arrive at the centre simultaneously with the caller. Each remaining skater in a combined figure must remember (1) to watch the caller and skate as he does, (2) to watch all the other skaters and skate so that his position relatively to them corresponds with Fig. 13—*i.e.* help to keep the figure "square," (3) to keep time with his partner, and not skate opposite to him unless the latter is "square" with the others.

Other simple calls belonging to Group I, sub-division *a*, are—"Forward entire," being a plain circle of outside edge forwards beginning and ending at the centre, "Inside forward entire," "Forward turn entire," "Inside forward turn entire," "Twice back and forward turn,"

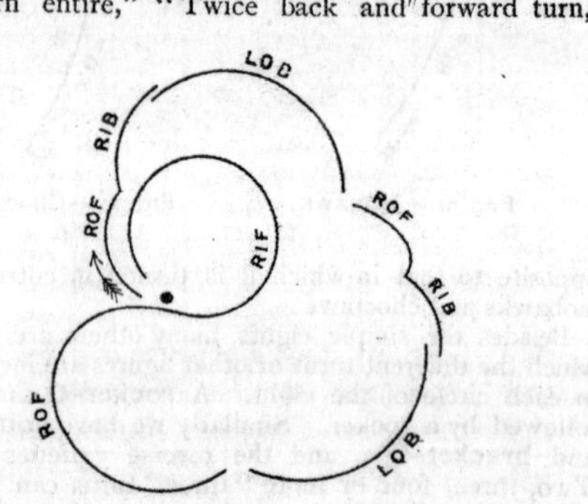

FIG. 15.—TWICE BACK AND FORWARD CENTRE-CHANGE ENTIRE.

"Twice back and forward and inside forward turn," "Twice back turn," "Twice back and inside back turn," and countless others.

Group I, sub-division *b*, may be further subdivided into three sections—(1) centre figures, (2) meet figures, and (3) pass figures.

Twice back and forward centre-change entire (Fig. 15) is an easy call belonging to section (1). After the "twice back," the skaters run up on the outside edge forwards to the centre, on the near side of which they change the edge, continuing back to the centre on the curve of inside edge forwards. A similar change can of course be made at the centre from the other three edges preceded by suitable movements.

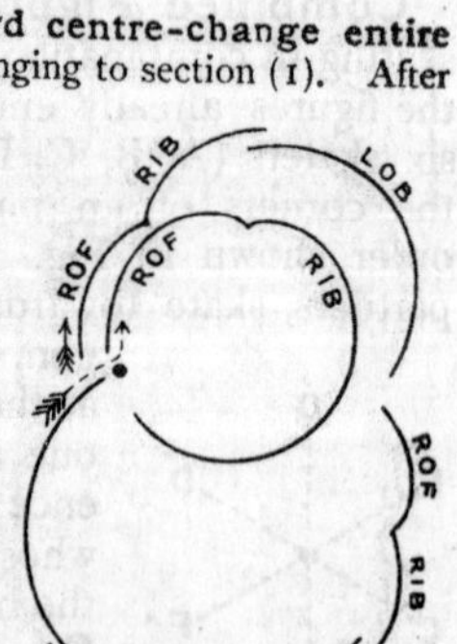

FIG. 16.—TWICE BACK OFF MEET AND FORWARD TURN ENTIRE.

Twice back off meet and forward turn entire (Fig. 16). This is one of the most familiar calls belonging to section (2). The skaters run up to the centre on the second "back" and take up the fresh stroke necessitated by the forward turn on the "off" side of the centre.

Twice back and forward and inside forward off

pass and forward (Fig. 17). This call belonging to section (3) is easily understood from the diagram.

Group II. consists of the "about" circling figures and the call, **Once back and forward turn about and**

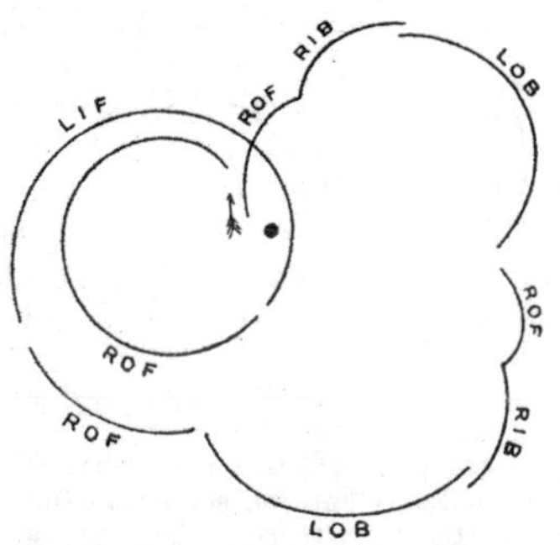

FIG. 17.—TWICE BACK AND FORWARD AND INSIDE OFF PASS AND FORWARD.

once back and forward turn (Fig. 18), sufficiently explains this variety of combined figure. The chief point to be noted is that the skaters must all skate the about forward turn simultaneously.

Group III. contains the "out and in" figures, and **Forward and forward turn out and forward in** (Fig. 19)

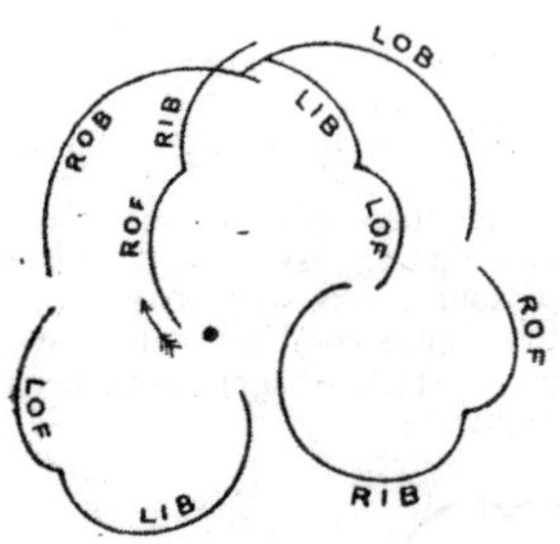

FIG. 18.—ONCE BACK AND FORWARD TURN ABOUT AND ONCE BACK AND FORWARD TURN.

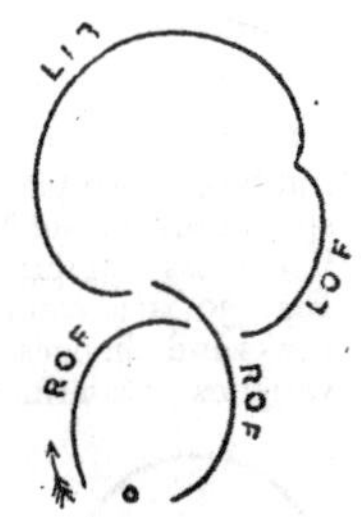

FIG. 19.—FORWARD AND FORWARD TURN OUT AND FORWARD IN.

is a typical call. It is one of the easiest and most commonly used on the ice, and the diagram fully explains it. Calls consisting of figures belonging to two or more groups are frequently skated. In fact, the number of combinations of figures making suitable calls is without limit.

Simultaneous Combined Figures—In these figures the same calls are skated as in the ordinary combined figures, but each skater is not paired off with a partner, as all the performers skate together simultaneously. To make this possible the skaters do not skate right up to the centre, but to the circumference of an imaginary circle surrounding the centre. This plan is useful when odd numbers are skating together.

Continuous Figure-Skating—This is the kind of figure-skating in which experts in the non-British style are proficient. The figures practised cannot be executed with facility in the British style, and so have not hitherto been introduced into combined figure-skating. Small circles and narrow curves are predominant, and for these the bent employed knee and non-quiescent unemployed leg are essential. The continuous figure-skater's aim, moreover, is to make sustained efforts on one foot, and to skate figures of a definite prescribed pattern, devised perhaps by himself, and often limited "to place" on the ice. Such "picture figures," as they are termed, composed generally of movements of exceptional difficulty, require constant persevering practice. The average English skating winter is never long enough to enable even our best men to attempt these figures with prospect of attaining even reasonable proficiency, but now that artificially frozen ice-rinks are open in London for

PLATE IV. NON-BRITISH STYLE OF FIGURE-SKATING.

six months of the year, many skaters are mastering them. Although the style adopted by most continuous skaters is the reverse of graceful to the English eye, it is certain that the most difficult continuous figures can be executed with perfect grace, as Herr Grenander, the World's Amateur Champion in figure-skating for 1898, and by far the most accomplished continuous skater yet seen in this country, has shown us. I am much indebted to Herr Grenander for permission to publish Plate IV., a portrait of himself just finishing a curve of inside edge forwards. A description of this distinguished

Swedish expert's style will be found in the *Figure-Skating* volume of the Isthmian library. A skater obtains the impetus necessary for progressing continuously upon one foot by means of a succession of "destroyals" and "rightings" of equilibrium effected at the moment of changing the edge or making a turn, and termed "the continuous stroke." When about to change, say, a forward edge, the skater leans strongly over, so as momentarily almost to lose his equilibrium, his body being in advance of his foot. To regain his balance, he turns his skate into a sharper curve, and brings the foot quickly forwards on the new edge so as to overtake the body. This rapid advance of the foot to catch up the body gives the skater added impetus. Similarly, when skating turns, the skater allows the body to get in advance of the foot, and at the moment of turning draws the latter rapidly after the body at an increased rate of speed.

Besides the changes of edge and different varieties of turns already enumerated in this article, the following miscellaneous figures are used in continuous skating :—

Loops are of three kinds—the ordinary variety, the turn loop, and the bracket loop. **Loops of the ordinary variety** (Fig. 20) are formed by suddenly converting a large into a small curve with an equally sudden return

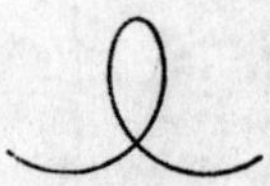

FIG. 20. LOOP.

FIG. 21. TURN LOOP.

FIG. 22. BRACKET LOOP.

to the large curve. They can be skated from all edges, those on the inside edge being the most difficult. **Turn loops** (Fig. 21) are turns worked into the form of a loop, and **Bracket loops** (Fig. 22) are brackets skated in a similar way.

Ringlets are circular loops.

Cross-cuts are of three kinds—the ordinary variety, the counter cross-cut, and the Swedish cross-cut. **Cross-cuts of the ordinary variety** (Fig. 23) are commenced in the same way as corresponding loops, but at the apex of a possible loop the skate is brought to a standstill (in the case of a forward cross-cut), and is then

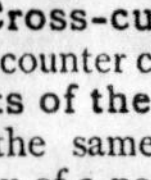

FIG. 23. CROSS-CUT.

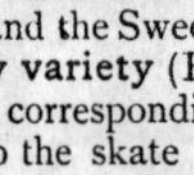

FIG. 24. COUNTER CROSS-CUT.

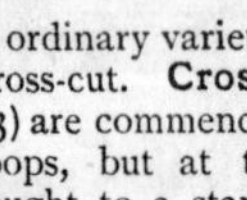

FIG. 25. SWEDISH CROSS-CUT.

drawn rapidly backwards to be again brought forward until the last curve cuts the first. The base of a cross-cut may be straight, as in Fig. 23, or curved. Cross-cuts can be skated from all edges. Fig. 24 is a diagram of the counter cross-cut, and Fig. 25 of the Swedish cross-cut.

Beaks resemble rockers and counters, since each figure is skated on one edge, and the foot is moved in the same direction as in the corresponding rocker or counter. In **rocker-beaks** (Fig. 26) the foot is moved rocker-wise, and in **counter-beaks** (Fig. 27) counter-wise.

Both rocker and counter-beaks can be skated from all edges. Beaks of both varieties can be made either narrow or broad, according as the two curves are near together or far apart. When the second curve is so near

FIG. 26. ROCKER-BEAK.

FIG. 27. COUNTER-BEAK.

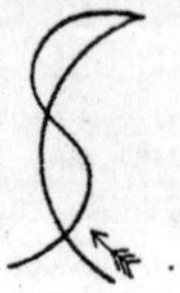

FIG. 28. PIG'S-EAR.

the first as to be practically superposed, a **hook** is the result—a most difficult figure.

A **pig's-ear** (Fig. 28) is a rocker-beak followed by a change, skated so that the serpentine line crosses the first curve of the beak twice. Figs. 29 and 30 are illus-

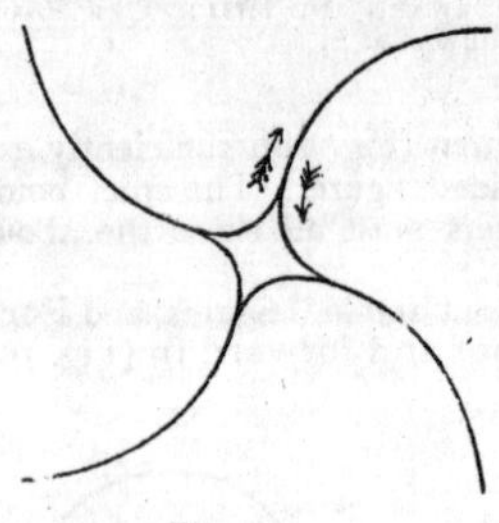

FIG. 29.

FIG. 30.

trations of two picture figures, both of which occur in the special test of the National Skating Association. Fig. 29 is a cross comprised of four hooks with changes, and Fig. 30 is a complicated figure consisting of counter-beaks and changes. Figs. 31–34 are diagrams of different varieties of continuous eights.

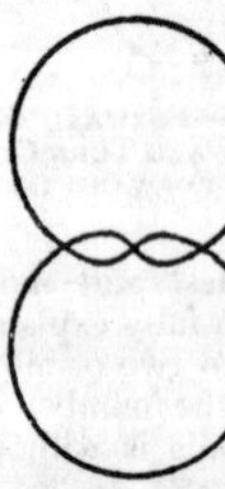

FIG. 31. CONTINUOUS EIGHT.

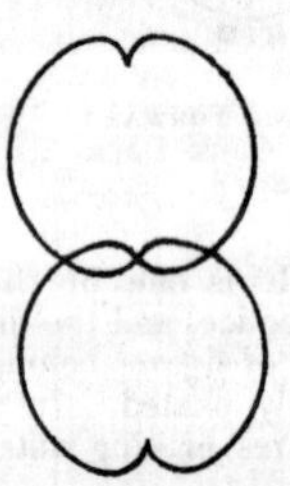

FIG. 32. CONTINUOUS CHANGE TURN EIGHT.

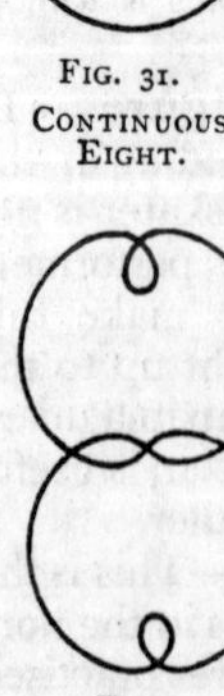

FIG. 33. CONTINUOUS CHANGE LOOP EIGHT.

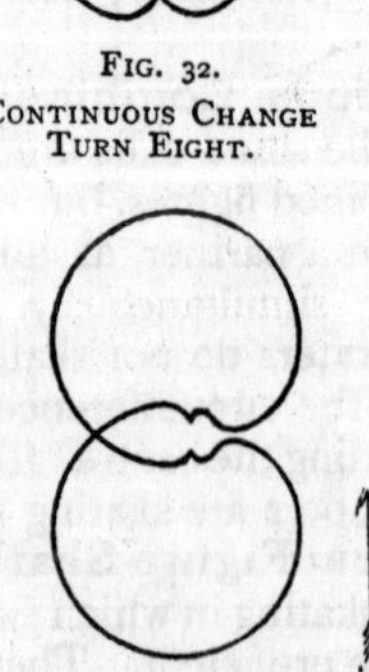

FIG. 34. CONTINUOUS COUNTER EIGHT.

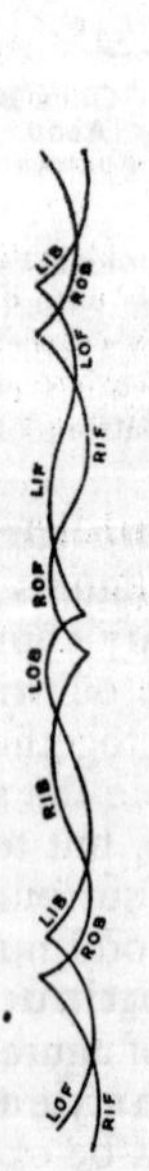

FIG. 35.

FIG. 36.

GRAPE VINES.

Grape-vines are two-footed Canadian figures of which here are a great many different varieties. Both feet are kept on the ice throughout, and the skater always progresses in one direction. The movements, though not hard to execute, are difficult to learn, as it is not easy to follow the complicated intertwining of the feet. I have only space to give diagrams (taken from Mr. Meagher's book on *Figure Skating*) of two of these figures—the single grape-vine (Fig. 35), which can be skated with the right or left shoulder leading, and the double grape-vine (Fig. 36), which can be skated forwards or backwards.

Hand-in-hand Figure-Skating—A large proportion of the figures enumerated in this article can be skated by gentleman and lady hand-in-hand. As a book has recently been published (*see* Bibliography) devoted entirely to hand-in-hand figures, it is unnecessary to give any detailed account of them here.

MONTAGU S. MONIER-WILLIAMS.

Bibliography—*The Art of Skating*, George Anderson ("Cyclos"), (London, Horace Cox); *A System of Figure-Skating*, T. M. Witham, formerly Vandervell and Witham (London, Horace Cox); *Figure-Skating, Simple and Combined*, M. S. Monier-Williams, W. R. Pidgeon and A. Dryden (London, Horace Cox); *Skating Volume of the Badminton Library*, J. M. Heathcote, C. G. Tebbutt and T. M. Witham (London, Longmans and Co.); *Figure-Skating Volume of the Isthmian Library*, M. S. Monier-Williams (London, A. D. Innes and Co.); *Skating Volume of the All England Series*, Douglas Adams (London, Bell and Sons); *Skating Volume of the Oval Series*, C. G. Tebbutt, A. Read, and A. Tebbutt (London, Routledge and Sons); *Figure and Fancy Skating*, G. A. Meagher (London, Bliss, Sands and Foster); *Hand-in-Hand Figure-Skating*, N. G. Thompson and F. L. Cannan (London, Longmans and Co.); *On the Outside Edge, being Diversions in the History of Skating*, G. H. Fowler (London, Horace Cox).

TESTS OF THE NATIONAL SKATING ASSOCIATION OF GREAT BRITAIN.

THIRD CLASS ICE FIGURE-SKATING TEST.

The judges will require the test to be skated in good form, the essentials of which are (1) Sideways attitude of body; (2) Face turned in direction of progress; (3) Uprightness of carriage; (4) Straightness of employed leg, and (5) Approximation of heels.

Test—(*a*) A forward outside 3 on each foot, the length of each curve being 15 feet at least. The 3 need not be skated to a centre. (*b*) The ordinary and cross outside roll forward and backward, the length of each curve being 10 feet at least. (*c*) A forward outside 8, the diameter of each circle being 5 feet at least.

In every case two of the appointed judges must be present at the examination of a candidate, and the candidate must satisfy both judges.

SECOND CLASS ICE FIGURE-SKATING TEST.

No candidate can be judged for this test unless he has previously passed the Third Class Test. The judges will require all turns to be skated clean, and all movements to be executed in good form.

Test—(*a*) The following figures skated on each foot: namely—1. Forward inside 3, the length of each curve being 40 feet at least. 2. Forward outside 3, the length of each curve being 50 feet at least.

(*b*) The following figures skated to a centre on alternate feet without pause, three times on each foot: namely—1. Forward inside 3, the length of each curve being 15 feet at least. 2. Forward outside 3, the length of each curve being 15 feet at least. 3. Forward inside two turns, the length of each curve being 10 feet at least. 4. Forward outside two turns, the length of each curve being 10 feet at least. 5. Forward inside three turns, the length of each curve being 10 feet at least. 6. Forward outside three turns, the length of each curve being 10 feet at least.

(*c*) Back outside two turns on alternate feet on the cross roll, three times on each foot, the length of each curve being 8 feet at least.

(*d*) The following figures skated on each foot: namely—1. Forward inside "Q," the length of each curve being 30 feet at least. 2. Forward outside "Q," the length of each curve being 30 feet at least. 3. Back inside "Q," the length of each curve being 15 feet at least. 4. Back outside "Q," the length of each curve being 10 feet at least.

(*e*) A set of combined figures skated with another skater, who will be selected by the judges, introducing the following calls in such order and with such repetitions as the judges may direct:—1. Forward 3 entire. 2. Once back—and forward. 3. Once back—and forward 3. 4. Once back off meet—and forward 3 entire. 5. Once back meet—and back—and forward 3.

When a stroke is taken in a combined figure from outside back to outside back it must be taken on the cross roll.

The whole of the above test must be skated on the same occasion and before two of the properly appointed judges, and the candidate must satisfy both judges.

FIRST CLASS ICE FIGURE-SKATING TEST.

No candidate can be judged for this test unless he has previously passed the Second Class Test. The first-class test is divided into two sections, A and B. The whole test must be passed before the same judges. The judges shall not be required to judge a candidate in section B, unless he has passed in section A.

SECTION A.

This section consists of a set of Combined Figures (skated with another skater who will be selected by the judges) introducing all the calls in Part I., and also such of the calls in Part II. as the Judges (for the purpose of alternating the feet, enabling the candidate to recover his position, or otherwise) may require.

The call "back entire" must be skated at least six times in succession on alternate feet, *i.e.* three times on each foot. Any other call in Part I. must be skated at least twice, beginning once with the right foot and once with the left. Subject to these conditions the calls shall be skated in such order and with such repetitions as the judges may, while the set is in progress, direct. In calls introducing "twice back" the candidate must recede at least 35 feet from the centre. The figure "back entire" must be 6 feet in diameter at least.

To pass thes ection the candidate must satisfy both judges in the manner in which he skates the set considered as a whole, and also in the manner in which he skates each individual call in Part I The judges may pass a candidate, notwithstanding a reasonable number of errors on his part in the course of the set, provided that he ultimately skates all the calls in Part I. to their satisfaction. Whenever a stroke is taken in a combined figure from outside back to outside back it must be taken on the cross roll.

Part I.—1. Twice back—and forward three—and forward inside three, off meet. 2. Twice back—and forward three turns—and back meet—and back two turns—and forward two turns. 3. Twice back—and forward reverse Q, meet. 4. Twice back—and back, off meet. 5. Twice back—and back inside reverse centre turn Q—and forward. 6. Twice back turn, centre turn entire, off meet. 7. Twice back centre change Q entire. 8. Once back—and forward—and forward inside two turns, centre change entire. 9. Twice back—and forward two turns, pass entire. 10. Twice back two turns, off pass entire, meet. 11. Inside twice back—and forward inside two turns. 12 Forward two Q's out—and forward reverse Q—and forward Q in, off meet. 13. Back entire.

Part II.—1. Forward entire. 2. Forward—and forward inside. 3. Inside forward—and forward. 4. Once back—and forward change.

SECTION B.

To pass this section a candidate must score 60 marks at least. No marks shall be scored in respect of any one-footed figure, unless it is skated on each foot, and in compliance (on each foot) with the printed conditions as to form and dimensions. A corresponding rule shall apply in the case of two-footed figures.

The number set against each figure represents the maximum that can be scored for that figure. Thus, for example, where the maximum for a figure is 10, a candidate who skates it to the complete satisfaction of the judges on each foot will score 10 in all, and not 10 for each foot. Subject to these conditions, the judges shall allot such number of marks for any figure as they consider proportionate to the merit shown in skating it.

The figures in the section are divided into groups, and a candidate shall attempt all the figures he proposes to attempt in an earlier group before attempting any figure in a later group, but he may resign marks scored in an earlier group for the sake of scoring for a figure in a later group. The judges may allow a candidate any number of attempts at a given figure that they consider reasonable.

In Groups 1—6 every loop must measure in its longest diameter between 6 inches and 1 foot 6 inches; and where more loops than one are introduced, the loops must not cut each other. The curve both before and after each trefoil, double loop, or loop, as the case may be, shall be 3 feet long at least

Group 1.—Continuous Trefoils, Six in Number.—In each trefoil the curve succeeding the last loop must cut that preceding the first. Forwards 18, backwards 26.

Group 2.—Double Loops.—A candidate shall not score for a figure in this group if he has obtained marks for the corresponding figure in Group 1. Forward inside 3, back inside 5, forward outside 3, back outside 5.

Group 3—Continuous Loop 8.—Six complete 8's must be skated, the diameter of each circle being 5 feet at least. Forwards 12, backwards 18.

Group 4—Continuous Loops.—Six loops must be skated. A candidate shall not score for a figure in this group if he has obtained marks for the corresponding figure in Groups 1 or 3. Forwards 6, backwards 10.

Group 5—Loops.—A candidate shall not score for a figure in this group if he has obtained marks for a corresponding figure in Groups 1, 2, 3, or 4. Forward inside 1, back inside 2, forward outside 1, back outside 2.

In Groups 6—10 every cross-cut must have a base at least 8 inches long, and where more cross-cuts than one are introduced the cross-cuts must not cut each other.

Group 6—Continuous Cross-cut 8.—Six complete 8's must be skated, the diameter of each circle being 5 feet at least. Forwards 9, backwards 15.

Group 7—Continuous Cross-cuts.—Six cross-cuts must be skated. A candidate shall not score for a figure in this group if he has obtained marks for the corresponding figure in Group 6. Forwards 5, backwards 9.

Group 8—Maltese Cross.—The cross-cuts must be approximately of the same size, and approximately at right angles to each other. Forward inside 5, back inside 8, forward outside 5, back outside 8.

Group 9—Inverted Maltese Cross.—The cross-cuts must be approximately of the same size, and approximately at right angles to each other, the bases being towards the centre of the figure. Forward inside 5, back inside 8, forward outside 5, back outside 8.

Group 10—Cross-cut. The curves before and after the cross-cut must be each at least 3 feet long. A candidate shall not score for a figure in this group if he has obtained marks for a corresponding figure in Groups 6, 7, 8, or 9. Forward inside 1, back inside 2, forward outside 1, back outside 2.

In Groups 11—16 the curve before and after each turn must be 6 feet long at least.

Group 11—Continuous Q 8.—Six complete 8's must be skated, the diameter of each circle being 5 feet at least. Inside turns 10, outside turns 10.

Group 12—Continuous Q's.—Six Q's must be skated. A candidate shall not score for a figure in this group if he has obtained marks for the corresponding figure in Group 11. Inside turns 4, outside turns 4.

Group 13—Continuous Bracket 8.—Six complete 8's must be skated, the diameter of each circle being 6 feet at least. Inside turns 15, outside turns 17.

Group 14—Continuous Brackets.—Six brackets must be skated. A candidate shall not score for a figure in this group if he has obtained marks for the corresponding figure in Group 13. Inside turns 9, outside turns 11.

Group 15—Brackets.—A candidate shall not score for a figure in this group if he has obtained marks for a corresponding figure in Groups 13 or 14. Forward inside 2, back inside 3, forward outside 3, back outside 4.

Group 16—Continuous Counter 8.—Six complete 8's must be skated, the diameter of each circle being 5 feet at least. Inside turns 18, outside turns 20.

Group 17—Continuous Counters.—Six counters must be skated, every curve being 9 feet long at least. A candidate shall not score for a figure in this group if he has obtained marks for the corresponding figure in Group 16. Inside turns 10, outside turns 12.

Group 18—Counter.—The curves before and after the turn must be 9 feet long at least. A candidate shall not score for a figure in this group if he has obtained marks for a corresponding figure in Groups 16 or 17. Forward inside 2, back inside 3, forward outside 3, back outside 4.

Group 19—Continuous 8.—Six complete 8's must be skated, the diameter of each circle being 5 feet at least. Forwards 4, backwards, 4.

In Groups 20—24 the curve before and after the turn or change of foot must be 30 feet at least.

Group 20—Rockers—Forward inside 4, back inside 3, forward outside 4, back outside 3.

Group 21—Counters.—Forward inside 3, back inside 4, forward outside 4, back outside 8.

Group 22—Brackets.—Forward inside 3, back inside 4, forward outside 4, back outside 8.

Group 23—Mohawks.—Forward inside 2, forward outside 3.

Group 24—Choctaws.—Forward inside 3, forward outside 2.

Group 25—Spread Eagle.—The curve must be 30 feet long at least. A candidate shall not score for more than one figure in this group. Inside with 60 feet radius 1, straight 3, outside with 60 feet radius 6.

Group 26—Toe Steps.—A candidate shall not attempt more than six varieties. Each variety 1.

Group 27—Grape-vines.—A candidate shall not attempt more than seven figures in this group. Each variety 2.

Group 28—Canadian 8.—One foot in advance of the other. Forwards 1, backwards 2.

SPECIAL ICE FIGURE-SKATING TEST

The test must be skated in London or the neighbourhood. All the figures must be skated to the satisfaction of three duly appointed judges. The whole test need not be skated on one day, but must be skated before the same judges within a period not exceeding one month. A candidate will be allowed a reasonable number of attempts to execute any particular figure.

No candidate shall be judged for this test unless he have previously passed the first-class test. No candidate who has failed to pass the test shall be permitted to make another attempt to pass in the same skating season, without the special written permission of the judges before whom he failed.

PART I.

This part must be skated in strict English form.

Section A.—The following set of combined figures must be skated in the order stated below:—1. Twice back and forward two turns, off centre turn, two turns, and forward inside turn off. 2. Twice back and forward off centre rocker entire off. 3. Forward bracket, turn entire. 4. Twice back centre bracket entire. 5. Forward inside turn, bracket entire. 6. Forward inside, and once back and forward, and forward inside three turns off centre change three turns entire. 7. Forward two counters out and forward inside two brackets, and forward mohawk and back inside off centre rocker entire. 8. Forward inside and once back and forward and forward inside off centre rocker entire.

Repeat beginning on left foot.

N.B. In the above calls "turn" means an ordinary or three turn.

Section B.—In Nos. 1 to 8, the turns are to be made at two oranges placed 50 feet apart, and the candidate must travel at least 50 feet before the first turn, and at least 50 feet after the second one. All threes and rockers to be done on the off side, and all counters and brackets on the near side of the orange. The cusps of all forward turns must be within 1 foot of the orange, and those of all back turns within 3 feet. In Nos. 9 and 10, the mohawks and choctaws must be executed at two oranges placed as before, and the length of curve, before and after the figure, must not be less than 50 feet. Outside mohawk and choctaw must be done on the near side, and the corresponding inside movements on the off side of the orange, the end of the forward curve being within 1 foot of the orange in every case. Each figure is to be skated on both feet.

1. Forward turn bracket. 2. Forward inside turn bracket. 3. Forward bracket turn. 4. Forward inside bracket, turn. 5. Forward two rockers. 6. Forward inside two rockers. 7. Forward two counters. 8. Forward inside two counters. 9. Forward mohawk, rocker, choctaw. 10. Forward inside mohawk, rocker, choctaw.

N.B. In the above list of figures "turn" means an ordinary, or three turn.

PART II.

This part must be skated in good style, having regard to the nature of the figures skated. The following will be regarded as points of good style:—(1.) Preservation of control over the body and limbs, whether the unemployed leg and arms are swung or not. (2.) Continuity of movement and uniformity of pace—*i.e.* the movement of the body and limbs should be such as to produce the effect of rhythm or cadence. Abrupt movements and sudden changes of speed, except such as are characteristic of the particular figure, should be avoided. The speed should be the same in the corresponding parts of the figure, whether on the same or different edges. (3.) Vigour.

The figures must be approximately symmetrical. In Nos. 1 to 7 the figure must be continued as long as the judges may require, the curves, turns, &c., being approximately superposed. In Nos. 3, 4, 6, 7, the turns and loops must be made approximately half-way round each circle of the eight. Every figure must either be executed on both feet, or, where a choice is given of edges, the figure may be skated on another edge on the other foot. No. 4 must be skated on the opposite edges to those selected for No. 3.

1. Continuous eight forwards. 2. Continuous eight backwards. 3. Continuous change, turn eight, inside *or* outside turns. 4. Continuous change, bracket eight, inside *or* outside turns. 5. Continuous counter eight, inside or outside turns. 6. Continuous change, loop eight, forwards. 7. Continuous change, loop eight, backwards. 9 to 12. Maltese cross on all edges. 13. Inverted Maltese cross on one edge. 14. Continuous counter cross-cuts, forwards *or* backwards. 15 and 16. Picture figure (1) on both edges (*see* Fig. 29). 17. Picture figure (2) (*see* Fig. 30). 18. Single grape-vine right and left shoulder leading. 19. Double grape-vine forwards. 20. Double grape-vine backwards. 21. Philadelphia grape-vine forwards. 22. Philadelphia grape-vine backwards. 23. Pennsylvania grape-vine forwards.

In addition to the above, the candidate will be required to skate three picture figures of his own selection on either foot to the satisfaction of the judges.

SPEED SKATING

SPEED SKATING—This sport, the national sport of Holland, does not seem, until of late years, to have been extensively practised elsewhere on the Continent or in Great Britain, with the exception of a district lying on the east coast of England, known as the Great Level of the Fens. This district, so like Holland in appearance and characteristics, has always been the home of speed skating, and has afforded skating in abundance and with a frequency unknown elsewhere in our island.

Fen Skating—The still waters of the Fen drains and of the sluggish rivers are readily frozen, and are traversed, like those in Holland, from village to village and from town to town by skaters. The washlands alongside the rivers, flooded and frozen, are used for races and in some places for bandy. The names of the fastest skaters are household words, their performances and styles the subject of great interest, and the result of races looked forward to with eagerness. Those who lived elsewhere had neither the skates nor the skill requisite for skating distances with ease and speed. On the rare occasions when an outsider, who found himself the fastest man of his locality, came to compete in the long races in the Fens, he was hopelessly beaten. And while the Fen skater could travel with ease at a speed of nine or ten miles hour after hour, and thus do forty, sixty, or seventy miles in the day with enjoyment, the athletic highlander would think a journey from Cambridge to Ely and back, some twenty-eight miles, a feat almost beyond his strength. Of late years, however, partly owing to the races held near Cambridge and London, Fen skates and the Fen style of skating have become better known, and are being gradually adopted in other parts of the country. The art has also become almost as popular with women as with men; and the former not only skate with speed and elegance, but accomplish journeys not much shorter than those above-mentioned.

The art of Speed Skating—The alternate movements of the legs of the skater are called "strokes." The skater runs or glides forward upon one leg—say the right—at first nearly upon the middle line of direction, but towards the latter part of this stroke he curves away towards the outer side, that is, in the case put, the right side. At the end of the stroke he thrusts his skate strongly against the ice, sideways and backwards, gripping the surface with the inside edge of the blade of the skate, and thus obtains the impetus necessary for driving him along during the next stroke. Meanwhile the other leg, the left, has been brought back from the final thrust of the previous stroke towards, and indeed over, the middle line, and has been drawn well under the body. As the stroke of the right leg is curving away from the middle line towards its finish, the left skate is placed upon the ice. The skater now makes the outward thrust on the right side, and throwing his weight forwards, rests it upon the left leg, upon which he runs in a manner similar to that already described for the right leg, and so on. During the time that the skater runs or glides upon his skate he maintains a steady balance upon it. To do this he leans over the leg upon which he is running towards the outside, so as to bring his centre of gravity immediately over his skate. When he is doing this the skate follows the direction of the body, and leans over towards the ice on the same side, and the skater runs upon the outside edge of the blade. The skater can thus run straight and steady, the edge of the blade acting as a guide, and preventing the skate from wobbling. Just before the final thrust the skater ceases to balance himself on the outside edge; his skate curves outwards, but his weight does not follow it, and he comes upon the flat of his skate and then finishes upon the inside edge. He thus prepares himself for transferring his weight to the other leg, which by this time is brought under him. It is in the ability to obtain and preserve a balance upon the outside edge after making a vigorous thrust with the other leg that the art of speed skating largely consists. It is impossible otherwise to make a long and steady stroke, or to skate with ease and speed for any distance, much more with grace. In easy travelling, say at eight or nine miles an hour, the stroke is considerably curved, the skater dwelling upon it as it turns outwards, and he thus starts the next stroke more or less on the *inside* of the middle line of direction. When this is carried to excess, the centre of gravity, instead of keeping in a steady line, follows a more or less wavy one, and we say that the skater rolls. When it is desired to increase the pace this tendency must be avoided, the body must be kept in the middle line, the stroke must be straighter and more forward. In racing, especially with the old Fen skate, the stroke is close to the middle line during most of its length, and the curve at the finish is not sustained. To make a vigorous backward thrust with one leg, and at the same time to place the other upon the middle line, and receive upon it, with steady balance, the weight of the body thus driven forward, and to run upon it along this line, is a feat requiring much practice and skill. In order to assist him in accomplishing it, the skater swings his arms across his body at each stroke to that side on which he is running, carrying them as far as they will go. This practice used to be invariably resorted to in racing when the old skate was used; but now, when the long Norwegian skates are used, the arms, except in spurting, are kept steady, usually behind the skater's back.

In making the outward thrust it is not necessary to raise the foot far off the ice. The thrust may be made and the skate brought back into position without being raised more than an inch or two. This gives much greater neatness to the stroke, and avoids unnecessary labour, and is the practice with most of our better skaters. But the Dutch raise their heels somewhat higher, and so also, when racing, do those, as a rule, who use the long-bladed skates. The former method is certainly more graceful for ladies.

Length of Stroke—Although a good skater is distinguished from a bad one by his longer and steadier stroke, still it is possible to dwell too long upon it. From 5 to 7 yards may perhaps be given as the average stroke of an ordinary man.

Stopping—The commonest way of stopping is to turn up the toes, thus forcing the sharp heels of the skate into the ice, at the same time arching the back, slightly bending the knees, and leaning backwards for the sake of balance. This way is effectual, but it cuts up the ice on limited spaces. Another way is to turn the toes inwards so as to put the skates athwart the ice. A third way is to turn both skates parallel to each other, and across the direction in which the skater is going. The skater should be master of all three methods.

In Holland the style is broadly the same as here. In travelling, ease is aimed at rather than great speed, and the skaters usually roll more from side to side of the course, and raise their heels higher after the thrust. A common practice is for two or more persons to join themselves by carrying a pole under their arms on one side. This enables them to swing along in file from side to side with great regularity and precision, and gives the foremost man assistance in facing the wind.

Skates—The ordinary English running skate has a wooden top, a steel flat blade about $\frac{1}{8}$ of an inch wide, with the prow turned up beyond the toe some inches above the ice. The wooden part is about as long as the foot. It is fastened on by leather straps, aided by an iron peg or screw at the heel, and short spikes on the fore

ENGLISH SKATE.

part. The bottom of the blade is only very slightly curved from end to end, rising about $\frac{1}{64}$ of an inch at each end. A good example is the "Standard" skate, known by the device of a flag and barrel, or of two crossed bandies upon the blade. For bandy, skating expeditions, and general purposes, no skates are more serviceable or reliable.

The rising prow carries the skate over rough ice and other obstacles, the blade is not easily broken, and the straps give a firm and comfortable hold without tending to pull away the sole of the boot.

Of late years the Norwegian racing skates have been introduced into this country. They are made entirely of metal, and are very light. They are rivetted on specially made boots, have a flat and very thin blade, from 16 to 18 inches long, projecting both behind and before. They are specially suitable for hard ice, and reduce friction to a minimum. They also run more easily than the shorter skate on ordinary English ice.

The skates used in Holland are somewhat milar to our own. They have, however, a thinner blade, which projects on the ice beyond the toe for some distance before curving upwards, and are tied on the foot with thongs, without the aid of any heel screw. They are seldom liked by strangers who try them. To combine the advantages of the Norwegian and Fen skates, a long-bladed skate with a wooden top, fastened on in the manner of the English

NORWEGIAN SKATE.

skate, has been brought out on the design of Mr. C. G. Tebbutt, and is worth a trial. In fastening on the ordinary skate, a hole is made in the heel of the boot to receive the heel screw. The position of this hole is usually at the centre, but may be put a little backwards or forwards according to the length of the skate. The forepart of the skate is usually placed under the inside part of the sole. This points the skate more towards the line of direction. The boots worn should be of fair thickness, so as to afford some protection to the feet from the pressure of the straps, which should be broad for the same reason. Of course ladies should not wear high heels.

Racing—Formerly races were held at various places in the Fen district under the promotion of local lovers of the sport. Latterly the best racing has been at Swavesey and Lingay Fen, near Cambridge, under the National Skating Association, and at Littleport, near Ely, under the Skating Club there. The championship course is a mile and a half,

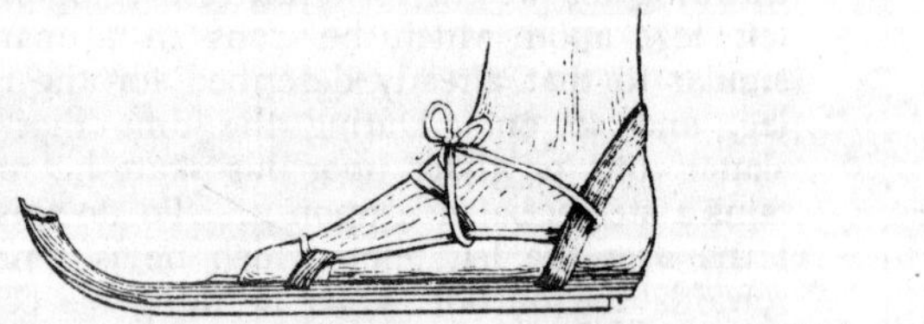

DUTCH SKATE.

with three (sharp) turns, that is to say, it is 660 yards long. The old method of racing was to run off the men in pairs, and then the winners of these heats, till the champion was arrived at, as in lawn tennis and golf. But now for some years the *time test* has been adopted; the competitors run in pairs, the four shortest times are chosen, and those who have made them are again paired with each other, and the event decided by the shortest times of these second heats. This system, though not perfect, seems the best that can be devised. Until quite lately the tracks of the race-course have been close alongside each other from end to end, passing at the turn round a barrel. But the oval-shaped course with wide, rounded ends, as used on the Continent, has been adopted on one or two occasions, and is favoured by some racing men. The art of rounding these wide ends is a special one, requiring the skater to bring the leg on the outside of the curve after each thrust over the other, and, when striking with the leg on the inside of the curve, to make the thrust quite under his body. In this manner, and particularly when using long-bladed skates, the racer can curve round at great, almost at full, speed. In his races with Hagen, in Norway, in 1891–1892, Smart, accustomed to the English courses, was seriously handicapped by the superior skill of his rival in this respect.

During the last twenty years the fastest skaters in this country have been George ("Fish") Smart and James Smart, of Welney (Norfolk), the former until 1888–1889, the latter since. Whether they are better or worse than L. Regester, William ("Turkey") Smart, and T. Watkinson, who came before them, it is hard to say, as when these latter flourished the courses were not measured, nor the times taken with any accuracy. In the last skating season, a man new to Englishmen but known abroad, H. Lindahl, a Norwegian now residing in this country, disputed the supremacy with Smart. These men are professionals. The amateurs have never equalled them in speed.

Great efforts of late years have been made to bring the best skaters of different countries together. In January, 1887, C. G. Tebbutt, of Bluntisham (Hunts), won the International Amateur Race at Leuwarden in Holland. A few weeks later J. Smart and G. See won the open race at Slikkerveer, and again in 1890–1891 at Heerenveen in the same country, making record times on the former occasion over the mile course.

In 1888–1889, at the International Amateur Races at Amsterdam, A. von Panschin, of St. Petersburg, won the mile, and J. F. Donoghue, of Newburgh, N.Y. (U.S.A.), won the two mile race. Two years later at the same place, after having just before defeated the amateurs of this country, Donoghue won every event from half a mile to five miles. In February, 1891, H. Hagen, the Norwegian champion, beat McCormick, the Canadian, at Christiania, over distances of one and three miles, and next season, at Hamar (Norway), beat J. Smart over various distances, varying from a half mile to five miles, both men beating previous records.

In the same season J. J. Eden, of Haarlem, who subsequently became international amateur champion in 1892–3 at Amsterdam, in 1894–5 at Hamar, and in 1895–6 at Petersburg, defeated our best amateurs at Lingay Fen (Cambs.).

Records—In considering records, regard must be had to the country skated in. The ice is better in Holland than in England, and better still in Norway, and the records are consequently better. Thus J. Smart did the mile at Hamar in 1891–1892 in 2min. 53secs., but his fastest time here is 3min. 8secs. Unfortunately there is reason to think some of the claimed records are untrustworthy. Subjoined are a few times.

RECORDS WITH ONE OR MORE TURNS.

Half Mile.

1m. 20⅕s. H. Hagen, Hamar, February 28th, 1892.
1m. 33⅕s. G. See, Lingay Fen, January 28th, 1887.

One Mile.

2m. 47⅖s. E. Halvorsen, Hamar, February 27th, 1892.
2m. 49s. Hagen, Hamar, January 3rd, 1892.
2m. 53s. J. Smart, Hamar, January 3rd, 1892.
2m. 53s. G. See, Slikkerveer, February 17th, 1887.
3m. 8s. J. Smart, Lingay Fen, December 24th, 1890.

Five Miles.

15m. 11s. Hagen, Hamar, December 27th, 1891.
16m. 2⅕s. J. F. Donoghue, Amsterdam, January 7th, 1891.
15m. 19⅖s. J. Smart, Hamar, December 27th, 1891.

One Hundred Miles.

7h. 11m. 38s. J. F. Donoghue, Stamford (Conn.), January 26th, 1893.

One Mile Straightaway (with Wind).

2m. 12⅖s. J. F. Donoghue, Newburgh (N.Y.), February 1st, 1887.

Straightaway (no Wind).

3m. 0s. G. Smart, Cowbit Wash, January 20th, 1881.

H. Hagen, G. and J. Smart, and G. See are professionals.

River and Canal Skating—The best, and almost the only place in this country where this can be enjoyed is the Fens. The large drains with which they are traversed, as well as the rivers Cam, Old Nene, and Witham, are locked at both ends, and, except when for drainage the locks are opened, or the pumping engines on their banks going, which is not often the case, these canals are quickly frozen. In addition, the rivers Ouse and New Nene are sometimes frozen and bear, the Ouse from above Bedford to Welney or even Deurer Sluice, the Nene to Guyhirn.

In such winters as 1890–1891 and 1894–1895 there are days when the whole district may be traversed on skates, and the towns of Peterborough, March, Wisbeach, Lynn, Ely, Ramsey, Chatteris, and Spalding, as well as the neighbouring ones of St. Ives, Huntingdon, and Cambridge, are connected by ice highways.

Unbroken runs of fifty, sixty, or even eighty miles over fresh ice have thus been obtained. In less severe seasons, fair runs may be had if the skater knows how and where to go. Of the three levels into which the district is divided, the "Middle Level" is perhaps the most likely, and the "Old Bedford" river, running twenty-one miles from Earith to Salters Lode, past Welney, the most likely drain for bearing. But the places where the ice is best depend on circumstances.

The tourist cannot expect to find, except rarely, a long unbroken run on the drains. He may have to get off more than once, and walk along the bank past weak places. Or he may find that the washes alongside the drain are flooded and bear, and may make a journey on them, hardly going on the drain at all. Or he may abandon his course altogether, and reach some other drain by walking, or by worming his way down some smaller cross drain or ditch. He may have to skate over much virgin ice. He should therefore be acquainted with the nature of Fen drains, with various kinds of ice, and with the topography of the district. For such expeditions it is almost essential to have a stout bandy or walking stick with which to try the ice. Familiarity enables him to tell pretty accurately by a couple of blows whether the ice is sound and will bear him. Hard black ice is usually the toughest, and two inches of it, or even less, will be safe for men of ordinary weight going singly. But with white snow-ice much greater thickness is necessary. The skater need not be alarmed by a lengthy single crack, accompanied by a rolling sound, running in the direction in which he is going. Such often occurs when the water beneath has slightly fallen, and may be quite consistent with strength and safety. Indeed, if the sound is deep it shows strength. The skater's saying "cracks she bears, bends she breaks" is broadly true. But if the ice begins breaking into many small cracks, or cross ones, it is time to be off. Of course the explorer should be master of his work, should be able to skate for miles on rough ice, or through an inch or more of snow, to go along the side of a drain on ice slanting towards the middle, to stop within three or four yards or less, and to accommodate his stroke to suddenly perceived obstacles. It is a good plan for a rope to be carried by one of the party, care being taken that he is the hinder, and not the foremost man. This precaution is too often omitted. Over deep and dangerous water the party should be roped together. If a long journey is intended, it is essential to start early, for winter days are short and exploration takes time, and it is dangerous to skate in the dusk even over a track, unless the frost has been very severe and the ground is well known.

Nor must it be assumed that because the drain bears one day it will do so the next with no change of weather. A lock opened or a pump set going may in a few hours spoil miles of good ice.

The scenery of the Fens is monotonous, though it has its charm. Unfortunately the tourist may see little of it, as many of the principal drains have banks too high to be seen over. This remark does not apply to the rivers Ouse above Earith, or to the Cam for some miles below Cambridge.

In severe seasons, good runs may be had upon canals in other parts of the country. Perhaps the most interesting and likely of these is the Basingtoke canal, running in a winding course from that town to the Wey at Weybridge, some thirty-five or forty miles. The route is picturesque, but the part between Basingtoke and the tunnel at Greywell is seldom safe, and much of the other part is crowded with locks. The Grantham canal, from that town to Nottingham, some thirty-two or thirty-three miles long, sometimes gives good skating. There are several other canals which in a good winter would afford fine skating if they were not broken up by steam tugs, and thus, even when bearing, rendered unskateable.

Unfortunately no arrangement exists for sweeping away the snow from the rivers, canals, or drains in this country, and when it falls heavily the skating is destroyed. This is the case with the Basingstoke canal, on which the snow soon gets trodden down.

Holland is par excellence the distance skater's home. The frost there, especially in Friesland, though somewhat more severe than here and lasting longer, is not accompanied by such heavy falls of snow as in Norway and Sweden. Moreover, every care is taken to preserve the ice and accommodate the skater. The drains are kept quiet and not allowed to be broken up by the vessels, warning notices are put up at dangerous places, and when snow falls a continuous track is everywhere swept. These frozen waterways are the winter roads, and are used by all classes as highways for business and pleasure.

The Dutchman and Dutch vrow roll along from side to side at an easy pace, but often for very long distances.

The Frieslanders are especially good and habitual skaters, going thus to market, work, or church. The tourist will find Amsterdam a good centre to stop at, and thence in a good year, excursions may be made in the day to Monickendam and the Isle of Marken, Haarlem, Leiden, The Hague, Gouda, Utrecht and other places. But there is more certainty of skating farther north, and those who like a rustic and kindly folk, quaint towns, and the "buried cities" of a maritime people will not fail to visit Friesland. A notable feat for Dutchmen is to skate a journey so as to visit the eleven cities of Friesland in one day, a distance of over 120 miles. This was accomplished for the first time by foreigners in 1890, by three well known English amateurs. Part of the

Zuider Zee becomes frozen in severe weather, and numbers of people thus visit the quaint little Isle of Marken lying some two or three miles from the mainland, having the novel experience of skating over salt water.

Except in Holland and the English Fens, there is little river skating. No other Northern country has the slow quiet waterways and the moderate fall of snow. The skating in Norway is on the lakes and fiords, and is soon limited by the snow to a swept track. The magnificent skating on the Hudson river in America is soon stopped by the same cause.

NEVILLE TEBBUTT.

ROLLER SKATING—Little more than twenty years ago the pastime of Roller Skating, which had previously been extremely popular in America, took England by storm; rinks sprang up in all the principal towns; to give but one instance, Brighton possessed at that period no less than six.

For a time the pastime flourished exceedingly, and numbered among its votaries many good ice skaters, and the *élite* of the fashionable world; the bad management of most of the rinks, however, eventually brought it into disrepute, and for some years roller skating languished until the opening of the large hall at Olympia, Kensington, by an American company as a roller rink in 1893. This company introduced a great improvement in roller skates, namely the Raymond Ball Bearing Skate, which, though in its main mechanical characteristics modelled on the older Plympton pattern, had the advantages of being lighter, and the addition of ball and cone bearings. The wheels, instead of being turned out of boxwood as formerly, were made of an extremely hard composition which prevented them from wearing into (so-called) flat edges. These improvements made roller skating on a good floor a delightful exercise, and one requiring but little exertion. The Plympton skate, with rocking foot-plate and four wheels working on rubber springs, was suggested by an ice skate of similar construction which Mr. Plympton had designed to overcome the difficulty of skating on a single blade. In the latter skate four small blades were introduced in the positions occupied by the wheels of a roller skate; it was not a success, however, owing to the difficulty of effecting turns on the small blades. The rink at Olympia was, for a time, very successful. Shortly after it opened, the National Skating Association took the sport in hand, and instituted 1st, 2nd, and 3rd class tests for proficiency in figure skating on rollers. These tests were modelled on the existing ice figure skating tests, with which they were almost identical, and the action did much to popularise the sport among good skaters, and those who saw in it greater possibilities than the somewhat mill horse exercise of circling a limited area. Many candidates were successful in passing the tests, and the judges appointed by the Figure Skating Department of the National Skating Association attended the rinks at Knightsbridge, the Aquarium, Lambeth, the Crystal Palace, Leeds, Brighton, and also at the Royal Normal College for the Blind, Norwood, which numbers among its many aids to physical culture two excellent rinks.

Mr. Guy Campbell, a son of the Principal of the College, was an enthusiastic skater, and the blind students, who were intensely fond of the pastime, made such progress under his tuition that two (one of them a lady) were successful in passing the 2nd class test, and eleven the 3rd class.

In this connection I may mention that the blind students, when skating the combined figures, were guided as to the position of their partners entirely by sound, and it was extremely interesting to observe the accuracy with which they timed their turns and returns to the centre by this method.

Two candidates only were successful in passing the 1st class test, the combined figures of which seemed to present a very serious obstacle to most of the competitors, probably from want of sufficient space for practice, as combined skating is really easier on rollers than on ice, owing to the greater certainty with which the skater can control his edges when leaving or approaching the centre.

While giving here some general directions, I may refer aspirants to proficiency in roller skating to the article by Mr. M. Monier-Williams on Figure Skating for information regarding form and the figures to be skated; these are practically the same in both branches of the art; indeed, certain figures, such as the Mohawks and Brackets, were probably discovered by roller skaters.

I believe that the Mohawk steps were first skated by the professionals Moe and Goodrich at the Crystal Palace Roller Rink in 1870, and were afterwards skated and named at the London Skating Club. The Brackets also were skated on rollers, and first described by Mr Witham in the *Field* of 1880.

A somewhat different method is necessary to acquire the art of roller skating as distinguished from blade skating.

The blade of an ice figure skate is always more or less curved, and consequently, when the skater is travelling on an edge, the point of contact with the ice will constantly shift as his body is inclined forward or backward, and, unless his weight is thrown well back, a weak and uncertain edge results. In roller skating there are four points of contact, which render the holding of an edge considerably easier, and the throwing of the weight on the heel is not so all-important, though always desirable. Moreover a much smaller impetus is required, a comparatively slight stroke of the unemployed foot being sufficient to secure a curve of 40 or 50 feet; indeed, the novice will do well to avoid taking a strong stroke, as he will find that the tendency of a good pair of roller skates is to run with such freedom as to leave him in a sitting posture. This free running tendency has, however, the advantage of rendering unnecessary the somewhat strenuous and violent stroke to which even the most proficient of ice skaters are occasionally compelled to resort.

One point that seems to have escaped previous writers on roller skating is the possibility and desirability of skating the turns (except loops) with all four wheels on the floor. This method, which one may term a flat foot turn, has the advantage of eliminating the clatter and shock incidental to the ordinary method of turning on the front or back wheels and dropping back upon the other pair.

The sensation produced by these flat foot turns is far more pleasing to the skater, and they present to the spectator the smooth and even appearance of a clean-skated turn on ice. The method must be acquired by gradually diminishing the lift of the heel, or toe, when turning, until the turn can be skated in the manner described, the weight of the body being thrown principally on the toe for forward turns, and on the heel for back turns. The toe or heel will then become a fixed point, the other pair of wheels being permitted to slide over the floor. They describe a segment of a circle in the same manner as the marking leg of a pair of compasses, which travels round the fixed point determined by its companion, on which the weight is principally thrown.

Considerable practice will be found necessary in order to skate these turns satisfactorily; but the result is so effective that they are well worth the extra work involved.

As regards that debated point, the comparative difficulty of ice and roller skating, I may say that in skating 3's, Q's, Brackets, Rockers and Counters on rollers, I have found the turns more difficult, but the edges preceding and succeeding them easier to hold than on blade skates, only a very slight effort being necessary to correct any momentary loss of equilibrium. The four points of contact formed by the wheels counteract the tendency to lean forward and to rock, which the novice finds it difficult to overcome on blade skates.

The loops are undoubtedly far more difficult to execute on rollers, and I found that it was only after the most persistent and persevering practice with a pendant rope that I was able to overcome their difficulties. The back loops, as in ice skating, are the most difficult; these I used to skate on the front wheels, the forward loops on the back wheels.

Cross cuts I have only once seen skated on rollers, by a professional at the Brighton rink, who used to skate them on the outside edge forward. The reverse, or Swedish cross cut, I have not seen attempted; indeed, it was but little known in this country even on ice at that time (1893).

In conclusion I may say that although the introduction of artificial ice rinks has caused roller skating to be neglected, it has still its votaries. Many of our best ice skaters of to-day learned their first lessons on rollers, and have still affection for their first love. I can conceive no more pleasant addition to the resources of a country house than a good roller rink with wooden floor, which could also be used for lawn tennis, &c. Such a one would provide amusement and healthy exercise during the many wet and dreary days of an English winter.

E. SYERS.

SKI—AND THEIR USE—Very few ever heard of ski in England until the appearance of Dr. Nansen's book on Greenland, and indeed it is only within the last two or three years that the public had any idea of what ski really mean. In northern lands, such as Norway, Sweden, and Finland, ski have always been a necessity; without their aid children could not go to school during the long and weary winter months, when the country is covered by many feet of snow; the farmer could not get from village to village, the postman would be unable to deliver letters, and life would be even more isolated than it is.

In Norway, amid the snow-clad mountains, the exercise has perhaps developed to its greatest perfection. The sport is encouraged in every way, prizes being given in each hamlet to the best skilöber, while the annual competition—a Norwegian Derby—for the greatest proficiency in the art is held on the first Sunday of February in Christiania.

An ordinary-sized man's ski are eight or nine feet long. They are only about four and a half inches wide, and an inch deep at the thickest part, that is to say immediately under the foot, but towards either end they taper to half this thickness. As a rule they are both the same length, and pointed upwards at the toes; but in some of the Norwegian valleys and in Finland one ski is much longer than the other, and that one is usually quite flat.

In the middle of this plank-like piece of wood, which is split with the grain to stand the great strain often imposed upon it, and never sawn at all, the toes are fastened by a leather strap. Another strap goes round the heel in a sort of loop fashion, securing the foot, but at the same time giving the heel full play. A special ski boot is worn over enormously thick horsehair stockings. This boot (lauparsko) has no hard sole at all, and, instead of being sewn at the sides, the large piece of thick leather which goes under the foot is brought well over the top and secured to what might ordinarily be called a leather tongue. At the back of the boot is a small strap, which is used to fasten the ski heel-strap securely to the lauparsko. Once fixed on the ski, the foot is so secure no fall can loosen it, and the only way to extricate the foot is to undo the three straps. Outside these huge ungainly hair stockings and strangely comfortable boots thick gaiters are worn. It is necessary to keep the feet and legs warm in such a cold land as Norway, where the mercury freezes in the thermometers, and snow six or seven feet deep covers the land sometimes for months together. Such cold sounds appalling, but it is quite the reverse. The air is absolutely dry, and there is seldom any wind.

The great annual competition at Christiania lasts two days; the first day is for distance, about twelve English miles; the second for jumping. About a hundred competitors come from various parts of the country to strive for these blue ribbons of the ski-racing world. The ascents and descents are about four hundred feet, the competitors having to cross clefts and ravines, hillocks and mounds in turn, a road with every possible kind of obstacle being chosen to tax the proficiency of the performers. Along the flat the skilöber shuffles, at each step accomplishing a distance of several feet; down the hill side they glide gaily over the crisp-frozen snow, keeping their ski as nearly together as possible and bending their knees; the speed becomes tremendous and would be dangerous could it not be lessened by thrusting into the snow a pole some six feet long which the skilöber carries, to act as a kind of drag. Going up hill—even to the initiated—is a trial of skill, as the general tendency of the ski is to slide backwards. The clever performer stamps the snow with his shoes so as to get a better bite.

LEARNING TO JUMP.

The twelve English miles are generally accomplished in about an hour and three-quarters, but, though that is amazing, it is nothing to the second day's competition, which is for jumping, an act which strikes terror into the heart of an onlooker. A very steep hill side is chosen for the purpose, half way up which a small platform built out in the snow enables the competitor to spring from its edge, eighty or ninety feet on to the sloping hill below.

The winter saw a hundred and five competitors at Holmentollen; at the given word a man rushed from the plateau on the hill top. Down the hill he tore, the pace in consequence of the steepness being tremendous. On he came till he reached the little platform built out from the mountain side; then, making a huge effort, his legs doubled up and his arms whirling like windmills in the air to keep his balance, he jumped.

Out of those competitors over sixty managed to regain their footing and complete their descent of the hill. The longest jump was nearly ninety feet!

A Ninety Foot Jump.

A man once sprang 120 feet, but he fell after landing in the snow; therefore 103½ feet is the record for a clean jump on ski.

Ethel B. Tweedie
(*Mrs. Alec Tweedie*).

SKITTLES—This is probably one of the oldest games on record, and used to be far commoner a couple of decades ago than it is now. Even now many village inns have a place set apart for skittles.

I have seen it played in three different ways. One consists of but four large pins, arranged on

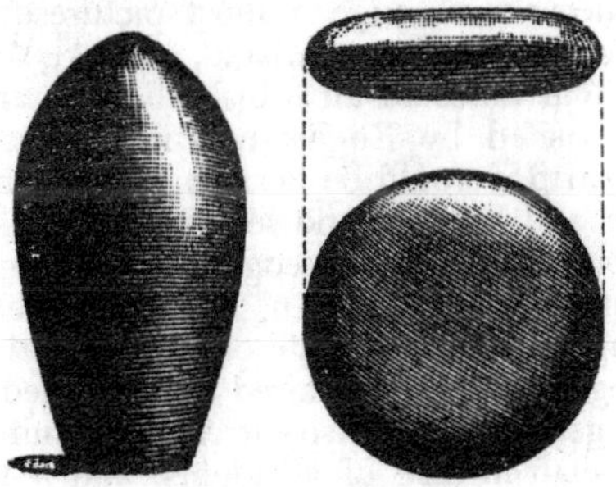

Pin and Bowl, or Cheese.

a square framework, one of the angles only being presented to the player. The bowl used is of the shape of a cheese and is made of the toughest, hardest, and heaviest wood procurable.

The bowl must be thrown upon the skittles and not rolled up to them: it thus requires more bodily strength than the variety in which nine pins are used and the ball rolled up to them.

The best mode of playing it is to throw the bowl with a round handed swing of the arm, so as to strike the nearest skittle at the right of its upper third. The bowl then springs on to the second skittle and from this generally twists on to the third, while the fourth skittle is sent down by the roll of the one first struck.

It is not at all easy to make this throw successfully, and many players prefer driving down the first and third skittles with a straightforward shot, and then making their second bowl spring across from the second to the fourth. This latter stroke appears very difficult, but is

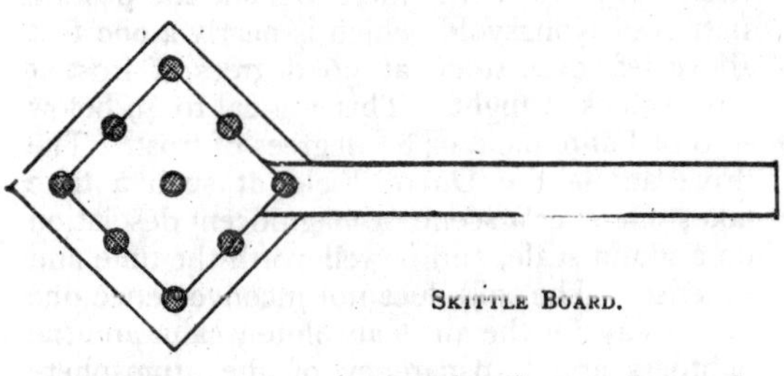

Skittle Board.

soon learnt; the great point is to throw the ball high, so that it may drop as perpendicularly as possible on the left of the upper third of the second skittle. By constant repetition of this, practice will overbalance mere occasional brilliancy of play.

Another form of this game is played with nine pins, which are set up in a regular order, the aim of the players being to throw down as many pins as possible in the fewest attempts. Each player is permitted to throw three times at the pins and if he can knock them all down in two throws, it is called a single and they are again set up for his last throw; if he can knock them all down in one throw, it is called a double, and they are set up again.

There is another form of this game called the American. The floor is planked in a line with the pins to where the thrower stands, a marker is used, and there is on one side a raised rectangular platform just large enough to hold the balls, sloping down towards the player; the balls are put in at the end near the pins and roll down to the player.

There is yet another form called the Dutch skittles. It is a modification of the nine pin skittles, the pins being higher and the centre one called a king, with a crown on its head. The great aim in this game is to strike the king out of the board without knocking down any of his subjects. If this be done, the game is won. In all other cases the king counts for no more than that of his subjects.

F. T. Pollok.

SLEDGING—As usually practised in the North of Europe, more especially in Russia and Scandinavia, sledging is a necessary and expeditious mode of locomotion for some six months in the year, since away from the railway tracks there are no other means of travelling over the snow-covered country, the use of wheeled vehicles being out of the question. In the large towns it is the fashion amongst the upper classes to make up sledging parties, and it is a most pleasurable and exhilarating sensation to find one's self on a still moonlight night gliding over well-kept frozen roads in a comfortable sleigh with plenty of fur rugs and drawn along by a pair of fast-trotting horses to the accompaniment of the cheerful jingling of sleigh bells. In Christiania. trotting races are often held in January at the time of the horse fair, on the Fjord, when the ice is in good order. The course being straight, as many as sixty or seventy sleighs will start in a row, making a very exciting spectacle to witness. Trotting matches also take place at Stockholm on the ice, but this city has not such a pleasant climate in winter, being exposed to strong cold N.E. winds from the Gulf of Bothnia. Petersburg is the city in which the finest sledges are to be seen, the fastest trotters and most luxurious and expensive furs. The Nevsky Prospekt (the Regent Street of Petersburg) on a fine afternoon in mid-winter presents one of the grandest sights in Europe in that respect. Moscow also should be visited at that time by sporting Englishmen who are able to afford the expense of a journey there. In Norway and Sweden, light single horse sleighs are used mostly for travelling up country, but double ones seating two persons are also to be found at the posting stations. The roads are kept in excellent order, rather better, as a rule, in the former country than in the latter, the snow-ploughs being in constant use, so travelling is expeditious and inexpensive even in the mountainous districts.

But on the Russian country roads the clumsy double sleighs with fixed leather hoods, which are ordinarily in use, necessitate the employment of more horses, three being generally used. These are harnessed to the vehicle in a ludicrous variety of positions, sometimes all three being tacked on to one another in single file, the "Yemtschik," or driver, riding on the fore horse, one of course being in the shafts; at other times two are yoked, one at each side of the shaft horse. Sometimes one is harnessed to the near side and the other in front; and again sometimes two are driven in front of the shaft horse. No regularity is observed, but they are ridden or driven according to the caprice of the yemtschik. The harness is of the most primitive description, and is patched and repaired with rope, string, and odds and ends of any kind of old leather available.

The smell of rancid birch bark oil with which the harness was originally cured and cleaned becomes intensely disagreeable after a time. The roads in winter, which one would naturally expect to be kept level and clear by the snow plough, are as bad as it is possible to conceive, for the snow plough is seldom in use, and the consequent joltings over the uneven surface are most unpleasant experiences for the traveller on a long journey; the scenery, too, owing to the flatness of the country and the denseness of the forests, is uninteresting and monotonous in the extreme, and not a source of pleasure to the traveller. The horses, driver and sledge are changed at each station, which vary in distance from fifteen to thirty versts (ten to twenty English miles); a verst = 1,167 yards.

About three kopecks (fivepence) per verst is the usual charge for horses, and one kopeck (about $1\frac{3}{4}d.$) per verst for driver. There is usually a tolerably comfortable guest room at the stations, and a "samovar," or tea urn, is always in readiness. Milk is generally procurable; but of course a well-furnished provision basket with wine, spirits and etceteras should be taken.

Norway presents a great contrast to Russia, owing to the vastness and grandeur of the mountain scenery, especially when it is enveloped in a mantle of snow. A very enjoyable trip may be made by a hardy sledge traveller, starting from Christiania in February as the days begin to lengthen, taking rail to Hamar on Mjösen Lake, and driving *viâ* Lillehammer up Gudbrandsdal over the Dovre Fjeld to Stören, about a 200 mile sledge journey, thence by rail to Trondhjem if necessary. The return journey south can be made by rail and sledge *viâ* Rendalen and North Österdalen to Koppang, thence by rail back to Christiania. Or one may take the rail from Stören to Röraas, thence to the north end of the big lake Faemund, driving down it from Nordvigen, on four or five feet of ice, to Elgaaen, some 20 miles distant; from there some 50 or 60 miles over the mountains to Idré in Vestradal, or Western Dalecarlia. One can drive down this valley *viâ* Lake Siljan in Dalecarlia through a most picturesque and interesting country to Carlstad, on Lake Wenern, some 650 miles in all; this valley is rarely or never visited by Englishmen in winter. For such a trip it would be best to buy (or hire) a sledge and harness, and sell them at the end of the journey. A long sledge coat and rug, both of fur, must be taken, and reindeer skin Komagers (with the hair outside) for the feet and legs (these can be hired and returned when no longer wanted); also fur cap and mittens, a spare shaft in case of accidents, and a ball of strong tarred marline for mending a broken shaft. Be sure to have some stout wire netting, with small meshes, fixed a good height above the dash board on the front of the sledge, to prevent the snow cast up by the horses' feet from hitting the face. The road stages average from about 6 to 15 English miles apart. The price for horses is from one kroner 50 öre, to two kroner per Norsk mile (7 English miles, 8·89 kilometres); a Swedish mile = 6 English.

It is usual for the traveller to drive himself in Scandinavia, the post-boy sitting behind; 30 to 40 öre (*3d.* or *4d.*) is enough for drink money. It is highly dangerous to drink spirits which have been exposed to the outside air at a low temperature, they should always be warmed. If a pocket flask is carried, it should be placed in an inner pocket near the body. The greatest cold experienced by the writer on any sledge journey in Scandinavia or elsewhere was once when crossing the Dovre Fjeld towards the close of December, on which occasion the Reaumur spirit thermometer outside the posting station of Kongsvold, which is nearly 4,000 feet above sea level, stood at 36 degrees of frost at nine o'clock at night. This is equal to 49 below zero of Fahrenheit, or 81 degrees of frost. The drive across the Dovre Fjeld at such a time takes one over a scene of magnificent desolation on a grand scale, and is well worth the time and expense. The cold does not inconvenience one in any way, for the air is absolutely calm and the lightness and transparency of the atmosphere most remarkable.

Frost bites are very rare in Norway, though common in Russia and parts of Sweden. The stations in the more frequented valleys are excellent, the accommodation very good, and the food plentiful of its kind, though a well-filled hamper should be taken and some old port wine and a bottle or two of Scotch whisky, and one or two of aquavitæ if required.

GERARD FERRAND.

SNAKES—Snakes are to be found in most parts of the world, and are the subject of unreasoning horror to many. On coming to know somewhat of their ways and powers, it will be found that they are not much to be dreaded, that they are very beautiful and interesting, and well worthy of the attention of sportsmen. They are difficult to find, the swift ones are hard to catch, and the large ones are immensely strong, and require great skill and strength to capture them alive.

In my experience of fifty years, only two Europeans of my acquaintance have been bitten—one by a cobra he caught by the tail as it was nearly buried in a rat-hole. Unfortunately the hole had a sharp turn and another exit, from which the snake got his head out and bit him in the thumb. He at once put a cord very tight above the bite and cut away the flesh, and lived for many years, although he suffered a great deal from abscesses, &c. The other case was a bite from an adder kept by one who collected live snakes and carelessly pointed his finger too near one. He also recovered after a good deal of pain.

In England there is more chance of being bitten by a mad dog than by an adder.

Although the number of natives reported to be bitten seems large, it is not so great considering the hundreds of millions in India, and that they have bare feet and legs, live in houses without doors, sleep on the ground, walk in the dark, and take practically no precautions.

Treatment of Snake Poisoning—Send at once for a doctor. Immediately tie a strong cord tightly round the finger or limb above the bite—also two or more a few inches apart, twisted as tightly as possible, higher up. Twist them tight with a piece of stick as for a tourniquiet, cut out the part bitten with a sharp knife, wash well, allow the wound to bleed, and squeeze to get out the poison. Cauterise with a red-hot iron, and thereby prevent absorption of poison into the blood. Give stimulants till surgeon arrives: fifteen drops of liquor ammoniæ in wineglass of water every twenty minutes—four doses. Brandy or other spirits in three times amount of water, but not sufficient to cause inebriation, should be taken, and food stimulants. Rest, coolness and good ventilation are important. The favourite remedy of keeping the patient moving about is wrong, as it only increases the exhaustion.

Of the numerous snakes that I have killed or caught alive none have had a chance to bite, except one at Lucknow, which was seen shining in the water outlet from my bath-room. When boiling water was put in, the snake came out at the outer end, where I took it up on a loading rod. I saw it was not a cobra by its small head and his colour, and took it to a tame mongoose. The beast had more sense than I, and at once took care not to be bitten. The snake began to yawn, and disgorged a snake nearly as long as itself. I then killed it, for it would have got more lively when relieved of its meal. On looking it out in Fayrer's book it turned out to be *Bungarus cæruleus*, a very poisonous sort. This made me more careful of snakes that I did not know.

Snake Capturing—A good way to catch them would be leave the drain from the bath-room open, or with a trap-door only opening inwards, taking care to secure any outlet. They require water, and in the dry season are often attracted by the flow from the bath or gussul khana.

Eggs are a very good bait, as most snakes like them and swallow them whole. One, the deirodon or anodon, has no regular teeth except modifications of the spinal vertebræ far back in the gullet as gular teeth; these break the shell as it goes down the throat. Snakes have been known to squeeze into a hen-house; they can flatten the ribs, but after swallowing some eggs are unable to get out. This might be used as means to trap them.

A Ten Foot Python.

It is not easy to run some snakes down. One evening I saw a cobra gliding over a walk in my garden at Secunderabad, and gave chase with one European and three active natives. It made very good running and was lost to sight several times, went up and through the branches of trees rapidly, and gave us all we could do not to lose it. After half an hour's hard work it all but escaped. I found it coiled up in a thick shrub growing in a large pot, poked it out and killed it. I now look on the skin—five feet—hung up in my room, with the skin of a python that has been tanned. This makes the very toughest leather, neatly marked with the scale-like indentations.

The capture of a large python would well repay a sportsman and be worth the work and cost if the snake were taken alive; if above twenty feet long, it would be of great value to any zoological collection. The best I killed was about sixteen feet long, in the Annamallys; it had just swallowed a large black lungoor, one of the most active of monkeys. Professor Owen says: "They can outclimb the monkey, outswim the fish, outleap the jerboa, and, suddenly loosing the coils of their crouching spiral, they can spring into the air and seize a bird upon its wing." Their strength is also surprising. Returning to my house at Kamptee at 3 o'clock a.m., the river being in high flood, I saw by the lantern light a snake in the verandah. By his fine marking I made out that he was a python, and therefore not poisonous, and went for him, got

SNAKE CHARMER.

my foot on his neck, and caught hold of him. Two sturdy native servants at once came to my help, and it was all we could do to get him into a strong cage, although he was only between seven and eight feet long, such was his muscular power.

In the morning the various birds came up to his cage, and stayed screaming so near that he could have caught them had he been free.

On one occasion a lad, fifteen years of age, was heard calling out; his comrades, thinking he was caught by a panther, were afraid to go to his aid, and ran for men; they found him killed by a python, and got it; it was fifteen feet long. This was near Hyderabad.

The Indian python *Molurus* is not known to exceed twenty feet. The python *Reticulatus* of Burma and the Malayan region is said to reach thirty feet; and the carpet snake, an Australian python, twenty-five and a half feet. I have seen tracks of apparently larger snakes in the Travancore forests, without being able to get up to them, as they led either into impenetrable swampy jungle or impracticable rocks. Had I a chance of snake-hunting, I would engage a snake-charmer, as they are experts, and can draw out cobras from their holes by music.

A large python when found gorged—a very rare event, as they get into such safe retreats—might be noosed with a strong rope, the other end having been made fast to a tree. One should be armed with a sharp hunting-knife, so as to cut him asunder in case of being caught in his coils.

To catch a small snake alive, push him from side to side with a slight, straight stick five or six feet long; this is a safe way of stopping without injuring him. Secure him with a landing net, as used for large fish, with a long handle.

A sharp stroke with a stick easily dislocates the vertebræ, and the reptile can be safely killed.

Books on Snakes—Sir Joseph Fayrer's *Thanatophidia of India*. *The Poisonous Snakes of India*, by Joseph Ewart, M.D. *Snakes: Curiosities and Wonders of Serpent Life*, by C. C. Hopley. *The Reptiles of British India*, by Dr. Günther. *Indian Snakes*, by Dr. E. Nicholson.

P. W. L'ESTRANGE.

SNIPE—The difference between a snipe and a woodcock is not merely one of size. Irrespective of the fact that the former rarely exceeds one-third the weight of the latter, the following characteristic distinctions may be noted. In the snipe the head is streaked or barred longitudinally, in the woodcock transversely; in the former bird the flight feathers are plain, in the latter variegated; in the snipe, also, the leg is bare above the tarso-tibial joint (popularly, though wrongly, termed the knee), while in the woodcock it is feathered to that joint. Inattention to these differences has given rise to many errors, amongst others to an announcement that the European woodcock had been met with in South America (*The Field*, 4th April, 1896)—a statement for which there is no foundation.

Of the twenty or more distinct species of snipe known to naturalists, three only are found in the British Islands, the remainder being natives of Siberia, China, India, Ceylon, the Malay Archipelago, Australia, New Zealand, Africa, Madagascar, North and South America.

The so-called "Common" or "Full" Snipe (*Gallinago gallinaria*), so much sought for by English sportsmen, has a wide geographical range. It is found throughout Europe (including Iceland and the Faeroes) and Northern Asia, up to about latitude 70°, and migrates southward in winter to North Africa, India, and the Malay countries. In India, China, and the Malay Archipelago its place is more or less usurped by two species of so-called **Pintail Snipe** (*Gallinago stenura* and *G. megala*), characterised by possessing respectively twenty-six and twenty tail feathers (instead of fourteen), and having the outside ones (eight and six on each side respectively) so attenuated as to consist of little more than pin-like shafts. In South Africa, Cape Colony, and Natal, the English snipe does not occur, its place being supplied by a larger and darker species, known as the Black-quilled snipe (*Gallinago nigripennis*), while in Madagascar and Mauritius is found a remarkably long-billed and long-toed snipe (*Gallinago macrodactyla*), in which the bill measures as much as 3½ inches.

The common snipe of North America (*Gallinago wilsoni*) is so like our English bird as to be scarcely distinguishable from it, except (it is said) by the possession of sixteen instead of fourteen tail feathers, though it is doubtful whether this alleged peculiarity is constant, or independent of moult.

In South America there are several species of snipe, some of which (as *G. frenata* and *G. paraguayæ*) so closely resemble our own bird and Wilson's snipe in colour and size—the measurements of bill, wing, and tarsus being nearly identical in these four—that to the majority of shooters they appear indistinguishable, while others (as *Gallinago imperialis, jamesoni, stricklandi, undulata*, and *gigantea*) are so conspicuous by their larger size and varying plumage as at once to attract attention. The largest known snipe is *Gallinago gigantea*, a native of Brazil and Paraguay. It is about double the size of our bird, being 19 inches in length instead of 10 inches, with a bill of 5 inches instead of 2·8 inches, wing 6·6 inches instead of 5·3 inches, and leg 2·2 inches instead of 1·3 inches.

In Australia there is a large snipe (*Gallinago australis*), measuring 11½ inches, with a wing nearly 1½ inches longer than in our bird, and having 18 instead of 14 tail feathers, the two outer ones in their attenuation resembling in character those of the pin-tailed snipe.

The snipe of the Auckland and Chatham Islands are about the size of our Jack Snipe, of a sandy brown colour above, mottled with darker brown; face, neck and underparts buff.

Painted Snipe—The Painted Snipe, so called from their variegated plumage, belong to a very different genus (*Rhynchæa*), and in their mode of flight, and actions generally, exhibit some affinity to the rails. From their sluggish habits and feeble flight they afford but poor sport to the gunner, who generally reserves his cartridges for something more worthy of his attention. Three species are recognised by naturalists; one which is common to Africa, India, Ceylon, Burma, China, Japan, the Malay Peninsula, Sumatra and the Philippines, and is known as *Rhynchæa capensis*, seu *bengalensis*; a second occurs in Australia, *Rhynchæa australis*, and a third in South America, *Rhynchæa semicollaris*, which is met with from Peru to Chili, Uruguay, Paraguay and Argentina.

Common Snipe—Of the three species of snipe found in the British Islands, the so-called "Common" or "Full" snipe is at all times the most numerous. A great many remain to breed with us, in haunts favourable to their mode of life, but the majority which are killed here in winter are immigrants from the Continent, and come to us about the end of October, or first week of November, those which escape the gun and the poacher's snare quitting the country in spring for more remote breeding haunts.

Those who delight in rural sights and sounds are familiar with the curious zig-zag flight of snipe in the pairing season, and the singular sound which is produced when the bird descends from a height with half-closed wings. This has been variously termed "humming," "drumming," and "bleating." Very different views have been expressed as to how this sound is produced, and it is disputed whether it is vocal or mechanical. One writer asserts that it is effected by the action of the wind causing a vibration of the outer tail feathers (See Meves and Wolley, *Proc. Zool. Soc.* 1858, p. 202.)

COMMON SNIPE.

In the opinion of the writer it is caused by a vibratory movement of the flight feathers in the downward descent of the bird (as happens with varying sounds in the peewit and rook); and this is the view taken by Naumann, Jardine, Hancock, Saxby, Chapman, and other observant naturalists. A long chapter on the subject reviewing the various theories will be found in the present writer's "*Essays on Sport and Natural History*," 1883.

Sabine's Snipe—When Vigors, in August, 1825, received from Queen's Co., Ireland, a very dark, almost black specimen of a snipe, he took it to be an undescribed species, and named it after a distinguished contemporary (*Trans. Linn. Soc.* vol. xiv. p. 557). At irregular intervals other specimens were subsequently obtained, and although in none of these did any of the measurements differ appreciably from those of the common snipe, the singular coloration seemed to justify its separation from that species. In December, 1870, there were at least five-and-twenty examples on record (*The Field*, 10th December, 1870), and since that date the number of recorded specimens has been more than doubled. In *The Irish Naturalist* for January, 1895, Mr. Barrett Hamilton, reviewing the records, remarked that out of fifty-five examples of Sabine's snipe existing in collections, thirty-one were obtained in Ireland, twenty-two in England, one in Scotland, and one in France. This bird is now generally regarded as nothing more than a melanic form of the common snipe.

Great or Solitary Snipe—Larger than the common snipe, and when in good condition double the weight, *Gallinago major* may be recognised not merely by its size, but by the white bar across the wing, white outer tail feathers, and more profuse spotting of the under parts. Its habits are altogether different. It does not breed in any part of the British Islands, but arrives from the north of Europe in September, long before the Continental common snipe make their appearance; it affects much drier situations than the better known bird, is generally solitary, rises heavily, and flies off silently.

Instances of the occurrence of the great snipe here in spring are very unusual; it is much rarer in Ireland than in England, and is equally rare in Scotland.

Jack Snipe—Less numerous than its larger relative, the jack snipe (*Gallinago gallinula*) is to be found generally distributed throughout the British Islands, in haunts congenial to its habits, between September and April; for it is only a winter visitor, never remaining to breed here as does the common snipe. In Europe its nesting haunts are in northern Scandinavia and Russia, whence it migrates in autumn to North Africa, visiting Egypt and following the course of the Nile to Abyssinia. In Asia it breeds on the tundras of Siberia as far north as latitude 70°, migrating to Japan and even to Formosa in the cold season, as well as to Tenasserim, India, Persia and Turkestan.

In its habits it differs considerably from the common snipe. As a rule it is very solitary, and lies so close as to be almost trodden upon, and then, instead of rising with a loud squeak and flying to some distance, it rises silently and, if not shot at, seldom goes far before alighting. It is only when deep snow lies in patches on the ground that the jack snipe show any tendency to congregate. At such times several may be found within a few yards of each other in sheltered situations, under tussocks, or to the leeward of reed-beds, where the snow has not covered the ground where any food can be obtained. Under such conditions the present writer once shot seven jack snipe in about half-an-hour on a small patch of bog land in the co. Kildare.

Snipe-shooting—How to make a good bag of snipe is a problem upon which many an opinion has been given. Whether to shoot over dogs, or without them; to walk down wind or up wind; to fire the moment a snipe rises, or to give him time; to use very small shot, or pellets of a medium size, in case of a chance at a duck or hare. These are some of the questions which perplex the tiro, and puzzle even experienced shooters to answer.

Those who have had much experience in snipe-shooting are of opinion that the sportsman should always, if possible, walk *down wind;* for the reason that as snipe, like other birds, generally rise head to wind, they jump *towards* the shooter, as it were, instead of away from him, and hang for a second in the air before going away. In so doing they offer a pretty cross-shot. This is all very well if the country be very open, and you can choose your direction, but in an enclosed country, where one has often to follow a winding stream, or go from one point to another irrespective of wind, one has to take one's chance how snipe may rise.

The argument in favour of walking *up-wind* is that the birds are less likely to hear your approach, and will therefore lie better. This course is doubtless preferable when a sharp frost has made everything very crisp, and the ground crackles at every step you take, thereby alarming the snipe, which are likely to rise out of shot.

Amongst ordinary game shots, not one in ten probably is a good snipe shot, and there is more knack required in killing a snipe than perhaps any other bird. The following practical hints for acquiring this knack are given in the Badminton volume on Shooting, *Moor and Marsh*, p. 146. "Always aim *above* a snipe; the bird is pretty certain to be on the rise when going away, though you may not think so. In the same way, if crossing, aim well forward, or one beat of the powerful pinion will put the bird three yards a-head while the finger is pressing the trigger. Let 'forward and high' be an absolute rule when pulling on snipe."

Dogs—As to dogs, setters are best fitted for such work, and are generally stronger in constitution than pointers, but it is doubtful if they ever attain the regularity and certainty in beating of the latter. Snipe lie in all sorts of out of the way places, often in the least expected spots. A setter will dash over them, rout them out, slash through the wet ground, spring the ditches, and leave and lose many a bird which the less hardy pointer will be almost certain to find. The latter will walk gingerly through the gorse, leap the wet ground cautiously, and, though moving with equal rapidity, will, as a rule, find more birds. Nevertheless, one of the best dogs for snipe which the writer ever owned was a red Irish setter, which he received as a puppy and trained to retrieve. On an Irish snipe bog full of soft places, this dog was invaluable, for he often had to pick up a bird which fell on spongy ground, which would not support his master's weight, and he would swim out to the middle of a pool for a duck or teal, even in the coldest weather. Sir R. Payne Gallwey is of opinion that the best dog for use in snipe-shooting is a small Irish water spaniel. Others maintain that a well broken retriever is all that can be desired.

Boots—As to the best boots for snipe-shooting opinions differ. Long boots that reach far above the knee like fisherman's boots are very tiring to walk in all day; ordinary shooting boots with or without gaiters will not always keep the feet dry, even if waterproof; sooner or later one is certain to get in over the tops. In the pursuit of home-bred snipe in the early part of the season, one may just as well wear these, and get wet as soon as possible, but one must move quickly, and so keep the feet warm. In mid-winter, when the water is icy cold, and there is perhaps a lot of snow lying about in patches, the best boots are those which reach only to the knee, not above it, and so do not interfere with the action of the knee-joint. These, if made in two pieces instead of three, so as to reduce the number of seams, and lessen the chance of leakage, may always be kept waterproof with a little care. The mud should never be scraped off when dry, but washed off with a brush and hot water. The surface of the leather is then undamaged, and in a sufficiently warm condition (after being wiped dry with a cloth) to receive the waterproof mixture, which should be well rubbed in with the hand. The following recipe is an old but a good one: Boiled linseed oil, one pint; beeswax, one ounce; Burgundy pitch, half an ounce; spirit of turpentine, two ounces. Melt the first three in an earthen pot, and then add the turpentine. This ointment well rubbed in before the fire will be found most efficacious.

Guns and Charges—The lighter the gun the better for snipe shooting, though we do not advocate a 16- or a 20-bore. They have too small a killing circle, and 12-bores nowadays are made sufficiently light to answer the purpose. A 12-bore weighing say 6½ lbs. with a charge of 2¾ drs. of Curtis and Harvey's No. 6. (or the equivalent in Schultze or E.C. powder) and an ounce of No. 8 shot will be found most effectual. A heavier gun than this handicaps the average shooter when out snipe shooting, although we have often seen professional coast gunners kill snipe and redshanks with a much heavier charge in a 10-bore gun. These men, however, in daily practice and in robust health, will carry all day with ease a gun that would tire an amateur in an hour.

Size of Shot—As to the best size of shot opinions differ. A wild-fowler of experience says No. 9 may be taken as the shot *par excellence* for snipe; No. 7 or 8 at farthest if the day be wild, but the first named will answer best at all times. True there are the chances of meeting with duck and teal in the very best places for snipe; but if No. 7 or 8 shot can bring one down No. 9 will do so with equal certainty, for not one of the three sizes will kill such large birds except under the alternatives a "short fair," or a "long chance" shot.

That most enthusiastic of snipe shooters, Colonel Peter Hawker, (the author of *Instructions to Young Sportsmen,*) thought there was nothing like No. 7. In his very entertaining *Diary* we find this remark:—"The difference between large and small shot in a gun is that the former goes in like the back of a knife and occasionally only; the other cuts like a razor with unerring certainty. No. 7 is best for everything unless you take a duck-gun."

Record Bags—For records of large bags of snipe in the British Islands the reader cannot do better than turn to the pages of the Badminton volume on shooting (*Moor and Marsh*, pp. 140–143) and to *The Fowler in Ireland*, pp. 205–211. The west of Ireland is by far the best part of our islands for snipe shooting. Snipe are more numerous and consequently larger bags are made in the counties of Cork, Kerry, Clare, and Mayo than elsewhere in the United Kingdom. Forty or fifty years ago Norfolk and other eastern counties of England afforded nearly as good sport as Ireland does now, or lately did, but the drainage and enclosure of marsh and waste land has interfered greatly with the snipe-shooter's sport.

For large bags of snipe the sportsman must go to Egypt or India. There are few localities perhaps better suited to this bird than the great marshes of Lower Egypt, where Captain Shelley states that in the month of February he has shot over forty couple in a day (*Birds of Egypt*, p. 249). In India, Colonel Peyton has killed between 80 or 90 couple of snipe before mid-day in the marshes on the banks of the Cabul River, where it debouches from the hills before entering the Peshawur river, and since his day even this record has been beaten by English officers in India and Ceylon, owing not merely to the abundance of birds there, but to the increased facilities for shooting them with central fire breech-loaders and improved ejectors. The largest bag of snipe shot in one day in Ceylon was made for a bet, some five-and-twenty years ago, when 110 couple were killed by one gun (*The Field*, May 14, 1898).

Weight of Snipe—Amongst the questions that periodically crop up for discussion in the columns of *The Field* and other journals devoted to sport, we are accustomed to read, "What is the average weight of a snipe?" The answer must depend upon circumstances. As soon as grouse shooting has commenced, a lot of home-bred snipe are moved from the moors and get scattered about the country. They are not then in the best condition, and often weigh no more than 3 oz. or 3½ oz. The foreign snipe come in about the first week of November, and are in the finest order within a week of a frost. The average weight then will be from 4 oz. to $4\frac{1}{2}$ oz., and perhaps one in a hundred will pull down the scale at 5 oz.; anything above this must be considered an unusual weight.

A solitary or great snipe will weigh from 7 oz. to 10 oz., according to its condition and the state of the weather at the time. A jack snipe is generally half the weight of a common snipe, and varies from 2 oz. to $2\frac{3}{4}$ oz.

Springes for Snipe—As a device for capturing snipe, a horse-hair noose at the end of a pliant wand, bent downwards and set in such a way that it flies upwards when the struggles of a captured bird release a wooden trigger, is very effective if set with judgment in the right spot by a skilful operator. But it is a poaching contrivance and scarcely deserves notice in an encyclopædia devoted to sport. It is mentioned here chiefly on account of its general adoption in some parts of Ireland, where large numbers of snipe, and woodcock also, are by this means captured for sale to the game dealers. Illustrations of a springe for snipe or woodcock will be found in *The Ornithology of Shakespeure*, 1871 (p. 229), in *The Fowler in Ireland*, 1882 (p. 218), and in Macpherson's *History of Fowling*, 1897 (p. 454). In the last-named work may be found also much interesting information relating to the methods of capturing snipe and woodcock in different countries, whether by springes in England and Ireland, by drag nets in France, by flight nets in Holland, or by tunnel nets in Sicily. The so-called "Polish snipe snare" is, perhaps, the simplest of all the devices mentioned, consisting of a number of horse-hair nooses attached to a line stretched between two pegs, which are driven into the ground at such a height that the lower half of the noose just touches the breast of any snipe that may approach it when feeding.

J. E. HARTING.

SOLITARY SNIPE IN RUSSIA—The Solitary snipe, or double snipe, a variety coming—in size and appearance—half-way between the ordinary or single snipe and the woodcock, is rarely met with in the British Isles, and when one is seen he is, as the name implies, a belated solitary specimen, driven to our shores by contrary winds or lost through temporary aberration of the instinct which should have carried him with his fellows in their customary line of flight south-eastwards. In Russia, which apparently lies in that line, he is seen for about a fortnight, during which space of time companies of his tribe pass like a great army over the region within, roughly, a hundred mile radius of St. Petersburg, billeting themselves upon the grass, stubble, and potato fields in batches of ten, twenty, or a hundred. The new arrival has come from his breeding grounds somewhere in the north, and is bound for Egypt and Asia Minor and beyond; he is weary, and arrives thin and quick on the wing, like his cousin the ordinary snipe; but a few days of rest and fat feeding by suction soon change all that, and at the end of the week or fortnight of his stay he is a very different bird—fat, lazy, loth to rise, and slow and heavy on the wing when rise he must.

Should any sportsman reading these lines, having friends in St. Petersburg, desire to make the acquaintance of this beautiful bird, let him be on the spot on or about August 31st, old style, which is, being interpreted, September 12th. That day is the central one of the red-letter fortnight of the doubles. They begin to arrive—a pioneer or two—some ten days before this, increasing in numbers up to the day indicated, and afterwards decreasing again until, by about September 25th, English style, if one belated specimen be still found in the fields he is probably wounded, or else he would have felt himself impelled by his instinct to move on. During his fatal fortnight of fatness there is no bird that flies more pitifully accessible and helplessly unable to avoid the sportsman's pellets. So fat has he become that he may occasionally be kicked with the foot before he will move, and when he does elect to fly he must soon alight again to take breath, even if shot at and missed.

Unfortunately for sportsmen, it is not every year that is a good "double" year. For, whether owing to an unfortunate breeding season among the birds themselves, or whether the vagaries of wind and weather have driven the flights to east or west of the usual course, it sometimes happens that the St. Petersburg sportsman is disappointed of his doubles. In that event the fortnight passes dolorously, with but here a snipe and there a snipe, and with no rich flights; whereas in a good double season a fair shot may bag his thirty or forty brace in a day.

FRED. WHISHAW.

SPORT, OBSOLETE—BADGER BAITING—Many animals, the fox, for instance, have to pay a price for their existence, and just a century ago this is what the badger had to pay for his.—"They dig a place in the earth about a yard long, so that one end is four feet deep. At this end a strong stake is driven down. Then the badger's tail is split, a chain put through it, and fastened to the stake with such ability that the badger can come up to the other end of the place. The dogs are brought and set upon the poor animal, who sometimes destroys several dogs before it is killed."—This is a friendly description, and conveys but little idea of the barbarities actually practised. That the badger was not alone the victim of this fiendish cruelty is evident from the concluding sentence of the above quotation. Often half-a-dozen dogs were maimed for life in the contest, a jaw torn away being a common

Tiger.

result. A glance at a badger's armed cranium suggests a good deal in this connection, the interlocking teeth—the "holders," and the way in which the lower jaw is articulated with the upper, explaining the hold which the badger is able to take and keep.

It may at once be stated that the older barbarous methods of badger baiting had nothing in common with badger hunting proper, or "digging the badger." If fairly pursued, this is a legitimate sport to every one concerned —including the badger. The method of hunting him nowadays is to wait quietly until he has left his "earth" on his nightly foray, then to insert a sack with a running noose in each of the principal entrances to his abode. Having given him a fair start, a scratch pack—and it matters little how this is constituted so long as the members composing it will give mouth—is laid on his trail, and *Meles taxus* is hustled unceremoniously homeward. If the plans have been properly laid, his reception is often of an undignified character, for he suddenly finds himself hopelessly involved in a sack—that is, unless he has gone clean through it. Once taken, he may be transferred to a new country to establish a new earth, may be conveyed home as an interesting pet, or, best of all, turned loose so as to afford another (or a series) of moonlight runs. Only those who have taken part can appreciate the fun to be derived from rushing the "brock" back to his dark retreat.

The above is one method of hunting. Badger digging proper is another. Here men, tools, and terriers are brought into requisition; and the badger is fairly (always laboriously) dug out of his rocky fastness. One of a team of reliable terriers marks the game—which has then to be dug up to. This may take two hours, but more often takes twelve—and I have known it to take twenty-four. The business of the terrier is to mark and bay the game, but unless compelled he should not tackle it. If, as occasionally happens, the badger charges home, the dog is compelled to act on the defensive.

BADGER.

Then the war becomes desperate. I have seen the jaw of a hard-haired terrier wrenched off and an eye torn out, but this, fortunately, very rarely happens. The dog or dogs having fixed their game, and its *locale* having been reached by digging, the badger is drawn by hand or with badger tongs. A badger's teeth can splinter iron, so that considerable care has to be exercised in handling him, especially as at this time his temper is considerably ruffled. I may mention a third method of hunting—that employed by a Cambridge undergraduate and his staff. This consisted of a badger, a beagle, and a bull-terrier.—"The badger was turned out, the beagle laid on after a certain amount of law, and the bull-terrier held in reserve to recover the badger should he go to ground. This sporting quartet thoroughly understood each other, and, as a rule, each kept to his own special department. The badger was expected, at least, to give a two or three miles run over a country, the beagle to speak to him all the way and to account for him, the man to keep the beagle in view, and the terrier to facilitate the operation of bagging the badger at the finish."

Even to-day there might be legitimate and illegitimate methods of badger baiting—only the former is never practised. For instance, but few terriers could "draw" a badger from a properly constructed badger-box. In this case the conditions would be something like equal. In the old badger baiting, however, the badger was often half-starved and maimed; the conditions under which the drawing was practised did not give it a chance, and after being placed in a tub, every dog in the neighbourhood was "tried" upon it. The poor imprisoned brute generally managed to leave its mark upon each of the snarling crew, and often had to be knocked on the head in the end. Public-houses in town and country were generally the scene of these barbarisms, and the week-end the chosen time for the "sport." The sickening scenes which were the sequels to these encounters did much to form public opinion against them, and in time the brutal exhibitions were proscribed. Subsequently the number of badgers rapidly declined, but now, thanks to the intervention of several landowners and country gentlemen, the species is again establishing a fairly firm footing. The badger is a harmless, unoffending creature, extremely interesting to watch and study, and long may it survive in the peace to which it is entitled.

J. W.

BEAR AND BULL-BAITING—It is not impossible that the chief performers in certain sports that rank as obsolete, such as badger-baiting and cock-fighting, might, if cross-examined under promise of indemnity, confess to some practical experience even now of pits and mains, of badger-bones and stakes; but the glories of bear and bull-baiting have now absolutely passed, without a possibility of return, in spite of the impassioned defence of a certain military member of the House which discussed the matter in 1809. He stoutly upheld the latter manly exercise as a prime cause of the growth of our population and a most necessary foundation of our militant spirit. Such an argument carried conviction to the mind of the House, and the Bill for the suppression of bull-baiting was thrown out by seventy-three votes to twenty-eight, and the militant spirit was saved for the moment.

The Reformed House, however, put a stop to the custom in 1835, to the intense disgust of the few faithful adherents, who frequently, as at Wokingham, were by no means satisfied by the mere present of beef which it had been hoped would be found full recompense for the loss of their sport.

As to the origin of the amusements, bear-baiting seems to have needed no other motive than ordinary cruelty, and the invariable desire on the part of the owner of a good dog to try its mettle to the full; but bull-baiting had excellent medical excuse. Bull's blood, as the ancients knew, was a swift and deadly poison; bull-beef, as Thomas Muffett explained (*Health's Improvement*, 1655), "unless it be very young, is utterly unwholesome and hard of digestion, yea, almost invincible. Of how hard and binding a nature bull's blood is may appear by the place where they are killed: for it glazeth the ground, and maketh it of a stony hardness. To prevent which mischief either bulls in old time were torn by lions, or hunted by men, or baited by dogs, as we use them: to the intent that violent heat and motion might attenuate their blood, resolve their hardness, and make the flesh softer in digestion. Bull's flesh being thus prepared strong stomachs may receive some good thereby, though to weak, yea, to temperate stomachs, it will prove hurtful."

The local authorities were much occupied in carrying out this regulation. At Leicester, "on Thursday before St Simon and St. Jude," an order was made at a Common Hall that "no butcher kill a bull till baited." At Southampton it was part of the mayor's duty to see that plenty of bulls were provided for baiting, and at Weymouth, in 1618, one Edward Hardy, butcher, "one of the searchers sworn and appointed for the viewing and searching of corrupt flesh killed within borough and towne, sayeth and presenteth upon his said oath that John Hingston, butcher there, upon Friday, being the fourteenth day of this instant month (August), did kill a bull unbaited, and did put the flesh thereof unto sale, and thereupon he is amerced by Mr. Mayor at iijs. iijd." Twenty-eight years later another Hingston, Justinian, was fined for the same offence.

Fitzstephen, in his well-known description of London about 1174, describes the amusements of the populace. It may be as well to give the original, for the translation is no way over-certain—"In hieme singulis fere festis ante prandium, vel apri spumantes pugnant pro capitibus et verres fulmineis accinctis dentibus addendi succidiae vel pingues tauri cornupetæ, seu ursi immanes, cum objectis depugnant canibus."

Bear-baiting appears always to have been an expensive amusement, and therefore was chiefly kept up by the Court, the royal bears giving displays from time to time during the 16th and

17th centuries. The London Bear Garden itself, situated in Southwark, was coupled by Sir Walter Ralegh with Westminster Abbey as one of the national sights to be shown to foreign visitors.

From 1550 to about 1680 seems to have been the palmy time of the sport, and Philip Stubbs, in his *Anatomy of Abuses* (1583), rails fiercely against it. "Is not the baiting of a bear, besides that it is a filthy, stinking and loathsome game, a dangerous and perilous exercise? Wherein a man is in danger of his life every minute of an hour, which thing, though it were not so, yet what exercise is that for any Christian? What Christian heart can take pleasure to see one poor beast to rend and tear and kill another, and all for his foolish pleasure."

It would seem that Philip somewhat exaggerated the danger, for the spectator, unless he were one of the enthusiastic owners who would rush in to rescue the dogs when they were in difficulties, would seem to have been as safe as the supporter of a modern bull-fight.

Again he denounces the bear-baiters—"And some, who take themselves for no small fools, are so far assotted that they will not stick to keep a dozen or a score of great mastives and bandogs to their no small charges, for the maintenance of this goodly game, (forsooth,) and will not make any bones of XX, XL, C, pound at once to hazard at a bait with 'fight dog, fight bear,' (say they,) 'the devil part all.' And to be plain, I think the devil is the master of the game, bearward and all."

Of course the sport was by no means confined to the rich, and one poet describes in rather hobbling verse the enthusiasm of the commons—

"And yet every Sunday
They will surely spend
One penny or two
The bearward's living to mend.
At Paris Garden each Sunday
A man shall not fail
To find two or three hundreds
For the bearward's vail.
One halfpenny a piece
They use for to give,
When some have no more
In their purse, I believe."

As to the dogs, we are told that "the force which is in them surmounteth all belief, and the fast hold which they take with their teeth exceedeth all credit: for three of them against a bear, four against a lion, are sufficient to try masteries with them." Mention is made of an English mastiff in France who pulled down successively a bear, a pard, and a lion in one day before the French king; but this record lacks detailed confirmation.

The passion for bear-baiting grew so fast that the Court of Aldermen of the City of London, in a reply to the Council in 1583, assigned the general desire for it as the prime cause for the neglect of archery, and deplored that even "the recent judgment in Paris Gardens," whereby seven or eight lives had been lost, had failed to check the popular liking. This judgment, on Sunday, January 13th, 1583, was caused by the collapse of a gallery when overcrowded, and gave emphasis to the denunciations of Stubbs and his sympathisers, and recalls Sir Thomas More's anecdote of what befell at Beverley, "when much of the people being at a bear-beating, the church fell suddenly down at Evensong time and overwhelmed some that were in it. A good fellow that after heard the tale told, 'Ho,' quoth he, 'now may you see what it is to be at Evensong when ye should be at the bear-baiting. Howbeit the hurt was not in being at Evensong but that the church was falsely wrought."

During the next century there was a steady opposition on the part of the Puritans to the whole practice of bear-baiting. It is to be hoped that the historian sacrifices strict truth to antithesis when he declares that they hated it, not because it gave pain to the bear, but because it gave pleasure to the spectators; but it must be confessed that the sport was usually stopped by the short and easy method of shooting the bears.

The Restoration naturally saw an enthusiastic revival. Pepys recounts his evening with his wife at the Bear Garden, and Evelyn was disgusted by the baiting of a gallant horse, upon which no dog could fasten till the assistants ran him through with their swords. On this occasion, however, even hardened baiters felt some excuse to be necessary, and they therefore pretended that the horse had killed a child, "which was false."

Suspended during the Plague, and deprived of Court patronage after the Revolution, bear-baiting sank out of fashion.

It cannot be denied, however, that the public was loath to let it go, and the Paris Garden was from this period eclipsed in celebrity by the "New Bear Garden" at Hockley in the Hole, a part of Clerkenwell.

At this spot bear-baiting was still kept up, but was no longer the chief feature. From an advertisement in 1709 we learn that, with other diversions, "there are two dogs to jump three jumps at the bear, which jumps highest, for ten shillings to be spent." Bears seem to have grown too valuable by this time to be baited to death, and the chief events of a Hockley entertainment were "trials of skill between masters of the noble science of self-defence." It is interesting to note the following advertisement in 1716:—"At the request of several persons of quality, on Monday the 11th of this instant of June, is one of the largest and most mischievous bears that ever was seen in England, to be *baited to death*, with other variety of bull-baiting and bear-baiting; as also a wild bull to be turned loose in the game place, with fire-works all over him." Efforts were made in

1724 to suppress the sport altogether; but they do not seem to have been wholly successful, for in 1730 the following advertisement was issued on behalf of His Majesty's Bear Garden:—

"A mad bull to be dress'd up with fireworks and turned loose in the game place. Likewise a dog to be dress'd up with fireworks over him, and turned loose with the bull amongst the men in the ground. Also a bear to be turn'd loose at the same time; and a cat to be ty'd to the bull's tail.

"*Note*:—The doors will be opened at four and the sport begin at five exactly, because the diversion will last long, and the days grow short."

The expense of the amusement and the growing sense of its brutality had done the work required before the eighteenth century was half completed, so far as the bear was concerned, but the bull was in a worse plight. The sport, for one thing, was cheaper, it improved the quality of the beef, as men were informed on the highest medical authority, and, which one may hope was the chief factor, the bull had a fair sporting chance of getting on even terms with his persecutors. Beyond question, he would have done ill to exchange his chance with the trapped pigeon or the enclosed rabbit of to-day. The bull could put down as paid not a few of his tormentors, including an enthusiastic publican of Stamford, who was driven into the river, when heated with liquor and the chase, and expired forthwith from apoplexy.

It is well to distinguish between the bull-running and the bull-baiting proper, of which the former was seen in its greatest perfection at Tutbury in Staffordshire and at Stamford.

The traditional origin at Stamford was a chance fight between two bulls in a meadow by the town. A dog interfered in the fight and drove one of the bulls into the town, where it was promptly beset by all the other dogs, and "became so stark mad that it ran over man, woman and child that stood in its way." The lord of the town, William, Earl of Warenne, was attracted by the tumult, and it appealed so keenly to his sense of humour that he bestowed the meadows in which the quarrel started upon the butchers of the town, upon condition that they should provide a mad bull for the continuance of that sport, every year on the day or week before Christmas.

The bull was always stabled overnight in an alderman's outhouse, and for the next day all shops were closed, all business suspended. The only rule of the game seems to have been that there must be no iron on the bull-clubs. The bull was turned out, and then, in Butcher's picturesque style, "hivie, shivie, tag and rag, men, women, and children of all sorts and sizes, with all the dogs in the town, promiscuously run after him, with their bull-clubs scattering dirt in each other's faces, as when Theseus and Pirithous conquered Hell and punished Cerberus. 'A ragged troupe of boys and girls doe follow him with stones; With clubs and whips, and many nips, they part his skin from bones.' And (which is the greater shame) I have seen both senatores majorum gentium et matrones (*sic*) de eodem gradu, following this bulling business."

The bull running at Tutbury was also not without its smack of quaint ceremony. Blount describes it in the *Tenures of Land and Customs of Manors* as follows:—

"After dinner all the minstrels repair to the Priory Gate in Tutbury, without any manner of weapons, attending the turning out of the bull, which the bailiff of the Manor is obliged to provide, and is there to have the tips of his horns sawed off, his ears and tail cut off, his body smeared all over with soap, and his nose blown full of beaten pepper. Then the steward causes proclamation to be made that all manner of persons except minstrels shall give way to the bull, and not come within forty foot of him, at their own peril, nor hinder the minstrels in their pursuit of him; after which proclamation the Prior's bailiff turns out the bull among the minstrels, and if any of them can cut off a piece of his skin before he runs into Derbyshire, then he is the King of Music's bull, but if the bull gets into Derbyshire sound and uncut, he is the Lord Prior's again. If the bull be taken and a piece of him cut off, then he is brought to the bailiff's house, and there collared and roped, and so brought to the bull-ring, in the High Street at Tutbury, and there baited with dogs; the first course, in honour of the King of Music; the second, in honour of the Prior; the third for the town, and if more, for divertisement of the spectators, and after he is baited, the King may dispose of him as he pleases. This usage is of late perverted; the young men of Stafford and Derbyshires contend with cudgels about a yard long, the one party to drive the bull into Derbyshire, the other to keep him in Staffordshire, in which contest many heads are often broken. The King of Music and the bailiff have also of late compounded, the bailiff giving the king five nobles (£1 13*s.* 4*d.*) in lieu of his right to the bull, and then sends him to the Duke of Devonshire's manor of Hardwicke, to be fed and given to the poor at Christmas."

The Duke of Devonshire in 1778 abolished the whole ceremony "respecting rather civility than antiquity."

The *modus operandi* of ordinary bull baiting was thus described by John Houghton in 1694:—

"I'll say something of baiting the bull; which is by having a collar about his neck, fastened to a thick rope about three, four, or five yards long, hung to a hook so fastened to a stake that it will turn round; with this the bull circulates to watch his enemy, which is a mastiff dog (commonly used to the sport) with a short nose, that his teeth may take the better hold. This dog, if right, will creep upon his belly that he may, if possible, get the bull by the nose, which the bull carefully tries to defend by laying it close to the ground, where his horns are also ready to do what in them lies to toss this dog; and this is true sport. But if more dogs than one come at once, or they are cowardly and come under his legs, he will, if he can, stamp their guts out."

According to a contributor to *Notes and Queries* the custom was for owners of dogs who wished to bait the bull to pay one shilling each entrance fee, and if the dog "pinned" the bull, they received five shillings.

As mentioned at the beginning of the article, bull-baiting lasted well into this century. The abandonment of Queen Caroline's trial was celebrated by a baiting at Aylesbury in 1820, and the jubilee of George III. in 1809 by a like performance at Windsor, and so late as 1828 there was a baiting at Oakley, for which the bull was dosed with beer and gin "to promote a little excitement in him."

Wokingham had always been proud of its bull-ring, and great resentment was felt when the Corporation suppressed the practice in 1822. Two bulls per annum had been bequeathed from 1661 to the populace by one George Staverton to be first baited and then distributed. The authorities decided to kill the beasts mercifully; but the poor resented deeply the loss of the sport. For several years they carried out informal baitings, breaking into the yard where the bulls were penned before the killing and dragging them off to the bull-ring. Actually as late as 1835, the year of the definite legal suppression of baiting, they broke into the place where one of the bulls was kept and baited him in the market-place. It is said that an enthusiastic amateur, lying on the ground, actually seized the poor brute by the nostril with his teeth! A sharp sentence of imprisonment on the ringleaders ended the sport as far as Wokingham was concerned, and though sporadic cases occurred for another year or two, by 1840 tethered baiting could fairly claim to rank as an obsolete sport.

The Stamford bull running also came to an end in that year, after a very animated fight for existence in the face, not only of local, but of national, authority. Lord John Russell as Home Secretary, a regiment of dragoons, and hundreds of special constables all took part in the efforts to stop it, but for five years local ingenuity managed to smuggle one or more bulls into the town and to let them loose in the streets. Legal penalties failed to secure their object, but on the 3rd November, 1840, the inhabitants of Stamford held a public meeting and decided that the enormous expense of their military garrison and of special constables obliged them to abandon their ancient custom. All that now remains of it is the bull-song, which for some time might be heard in the streets or in the theatre on great occasions, and may be heard even now.

C. S. COLMAN.

COCKFIGHTING—Although cockfighting must be classed among the obsolete sports, it is "obsolete" only in the sense that it is illegal. Nor—in the North and Midlands at all events—has its popularity greatly declined. True, "mains" are not now fought by the boys of the Free Grammar Schools, nor is the Master's salary made to depend upon the "cock-penny"; and it may be presumed that the cockpit at Rose Castle, Cumberland (the official residence of the Bishop of the diocese), is not now kept sodded. To a bygone generation the plucky "black-red" was supposed to set an example to virtuous youth; and to arouse a noble spirit of emulation in fighting the Gallic or other wide-throated cock that dared to crow defiance or flap his wings. The good Bishop probably fought his cocks from pure pleasure, as a rest from more serious labours—as, years later, did "Christopher North," at Elleray, his home on the banks of Windermere. Professor Wilson—Professor of Moral Philosophy and one of the representative men of his time—was wont to carry a game cock under his arm ready to pit against that of any of his neighbours. Once, at least, he indulged the pastime in his drawing-room on Sunday afternoon. He thought much of his fighting game, and an entry in his diary sets out a "list of cocks for a main with W. and T."—then follows an enumeration of the birds. His enthusiasm is equalled by that of an old lady of Houghton, who upon one occasion admitted she had "gone down on her bended knees," and prayed that a certain cock of her feeding might win at Newcastle. Although we do not now present boys who have won mains with Prayer-books "with an inscription suitable to the occasion," yet to-day the seal of a certain Northern School displays a "black-red"; but the motto "While I live I crow" is omitted.

In the cockfighting days the pedigrees of the birds were carefully kept; they were "taken up" at a certain time and fed with infinite care; and, needless to say, they were trained with great elaboration of detail. First, their wings and tail were cut, then they were carefully "conditioned," next they were sparred daily with tiny boxing gloves tied to their heels. The commonest fights were single battles for £5 or £10; or "four mains," in which the winners had to win two battles. These were individual contests, but when two districts pitted themselves against each other the number of cocks engaged was very large, and "mains" have been known to last for two or three days.

The sport had royal as well as episcopal patrons, and in the present century there were royal cockpits at St. James's Park and Westminster, the former being pulled down in 1824. Hogarth's and Cruikshank's pictures show the interiors of these, and the motley company which attended them. The mains were fought on raised circular platforms, and Hogarth depicts a man in a cage suspended from the ceiling, suffering the penalty of being a "blackleg." To these pits came peers and pickpockets, butchers and rat-catchers, gentlemen and jockeys, and gamblers of every description. Not only our own, but European monarchs visited them upon occasion, gracing the cocking with their presence. But all this pertains to the archæology of cockfighting, so to speak.

Of all the obsolete sports there can be no question that cockfighting was the most popular and the most widely practised. The pleasure to be derived from a Main of Cocks appeals to a wider class than is generally supposed; and among its upholders to-day are magistrates, tradesmen, farmers, and yeomen. It is indulged in quiet spots among the hills where the chances of molestation are small. Assemblages of surreptitious cockers are still not unfrequently pounced upon by the police; and certain classes of the community still stick to the sport in spite of all the efforts of the law to suppress it.

And there is perhaps a reason for this. Scientific cockfighting may be barbarous, may be debasing, but there is little of real cruelty about it. There is nothing in common, for instance, between cockfighting and badger baiting. A trained cock, either with natural or steel spurs, strikes straight home, and one clean blow generally suffices. At the same time, I do not wish to defend it. Its prohibition is on the statute books, and there it will remain.

J. W.

FOOTBALL IN THE STREETS—Amongst the Shrovetide attractions in many towns, a football match in the streets used to rank very high. Now that peaceful citizens are beginning strenuously to resent a faction fight only sanctioned by custom, it is to be feared that in a year or so the great contests will become wholly obsolete. The example of Dorking shows that the most stolid conservatism, and the keenest love of such football as unnumbered sides and undefined rules provide, are both unavailing against the yet more stolid resistance of an unhistorical police force.

On Shrove Tuesday it was the custom, after a sufficiency of cock-throwing and goose-riding, to start the great *mêlée*. Usually the town was conveniently split geographically into two sections, and the rules were simple. The ball had, by fair means or foul, to be carried to some prominent landmark in the rear of the enemy's quarters. Whether it were carried, thrown, or kicked there mattered not at all; but it was usually found out that straightforward pushing was of little avail when each side ran into three or even into four figures. Strategic retreats and flank attacks were adopted, and stories were handed down how the defences had been forced by swimming rivers, penetrating drains, and even, on one occasion, by breaking through a house wall.

As the ball was probably absent in nine out of ten of the places where the contest raged, and would be in any case invisible to the majority, the game fairly incurred the often repeated censure upon its "being meeter for the laming than the making able" of those that played thereat.

By a wise provision, the ball, at the beginning of this century, was usually filled with shavings, and thereby better able to resist rough usage; but even thus there are instances on record in which the Ulysses of one side has reversed the Trojan horse method by stripping the case of its interior, and carrying it in his own bosom within his opponents' lines.

Of recent years, however, as local feeling has grown less intense, and the growth of towns in one direction or another has spoiled the meaning of such old rallying cries as "St. James" and "St. Philip," the fashion of the game has changed; to a large extent the charge is true that tradition is made a mere pretext for rowdyism. Instead of the one ball round which the contest centred, half a dozen or more may be seen, driven in any and every direction by the band behind it, who prefer taking their own line to meeting the organised force of others.

PALL MALL—A paragraph is perhaps justifiable which recalls the famous game of pall mall, once the fashion of a brilliant Court, and, from what one can learn of it, a game that deserved to survive better than many another which has passed the test of time. Put briefly, and therefore, of course, inaccurately, it may be defined as golf played with a croquet mallet down an elongated skittle alley. The tools and implements were, by a happy chance, found in a house that was being pulled down in Pall Mall in 1845, and are now preserved in the British Museum. The head of the mallet is curved, and its ends are both sloped, the plane running back towards the shaft. The balls, which in the only surviving examples are of boxwood, are about twelve inches in circumference.

The aim was, as in golf, to drive the ball over the course in the fewest possible strokes, but instead of holing out, it was necessary to drive under hoops which were set down the alley.

From the scanty records of the game, it would appear that one feat required was to drive the ball through a ring of no great diameter, suspended, as would appear from one illustration, at the height of some eight or ten feet in the air. It is hard not to suspect that the artist, like others since his time, had trusted to imagination rather than actual inspection, for, apart from the enormous difficulty of driving a ball through the ring, there would be the absolute impossibility of persuading one's opponent that it had gone through and not outside. In the days when swords were worn, the closest friendships might have been permanently severed. In his course, the pall mall enthusiast had less variety than the golf player. With a floor of hard beaten sand, "dressed with powdered cockle-shells," says Pepys, there was every chance of a good lie, and the probability of being bunkered behind a hoop wire was extremely small. The alley itself seems to have varied, in the same fashion as a links, in its dimensions, but that at St. James's was about 800 yards long, and there were very few hoops in it, giving a very fair opportunity for a successful drive, considering the shape of the mallet. Side walls seem to have existed at Whitehall, but one cannot be sure whether they were a necessary feature or a luxury.

TOURNAMENTS — Under the head of Tournaments it has been customary to include many varieties of contests, the fact being that on the proclamation of a tournament different kinds of encounters were indulged in on succeeding days. We must be careful to distinguish between tournaments and pas d'armes, on the one hand, and the serious challenges which were often made to assert or refute the justice of an accusation, on the other. Accidents often occurred at the peaceful encounters, but they were not intended, and we do not propose to deal with the judicial combats and duels.

The contests at these tournaments may be divided into horse and foot encounters. The first would include **Tourneys** and **Jousting**, which later on became, at least in this country, tilting, and running at the ring; while the foot combats were generally fought out with axes, lances and swords, and eventually became the sport known as **Barriers**.

It is difficult to say if we can call the challenges which Jacques Lalain sent out to various countries, and which are so fully described in his Life by Chastellain and in the Memoirs of Ollivier la Marche, sports. Certainly the combats in which he took such a prominent part never actually led to fatal results, yet they were terribly earnest. So also, in the combat of Lord Scales and the Bastard of Burgundy, if it had been carried out to the bitter end, it is probable that the Bastard would have been slain. We are told that the English Duchess of Burgundy, sister of our Edward IV., never would attend at serious fighting, and Jacques Lalain was not allowed to spread his challenges in England, where the peace-loving Henry VI. evidently had quite enough of serious fighting without the fiery Burgundian's exploits.

Tournaments, on account of the many accidents attending them, were frequently denounced by the Popes, but for all that, and in spite of the accidents and deaths, we find mention of them continually.

As we have remarked, tourneys were one of the sports included in the term tournament, and we may as well proceed to give an idea of this class of game. For illustrations of the tourney the reader must refer to the numerous manuscripts, chronicles and histories, of which there are so many in our national collections. The MS. of Meliadus is full of pictures of tourneys, and gives us the appearance of them in the fourteenth century. Many illustrations from this MS. will be found in Cutt's *Scenes from the Middle Ages*, where also the student will see excellent reproductions of the warlike sports of those days. But in M. Quatrebarbe's handsome work, *The Tourney Book of King Réné of Anjou*, we get drawings of the whole of the incidents before and at a fifteenth century tourney. In one of these we see the knights with gorgeous crests on their helmets and trappers on their horses, armed, as usual in this sport, with wooden maces and blunt, pointless swords. The knights are in a large pen formed by posts and rails, and separated by two cords drawn across and forming a lane in which stand the heralds and others managing the tourney. When all is ready the officials withdraw, and men placed at the ends of the lane or passage cut the ropes with axes. Immediately the two parties engage and mingle and hammer away at each other till the judge or presiding officer commands them to desist. This was evidently not done at once, for the combatants soon became excited, and only those who got the worst of it would care to discontinue. In the drawings of Jost Ammon and others we see the "admired confusion" which prevailed, and in these German pictures we observe how a public square or place was often taken up for the sport. The successful combatants afterwards received the prize from the chief lady present, and the day's amusement would end with banquets and dancing.

Jousting, and its later form, tilting, was a more scientific and serious sport. Sometimes it was performed with sharp spears, and then accidents were pretty frequent, as we see in Rouse's *Life of the Earl of Warwick*, where that accomplished traveller is shown driving his spear right through the body of some unknown foreign knight in honour of his own lady.

Jousting was originally carried out in a large enclosed space, the riders fully armed and protected by armour, and their horses also wearing metal body and head defences. The two combatants rode straight at each other, and each endeavoured to dismount the other by striking him on the head or body. If the lances had blunt or rebated points, or were furnished with coronels, that is, heads with three or more short points to prevent slipping, a good blow would, if delivered straight, certainly shake, if not unseat, the person struck. If, however, the blow were not quite direct, the lance would be shivered. The terms of the challenge would decide how many courses were to be run and the nature of the weapons employed. This was generally arranged by those wishing to take part touching with their spears certain shields hung up near the lists. One shield would be for sharp lances, another for lances with coronels, and so on. If a knight and his friends issued the challenge to last for so many days, then as many knights duly qualified by birth, &c., as chose would ride against the challengers, who would be called the *Tenans*, while the others were the *Venans*. Prizes would be given to the most successful.

But it was found that some riders tried unfair means to unseat their opponents, jostling them, and otherwise departing from the true sportsmanlike practice. Accordingly, in 1443, we find a new style of jousting introduced, which in some places almost entirely superseded the open running. This was the running at the tilt. The tilt was originally a stout rope with a cloth (*toile*, Anglice *tilt*) hung over it, and stretched across the lists for some ninety yards.

The two riders were placed at opposite ends and at opposite sides of this *toile*, and then riding towards each other, each, with his left arm to the *toile*, endeavoured by a well-directed blow to dismount his opponent. Of course, in order to reach the other, each jouster had to place his lance on the left side of his horse's neck. It is clear that the right hand of each rider was at least three feet from the *toile* throughout the course, and the spear being but fourteen feet long from butt to point, it is evident that the spears were inclined at an angle of some 30° from the line of the *toile*. Thus no direct blow could be given, but, considering the combined weight of the two horses and their riders, a shock sufficient to break the spears, if they struck the head or body, was obtained. A rider might be knocked out of his saddle, but it was not likely, as the blow would be a very light one, and the lance would break before the person hit would be unseated. Soon the *toile* was changed into a wooden barrier, and in the challenge would be noted the height it was to be. It seems to have varied from five feet to six feet, and perhaps more. Now it is evident that two men riding in opposite directions, one on each side of a six-foot wall, would not see much of each other, and so it was. In the splendid tournament roll of the first year of Henry VIII., now preserved in the Heralds' College, we can only see the head of the knight who is charging along on the other side. The chances of hitting him would be small, except for very expert jousters. Then again it was sometimes difficult to get the horses to run close alongside of the barrier, and in that case the knights would be out of reach of each other. Sometimes double lists were used, forming a narrow lane for each horse to travel along. At the Field of Cloth of Gold, Henry objected to these double lists, but on one occasion at least he had to change horses, as the one he rode would not keep to the track. Besides this difficulty, a high wind sometimes quite prevented the lance being held steady, and such was the case more than once at the Field of Cloth of Gold.

FIG. 1.
From the Weise König, showing how by a toy the youth of the middle ages were instructed in the sport of Jousting.

The rules for the jousters at the tilt appear in England to have been drawn up in 1466 by John Tiptoft, Earl of Worcester. This was the year of the challenge of the Lord Scales and the Bastard of Burgundy, though the fight only came off the next year, and in that contest no tilt was used. These rules were, with slight differences, in use for many years, and are said to have been commanded to be observed and kept by an order in the fourth year of Elizabeth, 1562–1563. Generally speaking, they were as follows:—

Breaking a spear between the saddle and the fastening of the helmet to the breast-plate (for so we may interpret the *charnell* of the helmet)	1 point.
Breaking a spear above this spot	2 points.
Breaking a spear so as to unhorse the opponent or to unarm him so that he could not run the next course	3 "
But breaking a spear on the saddle caused a forfeiture of	1 point.
Striking the toile or tilt once	2 points.
Striking the toile or tilt twice	3 "

Breaking a spear on the sight of the helmet thrice, counted towards the prize before the breaking of most spears, and striking coronel to coronel was again better, whilst unhorsing the opponent was best of all. No prize would be given to the jouster, who struck a horse or a rider with his back turned, or who struck the toile or tilt thrice. Nor could a prize be won by a jouster who lost his helmet twice, except by fault of his horse. If the spear broke within a foot of the end, it only counted as a good attempt.

Now it is clear that in the later days of jousting, with a six-foot tilt, some of these conditions would never be fulfilled, as but little more than the head of the opponent could be seen or touched. And hitting the toile or tilt was a clumsy thing, like playing into the net at lawn tennis.

Of course, in the case of striking coronel to coronel, each rider was equally expert, and one may suppose points were allowed to each.

In the early days of jousting the ordinary armour for war was used, with the addition of the tilting helm, which, unlike the helmet, rested on and was fastened by staples and buckles to breast and back, and was large enough to allow of the head being moved inside it, as in the case of a diver's helmet. But as time went on, it was doubtless found more convenient to have stouter and richer armour for the showy occasions of the tournament, where the blows were more deliberate than in the field, and also where there were spectators who could admire at their ease. And in Henry VIII.'s time we find that, taking into consideration the fact that the lance blows could only be received on the side next to the opponent, that is, on the left, it was thought a good idea to strengthen that side of the armour by wearing additional pieces. The helm had its air-holes only on the right side, so as to avoid any chance of the lance-point or the coronel *biting* on the surface of the left side, and the rivet-heads were either flush with the surface, or so rounded as not to arrest the lance-head if it struck. For the defence of the left side of the rider the *volant*[1] piece was devised. This protected the left side of the helmet, and just came round the front medial line, the helmet being bolted to it, and the lower part of the volant piece bolted to the top of the breast. With this was worn sometimes a sort of shield of metal called a *manteau d'armes*; in other cases, as for the German jousting with sharp spears, a stout wooden shield, covered with small plates of bone, was fastened by a stout plaited thong to the breast-plate. This thong passed through the breast-plate, then through a wooden ball to keep the shield the proper distance from the body, and then through

FIG. 2.
George, Earl of Cumberland, temp. Elizabeth in tilt-yard costume. From his portrait at Skipton, Yorks.

the shield itself, the two points being tied on the outside of the shield and hanging down on its face. Yet another form of additional defence was used. This was a stout piece of metal, which stretched across the upper part of the body, turning forward on the right shoulder, but backward over the left, and reaching down the crest of the breast-plate to a point about four inches above the waist. To the upper part of this was riveted the volant piece, and a bolt passing through the crest of the breast-plate near the lower part attached this *grand-guard*, as it was called, to the breast-plate, to the curves of

[1] *Volant* is the term applied on the Continent to movable pieces.

which it closely conformed. On the left elbow also was fixed a pin, to which by a linch-pin could be fixed a large plate protecting the elbow and parts of the upper and fore arm. This was the real *pasguard*, though in modern times the heavy miton-shaped gauntlet with long cuff and no finger divisions. This covered the back of the hand and forearm, and, while not fitted for holding a weapon, was quite sufficient for the rein hand. This series of additional pieces is

FIG. 3.
Armour of Robert Dudley, Earl of Leicester, with the Grand-guard, Pasguard, and Main de fer for the tilt. This armour, now in the Tower of London, was made 1566–1588.

name has erroneously been transferred to the upright plates springing from the pauldrons or shoulder armour, and to a certain extent protecting the sides of the neck. Below this pasguard again was worn over the left gauntlet a large manifer, or *main de fer*. This was a seen in the armour of Robert Dudley, Earl of Leicester, made between 1566 and 1588 (Fig. 5), and similar pieces belonging to Henry VIII., are still at Windsor Castle and the Tower of London.

Now it is evident that when the jouster had

these pieces put on over his armour he was more helpless than ever. First his helmet was linched to the *volant piece*, which was riveted to the grand-guard, in its turn bolted to the breastplate. The rider thus had his head fixed in such a way that from his waist upward he was all one piece, and any movement to avoid an impending blow or for any other purpose was impossible. Nor could he see much —in fact, all the sight he had was through the slits in his helmet just above the volant piece. Considering this, we shall better understand the state of Charles Brandon, Duke of Suffolk, at the time of the accident described by Hall in the year 1524, when the king, having forgotten to close the vizor of a newly designed helmet, on the signal to go being given, the two jousters rushed along the course. It was too late to stop them, and Brandon shivered his lance on the brow-piece of the king's helmet. Brandon himself said that he was not only short-sighted, but that he could not see, for "my headpiece taketh from me my sight."

There was one unwritten rule, the non-observance of which cost Henry II. of France his life. That was that, after breaking the lance, the butt end should be cast away at once. Now, when Mongommeri, by a dexterous stroke, had shivered his lance and knocked off the king's plume of feathers, instead of casting away the stump, he rode straight on, and the splintered end of the stump, entering the sights of the king's helmet, pierced his eyes, and so led to the fatal termination.

From all this it will be seen that jousting at the tilt was a very peculiar sport. It required a good horse that would run truly along the course, and a steady hand; but there was a great deal of chance in it. If the opponent's horse swerved, however good one might be, one could not touch his rider, and one could not see enough to be able to vary by much the direction of the lance stroke. It was more a matter of the opponent riding on to the lance-head than of finding him by any movement of the lance itself.

In fact, the more one considers the conditions of jousting at the tilt, the more one is surprised that so much could be done. The jouster could not suddenly shift the position of his lance, nor follow the rider whose horse broke away from the track. What he had to consider was, where the opponent would come into contact with his lance-head, and, of course, two good riders with steady horses might score hits each course, whereas the best man in the tilt-yard would fail to hit a bad rider. Pluvinel gives a hint for overcoming the unsteadiness of the horses—namely, that each rider stood at his end of the tilt, but with his back to the course; then, on the word to go, he would make his horse wheel suddenly a half-turn to the right, and, giving the spur at the same moment, would drive the horse alongside of the tilt before he had time to swerve off. George Peele, in his *Anglorum Feriæ*, describing the jousting, 1595, on one of the many Queen's days in Elizabeth's time, speaks of young Dudley, whose "armed horse made dreadful harmony grating against the rails." This may sound well in poetry, but it could hardly have been pleasant for young Dudley. Certainly some of the valiant jousters of Elizabeth's Court took all precautions not to be hurt, for we see William, Earl of Worcester, esteemed the best tilter of his day, wearing a breast and back plate, which alone weigh upwards of 40 lbs. The suit is in the Tower collection, and seems more suited to keep out a musket ball than to guard the rider from a light deal lance. Such a suit would give every reason for the platform of three steps which Pluvinel tells us was erected at each end of the lists for the riders to mount their horses from after being armed by the armourer and his assistant. There would be no vaulting lightly into the saddle with such equipment, and it must have been more of an embarcation than a mounting. So also when the six or more courses were over and the knight had to be got out of his armour.

Illustrating the difference between the armour for the field, called "hosting harness," and that for the tilt yard, we have an interesting account written in 1547 by Sir H. Poulet and Sir J. Harington to the Protector Somerset, of a sort of Gymkhana got up by the gentlemen of the garrison of Calais to celebrate the accession of Edward VI. to his father's throne. Of course these gentlemen had only their war armour with them in that outpost of the English on French soil, so they had to do the best they could with what they had. The fête took place outside the town and though the old plans of Calais show a tilt within the walls, they had for want of one outside to "run at random." Young Henry Dudley and Jerningham determined to rehearse the sport and ran at each other in their hosting harness and with coronel staves, that is lances with coronels in place of the usual sharp steel head. At the second encounter "they met so freely that both went to the ground, their harness flying about the field and their horses astonished, but without hurt both leaped on horseback again and brake sundry staves very honestly." Of course the cause of this disarrangement of their armour was that while the portions of suits for the tilt yard were mostly bolted together, the war armour was to a great extent connected by straps. Sully himself tells us how at the assault on Rouen 1591, he got upset and all his armour disarranged, so that he had to withdraw to get it put in order again.

Although the word **Carrousel** has been in later times associated with the sport of running at the ring, it appears from the work *L'Arte del Cavallo* by Nicola Luigi Santa Paulina, published at Padua in 1696, that the original sport took its name from carosello, a hollow ball of chalk varying in size from a hen's egg to an apple. The persons taking part in the game were divided into two parties, each of which had a supply of these caroselli besides reserves held by attendants on foot. The sides then rode towards each other and threw them, each one guarding his head with a shield borne on the left arm. The encounters first took place by two against two, and then by squads. Paulina says this game was much played in Spain, where it was known as Alcançias, and often light canes were used for throwing instead of the chalk balls and then it was called the Feste di Cannas.

As late as 1760 we see, in the beautifully engraved work by Johann Elias Ridinger on the Manège, a gentleman in a three cornered hat and the costume of that date exercising with a tilting lance both at Turk's heads and also at the ring.

In the Armeria at Madrid is preserved the arrangement for the ring business, and Jubinal has figured it. There is a split tube, down which slides a spring holding the ring. The compression of the tube is sufficient to keep the ring suspended at the lower end until it is forced out by being caught by the lance-point. The lance for this ring running in the Tower has a small conical button on the point so as to prevent the ring slipping off the lance after it has been taken from the tube.

Running—If we may distinguish running at an inanimate object from the same at a living person, we shall find that the former was practised at a very early date and by the humblest classes as much as, if not more than by the wealthy. Thus we have the runnning at the quintain fixed or swinging, and the running, if we may so call it, in boats at a water quintain. Of these sports a famous MS. of the life of Alexander the Great in the Bodleian Library dated 1344, has supplied Strutt with illustrations for his work. We see boys and youths pushing with poles, now at a fixed mark on a post, at other times at a mark on the one end of a horizontal revolving bar, at the other end of which is suspended a sandbag. In other pictures we see an ambitious youth imitating his betters, being mounted on a wooden horse which two of his companions are pulling along, while the rider poises his lance at a fixed mark. In another picture some naked lads are about to charge against a tub of water set on a post. In the water tilting the lance bearer is on a small platform rigged up on a boat propelled by four or five of his companions, and the penalty of not striking the mark is apparently that the person so failing would overbalance and fall into the water. Then, again, in another MS. at Oxford we have a sort of inverted tug of war. Two boys, instead of pulling at a rope, are endeavouring to push each other backward, each having hold of one end of a pole.

As to the use of the swinging quintain, it is difficult to see what relation it bore to the jousting or tilting, for as the blow of the counterpoise could only be avoided by a quick movement of the body, a feat quite impossible in the later days of tilting, as we have already shown, it was evidently on quite different principles from the nobler variety of the sport. Plot, in 1677, mentions that at Deddington in Oxfordshire he had seen the running at the quintain, but that it was then only "in request at marriages." From what is said of the sport, it was evidently performed on horseback.

Running at the ring was an improvement on the above exercises and became a sport for the richer classes, who took to it very seriously. In time it became the sole surviving form of mounted exercises of this class and we may refer now to some notices of it in history.

The earliest mention of running at the ring in Hall's chronicles is on the occasion of the Spanish ambassadors being entertained in 1509 by Henry VIII. We are told that with other sports they witnessed Running at the Ring, when Henry and six courtiers ran against seven others. Each person ran twelve courses, but the king won the prize by taking the ring five times and touching it three times. Henry, however, seems to have preferred the rougher play of jousting, and the running at the ring does not often occur in his reign—at least Hall does not mention it.

In Elizabeth's time the sport was used, but probably more as practice for the nobler pastime of the tilt yard. With James's accession this mild exercise was more in favour than the manlier game, and in 1606, on the occasion of Christian IV. of Denmark's visit, we find the royal brothers-in-law excelling all their competitors. In 1612 the young Prince Henry and five others ran at the ring a match for a supper, which he won, and the next year, at Somerset's wedding, the King and the bridegroom also ran. So on during James's reign on state occasions running at the ring was one of the chief items of amusement, and, as might be expected, the Prince Charles generally took the prize. Pluvinel in his great work on horsemanship deals at length with the sport and gives most minute directions for the handling of the lance.

The Lists—As to the lists where the jousting took place, this was an enclosed space of ground with posts and rails and sometimes a bank and ditch round it. The ground was hard, even and firm, and in the preparation for the Field of Cloth of Gold Sir Nic. Vaux mentions that it will not do to scatter the earth from the enclosing ditch,

Fig. 4.

From a manuscript of Sir William Gregory, Garter King at Arms, and now the property of A. Wood Acton, Esq., of Acton Scott, Salop. The manner of the Tilt, the Tourney and the Barriers, as practised temp. Elizabeth, is well shown in this exceedingly interesting drawing.

over the lists, "for it will mar all the ground that none shall gallop nor runne surely upon it." Of course the arrangements varied with circumstances, but the general idea was to have stages for the spectators on each of the sides of the lists, and at each end entrances and exits for the jousters. There were also pavilions or chambers for the chief actors to prepare in, and the grand stand was richly furnished. The general shape of the lists was rectangular, but longer in breadth than in depth. At the Field of Cloth of Gold they were 150 paces long. In many towns there were places kept for the jousting, and could stand to have the finishing touches given, and the last strap or bolt arranged, and from which they got on to their horses. Representations of the tilt are to be seen in numerous manuscripts, and we may quote the fine Froissart in the British Museum, which was, however, executed some seventy or eighty years after the events therein recorded. Consequently we have the tilt shown at the joustings at St. Inglevert, though at that date, 1389, the use of this arrangement was not known. Then in Rouse's life of the Earl Warwick, which has been engraved by Strutt, in the 2nd volume of

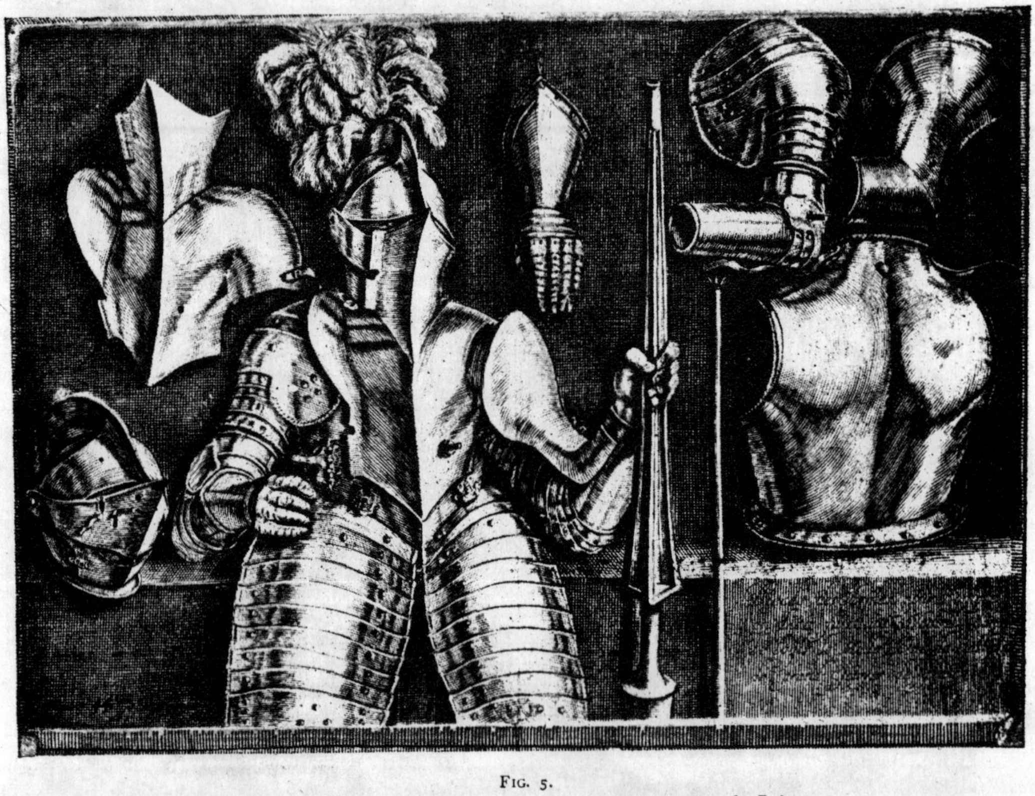

FIG. 5.
Tilting Armour of Lance (1627), from Pluvinel's *Instruction du Roi*.

in the Tilt yard at the back of the Horse Guards we have the survival of the name, this place being the site of the tilt yard in the latter part of the sixteenth century.

In some places we read of jousts taking place under cover, and in 1513 they were held at Lisle in a large chamber paved with black marble, the horses being shod with felt or flock (felto sive tomento) to avoid slipping. In other instances we read of stable litter being used. Across the lists, but not reaching to either side, ran the Tilt, and it is said that such a tilt still exists in Mantua. At each end of the tilt were the small platforms on which the jousters with their armourers and attendants Horda, we have good contemporary illustrations, and in the College of Heralds' Tournament Roll of the 1st year of Henry VIII we see the arrangements very clearly. Pluvinel and Perissem in their engravings also show the latest form of the tilt. In or near the lists would be arranged, on an artificial tree or mound, or in some such way, the shields, the touching of which by the "Venans" would indicate the class of combat in which they wished to engage. A very good idea of the whole arrangement may be had from the large picture at Hampton Court of The Field of Cloth of Gold, in the upper corner of which we see the lists, stands, tilt trees, &c. Of course in Germany, where these sports were very common, we find numerous illustrations by the hands of Jost Ammon, and by others, though Jost Ammon shows the jousters riding right arm and right arm along the tilt, which, if it ever took place, must have been peculiar to Germany.

It is quite clear that jousting was not an exercise to be taken up suddenly, but one which demanded a long course of training. We read of jousts held at Dijon in 1442 where jousting armour was used, but smooth saddles, *i.e.* without high backs. These were for new jousters to learn the business, and we are told that many of them were knocked out of their saddles. It is natural to find also that the older and more experienced knights scorned to take advantage of the young tyros, as in the case of Cotte Brune, a stout captain, who, when he learnt that he was to oppose the young Bastard of Bourbon in a match held in 1414 between Arras and Lens, with four jousters on each side to represent the French and Burgundians, managed to have *lances gracieuses* only used, and so no harm was done. St. Remy, who mentions the incident, uses the above term, but *lances courtoises* is also often met with.

The *ladies' lance* appears to have been an extra course at joustings and was run last, just as in Henry VIII's time, after a regular set of courses, we are often told that the jousters ran *volant*, *i.e.* without the toile or tilt, as a sort of extra show for the beholders.

Some of the blows given at these joustings were pretty severe, and the armour often was pierced and broken, though as some portions of the armour were attached by straps only, a man might have much of his panoply displaced without anything being broken.

The lances used for jousting were probably in the early days the stout war lances of every day use, but later on we find very light lances of soft wood used. These lances were made of little weight by being deeply fluted on the outside, or, in some cases, hollow for a considerable length. Of these lances the Tower collection fortunately possesses some specimens, and from the dimensions and the actual weights it will be seen how much lighter they were than they looked. When Hentzner the German traveller visited the Tower of London in 1598, one of the objects shown then, as now, was the lance said to have belonged to Charles Brandon Duke of Suffolk. Hentzner describes it as *tres spithamos crassa*, and in fact its girth at its largest part, that is, just in front of the hand grip, is 27½ inches, with 12 deep flutings extending some 6½ feet towards the head. The total length is 14 feet 4 inches, and its weight is but 20 lbs., showing what a large hollow space there must be. Two other lances of probably the same period are also in the Tower. One of these has been broken, and we are thus able to examine the construction of it. The maximum girth is 15 inches, and the total length is 12½ feet, the weight 10 lbs. From the broken specimen it can be seen that there is a hollow groove some 2 inches in

FIG. 6.
Tournament of St. Inglevert (1389), from the fifteenth century MS. of Froissart, Harl., 4379, British Museum.

diameter extending to about 1½ feet from the point.

There are several lances in the Tower, evidently of the Elizabethan period. They are 11 feet 7 inches long and weigh about 7 lbs. Externally they are fluted with 8 grooves. The section in front of the grip is octagonal, but none of the vamplates in the Tower have any but a circular mouth.

Sometimes jousters appeared in the tilt yard with abnormally large lances, as did Sir John Peche in 1514 at Paris where he ran a course with a spear "12 inches in compass." On the same occasion the Comte Galeas ran a course with a spear 5 inches square at the point and 9 inches square at the butt. At the Field of the Cloth of Gold the master of the horse of France ran a course with a spear four fingers in diameter at the point.

Philip de Commines refers to the large spears called Bourdonasses, which were hollow, and of which many were picked up on the field of battle of Fornoue. These were Italian, and in 1523 Henry VIII. received as a present four large Neapolitan and two Spanish spears. The military lances of the period were called chasing staves and punching staves, also Collen cleves, from their place of manufacture, Cologne.

The expression lance stroke is perhaps misleading. In war, a man riding at another with a spear would on some occasions move his spear arm freely so as to follow and reach his object, but with the jouster it was quite different. Having a stout substance to encounter, a strong resistance would either break or strain the wrist, or the lance would be driven backward through the grip. Now in the case of the jouster all this was avoided by the lance rest, a metal bracket (sometimes folding) which was fastened to the right side of the breast plate. The lance was held on this bracket and at such a point that the *burre* or ring of iron or leather, fixed round the lance just behind the grip, rested against the bracket and thus the force of the shock was distributed over the whole of the body of the jouster. With the heavy lances sometimes used in Germany the lance was further supported by the *rusthaken*, a long bracket reaching backward and curling over at the end so as entirely to support the spear in conjunction with the breast lance rests. The spear had then merely to be steadied by the right hand of the jouster. Any one couching a lance close up under the armpit will see how feeble the unassisted wrist would be in this constrained position to withstand any great resistance. Of course in old military pictures we see cavalry charging lance in rest, but for individual fighting the lance would have to be carried either under hand, as the English horsemen did in the Irish wars, or overhand, as their opponents are shown in the curious work Derrik's *Image of Ireland*, where we see the two methods of using the lance. Of course with running at the ring there was no occasion for the lance rest, except as a help to the hand in keeping the lance properly poised.

In Elizabeth's days the score was kept by marks on a series of lines opposite to the jouster's name on the roll, or cheque as it has been called, of the performers. Such a cheque is to be seen in the Bodleian Library and refers to a great match in 1570. The arrangement is as shown below, and seems to have been that in use in the early part of the sixteenth century also. The courses run are marked outside the figure, while the nature of the hits is shown by marks on different parts of the diagram.

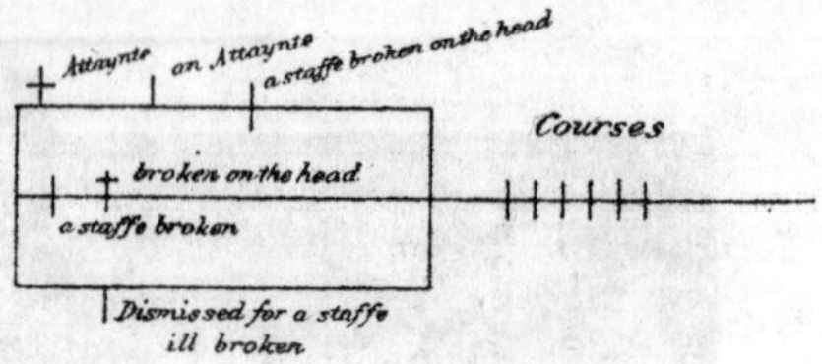

DIAGRAM OF SCORE.

Barriers—In volume xxix of the diaries kept by Sanuto of the events of the Field of Cloth of Gold, held in June 1520 on the selected site between Guisnes and Calais, we have an interesting description of the exercise of Barriers.

He tells us that in front of the Queen's stage was a square stockade with sufficient space for ten couple of men, and in its centre a long bar, about three feet high, with two side bars apparently touching the centre one. The opposing bands of men then fought two at a time, thrusting at each other with rebated spears until their weapons broke, and then they continued to cudgel each other with the fragments until separated by the smaller side bars being swung outward by four men, one at each end of each side bar. Even then they would hurl the fragments of their broken weapons at each other. The separation of the excited combatants could only be safely effected by these side bars, and wrestling was thus prevented. The fighting with swords at barriers was conducted in a similar manner.

In an engraving by Hogenberg, representing Spanish officers amusing themselves at Brussels, dated 1569, we have a good representation of the sport, though the side bars are not shown. The well-known engraving by Dunkarton after Passe shows Henry Prince of Wales in one of the postures adopted by those at barriers, though for portrait purposes the head is of course bare, the helmet lying on the ground.

For this exercise, a special form of gauntlet was often used. It resembled the manifer or left hand miton gauntlet, so often seen with mounted suits, but it had in addition small upright plates which, when the hand was closed round the spear or lance, fitted close to the wood and so prevented the opponent's lance point getting between the lance and the hand. This did sometimes happen with ordinary gauntlets, and in the very fine MS. of the life of Petit Jean de Saintré in the British Museum one of the illustrations shows a combatant whose hand is bleeding, the other fighter's lance having penetrated the palm and of course made him drop his weapon.

In the combat at barriers between Galiot de Baltasin and de Ternant, 1446, the latter held his lance with the butt end in his right palm and the left hand at the balance. Baltasin held his in the ordinary way. He broke a piece off his lance point when striking, and Ternant broke his helmet. The guards then interfered, and produced a knotted rope, to show the seven paces of two feet each, and the combatants were stationed at this distance from each other. They then advanced again and after seven strokes had been exchanged the combat ceased.

May 29, 1510. Luis Caroz de Villaragut writing to Ferdinand the Catholic from London says: "The King of England amuses himself almost every day of the week with running at the ring and with jousts and tournaments on foot, in which one single person fights with an appointed adversary. Two days in the week are consecrated to this kind of tournament, which is to continue till the feast of St. John, and is instituted in imitation of Amadis and Lanzilote and other knights of olden times of whom so much is written in books. The combatants are clad in breastplates and wear a particular kind of helmet. They use lances of fourteen hands breadth long with blunt iron points. They throw these lances at one another and fight with two-handed swords, each of the combatants dealing twelve strokes. They are separated from one another by a barrier which reaches up to the girdle in order to prevent them from seizing one another or wrestling. There are many young men who excel in this kind of warfare, but the most conspicuous among them all, the most assiduous and the most interested in the combats, is the King himself, who never omits being present at them."

FIG. 7.
Spanish Officers at Barriers. From Engraving by Hogenburg, 1569.

Barriers was no doubt a very exciting sport, and the separating bar was perhaps often the only thing which prevented the combatants from proceeding to more extreme measures when they had lost their temper. In 1515, at the barriers on the occasion of the marriage of Mary of England to Louis XII., Lord Gray fought with a big Frenchman who "tried to pluck him over the barrier."

In Hogenberg's drawings it appears as if the combatants at barriers had no upper part to their vizors, and, in fact, with the lower part covering the face, such an arrangement would be much more comfortable and nearly as safe. The blows would be given from below upward, and with the upper part of the vizor closed it is difficult to understand how there could have been much science or ability to see and avoid the opponent's strokes.

The rules of barriers forbade either of the combatants to touch the bar with the hand, to strike below the waist, or to use a closed gauntlet, or have any arrangement for fastening the sword or lance to the hand. Of course, thrusting under the barrier was also strictly forbidden.

DILLON.

SPORTING RIGHTS—Although there is considerable difference in detail in the law as to the rights of different kinds of Sporting, yet there are certain general rules that apply to all such rights, whether hunting, hawking, shooting, fowling or fishing. The law regards all such rights as belonging to the class known as *Profits à prendre*, and consequently the various special rules by which that class of rights is governed apply to all of them. Of these the most important is, that such rights cannot be possessed by the general public. The public can make out a title by long user to a right of way, but no length of use will give the public a title to sport in any form over land. The legal reason is that the public can acquire an easement, to which class rights of way belong, by prescription, but cannot acquire *Profits à prendre* in the same way. The ground for the distinction is not altogether obvious, but it is a well-settled law resting upon a decision in the time of Lord Coke (*Gateward's case*, 6 Rep. 596). The distinction has led to a great deal of litigation and disappointment, but it is at the present day recognised law and could only be altered by statute. It follows from it that all sporting rights must be owned by some definite person or body of persons, an individual or a corporation. Another consequence is that a landowner who has allowed time out of mind persons to sport over his land, and at their pleasure to hunt, shoot or fish, can at any moment take away his permission, and the public have no remedy nor cause of complaint, however much they may have used the permission, and however valuable it may have been to them.

Legally, there is no such thing as open fishing or shooting in England or Wales. There are places, every year becoming fewer, where the owner allows trespasses to be committed and says nothing, but there are no places, except the seashore and tidal navigable rivers, where the Queen's subjects have a right to sport as they have to pass over a highway. Sporting rights being therefore strictly private property, as much so as a man's house or his coat, and belonging to that class of property known as incorporeal, they can only be transferred from one person to another by the legal mode for transferring such property. This can only be done in one way by deed, by writing under seal; any other mode of transfer is invalid in law. This rule frequently causes great inconvenience in agreements for shooting or fishing, for if a person takes one or the other and signs an ordinary agreement, and soon after finds some one poaching and prosecutes him, the prosecution fails, on the ground that the tenant has no legal right to the sporting and so no right to prosecute, as he has no grant under seal. It should, however, be noticed that although he has not the legal right to the sporting and cannot act as legal owner, he is yet liable to pay the rent he agreed to pay, as that is payable in respect of the enjoyment of the property, not of the legal ownership of it.

Another general rule is that *prima facie* the sporting rights do not belong to the owner of the land, but to the occupier. He is the person in whom by law they are vested, and he as a rule need show no other title than that he is in the actual occupation of the lands; every one else must show some special title that prevails over the general one. The occupier stands on his legal right.

These rules apply to all sporting rights—(1) a definite owner, (2) who is presumed by law to be the occupier of the lands over which the rights are exercised, and (3) if owned by any one but the occupier, the owner must claim by deed.

The points to consider are—(I) The different kinds of sporting rights. (II) The places where. (III) The times when, and (IV) the mode in which they may be legally exercised.

I. Sporting rights are five in number:—(1) Hunting, (2) Hawking, (3) Shooting, (4) Fowling, (5) Fishing. All of them belong to the occupier of land by right of his occupation. If owned by any other person, whether he has all or only one or some of them, depends on the terms of his grant. Here the cases are legion, for each grant is a law to itself, and itself alone; the rule may be broadly stated that, while a grant of all sporting rights over land would include all five, a grant of shooting alone would not include fishing or hunting, a grant of shooting game would not include shooting birds not game. The safest and best term to use is the widest "all rights of sporting," for if once it is attempted to define the rights, and anything is left out, the grantee does not get it.

(1) As to *hunting*, strange as it may seem, it is in law clear that no one has a legal right, except it is reserved to him by deed, to follow hounds over enclosed lands. At any time an occupier can forbid all or any of the members of the hunt following a pack of hounds coming on his land, and can compel them, if necessary, by just as much force as may be required to make them do so, to quit his land, and he has a legal remedy for such trespass, if it is persisted in. It used to be said that the fox was a noisome beast, and any one was justified in going over a man's land to destroy it, but if this was ever law, which is extremely doubtful, it has been long ago exploded, and the rule is as stated, that all persons following hounds only do so on sufferance, and that whatever may be the animal hunted, whether stag, fox, otter or hare. If the occupier of the land so pleases, he can stop all or any of the persons following the hounds over his land. There is, however, one exception, but it is of such rare occurrence that in practice it is of small importance. If lands are within the bounds of a Royal forest, or if there is a right of free chase or free warren existing over the land, the holder of the Royal authority in a forest or a chace, or the owner of the franchise of free warren, can go over land within the limits of the forest, or chace, or free warren for the purpose of taking by hunting or otherwise, beasts of forest, beasts of chase and beasts of warren. Beasts of forest are hart, hind, bear, boar, wolf, and all beasts of Venery. Beasts of chase are buck, doe, fox, marten and roe. Beasts of warren are hares, roes and conies, and it would seem that the owner of these rights could take with him any one he thought fit for the purposes of hunting. It is said that there are sixty-three forests in England, but the hunting that is done in these privileged places is merely a fraction of the hunting that is done each season, and it only serves to justify a very small percentage of the persons who hunt, even if it legally justifies them; the broad rule is that all hunting is legally trespass, and is only carried on by the leave of the occupier, which could be withdrawn any day and at any time and without any notice. It makes no difference what is the animal hunted, or what is the mode of hunting, whether with a pack of hounds, or with greyhounds, or otter hounds, or in any other way, the law is the same. Hunting is only permitted trespass.

(2) *Hawking*—As to hawking, the broad rule is the same as to hunting. It can only be carried on with the leave of the occupier, but in hawking there is this im-

portant difference from hunting, that the owner or the servants of the owner of the hawk, if the quarry was started on land on which the owner had a legal right to go, would be entitled to go on the land on which the hawk killed the quarry for the purpose of getting it. The rule in hawking is the same as in shooting; the person who starts game on his own land and kills it while flying over another man's, may justify going on the land to pick up the game. But if the quarry is started on land where the owner had no right to go, he could not go on another man's land to pick it up. The term "quarry" has been used to include whatever it is that may be hawked, *e.g.*, larks or rooks, for although not game, the rule in this respect is the same as if they were. It will not be necessary to say any more about hawking here, for the rules as to it are the same as those as to shooting and fowling, except that a shooting tenant, unless either the words of his lease were general so as to include everything, or else the right of hawking was expressly included, would not be legally able to hawk, and it is quite possible that the owner of the shooting might object to the tenant hawking, unless he had expressly allowed it, on the ground that it might drive away the birds off the beat.

(3) *Shooting* is the right on which most questions as to sporting arise, but in law, with certain slight exceptions, there is no difference between shooting and other modes of exercising sporting rights, and no difference between whether the shooting is for game or beasts and birds not game. The right is now in the occupier, who, unless he is prevented by the deed under which he holds, or by the Ground Game Act, can, subject to the Game Laws as to the time for killing game, the Wild Birds' Preservation Acts as to the time for killing wild birds, and the Excise Acts as to gun licences and game licences, shoot and kill whatever he may find on the lands. He cannot, however, if he kills game, sell it except in accordance with the Game Acts. But the law, as long as the shooting takes place at legal times, and the shooter has the proper excise licence, takes no account as to the way in which the shooting is done. It is not illegal to shoot partridges on the ground, or pheasants running, or in trees, if the shooter is otherwise qualified, and it may be questioned whether under most shooting leases the tenant is not entitled to kill the game in any way he thinks fit. He may do it in an unsportsmanlike way, but that is not illegal. The only case in which it would seem the law would interfere is in the case of a man shooting on his boundary, not for the exercise of his rights, but to disturb the birds on his neighbour's land. The two cases that have been decided do not give a very clear rule. In the first a man shot near a decoy so as to disturb and drive out the birds in the decoy. This was held to be illegal, as the carrying on a decoy was a trade, and the shooting was in effect disturbing a man carrying on his legal trade. In the second a man shot so as to disturb and drive away his neighbour's rooks, and it was held no action would lie, the ground being that rooks were noxious birds not protected by law. So far the law is not settled as to whether a man can legally shoot on his boundary in such a manner as to drive away his neighbour's game. He certainly could not if it were a game farm, and probably not if his neighbour regularly sold his game, nor even if he regularly let it, for he would injure him in his trade, nor if the shooting drove the game from his neighbour's on to his land so that he could shoot it. But if it was merely to drive it away, it is doubtful if he could be legally prevented. For birds or beasts not game and that cannot be sold, it would seem that the person on whose land they are, if his neighbour deliberately frightens them away, has no legal remedy unless he could prove special damage.

The other exceptions as to the right to shoot are those imposed by the Ground Game Act. That Act gave to the occupier of land an inalienable concurrent right with the person who may be entitled to the sporting, to kill the ground game, hares and rabbits, but it limited the exercise of that right by providing that only one person on the occupier's behalf can use firearms to kill ground game. If the occupier lets his shooting, he still retains the right to the ground game, but if care has been taken to have the tenant of the shooting appointed the one person to kill ground game by firearms on the occupier's behalf, then the occupier, although he can still kill the ground game, cannot use firearms.

Subject to these exceptions the law does not interfere with the way in which shooting rights are exercised.

(4) *Fowling*, as opposed to shooting, would mean taking game and other birds by some mode other than shooting. Here again the law does not interfere with the exercise of the right except as to the times when it may be exercised. It cannot be used during close time, and a proper excise licence is also required to be taken out to use a gun or to kill game.

Game taken by fowling can only be sold in the way allowed by the Game Laws. But the person who is legally entitled can take the game and fowl by nets, snares and other devices, the only exception being poison and spring traps elsewhere than in rabbit holes. He can take his own game in his own way, however unsportsmanlike and however much his neighbour may dislike the methods he uses. The chief kind of fowling now carried on is at the decoys, where large numbers of wildfowl are taken. The professional bird-catcher also falls under the class of Fowlers. Nowadays fowling, except in decoys, is more or less a device to enable poaching to be carried on, but it is well to bear in mind that it is legal and can be legally carried out, and that it is important to a person who desires to acquire sporting rights that he should include the right of fowling, not for his own use, but to prevent it being given to any one else and used to his detriment.

(5) *Fishing*—The rights as to fishing are legally the same as the others, the law recognising no distinction between sporting over land and over water, in fact, regarding water merely as so much land covered by water. The rule is that in waters that are not tidal the soil of the river belongs to the owner of the adjoining bank, and he has just the same rights as if there was no water, and it was dry land. It is therefore a trespass to go on the water in a boat, it is a trespass to try and take the fish, as it would be to go on the land to take the game. The same rule as to the public being unable to acquire a right to fish by long user applies as in the case of shooting. However long an owner may have permitted the public to fish, he can at any moment withdraw his permission, and this whether the river is navigable or not, so long as it is not both navigable and subject to the regular flow of the tide, that is so long as the soil is not the public property of the Crown. It follows from this that there is really very little public fishing in the country, and if a person wants to fish he must either get leave or buy or rent fishing rights. Like other sporting rights, the right to fish will only legally pass by deed under seal. Fishing rights are, however, more restricted by legislation than other sporting rights. Game can be legally taken in any way but by poison and spring traps, but there are numbers of ways in which it is illegal to take fish, and some ways which are legal for certain kinds of fish are illegal for others. All these rules apply equally to public and to private fishing. A person cannot even kill the fish he has himself bred except in a legal way.

II. The next point to be considered is in what places the person entitled to sporting rights can exercise them. The broad rule is that his right is limited to the land over which he has the grant from the occupier. In a Royal forest or chace the right extends over all the lands within the boundary of the forest or chace, whoever may be the owner. The rights of the owner there are subject to the paramount right of the Crown, and this rule also prevails in the case of a right of free warren. This can be exercised over a defined tract of ground quite independently of the ownership of the soil. In a manor, the lord often claims the right of sporting over the lands within the manor, but as a rule the lord, in the absence of a grant of free warren, has no legal right of sporting over the enclosed lands, whether copyhold or freehold, only over the open unenclosed waste. The lord, however, may have retained the right to sport over the enclosed lands at the time of the enclosure, and if he has exercised it without interruption for a long series of years after the enclosure, it would be assumed in the absence of express evidence to the contrary that he had done so. In the case of a modern enclosure, the question whether the lord can sport over newly enclosed lands turns almost entirely on the construction of the document authorising the enclosure. As to the unenclosed wastes of the manor, the lord has the exclusive right of sporting over these, and could prosecute as a trespasser or poacher any tenant of the manor he found sporting on the waste. In strict law a commoner has no right to go on the waste except for the purpose of exercising his right of common. There may be a right in the commoner to the sporting on the waste, that is, such a right could legally exist, but it is of extremely rare occurrence, but common of fishing, the right of the commoner to fish in the waters in the manor is, although not usual, by no means unknown.

Subject to these exceptional cases of the existence of a superior right to that of the occupier, the sporting rights belong to the occupier of the lands. The exception that on the sea-shore the public can shoot or fish is not really an exception, for the land over which the public possess this right is only the land between high and low water mark, and is supposed to be in the occupation of the Crown, as trustees for the public, and therefore the public are entitled to go over it.[1] A distinction must be made between the land that belongs to the Crown, as such *jure-coronæ*, and the private estates of the Crown. Of these last, which are managed by the Office of Woods, the Crown is as much the private owner as any other landowner, and over them the public have no right of sporting. The right of fishing in a tidal navigable river is the same as shooting on the sea-shore. The soil of the bed of the river is by law in the Crown as sovereign of the country, or, as it is often said, as trustee for the public; here, therefore, the public can fish, but when once the place is reached where the tide ceases, the right of the Crown ceases and so do the public rights of fishing, however much the river may be navigable, for the soil of the bed of the river becomes the property of some one else.

An erroneous but very common idea exists that if a road crosses a river or runs along its bank, the public can fish from the bridge or the road, but this is not so, for (1) the public are only entitled to use the bridge or road for the purpose of passing along it, and (2) fishing from a road is really entering on the property of another without his leave. The case of the man who walked along a high road and shot the pheasants as they flew across, and of the man who walked up and down a road to obstruct grouse-driving, both of whom were held to be acting illegally, show this most clearly.

There are certain cases in which a person is justified in going on another man's land to seek for the game he has killed, such as if it was started on the sportsman's own land and fell dead over the boundary, or the case of where a man hooked a salmon, and while playing it, followed it into his neighbour's water; but all these depend on the special circumstances, and are an exception to the general rule, which is that to exercise sporting rights, the consent of the occupier, either implied from the sporting rights being reserved when he commenced his occupation, or existing by a paramount title, or expressly granted under seal by the occupier, is legally necessary.

III. When sporting rights may be exercised depends upon what they are. The Statute law has now laid down certain rules which apply to all sporting rights; there is a close season for game, a close season for birds not game, a close season for salmon and trout, and a close season for other fresh water fish. Whatever may be the rights of the owner, even if he is the grantee of the Forestal rights of the Crown, he can only exercise his sporting rights at a time the law allows. Close season applies equally to all the Queen's subjects. Besides close time there are prohibitions as to killing game on Sundays and Christmas Day and at night, and there are also in certain places prohibitions as to fishing at night, but subject to these the rule is that the owner of sporting rights can exercise those rights during the open season when he pleases.

IV. How can sporting rights be exercised? The answer is in any legal way. As to game, the only illegal modes are poison and spring traps; but as to fish, it depends on the kind of fish. For instance, it is illegal to use a fixed instrument to take salmon, and the size of the net that may be used is in many cases prescribed by local regulation, both as to the maximum and the minimum. In some cases a gaff used with a rod and line is prohibited either altogether, or at certain times of the year. Spearing salmon, trout or char is illegal, and these fish can only be taken by a properly licensed instrument, the difference between fish and game being here strikingly brought out. It is legal, if you take out a game licence, to kill game by any legal mode you like, while if you take out a fish licence you can only kill fish by the special instrument named in your licence. Thus, if you could knock a hare on the head with a stick, it would be legal if you had a game licence, while if you had a rod licence and did the same thing to a salmon it would be illegal. In the one case it is the person who is licensed to use any legal means to take game, in the other the use of a particular legal means to take fish only is given.

It may be said in conclusion that it is almost impossible to state concisely the different points that constantly arise in connection with the subject of sporting rights. It is only possible to state general principles, and it is the exceptions to these principles that create the difficulties; but the possessor of sporting rights must bear in mind (1) that such rights can only be legally acquired by a grant under seal, and that by this grant in some way, either expressly or as a consequence of law, the occupier must be bound. (2) That the rights do not generally, but only in very exceptional cases, extend beyond the boundary of the land of the person who makes the grant. (3) That they can be only exercised subject to the general law as to close time, licences, and employing legal methods of taking game or fish, and this even if the possessor of the rights buys or breeds his game, or hatches and turns out the fish. He will thus avoid many difficulties, and will not go very wrong.

J. W. WILLIS BUND.

[*See also* CLOSE TIME, GAME LAWS AND LICENCES.]

SPRING HARE, or **Jumping Hare** (*Pedetes caffer*)—This, the **Spring Haas**, of the Cape Dutch, is the largest and most remarkable of the African Jerboas. In general colour of a reddish-brown, slightly tinged with yellow upon the upper parts, and paling to greyish-white underneath, the spring hare is, about the head and body, not unlike our English hare. Here, however, the resemblance is at an end. The animal, with its semi-erect attitude, short fore-legs, strongly developed hind-legs and tail—the latter as long as the animal's body, covered with stiff hairs and black-tipped—is in other respects—although not, of course, a marsupial—far more like the kangaroo. Its leaping powers are extraordinary, and unless surprised or circumvented, it is not by any means an easy animal to come up with. Its habits are essentially

[1] Except when let or sold by the Crown to individuals or Corporations for some special purpose, such as oyster beds.

nocturnal, and it is seldom seen in daylight. Burrowing in sandy ground in large numbers, the spring hare issues forth soon after sunset, and if a farmstead or native location is anywhere near, at once devotes itself to an attack upon the crops and vegetables. It is in this way an extremely mischievous animal, and is hunted down as much as possible alike by white men and Africans. It is, however, from its nocturnal habits, a somewhat difficult beast to circumvent. On moonlight nights, in a locality where large numbers of these animals are known to attack the crops, a field can with great care and silence be surrounded and a good bag made with guns and knobkerries. The unaccustomed European, however, needs to keep a sharp look-out, or he may be knocked over and even partially stunned by the flying leap of a startled

SPRING HARE.

spring hare. Occasionally the natives pour a quantity of water into the animals' burrows, flood them out, and kill them with their knobkerries as they issue forth. The flesh of the spring hare is fairly good eating, and is much relished by natives. These animals are fond of the vicinity of hills, and upon hard, rocky ground their extraordinary jumping powers are best displayed. Their leap is said to cover in distance as much as from twenty to thirty feet. That is probably an exaggeration; but from fifteen to twenty feet may be put down as a not impossible achievement for the spring hare. The range of this animal extends from the Cape as far towards the Equator as Angola and Mozambique.

H. A. BRYDEN.

STABLES—In the construction of stabling many matters must be taken into consideration if the results of one's labours are to be an adequate and satisfactory return for the expenditure of time and capital. The first thing is to be absolutely certain as to one's requirements; second, to insist that these requirements are always used as the basis of construction from the time the foundations are laid until the last touch has been put to the completed work. Nothing spoils good work so much as chopping and changing, or departing from the lines of the original designs as the building progresses. Let the plans be drawn and approved and let the builder adhere rigidly to them.

In proposing to build a range of stabling, every man should know more or less what he requires. That is to say, he will have a general idea of how many horses he will want to accommodate. From this as a starting point, his architect will be able to supply him with plenty of details, some of which will probably be valuable, but, on the other hand, many of which will merit rejection. The latter will most probably refer to the inner construction of the stables, and as I attach much more importance to these details than to the outside appearance of the building, I will confine myself more particularly to them. The reason for this is obvious. The animals which will inhabit the new buildings will spend more of their time in the interior than on the roof. At the same time, no man should permit a building to be erected for him, the exterior of which would afterwards prove an eyesore. But before the point of fitting and arrangement is considered, a very important question arises as to the site.

Site—The best built and most scientifically arranged stable in the kingdom will be a comparative failure, unless built on a suitable site. Too much stress cannot be laid on this. A bad site is injurious to the health of horses and to that of the men employed with them. It creates endless annoyance and expense in this way, and generally gives rise to a very unsatisfactory state of affairs. A man who is contemplating the erection of new stabling knows his own ground; he should also know which is the most suitable for his purpose, and it is for him to choose the spot.

In considering this point, and in fact the whole question of stabling, I assume that the stables for a country gentleman's establishment are required. A certain number of carriage horses, hunters, and perhaps, in these days, a string of polo-ponies will be kept. These animals will spend more of their time in the stables than actually at work; therefore they will require better accommodation than, say, cab or 'bus horses. This follows quite independently of the fact that the difference in value between these classes would induce better treatment as a sort of insurance against monetary loss. In many instances the choice of the site will be, to some extent, limited by local conditions, but where it is possible every effort should be made to give effect to the following hints.

The site should be on high dry land, so situated that all surface water is carried away naturally; low-lying or marshy ground should be avoided under all circumstances. For subsoil nothing is better than gravel or sand; both are porous and lend themselves readily to nature's drainage system, ensuring a quickly drying surface after heavy rains. A clay formation or alluvial soils and *made* ground are of exactly the opposite quality, and should be avoided as being almost as objectionable as a swamp. Next to sand or gravel, a rocky formation such as granite, limestone or chalk is probably the best. The site being chosen, the next thing to do is to go thoroughly into the drainage question. With a sand or gravel subsoil all surface water will quickly disappear, but it is advisable and, in fact, absolutely necessary that the normal level of the land soakage or ground water should be kept at a certain depth below the surface. This depth I put as from five to six feet. Other points which must be taken into consideration in utilising the chosen site are light and ventilation. The building should have a south or west aspect, and be sheltered from cold northerly and easterly winds, but at the same time there should be no interruption to the free passage of air on all sides.

Walls—These points being satisfactorily settled, the main plan of the building may be considered. Whether brick or stone is to be used and whether solid or hollow walls are to be constructed are but matters of detail. If solid brick walls are decided upon, they should not be less than fourteen inches thick for externals; with stone the thickness should be at least twenty inches. A point in favour of hollow walls is that that they are warmer in winter and cooler in summer than solids.

Air-Space and Ventilation—My next point is the consideration of the cubic contents of the stable and its proper ventilation.

The cubic content, that is, the air-space contained by the building, is a most important point. Animals, as much as men, must have a sufficiency of air when kept in confinement. It is not enough to insist on plenty of outdoor exercise for horses that are not fully worked, if, when the exercise is ended, they are put into stuffy stalls or boxes which cannot contain a sufficient volume of air to ensure health. Taking a general average of stables in England, I find, from General Sir F. W. Fitzwygram's excellent book *Horses and Stables*, that the cubic contents range from 550 cubic feet in the case of the average cab-horse stables to 2,500 cubic feet per horse in the Royal Mews. Here we have a minimum and a maximum; the former is too low, the latter need not be insisted upon, though, if it can be allowed, there is no doubt that the increased air-space, unnecessary though it be for actual breathing purposes, facilitates ventilation. I would lay down the rule that the cubic content of a first class stable should be anywhere between 1,500 cubic feet and 1,700 cubic feet per horse. This gives ample breathing space, and should, in the majority of cases, give perfect control in the matter of ventilation. I am somewhat opposed to the idea of building to a greater height than 15 feet, inside measurement; air-space beyond that is not available for breathing, and, moreover, the superficial area of a stall is reduced should the building be carried higher and only the same cubic content retained as I suggest. If one takes 1,600 feet as the average and builds to 15 feet high, the result gives a superficial area per stall of 106·6 feet. This would not be altogether wrong, but a far better plan would be to reduce the height by two feet and increase the superficial area from 106·6 feet to 123 feet. Too much stress cannot be laid on the importance of floor area per horse as opposed to loftiness of the stable, but of course either point can be carried too far. I speak now of the ordinary stall; when the question of loose boxes is considered, the matter is considerably widened. In this case I would practically double my floor area and retain the maximum height of the walls at 13 feet. This would give the cubic content as 2,198 cubic feet, and both the air-space and superficial area would be ample for any horse whether sick or well.

The next point that arises is ventilation. By this I mean the complete changing of the atmosphere several times in the course of each hour. All the gaseous vapour, carbonic acid gas and organic particles given off by the animals must be cleared out of the stable almost as soon as they are formed. This can only be done by the complete changing of the atmosphere. Horses are not so susceptible to the effects of draughts as are human beings, so that the ventilation of stables is a somewhat easier problem to face than is the ventilation of houses. Speaking broadly, the scheme adopted should ensure a change of atmosphere every ten minutes or quarter of an hour. How this is to be brought about had better be left in the main to the architect. The great principle involved is the rising of the heated and vitiated air to the upper parts of the stable; outlets should thus be provided in the roof for the carrying off of this, whilst the fresh air should be admitted at a comparatively low level.

Another point of importance is that these outlets and inlets should not be under control of the stablemen. If valves are provided, these worthies will often close them to create a feeling of warmth in the stable, or they may be closed and forgotten for days at a time. If valves are provided, an unchecked arrangement of inlets and outlets, giving the *minimum* quantity of fresh air per hour, should also be added.

Paving—The last great point in the construction of new stabling is the paving or flooring. Many different materials have been used for this purpose, such as common and special bricks, wood blocks, flags, asphalt, many patent bricks or tiles, and concrete. Of them all, I recommend good Portland cement concrete; but, to be satisfactory in every way, it must be of the very best. I will state briefly my objections to the other materials mentioned: common bricks are by no means impervious to moisture; special bricks, usually glazed and very hard, contain small channels or grooves very difficult to keep clean and free from dirt; wood blocks are even worse absorbents than common bricks; both flags and asphalte form very slippery and dangerous floors.

Draining—Adopting, therefore, the very best Portland cement concrete, the only other thing to provide is sufficient slope of the fall of the floor to carry off urine and other liquids. I would recommend a slight fall from either side of the stall to a shallow channel running down the centre; this latter should have a drop of about one in sixty to a deeper channel at the end of the stall running at right angles to it, which might have a somewhat sharper fall to its point of connection with the main drainage system of the stables. This will insure the quick passage of all liquids and prevent objectionable smells and injury to the horses' health.

Under this head may be taken into consideration the matter of sanitary disinfectants, and for the comfort and well-being of the horses a liberal use of same must be made; when I say a liberal use, it must be understood that the medium must be taken, for to overdose the stable with a strong disinfectant means irritation to the animals, and the remedy in that case would be worse than the disease. Care should be taken to place such sanitary compound in places where most required—particularly when smells arise through liquid channels. Many of such compounds have come under my notice, and I have failed to find a better mixture than Jeyes' sanitary compound, which combines every ingredient necessary for the purification of stable air, and is not an irritant.

Renovation—An article of this description would hardly be complete if confined to new stabling only. In many places there are existing stables which require renovation, and this question I will now briefly consider. In the work of renovation, the first thing to be done is to take up all floors and pavements bodily; leave nothing to chance. Then examine, and, if necessary, remake and relay all drains, both land drains and sewers. Then look to the cubic content and superficial area. The roof may be raised with advantage, or a reduction in number of stalls may give all the superficial and air space that is required; then devote attention to the ventilation. This done, my remarks on new stables may be followed.

Stable fittings are matters of choice. It is hardly necessary to say that every owner of horses has his pet clothing for his favourites—clothing for one season of the year and clothing for another—and the health of the animals is no doubt preserved by the care taken in the judicious use of stable clothing, preventing chills and coughs, and rendering the horse more comfortable in its hours of rest. I have used many descriptions of horse covering, both when exercising and for the stable, and I have only words of praise for Jaeger's horse clothing in their varied forms and classes, the materials being scientifically woven, and prepared with every care in respect of healthy ventilation and warmth.

Coach-houses and harness rooms—These should be lofty and dry; well paved with cement, and well-ventilated; otherwise "must" will soon show itself. They should contain all the accommodation requisite to the demands that will be made upon them, and the fact must be borne in mind that the initial outlay of a few pounds may save money in the long run.

AUBREY WALLIS.

STILTS—In some parts of Switzerland and in several districts in France, especially in the Landes, walking on stilts is not only an amusement, but the usual way of locomotion. By means of these crane-like legs, men and women, and even children, transform themselves into the order of "Waders," emulate the long-legged storks and herons, and are able to cross over marshes and flooded grounds without wetting their feet.

There are various forms of stilts and modes of using them. Some, such as those employed by professionals, are strapped to the ankles and have no handles. Others have long handles, and the feet are received into leathern loops nailed on the stilt; but by far the best are those which, like the stilts used in the Landes, are furnished merely with two wooden projections on which the feet can rest.

The easiest way of mounting the stilt is to stand against a wall, and then take the handles of the stilts under the arms. Next, place the right foot on the step of one stilt; raise yourself with your back still leaning against the wall, and place the left foot on the step of the other stilt.

As the stilt-walker gets confidence and skill, he will be able to get on his stilts without needing the support of a wall, a short run and a spring being quite enough for the purpose.

In walking, raise each stilt alternately with the hands, lifting the foot with it. Having obtained some degree of proficiency, race with other stilt walkers. I saw a race in the South of France; the distance was a kilometre and a half over uneven country. Eleven competitors started and nine reached the goal. The other two came to grief; they were both leading, and were reckoned the most expert, but their fatal jealousy led to their overbalancing themselves as they were racing along neck to neck, though, when falling, they nimbly lighted on their feet.

There are experts who can ascend and descend steps on stilts, or pirouette on one stilt, holding the other over their heads, then replacing the feet without coming to the ground. It is said that accomplished stilt-walkers can even ascend and descend ladders laid at a considerable slope. The height of the feet from the ground rather diminishes than adds to the difficulty of walking on stilts.

F. T. POLLOK.

STOOL-BALL—The game of stool-ball was formerly a very popular game in England. Allusions are made to it in the writings of many authors in the seventeenth century, and it is probably of a much earlier date. Joseph Strutt describes it, and according to his description it was very much like what "rounders" is now. In his time it appears to have been dying out for he mentions it merely as "a pastime played to this day in the North of England."

The game probably never completely died out in the South of England, particularly in Sussex, and it has of late years changed considerably, owing to its increasing popularity. Thus, while formerly the hand was used to strike the ball, a bat is now used for this purpose. This bat is similar in shape and size to an ordinary fives bat, and is made of one piece of wood. The stools have been superseded by "targets," which are round boards, each one foot in diameter, fastened to posts, so that the lowest part of the target is four feet from the ground.

Judging from the references to this game, from the earliest to the latest, there seems always to have been a great amount of uncertainty about the rules, and this uncertainty has not ceased to exist, for there are still many differences as to the rules in different localities, even in Sussex, which is probably the county in which the game is most played.

The target has been described as being round, but many clubs have square targets. This instance alone will show that there is no very definite standard to go upon. However, it will be best to take what are apparently the best rules on each point, and treat them as being the general rules of the game. Most of the rules, of course, are generally accepted by all clubs, for it is only in small matters that differences still exist, and it is to be hoped that these differences will soon disappear.

The game is confined—in Sussex, at any rate,—to women, and there are eleven players on each side.

The targets are placed facing each other fifteen yards apart, and the sides toss for choice of innings. The striker's object is to guard the target from the bowler. The ball generally used is a tennis ball (not a lawn tennis ball). The bowler generally stands on a line half-way between the targets, but in some clubs the bowler stands beside the target, and bowls five times, when a change is made, and another bowler bowls five times from the other end, and so on, as in cricket.

If the ball is struck, the strikers are bound to run at least one run. To obtain a run, both strikers must tap the targets at their own end with the bat, run across, and tap the target at the opposite end. If one of the opposite side strike the target with the ball before the striker taps it with the bat, the striker who is nearest to that target is out. The striker is also out if the ball when bowled hits the target, or if the ball, after being struck, is caught by one of the opposite side before touching the ground. There is a rule, observed in most clubs, which is similar to "leg-before-wicket" in cricket. This is, that if the ball strikes any part of the body which happens to be in front of the target, excepting the hand holding the bat, the striker is out. The bowler must deliver the ball underhand, and may not throw or jerk it.

It is hardly necessary to say that the object of the game is to make runs, the side which makes the most being the winner.

To strike the ball, so that it will travel any distance, is extremely difficult, as will be seen on considering that the ball reaches the striker at a height of four feet from the ground. Besides this, the bowler is fairly close to the striker, who, as a rule, has not time to get the circular swing necessary for a hard hit between the delivery of the ball and its reaching the target. The difficulty of getting this swing is also increased by the striker being obliged to stand very close to the target, for if the target is not touched with the bat after the ball is bowled, and one of the opposite side touch it with the ball, the striker is out. If the striker stands sufficiently far from the target to get a good swing with the bat, and miss the ball, and if one of the opposite side standing behind the target caught the ball, there would be ample time to touch the target with it before the striker has time to touch it with the bat.

Notwithstanding this difficulty of striking hard, if the ball is hit, a run must be made or the striker is out, so it is not to be wondered at that the runs scored are not, as a rule, very numerous, and that the striker is not generally anxious to hit balls that are very wide.

It appears, however, that it is not wise to be too chary of hitting, but to strike the ball downwards, if possible, between the fielders.

Judging by the keenness shown by the players, stool-ball is evidently a very exciting and charming game, and, as it gives womankind another opportunity of combining outdoor exercise with rivalry, there is every probability of its maintaining a lasting position among the games of England.

CHARLES WALKER.

STUD BOOKS—**Horses**—*The Thoroughbred*—The originator of stud books, in connection with the breeding of the race-horse, is understood to have been Mr. Joseph Butler, of Killamarsh, Derbyshire, who in the "seventies" of last century had charge of the studs of Lord Fitzwilliam and Lord Lowther. He, in fact, prepared the material for a stud book prior to the publication of a volume in 1791, entitled *An Introduction to a General Stud Book*, and the latter was followed by the *English Stud Book*, in the preface to which it was stated that the "substance was collected solely for the private amusement of the editor." The editor was an ancestor of the Messrs. Weatherby, the officials of the English Jockey Club, and for very many years compilers of the present *Racing Calendar*. Coming to the present century, a volume appeared in 1803, containing pedigrees from as far back as the reign of Charles the Second. It was, however, in 1808 that the first volume of the present *General Stud Book* saw the light, embracing pedigrees, as set forth on the title page, "From the earliest accounts to 1807." This volume has run through several editions, the fifth having been published as recently as 1891. This, then, is the progenitor of the many stud books, devoted to the genealogy of the thoroughbred, which are circulated in other countries. It is compiled and issued every four years by the Messrs. Weatherby, and has reached eighteen volumes, not to mention annual supplements. A desire has been expressed that the interval between publication should be two years.

On the Continent, France has for many years had a stud book; while in Germany are the *Allgemeines Oesterreichisches und Ungarüsches Gestübuch* (Vienna), and the *Norddeutsches Gestut-Buchs* (Berlin). In Berlin also we have Freutzel's *Family Tables of English Thoroughbred Stock*. There is further a stud book, periodically published in St. Petersburg; and in Rome the *Libro Genealogico Cavalli di Puro Sanque Importati o Nati in Italia*, and we may add the *Stud Book Belge*, in Brussels. In the United States, the first volume of the *American Stud Book* was published in 1873, and South America is distinguished for its *Stud Book Argentino*, the official publication of the Jockey Club in Buenos Ayres; there is also the *Stud Book de la Republica O. de Uruguay*, belonging to the Jockey Club of Monte Video. Turning to Australia, as far back as 1859, a single volume was published by a Mr. W. Levy in Melbourne. This was followed by the late Mr. W. C. Yuille's *Victorian Stud Book*, which was eventually merged into the present *Australian Stud Book*, edited by his son, Mr. A. Yuille. The sixth volume, of over 600 pages, was issued in 1897, and was embellished with a large collection of tabulated pedigrees. Nearly thirty years ago there was a stud book published in Sydney, first edited by Mr. Fowler Boyd Price, and then jointly by Messrs. E. K. Cox and J. A. Scarr, both prominent New South Wales racing men. The little island colony of Tasmania is, as yet, content with a manuscript stud book; but New Zealand has issued the tenth volume, the present editor of which is Mr. G. Elliot, of Waganui, Canterbury.

There are also volumes, officially published and otherwise, in connection with hunters, hackneys, clevelands, polo ponies, the Yorkshire coach horse, &c.

Dogs—The *Kennel Club Stud Book* is the official record of the institution of that name, having its headquarters at 27 Old Burlington Street, London. The book covers every known species of the canine race, sporting and otherwise, and was first issued in 1874, the secretary and then editor being Mr. F. C. S. Pearce, who was succeeded by the present official, Mr. W. W. Aspinall. Originally circulated every four years, the *Kennel Club Stud Book* is now an annual publication, Vol. XXIV. being the last volume. The *American Kennel Club Stud Book* is a New York publication, and has reached thirteen volumes. The compiler is Mr. A. P. Vandenburgh, secretary to the A.K.C. On the Continent there are the *Svenska Kennel Klubbens Stambok*, published at Stockholm, and the *Finska Kennel Klubbens Kalendarsch Stambok*, published at Helsingfors. The *Italian Stud Book*, first published at Milan, in 1897, under the auspices of a club, is confined to pointers and English black and tan and Gordon setters. Of stud books devoted to special classes of dogs the *Greyhound Stud Book*, the official publication of the English National Coursing Club, was started in 1882, with the late Mr. David Brown as its compiler. It has now reached seventeen volumes. Prior to this official publication, there should not be omitted a stud book printed for several years by Mr. Goodlake (the very first stud book for greyhounds), in the early part of the present century. It was followed by one by Mr. Thomas Thacker, whose annual *Courser's Remembrancer*, of more than half a century ago, still finds a place in many a present day courser's library. To the foregoing may be added Captain Ellis's erudite *Bothal Stud Book*, printed for private circulation. There is also a *Greyhound Stud Book* published yearly under the auspices of the American Coursing Board, the editor of which is Mr. L. F. Bartels, Denver, Colorado. The third and last volume has an especial feature, namely, that the pedigree of every greyhound therein is displayed in tabulated form. Other stud books embrace foxhounds, harriers and beagles, fox-terriers, and breeds not connected in any way with sport.

W. F. LAMONBY.

SWAN, WILD—There are only about eight species of the genus *cygnus* known to naturalists throughout the world. They may be enumerated as follows:—The Mute, Whooper (sometimes spelt Hooper), Polish, and Bewick's swans; the Trumpeter and the Common American swan; the Black swan of Australia (*Chenopsis atrata*); and the Black-necked Swan of South America (*Cygnus nigricollis*). Of these the first four are claimed as British;

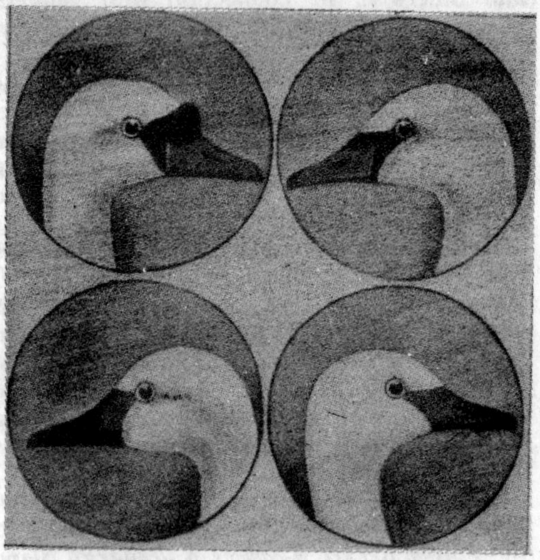

1, Mute Swan. 2, Polish Swan. 3, Bewick's Swan. 4, Hooper.

HEADS OF SWANS.

that is, as visitors occurring in the wild state, usually in the winter months only. It is not altogether improbable that the great North American bird, the Trumpeter swan, and also the lesser trans-Atlantic swan, *Cygnus columbianus* or *americanus*, have been similarly obtained; although in their case this would seem to be more open to doubt by reason of the fact that both species are kept in this country on waters where they are allowed more or less liberty. From such situations the cygnets are, of course, liable to escape, unless sufficiently early measures are taken to prevent them taking to flight. Neither is it unlikely that in severe winters, when their freshwater home has become untenable, they, like the semi-domesticated Mute swan, might occasionally be found on the tidal waters, in our estuaries, and even upon the open coast.

The Mute Swan (*Cygnus olor* or *C. mansuetus*)—As the semi-domesticated swan of our rivers and inland waters this bird is familiar to most people, and as its habits and life history are fully described in Mr. Harting's paper, it is unnecessary to touch further on these matters. It may, however, be as well to point out here that the Mute swan in a perfectly wild state is occasionally to be found on our coasts; indeed, the wonder would seem to be that wild Mute swans are not oftener found in British waters, seeing that they breed at large in the South of Sweden, in Denmark, and North Germany, much nearer, in fact, to our shores than any other wild swan. On being frozen out of the lakes and ponds, some of the semi-domesticated Mute swans do occasionally find their way to strange waters, where they are shot; but it is not quite fair to the wildfowler to assume that all the Mute swans he kills are birds that have escaped from protection.

The Mute swan has been introduced in the Outer Hebrides, and whilst visiting these islands last winter, the writer was informed by the gamekeeper on Benbecula that the swans were wild and bred on one of the lochs, but that they were sometimes molested by the boys, who took the eggs.

The Polish Swan (*Cygnus immutabilis*)—Naturalists are not agreed that this is a true species, specifically distinct from *C. olor*. Yarrell, however, described and figured this bird, and produced evidence which certainly carries the conviction that there are one or two clearly defined points of distinction. One of the most important is that the cygnets are white from the egg; whereas the young of the Mute swan are grayish-brown in colour. To compare the two species further, it may be pointed out that in the Polish swan the knob on the bill is not so large, whilst the feet and legs are ash or slate-gray instead of black. A strong argument, too, in favour of separation is the fact that Polish swans are occasionally shot out of strings flying Southward along the line of our East Coast, from Scotland to the mouth of the Thames. Yarrell lays stress on the circumstance of these herds being seen without any observable difference in the specimens obtained, all being distinct from the Mute swan, whilst the cygnets, so far as observed, were pure white, like the parent birds. The Polish swan is smaller than the Mute swan, its length being 4 feet 9 inches. The bill is reddish-orange, the nail, nostrils, and face black.

Is it recorded in the *Zoologist* of February, 1880, that a fine adult pair of Polish swans were shot on Wroxham Broad; both had perfect wings, and so presumably were wild birds, the male weighing 22 lbs., and the female 19 lbs., the former measuring 5 feet 2 inches, and the latter 5 feet in length. These weights and measurements accord pretty nearly with those given for the Mute swan. An immature female Polish swan killed at Wramplingham in March, some four or five years later, weighed 15 lbs.; measured, n length, 4 feet 8 inches, and, from tip to tip of fully extended wings, 7 feet.

The Whooper, Whistling Swan, Elk (*Cygnus musicus* or *C. ferus*)—This bird is not quite so large as the Mute swan, from which bird it may usually be distinguished, even at some considerable distance, by its different pose and upright carriage of the head and neck (*see* illustration). A closer examination of the two species reveals the fact that the Whooper has no knob at the base of the bill, this basal portion being flat and of a deep yellow colour, whilst the tip of the bill is black. The Whooper is reported to have bred in some of the Scottish islands towards the close of the last century. It now nests in Iceland, within the Arctic circle in Scandinavia, and in East Russia. A winter visitor to Great Britain, it appears abundantly only when the weather is severe in Northern Europe. In mild winters the Whooper is seldom seen on our shores. It is most numerous in Scotland, but in Ireland its smaller congener, the Bewick's swan, is the more plentiful of the two. The Whooper is our true wild swan, deriving its name from its loud call-note. In adult plumage the Whooper is pure white, with legs and feet dull black. The young birds in first plumage are pale brownish-gray, and the basal portion of the bill does not at first assume the deep yellow or orange colour of the old birds, but instead is of a pale yellow or flesh-colour, whilst the feet and legs are dark brownish-black. The cygnets attain adult plumage by the second winter. The Whooper is the same length as the Mute swan, both measuring about 5 feet, but in consequence of a somewhat slighter form or more slender build, it does not attain to the weight of the more familiar species. The average weight of the adult male Whooper in good condition is about 21 lbs., and an adult female weighs two or three pounds less.

Bewick's Swan (*Cygnus bewicki*)—This bird is the smallest of the British swans, and it, too, is a winter visitor. In severe seasons it is frequently found on our East Coast: is tolerably plentiful in favourable situations on the West Coast of Scotland, including the warm seas of the Outer Hebrides, and also the Orkneys and Shetlands, but is usually much more abundant in Ireland than elsewhere in our islands. To the latter place Bewick's swan resorts in far greater numbers than the Whooper, for it has been found there in frosty weather in herds of some hundreds. Bewick's swan has, from all accounts, a more westerly breeding range than the Whooper; nesting above the limits of forest growth, on the tundras of North-west Russia and Siberia, and on some of the islands in the Arctic Ocean. Bewick's swan may readily be distinguished from the Whooper by size and weight alone. Adult specimens measure from 46 inches to 50 inches in length, and weigh from 9 lbs. to 13 lbs., this being fully one foot less in length than, and only about half the weight of, the Whooper. In addition to this the coloration of the bill serves as a means of identification; the deep yellow of the basal portion of the smaller bird does not extend below the nostrils, as it does in the larger swan; the rest of the bill is black, and the legs and feet are dull black. The plumage of the adult Bewick's swan is pure white, and the young in first plumage resemble those of the Whooper, the basal portion of their bills being also flesh-coloured.

The Trumpeter Swan (*Cygnus buccinator*)—This North American swan, sometimes called the Hunter's swan, has been included in the list of British birds on the strength of a statement that four were killed out of a small herd of five which appeared at Aldeburgh, Suffolk, towards the end of October, 1866. One of these, now in the Ipswich Museum, has been identified by Professor Newton as of this species. Still, as the Trumpeter swan has been introduced and

WHOOPER. TAME SWAN.

has reared its young in the Zoological Gardens, Regent's Park, and elsewhere in this country, it is just possible that these examples may have escaped from confinement. An American authority, Dr. Elliott Coues, remarks of this swan that it chiefly inhabits North America, from the Mississippi valley westward, from Texas to the fur countries, Great Lakes, Hudson's Bay, and Canada. It occurs casually on the Atlantic coast, breeds from Iowa and Dakota northward, and winters southward to the Gulf. The bill and feet are entirely black. Adults measure 5 feet or more in length, and the enormous extent of their wings reaches to about 8 feet. The plumage is white, and some birds have a wash of rusty-brown on the head. The cygnets are smaller, with feet and legs not so dark, and plumage greyish, with upper neck and head rusty-brown.

Common American Swan or Whistling Swan (*Cygnus columbianus* or *americanus*)—Another North American swan, which is said to have occurred a few times in Scotland. There is, of course, nothing inherently strange or improbable in the supposition that swans breeding in Arctic America may reach this country. A slight divergence eastward from their usual line of flight, such as might be caused by wind or fog, when on their southward migration, would, in the case of birds of such powerful flight, soon see them well on their way hither. *C. columbianus* is rather smaller than his congener, the Trumpeter swan, being under 5 feet in length, and with a wing stretch of from 6 to 7 feet. Coues says that this is the species usually found along the Atlantic coast, and it is more numerous on either coast than in the interior of the United States. It is, however, somewhat rare in New England and eastwards, and breeds only in the high north. There is in this swan a yellow patch in front of the eye, but this is usually small and is not present in every specimen. The plumage of adults is white, and that of the young ashen-grey, with a reddish-brown tinge on the upper neck and head; the young have the bill in part flesh-coloured and the feet of a yellowish flesh colour.

With the Black swan of Australia most people in this country are now tolerably familiar; but as both it and the Black-necked swan of South America are not likely to travel to Great Britain of their own accord, neither need be mentioned further here.

SWAN-SHOOTING—All ardent wildfowlers are filled with the desire to shoot a wild swan sooner or later during their career; although, be it said, for the majority this longing never receives consummation. There is usually great excitement attendant upon the shooting of one's first wild swan, and once this is accomplished the true sportsman is generally content to leave the pursuit of these birds to others, whenever brent geese, duck, wigeon, teal, or any other better and more sporting fowl are about. Yet there is something very striking about the appearance of a herd of wild swans upon the waters, and certainly a company of Whoopers swinging along through the air in string or wedge-like formation is one of the grandest visions ever presented to the wildfowler. Then, too, the music of their cries is among the most inspiriting of sounds.

In their northern haunts wild swans are not so familiar with the sound of the fowling-piece or the sight of the gunner, and consequently on first appearing on our coasts they are somewhat careless in the matter of sentry duty, and are usually more or less easy to approach. The novice in swan-shooting should then with all speed make the most of his opportunities. At such times, by the exercise of a little judgment, and given a fair amount of good luck, he will be able to secure a swan or two before constant harassing by other gunners has rendered the birds perfectly inaccessible.

When the weather is exceptionally severe in Scandinavian waters and along the shores of the Baltic, the wild swans are much more abundant around our coasts and it is then that the best of the sport with them is obtainable.

The swan-shooter has two or three courses open to him, in accordance with the movements of the birds and their environment. He may elect to set up to them with the gunning-punt, when a well-directed charge of shot is certain to do some execution at fair range. Or, if the water is too rough to venture out in a punt, he may sail up to his quarry in some handy craft of light draught, with punt-gun fixed up with swivel or rope-breeching in the bow. If in this case the punt gun is not available, a heavy shoulder four-bore or double eight-bore will form a good substitute; the former throwing, perhaps, a quarter of a pound of AA or SSSG shot at a single discharge, and the latter 5oz. or so of smaller sizes of shot from the two barrels. If such means are not available, the gunner may have to make use of a sunken tub or a pit dug in the saltings where by patiently lying in wait he may now and again obtain a shot at passing swans. And lastly, where the situation will permit, he may attempt to stalk them along the shore of some loch or down the creek on the saltings, or the attempt may be made to secure a shot by driving.

When following swans, or indeed any wildfowl, amidst snow and ice it is advisable to put on a white cap and overall. That prince of wildfowlers, Colonel Hawker, taught us all these and many another dodge for getting at wary fowl.

Whilst going after swans in the gunning-punt, it sometimes answers to put two or three pieces of ice upon the fore-deck of the punt; this, however, requires careful manipulation, or the trim of the boat will be seriously disturbed. Still, something of the sort is more of a necessity in the case of Whoopers and their congeners than any other fowl for, by reason of their length of neck and height from the water, swans have an extended range of vision and thus are able to detect the movements inside a punt at some considerable distance. Over-anxiety has spoilt many good opportunities in swan shooting. Thus, when approaching swans in the water, the gunner should not be in too great a hurry to take a shot, for these heavy-bodied birds, unlike teal and some other ducks, cannot spring high into the air at one bound, but require both time and room to get under way. Thus there is ample time to tip the punt-gun and take a cool shot whenever they open their wings. It should, however, be remembered that swans rising from the ground are much quicker in getting well on the wing. In case the punt gun cannot be tipped, or the gunner doubts his ability to make the most of a flying shot, it is as well to remind him that the gun should be set high and that the heads and necks of sitting swans should be his target; moreover for this kind of shooting the mistake should not be made of using shot

Wild Swan

too large in size—B.B. will usually be quite large enough.

In shooting at flying swans with the shoulder gun the novice is liable to fall into error in two ways, first as regards their rate of speed, and next, in estimating the distance. The flight of a swan is very deceptive; the idea of speed is scarcely to be associated with the slow and measured beat of his huge wings, and yet the bird may actually be travelling faster than wild ducks or sharp-flying Brent geese. Inexperienced gunners often innocently open fire upon swans at from one to two hundred yards distance under the impression that they are well within gunshot. This, however, serves but to wound and to frighten birds, and care should be taken to estimate distances, if on land, by the bird's surroundings, or, if on water, by its eye, the marking on its bill, and the general distinctness with which it may be seen.

The head or the hollow underneath the wing are the most assailable targets at which to aim when shooting at a swan flying past.

Colonel Hawker speaks of a dodge for making a going-away swan "haul his wind" and so come across the gunner, and this is quite possible, as the following incident will show. In January, 1895, the last swan year of any account, I was wild-fowling off the Essex coast. It was in the early days of the memorable frost of that year, and on coming aboard the yacht from morning flight, preparatory to going afloat for the day and whilst swabbing the mud off my wading boots in the dinghey alongside, my man called attention to two swans flying up against the steady north-east breeze then blowing. As it was evident that the line of flight they were pursuing would bring them across the bow of the yacht not more than eighty yards away, I called to my man to hand me the double 8-bore he had just placed in the cabin, with some big shot cartridges. This he quickly did, and I fired two shots at the leading bird, a huge fellow, whereat he gave a heavy lurch and appeared to be coming down, but recovering, he hauled round, and in two seconds both were close alongside the boat, offering the best possible opportunity for a double shot, but the gun was not loaded, and by the time more cartridges were got out of the cabin the birds were 150 yards away, and the error was not retrieved, at all events just then.

Guns and Ammunition—Although not at all times absolutely essential, success in swan-shooting is usually best assured by the employment of heavy guns of wide bore. Swans have now and again been killed with ordinary game guns and No. 4 shot, by shooting at the head and neck or underneath the wing, but in a general way the range is so great as to necessitate the use of more powerful guns and weightier shot. In a punt gun of, say $1\frac{1}{4}$-inch or $1\frac{3}{8}$-inch bore, suitable charges of Curtis and Harvey's Colonel Hawker's punt-gun powder, and of BB shot of 58, or A shot of 50 pellets to the ounce, will do good execution at the heads and necks of sitting swans at 80 yards. But for flying shots at longer range, mould shot, SSSG of 17 pellets to the ounce, will be required; and with this size swans may be killed at 100 yards or over. For heavy shoulder guns of 4- or 8-bore, AA of 40, or AAA of 32 pellets to the ounce, may be used at fair ranges, whilst the mould shot already mentioned can be requisitioned for the longer shots.

Bibliography—Any one desirous of gaining further information relative to the habits and life history of the Swans will doubtless find what he requires in one or other of the following works: *A History of British Birds*, by Henry Seebohm (Porter); Yarrell's *British Birds*, 4th edition, the 1st and 2nd vols. of which were revised by Professor Alfred Newton, and the 3rd and 4th by Mr. Howard Saunders; *A Manual of British Birds*, by Howard Saunders; *A Handbook of British Birds*, by J. E. Harting; *A Dictionary of Birds*, by Professor Newton.

Then as to the shooting of wild swans, full directions for pursuing the sport in Great Britain are to be found in one or other of the following books: *Instructions to young Sportsmen*, by Colonel Hawker (Messrs. Longman). This, the standard work fifty or more years ago, ran through several editions; although of course the section treating of guns is obsolete, many of the instructions with respect to punts, sizes of shot, and the general methods of procedure when wildfowling, are as applicable now as on the day they were written. *The Wildfowler*, by H. C. Folkard (Longmans), a delightful book, holds first place as a history of the sport. *The Fowler in Ireland*, as also the section on *Wildfowling* in *Letters to young Shooters*, by Sir Ralph Payne-Gallwey, Bart., are extremely useful. *The Art of Wildfowling*, by Mr. Abel Chapman, a sound work; and *Practical Wildfowling*, by the present writer (L. Upcott Gill).

HENRY SHARP.

SWAN, TAME—From its size, its dazzling whiteness, and the gracefulness of its movements in the water, few birds are more attractive than the Mute Swan (*Cygnus olor*), which, having lived for centuries in a state of semi-domestication, has become in consequence one of the most familiar of waterfowl. The snow-white feathers in the wing receive additional beauty by the muscular power which the swan possesses of raising them without extending the wing itself, a habit which is technically termed "busking."

Anciently proclaimed a royal bird, it was ordained that when at liberty in a public river or creek no subject could claim ownership in a swan except by grant from the Crown. The privilege of keeping swans seems to have extended back as far at least as 1483, as appears by laws and orders made in that year, and in 1496. In creating this privilege the Crown granted **Swan Marks** (*cygni notæ*), notches or nicks on the bill to denote ownership; and the books, or rolls, of swan marks that have come down to us are amongst the most curious relics of the past.

Formerly no one might keep swans who was not possessed of freehold land of the yearly value of five marks (£3 6*s.* 8*d.*), and under a Statute of 22 Edw. IV., cap. 6, the swan, or cygnets, of any person not so qualified might be seized and became forfeited to the king. Every owner of swans, however, had to pay 6*s.* 8*d.* for a license to keep them, although this license did not require renewing, for it was available for the life of the holder. That being settled, the next point was to denote the ownership of every bird by causing a mark to be made upon its bill, and this had to be arranged with the royal swanherd, or, as he was then called the Master of the Game of Swans (*Magister deductus cygnorum*), who kept a book, or roll, for the purpose, in which the mark of every private owner was entered, and could be referred to at any time in case of dispute. From time to time commissions were issued for holding "Swanherds' Courts" or "Swan-mootes," at which orders were made "where and when they were fit and necessary for the preservation of swans." These orders were copied out and made known by proclamation in market towns; they purported to provide for every possible contingency that could arise in dispute regarding ownership and the proper protection of swans.

Swan Laws—The law relating to these birds, as appears by statutes of Edward IV. and Henry VII., was very severe. Any person killing a swan, or even driving one away from his own ground if it offered to breed there, was liable to a year's imprisonment, and fine at the king's pleasure of 13*s.* 4*d.*; and any one stealing the eggs incurred a penalty of 13*s.* 4*d.* for every egg taken. If a dog drove a sitting swan off her nest his master forfeited 13*s.* 4*d.*, and if the dog killed the swan, his owner had to pay 40*s.*, whether he was present or not.

Stealing the eggs of a swan from the nest was punishable under 11 Hen. VII. c. 17, by imprisonment for a year, and a fine at the king's pleasure; but this enactment was superseded by 1. Jac. I. c. 27, section 2 of which declared that any person so offending was liable upon conviction before two justices to be imprisoned for three months, unless he paid to the churchwardens, for the use of the poor, 20*s.* for every egg, or, after one month of his commitment, became bound with two sureties in £20 apiece never to offend again in like manner.

As to the present legal status of the birds themselves, the principle seems to be that when a swan is reduced lawfully into the possession of a private person, whether it be marked or not, he may be said to have a property in it for the purpose of an indictment at common law for larceny or otherwise; but that if the bird be at liberty, in the sea or in a navigable river, *prima facie* it belongs to the Crown. Although it is not larceny to take the eggs of swans, since the law has assigned a less punishment for the offence by statute, the eggs are protected under sect. 24 of the Game Act 1 and 2 Will. IV. c. 32, which enacts that "if any person not having the right of killing the game upon any land—nor having permission from the person having such right—shall wilfully take out of the nest, or destroy in the nest, upon such land the eggs of any bird of game, or of any *swan*, wild duck, teal, or wigeon, he shall on conviction thereof, before two justices of the peace, forfeit and pay for every egg so taken or destroyed, such sum of money not exceeding 5*s.* as to the justices shall seem meet, together with the costs of the conviction."

Cob and Pen—The origin of the names *cob* and *pen* for the male and female swan respectively, is traceable to those ancient "Laws and Orders for Swans" in which the sexes are invariably so designated. Thus, in 1598, we find it ordained that "if any brood be found being led by one swan, the swan and cygnets shall be seized for the king till due proof be had whose they are, and whose was the swan that is away, be it *cob* or *pen*"; for if the swan of one owner paired with that of another, there was a regulation as to the division of the brood in swan-upping time, when the cygnets were allotted and marked accordingly. (See "*The Orders, Lawes, and Ancient Customes of Swannes, caused to be printed by John Witherings, Esquire, Master and Governour of the Royal Game of Swans and Cygnets throughout England, published by August Mathewes*, 1632.") At the present day, in the case of a mixed brood, the cygnets are divided between the two owners.

Swan-upping—The practice of taking up swans at the end of July or beginning of August for the purpose of marking them so as to denote their ownership is a very ancient one, and originally was not, as now, confined to the Thames, but extended to all parts of England. Although no "Swanherds' Courts" are now held nor any proclamations made, and the office of "Master of the Swans throughout England" is abolished, many of the old orders are still adhered to for their own protection by those who keep swans upon the Thames. The owners thus privileged at the present day are Her Majesty the Queen, the Vintners' Company, and the Dyers' Company; and the old custom of marking the birds as soon as the young broods are sufficiently well-grown is annually observed. Each has his own swanherd, and at the appointed time they meet at London Bridge, and proceed up the river in boats by stages, the ceremony occupying four days, usually commencing on the third Monday in July. The stages are from London Bridge to Ditton, Ditton to Staines, Staines to Bray, and Bray to Henley; the number of swans upon the river is so great (between 400 and 500) that it is not possible to catch and mark them all in less time than four days.

The number of swans caught in 1897 between London Bridge and Henley was 481. Of these 168 belonged to the Queen, 181 to the Vintners' Company, and 132 to the Dyers' Company.

The swanherds report that, as a rule, the swans on the Thames are well treated by the public, who feed them frequently, and do not molest the young or take the eggs. This, of course has an important bearing in maintaining their numbers. Casualties unavoidably occur, such as the swamping of nests, and the consequent addling of eggs; the destruction of newly-hatched young by pike, or by accident, and deaths from cold and starvation in winter, although at that season many of the birds get housed in barns and fed by those who live near the river.

Nesting—Swans, it is said, pair for life, build a fresh nest each season, and if left unmolested, will keep pretty close to the same locality (Stevenson, *Birds of Norfolk*, vol. iii., p. 67). The same author remarks, "Young henbirds do not lay till their *second* year, some not until the third or fourth, and commence by laying from three to five eggs." The swanherd at Abbotsbury, after an experience of fifty years, declared in 1876 that they do not lay before their *third* year (Mansel Pleydell, *Birds of Dorsetshire*, 1888, p. 144).

The nest of a swan would fill an ordinary farm-cart. It is generally composed of a great mass of rushes, reeds, flags, and other coarse aquatic herbage, piled up in a heap at the water's edge, or carried for choice to some island for greater seclusion. On the top of this heap, and in a slight hollow, the *pen* will lay from five to ten greenish-white eggs, on which she must sit for six weeks before the cygnets are hatched. Although the nest is usually built of a sufficient height to escape the danger of a flood, many instances have been recorded in which swans have been seen to raise their nests suddenly when threatened by an unusually high tide.

During the time the *pen* is sitting, the *cob* is very pugnacious, boldly attacking any one who approaches the nest, and buffeting the intruder soundly. Although the late Mr. Stevenson has stated that he was never able to verify the assertion that a swan has been known to break a man's arm or leg, and that no such occurrence was known, even by tradition, amongst local Swanherds (*Birds of Norfolk*, vol. iii., p. 71), since his death a well authenticated case of this kind has been published. (See *The Zoologist*, 1896, p. 356.)

The *cob* is not merely the guardian of the nest he has helped to build, but usually sits for two or three days before the *pen* begins to lay, thus shaping and warming the interior at the same time. While the *pen* is laying her full complement of eggs, the *cob* sits upon them in her absence, appearing reluctant to leave them on her return; and although she will cover them with herbage when she goes oft to feed, he will uncover them, wholly or partially, before taking his turn at incubation. Moreover, instances have been known in which, on the accidental death of the *pen* before the eggs were hatched, the *cob* has continued to sit, and in due course has reared the cygnets.

Cygnets—The colour of the cygnets is at first sooty gray above, the neck and under parts of the body not so dark, the bill lead colour, and the line at the margin of the base black. At the end of October, when they almost equal their parents in size, the colour of the bill changes to light slate gray with a tinge of green. The sooty gray colour prevails uniformly over the head, neck, and all the upper surface; while the under surface of the body is uniformly of a lighter hue. The gray colour vanishes

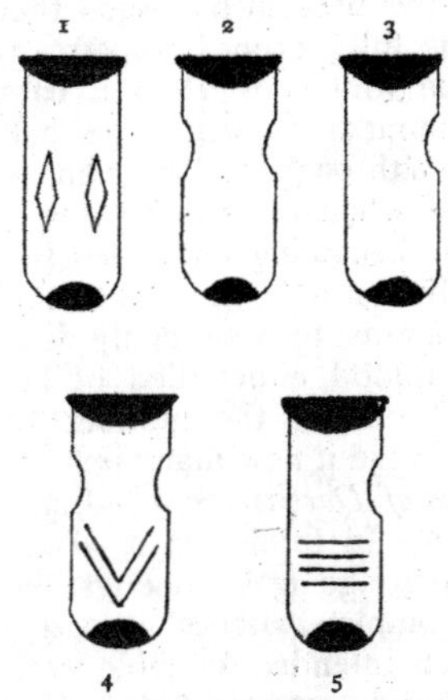

SWAN MARKS.

1, The Queen's; 2, the Vintners; 3, the Dyers; 4, the old mark of the Vintners; 5, the old mark of the Dyers.

almost entirely after the second autumn; and when two years old the cygnets have become quite white. In this respect the young of the mute swan (*Cygnus olor*) differ from the cygnets of the so-called Polish swan (*Cygnus immutabilis*), which are said to be invariably white from birth, a peculiarity which suggested the specific name *immutabilis.* Instances, however, have been recorded in which ordinary tame swans have been seen accompanied by white cygnets, and others which were followed by cygnets some white, the rest gray. (See the *Zoologist*, 1887, p. 463; 1888, p. 470.)

Swanneries—Anciently the Crown had an extensive swannery annexed to the royal palace or manor of Clarendon in Wiltshire, and another in the Isle of Purbeck (Hutchins, *Hist. Dorset*, vol. i. pp. 24, 171). In the Isle of Ely there was at one time a swannery belonging to the Bishop of Ely, whose swan mark appears in several rolls or books of swan marks compiled in the reigns of Elizabeth and James I. The Abbot of Glastonbury also, as appears by a survey of the temporalities of the Abbey after its dissolution in 1553, had a similar "game of swans" to the number of xl. couple upon a mere, which was five miles in circuit and a mile and a half broad. (See Phelps, *Hist. Somerset*, i. pp. 50, 578).

But the most famous swannery in the kingdom, and one which is still existing, is the swannery at Abbotsbury in Dorsetshire, at the western end of the Fleet estuary. There are records of a swannery here in possession of the abbot of the neighbouring monastery long previous to the Reformation. At the dissolution of the monastery, after some litigation it was surrendered to the king, who, in the thirty-fifth year of his reign, granted it to Giles Strangways, an ancestor of the present owner, the Earl of Ilchester. In April, 1878, the swanherd, who had held office there for more than fifty years, reported that the number of swans then under his charge was fully 1300 (*Zoologist*, 1878, p. 208). In the winter of 1880 a catastrophe reduced the number by nearly one half. The Fleet was frozen throughout during an extremely low spring tide, when the water plants growing at the bottom, becoming entangled in the ice, were torn up by the roots at the returning tide. Many of the swans, thus suddenly deprived of their supply of food, either died of famine, or migrated, and reduced the number to about 800, which average it now maintains (Mansel Pleydell, *Birds of Dorsetshire*, 1888, p. 144.)

Swan-Pits—In former days, when no city banquet or marriage feast amongst well-to-do citizens was complete without a roast swan or two, the cygnets intended for table were placed in a swan-pit and carefully fattened for some time previously. An interesting example of the kind still survives at Norwich, where the governor of St. Helen's Hospital, from the ancient swan-pit long-established there, supplies not only the tables of the mayor and corporation, but many private owners who consign their cygnets to his care for the purpose of being fattened. An interesting account of this "pit" will be found in Mr. Stevenson's work above quoted.

Wild Swans—During the winter months, when private lakes and pools on which swans are kept become frozen over, and the birds are no longer able to find their natural food in the shape of submerged vegetation, they betake themselves to the open waters of creeks and tidal rivers, where they often fall a prey to wildfowlers, who do not distinguish them from their wild relations. Of the latter three species, the Whooper (*Cygnus musicus*), Bewick's swan (*C. Bewicki*), and the so-called Polish swan (*C. immutabilis*) visit the British Islands in winter, and the plumage of all when adult being pure white the figures of the heads above given will afford the readiest means of distinguishing them.

J. E. HARTING.

SWIMMING—The exercise of swimming needs a regular action of all the muscles, for progress is brought about by the alternate movements of flexion and extension of the body and limbs. These movements begin in the legs, spread to the thighs, the vertebral column and the arms, promoting harmonious action between the muscles of both sides of the body, and consequently regular development and a straight figure.

The common idea is that swimming can be easily acquired. This in the abstract is true, but it is one thing to be able to keep afloat and propel yourself through the water, and quite another thing to do so correctly, with speed, and the least possible waste of power. Much depends on the teacher, for when once a bad style is contracted, it is with the utmost difficulty that improvement can be made. At the present time, any one can assume the title of "Professor of Swimming"; there is no recognised authority for testing the abilities of teachers, but hopes are entertained that the diploma examination instituted by the Life-Saving Society, which will be referred to later, will be the means of creating a much higher standard of education for the teaching of swimming than is now common.

Most persons who have learned to swim have a vivid recollection of the difficulties experienced in keeping themselves afloat when they first attempted the exercise. They especially remember the short, vigorous but flurried, misdirected, and consequently futile strokes which, instead of enabling them to skim the surface of the water, conducted them to the bottom. Impressed upon the memory, too, are the ineffectual attempts at respiration; the gasping and puffing and the swallowing of water inadvertently gulped instead of air.

Rapid progress is best secured by moving the limbs more slowly in flexion than in extension. Therefore, the general tendency of novices to bend the back, to make short sharp plunges with hands and feet and never to straighten the limbs, are faults which must be avoided by every one who wishes to become a swimmer. It should never be forgotten that every movement must be carefully executed, the circular sweep of the arms and legs properly defined, and all haste avoided.

The legs have the chief share in securing progress, and the greatest attention should be paid to this part of the stroke, so that the learner may be able to use his legs to the best advantage.

The best method of practising the leg stroke is to take hold of some support with both hands and bring the body into a horizontal position on the surface of the water, the legs extended close together and the feet turned slightly outwards, the heels touching. Then the legs should be opened and widened out at the knees, thereby drawing the feet well up towards the body, heels kept touching all the time. This movement should be freely practised before the next is

POSITION I.

entered upon, and on no account must the knees *be drawn under the body*. They are simply to be widened out sideways. As soon as the beginner fully understands this movement, he should, when the feet are drawn up, kick them wide out to each side and then close the straightened legs back to their original, horizontal position, with a strong stroke.

These are the essential actions of the legs in breast swimming, and, before the combined movements are practised, the beginner should be able to accomplish them with regularity and precision.

It is astonishing what confidence a learner will gain as soon as he begins to understand that he can regulate the movements of his limbs, and that as long as he keeps moving his legs in the manner described, his body will remain on the surface. Into these leg-actions he will almost imperceptibly glide; the feet are drawn up, then

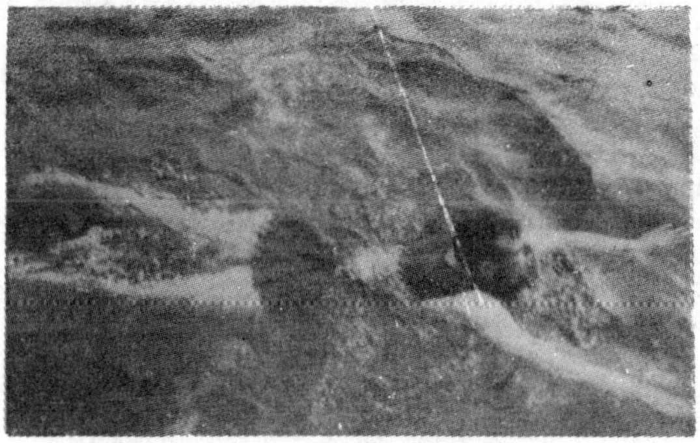

POSITION II.

the legs are swiftly extended and brought back together, with regular, rhythmical movement.

Expert breast-stroke swimmers, as they move the legs backwards, make a rounded sweep with the lower part of the leg and foot, causing a kind of flip or fin action, thereby adding to pace, by forming a series of irregular ellipses; as this comes with practice, the learner must first acquire the complete stroke.

Now for the arm movements. The arms should be flexed, with the elbows about four to six inches from the sides of the body; the hands should be brought up in front of the chin, thumbs touching and palms facing downwards. The hands should be near the surface and the body inclined forward, the head thrown slightly back. On no account must the hand be cramped, though the fingers should be fully extended and touching each other. In making the stroke, the arms should be shot out to their fullest extent, in line with the body; the hands then slightly turned outwards, the arms brought round by a steady pull until they are in line with the shoulder. The recovery is made by flexing the arms and bringing the elbows near the sides of the body, the hands coming almost naturally into position again in front of the chin.

POSITION III.

The combination of the arm and leg movements should next be practised.

The first difficulty will be that of breathing, but with a little careful attention that will soon be overcome. The inspiration must be made while the arms are being swept back from the extended position to the one in line with the shoulders; the expiration during the other portions of the stroke. Breathing should take place regularly every stroke, and not be suspended, as it very often is by beginners, during several.

When first attempting the combined movements, it is best to be held up by some one. At starting, incline the body to a horizontal position, with the back slightly hollowed, *not arched*, with arms and legs fully extended. Then the arms are brought backwards until in line with the shoulder; next, the elbows are flexed and the hands brought to the front in line with the chin. As the hands are brought to the front, the legs are drawn up and then quickly kicked out, swirled round and brought together again, as if in one motion, while at the same time the arms are shot forward. When the arms are fully extended, the hands should be about three inches, and the legs, when closed, about eight inches below the surface. On no account must there be haste in any part of the stroke, for the more careful his action at the outset, the quicker the beginner will learn. As soon as a few strokes can be accomplished, he should take up his position on one side of the bath at the shallow end, push off, and try to reach the other side.

With the acquirement of the breast-stroke will come the desire to learn the higher branches of the art, and for this purpose it is, in my opinion, desirable to master first the principles which govern floating, as thereby the beginner will soon understand how buoyant the human body is, how easily it can be made to remain upon the surface, and the position in which it should be placed to minimise the resistance offered it by water when travelling. The ability to float comes to you when least expected, or, rather, you suddenly find your proper balance after vainly trying to discover it for weeks. Some people there are who can float but not swim; while there are thousands of swimmers who cannot float at all. Their ignorance is largely due to lack of patience. They try once or twice, find it difficult to learn, and then turn their attention solely to racing for the rest of their career. In brief, floating is the balancing of the body on the surface of the water, and what the swimmer has first to find out is the exact position in which his arms and legs have to be placed in order to accomplish it. The learner should first stand erect in the bath with legs close together and then lean backwards, at the same time extending the arms beyond the head. After closing his mouth and taking a deep breath, a slight push from the bottom should be made, sufficient to bring the body to the surface in a horizontal position. Then, gently inclining his head back, holding his breath, and without troubling if his face go under water, he should first note which part of the body sinks first. If the legs sink, then either the arms are not fully extended, the head not sunk low enough, or the chest not properly inflated. The merest alteration of one of the limbs may suffice to keep the body on top. A good way of practising is to place the feet under the rail of the bath and then lie flat on the back with arms extended beyond the head, the whole body being kept perfectly straight, but not rigid. In getting into position, every movement should be made slowly, and, if the body descend a little, there should be no alteration in its position, as in any case there is slight sinking at every expiration, followed by a corresponding rise at each inspiration. Two great faults must be guarded against, (*a*) the almost uncontrollable desire to lift the head, and (*b*) *the contraction of the muscles before the whole body is rigid.*

Sometimes "sculling" is taught first, as this is the chief of floating and other surface feats. The body is kept straight, as previously described, but the arms, instead of being extended beyond the head, are placed at the side of the body, the hands palm downwards. By slight semicircular, wave-like motions of the hands from right to left, the recovery being made as if feathering an oar, the body is kept on the surface and motion also imparted to it. If a swimmer acquire this he can always keep his body in position for floating practice. In salt water it is much easier to balance one's self than in fresh, owing to the greater density of the water.

When he has acquired a knowledge of breast-swimming and floating, the beginner can then turn his attention to the speed strokes. With that familiarly known as the side stroke I do not intend to deal. It is practically out of date now, having been supplanted by the over-arm and Trudgen methods of progression.

The "over-arm" movement, which is a development of the old side stroke, is now used by almost every racing swimmer. The leg-kick is entirely different from that used in the breast stroke, and is more like that of a runner. The over-arm, the lower-arm and leg strokes combine in so uniform a manner that the body moves forward with a regular swing. The swimmer lies on his side, the majority preferring to turn on to the right, with the under or right arm fully extended beyond the head. He then pulls the under arm down through the water towards the hips, at the same time keeping the hand flat and the fingers closed. As soon as the stroke is finished, the arm is flexed and the hand shot forwards, until it again arrives in front of the head, ready for the next stroke. When the lower arm has nearly completed the downward stroke, the upper arm, slightly flexed so as to work clear of the chest, should be a little in front of the face, with the fingers closed together and hand pointing downwards. The hand is then swept through the water close to the body until opposite the waist, when it is brought smartly out and carried rapidly through the air to the front of the face, ready for the succeeding stroke.

The legs commence to work as soon as the upper arm is opposite the shoulder. They are then opened widely and should be ready for the kick when the upper hand leaves the water, the kick being completed before the said hand is ready for the next stroke. In this kick, the left leg is placed forward, knee slightly bent, while the right leg is carried far back and bent double. Then the left leg is smartly straightened and the right brought back to it with a determined swish as of a whip. In this stroke, as the body is on the side, the hands are worked in nearly a vertical plane, above and beneath the trunk, and not on either side of it, as in the breast stroke; but with regard to the legs the movement is different, for these are worked in the horizontal plane. The extremities and the body are consequently employed in the best possible manner for developing their power, reducing friction in the forward motion and preventing dead points.

In the over-arm stroke, three limbs move together in the same direction and keep time;

OVER-ARM STROKE.—I.

the fourth always moves in the opposite direction to the other three. The limbs which move together are the legs and over-arm; as the latter is advanced, the legs are drawn up and all three are forced backward with energy and rapidity, communicating to the body a forward impulse, and the body, being on the side, advances as on a keel to a considerable distance; the under-arm, which moves by itself, acts as a cut-water, assists in floating the body, and keeps up the momentum as the other limbs are getting into position for the next stroke, thus securing in a great measure continuity of movement. In order to get the greatest possible power from the kick, the legs should be made to diverge widely, and the greatest force should be imparted to them when pushed outwards and away from the trunk, the force being continued as the legs are converged upon each other, until the whole body is in a straight line.

Inhalation takes place during the forward movement of the over-arm.

The "Trudgen" stroke is so called because it was made popular in this country in the "seventies" by a swimmer of that name who had learned it while among the natives of South America. Though a fatiguing stroke for a long swim, it is of eminent service in "water polo," and, for a short distance, is perhaps one of the speediest known. The leg kick is essentially the same as in the over-arm stroke, the body being on the side when it is taken, but instead of the under-arm being moved in the ordinary way, it is brought out of the water beyond the head and swept round to the side, thus causing the body to turn on the breast. Then the upper hand is pulled through the water in similar manner and the leg kick taken, the body turning once more on the side. Trudgen swam on the chest always, with both arms out of the water, and this style is used in polo when dribbling the ball, but the double over-arm is the less exhausting of the two and just as speedy.

Swimming on the back is not much cultivated, but ability therein is of great assistance in the saving of life from drowning. The movements are similar to those of the breast stroke, the leg kick being identically the same. The arms are extended beyond the head, and then, with the palms turned outward, swept round to the body, and carried back out of the water to position.

When bringing a drowning person to shore, the hands are of course engaged, and the back-swimming has all to be accomplished with the legs. These are sunk at a far greater angle to the surface, so as to give freedom of action, and are moved from the knees downward in semi-circular sweeps, which not only propel the swimmer at a fairly rapid rate, but also tend, through the consequent swirl of water, to keep up the body of the person carried. When practising this stroke, the arms should be folded across the chest.

Under-water swimming competitions are not encouraged by any of the governing bodies, several fatal accidents having resulted therefrom. The breast stroke is ordinarily used, the head being depressed and the arms kept downwards. As soon as the swimmer is becoming exhausted, a warning pain, often described by swimmers as "a headache at the back of the neck," comes over the *medulla oblongata*. *He should immediately rise*, or insensibility, and possibly death, will ensue.

With ability to float is also acquired a sense

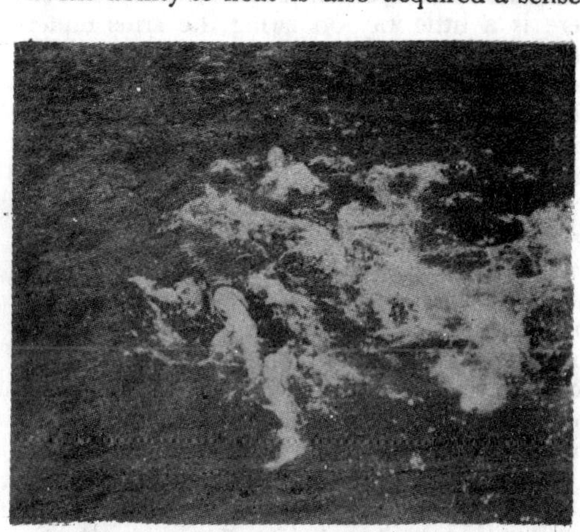

OVER-ARM STROKE.—II.

of absolute control over the water, and the swimmer soon learns how easily the body can be kept on the surface. Then arises the desire to accomplish some of the feats performed by experts. One of the simplest is that of treading water, which is useful when playing polo in deep water. The arms are extended at right angles, with palms downwards, and the downward action of the legs in the breast-stroke is used to keep the body off the surface, the hands being pressed down at each kick. When it is desired to move forwards, the legs are moved alternately, being thrust outward from the knees to the front and then drawn backwards, the sole of the foot striking the water; but the action is exactly the reverse when desirous of going backwards, the legs then being drawn alternately to the rear. When going forward, the hands are placed on the hips, but when returning they are folded across the chest. The "Pendulum" is a balancing feat which can easily be accomplished by one able to float. The body is first placed in a floating position, with the arms stretched out beyond the head, which is thrown well back. A good breath is taken, the head then inclined slowly forward, and the hands drawn very gradually and carefully towards the back of the head. As this action goes on the feet slowly sink until the body is perpendicular, with the face slightly out of the water. Then the head is sunk forward and the arms slowly extended, this bringing the legs to the surface in the backward direction, and causing the body to float face downwards. Similar actions in the reverse direction will cause the body to assume the perpendicular position, and ultimately float face upwards again, the body moving backwards and forwards like a pendulum, whence the designation of the feat. The "Propeller" and "Torpedo" feats are really variations of back-swimming—the one above, the other below the surface. For the propeller, the swimmer must first of all "scull," and then, when there is a little way on, swing the arms under the surface round to the head, beyond which they must be fully extended. The hands should then be moved from the wrists and fore-arms in wave-like sweeps, the palms being turned outwards, and the body can then be made to travel at a good pace. The body can be turned round by the slowing of the movement of one hand, the body turning to that side. The "Torpedo" feat is similar, except that the feet are raised above the surface, thus allowing the other portion of the body to sink slightly below the surface, while at the end of each stroke the palms are pushed slightly upwards and kept more in line with the body to prevent the head rising.

Revolving on the surface is allied to floating, as swimming actions are not required. The ordinary horizontal position is first assumed, the thumbs being locked. Then the lungs are fully inflated, the face is turned gradually to the right, and the muscular force of the right side slowly exerted. This will cause the body to turn over on to the face, and as soon as it does so the muscular force of the left side is so used as to cause it to revolve on to the back again. Once the body is in motion, the revolutions can be made in quick succession, but they must be performed neatly and without splashing.

Somersaulting, when properly performed, is very graceful. In the ordinary single backward somersault, the head is bent back as far as possible, and the legs drawn right up to the body, which is first of all steadied by the arms being carried out in a horizontal position and in the same straight line as the shoulders. The body is then turned on the back, the bent up legs being out of the water. A semicircular sweep of the hands towards the back, bringing them from palm downwards to palm upwards, turns the body completely over in a circle, the head sinking first. In the forward single somersault, the legs are doubled up and arms extended as before, but this time the chest is under the surface and the head well forward. Then a similar movement to that in the backward somersault is made with the arms, except that it is towards the front and not the back. This causes the body to rotate, the arms being the axis. Double somersaulting is rather more difficult. One swimmer stands on the bottom of the bath with legs extended and arms out at right angles. The second swimmer, after inflating his lungs, sinks, places his head between the legs of the first, and then brings his legs up until they can clasp the first swimmer's head, and also extends his arms, the two swimmers being back to back. As soon as the two are fixed, the backward somersault movement of the arms is commenced, and the men, if they know how to regulate their breathing sufficiently, can turn five or six times in this position, the head of one emerging from the surface as that of the other disappears.

Sinking to the bottom and rising again to the surface, without apparent motive power, is a feat which illustrates the difficulty experienced by an expert in staying under water, owing to the buoyancy of the body. First placing himself in a floating position, the swimmer, after carefully inflating his lungs, lifts his head slightly, at the same time slowly dropping the hips. This causes the body to sink gradually, and then, as the head goes under the surface, a small quantity of air is expired and the body descends to the bottom. In order to rise, the legs should be straightened, the abdomen contracted towards the chest, and the head inclined back. The body will then ascend slowly. As soon as the face appears above the surface a quick breath should be taken.

Diving, like floating, is not extensively practised in this country, and one has to go to Sweden to see this beautiful branch of the art displayed to perfection. There, somersaulting from great heights, and swallow-like flights of a whole team are common, but it is only of late years that such graceful forms of diving have been practised in England, and then only by particular clubs. More attention is now, however, being paid to the subject, and the general cultivation of this branch, and the inclusion of it in all tests of proficiency, is only a matter of time. The common forms are the "low dive" and the "plunge." The best way to learn is to stand on the side of the bath behind a towel held in front of the legs by two other swimmers,

SWEDISH DIVE.

this giving the learner an idea of lifting his legs as he makes the dive. He should then stoop the body forward until it is nearly double, stretch out his arms until they are in front of the head, and drop the latter between them. For the first dive he can let the body gradually fall forward and, as it goes over, throw up his legs. The swimmers holding the towel can assist him by raising it so as to throw up the legs properly. After a little practice, the nervousness consequent on the initial going into the water head first will be overcome, and the learner will soon be able to make a clean dive. Then he should stand erect on the edge of the bath with the legs close together and the arms swinging. After a few short inhalations, the arms should be swung forward and a spring made from the side. As the feet leave the edge they should be thrown above the head level, and the body straightened, while the head is sunk between the arms, which are kept fully extended, the thumbs touching and palms turned downwards. As soon as the water is entered, the hands should be turned towards the surface, and the diver will immediately rise.

Plunging is a standing dive from a firm take-off, the body, after entering the water, being kept motionless, face downwards. No progressive action is imparted to it other than the impetus of the dive, and the plunge terminates when the competitor raises his head above the surface. The ability to plunge is of good service to racing men and in saving life, as the body skims along the surface with speed for the first thirty feet, and is, soon after entering the water, in the right plane for fast swimming. Moreover, it is of service when entering water which may possibly be weedy, or whose depth is unknown. For this form of diving the swimmer first stands erect on the edge, then raises himself on the forepart of the feet, swings his arms from backward to forward, and then inspires deeply until the lungs are fully inflated. The body is shot out over the water, towards which it is only slightly inclined, and as the spring is made another deep breath is taken. The body should, when entering the water, be in one straight line, the head well sunk between the arms, and the feet turned back, so that when the body rises to the surface the soles should be nearly face upwards. During the first portion of the plunge, the body should not go more than a couple of feet below the surface, and the angle of entry should be such that it rises slowly at a very slight angle and not sharply. Otherwise much of the impetus gained by the dive will be lost, owing to the resistance of the water. After the first forty feet the body, as a rule, travels slowly along the surface, but there are several plungers capable of extraordinary performances.

In a plunging contest, where a time limit of a minute was imposed, Major W. Taylor, of Bootle, in 1897 covered 74 feet 11 inches, while in 1896 at Lewisham Bath Mr. W. Allason, of the Otter Club, traversed 80 feet 8½ inches in 98 seconds.

Sometimes plunging feet first is practised, the swimmer standing as before, first bending his knees and then leaping well out over the water. The arms are then quickly extended beyond the head, thumbs locked, and the body straightened and thrown back. The water is entered feet first and the body travels onward, face upward.

For high diving, coolness and keen judgment of the angle which the body should take when descending are essential, and these can be acquired by gradually increasing the height of the dive, a foot at a time. English divers commonly

SPRING-BACK DIVE.

drop the body from a height and throw up the legs in so doing; but this is a clumsy style and very often leads to the swimmer landing on his back. The better form is to leap into mid-air with the body almost horizontal, and then quickly decline the head and arms towards the water, so that the body comes down at so neat an angle as hardly to cause any disturbance when the entry is made. But the most graceful is that termed "swallow-diving," the body being shot out from the board, horizontally as in the style just described, but with the arms extended

SWALLOW DIVING.

at right angles. It is allowed to descend in that position until within about six feet of the water, when the arms are closed together under the body, the head smartly inclined into them and the legs thrown up. If performed properly this is a very pretty dive. Experts dive in this fashion from heights varying from forty to sixty feet, and when a body of them do it together, it greatly resembles the action of the swallow. Running headers and spring board diving can easily be learnt by those who can dive well from any height over six feet; but somersaulting, back-diving, cross-diving and the various other methods of entering the water, which are such charming features of a display by experts, require a considerable amount of careful practice, and should not be attempted until the diver is admittedly a good performer in the common styles.

SOMERSAULT DIVING.

Organisation—The management of amateur swimming in England is vested in a body known as the **Amateur Swimming Association**, and similar organisations exist in Scotland, Ireland, Wales, New South Wales, New Zealand, &c. The English body, which is the oldest of them all, was formed in 1869 with the ostensible object of promoting championships and legislating for the government of amateur sport. For many years its authority was not much recognised outside the southern counties; but since 1889, when England was divided into three districts, each of which has self-governing powers, it has become an important body and its suspensions are recognised by the governing associations of kindred sports. No person can be a member of its Council, or an officer, unless he be a dele-

NEARING THE WATER, SOMERSAULT DIVE.

gate from one of its three branches, *i.e.*, Northern, Midland, or Southern, and the representation in the Council of the district bodies is based on the number of clubs affiliated to each of them, so that, unlike several of the kindred associations, it is purely elective throughout. Its objects are (*a*) to promote and encourage the art of swimming and the game of water polo among both sexes; (*b*) to stimulate public opinion in favour of providing proper accommodation and facilities for acquiring and practising the art of swimming; (*c*) to promote and hold amateur championships; (*d*) to promote the uniformity of rules for the control and regulation of amateur swimming and water polo and the management of all competitions therein; (*e*) to enforce the observance of the laws and rules of the Association, and to deal with any infringement thereof.

Each district association is represented by its

president, six vice-presidents, hon. secretary and treasurer, and one delegate for every ten clubs affiliated, while the committee is composed of two representatives from each association and the officers *ex officio*. The annual meetings are held in each of the districts in rotation, and all resolutions adopted at the said meeting are binding upon every amateur swimmer, and apply to all districts. Sentences of disqualification are binding on all clubs, and are also recognised by the Amateur Athletic Association, the National Cyclists' Union, the National Skating Association, and the Scottish, Irish, and Welsh Associations, whose suspensions are in turn similarly recognised by the Amateur Swimming Association. In the event of a swimmer desiring to appeal against a sentence by either of the District Associations, he can do so to the Committee, whose duties include the hearing of such appeals, the passing of all amateur records, the selection of teams for the International and trial Water Polo Matches, the appointment of delegates to the International Water Polo Board, and the general management of the Association. The definition of an amateur is as follows:—

An amateur is one who has never competed for a money prize, declared wager, or staked bet; who has never taught, pursued, or assisted in the practice of swimming or any other athletic exercise as a means of pecuniary gain; and who has not, knowingly, or without protest, taken part in any competition or exhibition with any one who is not an amateur.

A swimmer ceases to be an amateur and becomes a professional by—

(*a*) Engaging in swimming, or any other athletic exercise, or personally teaching, training, or coaching any person therein, for pecuniary gain.

(*b*) Selling, realising upon, or otherwise turning into cash, any prize won by him or her.

(*c*) Accepting remuneration by way of expenses over and above the third class railway fare or otherwise.

(*d*) Accepting remuneration for swimming in public, or by being employed for money or wages in a swimming bath, or elsewhere as an attendant on swimmers.

There are, however, several vital exceptions to these rules; but the Association reserves full power to prevent any abuse of them. They are—

(*a*) Amateur swimmers shall not lose their amateur status by competing with or against professional football players in ordinary club matches, for which no prizes are given, or in cup competitions permitted by the National Football Associations or Rugby Unions of England, Ireland, Scotland, and Wales.

(*b*) Schoolmasters or school teachers giving instruction in swimming to their school pupils, and as part of their school duties, and receiving no extra remuneration therefor, shall not thereby endanger their amateur status.

(*c*) The fact of any payment being made to an instructor of life-saving shall not endanger the instructor's status as an amateur; but no such instructor can receive any fee or expenses for any meeting at which he competes for a prise of any description.

(*d*) A bath manager who is not a personal attendant on swimmers in a swimming bath (or otherwise ineligible to compete as an amateur under A.S.A. laws) does not, as such, endanger his amateur status.

By the laws of the Association every meeting, except those held by affiliated clubs, has to be registered and advertised as under their laws. Any amateur competing at an unregistered meeting is liable to disqualification.

Racing—As previously mentioned, the responsibility of dealing with and passing records rests with the Committee of the Association, who during the last few years have had to exercise constant care in checking times, owing to the vast improvement in speed rates.

The increased facilities for bathing and the great number of competitions which are now held have to a certain extent been the cause of this, for a swimmer has now far more opportunities of displaying his ability when in condition than was formerly the case. A mile race is considered the best test of swimming, and that is always the distance agreed upon for the World's Championship. For many years the record of 29 mins. 25½ secs. made by Mr. Horace Davenport, of the Ilex Club, remained the best known; but in 1892, S. W. Greaseley, of Leicester, who afterwards turned professional, swam the distance in 28 mins. 18⅖ secs. at Exminster. Since then it has been lowered to 26 mins. 46½ secs. by Mr. J. H. Tyers, of Manchester; while the professional, Joseph Nuttall, in a race at Rochdale on August 29th, 1893, against the American champion, J. McCusker, covered a mile in the marvellous time of 26 mins. 8 secs. In 1886 the half-mile record was 14 mins. 17½ secs., made by Mr. H. C. Schlotel, of Surbiton, in the championship of that year; but in 1891 S. W. Greaseley lowered it to 13 mins. 42⅖ secs. at Exminster. In 1895 Mr. Tyers was credited with the present record of 13 mins. 20 secs. The times for short distance races have been marvellously improved, no doubt largely through the better conditions for racing in baths which now prevail. In 1878 the hundred yards amateur championship was won in 1 min. 16¾ secs.; the standard time alone now is 1 min. 12 secs. J. Nuttall (then an amateur) won ten years later in 1 min. 6¼ secs., and this record was at the time considered extraordinary, but the time was gradually lowered until in 1896 Mr. Tyers swam a hundred yards in 1 min. 1⅖ sec. Similar improvements are noticeable in the times for the other championship distances. All amateur records must be made in A.S.A. or university costume, and in still water. For all distances up to and inclusive of 500 yards, baths of not less than 25 yards in length can be used, but records for distances over 500 yards must be made in open water over courses not less than 220 yards in length.

The present amateur records are :—

RECORDS.

Distance.	Time.	Made by	Club.	Date.	Venue
YDS.	M. S.				
100	1 $1\frac{2}{5}$	J.H. Tyers	Manchester Osborne.	June 11, '96	Burslem.
150	1 39	,,	Farnworth	Sept. 25, '97	Warrington
220	2 $38\frac{4}{5}$	,,	,,	June 26, '97	Nottingham
300	3 $56\frac{1}{5}$	,,	Manchester Osborne.	Sept. 30, '93	Bethnal Green.
440	5 $53\frac{1}{5}$	,,	,, ,,	Sept. 15, '94	Swindon.
500	6 45	,,	,, ,,	Aug. 20, '94	Sunderland
880	13 20	,,	,, ,,	July 13, '95	Bradford.
1,000	15 2*	,,	,, ,,	Aug. 18, '94	Southport.
1 mile	26 $46\frac{1}{2}$	,,	,, ,,	July 11, '96	Walsall.

A record can only be made in a scratch race or in an individual race against time duly fixed and advertised before the day, and included in the printed programme of some public gala or entertainment, upon which programme the name or names of the entrant or entrants must appear together with the name of the timekeepers. No competitor can start whose name is not printed, and no one, whether entered or not, can join in the competition after it has started. Records made in handicaps are not recognised.

Hints to Swimmers—1. When turning in a bath (swimming with over-arm stroke) place the hand of the lower arm flat against the side under water, and then take breath, swing the other arm round, dip the head and draw up the knees. This will turn the body. Then place both feet against the side, shoot the arms forward and push off, the head being under water as the turn is made.

2. When bathing in open water, look out for weeds and undercurrents. In the event of getting accidentally into weeds, stop kicking and simply move the hands as if "sculling." If you swim, the weeds will entangle round legs and arms.

3. If a current or tide be too strong for you, swim diagonally across it to a spot on either bank, or on shore.

4. Do not dive deep into strange water, especially a lock pool, unless you be an expert, or some one who knows the place be present.

5. To take a straight course in open water, pick out some prominent object on the bank and guide yourself by it.

6. Beware of broken bottles, tins, &c., in river beds.

7. When racing in the sea, you can ascertain the set of the current, and the best course to take, by throwing in a cork, or similar floating object, and closely watching its progress. The swimmer who swims straight from point to point, although perhaps speedier than others, very often loses by getting into slack water.

8. When stung by jelly fish rub the juice of a lemon well in, or use glycerine and rose water. When seized with cramp, turn on the back and rub the limb affected and kick vigorously. At the same time call loudly for help.

9. When in a rough sea, swim through each wave, not over.

10. Beware of barnacles, when pushing off from an old ship, the side of a pier, or sunken rocks.

11. When diving from a boat always go off the stern. When getting in a boat, lay hold of the stern close to the gunwale with one hand and catch the gunwale with the other. Kick hard and raise the body sideways until it rests on the edge of the stern, then quickly move the hand from the stern to the seat, and slide backwards into the boat.

12. Rub yourself well and take a brisk walk after every swim. When in good condition, bathe every day, and in open water for preference.

The diploma examination of the Life-Saving Society has been previously mentioned in relation to the teaching of swimming and the qualifications which should be possessed by instructors. The examination is divided into two parts, the one theoretical, the other practical. In the theoretical examination the candidate has to write an essay on the following subjects :—

(*a*) Importance and advantages of the knowledge of the art of swimming.

(*b*) Effect of swimming as an exercise upon the growth and development of the body.

(*c*) A short description of the lungs and respiration ; the blood and its circulation.

(*d*) The effect of excessive exercise or over-fatigue, and the physiology of breathlessness.

(*e*) Precautions as to loss of heat, and how to avoid cramp.

(*f*) The best method of teaching swimming.

In the practical examination (which may be taken in one or two parts) each candidate must perform in the presence of the examiners the following evolutions, in fresh water.

(*a*) To carry—dressed in a swimming costume, shirt, tie, collar, socks, boots, trousers, waistcoat, and jacket—a person by the second or third method of rescue a distance of at least 15 yards.

(*b*) To undress on the surface of the water.

(*c*) To swim continuously (*i.e.*, without any pause or rest) for twelve minutes in the following four positions : (1) on the breast, (2) on the back, using arms and legs, (3) on the back, the arms being folded on the chest, (4) overarm side stroke. Three minutes allowed for each position.

(*d*) To dive from the surface of the water to a depth of at least 5 feet and raise a weighted object.

(*e*) To float motionless on the surface of the water for at least 30 seconds.

(*f*) To dive from heights not exceeding 5 feet and 20 feet.

(*g*) To plunge a distance of not less than 40 feet.

(*h*) To swim by means of the propeller a distance of 30 feet.

(*i*) To turn from the surface of the water two somersaults forwards and backwards.

(*j*) To perform three voluntary movements illustrating fancy and scientific swimming.

(*k*) To illustrate, as may be required by the examiners, the best method of teaching swimming, diving, floating, and life-saving.

A maximum of ten points is allowed for each subject and movement. Any candidate failing to obtain 50 per cent. of the maximum for each subject or movement is disqualified.

ARCHIBALD SINCLAIR.

WATER POLO—Since the recognition of this sport in 1884 by the Amateur Swimming Association, it has become very popular, and, in addition to various national championships and league competitions, there is now established a regular series of annual international matches in which England, Scotland, Ireland and Wales all participate. On the Continent and in New Zealand, Australia, Canada, India, the United States, &c., it is also played, the English rules being those generally adopted.

The game is played with an Association football in a bath, or open water, the latter for preference, as the general idea of water polo is to increase the staying powers of a swimmer. In a shallow bath he can rest when not in possession of the ball, but in open water he cannot, and must exercise his knowledge of floating, treading water, &c.

A team consists of seven players, three of whom generally play forward, one at half-back, two at full-back, and the other in goal. The distance between the goals must not be more than thirty yards, or less than nineteen, and the width of the field of play not more than twenty yards.

The goal posts, which are fixed at each end of the field of play, must be ten feet apart, and when the water is over five feet in depth, the cross bar must be placed three feet above the surface; but when the water is less than five feet in depth, the cross bar must be placed eight feet from the bottom. In baths the goal posts are provided with flat metal foot, so as to rest firmly on the bottom, and the goals, which are usually of a permanent character, with goal nets attached, are drawn up by pulleys to the roof, when not in use. When in the water they are

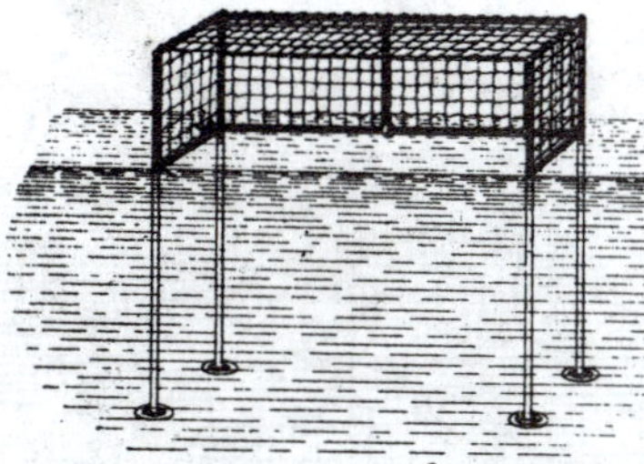

Goal-posts for Baths.

braced to the end of the bath by means of iron back stays and thereby made rigid.

In open water, in cases where the water is too deep to allow of the uprights being wedged firmly in the bottom, a different plan has to be adopted. Then a floating platform about twelve feet in width and four feet in depth is used. From the front of it project two stout pieces of battening, ten feet apart, and on them the uprights are raised to a height of three feet, with the cross bar fixed at the top, and from the two ends of the cross bar a frame-work is fixed to carry the goal net. The platform is moored securely at each end of the course, and the field of play marked out by flags on buoys, or poles lashed together along each side and end.

The game is started by the referee throwing the ball, which must measure between $26\frac{1}{2}$ inches and $28\frac{1}{2}$ inches in circumference, into the centre of the field of play. The teams, who have been

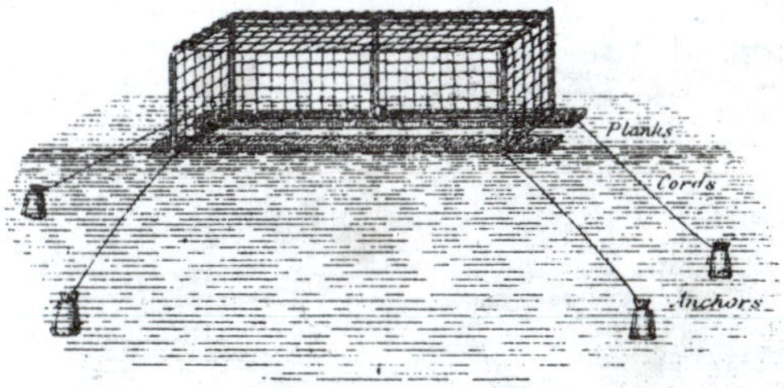

Goal-posts for Open Water.

previously lined up at their respective ends, immediately swim hard to their places, the centre-forward of each team usually going straight for the ball, and, if successful in reaching it first, passing back to one of his own side. The ball can be hit or thrown by any of the players, provided they are not standing and do not use both hands, and it can also be dribbled. For standing when playing the ball, touching the ball with both hands, holding the rail or side during any portion of the game, ducking an opponent when he is not in possession of the ball, retaining possession of the ball when ducked, holding, pulling back, or pushing off an opponent, or turning on the back and kicking off an opponent, fouls are awarded, the penalty being a free throw for the opposing side from the place where the foul occurred; but a goal cannot be scored from the said free throw, unless the ball has touched at least one other player. For fouls which the referee considers to be wilful, he can order a man out of the water after one caution, but many authorities are of opinion that for fouls committed close to goal, in order to prevent an almost certain score, a penalty throw, similar in character to the penalty kick at Association football, should be instituted. Beyond those just detailed, the rules are very simple. The duration of the game is fourteen minutes, seven each way, but time occupied in disputes or fouls, and the time from the scoring of the goal to the restarting of the game, are not reckoned in the time of play, so that a match with plenty of scoring often lasts close upon half an hour. A goal is scored by the entire ball passing beyond the goal posts and under the cross bar. Each side has then to line up at its respective end again and another goal cannot be scored after restarting until the ball has touched more than one player. Goal and corner throws are allowed on the same principles as Association football, and the goal-keeper is exempted from the rules relating to standing, using both hands, or jumping from the bottom when playing the ball, but he must not throw more than half distance under penalty of a foul to the opposing side, and can be treated as any other player when in possession of the ball.

The speediest swimmers and most reliable

TACKLING A PLAYER.

shots should be picked as forwards, while the captain, who should be good at passing, should play at half-back, the place of honour and hard work. Sturdy and cool players, with plenty of stamina, are best as backs. Each member of the team should have a knowledge of the "Trudgen" stroke, or be able to swim fast on the breast, as these accomplishments are of extreme value when dribbling. A good knowledge of swimming, and the proper methods of placing the body so as to get the best possible purchase when throwing the ball in the water, are indispensable before a man can rank as a good player. Constant practice is necessary, and this every captain should see that his team obtains.

Next to shooting, practice in passing is of most importance. Above all, a team should be a combination and not a mere collection of swimmers, each desirous of scoring. In shadowing their opponents, players should always be on the alert for possible passes, and when tackled should make quick short passes to one another. There must be no hesitation, for the man who is quick to see an opening and take advantage of it is the skilful player. One golden rule all players must observe, and that is never to pass direct to a covered player, for he is certain to be tackled, and their own goal may be in danger before they are aware of it. The proper place to pass is some distance from a covered player, particularly if he is known to be speedy, for then by superior swimming he can usually reach it quicker than his rival and possibly shoot a goal, or pass back, before his *vis-à-vis* is aware of the move. If the forwards are good swimmers, they will always keep in position for a few swift strokes, which at critical moments change the fortunes of the game and outwit opposing backs. Quick turning of the body and swift dribbling are of the highest importance. When dribbling, the forwards should work to the off side of the backs, so as to draw them wide of their goal, and when tackling seems imminent, pass sharply away. They should keep as far as possible from the opposing backs, except when the ball is on the goal line, when they should try and force a corner. On the half-back devolves the direction of the game. Against him he has opposed the centre-forward of the other side, and, as a rule, the most speedy swimmer in it. He must never let him go uncovered, and must also keep well in touch with his own backs. Except under special circumstances, he should never attempt to shoot goals, preferring rather to feed his forwards, or, when strongly attacked, to pass behind to his backs farthest from goal.

To the backs are relegated the duty of checking the play of the wing-forwards of the other side, who will try to swim round them, dribble, or pass just as they are being tackled. The backs must be alive to all these styles of play, as well as in touch with each other. Above all, they must avoid fouling, for so close to goal a foul is almost a goal thrown away. Rather should they concede a corner than duck an opponent when he is not in possession of the

BACK THROW.

ball, for this offence is likely to be considered by the referee a wilful foul.

The goal-keeper, though not necessarily a speedy swimmer, requires to be very quick; must know when to fist out, catch, or concede a corner, and what distance to throw out.

The ability to pass and throw accurately can only be developed by constant play and the careful watching of good men; but some useful hints can, however, be given on recognised styles of passing and throwing. First of all the player has to know how to dispose of his body, for on that depends to a large extent the force of his throw. In what is known as the forward shoulder throw, the ball is lifted from the water to the side of the head, the left arm is stretched out in front and the legs drawn up; then, as the ball is shot forward, the legs are forced rapidly down. When shooting at goal in this style, the player should be uncovered and make what is known as the *ricochet* throw, the ball touching the water with force a couple of yards in front of the goal-keeper, and rising over, or at the side of, him into goal. But for ordinary shooting the "back throw" is more commonly used. In this method the player seizing the ball turns rapidly on his back, brings his legs to the front, and, as the body advances, the ball can be shot forward with great force. But if the leg kick be not properly made, the body will sink and the throw prove abortive. It is when an opponent is making this throw that scientific tackling comes to the aid of the opposing side, effort being made to seize the upraised arm, or tip the ball out of the hand. Good passing is more difficult of accomplishment, particularly that termed the "Pass back." This is made when the player is in difficulty; but it is a style which should never be adopted unless the player can depend upon his own accuracy, for he does not see whither the ball is travelling and can only guess the position. Yet it is a common pass, and to such perfection has it attained that many men can place the ball behind them within a yard of where they judge their men to be. The hand should be placed under the ball and the latter quickly raised above the surface. Immediately it is clear, the ball is thrown back over the head, the disengaged hand being forced down into the water and a leg stroke taken. It is possible to make this throw with either hand, as well as to send the ball by deflections of the hand to right or left, high or low.

Then there are two other passes, developments of which come by practice. These are the "breast stroke" and "over arm." The "breast stroke" can be made with either hand, and is used when a player desires to pass to the right or left. When, for example, in dribbling up there is a likelihood of being tackled, the player passes on the side opposite to that on which the tackle is likely to occur, and so skilful can a player become with either hand, that while passing he is able to continue his swimming. In the "over arm" pass the ball is taken with the uppermost hand and passed either in the line of sight to the rear, or behind; but it is perhaps the most difficult of all to cultivate, though very useful to a half-back. By far the best passes are those which can be used with the "Trudgen" stroke, for, when that stroke is employed, the opponents can be seen all through the game, a matter of impossibility when the over arm stroke is used. It is invaluable when dribbling, as the ball may be driven along rapidly, passes made quickly, and either hand used. When a player is dribbling, the ball is allowed to drift between the arms, striking them or the chin as the player progresses, but never being actually held. The opposing side cannot then duck the swimmer without fouling, and must pick the ball out from between his extended arms.

The rules of the game, so far as Great Britain and Ireland are concerned, cannot be altered, except at the Annual Meetings of the International Board, which represents the English, Scotch, Welsh and Irish Amateur Swimming Associations. The first international match was one between England and Scotland at Kensington Baths, London, in 1890, when Scotland won easily. The same country's team proved successful the following year, but from that time until 1897 they never again managed to defeat England. Ireland first began to play International Matches in 1895, and Wales the following year. Inter-Varsity Matches, between Oxford and Cambridge, are now also annual fixtures. The results of the Internationals to date are here appended:—

ENGLAND *v.* SCOTLAND.

Played 8. Won 5. Lost 3.

1890, London,	S. 4—0	1894, Nottingham,	E. 4—1
1891, Glasgow,	S. 2—0	1895, Edinburgh,	E. 3—0
1892, Liverpool,	E. 4—0	1896, London,	E. 4—2
1893, Glasgow,	E. 3—0	1897, Edinburgh,	S. 2—1

ENGLAND *v.* IRELAND.

Played 1. Won 1. Lost 0.

1895, London, E. 12—0.

SCOTLAND *v.* WALES.

Played 1. Won 1. Lost 0.

1897, Newport, S. 3—2.

WALES *v.* IRELAND.

Played 2. Won 2. Lost 0.

1896, London, W. 3—0.
1897, Swansea, W. 3—2.

The English Championship competition was started in 1888 and was won in that and the following year by the Burton-on-Trent Club. In 1890 Hanley proved successful, but the previous holders once more came to the front the next year. Nautilus, a London club, won in 1892, and Tunbridge Wells in 1893. Since then Manchester Osborne have always proved successful.

In Scotland this game is named Aquatic Football.

WILLIAM HENRY.

AMATEUR SWIMMING ASSOCIATION.

INTERNATIONAL RULES FOR WATER POLO.

1. *Ball.*—The ball to be round and fully inflated. It shall measure not less than 26½ in., nor more than

28½ in. in circumference. It shall be waterproof, with no strapped seams outside, and no grease or other objectionable substance on the surface. The ball to be furnished by the home team.

2. *Goals.*—The width of the goals to be 10 feet, the cross-bar to be 3 feet above the surface when the water is 5 feet or over in depth, and to be 8 feet from the bottom when the water is less than 5 feet in depth. The goal-posts to be furnished by the home team.

NOTE.—Whenever practicable, nets should be attached to the goal-posts.

3. *Caps and Flags.*—One team shall wear dark blue caps and the other team white caps. Each goal-scorer shall be provided with a red flag, and the referee with a dark blue and a white flag and a bell.

4. *Field of Play.* The distance between the goals shall not exceed 30 yards, nor be less than 19 yards, the width shall not be more than 20 yards, and shall be of even width throughout the field of play. The goal-posts shall be fixed at least one foot from the end of the bath, or any obstruction.

5. *Depth.*—The water shall not be shallower than 3 feet.

6. *Time.*—The duration of the match shall be 14 minutes, 7 minutes each way. Three minutes to be allowed at half-time for change of ends. When a goal has been scored, the time from the scoring of the goal to the re-starting of the game, or time occupied by disputes or fouls, shall not be reckoned as in the time of play.

7. *Officials.* The officials shall consist of a referee, a timekeeper, and two goal-scorers.

8. *Referee.*—The referee's duties shall be to start the game, stop all unfair play, decide all cases of dispute, declare fouls, goals, half-time, and time, and see that these rules are properly carried out. He may proclaim a foul, without its being claimed by any of the competitors, and shall decide upon and declare all goals, whether signified or not. The referee's decision is final.

9. *Goal-scorers.*—The goal-scorers shall stand at the side near each goal, and when they consider that the ball has passed through the goal, at their respective ends only, they shall signify the same to the referee by means of a red flag. They shall not change ends, and shall keep the score of goals of each team at their respective ends.

10. *Teams.*—Each side shall consist of not more than seven players, who shall wear blue and white caps respectively, and drawers or costumes with drawers underneath the costumes. In baths no grease, oil, or other objectionable substance shall be rubbed on the body.

11. *Captains.*—The captains shall be playing members of the teams they represent; they shall agree upon all preliminaries, and shall toss for choice of ends. If they are unable to agree upon any point, the referee shall decide for them.

12. *Starting.*—The players shall enter the water and place themselves in a line with their respective goals. The referee shall stand in a line with the centre of the course, and, having ascertained that the captains are ready, shall give the word "Go," and immediately throw the ball into the water at the centre. A goal shall not be scored after starting or re-starting until the ball has been handled by an opposing player or by a player on the same side, who shall be within half-distance of the goal attacked. The ball must be handled by more than one player before a goal can be scored.

13. *Scoring.*—A goal shall be scored by the entire ball passing beyond the goal-posts and under the cross-bar.

14. *Fouls.*—It shall be a Foul: (*a*) To touch the ball with both hands at the same time; (*b*) To hold the rail or side during any part of the game; (*c*) To stand on or touch the bottom during any part of the game, unless for the purpose of resting; (*d*) To duck an opponent, unless he is holding the ball, or to retain possession of the ball when ducked; (*e*) To jump from the bottom or push from the side (except at starting or re-starting) in order to play the ball or duck an opponent; (*f*) To hold, pull back, or push off from an opponent; (*g*) To turn on the back and kick at an opponent; (*h*) To assist a player at the start or re-start.

NOTE.—Dribbling or striking the ball is not holding, but lifting, carrying, pressing under water or placing the hand under or over the ball when actually touching, is holding. Dribbling the ball up and through the posts is permissible.

15. *Penalties.*—The penalty for each foul shall be a free throw to the opposing side from the place where the foul occurred. A goal cannot be scored from a free throw unless the ball has been handled by at least one other player.

16. *Wilful Fouls.*—If, in the opinion of the referee, a player commits an ordinary foul wilfully, he shall be cautioned for the first offence, and for the second the referee shall have the power to order him out of the water until a goal has been scored. It shall be a wilful foul to start before the word "Go," to deliberately waste time, or for a player to take up a position within a yard of his opponents' goal.

17. *Declaring Fouls.*—The referee shall declare a foul by blowing a whistle and exhibiting the colour of the side to which the free throw is awarded. The player nearest to where the foul occurred shall take the throw. The other players shall remain in their respective positions from the blowing of the whistle until the ball has left the hand of the player taking the throw.

18. *Goal-keeper.*—The goal-keeper may stand to defend his goal and must not throw the ball beyond half-distance; the penalty for doing so shall be a free throw to the opposing side from half-distance at either side of the field of play. The goal-keeper is exempt from clauses (*a*) (*c*), and (*e*) in rule 14, but he may be treated as any other player when in possession of the ball.

19. *Goal Line and Corner Throws.*—A player throwing the ball over his own goal line shall concede a free corner throw to his opponents, but if the attacking side throw the ball over it shall be a free throw to their opponents' goal-keeper.

NOTE.—In the event of the ball having become dead by being thrown over the goal-line, it must not be considered in play until it has left the goal-keeper's hands.

20. *Out of Play.*—Should a player send the ball out of the field of play at either side, it shall be thrown in any direction from where it went out by one of the opposing side, and shall be considered a free throw.

21. *Declaring Goals, Time, &c.*—The referee shall declare fouls, half-time, and time by whistle; goals by bell.

22. *Leaving the Water.* A player leaving the water, or sitting or standing on the steps, or sitting on the side of the bath in which the match is being played, except at half-time or by permission of the referee, shall not re-enter it until a goal has been scored, or until half-time. Should a player leave the water he can only re-enter at his own goal-line.

AMATEUR SWIMMING ASSOCIATION.

HINTS FOR THE GUIDANCE OF REFEREES.

A (Rules 1 and 2, 4 and 5). See that the ball is of proper size and in accordance with Rule 1. See that the dimensions of the goal-posts are correct, and that they are fixed at least one clear foot from the end of the bath or any obstruction. Check depth of water, and measure the length and width of the field of play. See that the half-distance is clearly defined on both sides of the bath by towels or some visible marks.

N.B. Goal nets simplify the work of the Referee, and, wherever practicable, should be used.

B. (Rule 3). Distinctive coloured caps, as per Rule 3, should in every case be enforced.

C. (Rule 6). Be careful to have a proper time-keeper who is thoroughly conversant with the rules. An ordinary stop watch is the only one with which the time can be accurately taken. Note that when a goal has been scored, the time from the scoring of the goal to the re-starting of the game, and time occupied in disputes or fouls, must not be reckoned in the time of play.

D. (Rule 8). The absolute control of the game is in the hands of the referee. All cases of misconduct by players should be reported to the committee having control of the competition, so that they may be dealt with by the governing body. Further, any swimmer who may interfere with or insult the referee, either during or after the game, should also be reported.

The referee should, if possible, have one side of the field of play kept clear so as to be able to follow the game from end to end of the bath.

E. (Rule 9). See that the goal-scorers are in their places, and instruct them that their duties are to signify, by means of a flag, when the entire ball has passed between the uprights and under the cross-bar (no matter how passed through), and to keep the scores of each team at their respective ends.

F. (Rule 11). Ascertain that the captains have agreed upon all preliminaries; if not, give a decision as per Rule 11.

G. (Rule 12). Pay particular attention to see that the latter part of Rule 12 is not infringed. A goal shall not be scored after starting or re-starting until the ball has [also] been handled by an opposing player, or by a player on the same side (*i.e.*, the same side as the player who first handled the ball) who shall be within half distance of the goal attacked. The words within the brackets are explanatory, the spirit of the rule being: that until an opponent has handled the ball, a goal cannot be scored by the side which first gets the ball, except from within half-distance of the goal attacked.

H. (Rule 14). Be careful that no player other than the goal-keeper touches the ball with both hands. See that the "resting" clause be not abused. The rules only allow standing on the bottom for the purpose of resting, and players must not be allowed to walk about, stand with arms extended, with the object of shadowing or molesting any player, or be allowed to jump from the bottom.

Clause D. deals with the foul most often committed. Do not, on any account, allow a player to be interfered with unless he is holding the ball. For definition of "holding," see note at foot of Rule 14.

See that no player holds the rail or side during any part of the game. If this rule be infringed, no matter in what part of the field of play the ball may be, it must be brought back to where the foul occurred.

I. (Rule 16). Be particularly stringent with regard to Rule 16. Only caution the player once, and for a second offence enforce the penalty.

When advantage is taken of Clause D, Rule 14, in order to prevent the scoring of a goal, do not allow the goal, but caution the player, and for a second offence order him out of the water.

When once a decision has been given, do not allow any player or spectator to question the ruling: the laws of the Association definitely state how protests shall be made.

K. (Rule 18). When a free throw has been awarded, the ball must be considered dead until it has left the hand of the player taking the free throw, and on no account allow any player, other than the one taking the throw, to change his position.

L. (Rule 17). Goal-keepers must not be allowed to throw the ball past the half-distance mark. If the ball when thrown by the goal-keeper travel past the half-distance, even if it touch the water before reaching half-distance, the rule is thereby infringed.

M. (Rule 19). It is a corner throw when the ball is thrown by or passes off any player over his own goal line.

In the event of the ball having become dead by being thrown over the goal line, it must not be considered in play until it has left the hands of the goal-keeper.

N. (Rule 20). When the ball goes out of play, the last player it touches must be deemed to have sent it out.

O. (Rule 22). Note Rule 22 as to leaving the water and sitting or standing on the steps.

LIFE SAVING—It will not be out of place to give here a brief description of the methods of rescue, release, and resuscitation, recommended by the Life-Saving Society, and the special circumstances under which each should be put in practice. It must be remembered, however, that in order to qualify for the award of the proficiency medallion and certificate, and above all, to render himself thoroughly competent to put these methods into practical use should necessity arise, it is essential that the swimmer attend a class of instruction. He should by diligent practice endeavour to perfect himself, not resting content until quite efficient, giving particular attention to the water-drill.

Prior to the formation of the Society, the only attempt made to teach life-saving was by means of dummies. A heavy doll was made up of old clothes, &c., pushed a few yards out into the water, and the pupils jumped in and brought it to shore as best they could. The method of instruction advocated by the Life-Saving Society is conducted throughout with living subjects, giving the pupil a practical experience of what he has to do when called upon to render aid to those in danger of drowning.

The first method of rescue is for use when the drowning person is not struggling. Supposing the rescuer to approach him from in front, he grasps him by the arms just above the elbows and turns him round until he faces the same way as himself; then, passing his hands up to the side of the face, with the palms over the ears, and holding him firmly so, he swims on the back, drawing the patient after him. It will be found that there is but little difficulty in carrying a person in this manner.

In cases where the drowning subject is struggling it is, of course, necessary to obtain a firmer hold. In the second method, supposing the rescuer to have turned his patient as before, he then grips him by the arms just above the elbow, fingers inwards, thumbs outwards, and drawing the patient's arm up at right angles to his body, he swims on his back as before, keeping his own elbows to his sides. By this method, although not so easy for the rescuer, the drowning person is much more under his control, and he can to a great extent prevent him struggling.

The third method of rescue is for use in cases where the patient's arms are difficult or impossible to hold, owing to his violent struggles. It is somewhat similar to the second, but the rescuer's arms are, in this instance, passed under the patient's armpits and his hands folded across his chest; by squaring the elbows out the rescuer can prevent any danger of the patient, who is practically helpless, breaking away or clutching him; but the position renders his own task rather more difficult.

The fourth method has been devised to enable a swimmer to render assistance to another attacked by cramp or overtaken by fatigue; the rescuer in this case swims with the breast stroke, while the person in difficulties places his hands on his shoulders close to the neck, leaning his head well back and straightening his arms. His body floats easily under that of the rescuer, who can

RESCUE BY SECOND METHOD; SWIMMING ON THE BACK.

himself swim with as great freedom and almost as little exertion as he could had he not another dependent on him.

It sometimes happens that before the rescuer reaches the drowning person the latter has sunk and has not risen again. In that case the rescuer should look for air bubbles rising to the surface, before diving. In still water the bubbles rise perpendicularly and in running water obliquely. In diving from the surface in running water the rescuer must look for the body higher up the stream than where the bubbles appear. It is also possible that the body may be carried along by the stream, and the best plan is to look for it in a straight line in the direction in which the current is running. On reaching a person who has sunk to the bottom, the rescuer should seize him by the shoulders and push off smartly from the ground, when both will easily rise to the surface. When swimming back to shore, it is of vital importance that the face of the person in danger be kept above the water. The rescuer should swim with a wide, powerful kick and avoid tugging, so that the person assisted may be able to breathe freely. Care should be taken not to waste power by attempting to swim against the tide or stream.

It is difficult to over-estimate the danger incurred even by a skilful swimmer when clutched by a drowning person; but a knowledge of the Society's methods of release will render the task of getting free comparatively simple. Supposing the rescuer to be seized by the wrists, he should turn both simultaneously against the thumbs of the drowning person, and with a quick jerk bring his own arms at right angles to his body; by remembering to press against the thumbs, it is easy to break away, however firm the hold.

If clutched round the neck, the rescuer should lean well over the drowning person, place his left hand in the small of his back, and, raising his right arm in a line with his shoulder, pass it over the left arm of the drowning person, pinch his nostrils with his fingers, place the palm of his hand upon his chin and push him away from him until his head is under water. The nostrils being kept closed, the drowning person in attempting to breathe is compelled to open his mouth, water rushes in, choking ensues, and the rescuer will quickly find himself released.

The third method is for use when grasped round the arms and body. The rescuer should lean well over the drowning person and, withdrawing his arms in an upward direction, place his left hand on his opponent's right shoulder and the palm of his right on his chin, then, raising his knee as high as possible and placing it against the lower part of the drowing person's chest, he should simultaneously push hard in an outward direction with his knee and both hands, throwing himself back at the same time to increase the strain on the drowning person's arms to compel him to relinquish his hold. There should be no hesitation in adopting this method of release should necessity arise, for the rescuer's position is a perilous one, and to cope with the danger severe measures must be resorted to. It should be added, as a general rule for a swimmer's guidance, that in attempting a rescue he should utilise his knowledge by endeavouring at all times to keep above his antagonist, and whenever opportunity presents itself take a deep breath, for, if the struggle be severe, he will in all probability be forced under water.

There are three methods of resuscitation taught by the Life-Saving Society—the Silvester, Howard, and the Marshall-Hall; of these the Silvester is most strongly recommended for various reasons, among which may be mentioned the fact that it can be put in practice by one person without assistance; it is easily learned and the patient is not liable to injury while being operated upon.

The Howard method is used should the patient have lost an arm or his arms be injured; or should it be deemed necessary to put in force a more vigorous method than the Silvester. The Marshall-Hall is probably the least efficacious of the three methods, and as it requires considerable practice and care to be successfully put into operation it is not proposed to give a description of it here.

If a body has been recovered from the water, in which possibly life is not extinct, it is first necessary to clear the throat and then to ascertain if natural breathing is suspended; the clothing should be loosened at the neck and chest and the patient turned over until he is lying on his side with his head resting on his forearm;[1] the operator then removes any mud, weeds, or water which may have collected in the mouth and throat; afterwards the operator turns the patient on his back; he covers his thumb and forefinger with a handkerchief, draws forward the patient's tongue, and fastens it with a piece of string, or strip of cloth, to the lower jaw in order to prevent its falling back and so blocking up the air passages. This may also be accomplished by turning the patient's head well to one side. The tongue will then rest in the hollow of the cheek. The former is rather a difficult operation, but the position of the tongue should always be attended to. To ascertain if natural breathing is suspended, the operator places his ear to the patient's mouth and chest and listens for any signs of respiration, or a better way still, should a piece of bright metal (such as the inside of a watch-case) be at hand, is to place it just over the patient's mouth, when, if he still breathe, it will become clouded by moisture. Assuming that no signs of breathing can be detected, the operator, taking a coat or other garment, or a towel, makes a roll about 18 inches long and 3 in thickness, and places it under the shoulder-blades; he should then kneel down at the patient's head, lean forward and grasp his arms just below the elbows (fingers inwards, thumbs outwards) and draw them in an upward direction towards himself until they are in a line with the patient's body; they should then be bent and brought back to the chest and pressed firmly against the ribs and top for two seconds. The operator should continue these three movements at the rate of twelve to fifteen times a minute, and steadily persevere undeterred by the fact that a considerable time may elapse without any apparent success crowning his efforts.

LIFE-SAVING DRILL AT FRAMLINGHAM.

After natural breathing has been restored, promotion of circulation and warmth are the next care; this should be done by rubbing the patient's limbs and body with a cloth or flannel, and by placing hot water bottles or heated bricks to the soles of the feet, between the thighs,

[1] This position is shown in the photograph of over 100 boys under the direction of Mr. E. W. Lynch, who, as Hon. Life-Saving and Swimming Instructor, is teaching the boys resuscitation on the lawn at Framlingham College.

and at the armpits; the rubbing of the limbs should always be towards the heart.

In the Howard method there are but two movements: the operator, after clearing the throat and drawing forward and fastening the tongue, places the roll of clothing (which should be somewhat thicker than that used in the Silvester) under the lower part of the chest, draws the arms at full stretch above the head in line with the body, then kneels astride the thighs, and placing his hands upon the patient's lower ribs throws himself forward, pressing firmly in an inward and upward direction; he then springs back to his original kneeling position, removing his hands to allow the ribs to expand. The movements should be continued at the rate of fifteen times a minute. Care should be taken not to press the thumbs into the pit of the patient's stomach, and it should be remembered that too forcible pressure might result in some internal injury.

W. HENRY.
F. WYMAN BYLES.

TAHR—Nomenclature—Tahr or Ther (*Hemitragus jemlaicus*) are the names by which this distinctly Himalayan wild goat is most generally known to sportsmen; it is called *Jharral* in Nepaul; *Jagla* on the Pir Punjab range, and *Kras* in more northern and eastern parts of Kashmir, and by other strictly local denominations.

Although much smaller in body and in length of horn than its Himalayan congeners the ibex and markhor, the tahr is, in the writer's opinion, one of the most game of all Himalayan game animals in every respect.

Descriptions—An old buck stands well over three feet. Hair very long and shaggy, especially about the neck and shoulders. Its colour ashy brown, growing much deeper brown on the croup, hind quarters and sturdy limbs, and, when viewed from a distance, looking almost entirely black. Face longish, smooth-haired, and very dark brown, with paler markings about the muzzle and around the eyes. Ears small and tail short. No goat-like beard depends from the chin. The full-grown black horns of the buck are comparatively short but handsome withal. They seldom much exceed thirteen inches in length and about nine inches in girth, flattish on their sides but thick and rounded at the back. They are creased up to about two-thirds of their length, each crease terminating in a small sort of head on the angulated front margins of their horns, which rise in a line with the forehead and slightly diverge until they abruptly curve backward and rather downward for several inches in smooth and sharp points, which incline slightly inward. When viewed from the front the horns somewhat resemble a high coronet.

The female, called *Tehrny*, is smaller, lighter coloured and less shaggy than the full-grown buck. She carries horns of the same shape but of a much smaller size. She is said to have four teats instead of two, like the other female wild goats and sheep; but as the writer has seldom, if ever, shot a Tehrny he is unable to corroborate this statement.

Habitat—To find the old, black-looking bucks, one must hunt for them among the dangerous precipices and the steep, craggy, more or less pine and birch-clad gorges just below the limits of perpetual snow.

These old fellows live apart from and higher up than the females and young bucks from about February until October, when they promiscuously congregate in smaller or larger herds up to about twenty or so in number. On being disturbed or even shot at, they often stop to look back before getting beyond range of a second chance. It is best to stalk them from above, if possible, as they seldom look upward for danger.

The old bucks are much given to fighting

TAHR

Ht. at shoulder, 38 in. Max. horn. meas. 14⅝ in. Av. horn meas. 12 in.

among themselves during the rutting season in autumn, when numbers are said to be killed by falls. Some idea of the ground they usually affect may be formed when the writer mentions his having shot a buck that was standing on the brink of an almost sheer precipice, down which it fell so far that the aid of the glass was necessary to distinguish its form among the detached lumps of rock below, on which it lay dead. When with difficulty it was reached, the carcase was found all mangled and torn, and one of the stout horns was broken off at the root.

The tahr is more or less abundant along all the higher Himalayan ranges, and just below the snow-line, eastward from Cashmere, where the writer has found it on the Pir Punjab range on the same ground as the markhor. And on one occasion in October he shot a solitary "kras" on the same ground as the Hanjul or Kashmir stag, but the tahr was evidently a stranger in the land. It may sometimes be seen about the high, craggy crests of the middle ranges, but the bucks are never so big and black there as those of the higher regions.

The flesh is dry and coarse even to the taste of the hungry hunter, except perhaps when small fresh scraps of it are merely frizzled on the red-hot embers of a camp fire. The more eastern Himalayan Mountaineers, however, consider the meat to be an efficacious medicine for rheumatism, and transport it, when dried, and even the bones, to the plains of India as a remedy for that complaint.

Ammunition—A double ·450 bore express rifle, with its hollow fronted projectiles plugged with copper tube or bit of wood, is well adapted for shooting tahr, and boots or shoes, having their thick soles well studded with large hob-nails, are absolutely necessary for foothold on the ground which must always be worked over by those who expect to secure such a really handsome trophy as a big black tahr.

DONALD MACINTYRE.

TAPIR—The tapirs are a pachydermatous group of animals distributed over parts of America and Asia. They have short and movable trunks, at the extremity of which are the nostrils, and by the trunk they convey food to their mouth. The skin is hairy and very thick, the tail all but rudimentary. They inhabit vast forests, are nocturnal in their habits, and live principally on vegetable matter, though they are also said to be omnivorous, swallowing almost anything they come across.

The skull of an American tapir, seen in profile, somewhat resembles that of a hog, but whilst that of the pig has four faces, the tapir's has only three. The bones of the nose are articulated to the base of the triangle formed thereby, and here there is a point which penetrates between them. A deep furrow, produced by the upper border of the orbit, descends from the two sides above the orbit, which, approaching the sub-orbital hole, serves for the insertion of various muscles connected with the proboscis.

The skull of the Asian tapir differs from that of the American, the forehead being convex and rising higher than the back of the head. It is accompanied, in its rise, by the nasal bones, which give space for the comparatively large proboscis and add length to the furrows where the muscles are inserted. This organisation, according to Cuvier, explains why the Indian tapir has a more powerful and more extensile trunk than the American. There is also in the former, on the base of the nasal bones at their junction with the frontal bones and on each side, a deep fossa, or depression, which does not exist in the American. This elevation of the forehead is accompanied by a depression of the occipital crest, which, far from forming a pyramid, as in the American species, rather descends backwards. The aperture of the bony nostrils, enlarged by the prolongation of the maxillary bones, terminates below and forwards in more elevated premaxillaries, which are fused together in early youth, as in the American. In the upper jaw there are, in the adult tapir, on each side three incisors, one canine, four premolars, and three molars. In the lower jaw, on each side, there are three incisors, one canine, three premolars, and three molars; altogether making forty-two teeth in number. The bones of the extremities are very large and strong, resembling in many respects those of the rhinoceros.

There are three species of tapirs—the Ameri-

AMERICAN TAPIR.
Ht. at shoulder, 39 in.

can (*Tapirus americanus*), the hairy tapir (*T. villosus*) and the Asiatic (*T. malayanus*). Of the three species the American is the best known, and it is found extensively from Buenos Ayres to Central America, and from the Andes to the Atlantic. It spends the whole day in the shades of the densest forests, coming out to feed on the surrounding vegetation towards dusk. As it is a powerful beast, it forces its way with comparative ease through the brushwood and undergrowth of the forest, and it has regular paths which often assist the traveller in passing through the vast woods of the country it inhabits. It has a keen sense of smell, and will rush away into thickets where it cannot be followed. It is inoffensive and never comes to bay unless wounded and hardly pressed. It wallows a good deal, is very fond of water, and is a most expert swimmer.

The skin of the American species is of a deep brown approaching to black; but the sides of the lower lip, the under and middle part of the chin, upper edge of the ears, and the naked line at the bottom of the hoofs, are all snowy white. The scanty hair of the body is very short, and is hardly distinguishable at a short distance. The skin is of great density, and is seven lines thick on the back, but it offers no resistance to the bullets of a modern rifle. On the back of the neck there is a thick rounded crest, which extends from the forehead as low as the level of the eyes to the shoulders, and is beset with a comparatively thin mane of stiff blackish bristles.

The American tapir's flesh is not relished by Europeans, though it is by the natives; but the hide is valuable.

Although the lasso is the most popular instrument for hunting in South America, it is of very little use against the tapir, for their habitat almost precludes its use. A few have been captured by it, but even if the ground be favourable, its immense strength and impetuous rush often enable it to break the strongest lasso and to escape. The Guachos find out the animal's track, and with their dogs lie in wait until the tapir comes out for its evening meal and bath, and then interpose themselves between it and its bathing resort. It is not easily captured, and often kills several dogs during the encounter. Another mode of killing the tapir is to imitate its call and to shoot it on its approaching. This beast is easily tamed and is permitted to run at large in the streets in some of the towns of Guiana. It wanders into the forests to rest during the day, but returns again in the evening to the house where it is kept and fed. As it is capable of considerable attachment to its owner, it might be turned to good account as a beast of burden, possessing as it does docility, strength and patience.

The second of these species, the hairy tapir, inhabits the inner range of the Cordilleras; it has no mane, but its hair is longer and there are no wrinkles on the proboscis. In structural conformation it more resembles the Asiatic than the American, and is less common than the latter animal.

The third species, the Malayan, is found in the Tenasserim provinces of British Burma, in Malaya, Sumatra, Malacca, and the South West provinces of China. It is reported to exist in Borneo, which is more than likely, but the report requires confirmation. In size it is the largest of the tapirs known to exist, standing from 3 to 3½ feet at the withers and about 4 inches more at the rump; its length is about 8 feet. It has no mane, the hair is glossy black on the fore-part, but the back, rump, and sides of the belly are white. In its habits it is similar to its American relative, and in captivity it is mild and inoffensive and becomes as tractable as a dog.

There is a similar looking animal in the lagoons of West Africa, below the Congo. I saw one or two, but failed to bag them; but Captain Bailey mentions it in his book on sport on the Congo. Dr. Mason, a well-known naturalist, states that the natives assert that, when taking to the water, the tapir plunges in and walks along the bottom instead of swimming.

It has only one calf at a birth, but very little is known as to its breeding habits. The newly-born young are velvety black, marked with spots and longitudinal streaks of brownish yellow on the sides, and of white beneath; the change from the young to the adult coloration takes place between four and six months after birth. The chief sound uttered by the tapir is a shrill whistle of but little volume in comparison to the size of the animal.

F.. T. POLLOK.

TARPON—Habitat—The Tarpon (*Megalops thrissoides*), one of the Herring family, is a large sporting fish found in the Gulf of Mexico and its neighbouring waters. Its usual range is from Northern Florida down along the coast of South America. In summer it is sometimes caught in nets, even so far north as New York. It is, however, distinctly a warm water fish and prefers southern latitudes. It is known under various names, such as "Silver King," or "Grand Ecaille," along the Texas and Louisiana coasts; "Savalo" and "Sevanilla" in Cuba and along the Central American States to Venezuela.

Description—The tarpon ranges in size from the baby tarpon of 18 inches in length and 4 lbs. in weight, which can be caught on a fly, to the full-grown fish of over 200 lbs. in weight and 7 feet and more in length. Roughly speaking, the average size caught by sportsmen is about 6 feet in length and 100 lbs. in weight. The scales on a 6 feet specimen are about 3 inches in diameter, and on larger fish as much as five inches. These scales are tough, like thin horn, and are covered with a brilliant silver skin.

In addition to gills, it has two small blow holes on the top of the head, connected with what has been compared with a set of lungs.

The tarpon is a fish that spends a great deal of its time near the surface of the water, coming up often to blow, somewhat like a porpoise, but with less noise, although on calm days, or at night, this puff can be heard a considerable distance away.

Behind the dorsal fin, and forming part of it, is a long narrow fin, triangular in section, and about a foot long, looking like a bayonet, and so named. It would seem as if this long fin were meant for some special use, but no satisfactory explanation for it has yet been advanced.

Tarpon are supposed to run over 8 feet in length, but one of 7 feet 4 inches is the longest to my knowledge out of some 2,000 caught in the last ten years on rod and reel. I should think that 7 feet 6 inches or 7 feet 8 inches would be nearer the limit in size. A male fish is a fine gamey-looking brute, with large tail and fins. The female is somewhat deeper and heavier in proportion to length, and when in roe becomes somewhat pot-bellied.

When freshly caught, the tarpon is a most beautiful fish in appearance. The belly and sides are of a most brilliant silver. Along the back, the scales become dark green, showing purple iridescent colours, like mother of pearl. A specimen properly preserved and mounted will retain a great deal of its natural silveriness if the fat has been entirely removed from the inside of the skin.

Habits—The gameness of a tarpon varies a great deal, according as it is caught in salt or brackish water, and hooked in the mouth or throat. Those that frequent the brackish water of the creeks become rather dull in colouring and seem to lose a great deal of their fighting quality. A tarpon in good condition, on the other hand, will, if hooked in the throat, give a strong angler a hard time, for from half an hour to an hour and a half; the time depending a great deal on the strength of the angler and on how often the fish jumps. If hooked in the mouth or jaws, as the fish always is when caught trolling in the passes, he is not apt to jump so often, for he feels very little pain, but, as he does not bleed, he lasts longer.

A tarpon may jump only once or twice and then devote himself to rushing, sulking and towing. Such a fish may last anywhere from one to four hours.

A good and strong angler has been known to give up such a fish from sheer exhaustion after three hours of hard fight. A tarpon that will not jump is a very difficult customer to handle, and can easily tire out the average angler. As a rule, though, fortunately for the tarpon fisherman, the fish as soon as hooked will jump five or six times or more, and before he is landed may have jumped over twenty times. Of course the last jumps are not clear of the water; sometimes only the head appears, as the fish becomes exhausted. There is no fixed rule for the way a tarpon will behave when hooked; as no two in succession ever behave in exactly the same way, the sport is all the more interesting.

A MORNING'S CATCH.

Tarpon of 150 lbs. in weight have jumped twenty times inside of ten minutes and have been brought to gaff in twelve minutes all told; on the other hand, tarpon have been on the line for ten minutes without appearing once to let the angler know what he had hooked. It may take over an hour to land a fish, although he only weighs about 100 lbs.

As a rule the tarpon, as soon as hooked, comes out of the water with a great rush, jump and tumble, and continues to jump four or five times, generally clear of the water, after which he settles down to some long rushes.

Tackle—There are two ways of angling for tarpon, one called "still" or "bottom" fishing, the other "trolling" or "pass" fishing. For "still" fishing a rod about 7 feet to 7 feet 6 inches long is the proper thing.

The tip should be in one piece, the butt or handle being about 18 inches long, the tip from 5 to 6 feet long. Greenheart, lancewood, or split bamboo is the best material. The rod should be pretty stiff.

For pass fishing, or trolling, a still stiffer and shorter rod from 6 feet 3 inches to 6 feet 6 inches is necessary. Stiffness is essential, for the hook has to be driven with a strong, heavy stroke into the hard cartilage and the bony parts of the jaw of the fish as soon as he seizes the bait.

JUMPING TARPON.

The line used in still fishing may be 12 to 18 thread linen line; 12 is quite strong enough, but as the strength deteriorates rapidly when in use through chafing and damp-rot, it is safer to use an 18 thread line. In pass fishing it is a good plan to double the end of the line for about 50 feet. There are special lines, of which the last 50 or 80 feet are made double thickness, but any line can be strengthened by simply pulling out about 100 feet off the reel, doubling it up, and winding the end on to the line with a small linen thread. This can be done rapidly and answers the purpose well. The hooks used in still fishing and in trolling are quite different. That for still fishing is about the size of a large cod hook, the point turned slightly outward so as to catch in the throat. For trolling, a somewhat larger hook is used. In this case the point of the hook should turn in towards the top of the shank, so that when a strong strike is made the point may be driven in straight and not pulled sideways, and thus be either broken or bent. The barbed part of the hook should be short from point to barb. The point of the hook should be sharp and strong. The reel should be of the multiplying type, large enough to hold 200 yards of line. A strong gaff is also very essential.

Even with the hook now especially made for pass fishing, with a strong point and a short barb, it is rare that the point of the hook is driven in far enough to cover the barb. Many a fish has to be played and caught on a taut line with not over an eighth of an inch of the point of the hook buried in the jaw.

In pass fishing, on an average, about one out of four fish that strike is hooked, and one out of four fish hooked is landed. In a month's trolling a man will not average more than one fish landed out of ten that strike at the bait. By "hooked" is meant a fish that has to jump several times to get rid of the hook. Of course an improved hook that could be driven into the jaw with more certainty would greatly improve this average, but such a hook seems hard to devise.

In still fishing, a snell, snood or trace of cotton, wound with thin nickel piano wire, is used. This piano wire is not wound around in close coils, but in spirals about an eighth of an inch apart. Some such arrangement is rendered necessary by the rough and file-like jaws of the tarpon, which wear through any unprotected line. This snell works well. Leather and raw hide are also good. Snells should be about 3 feet long.

In pass fishing, no snell is used, but a piece of strong steel wire about 4 feet long is substituted. The reason is that the water where trolling is possible is generally clear, and the thick cotton snells are seen by the fish. Several swivels should be used on this 4 foot length of wire to prevent kinking.

The following is the usual method of making up a wired pass hook :—First the swivel is put through the eye of the hook ; on to this a piece of steel wire about a foot long is fastened, and another swivel is put on ; then a piece of wire about 3 feet long is fixed on, and then a third swivel to which the regular linen line is tied.

Some anglers use more than three swivels on the length, and some only use a wire two feet long. The long length of wire is chiefly of use in preventing the linen line from chafing on the scales of the fish.

A better method is to use a strong German silver chain with fine soldered links. About 6 inches of this chain is fastened to the eye of the hook, then a swivel, then 3 to 6 feet of steel wire, which may be divided into two pieces by another swivel. The chain should be tested to 50 or 60 lbs. strain.

Still fishing, or "ground" fishing, is carried on from a boat at anchor with cut mullet bait resting on the bottom. The fish is allowed to gorge the bait. This sort of fishing is generally done in the lagoons and up the estuaries and creeks.

Until 1895 this was the usual way of taking tarpon, as it was supposed to be impossible to get a hook to penetrate into the hard bony cartilage of the jaws and inner lining of the mouth.

For years in most of the Florida Passes (the narrow inlets from the Gulf of Mexico into the interior lagoons) large schools of tarpon could be found at times playing about and chasing small fish. The first tarpon ever taken was accidentally caught by a man who happened to be trolling in the Indian River Pass for channel bass, cravelle, or other fish. After losing large quantities of tackle, through tarpon taking the bait, he managed to hook and land one of them, much to his own amazement and delight.

Although tarpon were often seen in the Passes, and for years continued to walk off with spoons and other baits intended for small fish, no regular systematic pass fishing or trolling for them as a sport was known until 1895, when a couple of energetic anglers settled down at Captiva Pass with a large collection of different sorts of hooks and tackle and proceeded to experiment on the best method of hooking these big brutes in the mouth. It is largely owing to their experiments and perseverance that Pass fishing for tarpon has become practicable.

LANDED IN THE BOAT.

Pass fishing is far more exciting than still fishing, and much more of a sport. The excitement begins from the moment the bait is dropped over, and, as the fish has ten times the chance of escaping that he has in still fishing, the excitement lasts to the end. Still fishing is nevertheless much practised even now.

The Caloosahatchie River, in the neighbourhood of Myers, Florida, has so far proved to be the best tarpon fishing ground for bottom fishing, and it is the most convenient to reach.

It is forty-eight hours from New York; by rail to Punta Gorda, thence sixty miles by a small steamer.

There are several hotels at Myers where good guides may be engaged. The guide generally has his own rowing boat in which he rows to the fishing grounds. These are from two to six miles off. Most guides have a small sailing boat or sloop with which to tow the rowing boat backwards and forwards; this is the better way, as even an energetic angler becomes cramped after spending the day in a small rowing boat.

During the tarpon fishing season, which at Myers is March, April and part of May, there are regular bait men who catch mullet for anglers. A dozen to twenty mullet are sufficient for a day's bottom fishing. Tarpon grounds range along some fifteen miles of river, and the fish, as a rule, never stay more than two or three days in the same place.

Still fishing—The angler should have two rods and two reels, and use both when still fishing. Some use more, when tarpon are scarce, so as to increase their chance of a strike. Two rods are, however, all that one man should handle. If a strike is made the guide should immediately reel in the second line.

Jointed rods should never be used. An extra tip or two should be taken, as they are very apt to be broken when playing a jew fish, a saw fish, a shark, or any other of the brutes that may run to five or six hundred pounds in weight and often interfere with tarpon fishing. The quantity of tackle necessary depends upon the time the angler intends to devote to the sport. For a month's "still" fishing, eight 200 yard linen lines, two gaffs and eight to ten dozen hooks and snells are none too many, as the sharks and crabs cut off a lot of hooks and lines.

A start is made early in the morning. As a rule the guide will sail about for a while keeping a look-out for tarpon "signs," such as the blowing of the fish, and the swirl they make when seizing food on the bottom, or when scared by the boat passing near them. On a bright day one may see a tarpon sometimes a mile off, as he jumps clear of the water, his scales shining in the sun.

When a favourable position is reached the sloop is anchored. If the angler is not particularly energetic he may try fishing off the stern of the sloop, but generally the boat swings about a great deal. It is far preferable to get into the rowing boat and row off some distance from the sloop, until the water around is clear of any impediment, such as anchor ropes, which may interfere in playing a tarpon.

If the water is not over 8 feet deep, the guide will probably drive a pole into the soft bottom, which is generally sand, or mud mixed with sand, and fasten the boat to it; if deeper he puts out an anchor. The bait is the tail half of a mullet, and the hook is passed through the skin until the point emerges from the bait. The angler then casts out from one rod about 60 feet to the right of the boat, and from the second rod about the same distance to the left. Next he should from the tip of his rod pull off some 15 feet of line, which he can coil up on the stern seat, a small board placed across the stern of the boat; then he has nothing to do but wait. The waiting may last from ten minutes to ten days.

Were not every angler always confident that the next moment is going to be the critical one, this sort of fishing would be terribly slow. The excitement of expectation makes the time pass rapidly, especially if tarpon are blowing or swirling in the immediate neighbourhood. Then the cat fish, which in these creeks abound by thousands, and the crabs, which are there by hundreds, keep him busy renewing his baits and examining the line from time to time to see that it has not been bitten through. As a rule sharks do not interfere so much up the creeks. From time to time a jew fish or a bass, or even a large saw fish, may take the bait. Saw fish 14 feet long and 600 pounds in weight have been caught on tarpon rods and lines.

If it is good tarpon weather and the water is warm, and tarpon show themselves about, the angler may expect to get from four to ten strikes a day, sometimes even more. As a rule a tarpon, unless scared by some noise from the boat, takes the bait quite leisurely and swims off swallowing it. The angler should at once seize the rod, and as soon as the fifteen feet of slack have been taken out, and he feels the line grow taut, give a long steady strike.

The coiled up slack is used to give the tarpon time to swallow the bait, as he is apt to hold it in his mouth and swim off some feet before doing so. With the ordinary cut mullet bait and the hook used for bottom fishing, it is absolutely impossible to hook a tarpon in the mouth so as to hold. When the fish feels the hook in his throat he will at once rush the line off the reel at a great rate, and jump clear out of the water, fall back clumsily and continue to rush and jump for some time.

A cool head is all that is necessary for landing a tarpon in "still" fishing, as once hooked in the throat it is almost impossible for him to shake the hook out, and his only chance of escape is by breaking the line.

Trolling for Tarpon is quite another matter from bottom fishing, and is in every way far more exciting and sportsmanlike.

The Florida Coast is surrounded by a continuous line of long narrow coral islands covered witn mangrove trees and scrub growth. Inside these islands lie long lagoons connected with the waters of the open gulf and Atlantic by channels called passes, varying from 100 feet in width to a mile or more. These passes as a rule have, at certain times of the tide, a very swift current, sometimes over six miles an hour.

Tarpon are found to some extent in most of the passes. The best so far known in Florida is Captiva Pass, lying about half way between Myers and Punta Gorda. Undoubtedly there may be others quite as good or better along the Florida or Texas Coast, but they are somewhat out of the way and difficult to get at, and Captiva Pass remains the most convenient. The *modus operandi* is the same in all cases of pass fishing. A good stiff round bottom boat from 13 to 14 feet long is necessary. When the tide runs in or out strongly, the angler simply anchors his boat in the pass, for the tide runs swiftly enough to keep the small fish used for bait wriggling in the water as if swimming.

As a rule the tarpon are not all over the pass, but in certain fixed localities, either on the edges of eddies, or where the current sweeping in or out seems to carry the greatest amount of the small fish, crabs, &c., that float in and out with the tide.

At Captiva Pass, which is about half a mile or more in width, the best fishing is had in one channel, not over 200 feet wide, so that there is generally a rush for this place. An angler anchored over this stretch of water is apt to get ten strikes to an outsider's one, although the outsider may only be 50 feet off.

A long anchor rope about 70 feet long is necessary, as the water is deep, varying from 20 to 40 feet. The bottom being coral rock, a heavy weight is used in preference to an anchor, which is apt to catch in the rocks and stay there. A small buoy should be attached to the end of the anchor line so that, once a tarpon is hooked, the rope may be thrown overboard, as there is no time to haul it in.

The bait generally used is a small bright silvery fish. A small mesh net about 150 feet long should be brought to the pass for catching these small fish for bait. When small fish cannot be had, strips of larger fish, cut to imitate small fish, do very well. The white belly-skin of a small shark makes excellent bait.

BEACHED AT LAST.

If a small fish be used, the hook is passed through the end of the jaw and out at the top of the head.

The weight of the shank of the hook will keep the fish swimming, belly down, in a natural position. If the bait show a tendency to spin around, like a spoon bait, it should be stopped, for the tarpon will not strike such a bait so readily as a bait that merely wriggles steadily like a small fish swimming.

The best way to stop the spinning of the bait, which is generally caused by the fish getting stiff, is to cut the backbone in four or five places, then bend the fish backwards and forwards until it grows limp and will swim without revolving.

If the tarpon are seen swimming much below the surface, and if the current is very strong, it is a good plan to weight the end of the line with small strips of lead. Having anchored the boat, the angler drops his bait over the stern and allows it to fall back slowly with the tide.

If tarpon are plentiful, he is apt to get a strike before the bait has gone ten feet, if not, he should allow about 30 to 40 feet of line out, and then, with a firm hold on the rod, and his thumb on the break of the reel, he should be ready for the strike; this may come at any moment, and is sudden and strong.

Tarpon taking the bait give a sensation like a giant hand seizing the line and giving it a long, hard pull. The angler must be ready to strike at the exact second that the tarpon touches the bait, and to strike hard, even at the risk of breaking his rod. Unless he strike at the identical moment the fish bites, his chance is gone. Often even a good stroke will not drive the point of the hook up to the barb.

It is possible with careful playing, combined with good luck, to land a tarpon with only the point of the hook in, but as a rule the fish after a few jumps throws out hook and bait.

For this reason pass fishing is exciting and exasperating work.

The angler never knows how his fish is hooked, and always feels that in the first minute or in the last minute the fish may throw hook and bait into the air, without the least effort apparently. One is never sure of a tarpon in pass fishing until it is gaffed and hauled up on the beach.

As soon as the fish is securely struck, the guide should head the boat for the beach and row cautiously. There the angler lands and works the fish into the shallow water while the guide stands ready to gaff.

Tarpon may be on for forty minutes and during that time jump a dozen times or more, and may be got within a few feet of the beach several times, and after all the hook finally pull out as easily as if it had not a hold anywhere at all.

Of course this uncertainty adds greatly to the excitement of the sport. There are generally some pretty good-sized sharks on the look-out for tired tarpon, so that the angler even when he hooks his fish firmly, and plays him in the best of form, may end by supplying his quarry as lunch to a hungry shark.

Sometimes the point of the hook is driven right through the jaw of the fish, or works through it after playing him for a while. Often, just as a tarpon is hauled up on the beach, the hook drops out as he begins flopping about, showing that only the point of the hook had entered and not the barbed part.

The best time of the day for fishing in the passes is somewhat hard to decide upon. Tarpon seem very erratic in their habits. They have been known to stay in the pass and bite all day at both ebb and flood, and during slack tides. The best hours, though, for fishing at anchor in the pass seem to be the last three hours of the ebb. After that, as the tide slows down, trolling outside the pass at low slack water is good; then gradually working in as the flood begins, finally anchor again as soon as the current is strong enough to hold up the bait.

After the first hour or two of the flood, tarpon leave the pass and spread over the flats in the lagoons, coming back again towards the middle of the ebb tide. This seems to be the general rule. There are days, though, when the tarpon stay all day and night in the passes, and days also when none at all are seen there.

The best rods and tackle for tarpon fishing are to be obtained in New York. Some of the principal makers there have made a special study of the requirements of the sport, and their advice may be safely taken.

OTIS MYGATT.

TAXIDERMY AND MODELLING—Many people seem to think that taxidermy is but a higher sounding synonym of "bird-stuffing," but it has a far wider scope and includes the whole art of preparing or conserving skins throughout the vertebrate sub-kingdom. The word "bird-stuffing" is, or should be, a degrading libel on what is now an art which only the skilled modeller should attempt. It is easy to trace the genesis of the term "bird-stuffing," for no doubt the butchers and botchers had matters their own way formerly, and really "stuffed" or filled out skins by ramming the packing in until the bloated skin could hold no more.

The origin of taxidermy—*i.e.* the art of skin-preserving—lies in the very distant past. The earliest and most savage nations practised, and still practise, it for purposes of clothing or adornment. What profits the present article much more, however, is the consideration of what degree of antiquity can be assigned to the art of taxidermy as we now know it—the skinning, setting-up and mounting of mammals, birds, reptiles, and fishes as scientific objects or merely as trophies of the chase.

To quote from an article in the *Encyclopædia Britannica*, "Little is known of the beginning of the practice of the 'stuffing' or 'setting-up' of animals for ornament or for scientific purposes, and it is highly probable, from what we gather from old works of travel or natural history, that the art is not more than some three hundred years old. It was practised in England towards the end of the seventeenth century, as is proved by the Sloane collection, which, in 1725, formed the nucleus of the collection of natural history now lodged in the galleries at South Kensington."

It may be that a rhinoceros, originally set up for the museum of Ulysses Aldrovandus, removed from the Medicean, and still preserved in the Royal Museum at Florence, is the oldest specimen known, as it dates from the sixteenth century. Early in that century, about 1517-18, according to a French work of later date, some tropical birds were set up at Amsterdam.

In the University Museum at Pisa there are still preserved some fine groups of mammals, the work of Professor Paolo Savi in the beginning of the present century, which are as well executed as may be, and which have been commented on by English and other writers upon the subject. These are probably the first groups of animals portrayed in action which will bear criticism. After these came the work of Ploucquet, of Stuttgart, who contributed to the Great Exhibition of 1851 some finely-modelled groups of animals in action, which are still preserved in the Crystal Palace, but covered with dust through lack of proper glass protection. At the same time Ploucquet exhibited comic groups of animals engaged in impossible feats, which, it is sad to know, have been copied by others destitute of his humour and of his capacity for putting the proper half-human expression into their features. The province of taxidermy, however, is not to make hedgehogs play at cards in toy houses with toy furniture, nor rats engage in (toy) ball-room festivities, nor to find material for the antics of a "Comic

Naturalist." Such things may lend themselves to comic drawing, but they are distinctly out of place in taxidermic art.

Contemporary with Ploucquet were Jules Verreaux, John Wallace, and Edwin Ward, whose "Arab Courier attacked by Lions," "A Horseman attacked by Tigers," and "Lion and Tiger Struggle," were—the first especially—fine pieces of work, which vied with Ploucquet's in execution. Later came Rowland Ward's "Jungle" at the Colonial Exhibition, a large and ambitious work; and then museums awakened slowly to the need for more artistic and pictorial representations of natural objects. The small town of Ludlow had its birds mounted in its museum in a pictorial manner, and may have been, probably was, the first public museum to throw off the shackles which bound all museums to the principle that vertebrate specimens should be arranged on stands, or cross-sticks, all pointing one way, and all in one attitude; these essentials conducing, it was supposed, to British science, which should be, as every one knows, solid and severe. This was all very well, for no one supposes science can be anything but exact; but what was unnecessary to carry out the idea was the criminally inartistic and unnatural setting-up of the specimens, and the bounteous dust and dirt which rested upon and environed them, as if the custodians, with some dim and half-crazed idea of their functions as high priests of these sepulchres of the unnatural, had decreed that in the eternal fitness of things the dead should be carefully disregarded, and the funereal ashes sprinkled thickly around. In these days,—when, as is shown, the Italians first, next the French, and then the Germans have tried to teach the stupid and inartistic British taxidermist (with his American cousin) the way to be wise;—when one takes into consideration the example of foreign museums and the tardy yet thorough awakening of our own State museum to the principles which should underlie the presentation to the public eye of all natural objects, it will hardly be believed that any museums exist in which ill-made skins are fatuously wired bolt upright, and offered up in long rows of dreary monotony to a long-suffering people.

It might be of some avail to remind the inartistic or dirt-loving votaries of pure science, that it were far better that specimens should be left in cabinets than that well-made foreign skins (German, of course) should be dragged forth to be clumsily balanced upon sticks and chunks of wood, there to stare at vacancy with eyes too prominent for their attenuated and ragged outlines.

The literature of the subject is by no means meagre. In a recently published work of some 450 pages, foolscap quarto, over thirty pages are devoted to an enumeration of the abridged titles of works in almost every language, ranging in date through more than two and a quarter centuries, the earliest, by Bolnest, having been published in 1672. They are written from all points of view; from that of the man who knows nothing at all of any art or science, but who discourses fluently, as is his wont, upon any subject he can lay pen to, to that of the man who knows a great deal, but who either cannot or will not tell it. Intermediate are those who write up common or obsolete methods in a common and misleading style: the greatest offenders in this particular line of taxidermic infamy being our own countrymen and their American imitators. The reason is not far away: both strongly object to learning any language under the sun but their own, despise the teachings of foreigners, and generally avoid art and science in relation to all things, especially taxidermy, as if they were pestilences. Again, the exponents of this art seem sharply divided into two opposing factions—the scientific or semi-scientific men, who write taxidermic rubbish on their own account or for others, and the crassly ignorant "stuffers," who flout all teaching which does not travel on the lines of their respected, but obsolete traditions.

A remedy for this state of things has engaged the attention of educated naturalists from the days of Charles Waterton to those of the present. Early in the century Waterton wrote words of weighty warning and of import.

"Twenty years have now rolled away since I first began to examine the specimens of zoology in our museums. As the system of preparation is founded in error, nothing but deformity, distortion, and disproportion will be the result of the best intentions and utmost exertions of the workman. Canova's education, taste, and genius enabled him to present to the world statues so correct and beautiful that they are worthy of universal admiration. Had a common stone-cutter tried his hand upon the block out of which these statues were sculptured, what a lamentable want of symmetry and fine countenance there would have been. Now, when we reflect that the preserved specimens in our museums and private collections are always done upon a wrong principle, and generally by low and illiterate people, whose daily bread depends upon the shortness of time in which they can get through their work, and whose opposition to the true way of preparing specimens can only be surpassed by their obstinacy in adhering to the old method; can we any longer wonder at their want of sucess; or hope to see a single specimen produced that will be worth looking at?"

Years have passed, and the sting of his remarks is not blunted one whit by any special efforts which the Anglo-Saxon races have made to shake off the odium attaching to slovenly and unskilled work, and to justify themselves in the eyes of the nations. Indeed, how can this state of things be avoided, when our national museum, so careful and so worthy of imitation in other matters, has no efficient taxidermic staff employed, and is content to "put out" its work to be botched up by cheap and inartistic men, so that, on going around the galleries, one is impressed by the fact that the taxidermic work is uneven and the work of many hands, and that for every good man who has made his mark there are nine others who have egregiously failed? It is not too much to say that many of the groups are only redeemed from the contempt which their amateurish and careless handling calls forth by the beautiful modelling of the flower and foliage accessories, although, without being hypercritical, one might suggest that some of these accessories are more conventional than natural.

In these pages an attempt will be made to condense all that is known of the present state of taxidermy, with its little-known but indispensable ally—modelling. Needless to say, the future of the art will not be in the hands of the ignorant or pretentious, but will tax the fullest powers of a trained intellect, to which is wedded the manual dexterity of the artist and modeller. That—perhaps partly due to the writer's insistence and teaching—there is growing up a cohort of young men pledged to these principles, is a pleasing augury for success, and it may be, as a writer in the *National Observer* said:—

"Those who know good work will not be at all disposed to ridicule as exaggerated the contention that the good taxidermist should be an educated artist, designer, modeller, sculptor, biologist, and naturalist. The truth of the matter is that it creates a new career for youths with the necessary taste."

Methods of Setting-up and Mounting Mammals—In an article of this nature, it is a matter for grave consideration where to condense and where to expand, and at which end of the vertebrates to commence. For the purposes of convenience let the strict biological rule be ignored, and a beginning be made with the mammals, which are, after all, or rather *before* all, the most dear to the sportsman's heart. Lovely and lithe as most of them are in life, and graceful even in death, great skill is required to give even a semblance of life's vigorous reality to a skin by ordinary methods; so difficult, indeed, is it, that there are probably not more than six men, of various nationalities, who could satisfy a really competent and critical judge of the proper contours and finer shades of expression peculiar to any given mammal. Even the very best of those selected six will fail in some particular, or in some mammal not his forte; for one man may excel in the treatment of the Carnivora, and fail, say, in that of the Ungulata, whilst another may reverse those conditions, and so on. The secret, perhaps, of the success of the few and the failure of the many is two-fold. The first element is the undoubted fact that taxidermists are not usually well educated, and are usually very jealous and secretive: with no *esprit de corps*, and no inter-communication for purposes of teaching or criticism, as in the case of pictorial artists, their art must suffer. The second disturbing factor is that the general public is quite hopeless in artistic matters, and is inanely content with the crudest absurdities.

Antelopes with half-opened mouths, a general air of brazen defiance, and six well-defined and evenly-spaced ridges and depressions distributed on the neck like the gills of a shark; tigers smiling placidly, or bearing up bravely under the weight of unadulterated paint and putty which should, in all decency, choke, instead of accentuating, their ghastly grin; foxes with one eye nearly on the top of the head, the other near the angle of the jaw; domestic animals with one side bloated, the other atrophied; limbs placed in any position convenient, not to the animal, but to the tastes of the operator: these are criminalities which the public does not recognise, is satisfied with, or condones. Thus what should be an exact art is ruined by the ignorance of its exponents and their clients.

Failures in the treatment of mammals result from several causes, the most fruitful being the ignorance or want of special training of the operator. One need not imagine that, when one can set up a bird which is not absolutely a ragged bundle of feathered incongruity, and which may indeed be fairly natural in pose, that such slight knowledge assists with a mammal, which is, unfortunately for the student, not provided with a mass of comfortable fault-hiding feathers, but which has "points" all over its anatomy, and has a certain facial expression to be correctly represented.

Anatomy is the great stumbling-block. The ordinary "bird-stuffer" will not learn his bones, nor their relation to soft parts, and so long as a thing has a head and a tail and four limbs—one at each corner—that is sufficient, and any other points may be ignored.

The very rough and ready traditional methods of "setting up"—copied or translated *ad nauseam* from one old tome to another—have not smoothed the path, and the unfortunate student who attempts to put these directions into practice, very soon finds a skin far too long and wide, and wonders what he is to do with sundry flaps and bags of tegument which he had not previously noticed, and which do not appear to belong to the carcase before him. In the end he creates a boneless, but lumpy bag, and his admiration for his first effort is tempered with a growing awe for so supernatural a work, which can neither stand, sit, nor lie down, but holds an uneven and painful compromise between all three.

Perhaps something can be done for him in the following pages, and the preliminary is correct skinning, and by skinning is meant something in contradistinction to flaying. This latter is a butcher's method of removing the skin, and with some slight modifications its practice is good enough for those big-game hunters who wish merely to preserve skins as trophies, without reference to their subsequent "setting-up."

To skin a lion, tiger, or any big-game specimen, strong knives of suitable lengths and shapes, with a pair of strong shears, are all the tools absolutely necessary; but if a rope, pulley and beam can be provided in the case of weighty mammals, so much the better. In the field even, these may form a part of the outfit, but the comfort of a dissecting table must in most instances be dispensed with.

The subject—if it be impossible to skin it whilst warm, which is the easiest—should, as soon as *rigor mortis* has disappeared, be laid upon its back, the point of a knife should be inserted at the throat, and a cut be made extending in a straight line to the tail, care being taken not to cut into the flesh too deeply, if at all, and certainly not into the bowels.

As the operation of skinning a large mammal—when properly performed—adds no little to the subsequent correct setting up, some little detail will be necessary. Commence, therefore, by getting the carcase, when possible, upon a dissecting table, and let a beam, pulley and rope be provided, and fixed in a suitable position above. The subject being laid upon its back, a cut should be made, extending on the median line from the throat to the tail; another incision must be made from the chest to the arm-pit of each of the fore-limbs, and thence nearly to the end of the humerus, exactly following the course of the fore-limbs and running along just inside (in order to hide the finishing stitches) down to the manus, splitting the large central pad. At the hind-limbs the cut must follow the inner line of the limb, and divide the central pad. A rope tied to each fore-limb helps to stretch it out, and the first step towards the removal of the skin is made by flaying it back, and by carefully working around—cutting towards the body, to prevent the slipping of the knife and consequent cutting of the skin. When the skin is loose enough underneath, the foot of one side is disjointed at the second joint of the toes, as also is the fore-limb, the innermost toe being first detached. When skinned on one side, the operator continues the process on the other, extreme care being required in the management of the skin at the thin part of the flank.

When the skin is loosened sufficiently along both sides, and has been considerably relieved on the back, the lower parts, and the tail itself, must be carefully skinned around. In the case of small mammals, it may be pulled out without any cutting; if it should refuse to come out clearly, cut it near the tip, underneath, and flay towards the body. The hind-quarters should next be slung by a rope, and, the skin having been pulled from underneath them, the rope should be shifted to the fore-quarters, in order to raise the head from the ground or table. Skin the neck and throat, and, if there be reason why the skull should subsequently remain within the skin, which is not necessary with the skilled operator, disjoint it at the atlas vertebra; otherwise let it remain attached to the trunk. In either case, the ears, after being skinned a little distance towards their tips, should be detached close to the skull, leaving only small orifices, and one should be careful not to cut to their outsides.

One rule must be stringently observed, that, as there are many attachments in the region of the ear, the pupil must not cut on to the skin, but on the flesh, for any superfluous flesh left on the skin is very easy to remove, but holes are not so easily remedied. The same care must be used when skinning down to the eyes; the left-hand fingers must feel for the eye, and the skinning around the orbit of the eye must be done close to the bone, so as not to sever the membranous coats; that under the eye must be cut quite close to the eyeball, on the bone of the opposite ridge of the orbit. When this skin is freed, the next point is the loosening of that along the face underneath.

The other eye having been attended to in the same manner, the upper lip must be severed quite close to the teeth and the skinning carried on as far as the cartilage of the nose, which must be completely severed, causing the skin to drop and leave the front teeth uncovered. There now remain only the lower jaw and its large mass of muscles around the canine teeth, to be detached.

This being done, the skin falls entirely off, taking with it some of the inner skin of the lips, nose and eyes. The carcase being removed, and the skin replaced on the table, the lips should be "split." This operation must be commenced either at the side or under the nostrils, where the membrane of the lips reveals itself as a shiny skin, as the two skins meet. One must be skinned away from the other, quite close to the edges of the lips, until they are attached only by a thin edge and form a perfect bag. The under-jaw, nostrils and eyes are "split" in the same way, also the middle cartilage of the nose, to make less difficult the process of skinning out. Lastly the ears, on which some flesh was left as a safeguard, must be relieved of it, and must be skinned along the edges until they are turned completely inside out.

For a lengthy description of the skinning of

other and smaller mammals and horned heads, with their attendant differences, the reader may be referred to a recently published work.[1] Suffice it to say here that lesser mammals are not split up the limbs, and that their skulls are usually, although properly "trimmed," left attached at certain points to their skins.

Avoiding a poisonous preservative—usually inefficient—perhaps the best is that adopted by the present writer, viz.:—

Burnt alum	4 parts
Saltpetre	1 part

mixed and used dry or made into a paste with warm water, and in either case well rubbed into *all* the inside of the skin, and on all soft parts of the outside. The addition of a *small* quantity of carbolic acid, and also a small quantity of bichromate of potassa for very thick skins and in hot countries, is often beneficial. In all cases, the washing of the skin, *if quite fresh*, in strong salt and water (a saturated solution) to remove the blood, inside and out, before rubbing in the preservative, is of the highest importance. When not quite fresh, acetic acid (vinegar is a weak form of this) in varying strengths should be used with the salt and water.

The setting-up and mounting of mammals is, as may be conceived, determined by circumstances, and is varied in its methods.

To keep to the lion or tiger; such subjects are often mounted upon "mannikins," which are structures built up of board and iron rods covered with tow or with wood shavings (not hay nor straw, which probably mildew) worked into some resemblance of the carcase and finished up with modelling clay. The present writer invented what has been considered a more scientific and more correct method of getting the contours of all animals, by arranging the hardened carcase into the required attitude and casting therefrom, either as a whole or in parts, in plaster of Paris, and from the resulting moulds making paper models, upon which, when joined together, the skin is placed. These processes are substantially the same as those described in the following pages, dealing with the setting-up of an ostrich; but those who desire fuller information about the various processes connected with the modelling of mammals are referred to pages 116—160 of the work previously mentioned.

When the mammal's skin is sewn and pinned (with pointed wires) upon the model, the finer work of the colouring and insertion of the glass-spheres which replace the staring glass eyes—sold at so much a gross—and, after that, the filling and waxing of the soft parts takes place, and finally comes the question as to the "mounting," whether the animal shall be upon "rock-work" or what not.

Methods of Setting-up and Mounting Birds—Of all animated beings, birds have been the most hardly dealt with. The killing of the poor bird is not the worst fate that can befall it; it is its lamentable perpetuation as a highly embalmed caricature.

There are also, unfortunately, some clever colourists and draughtsmen who are unconscious of their absurdities. When dealing with feathered life, they will, with very few exceptions, copy from the ragged, moth-eaten, and limp mummies of the average bird-stuffer, instead of going direct to nature. When, as is often the case, flowers are correctly and beautifully drawn, as accessories to these bird studies, the incongruity is all the more painfully evident.

In five years, if the student works hard, he will recognise how little he knows, and in fifty he will know no more, *unless he learns how to draw correctly birds in any position*. That is the great secret, and the pupil, if he will not, or cannot, go to nature and draw creditably, will be a "bird-stuffer" all his life. In a greater degree, perhaps, this dictum applies to mammals, although with them there are the aids of casting and moulding which, except in the instances of large birds such as the ostrich, are unattainable.

As with mammals, so with birds—correct skinning is of the highest importance. Let a starling or a rook (both tough birds) be procured, or, if neither of these can be obtained, let a pigeon, which is easily purchased, take its place, the only drawback being that this latter bird is by no means so suitable for untrained fingers, and is indeed distinctly tender in such parts as those over the back and tail. Now, provided with the necessary scalpel, knives, and scissors, get to work by plugging the nostrils and mouth of the specimen with cotton wool. Lay the bird upon its side, with the head pointing to the right, and open it, *not* on the breast as most teachers and books recommend, but *under the wing*.

Skinning on the old lines is utterly incorrect both in theory and in practice, and is without one single recommendation, the disadvantages being that the bowels may be cut into by the learner, and so soil a white breast, and usually the skin is torn at the edges and stretched; afterwards comes the greater difficulty of shaping, and then the cut must be sewn up. After a time a rusty line of grease, drawn out of the skin by capillary attraction, declares itself.

With a pair of pliers in the right hand, take hold of the quill feathers with the left, draw out the wing as far as it will come, and, where it joins the body, put the nose of the pliers and break the bone. Do likewise with the other wing. Pick out that side of the bird which is the most badly muti-

[1] *Artistic and Scientific Taxidermy and Modelling*, by Montagu Browne. (A. and C. Black.)

lated and on it make the first cut (the state of the head should first be taken into account, as the head gives the bird nearly all its character). Turn the head diagonally toward the front, and, with the knife in the right hand, divide the feathers under the wing at the side of the breast and make a cut about half an inch long, through which the flesh of the body may be seen. Turn the body round in an exactly opposite direction, so that the tail points away, slip the point of the knife between the skin and the flesh, and cut as far as the femur, taking care to cut upwards, for fear that the skin may be damaged. With the knife-edge directed towards the flesh, relieve the skin over the back for about half an inch, do likewise along the opposite edge of the wing, breast and femur, and place some wadding between the skin and the flesh to keep the feathers clean. Loosen the skin around the broken wing bone, and detach it. If a little flesh still remain on the bone and skin in spite of all the care bestowed on it, it must be carefully removed to avoid making any holes. Leaving the wing, disarticulate the leg or cut the bone through at the junction of the femur and the tibio-tarsus; in the latter case the femur will remain joined to the body, and the tibio-tarsus will fall away with the skin. Pull the crop-membrane carefully back towards the body, take hold of it with the right hand, and with the left push the neck within the skin. Cut through the neck and windpipe, at the same time holding away the skin and feathers from the flesh. Let the head fall out of the fingers of the left hand and put a little wadding around the neck, or push a wire through it, in order that it may be the more firmly grasped. The skin is still attached to the wing, leg and tail. Take hold of the body with the left hand, and, while keeping the feathers from contact with the flesh, relieve the skin on the uncut wing and back. The student should notice that the skin on the back is exceptionally thin, and therefore must be scraped away and not pulled. This done, that on the breast or side may be loosened so as to come away easily from under the wing; and the knife being slipped in, the upward cut may be made which detaches the bone where broken. When the femur is exposed, push it up from the outside and cut through with the shears, being careful to exclude any skin.

The skinning of this part is a tiresome task until the tail is reached, as the skin is so very thin that, to detach it, it must be scraped from the bones. At the abdomen also it clings very tightly, and the knife must be used very sparingly, or the membrane over the bowels may be damaged, thereby endangering the feathers.

All this scraping and scarcely appreciable cutting over these parts will probably take a quarter of an hour, and must be continued until the pubes are passed. At this point it will be wise to let the bird lie supine on the table, merely supporting the tail above and below, and scraping until, in front, the vent is reached, and the oil-gland at the tail.

Slipping the knife underneath, and around, the final cut may be made which completely severs the skin from the body. Before the body is finally disposed of, it will be as well, of course, to take all the usual measurements and also determine the sex.

The skin being entirely detached from the body, it is necessary to start with the trimming of all flesh from the legs, wings, head and tail; the last, being already in the hand, may be operated upon first.

Carefully take away all flesh and fat with the scissors from both the tail and the skin which surrounds it. Now free the legs from skin down to the junction of the tibio-tarsus and the tarso-meta-tarsus. Take care not to pierce through to the outside when cutting away the ligaments; after the latter are cut away with a knife-point, the flesh may be removed from the bones with the finger and thumb.

The wings have now to be considered, and are decidedly the most troublesome. The flesh and pieces of broken bone must be removed, but the part still attached to the wing must be left untouched, as it furnishes something to take hold of.

The skin on the under side of the wing must be loosened until the flesh can be seen around the radius and ulna. Take away the broken bone, and remove all the flesh from the radius and ulna by cutting and scraping with scissors and knife. The head and neck now remain. Take the latter in one hand and press the skin over it, towards the beak, with the other, until coming to the place where the skin is found to adhere firmly to the ears, dip the finger and thumb in plaster or sand, and—preferably—pull the ears right out from their attachments, or, if they will not be persuaded, trim them out.

The skin around the eyeballs must be very carefully detached by cutting towards the back of the head, and when it is quite free a brain-scoop may be put into the orbit, pushed under the eyeball, and the latter pulled out without being burst. A plug of wool must be pushed into the orbit to clean it. The skin on the top of the skull must be loosened with a knife or the brain-scoop, well up to the base of the beak. Under and in front of the orbits, and at the side of the face, a little more skinning is required, to free the head from skin to the base of the beak.

If the tongue be not wanted within the beak, put the knife between it and the skull, then pull forward, when tongue and windpipe will come away. Where the neck joins the head disconnect it, but do not cut away the back of the skull, as the brains may be easily removed from the back of the eye-sockets.

Now take a preservative, and, if the student is wise, he will use a non-poisonous preservative in those initial stages which necessitate the handling of the skin, and afterwards follow with a mercurial solution. This is highly poisonous, and the only efficient protection known against the ravages of insects. It is applied with a brush *after* the specimen is "set-up," and permeates the skin, but is not handled by the operator.

The first is :—

Non-poisonous preservative soap—

Whiting or chalk	$1\frac{1}{2}$ lbs.
White Windsor soap (common curd soap) . . .	$\frac{1}{2}$ lb.
Chloride of lime	$\frac{1}{2}$ oz.
Tincture of musk	$\frac{1}{2}$ oz.

The price of musk of late years is so prohibitive that unless it becomes cheaper it must be replaced by Eucalyptus oil. The finishing wash, to be labelled "Deadly Poison," is :—

Alcoholic solution of mercury—

Methylated spirits or wine 90 per cent.	1 pint
Bichloride of mercury 50 grains	$2\frac{1}{2}$ scruples.

Paint every part of the skull and skin and the bones of the wings, legs, and tail well, but do not paint the feathers. Turn the skin back again to its normal position, with the feathers outside, and then proceed to "make a skin."

Through the opening made by the removal of the brain, fill the skull with chopped tow; and fill the orbits with wadding. (Note that where wadding is used the sharpest wire will fail to penetrate it.)

To prevent shrinking of the head, and to allow of any correction in shape that may be necessary when the head is returned, plaster it over thinly with soft pipe-clay or a modelling composition, forcing it in well above the beak and the sides of the face. Partially fill the throat with tow also.

Gather up the skin of the neck in the fingers of both hands and return the head through the neck, but be careful not to catch the bill in the skin and so tear it. This may be obviated in great measure by previously passing a thread through the nostrils and tying it around the bill. With care and by gentle pulling with the fingers, the head will, in the end, be in its natural position. Arrange the feathers with a fine needle and, if any ridges have been formed and held by the clay inside, bring them backwards, usually, sometimes forwards, by the aid of the needle. The hollows in the wings, caused by the removal of the flesh, are filled with tow, and a threaded needle is passed through between the radius and ulna, and around the radius of each wing, the ends of the thread being drawn until the wings are at their proper distance apart.

Around the leg-bones (tibio-tarsi), wrap tow to replace the flesh, and then pull them back into their proper places.

The next process is to make a false body—preferably of tow—about the size of, or a little less than, the natural one. This is done by taking a piece of wire of suitable gauge, long enough to reach from the inside of the skull to the beginning of the tail, and upon this wrapping tow at one end to form a neck, leaving unwrapped, however, as much wire as is represented by the depth of the skull. When this is done, wind the tow lower and bind firmly, copying the shape of the natural body. At the end of the wire the tow must be very thinly wrapped, and come to an apex to represent the narrowing at the tail. That there may be no slipping, turn the wire backwards on to the body.

If the false body be ill-shaped, bind it with hemp, and occasionally flatten it, until it becomes of a pear-shaped form.

To put the body into the skin, take it in the right hand, raise the skin with the left, put the uncovered point of the wire—unsharpened, if possible,—followed by the artificial neck into the palatal part of the skull, and then, with a little management, insert the whole body into the skin. Let the breast feathers lie over the breast of the false body, and let the tail touch the apex, settle the wings properly, distribute the feathers as in nature, get the whole of the back into good order, and fasten the wings in position by pins which pass from one to the other through the artificial body.

A trough should be made of board, with the sides of a height according to the size of the skin, and over it a piece of straw-board should be tacked. Place in the trough a thin layer of wadding, and on this lay the bird upon its back, so that the breast may be attended to. Settle the feathers properly (for this is final), cross or tie the legs, and arrange the head naturally, turning it to one side should it be long-billed. Any feathers which are untidy may be bound in place with cotton or hemp.

In place of this trough, skilled taxidermists use a paper strip, arranged around the bird after the final disposition of the feathers, and pinned at the ends.

There are other methods which the clever skin-maker will probably discover for himself, such as wrapping the skin in wadding or using two or three cross bands of tissue-paper, but, in any case, it is imperative to correct all irregularities before the skin becomes dry. A label should of course be attached to the legs, giving all information as to name of specimen, sex, locality, date of capture, name of collector, and colour of eyes and soft parts generally. A well-shaped skin should be indistinguishable from a dead bird, with feathers perfectly smooth, wings closed and legs crossed.

The skinning and making of a skin being disposed of, the important process of "setting up" comes next. Ordinarily, it is done either by wiring the legs, the wings, the head, and the tail, and filling in and shaping by cotton wool or tow—*i.e.*, the "soft-body" method—or by carving peat or cork into some semblance of a body, and thrusting wires therein, inserted from the outside through the legs and so on, or by making a "mannikin" of tightly bound tow or wood-fibre, placing it within the skin as a fictitious body, and arranging the wires in the best manner to do their supporting work. This "hard-body" method is, or should be, superseded, either by one adapted or by one invented by the present writer. The first deals with the question of retaining the whole of the skeleton of a small bird as a guide to its form, which has much to recommend it, especially as most taxidermists retain the bones of the legs, the wings, the tail and the skull, within the skin, thus leaving only the skeleton of the carcase or the "cage" undealt with. This, when freed from flesh, washed with strong carbolic acid and otherwise cured, worked over with tow and perhaps a little clay to replace the flesh removed, becomes the semi-artificial body to be replaced within the skin, and on this the skull, wing-bones, leg-bones and tail are wired in their exact positions, as in nature. Thus, if moderate care and skill follow in the final "setting up," the bird should be more life-like than it would become by ordinary methods. It has been urged against this process by those who have never tried it,—first, its difficulty, next, its liability to the attacks of insects. The first may be disposed of by saying that nothing is done, which is well done, or worth doing, without difficulty, and that it is not really so difficult as would appear; the second contention is disposed of, by the fact that all the bones are washed with carbolic, or creosote, or the non-poisonous soap, and the skin itself, *after* the bird is "set up" and finished, is washed by a solution of bi-chloride of mercury in spirits of wine. This, it need hardly be observed, is a deadly poison, and should not be touched by the hands. Arsenical or other poisonous soaps are painted *inside* the skin, and must be handled in "setting up," but the mercurial wash is applied *outside*, after the subject, be it bird or mammal, is finished, and therefore necessitates no handling.

This method of using the whole of the skeleton is, in the case of large birds, superseded by the other plan mentioned—the modelled body, which is used in the Leicester Museum for all mammals. The following description of the modelling and "setting-up" of an ostrich will, with modifications, do duty for the treatment of the vertebrate sub-kingdom.

At the outset, the specimen to be "set up," was measured, the colour of its soft parts and other details noted, and the feet, legs, thighs, neck, head, and other soft parts were washed in methylated spirits seventy per cent., to harden the skin generally, and also to fix the scales of the legs, which might otherwise have "slipped" in handling.

The bird was placed on its back on a dissecting table, being propped under the thighs, &c., with blocks of wood to maintain it in proper position. As it was intended that the bird should be mounted looking towards the left, an incision was made along the right margin of the central feathers, so that the ultimate stitching should not be seen. This was continued backwards to the tip of the tail, and forward, still following the edge line of feathers right round the sternum, down the under surface of the wing to the tip. Skinning was comparatively easy, until the masses of fat at the breast and round the base and sides of the tail were met with. As it was intended that a plaster cast of the body should be made, no more fat was left on the skin than was unavoidable. The whole side being laid bare, with the skin freed before and behind to its utmost limits, skinning was continued over the knee and down the leg to the junction of the heel, where it was disarticulated by means of an incision made from the outside. The skin of the leg was not in any way split except at this point. The tibio-tarsus was removed from the body at the junction of the femur, with all its relative muscles att[illegible]ed.

The same process was [illegible]e through with the other side, the whole front of th[illegible]ast being laid bare without any necessity for dividin[illegible] skin further. In undercutting the cloacal apert[illegible] it was found necessary to plug it with wadding and [illegible] tie the end of the intestine freed by this process. Ha[illegible]ng skinned down both sides, further operations were greatly assisted by partly hoisting the bird with a pulley, tail upwards, and commencing at that part, the skin by its weight assisting the process of freeing the back.

The neck was turned back as in small birds, the knife, however, being in constant use, to free it from the enveloping skin, and it was found necessary to make an incision on the side of the head near the top and to continue it for an inch or two up the neck to free and disarticulate it, after which the neck was easily got at. The left wing was cleaned by slitting it underneath from the tip to the point where it had previously been freed from the inside, thus avoiding the division of the skin across the breast. The wing-bones and head, the whole of the skin, and such bones as were attached, were thoroughly cleaned of flesh and fat, then well rubbed with the mammal preservative and left for some little time.

Afterwards, the toes and feet were slit up vertically, also the legs on their insides; the sinews, &c., were removed, and the bones and skin well rubbed with preservative. Next two iron rods (half an inch or five-eighths of an inch thick), tapped at one end for about six inches, were passed down the hollows of the leg-bones and out through the feet, the tapped portions protruding for some distance. The removed sinews, &c., were now replaced with pipe-clay, modelled to shape, and the skin carefully sewn up. A board or block of suitable size and thickness was now provided, having two holes bored for the reception of the protruding irons of the feet in such a position that these stood each four and a half inches from the median line, *i.e.*, nine inches apart, the right foot, however, being posed about six inches behind the left.

Whilst the skin was curing, the mould of the body was proceeded with, but owing to its bulk it was necessary to cast it in three separate parts, viz.: (1) neck; (2) body; and (3) right and left tibio-tarsi together. The first and third operations will be described later; the second is as follows:—

Three sacks of plaster—which were all used—were

obtained, and a galvanised iron bath with a handle at each end, holding about a pailful and a half, was found very convenient in which to mix the plaster with water. Another bath of water stood near for the necessary rapid washing and rinsing of hands and utensils, whilst the work was proceeding. Two operators were required, one to supply the mixing bath with the proportions of water and dry plaster, and the other to do the hand-mixing and actual casting.

The form of the specimen being studied, with a view to its proper relieving from the mould subsequently, it was found expedient to place the bird upon its back, raised from the bench by a small piece of wood, one inch

HEADLESS MODEL (BY THE DIRECT PAPER PROCESS) OF AN OSTRICH.

deep, placed under the lowest angle in the lumbar vertebral region. A four-sided wooden frame was constructed around, which cleared the specimen inside by an inch each way, and rose an inch above the level of the ventral surface; here n the carcase was temporarily propped in a manner similar to a vessel dry-docked. Cracks between boards were stopped with putty, and the inside of the frame was well oiled.

All being ready, the plaster was expeditiously mixed in successive bathfuls and poured into the box until the back was embedded, and until it reached the mid-level of the horizontally-placed tail and femora on both sides, leaving the top half of each exposed.

This constituted the first section of the cast, which, after a short time allowed for setting, was well oiled on its surface, and the next proceeded with.

First the spaces between the sternum and pelvis and their respective ends of the frame were divided by pieces of wood cut to shape and stopped with putty; these, of course, together with the exposed portion of the specimen, dividing the box longitudinally.

Into one of these divisions plaster was again poured to within three or four inches of the top of the ventral surface of the specimen, the wooden partitions were removed, and the other side similarly treated. A single cast was now made over the remaining exposed portion, similar to the back, although of course of much smaller bulk. Several hours were allowed to elapse before delivering.

The casting of the neck and tibio-tarsi was a more simple process. Wooden frames to hold them having been loosely constructed, so as easily to knock apart, plaster was poured in to a depth of from two to three inches, and, when this had set to a suitable density, known only by experience, the objects were gently laid upon it and pressed down to a level of half their thicknesses or more, according to necessity. When hardened, keyed, and oiled, the top cast was made, completing the operation.

Some little time elapsed before operations connected with the making of the paper model could take place, as all plaster moulds when first made are exceedingly damp, and, when required immediately, especially if in winter, must be artificially dried by placing near a fire or furnace, though not so close as to cause cracking, which would certainly result from overheating. In summer, however, exposure to sun and air would probably be sufficient, assisted by fire if wanted for immediate use. Into these moulds, when oiled, were pressed series of layers of paper in this order.

(1) A layer of white tissue-paper, pasted on under side only.

(2) Layers of cap or newspaper, pasted on both sides.

(3) Layers of moderately thick brown paper, pasted on both sides.

(4) Layers of stout brown paper, pasted on both sides.

By applying alternate layers of two differently shaded brown papers unequal distribution was obviated, thus ensuring uniform thickness and strength. After drying a few days the paper casts were relieved; irregularities of surface, caused by adhesion to the plaster, pasted down into place, overlapping edges trimmed, and the vertebral, or back portion, and two sides joined together with glued calico and paper strips, converting them into one piece.

The two neck-pieces were next joined together; they contained a stout wire, gauge nine, around which sufficient tow had been bound to fill the hollow model. This wire protruded at the lower end about eight inches for insertion and fixing in the body, which was effected by cutting a hole in the model and fastening the inserted portion with glued tow and calico strips. At the other end of the neck, about six inches of naked wire was left exposed as a subsequent head-support. The sternal portion was then fixed, thus completing the neck and body.

Next, the block on which the legs were fixed, with their long irons protruding upwards, was placed squarely under a beam which ran across the ceiling, from which was suspended the body at the correct angle and proper height from the surface of the block on which the feet rested, care being taken that the central axis of the body corresponded with the median line between the feet, the vertical position of the neck being ensured by a plumb line.

Next, the end of each leg-wire was pushed through the thickened end of its respective femur and filed off; and these irons, when bent at proper angles, severally formed the central axis and support of each tibio-tarsus, the inside half of which was first fixed in position and secured, and then the outer one. In the hollows of the thighs between the legs and the body was wedged glued tow, also well packed round about the irons, especially at their extremities. The model, now complete, received a coat or two of turpentine and flake-white and was allowed to dry.

Lastly, the skin, which during all the preceding processes had dried as hard as a board, was soaked in warm water, often changed, for two or three days, and was then scraped throughout to remove all fat and the hard inner layer of skin, until after some time it became as pliable as a glove. The feathers, cleaned somewhat by the soaking, were wiped down with benzoline and plaster

missing, replaced by modelling-composition, and the legs and all soft parts coloured according to the notes primarily taken.

Methods of "Setting Up" and Mounting Fishes—If mammals and birds have been badly used by the "stuffer," surely the fishes can bitterly complain of the indignities piled upon them by an attempt to resuscitate them by taxidermic processes, for no known processes of taxidermy, which necessitate the removal of cartilage and its substitution by a foreign material, can ever reproduce the gelatinous appearance which certain parts of fishes present. Supposing any fish be

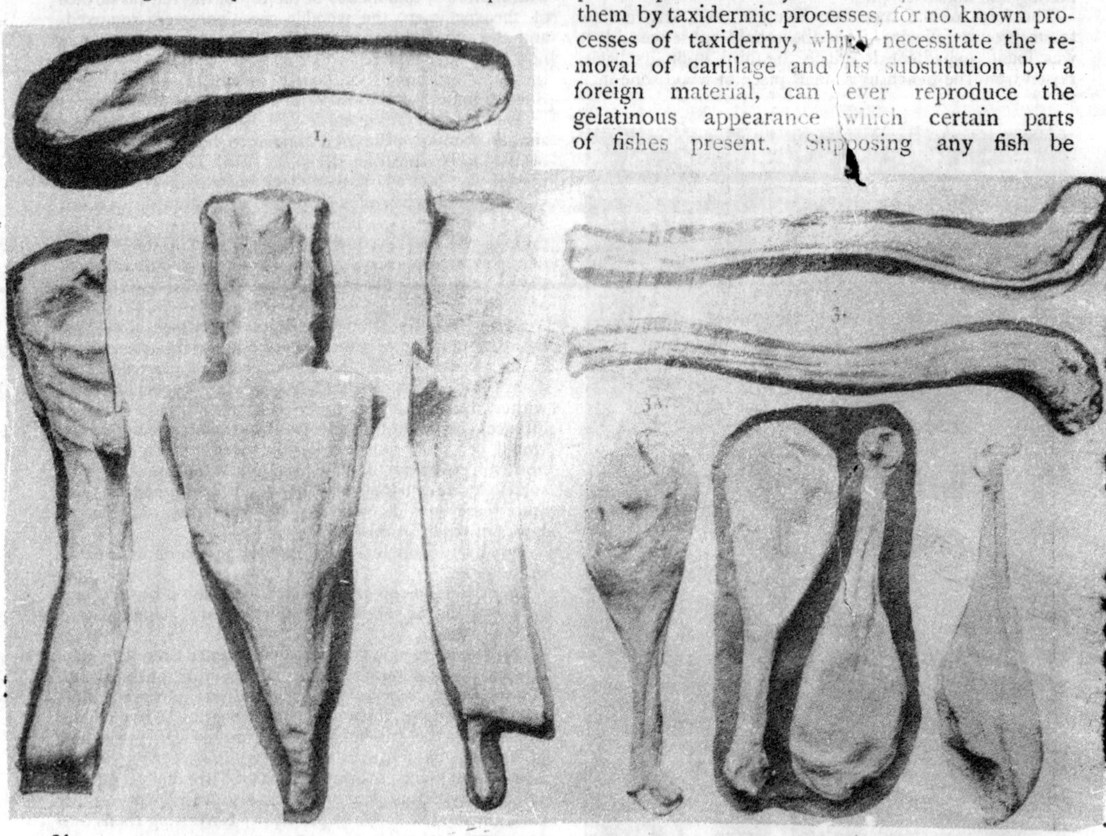

FIG. 1.—Represents a model, by the "direct paper process," of the sternum.
FIG. 2.—That of the back. FIGS. 2A AND 2B.—Those of the sides.
FIGS. 3 AND 3A.—Those of the halves of the neck.
FIGS. 4, 4A, 5, AND 5A.—Those of the legs.
All are untrimmed, excepting 4 and 5A. The moulds, being merely intaglios of the models, are not figured.

thrown on to clean and dry them still further. This done, all imperfect parts, or those not of a good shape, were modelled over with pipe-clay, worked very smooth with paste, and retained in position on the model by means of "cap-paper" pasted over all. The skull, still attached to the skin, was modelled up and placed upon the neck of the model, the skin of the neck being gradually drawn over it, and the remainder drawn over the model, one leg, the right, being further split for that purpose. The skin of the wings, legs, and body having been pulled into position and nicely adjusted, were carefully sewn together with skin-needles and strong thread. Then followed the adjusting of the face and eyes, and, more difficult still, the bringing together of the edges of the cut skin of the femur and reconciling it by means of a wax composition with the scutes of the tibio-tarsal joint. Finally, the feathers were cleaned and dried by being wiped down with benzoline followed by plaster of Paris, and well beaten out. All sewn edges were worked over with the wax composition, the scutes of the legs, where

skinned as recommended in most books, what is done with the face? Literally nothing, for there are certain parts which resist any tools, however cunningly fashioned, in their attempts to coax out the flesh, and the cleverest taxidermist, who fancies he succeeds, never awakens to the fact that, *outside* the head and other parts, great shrinkage and shrivelling of the tegument result upon drying, and therefore a stuffed fish is the most unnatural thing in the whole range of taxidermy, even if done in what is called splendid style. Such "splendour" means a nicely varnished and very plump body, with shrivelled bases to the fins, and wrinkles all over the skull. Wax superimposed is only a partial success, and if fishermen would be content with the actual form of their capture, correct in every particular, and with the finest markings shown upon the scales as in nature, and not "hanker" after the actual skin, with all its manifest imperfections and absurdities, there would be no taxidermic piscine mummies. The remedy for all this is casting from the actual subject as soon after capture as may be, which faithfully reproduces the exact form.

Really, taxidermy is powerless to represent fishes correctly, and the only method to secure exactitude is making a model in plaster or other media, and reproducing from that. In the first place a casting box should be provided, and this is quite simple in its construction, being merely four pieces of wood of any suitable lengths, two of which are not quite so wide as the others, the widest being slotted sufficiently at one end to allow the two narrower pieces to slide through them. By placing the wider pieces parallel to each other, slots downwards and at the contrary extremities, and then inserting an end of one of the narrower pieces in each slot, with the other end touching the inner face of one of the wider pieces, a square is formed, the size of which can be diminished or increased at will by merely sliding the narrower pieces through, and along the faces of, the wider ones.

There are three prominent methods of making moulds in plaster, *i.e.*, direct casting, waste moulds, and piece moulds.

Probably the best method of casting fishes in plaster is the following :—

Keep the specimen in a hardening solution for a short time, and afterwards well wash it. If flat, lay it on a slab of slate or glass; if not, on a board slightly larger than itself. Pu pieces of half-inch board underneath the dorsal, *lower* ventral, anal and caudal fins as a means of support, but not under the uppermost pectoral and ventral ones.

If any gaps occur between the ends of the pieces of wood, or where the sides of the fish do not quite touch the wood, fill up with putty. If the boards are too thin to hold up the fins to their ordinary height, elevate them with putty or by means of a second board of suitable thickness.

It is obvious that boards—used in preference to glass, cardboard, or slate—admit of the specimens being pinned to them, to prevent their being floated up by the plaster.

The pins used must be cut off quite close to the fins, in order that there may be no difficulty in removing them when the specimen is turned over, and all boards must be wetted or oiled and the fish kept damp—with water, or glycerin and water, put on with a soft brush—and clean, by taking off all dirt and putty.

If the pectoral or ventral fins are to lie flat on the fish when finished, they must be made to do so now; if to be raised, they must be held up, until set in the position decided on.

At this stage, build either wooden or zinc walls, stop up all cracks with putty, damp the fish, and pour in the plaster carefully. When it is dry, take away the walls, the boards and the putty, and turn the parts of the mould containing the fish upside down.

If the work has been done satisfactorily, the under half of the fish can now be seen, and should be gently brushed and wetted. The remainder is still in the mould, on the surface of which, now visible, keys should be cut, and, most important of all, it must be oiled.

Again build up the walls, fill up the cracks with putty, and pour on plaster.

In about a quarter of an hour, by gentle persuasion, the halves will come away from one another, and the fish can be taken out of its shell—care being required that the fins be not torn by the pins.

If the fins were raised, they must be protected from injury by supporting the mould on pieces of wood.

To make a cast of the pectoral and ventral fins, wash the fish, and replace it on the board with another board under the fins. Surround it with a little wall of putty and pour on plaster as usual.

Sometimes it is only necessary to make a cast of one side of the fins, on the side which is to be shown, but it is usual to take moulds of both sides, and of both sides of each right and left paired fin.

If the skeleton be not required and the fish be not lent solely for the purpose of casting, the above operation is unnecessary, and the following is preferable :—

Remove the ventral and pectoral fins after a cast has been taken, and put them by the side of the fish, which is set for casting, the result being that both surfaces of the fins will be seen on the same block as the fish; this is a capital safeguard against loss or error. In drying the mould, take care that it does not remain so long before the fire as to make it too brittle or too much like chalk, and, when dry, paint it over once or twice with colza-oil.

Many clever modellers think water preferable to oil with which to dress the mould, but oil at least obviates the difficulty of distinguishing mould from model when the edges are being trimmed.

A modification of "waste-mould" casting is to colour the plaster to be used for the first coat, and pour it very thinly over the specimen and let it set. Cover it with oil or soft soap and then pour on a thin coat of uncoloured plaster, oil and coat again, until of a thickness that will prevent the breaking of the mould when the specimen is removed. Remember how many layers were used, or introduce a different colour each time, soap or oil the mould, pour plaster into it, let it set, and then commence to take away—with a hammer, chisel, or with modelling-tools—the plaster layers one by one. When the last one is arrived at be very careful in removing it; this done, the whole object reveals itself.

Where either a fish, snake, or lizard is concerned, the edges of the mould should reach beyond the specimen to be cast to provide a tablet on which the model should rest, and this should be flattened and smoothed by suitable tools.

On the other hand, casting from a large specimen by means of piece-moulds is a much more difficult operation; and the subject, be it mammal, bird, or fish, must be carefully studied and looked over, with a view to "undercuts." These are certain portions that, when cast upon, would not "relieve" or come away without the breakage of the mould; this method has been sufficiently explained in the article upon the casting of the body of the ostrich, and is rarely required for the reproduction of fishes, save the very largest. With reptiles, however, it is different; they have limbs which do not readily relieve as do their analogues in fishes, and with them, and with many of the higher invertebrates, piece-casting must be resorted to, unless, indeed, they are sufficiently small to be covered with a glue, gatta-percha, or wax mould.

The first, or glue process, pre-supposes the possession of a good modelling-glue, and one adopted by the writer gives first-rate results :—

Glue (best Scotch)	16 parts
Water	1 part
Glycerin	7 parts
Linseed-oil	2 parts

The glue is wrapped in a cloth and broken very small, then melted in the ordinary manner in a glue-kettle, but with no more water added to it than the one part allowed. During the melting, the oil and glycerin are separately made hot, also in a water bath, taking care of fire.

The glycerin is added first in small quantities, and, when the glue has taken it up, the oil is added gradually and the whole is stirred and boiled together. Six hours should be sufficient to cause the whole to become intimately mixed.

This admirable preparation is not only of service for the making of moulds, but is of the highest value for the making of models also.

It has its limitations, however. It is not advisable to use it upon or within a damp object or mould, or upon either unoiled, and the size of the object to be represented must also be taken into consideration. It is not suitable for any natural objects of extreme size or over ten pounds in weight, but its advantages up to that are manifest in the ease with which, either as a mould or model, it "relieves." This is so marked that, as a mould, it is merely necessary to cover the object, and afterwards halve the glue covering wherever convenient.

As a model, its elasticity and toughness are such as to permit it to leave the most intricate undercuts with the greatest ease, and such things as frogs, snakes, and curiously-shaped fishes, fungi, and seaweeds are correctly expressed thereby, and when coloured to nature are indistinguishable from the originals.

Some few precautions are necessary, such as thinly varnishing the glue mould and letting the varnish set before plaster is poured in, and oiling a plaster mould with colza-oil before pouring in the glue, and, above all, painting the finished models as soon as may be with oil-colours. No change whatever takes place if this be done, and there are specimens finished and unfinished, the latter protected by a coat of oil-white, which have been in the Leicester Museum for five or more years without any shrinking or cracking.

For groups of small fishes, to be reproduced finally in plaster, paraffin wax is of the highest value, as it may be poured over a slightly damped surface, and, if it sets too rapidly, the addition of more wax causes it again to liquefy, and it flows over every part of the surface, and results as a perfectly hard mould with extreme definition in every part. When objects made of fine plaster do not readily relieve from a wax mould, it must be treated as a waste one, and be melted away from the plaster model by hot water, and the wax can be used again.

Up to the present, the processes described, with the exception of the passing mention of the glue composition, have dealt with the reproduction of forms in plaster. This, however, is heavy, and almost impossible to colour

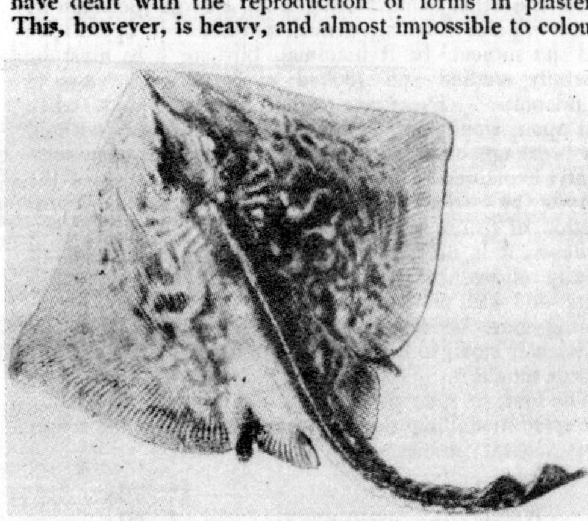

MODEL (BY THE PULPED PAPER PROCESS) OF A THORNBACK RAY.

so as to disguise its composition, and is, though of respectable antiquity and improved upon by modern methods, unable to bear comparison with methods invented or adapted by the writer.

"Carton-pierre" and its improvements are not limited by any considerations of size or weight, and the smallest and the largest objects can be perfectly represented, not only by exact form and definition but by colour.

There are several varieties of paper compositions, which the present writer has called the "Direct paper-process," "Pulped paper-process," and "Improved Carton-pierre." The first, used for representations of large fishes, reptiles, and for the models of the carcases of large birds and mammals, is that described when dealing with the model of the ostrich.

The second is made by taking certain proportions of flour mixed with water into a stiff paste, and flour mixed with linseed-oil, and combining them with tissue-paper by pounding in a mortar, the resultant mass being pressed into the oiled moulds and taken out when dry.

The very best of all paper pulps is the "Improved Carton-pierre," and this is of such extreme lightness

MODEL (BY THE IMPROVED CARTON-PIERRE) OF A LUMP-FISH.

when the model is dry, that it weighs but half an ounce to every pound of the original specimen.

Thus a twenty pound fish weighs ten ounces only in the completed model, the definition being extreme, and it takes colour beautifully. Indeed, it is not too much to say, that this and the glue process should for ever dismiss taxidermic processes in the reproduction of fishes, reptiles, and soft objects generally.

The figures represent a Thornback Ray, modelled by the oil, flour and water, pulped-paper process, and a Lump-fish done in the "Improved carton-pierre."

Mounting Natural Objects—The ordinary "mounting" is merely a sanded board, or a perch of wood. Extraordinary "mounting" is when the object is mounted with modelled "rockwork" or finely and correctly-modelled foliage and flowers.

Supposing a large wall-case be needed to hold animals in different attitudes, make a false bottom and join to it some upright boards which will be of the heights suitable to the rockwork. Old cardboard, in fact anything of paper sufficiently strong, can be bent into rough shapes suitable to the design decided on, and nailed on to the board, and brown paper should be glued all over the cardboard. To form rounded edges, make them up by roughly gluing on pieces of crumpled paper, or by laying on pieces of cardboard, and cover with glued or pasted paper. When finished, no wrinkles should be shown —fill them in, if any, with pasted or glued wadding,—and the whole should be glued and sanded. An artist with a fertile imagination may "create" a rock with some success, but it is best to go to nature for inspiration, and to take a rock of any size and make an absolute copy therefrom, and the result should be, not a weak and erroneous imitation, but a reproduction which should deceive even a geologist.

Oil the natural object well, and use for the base that side of the stone which is the least important. Paste tough brown paper over one side of the stone, thus transferring from the stone to the first layer of paper all its characteristics. Follow this only by a sufficient number of layers to prevent the paper from collapsing when dry, removing the stone when the model is dry or nearly so. A better method, which reproduces all detail, is to cast the rocks in plaster of Paris, and, if too large to cast in one piece, "piece-casting" is resorted to. When the mould is dry and oiled and the pieces are attached to one another, paste the paper inside the model; if necessary, the paper may be thickened considerably, for the finest markings are *on the surface* in this case, and not within the model as in the previous process.

If the original rock, from which models or copies were taken, have a sandy or rough surface, then glue and sand must be used to represent it faithfully, and the colouring may be accomplished by using tints of common powder-colours thinned with turpentine or linseed-oil. All finishing touches must be aided, if possible, by the rock itself as a guide.

If the rocks are smooth, they must be brushed over with a special preparation made by one part of each of powdered whiting and plaster of Paris, mixed with sufficient thin flour-paste and water to make it into a paint.

A white under-ground invariably adds lustre and purity of colouring, and, should the whiting develop small cracks, this may sometimes aid the general effect. If the stones themselves present a smooth surface, instead of whiting use dry flake-white mixed with turpentine, and, when dry, rub down with sand-paper till smooth; if it is inclined to crack, leave out the plaster altogether.

In reproducing rockwork the student should be careful not to cast from the *inner* and *newly-broken* faces of rocks to represent a weather-worn cliff face, nor to use plaster tablets, to be laboriously joined together, when the much lighter and more easily worked paper does so much better.

Artificial trees are ordinarily made by wrapping tow around wire until some kind of twig is fashioned; this, to make it more "life-like," is sanded or has sawdust glued upon it, and is coloured, sometimes a brilliant red, often a no less brilliant green, and results in a fancy conception utterly unlike anything in the botanical world. Sometimes a cylinder of paper is made, from which sprout excrescences intended to do duty for limbs; when, however—as is usually the case,—the "tree" does not measure more than a few inches in height, the absurdity is manifest, and the safer method is to take nature for a guide, and carefully copy from the tree or branch itself, making the foundation with cardboard or stiff paper, reproducing the "bark" by means of tissue-paper, and copying the colouring from the actual object. The only true representation, however, is that made in paper from a plaster of Paris mould—usually in several pieces—which is unmistakably correct in shape, and may be made correct in colour by any one possessing the requisite knowledge.

Natural trunks and branches of trees must be rigorously excluded from cases, as insects eventually appear, especially in birch trees, and are very destructive foes. They may be detected by the yellowish dust they make when boring through the wood. Mosses, used as accessories in cases, must be carefully dried, the dirt taken out of them, and they must be put into a bath of turpentine, to kill the larvæ of insects.

Sphagnum or bog moss, and beautiful lichens, of almost every colour, can be used advantageously for this purpose. Grasses, such as the sheep's fescue, several of the brome-grasses, the wall and sea barleys, and many other stiff kinds, dry without much shrinkage, and take colour well.

The colouring must be applied discreetly, and must be thinned with turpentine, and, if varnish be used, it must also be thinned, to give the grasses a silky appearance, but not a shiny surface.

Other grasses and reeds may be used, but bulrushes and sedges are of no value, and are distinctly out of place except in very large cases, and then they must be modelled in the art fabric used for flowers and foliage, the methods of which cannot, however, be described here for want of space, but are to be found fully detailed in the work previously mentioned.

No dried leaves, except as such, are permissible in cases; the fronds of fern (bracken) dry beautifully, and may with skill be made to look very well, if colour, as distinguished from paint, be discreetly used. Seaweeds are a hideous failure, unless cast from the original and modelled by the glue process; some of the corallines are permissible, and some sea-shells may be used, if the common error of making razor-shells adhere to rock, and such like absurdities, be eschewed.

"Groups," such as those in the British and the Leicester Museums, are the outcome of all taxidermic knowledge aided largely by the art of modelling—whether applied to the forms of the animals, or of their accessories, or both,—and their value, like that of a picture, depends upon a just conception and faithful delineation of form, colour, balance of light and shade, and composition, and, if these principles be properly taught and insisted upon, a great and glorious future awaits the art of taxidermy and its trained exponents.

MONTAGU BROWNE.

TEAL—Although one of the smallest ducks that fly, weighing no more than a partridge, the teal (*Querquedula crecca*) is one of the most attractive of wildfowl to sportsmen, not merely on account of the beautiful colours of the male bird, but because of the sporting shots it affords, and its excellence for the table.

Teal are generally easier to get at than ducks, and as they require but a slight blow to bring them down, it matters little what size of shot is used. Instead of rising head to wind like other wildfowl, they have an odd way of springing up vertically from the surface of the water, no matter what their position may be when discovered, and, the shooter not aiming high enough, the charge of shot often passes harmlessly below them.

Haunts and Habits—Quiet rushy pools which lie at a distance from any road, turf holes on a peat bog, and sluggish shallow streams with overhanging vegetation are favourite haunts of the teal. Of shy and retired habits, it shuns the more public ponds and rivers, and avoids the neighbourhood of man's dwelling.

On approaching the edge of a pond at a distance from a "spring" of teal (as a small flock of these birds is technically termed), they may be seen silently reposing on the water. Immediately the intruder is perceived, a harsh call is heard, and they jump suddenly into the air, wheeling round and about with amazing rapidity, now looking black, now white, according as the upper or under surface of their bodies is presented to the eye. Frequently, as though intending to alight, they fall through the air with a whistling sound, recovering themselves when apparently in the water, and rising again to a height. These manœuvres are repeated until the eye is strained in following them, and the entire flock at length settles down again in silence and repose as before. At such times it requires no small amount of caution to get near enough to them for a shot.

Col. Hawker, whose practical knowledge of wildfowl has rarely been equalled, has well described the habits of the teal in his *Instructions to Young Sportsmen*. "If you spring a teal, he will not soar up and leave the country like a wild duck, but will most probably keep along the brook like a sharp-flying woodcock, and then drop suddenly down. But you must keep your eye on the place, as he is very apt to get up again, and fly to another spot before he will quietly settle. He will frequently, too, swim down stream the moment after he drops; so that if you do not cast your eye quickly that way, instead of continuing to look for him in one spot, he will probably catch sight of you and fly up, while your attention is directed to the wrong place. If the brook in which you find him is obscured by many trees, you had better direct your follower to make a large circle, and get ahead of and watch him, in case he should slily skim away down the brook and by this means escape from you altogether."

Description of Plumage—For beauty of colouring the cock teal has scarcely an equal amongst wildfowl. The chestnut head with a patch of glossy green on each side, edged with buff; the neck, back and flanks beautifully pencilled with black and grey; the bright green speculum on the wing, broadly bordered above and below with velvet black; and the black and buff undertail-coverts present to the eye a perfect picture of harmonising colour which defies the imitative pencil of the artist.

The hen teal, like the females of all ducks, is of the usual sombre colour, her dusky brown and grey plumage being peculiarly well adapted to her concealment during the time she is engaged in incubation.

Nesting—Although usually placed in the vicinity of water, the nest is sometimes at a considerable distance from it, and always rests upon dry ground. A hollow is generally scraped out at the foot of some overhanging bunch of heather, or tussock of dry waving grass, and lined with fine heath stalks and bents. Here eight or ten creamy-white eggs are laid, in April, and as the hen bird covers them, she plucks from her breast and sides the soft brown down which underlies her feathers, and places it entirely round the eggs, filling up all the interstices, thus forming a warm bed for the young as soon as they leave the shell.

The old duck is very attentive to her young, leading them from the nest to the marsh, where they paddle about on the soft ground and shallow pools, snapping up flies and beetles with their tiny bills. They swim and dive well almost as soon as hatched.

Migration—Great numbers of teal pass southward for the winter, returning in the spring on the way back to their breeding haunts. In September and October they collect in large flocks, and, being very sociable in their habits, may often be found in winter in company with wild ducks. But although they mingle together when on the water, on being disturbed the two species always separate, the teal going off in one flock, the ducks in another. During the winter months teal may be found on the coast, in company with wigeon, but they apparently prefer the neighbourhood of fresh water, especially large quiet pools well sheltered by reeds or trees, to screen them from the wind.

Teal in Decoys—Teal are amongst the tamest of wildfowl, and are generally the earliest to come into a decoy. The decoy-man, aware of their market value (for they are highly esteemed for the table), knows better than to capture the first comers. He allows them to remain undisturbed for some time, in order to attract others of their kind. This policy sometimes proves very remunerative. It is on record that at certain decoys in Essex, from 200 to 400 teal have been taken in one day. At the celebrated Ashby decoy in Lincolnshire it was not an uncommon thing to take 1800 or 2000 teal in the course of a season, and in the winter of 1852–53 no less than 3279 of these little birds were thus captured. Folkard relates that at a decoy pond at Mersea in Essex a flock of about 400 arrived, the greater number of which were taken within a few hours. The Rev. Richard Lubbock, also, mentions an instance which occurred at a Norfolk decoy of 220 teal being taken at once.

Formerly the decoy season was from the 1st October till the 1st June: the statute 10 Geo. II. cap. 32 prohibited the taking of any wildfowl "by hays, tunnels, or other nets" earlier or later under a penalty of 5*s.* for every bird so taken, but that statute has been repealed, and now by custom the season for working a decoy is from October to February.

It is true that a few ducks and mallards come into the decoys in July and August, but they are generally birds reared in the neighbourhood, and are left alone to entice others. Teal come in about the first week of September. [See DECOYS.]

J. E. HARTING.

TENCH—MEASUREMENTS, &c.—Length of head $4\frac{1}{3}$ to $4\frac{3}{4}$, of caudal fin $5\frac{3}{4}$, height of body $3\frac{3}{4}$ to $4\frac{1}{4}$ in the total length. *Eyes*—diameter $6\frac{1}{2}$ to $7\frac{1}{2}$ times in the length of the head (but comparatively larger in the young), $2\frac{1}{4}$ diameters from the end of the snout, and from 2 to $2\frac{1}{4}$ apart. Interorbital space flat. The thickness of the head equals its length excluding the snout, while its height equals its thickness. Snout obtuse, mouth anterior, jaws anteriorly of the same length, gape wide, cleft rather shallow; the posterior extremity of the maxilla reaches to beneath the hind nostrils. Lips thick. *Teeth*—pharyngeal, in a single row, 4 or $\frac{5}{5}$ or 4, sometimes 4 on one side and 5 on the other. *Gill-rakers*—short. *Fins*—dorsal commences above the end of the base of the ventral, and is continued almost to above the origin of the anal: all the fins are rounded. In the males the first or even more of the ventral rays are thicker than in the female. *Scales*—about 18 rows between the lateral-line and the base of the ventral fin. *Lateral-line*—at first gradually descends and above the base of the ventral is continued to the centre of the base of the caudal fin. From the thickness of its skin it is termed the "shoe-maker" in Holland. *Colours*—leaden or greenish, lightest beneath; fins blackish. (Day's *Fishes of Great Britain and Ireland.*)

TENNIS—For the tennis-player imbued with the antiquarian spirit, the early history of this ancient, beautiful, and complicated game—the charm of which is indeed largely due to its complication—has much fascination. But when space is limited, it is impossible adequately to investigate the "palæontology" of a game which was played in France in some form or other so far back as the thirteenth century. In the following century it was introduced into many French towns, and buildings were adapted, or constructed, for the purposes of the game. These were called *tripots*, and we hear of the erection early in the fifteenth century of a *tripot* in Paris in the Rue Grenier Saint Lazare, called Le Petit Temple, in which one Margot, a woman, used to play about 1427, with such skill that she could hold her own with all but the best players of the opposite sex. The game in which she was so proficient is spoken of as "hand-ball," and there is other evidence to show that, up to the beginning of the sixteenth century, the hand had not been entirely superseded by the racket, as the weapon with which the ball was struck. The French names for "Tennis" and "Tennis-player" (*La Paume* and *Paumier* respectively) also indicate that the game was, in early times, played with the *palm* of the hand. The popularity of the pastime was on the increase during the sixteenth and seventeenth centuries. Of the French kings, Henri II. had the reputation of being a great player, and in England Henry VIII. and Charles II. were "distinguished amateurs." About the year 1615, there were fifteen courts in London—at present the number is five—and it is stated, on the authority of the Dutch Ambassador, that, in Paris in 1657, there were "only" 114 tennis courts! Most of these must have been uncovered buildings, roughly constructed, and having but little in common with the highly-finished and well-appointed tennis-court of the present day, the cost of erecting which may be safely estimated to be not less than £2,000.

Counting the two courts at the Queen's Club, two at Prince's Club, and one at Lord's, which is shortly to be taken down and transferred to a site behind the pavilion, there are, at the present time, twelve tennis-courts in England, which are either public or belong to clubs, and, in addition, there are not less than twenty-one private courts. In France the number of courts available for play is much smaller. In Paris there are two; at Fontainebleau, one; at Deauville, one; at Pau, one; at Bordeaux, one: or six in all.

In America there are five well-known courts; two at Boston; one at Chicago; one at New York; one at Newport. In Dublin there is one private court, and in Vienna there is another, but it is stated by a high authority that, "there is no such thing as a court known in modern Italy, Spain, or Germany."

Of the professional tennis-players, who, in modern times, have attained the highest distinction in the tennis-courts at home and abroad, the name of J. Edmond Barre, the great French player, stands pre-eminent. Mr. J. M. Heathcote, an accomplished writer on tennis, and perhaps the greatest of all amateur players of the game, has placed on record his opinion of Barre as being "the finest *all-round* player the world ever produced, or is likely to produce." Barre, who died in 1873, appears, indeed, to have been much superior to any of his contemporaries, and to have enjoyed a special reputation as a match-player of extraordinary staying power, and a remarkable giver of odds. Another great French player is Charles Delahaye, nicknamed "Biboche," who, in his prime, was inferior only to Barre. He has long since been on the retired list; and the leading professional players in Paris, at the present time, are Ferdinand, and G. Lesueur, known as "Le Biscon." Amongst English professionals famous for their achievements during the last fifty years, the names of Edmund Tompkins, George Lambert, Charles Saunders, and Peter Latham, the present champion of the world, may be specially mentioned. The first-named, who was a contemporary of Biboche, was reported to be the equal of the latter, though he never actually defeated and was indeed thrice beaten by, the Frenchman in a formal match. But there is no doubt that he was the strongest of English players for more than twenty years. A similar reputation was enjoyed by George Lambert for some fifteen years, and, in the seventies, the dedans of the tennis-court at Lord's was often crowded by spectators of the matches in which he took a part, and which were lit up by the extraordinary brilliancy of his execution. In May, 1885, Lambert was defeated by T. Pettitt, an Englishman by birth, but domiciled at Boston, United States of America. The match, a memorable one, was the result of a challenge by Pettitt, who was victorious by seven sets to five. In the following year Charles Saunders, at the time a young player of great promise at Prince's Club, Hans Place, became champion of England, as he succeeded in beating George Lambert, who by the way was then in his forty-fifth year. In May, 1890, a match between Saunders and Pettitt for the championship of the world and a stake of £500 was played in Lord Iveagh's court at Dublin, and was won by the latter by seven sets to five. Pettitt thus, for the second time, proved that he was the best player in the world; but in September, 1890, he announced that he should not defend his title of champion, and as at that time Saunders was indisputably second only to Pettitt, he naturally claimed the title renounced by the latter. In March 1895 he was challenged to defend it by Peter Latham, of the Queen's Club. The match was played in the new tennis court ("Prince's") at Brighton, and ended in a victory for the challenger, by seven sets to two. Saunders since then has been in failing health, and has not been able to take any part in public matches. He was never possessed of an exceptional physique, but he will always be remembered as an almost perfect exponent of pure tennis; the grace and finish of his play being especially memorable. Peter Latham, the present champion, is also champion at rackets. This supremacy at two quite distinct games is a special feature of his great reputation. Neither title is held merely because there is no one to dispute it. Last year (1897) the champion at rackets defended *his* title successfully in a home-and-home match with George Standing of New York for £2,000. This year the champion at tennis has been called upon to defend *his* title by F. Pettitt, and the match for a similar stake is to be played at Brighton about the middle of next October. It will be a great match, the result of which will confer, under the special circumstances of the case, an undying reputation on the winner.

For amateurs there are two competitions in which all tennis-players take a keen interest. One is known as the "M.C.C. Challenge Prizes." These were instituted in 1867 by the Marylebone Club. The prizes, known as the "gold" prize and the "silver" prize, are played for annually at Lord's in the months of June and July. In 1896 the competition, which up to that year had been limited to members of the club, was thrown open to the world. From 1867 to 1881 (fifteen consecutive years) Mr. J. M. Heathcote was the winner of the Gold Prize. In 1882 Mr. Alfred Lyttelton, who will always be remembered for his correct, graceful, and withal vigorous style of play, displaced Mr. Heathcote, only to be ousted by him in the following year. Mr. Lyttelton was, however, again the holder in 1884 and 1885, and from 1887 to 1895 retained the coveted distinction without a break. In 1896 he was defeated by Sir Edward Grey, but the latter, in 1897, had to lower his colours to Mr. E. H. Miles, who thus became the holder of the Gold Prize.

The following is a list of the holders of the Gold and Silver Prizes from 1867 to 1897:—

	Gold.	Silver.
1867	Mr. J. M. Heathcote	Mr. Julian Marshall.
1868	Ditto	Mr. G. B Crawley.
1869	Ditto	Hon. C. G. Lyttelton.
1870	Ditto	Ditto.
1871	Ditto	Ditto.
1872	Ditto	Ditto.
1873	Ditto	Ditto.
1874	Ditto	Mr. G. B. Crawley.
1875	Ditto	Ditto.
1876	Ditto	Mr. R. D. Walker.
1877	Ditto	Ditto.
1878	Ditto	Mr. C. E. Boyle.
1879	Ditto	Ditto.
1880	Ditto	Hon. Alfred Lyttelton
1881	Ditto	Ditto.
1882	Hon. Alfred Lyttelton	Mr. J. M. Heathcote.
1883	Mr. J. M. Heathcote	Hon. Alfred Lyttelton
1884	Hon. Alfred Lyttelton	Mr. J. M. Heathcote.
1885	Ditto	Ditto.
1886	Mr. J. M. Heathcote	Mr. B. N. Akroyd.
1887	Hon. Alfred Lyttelton	Mr. J. M. Heathcote.
1888	Hon. Alfred Lyttelton	Mr. A. J. Webbe.
1889	Ditto	Sir Edward Grey.
1890	Ditto	Ditto.
1891	Ditto	Ditto.
1892	Ditto	Mr. H. E. Crawley.
1893	Ditto	Sir Edward Grey.
1894	Ditto	Ditto.
1895	Ditto	Ditto.
1896	Sir Edward Grey	Hon. Alfred Lyttelton.
1897	Mr. E. H. Miles	Sir Edward Grey.

The other competition for amateurs is known as the Tennis Amateur Championship, which, since 1889 has been open to all amateurs. It is played annually at the Queen's Club, West Kensington, in the spring. The first prize goes to the winner, who earns the title of Amateur Champion, and the competitor who is unbeaten by any competitor, except the champion, is awarded the second prize. The following is a list of the winners of the first and second prizes since 1889:—

First Prize.		Second Prize.	
1889	Sir Edward Grey.	1889	Mr. E. B. Curtis.
1890	Mr. E. B. Curtis.	1890	Sir Edward Grey.
1891	Sir Edward Grey.	1891	Lord Windsor.
1892	Mr. H. E. Crawley.	1892	Sir Edward Grey.
1893	Ditto.	1893	Ditto.
1894	Ditto.	1894	Ditto.
1895	Sir Edward Grey.	1895	Mr. H. E. Crawley.
1896	Ditto.	1896	Ditto.
1897	Mr J. Byng Gribble.	1897	Ditto.
1898	Sir Edward Grey.	1898	Ditto.

Single-handed and four-handed matches at tennis between Oxford and Cambridge were begun in the year 1859, and, with the exception of the year 1864, have been annually played up to the present time. Up to this year (1898) Cambridge has won twenty-seven and Oxford twelve, of the four-handed matches; and of the single-handed matches Cambridge has won twenty-eight and Oxford eleven.

The Implements, the Court and the Game—The following is a drawing of the racket used at tennis. In the year 1857 a new method of stringing the racket was introduced, which materially increased its driving power, and was one of the first causes of the

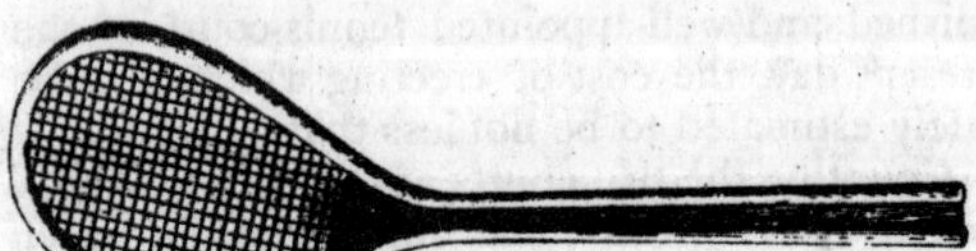

Tennis Racket.

very fast play, which is perhaps the distinctive feature of tennis of the modern type. There is no restriction as to the shape or size of the racket. But its length is usually about 27 inches, and its weight, when properly strung, about sixteen ounces.

Tennis-balls, as used in England, are made, nowadays, entirely of woollen material, and are covered with melton cloth. According to the "Laws of Tennis" they should not be less than $2\frac{1}{4}$ inches and not more than $2\frac{3}{8}$ inches in diameter. Their weight should be not less than $2\frac{1}{2}$ ounces and not more than $2\frac{3}{4}$ ounces. French and American balls are lighter, softer, and "slower" than English balls. It may here be mentioned that the great match, to take place next October at Brighton between Peter Latham the champion, and T. Pettitt of Boston, for the championship of the world and a stake of £1,000 a side, will be played with French balls.

The Court—The floors of the tennis courts at Lord's, the Queen's Club, and Prince's Club are made of blue lias, and as they have been

FIG. 1.—TENNIS COURT, LOOKING TOWARDS THE GRILLE.

much played on and have given general satisfaction, this limestone may be taken to be the most satisfactory material of which to construct the floor of a court. The walls can be built of brick, which should be coated about one inch thick with Portland cement, which need not be made as smooth as possible. It is the opinion of an expert in such matters, who was also a good tennis-player, that "both the floor and walls should have a high degree of elasticity, which is to be obtained by hardness and solidity; that the floor should be smooth, but not polished, and the walls should have a slight degree of roughness, sufficient to give full effect to cut and twist." A general idea of a tennis-court, which is usually a covered building, is given by the annexed sketches of the match-court at the Queen's Club as it is seen from the room or hall in which spectators assemble to witness a match (Fig. 1) and also from the opposite end of the court (Fig. 2). The term "dedans" is a name for this room, and also for the spectators in it, just as the expression "the pit" denotes a particular part of a theatre, and also the audience there seated. The wall marked A is called the main-wall; that marked B, the side-wall; that marked C, the end-wall (Figs. 1 and 2). An inner-wall, usually seven feet high, runs round three sides of the building, and is connected with the side-wall and end-walls by a sloping wooden roof, called the pent-house. The portion of the inner-wall under the end-wall, marked C, is named the *grille*-wall (Fig. 1). In the latter is a square opening called the *grille* (D). Between the grille and the *tambour* (E) the main-wall is thickened. The *tambour* is a kind of buttress, or projection, which, when struck, deflects the ball, and thus gives variety to the play. The openings in the inner-wall, under the side-wall, are called *galleries*. The opening (Fig. 2) at the end of the service-side of the court in the inner-wall, opposite the grille-wall, is called the dedans (F), along the back of which runs a stout net, behind which the spectators sit, in the room abovementioned. Across the court, at a point equidistant from the end-walls, and parallel to them, is hung a net (G), the height of which should be 5 feet at each end, and 3 feet at the middle. The half of the court between the end-wall over the dedans and the net is called the *service-side*: the other half is called the *hazard-side*. On the service-side the gallery furthest from the net is called the last-gallery, the one next to it the second-gallery, then comes the gallery called the "door," and then the first-gallery. In the space between the first-gallery and the post to which one end of the net is fastened, stands the marker. On the hazard-side there are corresponding galleries. Of these the one which is most remote from the net is often called the "winning-gallery," because a ball struck into it at once wins the

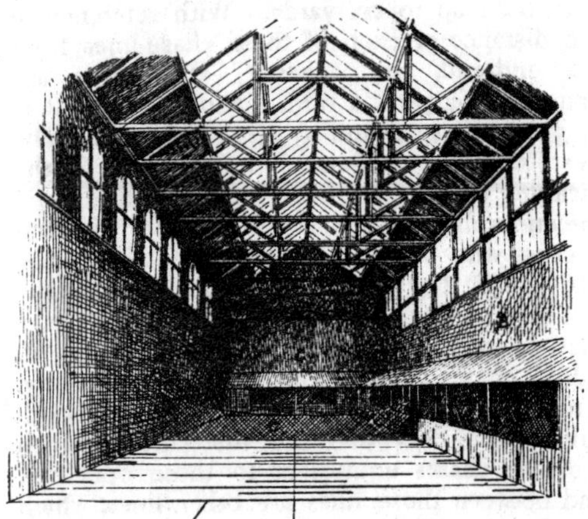

FIG. 2.—TENNIS COURT, LOOKING TOWARDS THE DEDANS.

stroke, just as it wins it when struck into the grille, or dedans.

Turning now to the floor of the court, the following lines painted on it deserve particular attention. (See ground plan.)

The half-court-line, drawn parallel with the side-walls, dividing the court lengthways into practically two equal parts.

The service-line, drawn parallel with the end-wall on the hazard-side, at a distance of 21 feet from it.

The pass-line, drawn from the service-line to the end-wall, parallel with the half-court line, at a distance of 7 feet from it. With reference to these lines, the service-court is the area enclosed by the service-line, the pass-line, the end-wall, and the side-wall. The pass-court is the area enclosed by the pass-line, the service-line, the end-wall, and the main-wall.

In addition to the above, lines are drawn on the floor parallel with the end-walls, which are termed the *chase-lines*. The number of these on the service-side exceeds those on the hazard-side, as there are none on the latter side, between

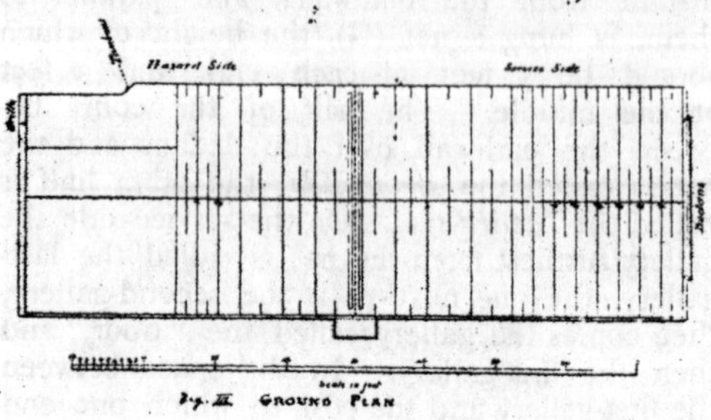

FIG. 3.—GROUND PLAN OF COURT.

the service-line and the grille wall. On the service-side the first chase-line is half a yard from the end-wall, the second one yard, the third a yard and a half, the fourth two yards, and so on up to six yards. With reference to the distance of each of these chase-lines from the end-wall, the "chases" themselves are named half-a-yard, a yard, 1 and 2, 2, 2 and 3, 3, 3 and 4, 4, 4 and 5, 5, 5 and 6, 6. The next chase is half-a-yard worse than 6, the meaning of "worse" here being "farther from the end-wall," just as the word "better" in connection with the chase means "nearer to the end-wall." The next lines are, one opposite the last gallery which denotes a chase equivalent to that opening, and another a yard beyond it, called chase a yard worse than last gallery. Similar lines are drawn opposite the second-gallery, the door and the first-gallery, which indicate chases equivalent to those openings, and between those lines are other lines, which enable the marker to pronounce whether a chase, for instance, is worse than the second-gallery, or better than the door.

The chases on the other side of the net are called hazard-side chases. They start from the service-line, and are named, the first half-a-yard, the second a yard, the third one and two, the fourth two. Then follow the lines which indicate chases equivalent to the openings, second-gallery, the door, and the first-gallery and, in addition, the line midway between those lines.

With regard to "the chase," Mr. J. M. Heathcote has humorously observed that it is "an expression which is to the uninitiated what the 'rule in Shelley's case' is to the law student." The expression is used with reference to the second contact of the ball with the floor, called the *fall* of the ball, at any point where chase-lines are painted, as distinguished from its first bound or contact, called the *drop* of the ball. A chase is also made if the ball enters any of the openings or galleries, except the dedans, grille and winning-gallery. Speaking of the chases on the service-side of the court, the author above quoted thus explains how they are played for and how the "winning" or "losing" of them affects the score.

"When the server mistrusts his ability to return the first or any subsequent stroke of a 'rest,' or when he perceives that the ball will 'fall' far before it reaches the main-wall, or will return far from it, making in either case what is called a 'long chase,' he makes no effort to return it; the marker observes where the ball 'falls,' and calls a chase at the spot where it has 'fallen,' *e.g.* if the ball falls on the 2 line, he calls 'chase 2'; if in the interval between '1 and 2,' and 2, he calls 'better than 2'; if in the interval between 2 and '2 and 3' he calls 'worse than 2,' &c.,; no stroke is scored, but the opponents 'change sides,' and 'play for the chase.' The player who made the chase—now the 'server'—tries to 'defend' it; his antagonist, now the 'striker-out,' tries to win it. A chase is *won* if the ball enters the dedans, or it it 'falls nearer to the end-wall than the ball which made the chase fell; it is *lost* if the ball 'falls' further from the end-wall than the ball which made the chase fell."

If the reader carefully reads the Laws of Tennis set out below, in connection with the above explanation and the description of the following illustrative "games," he will probably be able to understand and follow a match between two good players with little difficulty, and derive therefrom almost as much pleasure as if he were playing himself.

The three following "games" are meant for the "uninitiated," and are, therefore, not described in language of too technical a nature. They are intended to be fair specimens of games which might be played by any two players in a tennis-court.

GAME I.

(*In which no chases are made.*)

The players X and Y enter the court from the side-passage, by a door, in front of which the marker stands. X spins his racket on the floor for choice of sides, and Y calls "rough," that being the name for the side of the racket which shows the knots of the strings, while "smooth" indicates the other side. X, having won the spin, usually chooses the service-side of the court, and delivers the first service. Y fails to return the ball over the net. The marker calls out "15–love." X serves again. Y returns the ball. X striking the ball, on the volley or after the first bound, makes it enter the grille. The marker calls out "30–love." X now serves two faults. Y therefore wins a stroke, and the marker, who names first the last stroke won, calls out "15–30." Y now succeeds in striking the next service he receives into the dedans: 30 all. But in the next rest X "finds the winning-gallery," that is, succeeds in hitting the ball into that opening: 40–30. The next stroke, if won by X, would give him the game, but he loses it, as he hits the ball out of play (*see* Law 10) after Y has returned it. The marker therefore calls out "deuce." Neither player can now secure the game until he wins two consecutive strokes. The next stroke won by either player is called "advantage." If the same player wins the following stroke, the marker calls out "game." If he loses it the marker calls out "deuce." The score can thus alternate between "deuce" and "advantage" an indefinite number of times. X at last delivers a "nick-service," which Y cannot return, and then X finds the grille. The result is that X wins the game, and the players are left as they were when it was begun, that is, X is still the server and Y the striker-out.

Game II.

(*Illustrating "playing for chases" made on the service-side from the hazard-side.*)

X continues to serve. Y returns the first service so that X cannot reach the ball. The marker, seeing that it "falls" (*i.e.*, comes into contact with the floor for the second time) on the line numbered 2, calls out "chase 2." X serves again, and this time the ball from Y's racket enters the second-gallery. The marker calls out "chase second-gallery." Y has now made two chases, the first a good or "short" one, the second a bad or "long" one, and the players change sides to "play for them." Y is now the server, X the striker-out. The first chase made is the first played for, and the marker, to remind the players what they have to do, calls out, "chase 2." Y serves and X returns the ball. Y, watching the ball carefully, sees that it will "fall" further from the end-wall than 2. He therefore leaves it alone, and the marker calls out "lost it." This means that X has lost the chase, and Y's score is therefore credited with a stroke: 15–0. The second chase is now played for, and the marker again reminds the players what they have to do by calling out "chase second-gallery." This time X, either with his first stroke or (it may be) after several returns on both sides, strikes the ball into the "door." The marker calls out "lost it," and another stroke is added to Y's score: 30–0. Had X won both chases by succeeding in making his ball "fall" *better* (that is, nearer the end-wall) than 2, and better than second-gallery respectively, *his*—and not Y's—score would have been 30–0. With the strokes 30–0 in his favour, Y now delivers a service which X fails to return: 40–0. But off the next service X "lays down" or "makes" chase a yard. As the strokes are 40–0, and the next stroke may be decisive of the game, the players change sides again to play for the chase. The position now is that X is again the server, and Y has to try and win a very short chase. As X carelessly, or unskilfully, delivers a service which gives a good opportunity for finding the dedans with either a "straight" or "boasted" force, Y does not attempt to win the chase on the floor, but "goes for" the dedans, and if the ball enters it, he wins the chase, the stroke, and the game. If, however, X succeeds in "stopping" the ball, that is, prevents it from entering the dedans, and returns it so that his opponent fails again to return it, he is said to "successfully defend" the chase, and the marker calls the score 15–40. Assuming this to be the state of the score, X continues to serve, and Y establishes a short chase, viz., chase 1 and 2. With the strokes 40–15 in his favour, Y must now cross over to defend, and X to attack this chase. Y serves, and X's return of the ball "falls" in chase 2, that is, worse than the chase played for, and the marker calls out "lost it." Y therefore wins the chase, the stroke, and the game, in which his opponent has scored only one stroke.

Game III.

(*Illustrating "playing for chases" made on the hazard-side from the service-side.*)

At the beginning of the third game Y is on the service-side and X on the hazard-side. In the course of a rest, the former hits the ball hard on to the tambour. The ball is sharply deflected, and, after "dropping," rises from the floor, touches the battery-wall, that is, the wall under the galleries, and eventually "falls" on the line indicating chase a yard on the hazard-side. The marker calls out "chase hazard a yard." A similar stroke by Y results in the ball falling on the line which indicates chase half a yard on the hazard-side. The marker calls out "chase hazard half a yard." Two hazard-side chases have now been made by Y, and the players change sides to play for them. As was the case when chases on the service-side came to be contested, the marker, before X delivers the service, calls out distinctly the name of the first hazard-side chase, and when that is lost or won, the name of the second. Supposing that Y successfully defends both chases, his score stands at 30–0. He now, being on the hazard-side, makes chase better than 3, and X then from the service-side strikes the ball into the second-gallery hazard-side, thus making the chase so named. Though the first chase has been made by one player on the service-side, and the second by the other on the hazard-side, there are, nevertheless, two chases established, and the players must change sides to play for them. The reader and the players must remember all this time that the strokes, as the result of the play in connection with the first two hazard-side chases, are 30–0 in favour of Y, who has now first to defend chase better than 3. This he succeeds in doing by delivering such a service that X can with difficulty return it, and indeed only just gets the ball over the net, so that the chase is easily lost: 40–0. Y has now to attack the hazard-side chase. This he can best do by endeavouring to deliver a "nick-service," and, if he does so, he wins the chase, the stroke, and the game, in which his opponent has failed to score a single stroke.

To players, as distinguished from spectators, the following is tendered as practical advice, which may be of service to them when they first begin to play tennis.

(1) Remember always to serve carefully with reference to the chase which is being played for, whether it be a chase on the service-side which you are defending, or one on the hazard-side which you are attacking.

(2) Be on your guard against forgetting altogether in the excitement of a long rest, the fact that you are *defending or attacking a chase.* When defending chases, especially, beginners are liable, in their excitement, to return, or attempt to return, a ball which would have "lost the chase."

(3) Remember that a chase on the service-side is successfully defended by striking the ball into any of the openings on the hazard-side, and that a chase on the hazard-side is successfully defended by striking the ball into any of the openings on the service-side.

(4) Do not attempt to play games at all until you have had at least a dozen lessons from a competent teacher, who will show you how to hold your racket, how to hit the ball with the proper "stroke," and (a matter of the greatest importance) how to serve in one or more of the orthodox modes of delivering the service.

G. E. A. Ross.

The Laws of Tennis—(In force at Lord's and published with the kind permission of the M.C.C.):—

THE LAWS OF TENNIS.

The tennis court at Lord's is of the following dimensions:—

Area of floor—

Length	96 ft. 6 in.	}	ft. super.
Width	32 ft. 0 in.	} =	3088
At the tambour.	30 ft. 7 in.	} Ddt. tambour =	23
			3065

Area of court, including penthouse—

Length . . .	111 ft. 3 in.	} = 4338 ft. 9 in. super.
Width	39 ft. 0 in.	}

Height of court (to tie-beam) . . .	30 ft.	0 in.
Height of play-line	17 ft.	6 in.
Height of upper edge of penthouse .	10 ft.	9 in.
Height of lower edge of penthouse . .	7 ft.	1 in.
Angle of penthouse roof	29°	
Height of upper edge of openings	6 ft.	10 in.
Height of lower edge of openings	3 ft.	7½ in.
Width of dedans.	22 ft.	7 in.
Width of grille	3 ft.	1 in.
Width of last gallery (service side) .	9 ft.	9 in.
Width of second gallery ,, ,,	9 ft.	6 in.
Width of the door ,, ,,	3 ft.	5 in.
Width of first gallery ,, ,,	5 ft.	7 in.
Width of centre opening . ,,	7 ft.	11 in.
Width of last gallery (hazard side) .	9 ft.	6 in.
Width of second gallery ,, ,,	9 ft.	9 in.
Width of the door ,, ,,	3 ft.	5 in.
Width of first gallery ,, ,,	5 ft.	7 in.
The net is hung exactly across the middle of the court, from the centre post to the wall; its height at each extremity is	4 ft.	7½ in.
In the centre	3 ft.	0 in.

The last gallery line	21 ft.	5 in.	from dedans
The second gallery line . . .	30 ft.	4 in.	,,
The door line	36 ft.	2 in.	,,
The first gallery line . . .	42 ft.	7 in.	,,
The line.	47 ft.	4 in.	,,
The last gallery (hazard side) line	20 ft.	6 in.	from penthouse
The second gallery ,, ,, .	30 ft.	10 in.	,,
The door ,, ,, .	37 ft.	2 in.	,,
The first gallery ,, ,, .	43 ft.	8 in.	,,
The line ,, ,, .	48 ft.	4 in.	,,

The pass line is 7 ft. 8 in. from the main wall.

The fly nets are 8 ft. long and 4 ft. 7 in. high, with the exception of the one above the tambour, which is 10 ft. long and 4 ft. 10 in. high.

The racket is about 2 ft. 2 in. in length; the head 9 in. in length and 5¾ in. in width.

The balls weigh 2½ oz., and are 2¼ in. in diameter.

THE COURT, AND THE TERMS USED IN THE GAME.

1. The court is divided into two equal parts by a net, and a line painted on the penthouse. At one end is a gallery for spectators, open to the court, but guarded by a net, called the "dedans." The half court nearest the dedans is called the "service side;" the other half is called the "hazard side." The player on the service side is called "the server"; the player on the hazard side, "the striker out."

2. The court is also divided lengthways into two equal parts by a line painted on the floor and end walls.

3. The long side passage open to the court, and guarded by a net, is divided into a centre compartment, called the line (where there are the centre post, the marker's place, and the entrance to the court), and four other compartments on each side, divided by posts and nets. Counting from the line, the compartments are thus named—the first gallery; the door; the second gallery; the last gallery. Counting from the centre post, the posts are thus named—the line post; the first gallery post; the door post; the second gallery post.

4. Parallel lines for the purpose of marking the yard and gallery chases, and half lines for the half yard chases, are painted across the floor of the court.

5. The pass line is painted at right angles from the last gallery (hazard side) line to the end wall near the grille.

6. The "grille" is the square opening at the end of the hazard side of the court.

7. The "penthouse" is the sloping roof of the dedans, galleries, and grille, extending along three sides of the court.

8. The "main wall" is that opposite the penthouse.

9. The "tambour" is the projection in the main wall on the hazard side.

10. The line of play is defined by a painted line below the windows along the side walls. A ball which touches the walls above the line of play, or the roof or the rafters,

or the window nets (with the exception of the four double nets, called the fly nets, at each corner of the court), or the centre post, or goes over the rafters, is out of play.

11. In the following rules, the term "where a ball falls" is to be taken as meaning where the ball after being struck by one player falls untouched by the other on to the floor after its first bound.

12. To "return" a ball is to play it back over the centre net before it has touched the floor a second time.

13. The dimensions of the court and lines of play are given as they exist in the court at Lord's, but are not laid down as arbitrary.

The Game.

14. Tennis is played by the "set." The player who first wins six games wins the set.

15. A player who wins six games consecutively wins a love set, even though his adversary may have previously won one or more games.

16. The game contains four points, thus scored—15, 30, 40, game.

17. But if both players reach the third point or 40 together, the score is called "deuce." Another point called "vantage" is then introduced, and a player, in order to score "game," must win two points in succession, *i.e.*, "vantage" and "game." Otherwise, though he may have won "vantage," if he should lose the next stroke, the score returns to "deuce."

18. The vantage set is played on the same principle. When the players are at five games all, one player must win two successive games to win the set; otherwise, though he may have won the vantage game, if he should lose the next game, the score reverts to games all.

19. Vantage sets are only played with the consent of both players.

The Service.

20. The service shall be given from any part of the service side of the court.

21. The ball shall be served either directly on to the roof of the side penthouse, or the wall above it, so that it shall strike the roof of the said penthouse on the hazard side of the court, and shall drop on to the floor within the space formed by the penthouse walls and the "last gallery" and "pass" lines. It is otherwise a "pass" or a "fault."

22. If the service, though good in other respects, shall drop over the pass line, it shall be called a "pass."

23. A "pass" shall not neutralise a previous fault.

24. If the service shall bound untouched from the space above named and shall fall over the last gallery line or into any of the hazard side galleries (excepting the last gallery, when it shall be scored as a point to the server), a "chase" shall be called.

25. The server shall not serve until the striker-out shall be prepared, but if the striker-out shall take or attempt to return the service, it shall be treated as good.

The Chase.

26. When a ball shall fall on to the floor [excepting that part of it between the end wall and the last gallery "(hazard side)" line], a "chase" shall be called.

27. If a ball shall be struck, untouched, into any of the galleries [excepting the last gallery (hazard side)], a "chase" shall also be called.

28. The chase shall be marked according to the distance from the end wall, on that side of the court in which the ball shall have fallen, or the gallery into which it shall have been struck.

29. The nearer the ball shall fall to the end wall, the "better" shall be the chase.

30. The chase is a stroke left undecided until the players shall have changed sides and played for it.

31. The chase lines and half lines on the service side, counting from the dedans, shall be called in their order of merit:—

Half-a-yard.	Five and six.
A yard.	Six.
One and two.	Half-a-yard worse than six.
Two.	Last gallery.
Two and three.	Yard worse than last gallery.
Three.	Second gallery.
Three and four.	The door.
Four.	First gallery.
Four and five.	The line.
Five.	

32. Those on the hazard side, counting from the last gallery line, shall be called in their order of merit:—

Half-a-yard.	Second gallery.
A yard.	Door.
One and two.	First gallery.
Two.	The line.

33. When the ball shall have fallen on an intermediate space between any of these lines, the chase shall be called "better" or "worse" than the nearest line to which the ball shall have fallen, according as it may have been nearer or further from the dedans, or end wall on the hazard side. But with the exception of "better than half-a-yard" and "better than half-a-yard hazard side," chases shall not be called better or worse than the half lines.

34. When two chases shall have been made, the players shall change sides; but if one chase shall have been made when either player shall be at 40 or vantage, the players shall then change sides, because one point only is required to win the game.

35. To win a chase, a better chase (or a winning point) must be made by the player who did not originally make the chase which is being played for.

36. If the ball shall fall on to the same line, or into the same gallery as the chase which is being played for, it shall be called "chase off," *i.e.*, no point shall be scored, and the chase shall not again be played for.

37. If a ball shall be struck into the opposite court and, having touched the floor in that court, shall fall in the court from which it was played, it shall be called "chase the line."

Points.

38. The "server" shall win a stroke and score one point—

- If the "striker-out" shall fail to return his service (unless it shall have made a hazard side chase).
- If the "striker-out" shall fail to win a chase.
- If the "server" shall strike a ball into the "grille," or hazard side last gallery, or so that it shall fall within or on the hazard side last gallery line.
- If he shall win a chase.
- If in serving the ball shall drop into the hazard side last gallery.

39. The "striker-out" shall win a stroke and score one point—

- If he shall strike a ball into the dedans.
- If he shall win a chase.
- If the "server" shall make two successive faults.
- If the "server" shall fail to win a chase.

40. Either player shall win a stroke and score one point—

- If his adversary shall strike the ball in play without returning it over the net.
- If his adversary shall strike a ball so that it shall be out of play, or shall strike the ball twice.
- If his adversary shall strike a ball into the opposite court so that it shall return over the line without having touched the floor.
- If a ball in play shall touch his adversary on the hand or any other part of his person or clothes.

General Rules.

41. The players shall toss for choice of sides before the first set. In subsequent sets, they shall continue to occupy the positions they held at the end of the preceding set.

42. No ball shall be played after it shall have entered the dedans, grille, or any of the galleries or doors or touched any of the posts, or any article which may be in the dedans, grille or galleries.

43. If a ball shall touch the post of the dedans, it shall be marked as if it had entered the dedans.

44. If a ball shall touch the post of a gallery, it shall be marked as if it had entered that gallery.

45. The marker shall call the state of the game as it proceeds, so as to give the players continuous information.

46. He shall call each "fault" or "pass" as soon as it shall have been made; and in all cases of doubt shall instantly call "Play" or otherwise, as the case may be.

47. He shall call the chases to the best of his judgment as soon as made or decided; and shall direct the players when to change sides, again calling the chases to be played for, and the state of the game before another service is given.

48. His decision shall be final in all cases, unless, before the commencement of a match, either player shall require an appeal in doubtful cases against the decisions of the marker.

49. The appeal shall be to the dedans, or to an umpire or umpires.

50. The appeal shall be made before play is recommenced.

51. The marker shall be entitled, if in doubt, to appeal to the dedans or umpires.

52. The marker shall in no case be allowed to bet on the game he is marking.

The Rules for Double Matches

shall be the same as those for single matches, with the following additions:—

53. Unless agreed to the contrary, the partners shall serve and strike out in alternate games.

54. The partner who begins to serve shall continue to do so through that game, and the same rule shall apply to the striker-out, but this shall not prevent the latter from leaving the service to his partner if it can be more conveniently taken by him.

55. In other respects the partners shall play as they may think most advantageous to them.

Odds.

56. The following odds may be given in a set at tennis:—

57. A "bisque"—One point, which may be taken at the option of the player receiving it at any time during a set. One or more bisques may be given in addition to other odds, or may be received in reduction of odds, *e.g.*, half fifteen for a bisque. A bisque shall not be taken after the ball has been served, nor after a fault.

58. Half fifteen—One point at the beginning of the second game and every alternate game.

59. Fifteen—One point at the beginning of every game.

60. Half thirty—One point at the beginning of the first and every alternate game, and two points in the intermediate games.

61. Thirty—Two points at the beginning of every game.

62. Half forty—Two points the first and alternate games, three points the other games.

63. Forty—Three points in every game.

Cramped Odds.

64. Round services—The service of the player who gives these odds must strike both the side and end penthouses.

65. Half the court—The player who gives these odds may choose into which half of the court on either side he will play, and must play each ball so that it shall drop into this half court, or a point is scored to his adversary. His service is not limited to this half court. The post of the dedans and the line which divides the court are included in this half court.

66. Touch no walls—The player who gives these odds must confine his play solely to the floor (service only excepted) on penalty of losing a point.

67. Bar the openings—The player who gives these odds loses a point if he strikes the ball into the dedans, grille, or any of the galleries.

68. Bar the winning openings—The player who gives these odds loses a point if he strikes the ball into the dedans, grille, or last gallery, hazard side.

69. Side walls—The player who gives these odds must confine his play to the floor, the end walls and end penthouses, and dedans, or grille, or a point is scored to his adversary.

70. In giving cramped odds, a player does not lose a point if the ball goes out of his limits after it has touched the ground a second time.

71. The values of the several kinds of cramped odds vary according to the proficiency or style of the players. The following may be considered approximately their values:—

Round services = Half fifteen.
Half the court = Half thirty and a bisque.
Touch no walls = Forty.
Bar the openings = Half fifteen and a bisque.
Bar the winning openings = Half fifteen for a bisque.
Side walls = Half thirty and a bisque.

(Signed) Spencer Ponsonby.
J. M. Heathcote.
E. Chandos Leigh.
W. Hart Dyke.
C. G. Lyttelton.

April 24th, 1872.

TIGER (*Felis tigris*)—**Habitat**—The tiger is peculiar to Asia. It is not found in Ceylon, Afghanistan, Beloochistan or Tibet. It occurs in Northern Persia, Burmah, Java, the Malay Peninsula, Central Asia, Siberia, Manchuria and China, and is generally distributed throughout India in suitable localities. It has within living memory been shot in Sind, but is now extinct there, as well as in a great part of Western India, including Cutch, Kattywar and many of the Bombay districts. In the Island of Salsette, close to Bombay, there are still a few, and one was shot there in January, 1898.

India is the country above all others where tigers have been pursued and their habits observed by generations of sportsmen, and whence our knowledge of the animal is almost entirely derived.

Natural history—Indian tigers appear to be smaller than the tigers which inhabit the colder climates of Central Asia and Northern China; the latter carry much longer and handsomer coats than those inhabiting a hotter country, and the male tiger has a ruff of long hair on the neck, which the female is without. The pug or footprint of an old male tiger can easily be distinguished from that of a tigress, not only by its size, but by its squarer shape, that of a tigress being more oval. The footprints of a young male are of the same shape and size as those of an adult tigress. Those of a male cub are always a good deal larger than the footprints of his twin sister.

The period of gestation is stated to be fourteen or fifteen weeks, and I believe that more female cubs are born than males. There is no particular season for breeding, but in India most cubs are born from December to June. Tigers are monogamous, in the sense that they consort with one female at a time, but it is doubtful whether they live with the same tigress for any lengthened period. Though tiger and tigress are often together in a beat, they are more usually found alone. While the cubs are young, the male is not with them, indeed it is said that he will devour them; but when well grown, an old male will frequently be found with the tigress and cubs, though whether he is their father, or the expectant father of the next batch, it is difficult to say. A tigress seldom rears more than two cubs at a time. Occasionally they bring up three and still more rarely four. The late Major A. H. S. Neill, of the Central India Horse, told me he once cut out six unborn cubs from the body of a tigress that had been shot. The cubs stop with their mother till they are nearly, if not quite, full grown, and she is supposed not to breed again during this period, but I know of an instance of a tigress having cubs while her former family was still with her. I once saw four old male tigers together, amongst the same mass of rocks, to which they had evidently been attracted by a tigress. When they were shot, it turned out, on a *post-mortem* examination of their stomachs, that two had the previous night killed and eaten a sambur, the third had eaten a bullock, while the fourth was quite empty: there were thus three different sets of tigers that had met. In the beat the two that had eaten the sambur came together, the others separately. The tigress was heard calling the same day, and was killed two days afterwards. I have several times seen fresh claw and tooth wounds on tigers, but this particular lot of four had not been fighting.

Dimensions—Sportsmen are by no means agreed as to the length of tigers: there are some who maintain that tigers attain the length of 12 feet or more; others, of whom the writer is one, say that Indian tigers over 10 feet are very uncommon. In measuring, the tiger should be laid flat on its side and pulled out so as to lie as straight as possible. The tape should then be run from the tip of the nose over the head between the ears and along the backbone to the end of the tail, and it is allowable to follow any slight curve there may be of the body. It may confidently be asserted that the vast majority of tigers in the south of Bengal are under 9 feet 6 inches in length. Many are under 9 feet and not one in fifty is over 10 feet. The tail usually measures a little less than a third of the total length. The skin of a 10-foot tiger will, when properly stretched and dried, measure 12 feet or thereabouts. The skin of a 12-foot tiger would be upwards of 14 feet when stretched. Can any one produce the skin of an Indian tiger that measures so much, or even 13 feet? A very few inches in length makes a great difference in the bulk, weight and general appearance of a tiger, and one of 9 feet 6 inches looks far larger than one of 9 feet. The tigress measures from 8 feet 3 inches to 8 feet 9 inches; she is rarely over 9 feet, and occasionally a full grown one may be a little under 8 feet The skull of an old tiger is readily distinguishable from that of a young one. The older it gets, the more prominent is the ridge of bone that runs along the top of the brain pan. In a young adult this is hardly noticeable; in a very old one it is prominent. In an old skull in my possession it is an inch in height.

The canine teeth are also a sure test of age. In the young adult they are hollow throughout and the base is open. In an aged animal the base gets completely closed, and the fang, so far as it protrudes from the gum, is almost solid.

The weight of tigers is not often taken, for the necessary appliances are too cumbrous to find a place in the equipment of most shikaris. The Maharaja of Cooch Behar, in a letter to the *Asian* in 1893, gave the weights of twelve tigers which varied from 445 lbs. to 536 lbs., the latter being the weight of a 10 feet tiger. Another 10 feet tiger weighed 453 lbs.; a 10 feet 2 inches tiger weighed 445 lbs.; two tigresses weighed 360 and 343 lbs. respectively. No two tigers are marked alike; young tigers are handsomer than old ones; their colouring is more vivid and the stripes darker and closer together. A very old tiger has fewer stripes and these are more faintly marked. The rich tawny orange colour, too, becomes of a pale yellow.

Man-eaters—Man-eaters are erroneously supposed to be old and worn out tigers that are unable to catch their ordinary prey, and the legend runs that a human diet has the effect of making their skins mangy.

No doubt some old tigers, or those that have been partially disabled by a wound, take to man-eating, but many man-eaters are in the prime of life and have splendid coats. Man-eaters do not confine themselves entirely to human food, but prey on animals as well, and are not more dangerous than any other tiger to beat for. They develop wonderful cunning, and evade pursuit in an astonishing manner. The natives believe that the ghosts of his human victims ride on the man-eater's head, to point out danger; and in one instance where a shikari had been a victim they were convinced that it was useless to try and circumvent the animal, as the shikari's ghost was up to all the dodges.

Methods of seizing the prey—Opinions

differ as to how a tiger seizes his prey, some alleging that he seizes by the throat, others by the back of the neck. My own view is that they usually seize by the throat, and occasionally by the nape of the neck. In the latter case the kill is of small height, such, for instance, as a pig. I only once remember seeing a bullock that had been seized by the back of the neck.

As might be expected, the throat is not always seized with mathematical accuracy. The holes made by the fangs on one side may be found close under the ear, while on the other side the holes will be near the bottom of the jaw.

Tigers occasionally attack powerful animals. I know an instance of an old solitary bull bison (the Gaur) killed by one, and I shot a solitary old bull buffalo that a few days previously had had a tiger on his hind quarters; in this case the tiger's teeth had been fixed into the back near the tail; and the claws on each quarter. Tigers frequently kill the wild boar, and cases have occurred where both boar and tiger have been found dead together. A tiger, when he kills, seldom eats at the spot, but drags away the animal for some distance. I do not think he ever lifts a heavy animal off the ground. He begins to eat at the hind quarters, and will often finish both hind legs of a bullock at one meal. The Indian bullock, however, is not a large animal. If there is good cover and water near, he will lie up all day close to the kill, but sometimes a tiger will go a long way from his kill to quite another jungle. The next night he returns and drags the remains of the carcass forty yards or more from where it lies, and eats most or all of what remains. He stops about in the neighbourhood for two or three more days, and does not trouble to hunt for some time, though, if he gets the chance, he will kill again. Tigers will eat a dead animal they may find, although they have not killed it themselves. Though this has been disputed, it is beyond doubt. They take readily to water, and are fond in hot weather of lying in shallow pools.

Tiger-hunting—When after tiger, it is usual to tie out bullocks or young buffaloes in several different directions within a radius of ten miles or so from camp. These are visited in the early morning, and news of a kill (if there be one) should reach the camp by 9 a.m. The best time for the beat is in the heat of the day. If the kill is in cover, the vultures will not have found it; if visible to them they will have collected. If they are on the kill, the tiger is sure to have gone, for they do not venture to descend if the tiger is anywhere near, but patiently wait on the trees around. The tiger sometimes kills a rash one that alights.

To arrange the beat properly is more than half the battle. The first thing to consider is the point for which the tiger is likely to make, for when moved he will not rush off aimlessly in any direction, but is sure to have some other resort, to which he will make his way, and he is more easily driven in this direction than in any other. The guns should therefore be placed on his presumed line of retreat. It is necessary to place stops on each side of the beat about seventy yards apart, so as to form a funnel, as it were, leading up to the gun. With a knowledge of the ground and the stops well placed, it is quite feasible to bring the tiger up to within twenty yards of a single gun, and that from a distance of half a mile or more. Of course, the more guns there are, the easier it becomes to bring the tiger within shot of one or other of them. (Trees will occasionally be seen clawed by a tiger to the height of ten feet or so. He rears himself against the tree, and draws his claws down through the bark, in order, it is said, to clean them, though I incline to think it is done in play.) The stops are men placed in trees, whose duty it is to remain silent as long as the tiger is taking the proper direction, but, should he attempt to pass through the line of stops, the stop he approaches gives two or three quiet taps with the back of his axe on the tree, which usually turn the tiger back; he may then try the other side, when, again hearing a tap, back he goes. Should, however, he persist in breaking out, the stops on the side through which he is going, set up a perfect rattle of taps and shouts, which often sends him back with a roar. Sometimes he breaks through and escapes: but if all goes well he comes up to the gun, probably at a walk or a slow trot, stopping every now and again to listen to the beat, affording an easy shot. Should he have been turned by the stops nearest to the gun he may pass at full gallop. The most difficult shot is when he comes full speed immediately under the tree in which the sportsman sits. As soon as the shot is fired, the shouts of the beaters redouble. They should then be quiet for a few minutes, so as to hear a whistle which the sportsman should blow, if the tiger is not dead, or has not passed him. If no whistle is sounded, they can safely come on and beat the jungle out. On no account should the beat be allowed to come on if the tiger has gone back, or is lying wounded between the gun and the beat. If the tiger is lying wounded beyond the gun, the beat should be stopped 150 yards from where one sits. No attempt should ever be made to beat out a wounded tiger, nor any beaters allowed to go near any jungle where he may be. Two or three men should have been placed in trees 200 yards behind, who will be able to give valuable information as to whether the tiger has gone on, or (as often happens when he is badly hit) lain down soon after passing the gun. When the beat is stopped, your head man will approach, and, standing far off, receive instructions in what direction he can safely come to you. Now comes the only dangerous part of tiger shooting,

—tracking a wounded one on foot. One should wait half-an-hour before commencing to do so, as this gives the tiger an opportunity of expiring. Some advocate following up a wounded tiger with a number of men in a close group immediately behind the gun, the idea being that a tiger will not charge home into a crowd. This is true enough, but at the first growl your group bolts. Personally I prefer three or four reliable men who will move on quietly with you. If a tiger has merely a flesh wound through the leg, or one that does not sicken nor partially disable him, he probably will not charge until he has been put up several times; he sees you long before you are near him, and moves quietly off, leaving a blood-stained patch where he has lain down. If shot through the stomach he is pretty sure to charge. As he sees you getting near where he is lying, he usually growls, the sound appearing to come from quite a different direction from the real spot. He may move on, but if not he comes at you with a "wouf, wouf" at full speed, and it is then that accidents happen. Sometimes a tiger will charge from 100 yards, but more frequently he waits till one is quite close before he charges. It is very difficult to see a tiger in jungle before he moves. Nine tigers out of ten are killed at the first shot, for they are usually fired at from a secure position at very close quarters.

When a tiger is shot at, he bolts forward in the direction in which his head points; and it is a safe rule, if on the ground, to let him pass you before firing, as he then goes straight on. If the shot knocks him down, he rolls about on the ground, and, if he is able to get up again, his head may be pointing in any direction and you may find yourself right in his path. This is one reason why the gun should always be posted on a tree or a rock if possible. Another reason is that when one is ten feet or so off the ground, one has a much better view of the jungle and is also more out of the line of sight of the tiger. If one is on the ground in front of him, he will see the slightest movement and turn off. As a rule they do not look upwards, but even in a tree a sudden motion may attract his attention, and I have seen a tiger that has been turned by stops standing and looking up into the trees before him as he came on. Again, if two guns are posted on the ground the one that fires the shot is safe, but the other may be directly in the path of the wounded tiger bolting.

A comfortable seat in the tree is necessary for good shooting, as one may be an hour or more in position before the beat commences. A native charpoy or bedstead tied up makes a good one. Another, which is put up easily and with less noise, is a piece of thick leather two feet square, in the middle of which is sewn a cushion of raw cotton covered with canvas. Eyelet holes are made in the edges, through which a rope is passed, leaving a long piece of rope four feet long at each corner, by which it can be tied to the branches. There is some art in tying it so as to be quite firm.

Here one can sit with the legs dangling until the beat commences, when the best attitude is to sit on the heels or kneel on one knee, so that one can wheel round to right or left as occasion may require. The beat itself is well supplied with tom-toms and other native musical instruments, and with the noise so made and with plenty of shouting and throwing of stones into the thick places as they advance, the tiger—especially if he is being beaten in the right direction—will come on a long way in front of the beaters. Sometimes it is advisable to have a silent beat, that is, the beaters do not shout, but merely tap the trees as they walk through the jungle. This plan is adopted for the first beat, if the jungle behind the guns is to be afterwards beaten. One great secret of successful shooting is to remember that one is not bound to fire at a tiger the moment one sees him. If he is going so as to pass one within ten yards, it is a mistake to fire at him fifty yards off. Should he be heading so as to pass closer to another gun, the rule is that you must leave him to the other gun. A shot through the lungs is fatal in a few seconds. A tiger so shot with a ·500 Express, the weapon always used by the writer, seldom drops on the spot, but gallops 100 yards or so, stops, falls over and expires with a growl or two. When shot through the liver they go rather farther before dropping. Tigers generally roar when hit, and often turn to bite the wound. Even when missed they often roar to the shot. If you are tracking a wounded tiger and take the track more than 300 yards you may be certain that the wound is not one that will be speedily fatal.

In hilly, rocky ground, tigers are very fond of lying up in caves. A cave, however, is not a large opening that can be walked into, but consists of one or more narrow tunnels barely sufficient to let the tiger through into a mass of rocks piled over each other. Somewhere inside, no doubt, there is more room, and hither the tiger, panther and bear retreat out of the heat.

The best way to start him out is to collect the beaters on the top of the rocks, usually at the summit of a hill. At a given signal tremendous yells, beating of tom-toms and other noises burst forth, and out darts the tiger with a roar. But sometimes he refuses to move, and in that case you can look into the different holes and crevices in the rocks; if he is to be seen, his two eyes, glowing like lamps, are plainly visible in the darkness. A curious effect is produced by his winking, as the two shining eyes are for a moment extinguished. The bullet should be placed about an inch above the eyes. He is generally, however, out of sight, and as a last resource an attempt may be made to smoke him out by filling one of the entrances with grass and firing it, but I have never myself found this to answer. The gun should be placed at least 200 yards from the cave, to give the tiger time to subside into a walk, for he always comes out fast at first. Should a tiger go into a cave in the course of a beat he will never be driven out of it, if the cave is of any extent.

Sometimes accidents happen with an unwounded tiger; if he breaks back through the beat he may maul some one on the way. The cause of his so doing is that he is being driven in a direction away from the point for which he wishes to make, or, if he is often turned by stops, he gets suspicious, lies up, and charges the beat when it gets near.

An elephant is sometimes used to follow up a wounded tiger. In Bengal and Northern India tiger-shooting is always carried on with the aid of elephants, the long grass rendering their use a necessity. The beat is composed of a line of elephants, on some of which the guns are seated in howdahs. One or more guns seated on elephants may be posted in advance of the general line of beat to intercept the tiger making off, but, as a rule, the shots are fired from the advancing line. A good Shikaree elephant will neither run away from, nor attack a tiger, but stand still even if the tiger charges it. It is dangerous to be on an elephant that bolts in a tree jungle, as the howdah and its occupant may be swept off by the branch of a tree. An elephant that charges at the tiger is as bad.

Sitting up over a tiger's kill at night is very interesting, although frequently unsuccessful. As a tiger almost always returns to its kill when no one is there and often fails to turn up when you are waiting for him, the inference is that he finds you out and departs oftener than you suspect. A native charpoy or bedstead should be tied up in a tree over the kill, and a screen of grass or branches made all round it. This should be occupied about 4 P.M., for the tiger may return before sunset; the most usual time, however, for his return is about an hour after sunset, but he may not come till midnight or later, in fact it is quite uncertain when he will come. If there is no moon it is hopeless to try to shoot at night. Even if the tiger does not return, there is much to interest one before it gets dark. Sand grouse and peacock come down to drink at the water near which the kill probably is. The call of a cheetul or sambur breaks the silence. Every rustle of the leaves brings the heart into your mouth with the expectation that it is the tiger's tread. Sometimes the tiger himself will speak, with quite a different sound from that which he makes when charging. If he comes to the kill, you hear his footfall among the leaves, or on the gravel of the stream. He is by no means certain to come at once to the kill—he often lies down near it for a long time, or walks round growling to himself. When he seizes it he gives a "wouf." Sometimes he comes so quietly that not a sound is heard before he seizes the kill. The best plan is to lie perfectly still until he begins to eat, as any little sound you may make when getting into position is then covered by the noise he makes crunching. Should the tiger observe you he gives a roar and bolts. Instances have been known of a tiger returning to a kill the same night after being fired at on it, but, as a rule, the least thing which causes him suspicion will send him away for ever. Should you drag a kill a few yards to a more convenient place, if it is out of sight of its original position the tiger seldom comes to it; not finding it where he left it, he walks off. As a tiger always drags the kill away before eating, it should be securely tied by a stout rope to a tree, otherwise the tiger drags it off at once. You may also have a chance at a tiger by stalking the kill at dawn, when he may be on it, or, more likely, sitting close to it. It is better, however, to trust to driving him out during the heat of the day, for if disturbed in the cool morning, he may go off for miles instead of stopping near the kill. Tracking tigers up to the very spot where they are sitting, and shooting them as they get up, is rarely possible; when it is possible, there is great satisfaction in getting a tiger in this manner, but the ground in most places is too hard for continuous tracking. In April and May, the hot weather, the best time for big game shooting, a great deal can be done in locating tigers for a beat, by tracking. Year after year tigers occupy the same hill, the same ravine or other well-known spots in the jungle. If there is a tiger about, his tracks are in the river bed, along the jungle roads, and in the sandy bottoms of the nullahs. When you lose the track, you make a cast forward to the next nullah—half a mile each way will show if the tiger has crossed it. If not, you must try in another direction. The best part of a day can be spent in this way, often without success, often losing the track altogether, but sometimes the track leads into a hill or thick jungle, out of which there is no track, and you know the tiger is there. Many tigers can be got without a kill, by tracking them, and to my mind there is an additional charm in the sport where you have had to work for it. I am informed that in the Central Provinces, the authorities have made a rule by which one is prohibited from having a beat for tiger without a kill. A more vexatious and ridiculous rule it would be difficult to conceive.

When beating for tiger, the rule is not to fire at panther, bear, or other animal that may be in the beat, for the tiger may be turned by hearing a shot in front of him, or, worse still, may break through the beat and perhaps maul a man on the way. When the beat is over, the beaters should be paid at once on the ground; the usual rate of pay is 2 annas (*2d.*) a day, and

Snipe.

double pay if a tiger is shot. They sit round according to their villages, and you should pay them yourself, for otherwise it is probable they will not get their due. A large supply of small coin should be taken.

When the tiger is skinned, the ground where the skin is to be pegged out should be covered with wood ashes to the depth of half an inch or so, as this is a sure protection against white ants, who will destroy a skin in a few hours if they can get at it. The skin is placed on the wood ashes hair downwards, always in the shade. Wood ashes should be rubbed on the inner side, which should be left covered with the ash till the skin is quite dry. The ashes absorb the grease out of the skin. The whiskers become very brittle and and are sure to break off. They should be pulled out and kept if it is desired to stuff the head. The lips and ears are the parts most difficult to clean; the ears especially should be skinned down to as near the tips as possible or the hair will come off them. Near the shoulder, embedded in the flesh, will be found a small bone, in the language of zoology a rudimentary clavicle, really the remnant of a bone once functional and useful in some ancestors of the tiger in bygone ages.

The Europeans at Amoy, China, have shot a good many tigers there. Mr. R. P. Bruce has kindly furnished to me some information about the tigers in that neighbourhood. He writes: "Tigers in the Amoy district lie up in rocky ravines, having long underground tunnels or caves, into which they penetrate even as far as 150 to 200 yards from the opening. There is no game; the tigers hunt round the farms and villages for any domestic animal. During these night hunts, they occasionally get men, cows, pigs, and goats, but much oftener dogs, for the more valuable beasts are carefully enclosed every evening. Tigers are numerous. All the tigers are man-eaters in the sense that they readily go for men, and as they hunt so near the haunts of man they have no regard for human scent. They are bagged in many ways, up a tree, or rock, in moonlight with a fastened goat. This last mode is very unsuccessful; with a bright moon the tiger does not come, but if the moon goes down he has the goat at once and the shooter cannot see. Another way is to take up a position at 5 A.M. or sooner, commanding the entrance of a cave where a tiger is known to live. If he returns from his hunt after daybreak you get a good chance. It is dangerous getting to the place in the dark, but we have got several this way. However, 75 per cent. of our tigers have been bagged since we discovered a party of Chinese hunters who would enter the caves behind a torch lashed to a 10 foot bamboo; about six of them go in, all armed with three-pronged spears. They are in no danger while the passage is small, but if it opens into a chamber they are very careful to see that the beast is not there before they pass through to the exit passage. Any bifurcations of the passages are either carefully explored by half the force or built up before they move forward. The tiger retreats before the glare of this unusual intrusion, and, if there is a bolt hole, he comes out to the guns and gives grand sport. Unfortunately, however, it happens oftener than not, the tiger retreats to a *cul-de-sac*, and there stands at bay. When this is notified to the shooter, he crawls in, gets in front, manœuvres the torch till he gets a good view and kills at 10 yards. The only thing calling for care is to kill dead by head or chest shot, for the concussions underground extinguish all lights, and a wounded tiger in the dark is no fun, however small the passage. As a novelty, this entering the cave business was very exciting, but as a matter of fact it is poor sport. The beast is completely cowed, and in a crawling hole can do nothing brilliant. I have known them show fight, but a couple of crossed spears with the butts jammed to the sides of the cave and the torch rammed into the tiger's face kept the men safe. The only accident was when the tiger rushed out before the men entered the cave.

"We measure straight from peg to peg at head and tail. In this way we have never got a tiger of 10 feet. I think 9 feet 6 inches is the biggest. The largest tiger I ever saw had a stump for a tail, and measured 9 feet 2 inches. They are said to be much larger in Northern China. I doubt if ours are bigger than, or as big as, some of the Indian tigers."

Mr. F. Leyburn of Amoy has sent me measurements of thirteen Amoy tigers. They vary from 7 feet 9 inches to 9 feet 5 inches; of these five are 9 feet and upwards; also of fifteen tigresses which vary from 7 feet $6\frac{1}{2}$ inches to 8 feet 4 inches; of these six are 8 feet and upwards. If measured in the Indian manner (by following the line of the body and not in a straight line from peg to peg, as seems to be the Amoy method), the measurements would be from 4 to 6 inches more. This bring out the size of the Amoy tiger to be very much the same as that of the Indian tiger.

Other Amoy measurements are, of the 9 feet 5 inches tiger, tail 3 feet 4 inches, shoulder height 41 inches, chest girth $45\frac{1}{2}$ inches, skull length $13\frac{1}{2}$ inches, skull breadth $9\frac{2}{3}$ inches, the skin 11 feet 7 inches. Of a 9 feet tiger, shoulder height 43 inches, chest girth $39\frac{1}{2}$ inches: skull length 13 inches, skull breadth $8\frac{5}{6}$ inches, skin 10 feet $10\frac{1}{2}$ inches. Of an 8 feet tigress, tail 2 feet $9\frac{1}{2}$ inches, shoulder height 35 inches, chest girth 35 inches, skin 10 feet.

The Maharaja of Cooch Behar gives, in the letter to the *Asian* previously quoted, the height of fifteen Indian tigers which vary from 36 inches to $44\frac{3}{4}$ inches, and of two tigresses 34 inches and $38\frac{1}{2}$ inches. The girth of the fifteen tigers varies from $48\frac{1}{2}$ inches to $54\frac{3}{4}$ inches, that of the two tigresses being 41 inches each. These measurements are on the whole larger than the Amoy ones.

J. D. INVERARITY.

TOBOGGANS AND TOBOGGANING —The word "*toboggan*" is a corruption of the American Indian "*odabaggan*," a sled. No country in particular can claim to have been the first to adapt a vehicle for the express purpose of carrying heavy weights over snow; but the peculiar form of sled known as a "toboggan" owes its origin certainly to Canada.

The North American Indians recognised the difficulties which attended the transport of their goods across large areas of snow, and placed these goods upon long strips of thin wood, turned up at the ends, the better to enable them to glide over the frozen surface. On reaching a declivity the Indian allowed his toboggan to descend by means of its own gravity, and directed its course by sitting at one end and steering with sticks.

In recent years this gliding down hills has been indulged in as a pastime and sport. The original rough birch-wood sleds of the Indians, which were bound together by deer thongs, have given place to light and elegantly made toboggans constructed of birch, maple, hickory, or bass wood, in strips bound together by metal rivets.

In Canada, the United States, and Russia, special slides have been built with the view of directing the course of the toboggan, increasing the pace, and avoiding the unforeseen leaps and drops, or "*cahots*" as they are called, which upon the natural course frequently caused injury to the toboggan and its occupants.

These slides, which were copied from those in Russia, commence on a raised scaffolding so as to afford a steeper incline at the start, and continue over more gentle and natural slopes to the finish. The scaffolding rises from the ground to a height of 40 or 50 feet and supports the slide, which starts from a platform at the summit and descends at an angle of about 45° to the ground. The platforms of the Turque Bleue Club at Montreal, and that at Woodlawn Park, Saratoga, were raised 40 feet from the ground, the descent being 120 feet long.

The slides, for a considerable distance, are divided into two or more parallel courses or "*chutes*," which are separated from each other by low banks of snow, so that the toboggans can descend side by side without danger of collision. The breadth of each chute is only slightly greater than that of the toboggan, and very little skill in steering is required, except, perhaps, at the lower part of the course, which is not protected in the manner described. Now, whether these slides are constructed at more or less the same angle throughout as in Canada, or with alternate rises and falls, as in Russia, the ordinary type has a straight course with no corners. This, as we shall presently see, is the essential difference between these old-fashioned slides and the more recently constructed toboggan runs of Switzerland.

The slides, or chutes, are sometimes made of snow beaten down hard and iced so as to give a glassy surface, and sometimes of blocks of ice laid side by side and planed.

The Canadian toboggan is from 4 to 8 feet long, and from 16 to 24 inches wide, and will accommodate from one to six persons. It generally presents the whole under surface to the snow over which it glides, but some toboggans are made with low runners which raise them about an inch from the ground. Formerly two sticks were held, one in each hand, for the purpose of steering, but it was soon found that a recumbent position was the best for the steerer to adopt, and he now either kneels, sits low, or lies at the end of his toboggan and directs its course with the toe of one foot, trailing it behind upon the ice. It is remarkable how responsive the toboggan is to the slightest touch of the toe, and many riders are able to steer by merely swaying the leg from side to side without actually coming in contact with the snow. The pace attained upon one of these straight courses is very great indeed, being limited only by the weight of the toboggan, and by the resistance due to friction against air and ice.

It is probably owing to the fact that the sport, as it obtains in North America, does not admit of much opportunity for the exercise of skill, that tobogganing as a pastime is on the decline in the large cities of Canada and the United States. Within the last few years several of the chief runs have been closed, and the sport is in danger of extinction unless our cousins across the water introduce the same surmountable difficulties as, in the Engadine in Switzerland, have encouraged and improved the sport.

In Switzerland the sled most used by the country people is the "*schlitti*." This is a much shorter sled than the Canadian type, and is raised about a foot from the ground upon flat wooden runners shod with iron.

When it became fashionable for persons suffering from pulmonary complaints to spend the winter months in Switzerland, the English and American visitors to St. Moritz and Davos introduced tobogganing as a sport, and set to work to construct both toboggans and runs. Not content with the Canadian or the Swiss type of machine, they adopted the best qualities of each, and after continual experiment and thought, the present type of toboggan has been evolved. The Swiss type was found to be too short for steering and too high for stability, while the Canadian type was too long to be guided successfully round corners, and too low to admit of what is known as "body steering" or balance. Above all, experience proved that the curved runner was the more resilient, and that the rounded runner was faster than the flat.

While the type of toboggan was being altered, the slide, or toboggan run, was at the same time undergoing a complete revolution, and there can be no doubt that the chief cause of the improvement in the sport is due to the substitution of a crooked run for a straight, and to the introduction of difficulties which call for an extra amount of skill on the part of the rider. The chief of these difficulties are the corners and the width of the course, for, with regard to this last, the chutes of the Canadian course have been discarded, and the rider is obliged to select for himself that particular route which affords him the highest rate of speed.

The Buol run at Davos was the first attempt at carrying out the new principles; but owing to want of experience the engineers of this run constructed the corners too sharp and the banks too steep and high. A toboggan, if released from the top of this run, would, unless upset by the inequalities of the surface, find its way to the bottom. The Buol run resembled an exaggerated Canadian chute with the addition of corners. The engineers of the Cresta run at St. Moritz have worked on a different principle. It has been their aim to construct the banks at the corners in such a manner that, although a novice when travelling at a moderate paçe will probably run off the course, yet a more skilled rider will negotiate the corners with safety, and the best riders will descend at a very high rate of speed.

The Cresta is a run of infinite variety. Throughout its entire length of three quarters of a mile, in which it descends 500 feet, there are no two corners alike, no two consecutive gradients which are similar, and no section which is actually straight.

Of the corners, several are almost right angles, and one, at least, is hardly more than a prolonged curve. Where the corner is most abrupt, there we find the steeper and higher bank, which is accentuated if at the same place the course descends with greater rapidity: and, conversely, where the corner is comparatively flat, and the gradient slight, there we find little or no bank. The run is made of snow well trodden down and packed, and is afterwards covered throughout its entire length by a veneer of ice. This veneer is made by throwing water on the snow, and varies from an inch to several inches in thickness, being thinnest on the straighter sections of the run, where the friction is least, and thickest upon the banks at the corners. This run takes six weeks and more to build, but this length of time is due in part to the want of skilled supervision, the scarcity of labourers, and to the very great perfection of detail which is given to it.

Unless these difficulties can be overcome, the Cresta run itself bids fair to become a thing

SECOND BANK OF "CHURCH LEAP," ST. MORITZ.

of the past, and with it will go the perfection of tobogganing as a highly-skilled sport. The old Buol run erred in being under-constructed. The Cresta errs in the opposite direction. Each consecutive winter sees the corners made more mathematically perfect, and the straighter sections approximating more to the actual straight. The truer the curves and the straighter the course the easier becomes tobogganing, and the writer believes that the time has now arrived to say "enough." If we continue to "improve" we shall "improve" to excess, and ultimately revert to the Canadian "chute."

Now, what are the qualities of a good tobogganer? To quote from Mr. Gibson,

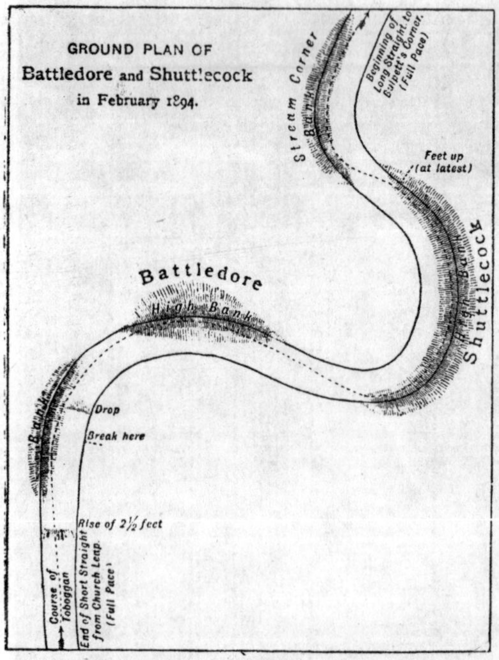

GROUND PLAN OF CRESTA COURSE.

"Tobogganing is a sport which appeals to all Englishmen, as it calls into play all those qualities for which England as a nation is famous. The decision quickly called for and instantaneously carried out, the opportunity of exercising pluck, nerve, resource, and activity, the quick eye for a curve, the necessity for hand and eye to work exactly together."

Great bodily strength is not necessary, although no doubt an advantage if accompanied by agility: and it is this fact which renders the sport possible both to the weak and to the strong, to ladies, children, and men of mature years.

In racing on the Cresta, the winner is not necessarily he who makes the fastest course. The prize goes to him who makes the shortest aggregate time on three heats. Now, as each competitor is obliged to run three times, his place in each heat being drawn by lot, and as the course varies, not only day by day but hour by hour, owing to variability of temperature and other causes, a great deal of judgment is required on the part of the rider. Experience alone can teach him which of several toboggans to select on such and such a day, for a toboggan which will suit a very hard course will be useless upon a soft. Again, it must be remembered that the grooves which are necessary at the rear of the steel runners to enable the rider to get a grip upon a hard ice corner, and to prevent skidding or slipping down the banks, will be found to impede the pace when the course is soft. In order to give these grooves their full value, the rider should shift his position on his toboggan, getting back as far as he can, and thus transfer his weight to the rear of the machine. He will then be able also to jerk or swing the front part of the machine from side to side and force it to describe a different course from that which it would otherwise follow. This is known as head-steering, and is exceedingly difficult to do well.

As soon as a corner is turned and the course becomes somewhat straighter, the rider will distribute his weight the full length of his machine, or throw it perhaps into the bows in order to prevent the grooves, for which there is now no further use, from retarding the pace. In steering, the feet are seldom, if ever, used, but they are of the greatest possible service in steadying the toboggan on the banks, and in diminishing the pace when approaching a difficult corner.

For this purpose a very strong iron toe furnished with sharp teeth is screwed on to each boot. In the judicious application of this power of breaking lies one of the chief differences between a good and a bad tobogganer, for we must remember that the winner seldom wins by more than a few fifths of a second, and that the loss of a fifth by over-breaking may prove fatal to the rider.

The selection of a toboggan is a thing of the greatest importance. It must suit the rider in every respect—in length, width, height, and weight.

For example, if too heavy, it will be unmanageable on the banks at the corners and run away down the straighter sections of the course. The runners, also, of the toboggan must be exactly parallel, and every part of the machine must be most carefully put together. The best rider upon a good machine ought to win his race; he will probably lose it if his toboggan does not suit him in every respect.

The type of toboggan now used upon the Cresta and other ice runs is known as the "steel *skeleton*." This will be best described by the engraving with its accompanying letterpress, which I borrow from Mr. T. A. Cook's book on tobogganing :—"Length over all on the top, including centre-board and 2 inches of counter-board at the back, is 4 feet 1 inch. Length of runner on the ground, 3 feet 6 inches, *with a spring of about* 10 *millimetres.* Height of machine (without cushion on centre-board), 5 inches. Diameter of runners, 18 millimetres. These are the measurements which, after many trials, have produced the highest average of success, and are properly pro-

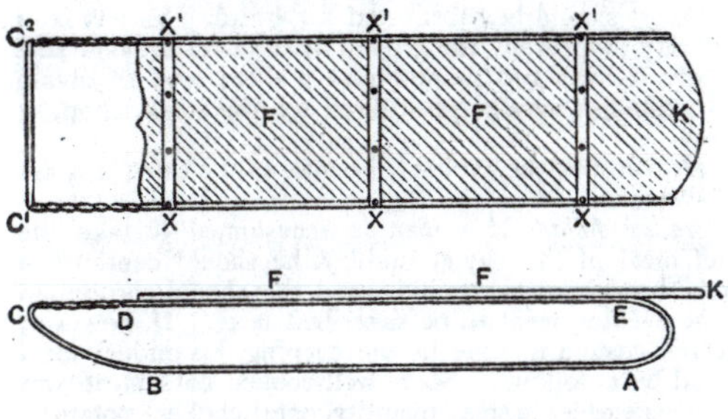

PLAN AND ELEVATION OF STEEL "SKELETON."

A to B, 3 feet 6 inches; total length, 4 feet 1 inch; C¹ to C², 12 inches; F, wooden centreboard; K, counterboard; X X¹, bars holding F and riveting runners.

portioned to a man of 5 feet 11 inches. Narrower machines may certainly be said to have failed. Lower ones are very difficult to ride. Longer runners are very hard to steer."

The counter-board mentioned in this description is a device for the purpose of affording to the rider a greater power of leverage over his machine.

The toboggan is constructed entirely of English steel, the various parts being strongly riveted together.

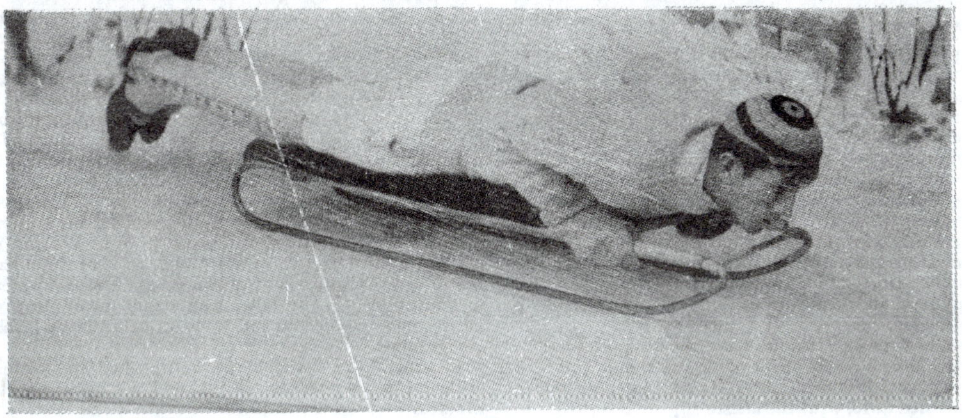

A RUN.

Upon such a course as the Cresta run it is not only too dangerous, but also next to impossible, for more than one rider to descend at a time. The racing, therefore, is judged entirely by time. Each tobogganer breaks or connects an electrical circuit automatically as he passes the starting and winning posts. The timekeepers have therefore merely to read off the results as given by the clock upon the circuit.

A good average run down the Cresta course takes 75 seconds, but during the winter of 1896–97 the record was made of 69·2 seconds.

Over the last 210 yards (and these contain at least two corners) the pace has been timed electrically at a fraction over 68 miles per hour.

The pace obtained upon a snow course or a road is necessarily not so great. The Klosters road, near Davos, winds down from an upper into a lower valley. That section of the road which is used for racing is two miles (less 160 yards) long, with a fall of 860 feet, and there is one bend at least which is at so sharp an angle as to compel the tobogganer to come nearly to a standstill to turn it. The record for this course is 4 minutes 34 seconds The type of machine used for road-racing differs from that used upon an ice course, in being much longer, and in being without grooves. To increase his pace, a strong rider will make use of his hands with which to thrust himself along, and will at times kneel upon his machine and punt with one foot. A weak rider is therefore at a disadvantage upon a road course, although his skill may be even superior to that of his more athletic opponent. For this reason, and because the surface of a road cannot be controlled to the same extent as can that of an ice course, toboggan-racing on roads is not a satisfactory sport.

Bobsleighing, another form of tobogganing, is a very much more sociable amusement. A bob-sleigh consists of a plank resting upon two small toboggans placed one in front of the other. The front toboggan turns upon a pivot and is used for guiding. From two to ten persons can sit upon the plank. The man in front steers, and the brake is applied by the man at the stern. Bobsleighing is usually indulged in upon a road, as an ice corner is undesirable, but a great pace is obtainable, and much dexterity is therefore required.

HAROLD W. TOPHAM.

TRAINING — Under the headings of the various sports there has already appeared the necessary information required by a man to become "fit" to excel in that particular department. All that is now required to fill in the gap is a general summary of the rules by which a man must be guided—rules bearing largely on his mode of life and surroundings; in short, the means by which he may "maintain his general health in the best possible state of efficiency."

First and foremost, his life must be one of absolute regularity. On this the success of all his efforts will largely depend. Of almost equal importance is moderation in all things, food, sleep, and muscular exercise. These two—moderation and regularity—form the keynote of all training.

Whatever be the particular form of muscular work to be undertaken, undoubtedly the best preliminary training is walking.

By walking, the muscles of the trunk and legs, the latter more especially, are hardened and rendered more efficient, the respiratory apparatus is stimulated and, perhaps of greater importance, the heart and blood vessels are braced up, and so prepared to withstand the more arduous labour presently to be thrown upon them.

An enormous difference can be wrought in the physical condition of a man by graduated walking exercise, of which fact advantage is being day by day more largely taken. By beginning on the flat and then taking more hill work into the daily routine, in a short time there will be a considerable increase in chest expansion and muscular development.

Walking, again, is far the best method for removing superfluous fat. Clad in thick and numerous woollen garments, a man may rapidly reduce his load of fat by brisk and continued walking.

Either at the very commencement, or as soon as walking has sufficiently raised the tone of the body, the aspiring athlete must strictly regulate his mode of life. This we may consider under the heads of *hours, food, drink, baths and clothing, surroundings.*

Hours—The vitality of the body is at its highest between the hours of 6—12 A.M., and at its lowest between 12 P.M. and 5 A.M., and from this we must conclude that "early to bed and early to rise" is a good rule, for the athlete at any rate. Bed should be left at 7 A.M. in summer and 8 A.M. in winter; and a bath, of which more later, should be taken at once.

Then should follow a smart run in flannels, at the end of which a rub down with a rough towel is a *sine quâ non.*

Three-quarters of an hour after leaving bed breakfast should be attended to. After this, as after every meal, should come half an hour's rest, but not a nap.

The morning should then be devoted to the serious business of the day, be it rowing, cycling, running, or what not.

In the height of summer these times may be advanced an hour, to avoid the extreme heat of midday. At 12.30 or 1.30, according as the day started at 7 or 8, the midday meal should be taken, followed as before by a rest of half an hour.

Then a portion of the afternoon should be devoted to work again, and finally the working day should end with a brisk walk, after which the evening meal should be taken. Bed at 10.30 at the latest.

In ordinary life many men are satisfied with 6—8 hours' sleep; but, in a course of training, there is far greater energy expended by the body, so that longer time of physiological rest must be given to it to repair the waste of the day's toil.

Food—At one time the diet was considered to be the most important element in a course of training, but modern theories rather tend to the belief that so long as the food is assimilated with no undue tax on the digestive apparatus it is good.

Too much insistence cannot be laid on the importance of meals being taken at regular times.

It is still a vexed question whether the morning run should be taken on an empty stomach or not, but probably an absolutely empty stomach is not the best.

Immediately after the bath a plain water biscuit, washed down with half a glass of milk, will prevent that giddiness which is a frequent source of trouble when exercise is taken on an empty stomach.

Breakfast—A plateful of porridge and milk, followed by some well and plainly cooked dish of meat. Should the appetite permit, a lightly boiled or poached egg may be added, and, to finish up, some stewed fruit or marmalade.

Hot rolls, fat bacon, or ham are to be avoided, and cold toast should be substituted for bread. Variety is of necessity to prevent the growth of distaste for food that rapidly follows too monotonous a diet; and to obtain this white fish may be substituted for the steak, chop, or mince.

Salt fish must be avoided, because of the thirst it is apt to produce.

Midday Meal—If a man is accustomed to take the chief meal of the day at midday, he should continue to do so throughout his training, and this should correspond to the evening meal to be described later. If, however, it is his custom to dine in the evening, his midday meal should be as follows. Some well-cooked cold meat with green vegetables in small quantity, or artichokes; potatoes, carrots, or parsnips are best left out of the dietary, for they take a long time to digest and are fattening.

For sweets, a milk pudding, with stewed fruit or jam, will suffice. Cheese should be tabooed by reason of its slow digestion. There is no objection to a cup of well made tea and a slice of bread and butter in the afternoon.

Evening Meal—Six to seven is the best time for this. It should begin with a small quantity of clear soup; thickened soup should be completely barred. White fish may be taken, but the oily sorts must not.

The principal dish should be "butcher's meat." This should be well cooked, but not dried up nor yet raw.

When muscular effort is demanded, there is no doubt that the average Englishman requires meat and meat in large quantities. It has again and again been proved by experiments on groups of men that the best work can be done on a diet that largely consists of meat.

The best is beef, and this should form the staple article of the chief meal, but it may be varied by mutton occasionally.

Dinner should end with a light pudding and stewed fruit. Of puddings, the best of all is ground rice.

Fruit can almost always be had, and when fresh fruit is not in the market prunes are always obtainable. Fruit should not be eaten raw, and nuts must be faithfully shunned.

The man who likes his principal meal in the middle of the day must follow the above rule, and for his evening meal should content himself, about 5—6, with a cup of tea and a slice or two of toast, and, an hour and a half before bed time, take a meal similar to the midday meal first mentioned. The other man should take a cup of unsweetened pure cocoa and a biscuit immediately before going to bed.

In general, food should be well cooked and plainly cooked. Spices, sauces, pickles, and relishes are to be avoided.

Pastry and heavy things are bad, for they are not easily digestible and cause considerable distention of the stomach, and so impede the breathing. Bread should always be at least one day old, and for the most part should be toasted. Butter may be taken in moderation.

Drink—The reduction of the quantity of fluid taken to the proper amount is a source of great discomfort to very many in training.

With care a balance may be struck between the amount taken and that lost by the ordinary natural means, so that the sweat glands are not called upon to exercise their function.

The ideal method is to drink nothing between meals

and nothing while actually eating, but to end each meal with a reasonable quantity of fluid.

This happy state cannot be reached at once, but by gradually tending that way it may be reached by all in a very short time.

Probably one large cup of tea or coffee at breakfast, one tumblerful of some fluid at the midday meal, a small cup of tea in the afternoon and 1½ tumblerful at the evening meal, added to the half-tumbler of milk or the cocoa, will be ample.

What to drink—It is certain that alcohol is not a necessity for training, and it is equally certain that it is not in many cases harmful.

The man who is not accustomed to the daily use of alcohol should leave it absolutely alone.

The man in whose dietary alcohol has a regular place may still continue to take it with his principal meal, but he must rigidly exclude it at all other times. As to the form, a light table beer or claret is the most suitable.

With alcohol we may consider tobacco. For the man in training tobacco is bad, in itself and from its haunts. Even in strictest moderation it causes the throat to be less moist than it should be, and so impedes respiration. Then again, the non-smoker seldom cares to stay in a room full of tobacco-smoke, and so the stuffy smoking-room atmosphere is avoided. Should, however, it be impossible to forego the weed, smoking should be strictly limited to the period of rest after meals, and, if possible, to the open air.

The best form of tobacco is a light flake, the pipe briar and freely drawing. Cigarettes and cigars are more deleterious than a pipe.

A pipe in the smoking-room before going to bed should be absolutely forbidden.

Baths—For ninety-five men out of a hundred the early morning cold tub is excellent. It should be taken immediately on rising, and a good rubbing with a rough towel given after it. The other five men who cannot stand a cold bath must take a hot bath.

A *warm* bath is bad, but a short plunge in a bath at a temperature of 112–115° is almost as beneficial as a cold bath; experience has shown that in hot climates it is even better. The danger of a hot bath is the tendency to stay too long in it, with the result that the bracing effect is lost and muscular slackness ensues.

For **clothing**, some form of woollen garment must be worn next the skin constantly.

After each period of exercise all clothing should be changed and the body rubbed dry with a rough towel, and the discarded clothing thoroughly dried and aired, in the open air if possible. In this way several sets of flannels may be required; but the advantage of always starting in dry, well-aired clothes is too great to be omitted in view of the constant danger of chills from damp clothing.

At night flannel pyjamas should be worn; the bed should be a reasonably hard spring mattress, and the bed-clothes light.

Surroundings—Undoubtedly the final training should take place in the locality of the event to be competed in. By this means the system becomes accustomed to the difference in atmosphere and other local peculiarities, including the drinking water, which is of some importance to the digestive apparatus.

For the man who till shortly before his race has been confined to a town, a short stay at the seaside is an excellent beginning to a course of training, but to continue throughout at the seaside is unwise, in view of the less bracing air in towns situated inland. An important item is the ventilation of the bedroom. Within reasonable limits it cannot be too cool; a hot, stuffy room contributes as rapidly to staleness as any other single factor.

Finally the man in training should have some mental occupation, not too absorbing, in order to keep his mind from dwelling too constantly on his chief business of the moment; a game at whist or chess in the evening is an excellent aid to sleep, but this must depend on individual idiosyncrasy.

Staleness—Pages may be written on the various causes of this bugbear of training, and pages more on its course and treatment. In a few lines it is impossible to do more than hint at these. Of causes, overwork, monotony of work and mental worry are perhaps the principal. The last is largely out of control of the trainer, but a judicious man may with care prevent his pupil falling a victim to the other two.

As to treatment, probably the best is complete rest from the matter in hand.

By this is not meant doing absolutely nothing, but the boat or track, or whatever it may be, should be left alone for a day or two, and some form of exercise different and less arduous taken up. For instance, the boating man may try a round of golf or tennis and so on, and equally valuable is a change of scene.

In conclusion, it must be remembered that no two men can train in absolutely the same way, but the general laws here laid down will form a guide by which any man may hope to achieve success.

HORACE C. COLMAN.

TRAPPING

TRAPPING—Fur-bearing animals have enormously decreased in the more civilised portions of America, but, taking the Canadian Pacific Railway as a rough boundary, they are steadily on the increase to its north and west. This satisfactory state is owing principally to the fact that the Indians, their former persecutors, have for many years forsaken ancestral pursuits for the more remunerative occupation of packing provisions into the ever-increasing mining districts. The old time trapper is almost a thing of the past, only represented here and there by a frozen out miner whiling away the winter with a dozen or so of steel traps.

Along the coast-line, most fur is coarse, light-coloured and comparatively worthless, with the exception of that of the bear, which appears to thrive on the abnormal rainfall of the North Pacific coast.

The **Sea-otter**, the most valuable of all fur-bearing animals, deserves some mention. Although now rare, it is still found along the coast of Alaska and about the Aleutian Isles.

Its capture was formerly only undertaken by Indians under perilous conditions. During a gale, a crew of Indians in a dug out canoe would put to sea, making for some well known rock where sea-otters sheltered; on approaching this, a single Indian armed with a club would make a jump for it. If he missed his footing, one more "good Indian" would be the inevitable result; but, if successful, he would club to death perhaps six otters, and secure a prize he considered well worth the risk.

The present mode of killing sea-otters is to chase a solitary individual with three canoes arranged in a triangle, one canoe being on either side of the otter, and the third behind it. Whether within shot or no, every time it comes up to breathe it receives a volley and dives again with shortened breath. The pursuit is prolonged until, being thoroughly exhausted, it finally receives at close quarters either shot or bullet. This form of hunting necessitates a fairly calm sea, otherwise so small a mark could not be kept in view.

The skin is sufficiently elastic to stretch to double its natural size, which has caused an erroneous impression as to the dimensions of this rarely observed animal.

The primest fur is only to be obtained in the interior, and the best and darkest Marten or Sable will be found among the densest and largest timber. The trapper therefore selects what he considers the most likely looking country for a winter's campaign, and, after building himself a shanty, gradually sets out some fifty miles of traps over mountain and valley, composed of deadfalls, snares, and steel traps at intervals of a third of a mile apart, with a rough lean-to every twenty miles to sleep under and to *cache* a few provisions in. The trapping season lasts from November to April, but January and February are the least productive months.

Taking in rotation, somewhat according to their market value, those animals likely to be obtained during a winter's trapping, we commence with the **Silver Fox** which, like all its tribe, dreads the smell of iron, and is most difficult to capture in a steel trap. A successful capture may be effected, and all scent obliterated, by setting the trap just under water in one of the numerous warm springs often found in the north, and covering the pan with moss. Beyond the trap a grouse should dangle from an upright stick, and the fox, rather than wet its foot in this cold climate, will, in order to reach the bait, place it upon the deceptive moss and become caught.

LEAVING THE HUT.

The **Cross** and **Red Fox** may be captured by the spring pole, which consists of any convenient young tree cut of sufficient weight at the butt to suspend the animal for which it is set. This should be fixed to another tree beside the trail in such a position that the string loop, attached to the lighter end, hangs above the trail at the height of the animal's head. The pole is held there by a portion of the noose attached with a jam round a peg driven in the ground ; on a tug at the noose, this releases itself and the pole, which immediately hoists the animal aloft to choke.

Beaver can be taken in steel traps throughout the winter, but autumn and spring are the times when every beaver in the district may, with a few exceptions, be secured by a competent trapper.

A beaver trap is a very formidable instrument with double springs. It needs considerable experience to set, especially in deep snow, where feet, hands, and a man's entire strength are called into force. Like all American traps, although formerly constructed in England, they far excel anything of the sort in use by us both in strength and lightness. They are toothless, and consequently it is very exceptional for any animal but a beaver to twist off a foot. They, owing to their great weight, of sixty pounds and upwards, almost invariably, if caught by a fore foot, wrench it off and escape.

Beavers, in their constant excursions ashore after tree limbs and berries, wear deep grooves in the banks, and the trap should be set under water at the foot of one of these. A pole fourteen feet long should be inserted through the ring of the chain and pushed into the mud far out in the lake, with the upper end fastened to the shore, so that when the beaver dives on being caught, the ring slips down the pole and he becomes anchored to drown in deep water; the pole must be of dead wood, for otherwise it will be cut off and carried away as food, beaver and all.

A CAPTURED MARTEN.

A very attractive bait is beaver castor, the secretion from which is sprinkled on land above the trap and the earth scratched up. All footmarks and the taint of anything handled must be thoroughly effaced by water. If this is attended to, with a properly set trap there is no difficulty in taking beavers, which may also be trapped in the dead of winter by chopping through the ice and fixing a trap on a platform close to a beaver house. A piece of willow thrust under the ice above the trap will, on being discovered, induce the beaver to seek a footing on the trap while gnawing it off.

If a portion of their dam be chopped away, the beavers, on finding the water lowering, will soon seek out the break and may be trapped when repairing it.

Another method of trapping beaver is to set beneath the ice, in front of their play-holes situated in the bank, a raw hide net of about 12 yards in length with a bell attached. The net is set by chopping holes through the ice and passing it in a straight line with the bank from one hole to another by the aid of a long willow.

The nearest "house" is sought, and by hammering or chopping the roof, the alarmed inmates are driven out to take refuge in their play-holes and become entangled in the impeding net. The bell rings, and the trapper hastily hauls up the net and gaffs the beavers, finally clubbing them to death. A very short period suffices for a beaver to cut itself free and escape. Beavers' pelts take time and trouble to clean from fat, and are opened and stretched on willows fixed hoop fashion. All other pelts are cased, that is, they are cut from one hind leg to the other and the body drawn out, a split board being inserted in its place and wedged open.

Where beavers exist, the **Musk rat** or **Musquash** of the fur dealers is often plentiful. They cause constant disappointment by taking the place of more valuable fur in the traps.

Under certain conditions of early ice, much sport may be experienced by driving these rats out of their houses and chasing them as they swim beneath the ice, striking a sharp blow with the back of an axe above them every time they stop to renew their breath, which they effect by blowing out a bubble of air from the lungs, and waiting until it regains its oxygen before again inhaling it; on being driven away they quickly become exhausted and sink; a hole is then chopped and the body recovered with a gaff.

Musk rats may also be speared by driving the weapon through their houses, or they may be caught in traps set inside them.

The Otter may be taken in several ways with steel traps. But the most successful is at the slides where they play in winter, at the outlet of some warm mountain-stream where it flows into the main river and remains unfrozen. Here, if there be a steep cliff, they will form a slide from the top into the water, whence they emerge at some easier grade to re-ascend and again slide down. Where they leave the water is the best place for the trap, which should be set as for beaver, but they may be taken at the top of the slide. Twigs or branches should be arranged to guide them into the trap, which should be placed well on one side, for otters walk very wide. After the trap has been carefully covered over, all taint must be obliterated with water.

A specially constructed claw trap is made for catching otters across the centre of the body as they slip down their slides, with fore-feet tucked backwards under them, in which position no ordinary trap would be of service. They can also be trapped by constructing a nest of twigs fixed to the top of a pole driven into the bottom of the river, and standing a few inches above the water close to the ice, with the trap in the centre and a sliding ring on the pole. They make use of this nest as a means for gaining the ice. Although otters do not habitually eat animal flesh, there is little doubt that they sometimes do so, and a trap baited with meat will often catch them.

ERMINE IN STEEL TRAP.

Wolverine or **Glutton**—This ravenous animal will certainly put its foot on the first opportunity into a reasonably placed trap in front of any bait; travellers' tales of its cunning are mere inventions devoid of foundation. Much the same may be said of the *Fisher*. They are together a couple of lawless tramps, robbing the trapper of valuable fur on every occasion, and invariably paying the penalty.

The **Lynx** is a stupid and harmless cat, which willingly thrusts its handsome head through a noose, or its woolly paw into a trap, although it be unbaited, except for a covering of feathers, which it always tries to scrape away. Feathers make a good covering for traps, and often, in deep snow, nothing else is available; but when these do not exist, a good plan is to lay a piece of thin paper over the trap and sprinkle it lightly with snow.

The majority of animals secured during a season's trapping will usually consist of **Martens**, which are easily caught with any description of bait, be it even one of their own kindred. The trap should be set at the foot of a pine or cedar in a small house constructed of bark or boughs; in fact all traps should have, when practicable, some covering, both as a guide to the animals and to keep off the snow and hide the bait from jays, whiskey jacks, Clark's crows or squirrels. The lighter the fabric, the better; for should a larger animal come along, it will trample through the frail structure where something more formidable would prevent it placing a foot in the trap, and a little Marten trap will well hold a Wolverine or Lynx, even though it grip but two toes.

Martens are easily taken in deadfalls constructed as follows. A house of bark about a foot high is built strongly against a tree, and across the opening of this is laid a pole six inches in diameter, fixed with four long pegs. On the top of this is laid another similar pole, one end of which is raised sufficiently to admit the animal, and is kept in position by an upright stick about six inches long from pole to pole. Between this stick and the lower pole is placed another stick, of about seven inches in length, protruding into the house, where a bait is tied to the end of it, which, when pulled releases the upright stick, when down comes the upper pole across the victim's back.

A less troublesome trap on the same principle can be arranged by laying the poles at an angle from the ground to the fork of a tree about ten feet high. In this trap the bait is fixed as before, but high up, and as there is no house it sticks out on one side in the open.

A somewhat brutal Marten trap is constructed by boring a hole in the foot of a tree with a two and a half inch auger, and hammering a long French nail through the top at an inward angle into the hole, through which it protrudes about an inch; the bait is placed far back in the hole, and the marten, thrusting in its head, is unable to withdraw it on account of the nail, which penetrates the nape of the neck further and further the more it struggles.

Carnivorous animals very rarely bite off a foot, and then only when it may have become so frozen as to be mistaken for the trap. In deep snow, martens seldom appear above the surface, being enabled to travel below among the fallen timber, where mice are plentiful.

Mink frequent the banks of rivers and lakes, and are captured by the same means as marten;

but after the river is frozen up, they travel between the ice and the river bed. Traps may advantageously be set in these places.

Skunks are mostly found on low lands and caught in steel traps baited with any meat and flesh. Needless to say they are very objectionable to skin, but all animals appear fond of their flesh.

Wolves and **coyotes** are the most difficult to trap, and are, on account of their enormous destruction to deer, the only animals it is really legitimate to poison; but too much care cannot be exhibited when poisoning. Every bait should be accounted for, and even then endless harm and destruction may ensue.

Wolves are sometimes destroyed in a most barbarous fashion. A knife blade, sharpened back and front, is fixed upright in the ground or snow, and smeared with grease which freezes on the blade; the wolf, in licking this off, so lacerates his tongue as eventually to cause death.

Raccoons may be easily trapped. They often frequent lakes, rivers, or sea-shores, where, if a small hole is scooped out and allowed to fill with water, the trap being placed at the bottom, they will be certain on discovering the hole to poke down a hand and begin feeling around for a crab or a clam. Traps set in the ordinary way, baited with fish for preference, will surely take them.

Ermine constantly get caught in traps set for all other sorts of fur, but scarcely repay the trouble of skinning.

Bears are captured in snares, deadfalls, box traps, and steel traps, baited with deer, salmon, or almost anything. Snares must be set on much the same principle as those previously described, but proportionately larger. The noose should be composed of twisted entrails or hide, and frequently examined to see that no squirrel has gnawed it half through. Instead of a pole a heavy tree is used, poised in a forked branch of some birch or other tree conveniently near the trail. The heavy end is supported by two poles, but, as a bear is too heavy to be hoisted bodily into the air, it is sufficient to raise him off his fore legs, when he will quickly choke himself. A deadfall must be set on the ground and constructed of trees as large and heavy as can be fixed in position. The object is to catch the bear across the back, and not across the neck; in the latter case he might pull himself out.

BEAR WITHDRAWN FROM DEADFALL.

Box traps are built of heavy logs dovetailed at the ends, like a small flat roofed hut, with a falling door, mouse trap fashion.

The iron spring traps used for bears are not so cumbersome as might be supposed. They should be fixed to a heavy log by the chain to lessen the strain of the Bear's plunges. An entire deer makes a good bait in all cases, but they have no objection to one of their own species, if it be not a grizzly, which scarcely anything will touch.

Skins, when prime, peel off white and clean, needing no further cleaning. They must not be dried by sun or fire, but must be hung in a dry draughty spot. Beaver and bear skins require much care and labour to remove all fat, which, if allowed to remain, will cause the hair on the opposite side to slip ; they should be stretched on a frame or between trees until dry.

J. TURNER TURNER.

TROTTING—As a sport trotting has always occupied in Great Britain a very minor and subordinate place among the recognised pastimes of the people, it having been overwhelmingly overshadowed by thoroughbred racing. In America the positions are almost reversed for, though the thoroughbred is popular, the national race horse is the trotter. As all foreign countries which need thoroughbred blood for racing purposes send to England for it, and use English racing rules as the foundation of their turf law, so all countries that desire to introduce trotting sport and blood go to America for their foundation stock and take its trotting rules for their guidance. The American trotter at all distances is the fastest horse at his gait and, having been bred for half a century on well established lines of blood and performance, has become a distinct breed with a stud book which has already reached its fourteenth volume and which goes back to the foundations of the race. As every incident in connection with trotting sport down to the minutest details receives the same attention that thoroughbred sport does in England, trotting sport in America will occupy the principal space in this article.

To secure a high rate of speed, science has been brought to bear in the construction of the tracks or courses on which trotting races are held, so as to reduce to a minimum the friction and resistance to extreme speed. A modern trotting track requires not only a competent surveyor but an experienced track builder. A regulation track must be either exactly a mile from wire to wire, measured three feet from the inside fence, or exactly half a mile with the same measurement. A plot of ground as nearly level as possible is selected, and the natural ground is cut down a foot. The level is regained by packing ordinary grass sod 12 × 4 inches upright. On the top of this natural sponge and spring six inches of earth is placed, which, if of too loose a nature, is mixed with clay. The result is a track smooth and elastic, yet so porous that it quickly absorbs water, retaining it in the sod and thus preventing the upper crust from getting hard. A careful track master sees, however, that by the aid of a track harrow, roller and a leveller the surface is kept as smooth as a billiard table. A half mile track of the best class is constructed in the same manner.

In many cases where an association cannot afford the expense the surface is simply ploughed up and levelled, but in all cases the surface is earth. There are no grass tracks in America. The illustration, with measurements, shows a regulation American half mile track. In all cases the track must conform to the imperative rule of being exactly one mile, or half a mile, measured three feet from the inside fence.

The modern sulky is the lightest and at the same time the strongest that modern mechanism can devise. The old high wheel sulky weighed in 1860 about 75 lbs., but was gradually reduced in weight to 40 lbs., while the wheel with steel tire had a diameter of 54 inches. The modern bicycle-wheeled sulky weighs about 25 lbs., and the wheel has a diameter of 28 inches. The general consensus of opinion is that a horse can go five seconds to the mile faster with a bicycle sulky than he can with the old vehicle. The smaller bicycle wheel can hug the fence closer, has less resistance, and is therefore faster.

The American method of conducting trotting races is by heats, and, unless otherwise specified, a horse has to win three heats to win a race. In order to prevent a race from being too long, horses in a race who have not won one heat in five are out of the race. The winners of the heats then trot till one of them has won three, which terminates the race. The following summaries of races illustrate the system.

FRANK FEHR STAKE, value $1,000 ; 2.11 class, trotting.

Elloree, chestnut mare, by Axtell, dam Flora McGregor, by Robert McGregor—Sanders	1	1	1
Fred B., brown gelding—Whitney	4	2	2
Grace Hastings, chestnut mare—Spears	2	4	3
Athanio, brown horse—Geers	3	3	4
Pilot Boy, grey gelding—Wells	dis.		
Dick Hubbard, grey gelding—Macy	dis.		

Time, 2.10½—2.12¼—2.09¾.

NEW YORK, Oct. 21 and 22.—Purse $300 ; 2.30 class, trotting.

Allie Tare, black gelding, by Alcantara—Devy	3	1	3	2	2	1	1
Lucy M., chestnut mare, by Repetition—Rathbun	5	2	2	1	1	3	3
Legend, chestnut mare, by Melville—Coates	1	4	1	4	4	2	2
Harry P., black gelding—Hurd	2	3	4	3	3	rd.	
Lonely Girl, black mare—Whelpley	4	9	6	7	6	rd.	
Hazel, black mare—Wilkinson	6	7	9	5	5	rd.	
Hattie D., black mare—Miller	7	5	5	6	dr.		
Highland Girl, chestnut mare—Doncourt	8	6	8	8	dr.		
Formosa, black mare—McGuire	9	8	7	9	dr.		

Time, 2.22½—2.22¼—2.25—2.23¼—2.24¼—2.24¼—2.24½.

In the first race Elloree won in straight heats and the four moneys in which a purse is usually divided, 50, 25, 15, and 10 per cent., go to the horses in the order in which they appear. In the second race it will be noted that at the close of the fifth heat no horse had won three heats and three horses were retired, the other three having been previously drawn. In this case, as only three horses were left to fight the race out to a finish, Harry P., though not allowed to compete further, got fourth money.

In all trotting and pacing races the time record of the horse is his handicap, and indicates the class to which he is eligible. A horse with a record of 2·30 can compete in any faster class, but he cannot be entered in a slower class, but all horses are allowed a margin of three-quarters of a second. For instance, a horse with a record of 2·29¼, is eligible to the 2·30 class. A horse with no record, who has not been started in a race, is naturally entered in what are called the slow classes, *e.g.*, the 3·00, 2·50, or 2·40 classes. There are also classes where age determines the eligibility to enter, *e.g.*, two, three and four year old classes, but these are rare. Two year old races are usually decided in mile heats, best two in three. The vast majority of races and matches against time for a distance of over a mile have been decided in one effort.

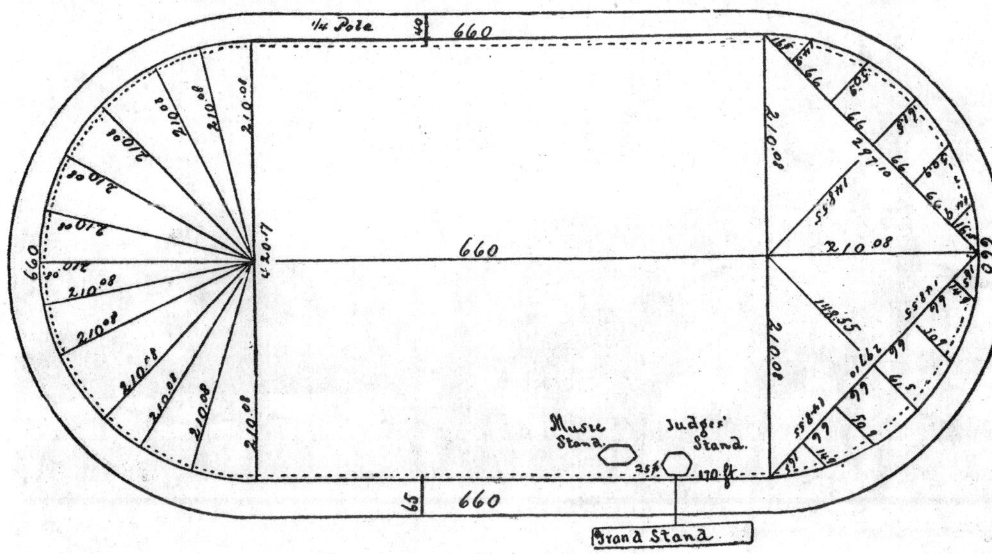

HALF MILE TRACK.

Left End: Method of Laying Out recommended to Amateurs. Right End: Method recommended to Surveyors.

The government of the trotting turf is provided for by two organisations, respectively called the National and the American Trotting Associations, and under their control are fifteen hundred trotting associations and driving clubs, ruling off for fraud being recognised by both. Ruled off horses are not eligible to compete either in England or the Continent, English and European expulsions being equally effective in America. Every reputable trotting club is a member of one of these associations, and is entitled to send a delegate to a biennial congress which makes such amendments to the rules regulating trotting races as it may deem advisable. The Congress also elects a Board of Review, of which the president of the association is the chairman. This board sits twice a year, in May and December, and decides on all questions in dispute which have been appealed from the trotting meetings. About $5,000,000 (£1,000,000) are annually competed for in purses and stakes.

While to America belongs the credit of having made trotting a great national sport, the honour of providing the foundation blood of the breed belongs to England, and, strange to say, the pedigrees of the vast majority of the fast trotters and pacers may be traced directly up to the thoroughbred horse Messenger, who was imported to America in 1788. He appears in the English thoroughbred stud book as a grey, foaled in 1780 by Mambrino, dam by Turf; second dam by Regulus, etc., though many able writers have maintained that he was not strictly thoroughbred. One important fact strongly favours this contention. Messenger as a progenitor of thoroughbreds was a distinct failure, so much so that the line is extinct, while he is the founder of the greatest trotting family in the world. A second fact is that contemporaneous with Messenger were a large number of thoroughbred sires in America, which had the same facilities as Messenger, yet not one of whom has left any impress upon the trotting breed. In the male line Messenger is without a peer. He died in 1808.

The two great descendants of Messenger, from which the modern trotting family principally comes, are Hambletonian and Mambrino Chief, and an examination of their pedigrees will show how far the blood of Messenger predominates. Hambletonian's tabulated pedigree is as follows:

HAMBLETONIAN (Founder of the Hambletonian family).	ABDALLAH I.	MAMBRINO . . . . Thoroughbred.	MESSENGER.
			Daughter of SOUR CROUT.
		AMAZONIA	Son of MESSENGER.
			Unknown.
	CHARLES KENT MARE	IMP. BELLFOUNDER	BELLFOUNDER, an English Norfolk trotter.
			Unknown.
		ONE EYE	Bishop's HAMBLETONIAN, thoroughbred son of Messenger.
			SILVERTAIL, daughter of Messenger.

It will be seen at a glance that Abdallah, the sire of Hambletonian, was a grandson of Messenger, and that his dam, Amazonia, was by a son of Messenger. The dam of Hambletonian was by Bellfounder, a Norfolk trotter whose name is found in the top crosses of many leading hackneys, both in England and America; but her dam was One Eye by Bishop's Hambletonian, a son of Messenger and Silvertail; the dam of One Eye was also by Messenger. It may also be pointed out that Bellfounder was a failure as a speed producer, when his blood did not mingle with that of Messenger. The enormous influence which Hambletonian has exercised as a producer of trotting speed is shown in the following results. At the close of 1896, 148 of his sons had produced 1,398 trotters and 155 pacers, with records from 2·04 to 2·30, while 80 of his daughters produced 104 trotters and 8 pacers, who have taken records of 2·30 or better. Up to the close of 1896, 16,207 trotters and pacers have made records from 2·00½ to 2·30, and at least 80 per cent. carry the blood of Hambletonian by from one to five crosses. Later on the Hambletonian blood in the trotting and pacing champions will be discussed.

Mambrino Chief, by Mambrino Paymaster, he by Mambrino, son of Messenger, is the founder of a great brood mare's family, the mares to the cover of the male descendants of Hambletonian producing the highest speed results. There are several other minor families, such as the Bashaws, descended from a horse called Grand Bashaw, imported from Tripoli early in the century. American Star, Pilot Champion and Norman, all native horses of obscure or unknown pedigree, had daughters who to Hambletonian or his male descendants produced notable trotters, but as they failed to produce any sires of note who in the male line founded families, the racing success of their offspring must be placed to the credit of the predominating virility of the Messenger family.

TROTTING PAIR OWNED BY MR. W. WINANS.
Blackstone, 2.20. Lake Erie, 2.13½.

America for the last fifty years has devoted attention and capital to developing the trotter. In the early days of breeding, performance was the sole test, and only those trotters or pacers who obtained records of 2·30 or better, or horses or mares who had produced trotters who had made such records were declared standard.

This test of performance is the condition for registration in the stud book and its practical effect has been to make a distinct breed which has shown a continuous speed progress to the present time.

In this connection it will be interesting to note by decades the progress obtained by breeding and training. In 1845 the grey mare, Lady Suffolk, trotted in 2·29½, being the first trotter to get a record below 2·30. She was by Engineer II., a grandson of Messenger, while her dam was by Plato, a son of Messenger. In 1859, Flora Temple, by One Eyed Kentucky Hunter, dam by an Arabian horse, trotted in 2·19¾, and was the first horse to trot below 2·20. In 1867 the brown gelding Dexter cut the record to 2·17¼. He was by Hambletonian. Between 1870 and 1880 there was a notable reduction in the record. The bay mare, Goldsmith Maid, trotted in 2·14. She was by Alexander's Abdallah, a son of Hambletonian, her dam being a daughter of Abdallah, the sire of Hambletonian. This remarkable mare made her record when seventeen years old, and during her racing career had to her credit 332 heats of a mile each on 2·30 or better. Between 1880 and 1890 St. Julien, by Volunteer, a son of Hambletonian, put the record down to 2·11¼; Jay-Eye-See, a black gelding by Dictator, another son of Hambletonian, cut it to 2·10, and the chestnut mare, Maud S., by Harold, also by Hambletonian, placed the trotting record at 2·08¾. The record of Maud S. deserves special mention as it was made to a high wheel sulky over a regulation track, and has not been beaten under the same conditions. The dam of Maud S., Miss Russell, was by Nutwood, a great grandson of Hambletonian.

The bicycle-wheel sulky came into use in 1892, and a general reduction in records ensued. On September 28th, 1892, the brown mare Nancy Hanks put the trotting record at 2·04. This mare is inbred, for her sire is Happy Medium, and her dam Nancy Lee, by Dictator, both sons of Hambletonian. This record has been only beaten by a quarter of a second, the present champion being Alix (2·03¾), by Patronage, dam Atlanta, by Attorney. This pedigree traces up to Mambrino Chief and Hambletonian. It will be noted that in fifty-two years the trotter has progressed from 2·29½ to 2·03¾. As the best judges place the speed limit at the trot at 2·00, the perfection of the breed is a question of the near future.

How do values compare between the trotter and the thoroughbred? An absolutely accurate solution of this question is impossible, but a few simple figures will give a good idea of the value of the high-class trotter. The two-year-old colt Arion, after he made his record of 2·10¾ (which is still the champion record for that age), was sold for $120,000 or a little over £25,000. The three-year-old colt Axtell, also a champion, was sold for $105,000, or £21,000. Bell Boy at three years old sold for £17,000; Stamboul (2.07½) for £10,000; Nancy Hanks for £9,000; Maud S. £8,000; Dexter £6,000; while £2,000 for a high-class performer or a brilliant prospective one was an average figure up to 1893, when the financial depression caused a heavy fall in all prices.

An article on the trotter would be incomplete without a reference to the pacer, for with many horses the gaits are interchangeable, and the vast majority of trotting sires begat a certain proportion of pacers. The pacers, with a few notable exceptions, are all trotting bred. Star Pointer, the champion pacer, with a record of 1·59¼ is the grand exception, as he is a member of a pacing saddler family long famous in Tennessee, but he is the one exception to a thousand pacers, who are by trotting sires out of trotting

MR. L. WINAN'S MOXIE.
Mile Record, 2.12

dams. John R. Gentry 2·00½, ex-champion, traces on both sides of the line to Hambletonian. Joe Patchen, 2·01¼, is by George Wilkes, son of Hambletonian, while on the dam's side he is strongly inbred to Mambrino Chief. It is also a common incident for a trotter, when he has got to the limit of his speed at the trot, to be put to pacing, and there are many horses who can go at either gait, as the following sample list will show:—

	Trotting.	Pacing.	Average.
Jay-Eye-See	2.10	2.06¼	2.08⅛
Heir-at-Law	2.12	2·07	2.09½
Ottinger	2.10¾	2.11½	2.11⅛
Direct	2.18¾	2·05½	2.12⅛
Connor	2.13½	2.11¼	2.12⅜
George St. Clair	2·15¼	2.10¼	2.12¾
San Pedro	2·14½	2.10¾	2.12¾
Red Bud	2.14½	2.12½	2.13½
Bert Oliver	2·19¼	2.08¾	2.14
Monbars	2.11¾	2.16¾	2.14¼
Vassar	2.21¾	2·07	2·14⅜

and there are scores of others.

Trotting in England, as a racing pastime, is in its infancy. Of late years, under the fostering control of the Trotting Union of Great Britain, the sport is assuming a higher plane, and at Manchester, Liverpool, and many northern cities, in Scotland and Ireland, meetings are held, but with the immense hold which the thoroughbred has upon the British public, it is questionable whether it will ever become a leading sport. This is to be regretted, as, with the finest roads in the world, the trotter should be a popular horse in England, and if the breed were carefully cultivated, as it is in America, and tested at the race track, it would be a vast source of wealth to the breeder. As in America, the fast performers after their racing days are over are sold for road purposes, while the large and handsome slow ones are sold for the carriage, the inferior individuals going into the ordinary avenues of commerce; thus the English breeder would find no absolutely bad stock on his hands. But trotting races must became popular before it will ever be profitable to breed trotters on a large scale.

Breeding the trotter and trotting races in France are fostered and encouraged by the Government, which contributes a certain sum of money annually for purses and stakes, to be competed for at the various meetings. The majority of the races take place on grass race-courses at various distances, and, as the tracks are not constructed for speed, fast time is out of the question. The French Government encourages the sport, as it relies largely upon trotting-bred horses for the cavalry service. In many purses which it offers it reserves the right to purchase the winner at a price stipulated in the conditions of the purse or stake.

Russia is the only country in Europe which can claim that it has a distinct trotting breed. It is called the Orloff, after Count Orloff, who, after defeating the Turks in 1772, on his return home brought with him some Arab stallions and mares. He also imported from England twenty thoroughbred stallions and thirty mares. By breeding with native mares and applying the doctrine of selection, the Russians have developed a breed of trotters which has not the speed of the American, but is possessed of great endurance, and is a very superior carriage horse. The great season in Russia is in the winter, and the races take place on the ice. These races were originally on sleighs but, as the rubber-tired wheel is faster, sulkies are now used.

Germany and Austria have taken kindly to trotting sport, and at Berlin and Vienna spring and autumn meetings are held, the purses ranging from £100 to £1,000 each. In Europe the fastest time has been made in the international races, and the European record is now held by the brown horse, Colonel Kaser, who on October 3rd, 1897, at Vienna, Austria, won the Prix d'Automne, worth 10,000 crowns, his fastest heat being 2·14$\frac{1}{10}$. Colonel Kaser was bred in America, and is by Stranger, by General Washington, dam Goldsmith Maid by Alexander's Abdallah; second dam by Abdallah, sire of Hambletonian. In Europe the majority of races, as in England, are distance handicaps, the handicap being based on the records or the sizes of the contestants. The majority of the international races are decided in heats, best two in three, or three in five.

In the British colonies trotting flourishes in Canada, and it has numerous stock farms, but its leading sires and dams are bred on the same blood lines as those which flourish in the United States. In justice to Canada it must be said that, in the early days of breeding the trotter, it contributed more than its share of brood mares. In Australia and New Zealand the sport is in its infancy, the local record being held by a horse called Fritz, with a record of 2·14$\frac{1}{5}$. He is native bred, but is by an American sire and dam.

Below are tables which show the highest rate of speed at various distances, with all the dates and minor details which it is possible to obtain.

Fastest Records—At the trotting and pacing gait at all distances up to the close of 1897, the fastest authenticated records in the world.

TROTTERS.

Fastest Yearlings—Colt and Filly.

Adbell, brown colt, by Advertiser, dam Beautiful Bells, by The Moor; San Jose, Cal., Sept. 28, 1894; time, regulation 2.23

Pansy McGregor, chestnut filly, by Fergus McGregor, dam Cora, by Corander; Holton, Kan., Nov. 18, 1893; race, kite 2.23¾

Two-year-olds—Colt and Filly.

Arion, bay colt, by Electioneer, dam Manette, by Nutwood; Stockton, Cal., Nov. 10, 1891; time, kite track 2.10¾

Jupe, bay colt, by Allie Wilkes, dam Annie Patchen, by Mambrino Patchen; Boston, Mass., Sept. 29, 1896; race, regulation 2.13¾

Janie T., bay filly, by Bow Bells, dam Nida, by Monon; Lexington, Ky., Oct. 15, 1897; race, regulation 2.14

Three-year-olds—Colt and Filly.

Fantasy, bay filly, by Chimes, dam Homora, by Almonarch: Nashville, Tenn., Oct. 17, 1893; race, regulation 2.08¾

Arion, bay colt, by Electioneer, dam Manette, by Nutwood; Nashville, Tenn., Nov. 12, 1892; time, regulation 2.10¾

Four-year-olds—Colt and Filly.

Directum, black stallion, by Director, dam Stemwinder, by Venture; Nashville, Tenn., Oct. 18, 1893; race, regulation 2.05¼

Fantasy, bay filly, by Chimes, dam Homora, by Almonarch; Terre Haute, Ind., Sept. 13, 1894; time, regulation . . . 2.06

Five-year-olds—Colt and Mare.

Ralph Wilkes, chestnut stallion, by Red Wilkes, dam Mary Mays, by Mambrino Patchen; Nashville, Tenn., Oct. 19, 1894; time, regulation 2.06¾

Fantasy, bay mare, by Chimes, dam Homora, by Almonarch; Des Moines, Ia., June 21, 1895; time 3.07

World's Record.

Alix, bay mare, by Patronage, dam Atlanta, by Attorney; Galesburg, Ill., Sept. 19, 1894; time, regulation 2.03¾

Stallion Record.

Directum, black stallion, by Director, dam Stemwinder by Venture: Nashville, Tenn., Oct. 18, 1863; race, regulation 2.05¼

Gelding Record.

Azote, bay gelding, by Whips, dam Josie, by Whipple's Hambletonian; Galesburg, Ill., Sept. 5, 1895; time, regulation 2.04¾

Race Record to Sulky.

Directum, black stallion, by Director, dam Stemwinder, by Venture; Nashville, Tenn., Oct. 18, 1893; regulation . . 2.05¼

Alix, bay mare, by Patronage, dam Atlanta, by Attorney; Terre Haute, Ind., Aug. 17, 1894; regulation 2.05¼

To Wagon—Race.

Elloree, chestnut mare, by Axtell, dam Flora McGregor, by Robert McGregor; Cleveland, O., Aug. 28, 1897; regulation 2.10

To Wagon—Time.

Guy, black gelding, by Kentucky Prince, dam Flora Gardener, by American Star; Detroit, Mich., July 18, 1893; regulation 2.13

Under Saddle—Race.

Great Eastern, bay gelding, by Walkill Chief, 330, dam by Consternation; Fleetwood Park, New York, Sept. 22, 1877; regulation 2.15¾

Fastest Race in Straight Heats.

Alix, bay mare, by Patronage, dam Atlanta, by Attorney; Terre Haute, Ind., Aug. 17, 1894: time 2.06, 2.06¼, 2.05¼

Team Record—Race.

Sally Simmons, brown mare, by Simmons, and Roseleaf, black mare, by Goldleaf; Columbus, O., Sept. 27, 1894; regulation 2.15¼

Team Record—Wagon Time.

Honest George, bay gelding, by Albert, and Belle Hamlin, bay mare, by Almon Jr.; Providence, R.I., Sept. 23, 1892; regulation 2.12¼

Trotter with Running Mate—Wagon Race.

Frank, bay gelding, by Abraham, dam by Green Mountain Boy; Prospect Park, L.I., N.Y., Nov. 15, 1883; regulation 2.08½

Trotter with Running Mate—Wagon Time.

Ayres P., chestnut gelding, by Prosper Merimee, dam by Rustie; Kirkwood, Del., July 4, 1893; kite 2.03½

Tandem—Time.

Mambrino Sparkle, bay mare, and William H., bay gelding; Cleveland, O., September 16, 1886; regulation 2.32

A Team of Three Trotting in Harness Abreast—Time.

Belle Hamlin, bay mare, by Almont Jr.; Justina, bay mare, by Almont Jr.; and Globe, bay gelding, by Almont Jr.; Cleveland, O., July 31, 1891; regulation 2.14

Four-in-Hand—Race.

Frank Rose, roan gelding; Peculiar, bay gelding (leaders); Rumps, bay mare; Tom Bradley, brown gelding (wheelers); Cleveland, O., Sept. 7, 1882; regulation 2.40¾

Four-in-Hand—Time.

Damania, Bellnut, Maud V., and Nutspra, all by Nutmeg; Chicago, Ill., July 4, 1896; regulation 2.30

Six-in-Hand—Time.

Fleetwing, Lamar, Flora, Hugie, Dexter, and Pete; New York, N.Y., Nov. 9, 1896; regulation 2.56¼

Two Miles—Race.

Nightingale, chestnut mare, by Mambrino King, dam Minnequa Maid, by Wood's Hambletonian; Buffalo, N.Y., Aug. 9, 1894; regulation 4.36½

Time.

Greenlander, black stallion, by Princess, dam Juno, by Hambletonian, 10; Terre Haute, Ind., Nov. 4, 1893; regulation 4.32

Under Saddle—Race.

George M. Patchen, bay stallion, by Cassius M. Clay, dam by Head 'em; Fashion Course, L.I., June 18, 1863; regulation 4.56

Three Miles—Race.

Fairywood, black gelding, by Melbourne, dam Gona Fay, by Fairygift; Minneapolis, Minn., July 1, 1895 . . . . . 7.16½

Three Miles—Time.

Nightingale, chestnut mare, by Mambrino King, dam Minnequa Maid, by Wood's Hambletonian; Nashville, Tenn., Oct. 20, 1893; regulation 6.55½

To Wagon—Race.

Prince, chestnut gelding, by Woodpecker; Union Course, L.I., N.Y., Sept. 15, 1857; regulation 7.53½

Under Saddle—Time.

Dutchman, bay gelding, by Tippoo Said Jr.; Beacon Course, N.J., Aug. 1, 1839; regulation 7.32½

Four Miles—Race.

Senator L., bay stallion, by Dexter Prince, dam Fanny Bayswater (thoroughbred), by Bayswater: San Jose, Cal., Nov. 2, 1894; race (walk over); regulation 10.12

Time.

Satellite, chestnut gelding, by Tempter, dam Lucy; Keokuk, Ia., Aug. 12, 1887; regulation 10.52½

Five Miles—Race.

Bishop Hero, roan gelding, by Bishop, dam Lida Kendall, by Hero of Thorndale; Oakland, Cal., Oct. 14, 1893; regulation 12.30¾

To Wagon—Race.

Fillmore, chestnut gelding; San Francisco, Cal., April 16, 1863; regulation 13.16

Ten Mile—Race.

Controller, bay gelding, by General Taylor; San Francisco, Cal., Nov. 23, 1878; regulation 27.23½

Time.

Pascal, black gelding, by Pascarel, dam by Leamington New York, N.Y., Nov. 2, 1893; regulation 26.15

To Wagon—Race.

Julia Aldrich, chestnut mare; San Francisco, Cal., June 15, 1858; regulation 29.04½

Twenty Miles—Time.

Captain McGowan, roan stallion; Boston, Mass., Oct. 21, 1865; regulation 58.25

Thirty Miles—Time.

General Taylor, grey stallion, by Morse Horse, dam Flora; San Francisco, Cal., Feb. 21, 1857 . . . . . 1.47.59

Fifty Miles—Time.

Ariel, bay gelding, Albany, N.Y., 1846 . . . . . 3.55.40½

One Hundred Miles—Time.

Conqueror, bay gelding, by Bellfounder (Latourette's), dam Lady McClare, by Imp. Bellfounder; Centerville, L.I., Nov. 12, 1853 . . . . . 8.55.53

PACERS.

Yearling Colt and Filly.

Belle Acton, bay filly, by Shadeland Onward; Lyons, Neb., Oct. 14, 1892; time, kite 2.20¾

Rosedale, bay colt, by Sidney, dam Rose Leaf, by Buccaneer; Stockton, Cal., Nov. 8, 1893; time, kite 2.22

Two-year-olds—Colt and Filly.

Directly, black colt, by Direct, dam Mabel, by Naubic; Galesburg, Ill., Sept. 20, 1894; time, regulation 2.07¾

Lena Hill, brown filly, by William M. Hill, dam Possum Pie, by Octoroon; Dallas, Tex., Oct. 28, 1893; race, regulation 2.12¾

Three-year-olds—Colt and Filly.

Search Light, black colt, by Dark Night, dam Nora Mapes, by Furor; Santa Anna, Cal., Oct. 30, 1897; time, regulation 2.05¾

Miss Rita, chestnut filly, by J. J. Audubon, dam Lady Garfield, by Jupiter; Galesburg, Ill., Aug. 31, 1895; race, regulation 2.09¾

Four-year-olds.

Online, bay colt, by Shadeland Onward, dam Angeline, by Chester Chief; Sioux City, Ia., Oct. 12, 1894; time, regulation 2.04

Aileen, bay filly, by Gazette, dam Hernia, by Nuncio; Freeport, Ill., July 26, 1895; race, regulation 2.07½

World's Record.

Star Pointer, bay stallion, by Brown Hal, dam Sweepstakes, by Snow Heels; Readville, Boston, Aug. 21, 1897; time, regulation 1.59¼

Stallion Record.

Star Pointer, bay stallion, by Brown Hal, dam Sweepstakes, by Snow Heels; Readville, Boston, Aug. 21, 1897; time, regulation 1.59¼

Gelding Record.

Robert J., bay gelding, by Hartford, dam Geraldine, by Jay Gould; Terre Haute, Ind., Sept. 14, 1894; time, regulation 2.01½

Mare's Record.

Lottie Lorine, bay mare, by Gambetta Wilkes, dam Lady Yeiser, by Garrard Chief; Terre Haute, Ind., Sept. 30, 1897; race, regulation 2.05¾

Bessie Bonehill, grey mare, by Empire Wilkes, dam Arab Girl, by Crittenden; Terre Haute, Ind., Sept. 30, 1897; race, regulation 2.05¾

Race Record to Sulky.

Star Pointer, bay stallion, by Brown Hal, dam Sweepstakes, by Snow Heels; Springfield, Ill., Oct. 1, 1897; race, regulation 2.00½

To Wagon—Race.

Joe Patchen, black stallion, by Patchen Wilkes, dam Josephine Young, by Joe Young; Boston, Mass., Nov. 3, 1896; half mile track 2.11

To Wagon—Time.

Joe Patchen, black stallion, by Patchen Wilkes, dam Josephine Young, by Joe Young; Joliet, Ill.; Oct. 20, 1897; regulation 2.04¼

UNDER SADDLE.

Johnston, bay gelding, by Joe Bassett; Cleveland, O., Aug. 3, 1888; time, regulation 1.13

TEAM RECORD—TIME.

John R. Gentry, bay stallion, by Ashland Wilkes, dam Dame Wood, by Wedgewood; and Robert J., bay gelding, by Hartford, dam Geraldine, by Jay Gould; Glens Falls, N.Y., Oct. 8, 1897; regulation 2.08

PACER, WITH RUNNING MATE—TIME.

Flying Jib, bay gelding, by Algona, dam Middletown Mare, by Middletown; Chillicothe, O., Oct. 4, 1894; kite . 1.58¼

TWO MILES—RACE.

Defiance, bay gelding, by Chieftain; and Longfellow, chestnut gelding, by Red Bill; dead heat; Sacramento, Cal., Sept. 26, 1872; regulation 4.47¾

TWO MILES AGAINST TIME.

Chehalis, black stallion, by Altamont, dam Tecora, by Cassius M. Clay Jr.; Salem, Ore., Oct. 6, 1897; regulation 4.19¼

UNDER SADDLE.

James K. Polk, chestnut gelding; and Roanoke; dead heat; Philadelphia, Pa., June 30, 1850; regulation 4.57½

THREE MILES—RACE.

James K. Polk; chestnut gelding; Centerville, L.I., N.Y., Sept. 13, 1847; regulation 7.44

TIME.

Joe Jefferson, brown stallion, by Thomas Jefferson; Knoxville, Ia., Nov. 6, 1891; regulation 7.38¼

UNDER SADDLE—RACE.

Oneida Chief, chestnut gelding, by Kentucky Hunter; Benson Course, N.J., Aug. 14, 1843; regulation 7.44

TO WAGON—RACE.

Longfellow, chestnut gelding, by Red Bill; Sacramento, Cal., Sept. 21, 1868; regulation 7.53

FOUR MILES RACE.

Longfellow, chestnut gelding, by Red Bill; San Francisco, Cal. 1869; regulation 10.34½

TIME.

Joe Jefferson, brown stallion, by Thomas Jefferson; Knoxville, Ia., Nov. 13, 1891; regulation 10.10

FIVE MILES—RACE.

Fisherman, bay gelding, by Lightning; San Francisco, Cal., Dec. 19, 1874; regulation 13 03½

TO WAGON—RACE.

Lady St. Clair, by St. Clair; San Francisco, Cal., Dec. 11, 1874; regulation 12.54¾

FASTEST RACE IN STRAIGHT HEATS.

Star Pointer, bay stallion, by Brown Hal, dam Sweepstakes, by Snow Heels; Indianapolis, Ind., Sept. 18, 1897; regulation 2.04¾, 2.03, 2.01

HALF-MILE TRACK RECORD.

Joe Patchen, 2.03, black stallion, by Patchen Wilkes, dam Josephine Young, by Joe Young; Combination Park, Boston, Oct. 28, 1896 . . . . 2.04½

In explanation of the above table, unless otherwise stated, the records have been to sulky. The term wagon means a four-wheel skeleton buggy. Time means that the record has been made against the watch, and not in a race, and "regulation" that the track is a regular mile track, three feet from the inner fence. All records made since 1891 have been made to bicycle-wheel sulky unless otherwise specified.

AUTHENTIC ENGLISH TRACK TROTTING RECORDS TO DATE, OCT. 8, 1897.

Miles.		Time.
¼	Lake Erie, by Cadmus Hambletonian, dam Daisy Dayton (American bred); Crystal Palace, Sydenham, May 28, 1898	42 sec.
½	†Rowley, black gelding, by Clear Grit, dam thoroughbred (bred in Canada); Alexandra Park, London, May 1, 1893	1.09¼
1	†Rowley; Greenwich Park, Liverpool, March 20, 1893	2 24¾
1½	Rowley; Alexandra Park, London, June 10, 1893	3.41⅗
2	Rowley; Greenwich Park, Liverpool, April 24, 1895	5.00½
2½	*†Rowley; Alexandra Park, London, June 12, 1895	6.27⅗
3	Benny C., black gelding, by Indianapolis, dam Clipper, by Albert (American bred); Manchester Racecourse, April 16, 1897	7.49
4	†Ellia McKay; black mare, by Ansonia, dam Shelburne Girl, by Highland Boy (bred in Canada); Manchester Racecourse, June 1, 1896	10.37⅘
5	†De Brino, black gelding, by Detractor; Ashtown Park, Dublin, Sept. 1, 1895	13.13
6	*†Lady Combermere, chestnut mare (Canadian); Manchester Racecourse, July 16, 1894	17.46¼
7	Do. do. do. do.	20.46¼
8	Do. do. do. do.	23.45
9	Do. do. do. do.	26.45½
10	*†Benjamin, brown gelding (Canadian bred); Paisley Recreation Ground, Sept. 19, 1896	28.30
11	*†Lady Combermere; Manch'r Racecourse, July 16, 1894	32.44½
12	Do. do. do. June 10, 1895	35.47¼
13	Do. do. do. do.	38.46½
14	Do. do. do. do.	41.50¾
15	Do. do. do. do.	44.48
16	Do. do. do. do.	47.51
17	Do. do. do. do.	50.50¼
18	Do. do. do. do.	53.49¼
19	Do. do. do. do.	56.55
20	Do. do. do. do.	59.59⅘

(Records not marked made in races.

† Flying starts. * Against time.

E. B. ABERCROMBIE.

Pacing—Four modes of progression are natural to the horse: the walk, the trot, the pace and the gallop, the so-called "canter" being only a slow gallop. The pace, though known in some Welsh breeds, is, curiously enough, not distinguishable by the average Englishman from the trot, with the result that for some years American pacing horses were allowed to compete in English trotting races as trotters.

Yet the distinction is patent. A horse trots when his off fore and near hind legs strike the ground simultaneously, and it paces when the legs *of a side* move in unison, like those of two riders on a tandem bicycle.

Certain drawbacks attach to either action. Thus, a trotting horse is apt to "over-reach," that is to say, the hind heels may step on those in front, which is obviously impossible in pacing, where the fore foot moves out of the way as the hind foot of the same side advances. It is for this reason that the speed of pacing is so far above that of trotting, so that the pacing record stands at 1 min. 39½ secs. (Star Pointer's time), as against a trotting record for the world (Alix) of 2 min. 3¾ secs.

Although, however, a pacer cannot "over-reach, he is more apt than the trotter to "knee-bang," *i.e.*, hit his knees or fetlocks (a proceeding against which he is protected by "booting"), as well as to "cross fire," or hit the heel of his off fore with the toe of the near hind foot.

Pacing has two forms. In one, the whole animal rolls from side to side, after the fashion of a skater doing the Dutch roll: and such a pacer can be distinguished when in motion even with no more than the top of his body visible. The other kind of pacer (to which belongs Mr. L. W. Winans' Jack Bowers, with a record of 2 min. 9¼ secs. for the mile, trial 2 min 7 secs.)

keeps the body still, merely swinging the legs slightly from side to side. It is this sort of pacer that looks to the casual observer as if it were trotting. It should be sufficiently apparent from the tables appended to this article that the faster records have almost invariably been held by the pacers, and it may fairly be inferred that the trotters will never have their chance in English trotting races until a separate class altogether is made for pacers.

Pacing is no modern artificial action, as some would have us believe, but may be traced in the horses of many nations of antiquity that rode without stirrups (examples may be seen in the casts of Egyptian sculptures, at the Crystal Palace), and is perhaps identical with the "ambling," so freely alluded to in the literature of the Middle Ages, while it is noticeable to-day in many of the Cossack horses. Of late years a great number of American pacers have been imported into England, and they may be seen any day in cabs and carts; indeed, the writer has even seen a pacer and trotter, both high steppers, in a phaeton in the Park, the coachman being under the impression that he had to handle a pair of trotters, and marvelling no doubt at the "rolling" of his near horse. It is important to bear in mind that many American horses are able to move with either action, a set of lighter shoes often sufficing to convert a trotter into a pacer, indeed it is customary to force such animals to keep to the pace by hobbling the legs of a side with elastic cords. Pacing is, in fact, less wearing to the animal's feet, as was proved in the case of Jay-Eye-See, which made a pacing record of 2 min. 6½ secs. after its feet had given out in trying to beat its own trotting record of 2 min. 10 secs. In the accompanying drawing of a trotter and pacer, it may be pointed out that in the pair coming towards the spectator the pacer is purposely made to incline rather more to one side than would actually be the case, in order to emphasise the difference between the two modes of action.

TROTTING. PACING.
(From a sketch by Mr. W. Winans.)

TABLE SHOWING EACH HORSE THAT HAS HELD THE "PACING" RECORD FROM THE BEGINNING OF THE CENTURY TO DATE, FOR A MILE.

(All these records were made "in harness," *i.e.*, to two-wheeled sulky, driver weighing 10 st. 10 lbs., except Pocahontas, who went to "wagon.")

The first pacer to do a mile in three minutes is not recorded, as the pacer is so fast that that rate of speed would be too slow to attract any attention.

The first pacing record which has been preserved is in 1835, when Oneida Chief, chestnut gelding, by Kentucky Hunter, dam unknown, went in 2.31.

Four years later, in 1839, Drover, black gelding, pedigree unknown, went the mile in 2.28.

In 1845, James K. Polk, chestnut gelding, pedigree unknown, went in 2.27.

Next year, in 1844, Unknown, chestnut gelding, pedigree unknown, went in 2.18½.

In 1852 Pet, roan gelding, pedigree unknown, went in 2.18½.

In 1855 Pocahontas, chestnut mare, by Iron's Cadmus, dam by Big Shakespeare, went in 2.17½.

In 1868 Billy Boyce, black gelding, by Corbeau--McGinnis Mare, by Tom Hal, went in 2.14¼.

In 1879 the blind horse, Sleepy Tom, chestnut gelding, by Tom Rolfe, dam by Sam Hazard, went in 2.12¼.

In 1881 Little Brown Jug, black gelding, by Hal Jr. — Lizzie, by John Netherland, went in 2.11¾.

In 1884 Johnstone, black gelding, by Joe Bassett, dam Cary Mare, by Ned Forrest, went in 2.6¼.

In 1892 Hal Pointer, black gelding, by Tom Hal—Sweepstakes, by Snow Heels, went in 2.4½. Later in 1892 Mascot in 2.4.

In 1894 Robert J., black gelding, by Hartford—Geraldine, by Jay Gould, went in 2.1½.

In 1896 John R. Gentry, black horse, by Ashland Wilkes, dam Dame Wood, by Wedgewood, went in 2.0½.

And in 1897 Star Pointer in 1.59¼, which is the record to date.

W. WINANS.

TROUT (*Salmo fario*)—Omitting the roach, so dear to the artizans of London and the great midland towns, the trout is beyond question the most popular and sport-giving of our fresh-water fish. It was a craze with the older naturalists to divide him into numerous species, but the modern, and without doubt the better, opinion is that all the different forms of trout found, at any rate, in fresh water, belong to one species; and high authorities now unhesitatingly assert not only that sea-trout and our common river and lake trout both sprang from one common ancestor, but that they are very closely allied to the salmon.

From the sportsman's point of view, which is, after all, the one with which we are more immediately concerned, these fish divide themselves up into two large classes :—(1) Sea or salmon-trout (*Salmo trutta*), called *white trout* in Ireland, with their variety, the bull-trout (these fish are dealt with in a separate article), and (2) the brown-trout, called yellow-trout in Scotland (*Salmo fario*), which varies a good deal in its appearance and habits, according as it may be found in large rivers, brooks, large lakes, and small lakes. Food, age, sex, growth-rate, and the soil over which it swims also have their effect on its colouring, spots, and general markings. With age, for instance, the spots often become almost imperceptible, and the fish grows long, lank, and ugly. Many such a trout has been foolishly returned to the water by well-meaning anglers, who thought it was merely out of condition, and would grow into a lusty, silvery-sided, big-spotted, small-headed fish later on in the season.

The variations in the size, number, and position of spots on trout are very remarkable. I have taken fish on the sides of which were two rows of spots placed at equal and regular distances, while the very next fish which found its way into my creel would be covered with spots as if they had been sprinkled over it out of a pepper pot. In quickly grown, healthy, lake trout the spots are often few and very large, with a kind of halo round them.

The colours on the scales of the fish depend very much on its surroundings. A trout taken off a muddy, weedy bottom will often have a general shade of rich yellow over its sides and belly, while even in the same lake a trout taken from the opposite shore which, let us say, is rocky and sandy, will be of a steely blue colour. A trout swimming in deep water over a peaty bottom will have a dark back, while fish which inhabit shallow, bright, gravelly streams, will have a light brown back, in fact almost gravel colour. This is without doubt a provision of nature to disguise the fish as much as possible from the keen eyes of herons and other fish-eating birds.

The life history of the trout is now well known. It commences, of course, with the egg, which is deposited by the female on a gravelly shallow in a river or brook. Its size may equal that of a pea if deposited by a large, healthy, and not too old fish, while the eggs from small burn trout are a good deal smaller. As the female sheds her eggs, the male fish extrudes a few drops of milt in the water, which may, or may not, reach the eggs and fertilize them. The fish, with a vigorous sweep of the tail, then throw up some gravel behind them, which is intended to, but does not always, cover up the eggs which have just been laid. The waste, of course, is enormous. A trout yields roughly about 1,000 eggs for every pound avoirdupois of its weight, but of these probably not one-tenth hatch and ultimately produce adult fish.

TROUT.

The fish culturist, on the other hand (see PISCICULTURE), hatches out ninety-five per cent. or more of the eggs which he takes from the hen fish, and with good luck will rear fifty per cent. of the young fry. With him the great mortality is in the fry stage. In due course the eggs deposited by the trout hatch. If the temperature of the stream is sixty degrees, the period of hatching will be about sixty days; but in lower temperatures longer. Out through a crack in the shell of the egg struggles the alevin, a little fish which has a preposterous bag of yellow-looking fluid attached to its stomach. This feeds it for some weeks, during which it lies hidden among the stones. Then by degrees it begins to feed itself, and at the end of a year may be a fish of any size between two and ten inches in length, the latter, I need hardly say, being an extremely large yearling. In a Devonshire brook or Highland burn, the little fish may never exceed four or five inches in length, but in a large lake or river, and particularly if placed in a lake which has never before contained fish, and in which fish food has therefore increased to an enormous extent, it will grow in the course of a very few years to weigh four or five pounds, or even more.

Trout can now be bought so cheaply from half-a-dozen or more firms of pisciculturists, that almost any river, lake, or pond can be stocked with them at more or less expense, provided only that there is no pollution which will destroy the fish. But the advisability of turning rivers which produce quantities of excellent coarse fish into trout preserves is open to question. At the same time, it should be mentioned that many a river in which, owing to pollution, no trout can *breed*, can be made to afford sport by re-stocking it from time to time with fish obtained from the fish-culturists. The Wandle in its lower reaches is an instance of what has been, and can be done in this direction. The pollution in that stream is sufficient to destroy the eggs of trout, but not the fish.

Every fly-fisherman should have some general idea of the habits of trout, which vary somewhat according to the nature of the water and the size of the fish. Trout feed on the bottom, in mid-water, and take flies and insects from the surface; but generally speaking large trout are not ready feeders on, to them, such insignificant items of food as are found floating on the face of river or lake. To this rule, however, there are several exceptions. Where flies hatch out and come floating down stream in great numbers, large trout leave the bottom, and, poising themselves in the water, suck down hundreds of the insects which are passing over them, though the flies may be very small indeed. This is the case in the chalk-streams of Hampshire. In some other rivers which are very similar in character, the larger trout rise very badly to the fly, because there is not a sufficient quantity of flies to tempt them to the surface. Thus, while in the Test a fly-fisher will stand a fair chance of hooking trout weighing three or more pounds on a minute imitation of the Blue Dun, on some portions of the Kennet he may fish a whole season without getting a fish of this size, unless he resorts to larger and more substantial baits, such as a small gudgeon or bleak. The second exception, which is a very similar one, occurs in the season of the May-fly, when, on those rivers which produce this beautiful insect, large trout come to the surface during the May-fly carnival, and become fly-takers then, but at no other period of the year. Sometimes, too, large trout may be caught at night close to the sedges by fishing with a very large imitation moth or sedge-fly.

In the smaller and shallower streams, unless food is exceptionally abundant, trout run small, and take the fly readily enough when in the humour. And that trout humour is a very strange thing. During a portion of the day the fish lie hidden in holes in the bank, under the shelter of rocks and stones, or under over-hanging bunches of weeds, and the cleverest fly-fisher in the kingdom will fail to obtain any sport worthy of mention. But suddenly some mysterious change takes place; quantities of fish leave their hiding places and commence to feed, and for a time the sport may be fast and furious. These feeding times of trout may be owing in a large measure to changes of temperature. They may, too, be connected with some subtle electrical or other atmospheric condition of which we know nothing. In fly-producing rivers, if the term may be allowed, the rise of fish very often commences with the rise of fly. The word seems to be passed round that there is a banquet being spread on the surface of the water, and up rise the trout to partake of it.

Generally speaking, the morning and the evening are the best times of the day for fishing; but here again much will depend on the weather. In early spring a sharp frost in the small hours of the morning may prevent the fish from feeding much before ten o'clock. On the other hand, I have often known a morning in spring when all the fish were caught between seven and eleven and no sport worthy of mention was had during the rest of the day, though the evening seemed suitable enough for it. In lakes, this uncertainty of feeding-times is much more pronounced than in rivers. It is least noticeable of all in small brooks or burns where the trout are small, numerous, and hungry. A cold mist spreading over the water in the evening usually causes the trout to stop rising.

Fly-fishing for trout is, broadly speaking, divided into two branches: fishing with the Wet Fly; and fishing with the Dry or Floating Fly. For both forms of fishing I should recommend a rod not more than ten feet in length, fairly powerful in the top joint, and not too stout in the butt, playing well down to the hand. The best tackle-makers have devoted such pains to improving the fly-rod of late years that the reader can safely place himself in their hands, but may, with advantage, take an experienced friend with him when making his purchase. One of the best and cheapest forms of fly-rod is made of green-heart. Still better, but very much more expensive, is a rod of solid pieces of cane built up in sections. But whole-cane rods are also a good deal used, and may be recommended to ladies for their lightness. The rings should in every case be upright, and err, if anything on the side of largeness.

The line is a matter of some considerable importance. It should invariably be tapered—at both ends for preference—and be of eight-plait silk, round, solid, and dressed with linseed oil which has been forced into it by placing the line in the oil under an air-pump, and exhausting the air. Several dressings are necessary, and many rubbings down to obtain that beautiful smooth surface which is so invaluable when shooting the line through the rings in order to make an extra long cast. A guinea is not an extravagant sum to pay for 45 yards so prepared. The stoutest part of the line should be nearly as stout as a salmon line. This size is of course not necessary for the purpose of holding a fish, but to give the weight which ensures great precision in casting and enables the angler to get out a fly in the teeth of a considerable breeze. Where the line joins the gut it is, of course, tapered very fine, and there is nothing to alarm the fish. I have not much doubt, however, that these very heavy lines do have the effect of scaring other fish than the one the angler is intent on catching. In dry-fly fishing the line is greased with kidney suet of the red deer or the sheep—the former for preference—vaseline, or other grease, and floats on the surface of the water; but in wet-fly fishing, where the line sinks slightly, there are not a few anglers who use an undressed line which, on getting soaked with water, is sufficiently wet to enable satisfactory casting to be done with it, with the additional advantage of not flailing the water over much.

With regard to the reel, or winch, I personally have a strong preference for one of the Nottingham type with what is termed a "Bickerdyke" guard, or one of Slater's guards, and fitted with a light check. It has all the advantages of the ordinary check brass winch, but, thanks to its large diameter, it enables the angler to wind up the line almost as fast as if he had a multiplying winch, which is often of immense importance when playing a difficult fish. By placing a finger on the rim of the reel the check can be increased when needed.

At the end of the line comes the gut cast. This should always be tapered from medium gut to a very fine point, and be made of long pieces of gut—fifteen inches or so between the knots. The usual length is three yards, and this is a good length for wet-fly fishing where two, and sometimes three flies are used; but for dry-fly fishing, where a single fly is used, two yards and a half is sufficiently long, and when it becomes necessary to cast against a strong wind it is sometimes desirable to reduce the length of the cast to as little as a yard.

With a proper rod and line the beginner will soon learn to cast a fly fairly well, but with a weak, whippy rod and a heavy line, or a very light line and a stiff rod, even the most experienced fly fisher will make bad practice. Perhaps the best way to commence is to omit the cast, and, standing in an open meadow or grass-plat, wave the line backwards and forwards over the head, fully extending it, or endeavouring to, at each backward and forward cast. The wrist then soon acquires the knack of *making the rod do the work*, which is a point of considerable importance. The length of line can be gradually increased, and, when eight or nine yards of line can be extended straight on the grass, then the gut cast with the fly at the end of it may be added.

A common mistake of beginners is to make the forward cast too quickly, with the result that the line behind snaps like a whip, and the fly is cracked off. In making a backward cast the rod should be pointing a little towards the right, and then be brought forward almost perpendicularly over the shoulder. This causes the line to follow an abrupt curve, and the more abrupt this curve is, the longer it is necessary to give the backward cast. A common method of casting in Ireland is to make a very bold curve with the point of the rod, giving no time whatever for the backward cast. This is done by bringing the rod backwards almost horizontally with the earth, and without hesitation casting it forward perpendicularly over the shoulder—in short, something like the Spey cast. But there is no cast by which the fly can be placed so accurately as the one I have first described. The secret of allowing the fly to alight softly on the water is to aim at an imaginary point in the air about three feet immediately above the point on the water where it is desirable to place the fly. The fly will then reach this point, stop for a fraction of a second, and descend by its own weight.

Wet Fly-Fishing—I personally never use more than two flies for this branch of fly-fishing, and when the water is low and bright find I have infinitely better sport with a single fly than with two. What is called the dropper-fly should be placed on the cast about three feet, or a little less, from the tail-fly (less in small streams, more in large streams or lakes). For stream fishing the following is a useful list of flies:—march brown, hare's ear, red spinner, alder, cochybondhu, red palmer, black palmer, black gnat, sedges, may-fly, spent gnat. *Special flies for Yorkshire*:—Broughton's point, water-hen bloa, woodcock, dark snipe, march brown, iron blue dun, orange partridge, brown owl, poult bloa, knitted midge, yellow dun, dark needle, fog black. *Devonshire flies*:—blue upright, cowdung, silver twist, red upright, march brown without wings, etc. *Derbyshire*:—the cockwinged dun, darkwinged coachman, honey dun and other bumbles, and the flies recommended for dry fly-fishing.

Speaking generally, larger and brighter flies may be used at the commencement of the season than in July or August. Hackled-flies with *soft* hackle obtained from the neck of the hen, are preferred for wet-fly fishing, but many good trout are caught with winged flies sparsely hackled by cock's hackles.

Years ago controversy raged round the great question whether up-stream fishing or down-stream fishing leads to the best basket. Without the least doubt up-stream fishing is best where the water is bright and the fish educated, but in a Scotch or Irish rivulet, or in Norway, or any places where the fish are very unsophisticated, and rise freely, most fish will be killed fishing down stream provided a sufficiently long line can be cast. The difficulty in up-stream fishing is to strike the fish when it rises, and, indeed, to see or feel the rise, for the flies, as soon as they reach the water, are brought back by the current towards the angler, and the line sags. The experienced fly-fisher will keep one eye on the line and one eye on the water, and on the slightest check to the line or break of the surface, will strike.

Wet-fly fishing is by no means a "chuck-and-chance-it" operation, as it has been somewhat foolishly described. The angler must have a considerable knowledge of the most likely places to find the fish before he will have much success, and even then must cast with considerable accuracy, behind rocks, in tiny runs, on the edges of eddies, under overhanging trees and bushes. He must in addition have a very sharp eye for the rise of the fish, and a very keen sense of touch. Fishing up-stream is best done with a short line, and, when the water gets low, by pitching a single fly into tiny pools and runs between rocks, good sport may sometimes be had when the angler of average ability will declare it absolutely impossible to catch trout owing to the state of the water.

Wading is often necessary to enable the angler to keep sufficiently low. When standing on the bank he is probably in sight of the fish, while when he is knee-deep in water they hardly notice him. By entering the water the angler can also, of course, reach portions of the river which are beyond his casting powers so long as he remains on the bank.

The waterproofers now turn out such excellent goods that advice on waders is hardly required; but men of middle age and upwards, or those subject to rheumatism, should bear in mind that though waders made of light material are less fatiguing to carry than heavy ones, those of stout material, particularly if lined with tweed or some other woollen substance, afford very valuable protection from the cold, and are advisable in streams rising at considerable elevations. What I may term lowland streams often reach such a temperature in summer that very thin waders may be worn with impunity. Stockings are, generally speaking, better than boots, because they can be turned inside out, and they are all the better for being washed inside occasionally, and then dried, as the perspiration from the feet rots them very quickly. Thick woollen socks or stockings should always be worn inside the wading stockings, and another pair over the stocking to prevent any stones or grit which may enter the brogue, or shoe, from cutting into the indiarubber and causing a leak.

When fishing down, or across the stream, the dropper-fly can be worked to great advantage. Unless the cast is a very long one the dropper-fly may be dribbled along the surface of the water, and will often catch fish when the tail-fly is useless. On other days the fish may show a preference for the tail-fly, which is sunk an inch or two below the surface.

Dry-Fly Fishing, or fishing with a floating fly, may be carried on successfully wherever the water is fairly smooth and the trout are rising. It will kill fish on calm days when the wet-fly is absolutely useless. In those southern streams which are much fished, and where the trout feed mostly on flies such as duns, which float on the surface, a wet-fly is of little use except in the rapids below weirs and in mill tails, at night, during rain, or when the water is roughened by a strong breeze.

Dry-fly fishing is almost a cult in itself, and enthusiastic users of the floating fly are apt to condemn, and somewhat look down upon other methods; but a long experience of every kind of fly-fishing has taught me that the amount of skill and knowledge of the habits of the fish required is about equal whether the dry or wet fly be used. In dry-fly fishing it is usual to mark down a rising fish before casting the fly on the water, and then approach him very cautiously. On arriving within casting distance, being careful to be somewhat below the fish, a few false casts are made in the air. When the angler is confident he has the right amount of line out, the fly is dropped lightly as thistledown about a yard in front of the fish, and allowed to float over him without the slightest drag. The water in our southern chalk streams is usually clear, and as likely as not the fish will be seen if the light is right, and immediately on his taking the fly he is struck and played. It is of great importance that the line should not drag, but float naturally down the stream; and in selecting a fish, one rising close to the bank should always be preferred to one rising in the centre.

Greasing the line to make it float I have already described and recommended. It is also the custom to touch the body and hackles of the fly lightly with odourless paraffin, which is now kept in suitable bottles, fitted with cork and brush, at most tackle-shops. Any excess of paraffin on the fly should be removed with the pocket handkerchief.

Considerable difference of opinion exists among fly-fishers of experience as to whether a fish should be cast over repeatedly, or given up as hopeless after three or four casts. When fish are very numerous, and rising freely, if one is disinclined to take the artificial fly he may be regarded as shy, and best left alone (his mouth may be decorated with a fly or two), and it will be good policy not to waste time over him, but to seek another less sophisticated. But in the generality of rivers I have always observed that the fishermen who stick persistently to a rising trout, assuming that they can cast sufficiently well not to put him down—that is to say, frighten him and make him cease rising altogether—eventually get their fish. I remember spending the best part of two hot sunny days over a large trout in the Kennett. There was a great glut of May-flies, and he was rising freely all day long. I was rewarded for my patience by eventually catching him. He weighed between four and five pounds, so was worthy the trouble.

There are many points of great importance to be borne in mind when fishing with the dry-fly. In the first place it is most important not to allow the gut attached to the fly to float over the fish. In other words, it is better to make an over-short than an over-long cast. In selecting a fish care should be taken to cast over one that is really feeding on flies, and not merely "tailing," that is, burrowing its head in the weeds searching for fresh-water shrimps and other insects, while the tail, its head being depressed, breaks the water and gives the appearance of a rise.

"Bulging" is another term used by dry-fly anglers, and means the commotion in the water caused by a fish as it swims after and seizes the larva of the fly on its way to the surface. When the fish are "smutting," or rising at swarms of tiny black midges which are sometimes found on the river, they are often very difficult to catch with the artificial fly.

Both on wet and dry-fly streams trout are usually caught in the late evening, and even at night, with big flies dressed to imitate sedges and night moths. There is also a well-tried artificial fly, the Coachman, which is not only useful at night, but often accounts for a good fish in the day time. The following is a useful short list of flies for chalk streams.—*Small flies*:—Gold ribbed hare's ear, dark olive dun, iron blue, medium olive quill, red quill, blue quill, detached badger, Wickham's fancy, black gnat, little chap, and on some rivers the grannom. *Large flies*:—Orange sedge, silver sedge, alder, May-fly, spent gnat.

Loch Fishing—In well-stocked lochs, trout frequently swim in shoals, and are found mostly at the mouths of the streams, or at the outfall of the loch, over shallows and projecting rocky points, or spits of land, and in particular where the shallow water of the loch suddenly breaks into deep water. All these places can be fished from a boat which drifts broadside with the wind, one angler being in the bows, the other in the stern; and the speed of the boat may be retarded if needful by a stone attached to a rope, which drags along the bottom. Sometimes what is termed a floating anchor is used for the same purpose. If the best spots cannot be fished by drifting, the angler must of course be rowed to them, and the boat checked so long as appears desirable. On very rough days I have had my boat worked from the bank by a gillie, letting it out by means of a rope, and have so obtained fishing when it was almost impossible for a man to row against the wind and waves. Where there is no boat, salmon waders are often extremely useful. A great variety of loch flies is not required, but the size varies in different lochs. Where the water is dark and peaty, strong contrasts of colour are desirable, nothing showing better in such cases than the fly called the zulu. I prefer those with seals' fur body (dyed various colours). On calm days the dry-fly may be used. It should be cast into ripples left by rising fish. Another method, when there is no ripple, is to cast out the fly, let it sink to the bottom, and then draw it slowly to the surface, in which process the trout will often take it. Some lake trout rise very well at night. I never used more than two flies myself, nor do I advise them, but three are very commonly used.

Spinning for Lake Trout—This is generally done by rowing the boat and trailing the spinning tackle after it. The best baits are minnows, gudgeon, loach—in fact, any fish which will spin well, and is not too large. Probably the best artificial bait is the well-known phantom minnow. The Devon minnow is also very successful. For mounting the natural bait there are many forms of spinning flights sold in the shops, most of which I have carefully tried, and have come to the conclusion that none is so useful as some form of the Chapman spinner which, for this purpose, should have no lead on its spike. It never fails to spin a bait, unless the bait is too large for the fans. The tail triangle should be at least level with the tail of the bait. The archer spinner, the Bedford spinner, and crocodile spinner are all good forms of this tackle. About 36 inches from the spinning-bait should come a small double swivel—of brass for preference—and then a small lead hung *below* the level of the line. Then 24 inches more of gut, at the end of which the line is made fast. The spinning line, by the way, should be of solid, eight-plait silk, dressed, and as fine as can be used, having regard to the size of the trout likely to be caught.

Dapping the natural May-fly is carried on in some of the Irish lakes and elsewhere. It only lasts a few weeks. The tackle consists of a light 18 foot rod, a long and very fine undressed silk line, about two yards of fine undrawn gut, and a single hook, on which one or two May-flies are impaled. The angler sits in a drifting boat, the line is carried out by the wind, and success depends on keeping the May-fly just touching the water, without allowing any of the gut to alight on the surface. As the wind increases the rod must be lowered; as it decreases it has to be raised.

Thames Trout Fishing is a thing of itself. The fish grow to a great size, very rarely rise to a fly, and are mainly got by live bait, or spinning bait. In the early part of the season success depends in a large measure on knowing where to find individual fish. Later on, the trout work up into weir-pools. The most successful trout fisher I know uses exactly the same spinning tackle as that I have described for loch trout-fishing, but in the Thames it is not trailed, but cast out some distance, and then drawn rapidly in with alternate draws of the line and pulls of the rod, so as to keep the bait continually moving. The spinning should be done far more rapidly than for pike. The comparatively quiet waters of a reach are soon spun over, but the rough waters of the weir may be worked for a long time without disturbing the fish, and with some chance of success. One of the best spinning baits on the Thames is a small bleak or dace, and gudgeon are also used with much success.

Live-baiting for Thames trout requires more skill than most people would imagine. The line should be fine, and greased to make it float. At the end of it should be two yards of fine round gut, terminated with a small triangle. Above the triangle is the lip-hook. The lip-hook is put in the upper lip of a small bleak, gudgeon, or dace, and the triangle caught in its side not far from the tail. At the other end of the gut is a single shot, which keeps the tiny fragments of lead from slipping down the line, and a foot above this the line passes through a slit in a small cork, taken from a six-ounce medicine bottle.

In quiet reaches, the boat or punt is moored thirty or forty yards above the spot where the fish is supposed to be, and the live-bait is taken down over the fish by the stream. Then the angler waits patiently, reeling up slowly if he sees a fish feeding. In the weir pools the live-bait is worked into every eddy and spot likely to contain a fish, and is kept for ever moving. In rather calm water two minnows on single hooks will sometimes succeed better than the bait mentioned, but very large fish usually show a preference for a very large bait.

"Fly-tying" is dealt with in a separate article, and I would recommend those who seek to know further of this, the most delightful form of fishing which we can enjoy in British waters, to read the subjoined books on the subject.

JOHN BICKERDYKE.

Dry-fly Fishing, F. M. Halford; *Angling*, Francis Francis; *Angling for Game Fish*, John Bickerdyke; *Yorkshire Trout Flies*, T. E. Pritt. *Book of the Dry Fly*, G. A. B. Dewar.

TROUT—MEASUREMENTS, &c.—Length of head 4¼ to 4¾ (in old breeding males 3½), of caudal fin 7 to 7½, height of body 4¼ to 5 in the total length. Head much more pointed in some forms than in others. *Eyes*—diameter 4½ to 6 in the length of the head, varying with the size and age of the specimen, 1¼ to 2 diameters from the end of the snout and the same apart. In old breeding males the eyes are comparatively smaller, and as much as 3 or 3½ diameters from the end of the snout and also apart. *Teeth*—in a double zigzag row along the body of the vomer, and in a transverse row across the anterior portion of that bone where it is joined with the palatine arch. *Fins*—the first dorsal (except in old breeding males), as a rule, commences somewhat nearer to the snout than to the base of the upper caudal ray; the height of the anterior ray usually exceeds the length of its base. Origin of adipose dorsal fin about midway between the anterior insertion of the base of the rayed dorsal and the posterior extremity of the upper caudal lobe. Pectoral as long as the postorbital portion of the head, or even of the entire head excluding the snout, in some examples it is more pointed than it is in others. Ventral inserted beneath the middle or last third of the base of the dorsal fin. Caudal forked in the very young, emarginate in those of a medium size, becoming square in large examples, or even rounded. *Scales*—from 13 to 15 rows between the hind end of the adipose dorsal fin in a row passing downwards and towards the lateral-line. About 26 or 27 rows from the lateral-line to the base of the ventral fin. *Cæcal appendages*—these differ considerably, apparently being influenced to a great extent by the locality they inhabit and the food which they can obtain. *Colours*—these vary, as has already been observed, not only with locality but also owing to changes of food. Those from Wales and along the S.W. coast are of a somewhat darker appearance than those from the Midland counties and towards the north, and have rather more black but less red spots.

Day's *Fishes of Great Britain and Ireland.*

TROUT, RAINBOW—There are several varieties of the rainbow trout (*Salmo irideus*), but the rainbow of pisciculturists, which has been acclimatised in the Southern States of Eastern America, in the North Island of New Zealand, parts of Germany, and which is now being tried in England, is the *S. irideus* var. *Shasta*, which is found in the McCloud river.

It differs from our own trout principally in having smaller scales, a shorter head, a smaller mouth, and in being differently coloured. The gill covers are brilliantly coloured with carmine, and this colour extends along the middle of the side of the body in a broad line. The back is very dark, and is covered with black spots. The abdomen is almost white and is also spotted with black, though these spots are very much smaller and less numerous than those on the back. The head, tail, and fins are also spotted, and the ventral and anal fins are usually tipped with white, as are also sometimes the other fins. The eyes are larger than those of our own trout.

The rainbow probably rises more freely to the fly than any other salmonoid. It is extremely game, and has retained its high sporting qualities in all the countries into which it has been introduced. The opinion of most fishermen who have caught it in its own home, in the Eastern States, in New Zealand and in Germany, is that it fights better than the *fario*, Loch Leven or American brook trout. It is also "an excellent and delicate table fish."[1] It seems to attain a maximum weight of about 9 lbs, in New Zealand, America and Germany, and fish

[1] See Report of Rainbow in Bulletin of United States Fishery Commission, 1897.

of 5 lbs seem to be fairly common. It shows very little tendency towards cannibalism.

The rainbow trout is much more easy to rear than any other salmonoid which has come under my observation. They are practically free from attacks of fungus, and the young fish feed more freely than any other fry. They seem to be altogether the hardiest of any trout. This is a great recommendation to the pisciculturist, for the percentage of deaths among them should be less than with any other trout.

Angling writers seem to differ very much as to whether this fish will prove a success in our own waters, which fact is probably due to the very contradictory reports concerning it which come from the different places in the United Kingdom where it has been introduced. But little discrimination has hitherto been shown as to the relative value of these reports. Wherever the rainbow has been tried, the same results have followed. When it has been introduced into warm waters, as in the North Island in New Zealand and in the Southern States of Eastern America, it has done well; when it has been put into cold waters, as in the South Island in New Zealand and in the Northern States of Eastern America, it has disappeared. It seems also to disappear from shallow swift streams when introduced into them.

Were these facts kept in mind by those who stock waters, and those who publish and comment upon the reports of such attempts, much of the confusion and mystery which now apparently surrounds the rainbow would disappear. The probability is that in warm lakes and ponds and deep sluggish rivers, which do not get a rush of snow water in the winter, this fish will do well in the South of England, but it is still more probable that it will never thrive in the North. Lakes and ponds of from four to six feet deep with a stream, no matter how small, running in, seem to be the most favourable kind of waters. A good supply of food and of suitable weeds is absolutely necessary in a water which is to be stocked with rainbows.

In favourable waters, however, it should be a boon to the fisherman, as it thrives in waters where the *fario* would not do nearly so well, if at all. A mere trickle of water through a pond seems to be all that is necessary to its well-being, and it grows much more quickly than other trout.

The same patterns of flies as are used for other trout should be used for the rainbow, and in the waters stocked with them in England they seem to rise freely and boldly.

As the rainbow spawn usually in February and March, they should not be fished for from January to June. They recover from spawning, however, much more quickly than *fario*. This fact as to the time of their spawning has been brought forward as an argument against their introduction into our waters. There is no doubt that they would probably eat the spawn of the *fario* if they had an opportunity, but it is improbable that they would have one, as they would not go up stream to the spots where the spawn of the *fario* was deposited until most of the ova of the *fario* were hatched out. Besides this, the rainbow will probably thrive best in waters which are not suitable for the *fario*.

CHARLES WALKER.

RAINBOW TROUT.

FLY DRESSING FOR TROUT AND GRAYLING—WET-FLY AND DRY-FLY—The dressing of flies is not a modern invention. Ælian, writing about the end of the second century of our era, describes fishing with the artificial fly as practised in Macedonia; and Oppian, writing about 176 A.D., refers to the practice of flyfishing for a sea-fish called the scarus. And though the next reference to the subject in literature occurs in the book *On Fysshynge with an Angle*, published in 1496, and ascribed to the legendary Dame Juliana Berners, yet, judging from what was known of it in Izaak Walton's day, the art was even then encrusted with tradition. It had probably been introduced into England by the Romans, and had come down from mouth to mouth, or from manuscript to manuscript, largely, no doubt, through the monks.

On Fysshynge with an Angle gives certain particulars of dressings of flies, but no instruction in the methods of tying. Walton himself, in his first edition (1653), gives a transcript of the instructions in Barker's *Delight* (1651); and in his second edition (1655) he falls back on Leonard Mascall's *Booke of Fishinge with a Hooke and Line* (1590), and copies Mascall's instructions verbatim. Walton was therefore no inventor or refiner.

The advance in the art during the succeeding centuries has been slow, many writers who pretended to authority contenting themselves with merely copying from previous authors. In the *Compleat Fisherman* of James Saunders (1724) there is the first mention of silkworm gut. Successively there followed Bowlker's work, *The Universal Angler* (1766), Best's *Concise Treatise* (1787), T. F. Salter's *Angler's Guide* (1814), Geo. C. Bainbridge's *Flyfisher's Guide* (1816), Ronald's *Flyfisher's Entomology* (1836), Hewett Wheatley's *Rod and Line* (1849), which advocates eyed hooks; and several other crude, was made to imitate natural insects, yet Ronald (*Flyfisher's Entomology*) was the first, in 1837, to set side by side upon the same page pictures of the natural flies and the dressings claiming to represent them, and to append to the descriptions the scientific names of the

LARGE AND SMALL PHRYGANIDS.
(Two-thirds natural size.)

various insects depicted. Bainbridge's work in 1816 had given certain coloured pictures, more or less meritorious, of some of the natural insects, but not of the dressings representing them. Theakston's work gave minute verbal descriptions of some ninety different insects, with a careful

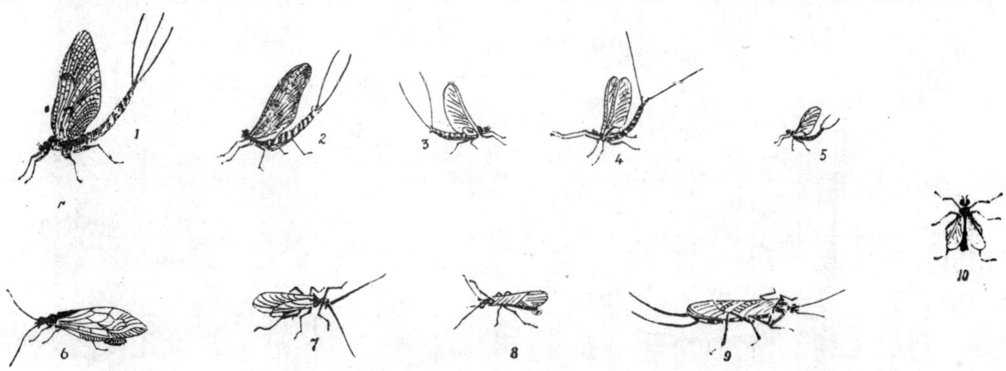

1. GREEN DRAKE. 2. MARCH BROWN. 3. OLIVE DUN. 4. RED SPINNER. 5. IRON BLUE.
6. ALDER. 7. FEBRUARY RED. 8. WILLOW FLY. 9. STONE FLY. 10. HAWTHORN FLY.
(Two-thirds natural size.

improvements much in advance of his time; John Jackson's *Practical Flyfisher* (1853), Blacker's *Art of Flymaking* (1855), Stewart's *Practical Angler* (1857), and Theakston's *British Angling Flies* (1862). In Francis Francis's *Book of Angling*, published first in 1867, the art of fishing with a dry-fly is first touched on by a standard author, though a century earlier the method had been suggested for casual use. Indeed, in the same century appeared eyed hooks and the Pennell jam knot. In 1876 appeared *A Quaint Treatise of Flees and the Art of Artyfychall Flee Making*, Mr. Aldam's reprint of an old Derbyshire manuscript describing the dressings of some twenty-five flies, with addenda by Mr. Aldam. The feature of this work was that a representation of every fly described was mounted in sunk panels, with examples of the materials from which it was made. It is said that there are several old manuscript copies of the same original MS. transmitted from father to son in the midland and northern counties.

In 1885 appeared Mr. F. M. Halford's *Floating Flies and How to Dress Them*, a work in which the first serious and adequate attempt was ever made to describe the minute processes of fly dressing. And although it purports to be confined to giving instructions in dressing floating flies, yet it is so clear, so careful and so exhaustive that the art of dressing sunk flies may readily be picked up from its pages. An extension of the subject, bringing it down to date, entitled *Dry-fly Entomology*, has lately been published.

Though doubtless from the first some effort, more or less black and white life-size drawing of each. These works gave a great stimulus to the study of angler's entomology, and led incidentally to a steady improvement in the dressing of flies.

The classes of natural flies imitated are :—

I. The Ephemeridæ, comprising the Green Drakes, the March brown series, the blue, olive, and yellow dun series, the blue winged olives and the iron blue series with their respective spinners.

II. The Sialidæ, comprising the Alder fly.

III. The Phryganidæ, the caddis or case flies.

IV. The Perlidæ or stone flies.

V. The Tipulidæ or saw flies.

VI. The Cecropidæ, comprising only the Froghopper.

VII. The Empidæ, comprising only the Early Black Gnat.

VIII. The Tenthredinidæ, comprising only the Great Dark Drone.

IX. The Hemerobiidæ, comprising only the Gold-eyed Gauze-wing.

X. The Diptera, comprising house-flies, blue-bottles, and the like.

XI. The Coleoptera or beetles.

XII. The Hymenoptera, comprising ants, bees and ichneumons.

In addition, anglers dress imitations of caterpillars and of some of the above insects in their larval and pupal stages, and flies typical of a class which we may call general flies, and flies which may be termed fancy flies, resembling no insect except in shape; for even where no particular insect is imitated, the aim of the dresser is to suggest an insect of some sort. The cuts have giver an idea of the shapes of the principal natural flies. The methods of imitating them are very various; and in deciding whether to adopt one method rather than another the dresser should ascertain the character of the water to be fished with it.

The aim being to suggest some living insect, the dresser must seek to present to the fish the colours, the shadings, the harmonies, the attitudes and the motions of life. Thus, where the surface of the stream is smooth, so that the natural flies float down on it without danger of immersion, the best imitation the angler can offer to the fish is one as precise in colour, size, shape, and attitude on the water as can be contrived consistently with strength and durability. Motion must be omitted. Here what is known as dry-fly fishing comes into play. In tumbling, shallow mountain streams, the colour and action of life only can be suggested, as any attempt to portray the attitudes of the natural insect as it is when at rest would be thrown away; and the action of something struggling for life in a boiling torrent is much more likely to be attractive to the fish. Hence the Yorkshire school, addicted to the use of soft hackles and discarding wings, and the Devonshire school, which employs brilliant cock's hackles, again without wings. For big heavy waters, such as Tweed and Clyde in spring, strongly built flies with divided wings of several thicknesses of feather are often employed. Derbyshire affects lightly built floating flies and bumbles; the Usk, big spare lightly dressed winged flies with a very knowing rake. There are in fact endless varieties in detail in the dressing of flies to suit the various rivers of these islands; and that is why it is well to get flies of a local dresser, or, better still, to be master of all modes of dressing them. Above are seven styles of dressing the common blue dun.

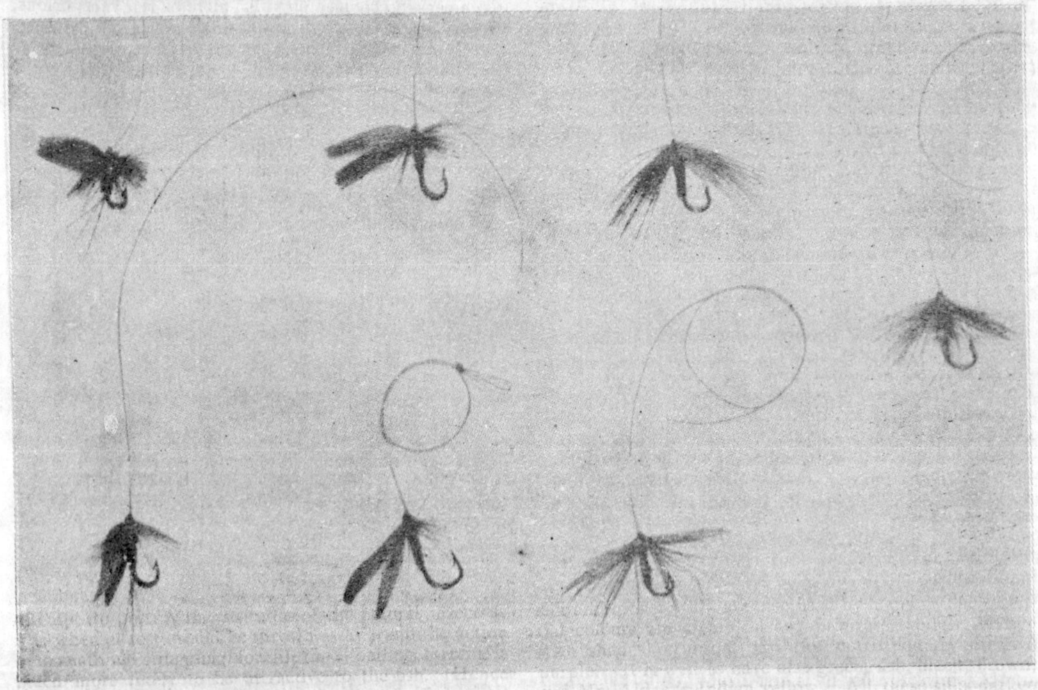

Implements.—It is only possible to few to make firm work on small eyed hooks without the assistance of a vice; and most amateurs will find a vice an advantage in dressing sunk as well as floating flies. The form is not very important, provided that the jaws are strong and well tempered, yet small enough to allow the forefinger and thumb to come down upon and grasp the hookshank in the operation of winging. The vice should be provided with a clamp for fixing it to a table. The most beautiful vice is Mr. Hawksley's, made by Messrs. Holtzapfel, of Cockspur Street, price 35*s*. In addition, the operator needs a pair of straight fine-pointed dissecting scissors, a pair of curved oculist's or manicure scissors, one or more pairs of hackle pliers, a watchmaker's pliers, a sharp penknife, and a dubbing needle. A stout needle, fixed in a wooden shaft, makes an efficient dubbing needle.

Materials—The dresser must have tying silks of various colours, wax, gut, hooks, varnish, floss silk, dubbings, herls, tinsels, wires, hackles both from poultry and other birds, wings and other feathers of various birds, and dyes.

Tying silks—Pearsall's gossamer silk, spun for the purpose, are the most convenient on the whole. Naples silk and glover's silk are also used by many. The essential colours are cream, straw, primrose, yellow, orange (two shades), crimson, and (for north country streams) purple. It is well to have also green, ash, black, brown, and Mr. Aldam's Indian yellow. All these silks darken very much when waxed.

Wax—It is therefore desirable to have some transparent wax in addition to some ordinary harness maker's wax.

Gut will be required, if the flies are not dressed on eyed hooks, and of fineness appropriate to the work in hand.

Hooks—These are either eyed or ordinary, and are to be had blue, bronzed, or japanned. The bends used are Limerick, Sneck, Kirby, and Round, and the sizes run from 000 new scale (the smallest) to No. 4, and very occasionally to a larger size for trout, grayling, and dace, but much larger sizes are used for chub. Eyed hooks have either upturned or downturned or straight eyes. Sizes under No. 4 are not found to hook well in wet fly-fishing, and it is better for this purpose to dress flies on gut. On the other hand, for dry-fly fishing eyed hook present enormous advantages. Mr. H. S. Hall's

Snecky Limerick bend with upturned eye is probably the best bend for this style of fishing.

Varnish—A small bottle of ordinary spirit varnish, very thin, and stoppered with a cork rubbed with mutton fat to prevent it from sticking to the bottle, answers all purposes. The varnish is applied with a fine porcupine quill, or a needle mounted like the dubbing needle.

Floss Silks—These must be bought of tackle-makers, and a large variety of colours is of service. The essential colours are white, primrose, yellow, orange, and claret. All shades of green and olive, ash, red-brown, and purple are desirable. Floss silks are used for wrapping round hooks to imitate the bodies of flies.

Dubbings are used for similar purposes, only they have to be spun on the tying silk to make them adhere. Crewels, wools, baize, furs of various animals (hare, rabbit, fox, squirrel, mole, water-rat, opossum, &c.), mohair, seal's fur, and pig's-wool. The function of dubbing is to represent the filmy semi-transparent covering which modifies the base colour of the natural fly. Thus the mole's fur or water-rat's fur, with which the iron blue dun is dressed, serves to indicate the soft inky envelope which in the sub-imago covers the delicate claret spinner within. So this fly is properly dressed with a plum or claret coloured silk, which shows through the envelope of dubbing. It should be noted that in a wet-fly, where the body is dubbed, it is of great importance that the tying silk should be of the right colour, for when the fly is wet, the silk will, especially in bright sunlight, show right through the dubbing in a most incomprehensible manner; and if the colour of the silk be wrong, the fly will not do. It is better to be wrong over the dubbing than over the base colour.

Waxing has a very modifying influence upon the colours of silk, greater or less according to the nature of the silk and the wax. With ordinary harness-maker's wax, white silk becomes dark leaden dun, cream a dark olive, primrose and yellow other and lighter shades of olive, olive nearly black, orange a dirty yellow brown, and crimson a deep red. Dubbings cannot, unless they be composed of one fur only (and even then not always), be successfully described on paper. The dresser should, if possible, match the dubbing with the natural fly, wetting the material and holding it to the light. If dubbing be made of more than one material, it should be well mixed by pulling and tearing until the colour is uniform throughout. This process is called "testing."

The dubbing is applied thus. A sufficient portion and a little over is taken in the hand and picked out so as to form a long fine taper. This is rolled in the palm of the left hand with the two middle fingers of the right. The taper roll is then placed along the tying silk, with the fine end towards the fly, close up to the hook, and is rolled on to the silk with the forefinger and thumb. The silk is then twisted tightly from right to left (assuming that the dresser is winding over the hook and away from him), until it has taken hold of the dubbing for a sufficient length. The silk with the adhering dubbing can now be wound on to the hook. The object of twisting the silk from right to left is to prevent the dubbing from working off the silk. If twisted in this way, each lap of the dubbed silk serves to fix the dubbing tighter. In some flies only a little dubbing is put under the breast or round the shoulders. In other patterns the dubbing is used to represent the legs of the fly only. In dressing duns, it is well to pick over the dubbed body with the pliers to remove any inequalities.

Herls—Green and bronze peacock herls, including the eye feathers, and black ostrich herls are essential, with wing and tail feathers of adjutant and condor for those who can get them. Strips from the tails of golden pheasant, cock-pheasant, turkey, blue macaw, magpie, and others, breast feathers of the common goose, wing and back feathers of the heron, lapwings' toppings, and many more, are useful at times.

Tinsels—Flat gold and silver tinsel of two widths, fine gold wire, fine gold and silver twist of two thicknesses, and (for chub flies) stouter oval gold and silver twists should be procured.

Hackles are the most important part of the fly-dresser's equipment. They are procured from the necks and saddles of poultry, and from the necks, breasts, backs, rumps, and wing coverts of numerous other birds. The following are the most important:—corncrake (shoulder and under wing), young curlew (shoulder), dotterel (shoulder), golden plover (shoulder and breast), red grouse, moorhen (under wing), brown owl (shoulder), partridge (breast, back, and rump), pheasant, cock and hen (neck and breast), sea gull and sea swallow (shoulder), snipe (shoulder and under wing), starling (neck, crest, back, shoulder, and under wing), thrush (under wing), and wren (tail). They are all easily procured, except the young curlew, the dotterel, and the sea swallow. Many others are mentioned in books on fly-dressing, but are only of occasional service.

Poultry hackles are had from the necks and saddles of domestic fowls, both cock and hen. The colours needed are badger (black centre and cream-coloured points) to be had from Dorkings, black, blue (the smoky dun colour known as blue by fishermen), and as many shades as possible from nearly black to the palest smoke colour, to be had from Andalusian and blue game fowls; cinnamon, cochybondhu (a hackle with black centre and list, and red in the interval), cream, cuckoo (a freckled hackle from the Plymouth rock), furnace (black centre and red points), ginger (a series of shades from cream to light red, including ginger cuckoo), grizzle (a freckled or spangled sandy or rusty blue dun), honey dun, yellow dun, and copper dun (blue duns of all shades edged or freckled with sandy or rusty ginger or red of all shades), from cross-bred Andalusians and blue game fowls, red of all shades, from a hot orange, ginger to deep mahogany, and white.

In addition, white, ginger, or blue hackles dyed in canary, onion dye, green olive, brown olive, and medium olive (a good variety of shades), and white and black hackles dyed claret.

Blues, honey duns, sandy gingers, and badgers are the most difficult to procure good.

Few hackles approximate to perfection, but there are innumerable useful hackles falling short of that degree of excellence. Good hens' hackles are easier to get than good cocks'. Hackles, and indeed all birds' feathers (except rusty duns), are in best condition from December to March. For floating flies, cocks' hackles are immensely superior to hens'. Cocks of two years old and upwards yield the best hackles for that purpose. For wet-fly work softer hackles are better than stiff ones. Poultry hackles should be fine and clean and bright in the fibre, and as much as possible of the same colour back and front.

The large saddle hackles of cocks, their beard hackles, and the broad glossy hackles on their shoulders are used for representing the whisks or tails of upwinged flies (Ephemeridæ). These are also represented by the white and blue feathers from the neck and breast of a guinea fowl, dyed or plain as required.

Other feathers—Wings of the hen, blackbird, bullfinch, chaffinch, coot, corncrake, fieldfare, grouse, common gull, jay, lark, partridge, peahen, cock and hen pheasant, snipe, jacksnipe, starling (old and young), thrush, and woodcock should be had. Also tails of the great tit, partridge, pheasant (cock and hen), some broad glossy feathers from under a cormorant's wing, and some loose fibred feathers from a moorhen's breast.

Dyes—Crawshaw's dyes or the Diamond dyes in the following colours: magenta or wing, red spinner, orange, canary, green olive, brown olive, and medium olive, green drake, slate, and iron blue.

With the above equipment the amateur will be well set up. Few more feathers are required, but a piece of bottle rubber should be procured, some white horsehair, and some tawsy ends of gut for dyeing, some chaffinch quills, and some pike scales to wing black gnats.

General Principles—In spite of the numerous

insects imitated and the innumerable patterns to be found described in books, there are structurally only two types of artificial fly, viz., (1) those hackled at the shoulder only, with or without wings, and (2) those hackled all down the body, or the palmer or bumble class, again with or without wings. These are the essential characteristics, and whether the hackle be soft and mobile or stiff and glassy, whether the fly be winged or wingless, fat, thin, or medium, whether it be heavily or lightly dressed, whether it has quill or herl or dubbing for body, ribbing, tag, or whisk, are matters of detail. The tying silk is the structural basis or skeleton of the fly. The rest, wings, hackle, whisks, dubbing, quill, floss, and what not, are all accessories which are fitted into the silk at various stages according to the type of fly to be dressed. Experience only, and the study of good models, can teach the novice how and when to fit these accessories to the best effect for the special purposes of the water for which the fly is required.

Processes in Outline—A fly may be begun in four different ways, viz. :—(1) At the shoulder, (2) at the middle of the hook, (3) at the tail, and (4) in the case of an eyed hook only, at the head. And it can be finished in three places, viz. :—(1) At the head, (2) at the shoulder behind the hackle, and (3) at the tail.

Beginning at the shoulder one can work to the tail and back to the head and finish there, or return to the shoulder and finish there, or the process may be reversed. Beginning at the middle one can work to the head and back to the tail and finish there, or return to shoulder or head and finish there. Beginning at the tail one can work to the head and finish there or at the shoulder. Beginning at the head of an eyed hook, one can work to the tail and finish there, or return to shoulder or head and finish there.

In any case these two rules should be observed. (1) That there should be no knot or hitch in the tying silk from the start until the finish, and (2) that that finish should be the whip finish here described. It is the only safe finish, and is executed as follows.

The Whip Finish—The fly being finished all except the fastening of the silk, take the silk between the forefinger and thumb of the right hand, about two inches from the hook, bring the loose end round the little finger of that hand and over the backs of the fingers, and lay it along the hook so that it will be tied down by the next lap of the silk. Then go on winding the silk for three or four laps over the loose end, extricate the gut, if any, from the successive turns of the silk, and taking the loose end of the silk in the left hand, draw it towards the left till all the silk has been drawn through and the finish is quite firm. Then varnish the finish. The varnish may also be applied by putting a drop on the silk near the fly just before pulling through.

The dressing of flies upon eyed hooks is dealt with separately from dressing upon gut. The dressing of flies on gut is primarily for wet flies, and that of flies on eyed hooks for dry flies. But if any one desires to dress floating flies on gut or sunk flies on eyed hooks, he can do so from the following descriptions, the difference between wet and dry being largely a matter of the amount and quality of wings and hackle.

The Parts—Wings for Wet-flies—Wings are of many types. They are either split, solid, or rolled; single, double, or treble, or even thicker; and they either show the upper or under surface of the feather on the outside. They can, within limits, be of any degree of fineness or breadth. Rolled wings, reversed wings, Tweed upright wings (to coin a term), Irish wings, and Drake wings require special methods of tying. All other wings are here classed as ordinary. Wings are usually cut from the quill feathers (primary or secondary) of birds, but in some birds, where the primaries and secondaries are of too coarse a texture, smaller feathers of suitable quality are found.

Split wings, and indeed most wings, are best dressed from corresponding feathers taken from opposite sides of the same bird; but many dressers merely double the fibre cut from one feather, and coax it into shape when tied on. Ordinary wings are tied in at the head projecting over the bend of the hook; and where feathers from opposite sides of a bird are used, the part of the feather which was nearest the root of the stalk should be nearest the head of the fly.

In tying on ordinary wings the fibre used for the wing is grasped firmly in the forefinger and thumb of the left hand, and brought down on the hook so that the fibres are nearly as possible parallel with the shank. The silk is then brought up between the thumb and the hook, over the silk and down between the hook and the forefinger; the fibre and the hook are again grasped firmly and the silk is brought down with a firm pull, and round again and over the fibre lapping, three or four turns closely towards the head.

Rolled wings, reversed wings, and Irish wings are tied in, projecting over the head of the fly.

Rolled wings are made of two little rolls of fibre from the wing of a bird, and it is distinctive of this method that they must be tied on on a silk basis, all other wings being tied on the bare hook.

Reversed wings are merely ordinary or rolled wings tied on projecting over the head of the fly.

What are here called Tweed upright wings are made of two or more thicknesses of feather laid one over another, doubled, and then tied on as ordinary wings. The fibre is then divided into two equal parts and the silk passed between the two parts and round under head and shoulder to keep the wings apart. Rolled wings and reversed wings are kept apart in the same way.

Irish wings are made of a doubled slip of feather tied in projecting over the head of the fly. The rest of the fly is then dressed and the wing feather is then brought back to slope over the tail, and bound down with the silk and secured by the whip finish.

The wings of May-flies or Drakes are from the breast feathers of mallard, Canadian wood duck, Rouen drake, or Egyptian goose, and are tied in by the stalks.

Wings for Dry-flies—Wings for floating flies are of three kinds besides May-flies—all split and all put on more or less upright—ordinary, reversed, and rolled. They are also single or double (except the rolled, which are manifold), and they present either the upper or under side of the feather on the outside. The upper side is the more usual side to show, as the outward curve of the feather thus tied makes the wings sit like a V, and they serve as a parachute to let the fly down cocked upon the water. The detailed manipulation of these wings is dealt with later in the section devoted to dressing floating-flies on eyed hooks.

Bodies—The bodies of flies are simulated either with plain tying silk waxed with dark or colourless wax, or with the same covered or partly covered with dubbing, floss silk, quill (so called—the strands from the eye or tail herl of a peacock stripped of its metallic flue or the enamel of the stalks of feathers), herl and tinsel, and are ornamented with ribbings of silk, gold or silver wire or tinsel, or with tags of gold or silver tinsel. The method of winding-on dubbing has been previously described. The material for winding-on for bodies is usually tied in at the tail projecting to the left, and is thence wound to the shoulder and secured. Herl is usually tied on three or four or more strips together, and then the strips are twisted from right to left round and so as to adhere to the tying silk, and so wound up the body and secured at the shoulder.

Legs—These are simulated either with hackles, or by picking out dubbing. Poultry hackles require no preparation except the stripping of the down at the root. But the soft hackle of other birds must be stroked backwards to enable the fibres to separate freely as the hackle is being wound. Cock hackles are sometimes doubled by drawing all the fibres to one side of the stem, the stem being held by one end in the vice and the other in the hackle pliers. Soft hackles, if too thick or of irregular shape, are often stripped of the plume on that side which will be under when the hackle is wound. Every hackle should be tied in so that it can be wound on its edge, and with the best side towards the head of the fly.

Hackles are tied in by either the stalk or the point. Most modern dressers tie in the stalk and wind the hackle by the point, which is seized in the pliers for the purpose. Every hackle should be wound in the same direction as the silk is wound. Thus if the silk is whipped over the hook and away from the operator, the hackle should be wound in the same direction, and *vice versâ*.

Whisks.—Three or four fibres of saddle or beard hackle of a cock, soft and flexible for wet flies, stiff and glassy for floating flies, or two or three fibres of a gallina neck or breast feather dyed or plain for floaters, are taken in the left hand when the whipping approaches the bend of the hook, and the butt ends being passed under the hook the silk is brought over the hook and round underneath again ; then under the whisk fibres, close, to make them sit up.

PROCESSES IN DETAIL.—DRESSING FLIES ON GUT.

First Series.

To Tie a Hackle Fly hackled at Shoulder Only.—*Process I*—Fix your hook firmly in the vice by the barb and the lower part of the bend, with the shank end projecting to the right. Double 15 or 18 inches of tying silk round the hook and twist the ends lightly together, and then wax the silk by rubbing the wax up and down the doubled and twisted length two or three times. Then separate and untwist the silk at the eye and draw it apart against the hook. Take a length of gut and bite one end so as to make a few indentations for the silk to grip. So far the process is alike for all flies to be dressed on gut. Then, holding one end of the silk in the left hand and taking the silk in the right 3 or 4 inches from the left, pass it over the hook, and holding firmly by the left hand, whip under and round the hook, beginning where the shoulder of the fly should be (leaving about one-sixth of the shank bare to take the hackle and the head), and bind down the short length of the silk with three or four successive lappings, close together, but moving towards the bend of the hook. The short end may now be taken off by a smart twitch towards the head of the hook. Next pass the bitten end of the gut athwart under the hook, bring the silk firmly round it for the next turn, and it will lie straight under the hook. Pull it until the bitten end is under the middle of the hook, and then whip in close firm turns to near the bend. Bind on the whisks, if any, as described. Then the silk or floss or quill or herl for the body and the rib, if any, or roll on the dubbing as described, and lap firmly back to the shoulder. Then take the hackle, prepared as described, a little longer in fibre than the hook shank, and lay it face downwards on the hook with the stem towards the bend, and the plume projecting over the gut, and bind the stem down firmly with two or three turns of silk. Twitch off the stump of the stem, wind the body material or ribbing or both to the shoulder and secure them with two turns of silk, and cut away the waste. Then taking the point of the hackle in the hackle pliers, and passing the middle finger of the right hand through the ring of the pliers, hold the stem of the hackle at right angles to the hook, and turn the hackle on its edge in the same direction as the silk is wound, two, three, or four times round the hook, each turn close in front of or behind the last. Wind the silk through the hackle so as to bind down each successive turn and, having reached the head, either finish with the whip finish, or, after three or four turns to form the head, whip back through the hackle and finish with the whip finish behind the shoulder. Cut away the point of the hackle and varnish the finish, and the fly is complete. A variant of this method of finishing behind the shoulder is, after binding on the hackle to whip under the hackle up to the head, to take two turns back from the head, wind the hackle up to the silk, whip the silk through it, and finish behind the hackle.

Process II—Commence as before, but in the middle of the hook, lay the gut under, whip in close turns to the head, binding down the hackle stem on the bare hook, pass the silk under the hackle and whip to the head. Thence whip to the hackle, turn it as before, and whip carefully through it. If the body is to be plain silk, the dresser may now either whip to the tail and finish there or return to the shoulder and finish there. If the body is to be dubbed and finished at the tail, the dubbing can be rolled on immediately after the hackle has been wound, care being taken to have the dubbing thickest at the shoulder, and tapered to the tail. Or if the body is to be floss or quill, the material can be tied in at the shoulder, projecting over the head, and wound to the tail and secured, the waste end cut off, and the fly finished with a whip finish. But if the body will not be made too thick, it is better to whip the bare silk from the shoulder to the tail, and there bind in whisks and body materials as may be, and thence work back to the shoulder and finish behind the hackle. This method makes a strong and workmanlike fly, and is preferable to the finish at the tail because (1) the latter is liable to be torn by the trout's teeth, (2) the former is susceptible of more elaboration in the way of body materials than the other.

Process III—Laying the bitten gut under the hook, hold it there with the forefinger and thumb of the left hand, and beginning near the head lap in open folds to the tail, and take one or two turns back towards the head. Bind in whisks, quill, herl, or other body material, and whip in close laps to the shoulder. As soon as the first two turns over the gut are taken, the open coils of silk may be unwound and twitched off as waste. The hackle is then tied on, and the body material is wound to the shoulder and made fast, the hackle wound and the fly finished at head or shoulder as before.

Second Series.

To tie a Fly hackled all down the Body—a Palmer or Bumble.—*Process I*—Beginning at the shoulder and whipping to the tail, bind in at the tail, projecting to the left the tinsel wire or other ribbing and the body material (unless it be herl, which will be rolled on as described), and whip to the shoulder. Bind in the hackle or hackles by the stalk firmly, and cut or break off the waste end. Wind the body material to the shoulder, secure and cut off waste. Wind the hackle in close coils at the head and more open coils to the tail, and leave the pliers hanging to the end. Then bring the ribbing in even open coils through the hackle, secure at shoulder and cut off. If two hackles are used, the front one may now be turned and the silk wound through to the head, when the whip finish completes the fly.

Process II—Commence at the middle of the hook and binding in the gut, whip to the shoulder, tie in the hackles, whip to the tail, and complete as in Process I.

Process III—Before whipping to the tail, bind in body materials and ribbing projecting to the right. Whip to the tail, wind on the body material, secure at tail with two turns, and cut off neatly. Turn the hackle to the tail as before, secure with turns of the ribbing material, and cut off, neatly finishing at the tail with the whip finish.

Stewart's Scotch spider patterns are a variant of Process II. The hackle being soft is rolled round the silk before being wound. The silk is then whipped to the tail and the fly finished there.

Third Series.

To dress a Winged Fly hackled at Shoulder only.—*Process I*—Is identical with Process I of the First Series, except that a little more space is left at the head for the wings, and as a last step before the whip finish, a pair of ordinary wings are whipped on with several firm turns of silk, and the fly is finished with a whip finish at the head or behind the hackle, and the wing stumps are cut off close.

Process II—Is identical with Process II of the First

Series, except that a pair of ordinary wings or Tweed wings are whipped on before tying on the hackle.

Process III—Is identical with Process III of the First Series, except that a pair of ordinary Irish or Tweed wings may be tied on before the hackle is tied on, or a pair of ordinary wings may be tied on just before the whip finish.

Process IV—Commence at the middle and whip to near the head, tie in rolled reverse or Tweed upright wings as before described, bind on the hackle behind the wings, whip to the tail and back to the shoulder, putting in any necessary materials as before. Turn and secure the hackle, and finish at the shoulder. Or Irish wings may be used with the finish at the head.

Fourth Series.

To dress Winged Palmers or Sedges.—*Process I*—This is identical with Process I of the Second Series, except that ordinary wings are whipped on before the hackle is bound in.

Process II—Beginning in the middle of the hook, wind to the head, binding in the gut. Here tie in rolled, reversed, or Tweed upright wings, cut away the stumps, form the head, and tie in the hackle or hackles behind the wings. The rest of the process is identical with Process III of the Second Series.

Substantially and in principle the foregoing are all the methods for tying small flies on gut. May-flies do not differ in principle from small flies, and the methods of tying on eyed hooks can readily be learned by discarding so much of the above processes as is devoted to securing the gut to the hook, and by a modification of the processes described next for dry flies.

Floating Flies—For floating flies, eyed hooks present such advantages that it is proposed to treat the subject as synonymous with floating flies on eyed hooks. For those who prefer to dress them on gut, it is only necessary so to bind on the gut as to leave the silk in position to proceed with the rest of the fly in the same places, as one begins on an eyed hook in the following methods.

The insects imitated are the same in both methods save that the March brown is never seen on many dry-fly waters. The artificial patterns differ from wet-fly patterns (1) in being more thickly dressed in hackle and wing, (2) in being as far as possible so constructed as to absorb little water and to throw it off readily in drying, and (3) in the winged patterns in the wings being split and so built as to let the fly down on the water with the wings upright and cocked.

The types are four, viz., (1) wingless flies hackled at the shoulders only, (2) winged flies similarly hackled, (3) palmers or bumbles, and (4) winged palmers or bumbles, usually called sedges.

Types 1 and 2 have sometimes detached bodies.

May-flies differ somewhat in detail, but in no essential point of principle from smaller flies, but the spent gnat requires a special description.

It will be convenient first to describe the process of winging, of which there are several varieties, but all are available for every kind of winged floater except May-flies.

Beginning near the eye, but leaving room for the head and wings, whip towards the tail six or seven turns, binding down the short end and thence back to the starting point. Twitch off the short end. Take corresponding feathers from opposite sides of the same bird, and cut slips from each to form single or double or rolled wings as the case may be. If the wings are to be double lay two slips from the same feather or from adjoining feathers from one wing and lay one on top of another so that the points and edges correspond. Do likewise with the other wing. Then lay the feather for one wing precisely on the top of the feather for the other, and take them up in the pliers, place them crosswise between the finger and thumb so that, if the wings be ordinary, they slope backwards with the natural curve of the feather towards the tail, and if they are to be reversed or rolled they project over the eye and bring down the feather on to the hook. Bring the silk up between the thumb and the feather, down again between the feather and the finger on the far side, hold the feather firmly with the finger and thumb and draw down the silk firmly, pass it once round, and behind or in front of the wing according to the nature of the wing, and release the feather. The wings should now set apart in a V shape. Bring the silk up between the near stump and the metal, pass between the wings and down on the far side, round under the hook, back between the wings, and down between the wire and the further stump, then back to the other side of the wing. If the wing be ordinary, draw back the stumps, bind them under the hook, and in any case cut off slantingly so as to taper the body towards the tail. There are many variations in this method for which space is not available.

To dress a Wingless Fly hackled at Shoulder only—Fix the hook in the vice as before. Wax a length of silk, commence whipping near the shoulder and whip to the shoulder, leaving space to wind the hackles on bare metal, and finish at the eye. Bind on one, two, or three hackles according to need, and whip back to the bend, taking off the stumps so as to taper the body. Here bind in whisks if they are required, quill, floss, or herl for the body and any ribbing material required. If the body be dubbed, roll on the dubbing. Whip to the shoulder, wind in the body and ribbing, and secure it. Then wind the hackle or hackles, the hindmost first, securing them by bringing the silk through each, binding down the successive turns of hackle. Finish at the eye with the whip finish.

To dress a Palmer or Bumble—This is dressed precisely like the last, except that the last hackle, instead of being turned at the shoulder, is wound in open folds to the tail, and there secured by two turns of gold or silver wire or twist. The twist is then wound in similarly spaced laps to the shoulder and there secured, and the waste end cut off. The remaining hackles or hackle are then wound at the shoulder and secured, and the fly finished with the whip finish at the eye. That is the soundest method. But another plan is to tie in body materials and ribbing at the shoulder, wind and secure the front hackle, whip the silk to the tail, wind on the body material and secure it at the tail, bring down the last hackle in open laps to the tail, and secure it. Wind the ribbing down the body so as to support and secure the turns of the hackle; secure it at the tail, cut off the waste end, and finish at the tail with the whip finish.

To dress a Winged Floating Fly hackled at the Shoulder only—Having tied on the wings as previously described, next tie in at the shoulder so as to pass when wound either in front of the wings or immediately behind them one cock's hackle, in the former case face or bright side downwards, in the latter case with bright side flat against hook and wing. Tie in a second cock's hackle to wind behind the wing, whip to near the bend of the hook, breaking or cutting off the roots of the hackle *en route* so as to taper the body. Bind in the whisks at the tail and take one turn under them. Then tie down herl, quill, floss, tinsel, or whatever the body material is to be (except dubbing), and the ribbing, if any, and whip back to the shoulder. If dubbing be used, spin on the dubbing before whipping back. Wind the body material and ribbing, if any, to the shoulder. Make fast at the shoulder with two turns of silk. Wind the hinder hackle so as to force the wings upright and bring the silk through so as to secure the turns. Wind the front hackle, secure it in like manner, and finish at the head with the whip finish. Some dressers only use one hackle wound altogether in front of or altogether behind or partly before and partly behind the wings, and they finish with the whip finish, or two turns behind the wings. The latest novelty is to use yet a third hackle, a hen's or other soft plumaged bird's in front of the wings, or, in wingless hackled floaters, instead of them.

To dress a Winged Palmer, Sedge or Rail—

Wild Turkey.

Having tied on the wings as before described, tie in two cocks' hackles as described in the last method, and a third for winding down the body, whip to the tail, tie in the body material, unless it be dubbing, and some fine wire, and twist and whip back to the shoulder. Wind on the body material and secure at the shoulder, cutting off the waste ends. Wind the hindmost hackle in open laps to the tail, secure with a turn or two of the wire or twist, and bring that through the successive turns of the hackle to the shoulder. Here secure it and cut away the waste. Wind the second hackle close behind the wings, and the first close in front securing each as before described, and finish with the whip finish.

To dress Detached Bodied Flies—Detached bodies are usually of india-rubber, gut, or hair wound on a split hog's bristle, doubled round a hook, the whisks being bound in at the tail. The bristle is subsequently set astride the eyed hook, behind the wings if the fly be winged, otherwise behind the hackle and there bound on and the binding covered by the body material. The waste ends of bristles are cut off and the fly is then finished in the ordinary way.

But detached bodies are of less importance than they were, for almost as good an effect can be had by using dyed or plain horsehair or gut on the bare hook, tying it in at the shoulder and winding to the tail, binding in the whisks in so doing, and thence winding back to the shoulder.

To dress Floating May-flies—These are either hackled at shoulder only or down the body and are either winged or wingless. If they are winged the winging is performed just as in the case of small flies, substituting the stalk of the mallard breast or other similar feather for the stumps of the small feather. The methods of forming the body and putting on the hackles, ribbing-tags, &c., do not differ in principle from those applied to similar ends for small flies. Straw bodies used to cause much heart-breaking, but rofia grass can be wound like a quill and serves the same purpose.

Spent Gnats (representing the dying or dead spinner of the May-fly) are hackled all down the body and are winged with two pairs of dark blue or black glossy cocks' hackles, tied so as to project horizontally to right and left of the hook, with a slight backward slope from the shoulder.

G. E. M. SKUES.

TSINE (*Bos sondaicus*)—The tsine are true wild cattle, and extend from the hill tracts of Chittagong downwards, and are found in Java, Sumatra, Borneo, and the Celebes. They are very wary, graze in the open *quins* or plains, and are not easy to circumvent.

A bull tsine that Captain Chas. Hill and myself once killed, was very handsome, of a deep red colour (the old bulls get almost black in their second childhood), with white rings round the eyes, white under the belly, under the tail. and along the buttocks. Below the knees they have dirty white stockings, somewhat similar to those of the gaur and gayal. A slight hump, which is lost in the ridge, a slight dewlap, not always apparent, is also characteristic of them. The head is very like that of a wild stag, the facial angle being quite straight. They are fairly plentiful in Burma, and the native shikaries, although forbidden by their religion to take life, and though all cattle are particularly sacred, often pot them by sitting in the branch of a tree overlooking a path along which they travel to and fro from their feeding grounds, and sell the meat to the villagers. I often tried to get near them, but seldom succeeded, but in one of my wanderings in Burma I came across an open space on the Yomah range of hills and found that a herd of tsine retired to a belt of the jungle in it daily. Getting up at 3 a.m. one day, I walked to the grove, getting wet through for the dew was very heavy, and the grass long. There were many tigers about, too, which did not make it the more pleasant to go through such jungle. We ensconced ourselves in the brushwood, and sat there shivering for hours before the tsine appeared. At last several cows came and then later on two bulls, but I did not get a shot till near 11, for the day was cloudy and the cattle in no hurry to take their mid-day siesta. I killed one and wounded the other. In following him up I found he had turned off near a nullah with a steep bank; the grass was not heavy, and I thought I should see the beast as soon as he could see me. I came to a river bank, steep and with fully ten feet sheer drop to the water, at which there was a fallen tree alongside. I was about to sit down, when there was a rush and the head and pair of horns of a tsine were all but on me. I threw myself backwards, holding on to a branch of the prostrate tree, and so hung over the bank. The impetus of the bull carried him clean over me and he fell with a splash into the pool, where he was speedily killed.

F. T. POLLOK.

TURKEY—The wild turkey is the king of the game birds of North America. It was formerly very abundant throughout most portions of the United States, but it is almost as eagerly followed as the deer, and is less well able to protect itself, so that it has now been practically exterminated from most of the Northern States. In the Southern States, however, there are still plenty of places where excellent wild turkey shooting can be obtained. The sport is carried on in several different ways. Sometimes the shot-gun is used, and sometimes the rifle. The birds are sometimes baited, corn being scattered about in some place until they get into the habit of going there, and the shooter then lies in wait for them. More often they are called, a peculiar little whistle being used, and the hunter lying concealed while he imitates the notes either of the gobblers or of the hens. In its essence this is a repetition of moose calling on a small scale, and almost as much skill is necessary, for the wild turkey is an extremely wary bird, and only an expert can call an old gobbler up to a blind.

In the wildest regions it is still possible to enjoy the fun of shooting turkeys on their roosts. Frequently large flocks will make an habit of going to one place to roost, and the hunter can, by taking proper precautions, lie hidden there until they have settled down and night has fallen The turkeys are then very loth to leave, and frequently a goodly number can be shot, especially if those lowest on the branches are selected, before the others will take flight.

The most sportsmanlike way of killing turkeys, however, is by fair still-hunting with a small calibre rifle. Turkeys are quite noisy. especially in the early morning, and if the still-hunter is out early enough, he can hear them as they fly off from their roosting trees or settle on their feeding grounds. Extreme caution is necessary, for the turkeys are very wary, and the man must be both a good and a quick shot with the rifle.

An even more sporting way of chasing wild turkey is with greyhounds. This is of course only possible in country which is open, interspersed here and there with groves, or gullies filled with brushwood; and of course turkeys are much more quickly killed off in such places than in regions of dense forests, so the sport is necessarily evanescent. It was at one time followed a good deal by the Army officers, and some of the ranchmen, in Texas. The method was to start out quite early in the morning to some ground where the birds were known to be feeding away from thick timber, and to get between them and the cover. Then all possible care was used to bring the dogs as near the birds as possible before the latter took alarm. As the turkey sprang into the air the greyhounds raced after him, for they speedily grew to understand their work, and kept an eye on the bird in front of them. If the turkey managed in his first flight to get to cover, or if he crossed such difficult country that the greyhounds were thrown out, the hunt was over; but if the ground was open and fairly level, and the dogs good, they kept him in sight until he lit. The heavy bodied, short winged turkey is not a bird of strong flight; it gets very tired after going about a mile, and lights. If the greyhounds had been favoured by fortune they were near enough to see the bird as it lit. The turkey then began to run along the ground, but in a minute or so the greyhounds were on him and put him up again. His second flight was always much shorter and slower than the first, for he was now tired. Probably, however, he still kept ahead of the dogs. If he did not distance them at the outset they gained on him towards the end of his flight as he came toward the ground, and ran underneath, making wonderful springs at the spent bird as he sailed along fifteen or twenty feet above their heads. Sooner or later, as the bird became exhausted and sank nearer the ground, one of these springs would be successful, the sharp teeth would close on the old gobbler, and the chase would be at an end. Even if the turkey distanced his pursuers the second time, they would be on him again very soon, and the third flight was so weak that only the close proximity of cover gave the quarry any show at all. It was usually too exhausted to try a fourth flight.

In some old European hunting book I have read of taking the great bustard with greyhounds, and I have elsewhere seen it stated that this was an impossibility, as the bustard was a bird that flew well; but on reading Mr. Abel Chapman's very interesting book on Wild Spain, I was struck by his account of his experience with bustards, and how he followed them on horseback, with the result of finding that after one or two flights the usually wary birds would lie close to the ground and seek to escape observation instead of trusting again to their wings. Under such circumstances it is evident that good greyhounds might take them just as they take wild turkeys.

THEODORE ROOSEVELT.

TURTLE COURSING—In the lagoons of the Laccadive Islands of the Arabian Sea, the turtle is coursed in a sporting fashion that could doubtless be followed in all coral islands. On a still day, when there is no breath of air to ripple the surface and hinder one from readily seeing to the bottom of the clear water of the lagoon, a line of well-manned light rowing boats is formed, with a steersman in the stern, steering with a paddle, and a spearsman standing in the prow. Slowly and silently the line advances, the boats abreast at short distances, and keeping the strictest line, an erect spearsman in the prow of each peering diligently into the clear depths ahead, till he sees a dark object on the white sand of the bottom, and points the direction with his spear. At the same moment the turtle, seeing the boats against the light, makes off, but being clearly visible against the white sandy bottom of the clear lagoon, the viewing spearsman gives the equivalent to a tally-ho, and the pursuit is commenced. Every oarsman strains at his oar with all his might, and the steersman, taking the direction of the turtle's flight from the pointing of the spear in the hand of the prominent figure standing in the prow, follows every turn in the turtle's flight just as if he saw it himself, the spearsman the while excitedly gesticulating, and shouting out whether they are gaining on the turtle or the reverse. Meanwhile, at the first tally-ho, all the other boats have taken up the chase and are racing like greyhounds for the lead, till a turn in the course gives one or other of the boats an advantage, and one and another fresh spearsman takes up the view, his steersman then being guided by his gesticulations. And so the chase proceeds, every oar pulling its very best, or they will hardly keep the turtle in view, every spearsman and every steersman shouting to them to pull better, and creating an Asiatic babel. Sometimes by a lucky turn one boat only is up, and the spearsman plunges head first with his spear. But more ordinarily the turtle, seeing that he is followed on both sides, ceases turning, and keeps a straight course, till his pace slackens, and the boats are closing up to him.

Then, by common consent, each spearsman lays aside his spear, and, still pointing out the direction with outstretched arm, watches his opportunity for a plunge. This he must take to a nicety, so as not to overshoot or fall behind his point, which is the outstretched neck of the swimming turtle. With one hand he has to seize this firmly just behind the head, before the turtle has time to withdraw it, and with the other hand to grip the shell by the edge and turn the turtle belly upwards, so bringing him to the surface. But if he has misjudged his spring he has lost his chance, and the sea is alive with others plunging in after him. These turtle frequently measure 3 feet by 2½ feet, and have a razor-like powerful beak and flippers that can give an ugly scratch. Englishmen have taken their place as prowman and successfully captured turtle by hand in this sporting fashion.

H. S. THOMAS.

UNIVERSITY CONTESTS—The following tables give the results of contests between the two Universities, and there are one or two points upon which remark may be made.

Date—The priority in date must be granted to the Cricket Match which was arranged by the energy of the late Bishop Wordsworth, then at Christ Church, Oxford, in 1827, and was played at Lord's. In 1829 the teams met at Oxford; but for the next contest, in 1836, they reappeared at Lord's. Meanwhile, in 1829, the first boat race had been rowed. The Sports followed in 1864, and the five "blue" events were completed by the Rugby match, first played at the Oval in 1872, and by the Association match in 1874 upon the same ground.

Colours.—There appears to be no evidence as to the colours worn by the Oxford cricket team in 1827; but, from the facts pointed out later, it is certain that Cambridge did not wear light blue. At the first boat race, in 1829, "Oxford blue" was adopted as the colour for the crew from the Isis. In all probability this colour was taken from the Horse Guards' Blue, for the designation of that regiment was originally "The Oxford Blues," and the shade of colour is almost identical. At any rate, the resemblance is suggestive.

Cambridge, on the other hand, rowed their first race in pink, and there is a definite tradition as to the cause of their adopting the light blue. Just before the second race, in 1836, the crew realised that they were unprovided with colours, and at the last moment a Mr. R. M. Phillips was hurriedly requested to get them some ribbons, no particular shade being specified. Accompanied by an Eton man, he went to the nearest shop, and at his friend's suggestion purchased a supply of Eton blue ribbons, a chance choice to which future generations adhered.

When the Sports were started in 1864, athletic blues were granted without opposition to the first strings on either side, Oxford being the first to make the concession. A half blue was also granted to the second strings, which became a full blue if they won the event in which they competed.

The struggle for the football blue was more exciting, at Cambridge at least.

After the football teams had played matches for some considerable time, at the request of the Oxford Association captain, the Oxford Rugby captain wrote to the President of the O.U.B.C., requesting that a blue should be granted to both football teams, the eleven and the fifteen. The latter was laid before a meeting of blues, that is, of the cricket team, the athletic blues, and the crew of the boat, and the request was granted at once.

At Cambridge matters were not so easily settled. Towards the close of 1883 the question of granting blues for Rugby and Association was mooted. Application was made and was refused by the then blues, although they offered as a compromise that a certain limited number of blues should be shared between the teams. This was promptly rejected. Next season, on December 10th, 1884, the Cambridge Rugby Union XV. assumed the blue at Blackheath. Naturally a very heated controversy arose, which culminated in a debate at the Cambridge Union, of which full details may be found in the Rev. F. Marshall's book on Rugby football. On a division, the supporters of the football blue were victorious by 707 to 466.

Since this time, certain half blue distinctions have been invented, but they differ at the two Universities. No other full blue exists than the five above mentioned.

All questions connected with the awarding of blues and half blues, the general arrangement of contests, and their dates, come before the Blues Committee, composed of the presidents and captains.

C. R. B. BARRETT.

RESULTS OF CRICKET MATCHES.

1827	Drawn.
1829	Oxford won by 115 runs.
1835	,, ,, 121 ,,
1838	,, ,, 98 ,,
1839	Cambridge won in 1 inn. by 125 runs.
1840	,, won by 63 runs.
1841	,, ,, 8 ,,
1842	,, ,, 162 ,,
1843	,, ,, 54 ,,
1844	Drawn.
1845	Cambridge won by 6 wkts.
1846	Oxford ,, 3 ,,
1847	Cambridge ,, 138 runs.
1848	Oxford ,, 23 ,,
1849	Cambridge ,, 3 wkts.
1850	Oxford ,, 127 runs.
1851	Cambridge ,, in 1 inn. by 4 runs.
1852	Oxford won in 1 inn. by 77 runs.
1853	Oxford won in 1 inn. by 19 runs.
1854	Oxford won in 1 inn. by 8 runs.
1855	Oxford won in 1 inn. by 3 wickets.
1856	Cambridge won by 3wkts.
1857	Oxford ,, 81 runs.
1858	,, ,, in 1 inn. 38 runs.
1859	Cambridge won by 28 runs
1860	,, ,, 3 wkts.
1861	,, ,, 133 runs.
1862	,, ,, 8 wkts.
1863	Oxford ,, 8 wkts.
1864	,, ,, 4 ,,
1865	,, ,, 144 runs.
1866	Oxford won by 13 runs.
1867	Cambridge ,, 5 wkts.
1868	,, ,, 168 runs.
1869	,, ,, 58 ,,
1870	,, ,, 2 ,,
1871	Oxford ,, 8 wkts.
1872	Cambridge ,, in 1 inn. by 166 runs.
1873	Oxford won by 3 wkts.
1874	,, ,, in 1 inn. by 92 runs.
1875	Oxford won by 6 runs.

RESULTS OF CRICKET MATCHES—*Continued.*

1876	Cambridge won by 9 wkts.	1888	Drawn.
1877	Oxford ,, 10 ,,	1889	Cambridge ,, 1 inn. by 105 runs.
1878	Cambridge ,, 238 runs.		
1879	,, ,, 9 wkts.	1890	Cambridge won by 7 wkts.
1880	,, ,, 135 runs.	1891	,, ,, 2 ,,
1881	Oxford ,, 135 ,,	1892	Oxford ,, 5 ,,
1882	Cambridge ,, 7 wkts.	1893	Cambridge ,, 266 runs.
1883	,, ,, 7 ,,	1894	Oxford ,, 8 wkts.
1884	Oxford ,, 7 ,,	1895	Cambridge ,, 134 runs.
1885	Cambridge ,, 7 ,,	1896	Oxford ,, 4 wkts.
1886	Oxford ,, 133 runs.	1897	Cambridge ,, 179 runs.
1887	,, ,, 7 wkts.	1898	Oxford ,, 9 wkts.

RESULTS OF FOOTBALL MATCHES.

Rugby.

1872	Oxford won by a goal from a try.	1885–6	Cambridge, 2 tries to nil.
1873–4	Drawn, 1 try each.	1886–7	,, 3 ,,
1874–5	Drawn, 0—0.	1887–8	Cambridge, 1 goal and 2 tries to nil.
1875–6	Oxford, 1 try to nil.	1888–9	Cambridge, 1 goal and 2 tries to nil.
1876–7	Cambridge, 1 goal 2 tries to nil.	1889–90	Oxford, 1 goal and 1 try to nil.
1877–8	Oxford, 2 tries to nil.	1890–1	Drawn, 1 goal each.
1878–9	Drawn, 0—0.	1891–2	Cambridge, 2 tries to nil.
1879–80	Cambridge, 2 goals to 1 goal.	1892–3	Drawn, nothing scored.
1880–1	Drawn, 1 try each.	1893–4	Oxford, 1 try to nil.
1881–2	Oxford, 2 goals and 1 try to 1 goal.	1894–5	Drawn, 1 goal each.
1882–3	Oxford, 1 try to nil.	1895–6	Cambridge, 1 goal to nil.
1883–4	Oxford, 3 goals and 4 tries to 1 goal.	1896–7	Oxford, 2 goals (1 dr.) to 1 goal 1 try.
1884–5	Oxford, 3 goals and 1 try to 1 try.	1897–8	Oxford, 2 tries to nil.

Oxford 10; Cambridge 8; drawn 7; total 25.

Association.

1873–4	Oxford,	2 to 0	1886–7	Cambridge,	3 to 1
1874–5	Cambridge,	2 ,, 0	1887–8	Oxford,	3 ,, 2
1875–6	Oxford	4 ,, 1	1888–9	Drawn,	1 ,, 1
1876–7	,,	1 ,, 0	1889–90	Cambridge,	3 ,, 1
1877–8	Cambridge,	5 ,, 1	1890–1	Oxford.	2 ,, 1
1878–9	,,	2 ,, 0	1891–2	Cambridge,	5 ,, 1
1879–80	,,	3 ,, 1	1892–3	Oxford,	3 ,, 2
1880–1	,,	2 ,, 1	1893–4	Cambridge,	3 ,, 1
1881–2	Oxford,	3 ,, 0	1894–5	Oxford,	3 ,, 0
1882–3	Cambridge,	3 ,, 2	1895–6	,,	2 ,, 0
1883–4	,,	2 ,, 0	1896–7	,,	1 ,, 0
1884–5	,,	1 ,, 0	1897–8	Cambridge,	1 ,, 0
1885–6	,,	1 ,, 0			

Cambridge 14; Oxford 10; with one drawn game in 1888–9.

OXFORD AND CAMBRIDGE SPORTS.

100 Yards Flat Race.

Year	Winner	Won by	Official Time. Sec.
1864	S. B. Darbyshire (Wadham, Ox)	½ yd	10½
1865	H. C. Jollye (Merton, Ox)	½ yd	10¾
1866	R. W. Vidal (St. John's, Ox) / T. M. Colmere (B.N.C., Ox)	Dead Heat	10⅕
1867	E. A. Pitman (St. John's, Cam)	2 ft	10⅖
1868	J. P. Tennent (Wadham, Ox)	2½ yds	10
1869	J. G. Wilson (Worcester, Ox)	2 yds	10⅕
1870	J. G. Wilson (Worcester, Ox)	1½ yds	10
1871	J. G. Wilson (Worcester, Ox)	6 ins	10⅖
1872	W. A. Dawson (Trin, Cam)	2 yds	10⅖
1873	G. H. Urmson (Ch Ch, Ox)	2 yds	10
1874	E. J. Davies (Pem. Cam)	1 yd	10⅕
1875	C. C. Woodland (Corpus, Cam)	1 yd	10⅕
1876	M. Shearman (St. John's, Ox)	3 yds	10⅕
1877	E. C. Trepplin (B.N.C., Ox)	2 yds	10⅕
1878	E. C. Trepplin (B.N.C., Ox)	3 yds	10⅕
1879	E. C. Trepplin (B.N.C., Ox)	1 yd	10⅕
1880	E. L. Lucas (Jesus, Cam)	1¼ yds	10⅕
1881	L. Carter (Corpus, Ox.)	1 yd	10⅖
1882	L. Carter (Corpus, Ox)	¾ yd	10⅖
1883	W. G. Mosse (Corpus, Cam)	1 ft	10⅗
1884	L. Carter (Corpus, Ox)	1 ft	10⅗
1885	H. E. Booty (Clare, Cam)	½ ft	10⅘
1886	H. C. L. Tindall (Christ's, Cam)	4 ft	10¼
1887	E. S. Fardell (Trin, Cam) / H. M. Fletcher (Trin, Cam)	Dead Heat	10⅘
1888	H. M. Fletcher (Trin, Cam)	1 ft	10⅘
1889	R. W. Turner (Trin. Hall, Cam)	2 ft	10⅗
1890	E. O. B. Prest (Trin. Hall, Cam)	6 ins	10⅘
1891	A. Ramsbotham (Exeter, Ox) / C. J. B. Monypenny (Jesus, Cam)	Dead Heat	10⅖
1892	A. Ramsbotham (Exeter, Ox)	1 ft	10⅖
1893	A. Ramsbotham (Exeter, Ox) / C. B. Fry (Wadham, Ox)	Dead Heat	10⅕
1894	G. Jordan (Univ. Ox)	½ yd	10⅖
1895	G. Jordan (Univ. Ox)	9 ins	10¾
1896	G. Jordan (Univ. Ox)	2 yds	10¼
1897	C. R. Thomas (Jesus, Ox) / F. L. Carter (Caius, Cam)	Dead Heat	10⅕
1898	C. R. Thomas (Jesus, Oxford)	1½ yds	10⅖

Quarter Mile Flat Race.

Year	Winner	Won by	Sec.
1864	S. B. Darbyshire (Wadham, Ox)	2 yds	56
1865	Hon. F. G. Pelham (Trin, Cam)	20 yds	55½
1866	Hon. F. G. Pelham (Trin, Cam)	3 yds	54¼
1867	E. A. Pitman (St. John's, Cam)	2 yds	52
1868	J. H. Ridley (Jesus, Cam)	3 yds	51
1869	A. B. Upcher (Trin, Cam)	4 yds	53
1870	R. V. Somers-Smith (Mer, Ox)	1½ yds	51⅘
1871	R. Philpot (Trin, Cam)	2 yds	50½
1872	R. Philpot (Trin, Cam)	2 yds	51⅖
1873	G. H. Urmson (Ch Ch, Ox)	10 yds	51
1874	G. A. Templer (Trin, Cam)	4 yds	51⅕
1875	T. Snow (New, Ox)	1½ yds	51⅗
1876	A. R. Lewis (Corpus, Cam)	8 yds	52⅗
1877	W. H. Churchill (Jesus, Cam)	2½ yds	52⅗
1878	W. H. Churchill (Jesus, Cam)	3 yds	51⅘
1879	M. R. Portal (Balliol, Ox)	6 yds	52⅕
1880	R. H. Macaulay (King's, Cam)	4 yds	51⅖
1881	R. H. Macaulay (King's, Cam)	2 yds	50⅕
1882	R. H. Macaulay (King's, Cam)	5 yds	50⅗
1883	E. P. Powell (Trin, Cam)	3 yds	52⅗
1884	M. H. Paine (Merton, Ox)	½ yd	51⅕
1885	A. S. Blair (B. N. C., Ox)	½ yd	51⅘
1886	H. C. L. Tindall (Christ's, Cam)	9 yds	51
1887	H. M. Fletcher (Trin, Cam)	1 yd	53⅖
1888	A. G. Lemaitre (St. John's, Ox)	2½ yds	51⅘
1889	R. W. Turner (Trin. Hall, Cam)	10 yds	51⅖
1890	W. B. Thomas (Ch Ch, Ox)	9 yds	50⅕
1891	P. R. Lloyd (Pem, Ox)	6 ins	50⅗
1892	C. J. B. Monypenny (Jesus, Cam)	8 yds	49⅘
1893	A. Ramsbotham (Exeter, Ox)	4 yds	50⅖
1894	G. Jordan (Univ. Ox)	4 yds	50⅘
1895	W. Fitz-Herbert (Trin. Hall, Cam)	4 yds	50
1896	W. Fitz-Herbert (Trin. Hall, Cam)	4 ft	49⅗
1897	G. Jordan (Univ. Ox)	8 yds	49⅘
1898	E. L. Carter (Caius, Cam) / C. G. Davison (Sidney, Cam)	Dead Heat	51

One Mile Flat Race.

Year	Winner	Won by	Min.	Sec.
1864	C. B. Lawes (Trin, Cam)	4 yds	4	59
1865	R. E. Webster (Trin, Cam)	40 yds	4	44¼
1866	J. W. Laing (Ch. Ch., Ox)	20 yds	4	46
1867	S. G. Scott (Magdalen, Ox)	6 yds	4	40⅖
1868	W. C. Gibbs (Jesus, Cam)	20 yds	4	28⅘
1869	E. Royds (Trin. Hall, Cam)	3 yds	4	35
1870	R. H. Benson (Balliol, Ox)	1 yd	4	32⅖
1871	T. Christie (Lincoln, Ox)	6 yds	4	34
1872	T. Christie (Lincoln, Ox)	3 yds	4	38⅖
1873	C. E. Gunton (Trin, Cam)	10 yds	4	28⅗
1874	E. A. Sandford (Ch. Ch., Ox)	3 yds	4	39⅕
1875	E. A. Sandford (Ch. Ch., Ox)	½ yd	4	34⅘
1876	E. R. J. Nicholls (Ch. Ch., Ox)	6 yds	4	27⅕
1877	W. Cunliffe (Trin, Cam)	3 yds	4	32⅘
1878	D. L. Clarke (Magdalen, Ox)	1½ yds	4	31⅖
1879	B. R. Wise (Queen's, Ox)	5 yds	4	34⅗
1880	B. R. Wise (Queen's, Ox)	25 yds	4	28⅘
1881	T. E. Wells (Magdalen, Ox)	25 yds	4	36⅕
1882	T. E. Wells (Magdalen, Ox)	50 yds	4	30⅘
1883	W. D. LaTouche (Pem, Cam)	18 yds	4	34⅘
1884	G. E. H. Pratt (St. John's, Ox)	3 yds	4	26⅖
1885	E. R. Holland (Pem, Ox)	12 yds	4	37⅗
1886	F. J. K. Cross (New, Ox)	8 yds	4	28⅗
1887	F. J. K. Cross (New, Ox)	40 yds	4	25⅖
1888	F. J. K. Cross (New, Ox)	25 yds	4	29⅘
1889	F. J. K. Cross (New, Ox)	20 yds	4	28⅗
1890	W. Pollock-Hill (Keble, Ox)	60 yds	4	21⅗
1891	B. C. Allen (Corpus, Ox)	3 yds	4	26⅗
1892	W. E. Lutyens (Sidney, Cam)	6 yds	4	24⅗
1893	W. E. Lutyens (Sidney, Cam)	25 yds	4	22
1894	W. E. Lutyens (Sidney, Cam)	10 yds	4	19⅘
1895	W. E. Lutyens (Sidney, Cam)	60 yds	4	23⅖
1896	H. F. Howard (Trinity Hall, Cam)	13½ yds	4	29⅖
1897	H. F. Howard (Trinity Hall, Cam)	12 yds	4	27⅗
1898	A. L. Danson (Balliol, Ox)	6 in.	4	25⅘

Two Miles Flat Race.

Year	Winner	Won by	Min.	Sec.
1864	There was no race.			
1865	R. E. Webster (Trin, Cam)	40 yds	10	38½
1866	J. W. Laing (Ch. Ch., Ox) / C. H. Long (Trin, Cam)	Dead Heat	10	20
1867	R. L. N. Mitchell (Ch. Ch., Ox)	1 ft	9	59

In 1868 a Three Miles Race was substituted.

THREE MILES FLAT RACE.

Year	Name	Won by	Official Time Min.	Sec.
1868	J. H. Morgan (Trin, Ox)	200 yds	15	20¼
1869	J. H. Morgan (Trin, Ox)	200 yds	15	35
1870	J. H. Morgan (Trin, Ox)	100 yds	15	40
1871	A. F. Clarke (Trin, Ox)	100 yds	15	23
1872	R. H. Benson (Balliol, Ox) / E. M. Hawtrey, St. John's, Cam)	Dead Heat	15	44⅗
1873	W. M. Smith-Dorrien (Mag, Ox)	100 yds	15	8⅗
1874	W. R. H. Stevenson (New, Ox)	220 yds	15	46
1875	W. R. H. Stevenson (New, Ox)	25 yds	15	30⅗
1876	A. Goodwin (Jesus, Ox)	40 yds	15	12
1877	W. R. H. Stevenson (New, Ox)	190 yds	15	38
1878	A. Goodwin (Jesus, Ox)	25 yds	15	50⅗
1879	A. F. Hills (Univ. Ox)	150 yds	15	14⅗
1880	W. W. Hough (Corpus, Cam)	85 yds	15	1⅕
1881	F. R. Benson (New, Ox)	280 yds	15	5⅕
1882	W. W. Hough (Corpus, Cam)	180 yds	15	27⅕
1883	W. W. Hough (Corpus, Cam)	160 yds	15	29⅕
1884	T. C. Toler (Ch. Ch., Ox)	10 yds	15	24⅗
1885	E. F. W. Eliot (Trin, Cam)	10 yds	15	27⅘
1886	J. H. A. Marshall (Univ. Ox)	150 yds	15	11¼
1887	F. M. Ingram (Magd, Ox)	7 yds	15	25⅘
1888	W. Pollock-Hill (Keble, Ox)	50 yds	15	28⅕
1889	W. Pollock-Hill (Keble, Ox)	70 yds	15	20⅗
1890	W. Pollock-Hill (Keble, Ox)	80 yds	15	20⅗
1891	C. Ekin (Clare, Cam)	8 yds	15	12⅕
1892	B. C. Allen (Corpus, Ox)	60 yds	15	13⅘
1893	F. S. Horan (Trin. Hall, Cam)	80 yds	14	44⅗
1894	F. S. Horan (Trin. Hall, Cam)	20 yds	15	7
1895	F. S. Horan (Trin. Hall, Cam)	150 yds	14	50⅗
1896	J. M. Fremantle (Hertford, Ox)	10 yds	15	12
1897	J. M. Fremantle (Hertford, Ox)	50 yds	15	7⅕
1898	J. M. Fremantle (Hertford, Ox)	100 yds	15	34

120 YARDS HURDLE RACE (10 HDLS.).

Year	Name	Won by	Sec.
1864	A. W. T. Daniel (Trin, Cam)	6 yds	17¾
1865	T. Milvain (Trin. Hall, Cam)	1 yd	19
1866	D. Morgan (Magd. Hall, Ox)	2 yds	18¼
1867	C. N. Jackson (Magd. Hall, Ox)	3 yds	17⅕
1868	C. Pitt-Taylor (Trin, Cam)	3 yds	16¾
1869	F. O. Philpott (St. Edm. Hall, Ox)	3 yds	17½
1870	J. L. Stirling (Trin, Cam)	8 yds	16¾
1871	W. C. Davies (Trin, Cam) / E. S. Garnier (Univ. Ox)	Dead Heat	16⅗
1872	E. S. Garnier (Univ. Ox)	1 ft	16⅘
1873	H. K. Upcher (St. John's, Ox)	1 yd	17⅗
1874	H. K. Upcher (St. John's, Ox)	5 yds	16⅕
1875	A. B. Loder (Jesus, Cam)	1 ft	16⅘
1876	A. B. Loder (Jesus, Cam)	8 yds	16
1877	S. F. Jackson (St. John's, Ox)	1½ yds	17
1878	S. Palmer (Corpus, Cam)	6 ins	16⅖
1879	L. K. Jarvis (Trin, Cam)	1½ yds	16⅗
1880	G. P. C. Lawrence (Corpus, Ox)	1½ yds	16⅖
1881	W. E. Bailey (Trin, Cam)	2½ yds	16⅗
1882	C. L. Des Graz (Trin, Cam)	3 yds	17⅕
1883	C. L. Des Graz (Trin, Cam)	1 yd	17⅕
1884	W. R. Pollock (Trin, Cam)	5 yds	16
1885	A. McNeil (Trin, Ox)	8 yds	17⅖
1886	A. C. M. Croome (Magd., Ox)	3 yds	16⅖
1887	J. Le Fleming (Clare, Cam)	1½ yds	17⅗
1888	J. Le Fleming (Clare, Cam)	2 yds	17⅕
1889	J. L. Greig (Clare, Cam)	1 ft	16⅗
1890	J. L. Greig (Clare, Cam)	5 yds	16⅘
1891	H. Le Fleming (Clare, Cam)	3 yds	16⅖
1892	H. Le Fleming (Clare, Cam)	1½ yds	16⅖
1893	H. T. S. Gedge (Keble, Ox) / E. L. Collis (Keble, Ox)	Dead Heat	16⅖
1894	W. J. Oakley (Ch. Ch., Ox)	1 yd	16⅗
1895	W. J. Oakley (Ch. Ch., Ox)	1 yd	16⅘
1896	E. T. Garnier (Oriel, Ox)	6 ins.	16⅗
1897	E. T. Garnier (Oriel, Ox)	2½ yds	16⅖
1898	E. T. Garnier (Oriel, Ox)	6 ins	16½

200 YARDS HURDLE RACE (10 HDLS.).

Year	Name	Won by	Sec.
1864	E. Wynne-Finch (Trin, Cam)	6 ins	26¾

This race has not since been run.

STEEPLECHASE (ABOUT 2 MILES).

Year	Name	Min.
1864	R. C. Garnet (Trin, Cam)	10

This race has not since been run.

LONG JUMP.

Year	Name	Distance	ft.	in.
1864	F. H. Gooch (Merton, Ox)		18	0
1865	F. H. Gooch (Merton, Ox)		18	9
1866	T. G. Little (St. Peter's, Cam)		20	4
1867	C. A. Absolom (Trin, Cam)		20	2
1868	A. C. Tosswell (Oriel, Ox)		21	0¼
1869	R. Waltham (St. Peter's, Cam)		20	8
1870	J. A. Ornsby (Lincoln, Ox)		20	3¾
1871	E. N. Hodges (Queen's, Ox)		20	2
1872	E. J. Davies (Pem, Cam)		21	5
1873	E. J. Davies (Pem, Cam)		21	8
1874	E. J. Davies (Pem, Cam)		22	10½
1875	H. K. Upcher (St. John's, Ox)		21	0
1876	M. J. Brooks (B. N. C., Ox)		21	8½
1877	C. M. Kemp (Oriel, Ox)		20	1¾
1878	C. M. Kemp (Oriel, Ox)		22	2¼
1879	E. Baddeley (Jesus, Cam)		20	10¾
1880	H. S. Wood (Queen's, Ox)		20	11¾
1881	E. Storey (Trin, Cam)		21	0½
1882	H. S. Wood (Queen's, Ox)		20	1¾
1883	M. B. Peacock (Trin, Ox)		20	3¼
1884	O. Grabham (Jesus, Cam)		20	11½
1885	A. G. Grant-Asher (B. N. C., Ox)		19	10
1886	F. B. Roberts (Selwyn, Cam)		21	9½
1887	F. G. Tuck (Trin, Cam)		20	2
1888	W. C. Kendal (St. John's, Cam)		20	10¾
1889	J. L. Greig (Clare, Cam)		21	0½
1890	J. L. Greig (Clare, Cam)		22	7¾
1891	T. Jennings (Caius, Cam) / R. J. Leakey (Corpus, Cam)	Dead Heat	20	7½
1892	C. B. Fry (Wadham, Ox)		23	5
1893	C. B. Fry (Wadham, Ox)		23	0½
1894	C. B. Fry (Wadham, Ox)		22	4
1895	W. Mendelson (Jesus, Cam)		22	5½
1896	E. Batchelor (Caius, Cam)		22	7
1897	G. C. Vassall (Oriel. Ox)		22	7
1898	G. C. Vassall (Oriel, Ox)		22	5¼

HIGH JUMP.

Year	Name	Height ft.	in.
1864	F. H. Gooch (Merton, Ox)	5	5
1865	F. H. Gooch (Merton, Ox)	5	5
1866	J. H. Roupell (Trin. Hall, Cam)	5	6
1867	T. G. Little (St. Peter's, Cam)	5	9
1868	Hon. F. S. O'Grady (St. John's, Ox)	5	7
1869	R. L. N. Mitchell (Ch. Ch., Ox) / J. G. Hoare (Trin, Cam)	5	5
1870	E. Bergman (St. Edmund's Hall, Ox) / J. H. Gurney (Trin, Cam)	5	4½
1871	J. H. Gurney (Trin, Cam)	5	5½
1872	J. H. Gurney (Trin, Cam)	5	5
1873	J. H. Gurney (Trin, Cam)	5	6
1874	Mr. J. Brooks (B. N. C., Ox)	5	10
1875	M. G. Glazebrook (Balliol, Ox)	5	9
1876	M. J. Brooks (B. N. C., Ox)	6	2½
1877	G. W. Blathwayt (Corpus, Cam)	5	7
1878	G. W. Blathwayt (Corpus, Cam)	5	8
1879	R. H. Macaulay (King's, Cam)	5	8¾
1880	R. H. Macaulay (King's, Cam)	5	9
1881	H. R. Cooke (Trin, Cam)	5	6
1882	G. L. Colbourne (Corpus, Cam)	5	8¼
1883	G. L. Colbourne (Corpus, Cam)	5	8¾
1884	G. L. Colbourne (Corpus, Cam)	5	9
1885	G. F. Hornby (Corpus, Ox) / W. P. Montgomery (Merton, Ox) / S. O. Purves (Queen's, Cam)	5	6½
1886	W. P. Montgomery (Merton, Ox)	5	8½
1887	W. P. Montgomery (Merton, Ox)	5	8¾
1888	W. P. Montgomery (Merton, Ox)	5	10½
1889	H. J. Scott (Merton, Ox) / E. B. Badcock (Trin, Cam)	5	8
1890	T. Jennings (Caius, Cam)	5	8¾
1891	H. Le Fleming (Clare, Cam)	5	9½
1892	H. Le Fleming (Clare, Cam)	5	9½
1893	E. D. Swanwick (Univ. Ox)	5	11
1894	E. D. Swanwick (Univ. Ox)	5	10½
1895	G. A. Gardiner (New, Ox)	5	9
1896	E. O. Kirlew (Ch. Ch., Ox)	5	8½
1897	E. O. Kirlew (Ch. Ch., Ox) / E. H. Cholmeley (Jesus, Cam)	5	7⅝
1898	H. S. Adair (Oriel, Ox)	5	8

THROWING THE CRICKET BALL.

Year	Name	Yds.	ft.	in.
1865	E. A. Gray (Trinity Hall, Cam)	103	2	8

In 1864 and since 1865 the Ball has not been thrown.

THROWING THE HAMMER (16 LB.).

Year	Name	ft.	in.
1866	G. R. Thornton (Jesus, Cam)	87	7
1867	J. R. Eyre (Clare, Cam)	98	0
1868	T. Batson (Lincoln, Ox)	99	6
1869	H. Leeke (Trin, Cam)	103	11
1870	F. U. Waite (Balliol, Ox)	107	2
1871	A. W. Churchward (Pem, Cam)	105	5
1872	J Paterson (Trin, Cam)	105	2
1873	S. S. Brown (St. John's, Ox)	122	6
1874	G. H. Hales (Trin, Cam)	126	9
1875	G. H. Hales (Trin, Cam)	127	0
1876	G. H. Hales (Trin, Cam)	138	3
1877	G. H. Hales (Trin, Cam)	138	0
1878	E. Baddeley (Jesus, Cam)	106	2
1879	A. H. East (St. John's, Cam)	117	1½
1880	A. H. East (St. John's, Cam)	116	0
1881	W. Lawrence (St. John's, Ox)	120	2

Year	Name	Distance ft.	in.
1882	H. H. Birley (Jesus, Cam)	101	10
1883	F. P. Le Marchant (Queen's, Ox)	95	8
1884	F. P. Le Marchant (Queen's, Ox)	107	4
1885	J. R. Orford (King's, Cam)	99	7
1886	J. H. Ware (B. N. C., Ox)	96	11
1887	H. Neilson (Clare, Cam)	94	10
1888	H. Woolner (Trin, Cam)	93	10
1889	K. L. Macdonald (St. John's, Ox)	91	5
1890	N. M. Cohen (Jesus, Cam)	94	2
1891	T. Jennings (Caius, Cam)	102	10
1892	H. A. Cooper (Trin. Hall, Cam)	96	4
1893	G. S. Robertson (New, Ox)	105	1½
1894	G. S. Robertson (New, Ox)	101	4½
1895	G. S. Robertson (New, Ox)	116	7
1896	A. B. Johnstone (Pembroke, Cam)	107	7
1897	J. A. Halliday (Trin, Cam)	97	9
1898	L. O.-T. Baines (Trin. Hall, Cam.)	102	6

In 1864 and 1865 Hammer throwing was not in the Programme.

Putting the Weight (16 lb.).

Year	Name	Cam. style. ft.	in.	Ox. style. ft.	in.	Total dist. ft.	in.
1865	G. W. Elliott (Trin, Cam)	31	4½	33	10	65	0½
1866	G. W. Elliott (Trin, Cam)	32	10½	—		—	
1867	R. Waltham (St. Pet, Cam)	34	9	—		—	
1868	R. Waltham (St. Pet, Cam)	34	3	—		—	
1869	R. Waltham (St. Pet, Cam)	34	4	—		—	
1870	S. F. Lucas (Exeter, Ox)	36	2½	—		—	
1871	H. W. R. Domville (Pem, Ox)	35	3½	—		—	
1872	H. W. R. Domville (Pem, Ox)	37	5½	—		—	
1873	S. S. Brown (St. John's, Ox)	35	2	—		—	
1874	S. S. Brown (St. John's, Ox)	37	11	—		—	
1875	S. S. Brown (St. John's, Ox)	36	2			—	
1876	C. H. Hodges (Queen's, Ox)	36	0	—		—	
1877	H. O. D. Davidson (Trin, Cam)	35	0½	—		—	
1878	A. H. East (St. John's, Cam)	36	7½	—		—	
1879	A. H. East (St. John's, Cam)	36	2½	—		—	
1880	A. H. East (St. John's, Cam)	37	5	—		—	
1881	W. Lawrence (St. John's, Ox)	36	5	—		—	
1882	A. M. Evanson (Jesus, Ox)	35	11	—		—	
1883	J. H. Ware (B. N. C., Ox)	37	10½	—		—	
1884	J. H. Ware (B N. C., Ox)	37	6	—		—	
1885	J. H. Ware (B. N. C., Ox)	36	11	—		—	
1886	J. H. Ware (B. N. C., Ox)	39	1	—		—	
1887	E. O'F. Kelly (Caius, Cam)	36	3	—		—	
1888	E. O'F. Kelly (Caius, Cam)	37	0	—		—	
1889	C. Rolfe (Clare, Cam)	35	6½	—		—	
1890	M. B. Elder (Jesus, Cam)	37	5	—		—	
1891	S. H. Barber (King's, Cam)	35	7	—		—	
1892	C. A. White (New, Ox)	36	2½	—		—	
1893	E. Hind (Keble, Ox)	34	11½	—		—	
1894	C. H. Rivers (St. John's, Cam)	37	8½	—		—	
1895	E. J. Watson (Trin, Cam)	37	9	—		—	
1896	J. H. Bulloch (Trin, Cam)	38	2	—		—	
1897	J. H. Bulloch (Trin, Cam)	37	6½	—		—	
1898	F. E. Snowball (Queen's, Ox)	37	4	—		—	

The Sports have been won on 15 occasions by Oxford and on 19 occasions by Cambridge.

There has been one tie, and if on that occasion the Sports had been decided by seconds, Cambridge would have won.

Since the commencement of the Sports, Oxford has scored 159 firsts and 158 seconds, and Cambridge has scored 155 firsts and 149 seconds, out of 314 events.

For the Boat Race results, see Vol. II., p. 296.

UNIVERSITIES, SPORT AT AMERICAN—At an American University all forms of sport are taken far more seriously than is the case at Oxford or Cambridge. In comparing my Harvard friends with those far more numerous companions who were my contemporaries at Oxford, I find it difficult to realise that both were undergraduates. The differences are emphasised with a keenness that is reflected in the men themselves, in every branch of sport which they affect, in the very point of view from which they regard their time at a University and their lives afterwards.

Climate, to begin with, is a very vital factor in the problem of describing either an English undergraduate to an American student, or a Cambridge "man" to him of Yale or Harvard. Abuse the English climate as you may, there is yet in it that saving quality of moderation which escapes the deadening extremes of heat or cold. A Thames that will bear a coach and four is as rare as a Henley that produces sunstroke in a single crew. Rowing is indeed not only a possibility, but in almost every year a recorded fact on English rivers from the first day of January till the last day of December. And since few Englishmen are content with merely practice, you shall find an energetic wet-bob within sight of a good race from one end of a year to the other.

Take the career of a freshman, for instance, who goes up to Christ Church with a reputation from the Eton eight, perhaps as captain of the winning crew in the last Ladies' Plate. He probably rows for his college in the University Fours in his first term; he certainly is sent up for the University Trial Eights, and before the next term begins he will have had a chance of several good races and at least two victories to add to his experience. If his excellence is already proved to be first class, he goes at the end of January straight into the University crew, and finishing the last part of his training upon tidal waters, he races at Putney against Cambridge early in April. If this has as yet proved impossible of attainment, he has at least rowed in his College Torpid, and very possibly put seven hard bumping races to his credit, without counting other minor college competitions that may come in his way. In the summer term the rowing calendar grows yet more thickly studded with "important fixtures." His college eight often begins training before the rest of the University are in residence. Soon after the middle of the term his crew has made its bid for the headship of the river, ousted its rivals, or maintained its place, and he sees his way clear to the possible entry for a cup at Henley. But there are University Sculls and Pairs to be won before the Isis is deserted, and the lesser triumphs of his college regatta to achieve, and a short period of rest (if his captain be a wise one) enjoined before the Henley training starts. After all that has gone before, about three weeks only is required (except in rare cases), either to accustom a college eight to the lively water of the lower reaches, or to weld into a crew the various oarsmen picked from the best of either University, who represent such a combination as Leander; for at Cambridge the rowing season has been, to all intents and purposes, identical.

Imagine, then, the American crew whom our three-weeks Leander eight find ready for them at the Temple Island. Whether they hail from Yale or Harvard or Cornell, they are eight as big and strong and handsome men as ever sat in a boat on either side of the Atlantic. You notice particularly the fine development of their arms and the sunburn of their skins; for their habit of rowing naked to the waist at home has coloured them like so many bronze statues. But the greatest difference of all you will not see, for it is rather mental than physical, rather moral than material; it has nothing to do with *papier maché* boats and central seating, with swivel rowlocks or new-patterned blades; it is a matter of the "point of view," and a result of training, or—if you will—of nationality. Six months ago these eight devoted boys were practically certain that they would represent their University at Henley. Six months ago they toiled in a gymnasium at appointed tasks; they worked at an accurately calculated piece of machinery in a tank; they thought and slept, and dreamt and lived on rowing. If the contest in question had been one of Yale against Harvard, the eight would have devoted their entire nervous energy for a very considerable period not to rowing merely, but to the problem how most decisively to beat their rivals. The prospect of defeat has filled them with the bitter conviction that their whole after life would be a disgusting dreary desert. The vision of success has brought with it plans for extended journeying around a sympathetically joyful universe. Exile in a hard-worked West, where alone the vanquished may hide his humbled head from a world that echoes with derisive scorn, is their only alternative. The thing began very seriously indeed; it went on with dogged resolution; it has ended in a nervous tension that wears every member of the crew to fiddle-strings. And this is not merely the result of a necessarily peculiar preparation; it has been caused by intense mental preoccupation, only interrupted by examinations far more severe and far more frequent than any Blue at either English University is called upon to face. But it is caused more than all by a conviction that nothing—absolutely nothing—will atone for the bitterness of defeat. How different all this is from the "mental attitude" of the English crew beside them, must be clear from what has been already said. Whether from Oxford or from Cambridge, the English oarsman has had far more things than rowing to occupy his attention in the year that lies behind; even in rowing alone, so many varied interests and so many different races have taken up his time, that this international contest which winds up his summer season is itself but the final incident of an excellent good time.

Because I have so far confined myself to rowing, it must not be thought that this is the only sport in which the American undergraduate has a far harder time than we do. It was once actually said that the English took their pleasures seriously. That critic can never have had the advantage of visiting an American University. Sadness is no word for the feeling with which a Yale or Harvard captain approaches any contest against his hated rivals. He is filled with a serious and solemn realisation that out of an infinity of possibilities it lies upon him to choose that special combination which shall ensure success. He has no joy in practising save as a means to the perfection of that end. He takes no delight in the actual contest till the final record proves him incontestably—nay, overwhelmingly—the victor. This feeling finds its expression in the rigid formation of a certain style, that after long study has been judged to be most likely to succeed. That is why you hear strange terms like the "Abraham Lincoln" stroke, or the "George Washington" style in various Universities. The gentlemen whose names are thus immortalised are supposed to have invented a particular manipulation of the arms and body, which will apply the blade in a manner absolutely invincible, and—most important of all—absolutely unknown to any rival prophet. That is why American football teams practise in the darkest secrecy behind high palisades with posted scouts to ward off spies from any hostile camp. The rival team or eight might possibly discover the talisman of victory and put the secret of their opponents' lively combinations to their own base uses. I shall never forget the horror of an American University friend of mine when he first realised that Oxford were about to accompany the Cambridge coach in his own steam launch while he shouted instructions to the light blue crew. His state of mind then was only surpassed by the blank amazement with which he learnt one night at Putney that Cambridge were beguiling the after-dinner tedium of their training by inviting the Dark Blues to see—and loudly laugh at—a moving picture of the Cambridge crew at work near Mortlake thrown upon the screen by the merciless animatograph.

He was almost as much confused to hear the independent fashion in which the rival captains settled the details of the coming race. For no American undergraduate, however exalted his position among his fellow-sportsmen, can dare to settle the details of an athletic fixture of his own mere motion. The love of legal quibbling—which I have already noticed in another article upon their football—may perhaps go for something in accounting for this. But a very direct—and to my mind a very unfortunate—cause, is the way in which graduates are allowed the control of these affairs; not younger men only who have just taken their degrees, but men whose only excuse for being connected with University sport is the fact that they have grown old in delivering University lectures. I must not be so misunderstood as to be charged with ingratitude to the many—who shall be nameless, for their fame needs no advertisement and does not seek it—who have lived on at Oxford and Cambridge doing such good service to their various athletic institutions that we almost forgot they were "Dons" at all. But not one of these public-spirited gentlemen interferes with athletic details in the manner common in America. A conspicuous instance occurred at the last University boat race (1898). Not a man present had any voice in the matter save the two presidents. Many were of the opinion that a race in such weather was not only unwise but impossible. Yet the captains wished to row, and they did. The men who run, or play cricket and football, or row are accustomed to manage their own affairs in this manner, and it is a very good thing for them. Financial matters are often left—and with great advantage—to permanent and older officials of the kind I have mentioned. But it is no small part of the valuable training of English University life that the undergraduates have so much of the management of their own affairs in their own hands. Even a college captain tastes the joys of leadership and is stiffened by responsibility. The captain of any University team is a far more important member of society. The honour of his University in some particular direction is in his hands to make or mar. He is not judged merely on results, but he is asked to make the best use of his material, and he is conscious that every man behind him backs him up. The lessons in personal self-control, in the conduct of affairs, in the treatment of other men, that are thus acquired, are of the highest service afterwards, and even at the Universities their effect is to turn out men much more in contact with the realities of life, as represented by the surroundings of a larger world than is the case in America.

For at Harvard, to take an instance typical of the rest, the governing body of the university (called the "Faculty") has controlled its sports from the beginning: a system that has some excuse with schoolboys, or even at the outset of a very small University, but is antiquated and unnecessary now for Yale or Harvard or their rivals. Imagine the Senate or the Hebdomadal Council arranging the details of the 'Varsity sports and deciding to abolish the hundred yards! Yet the Harvard Faculty has always been accustomed to issue ordinances allowing or forbidding certain competitions, deciding the number, the date, and the place of various matches, controlling the movements of the members of the teams. Though undergraduates now go up a little older than they used to do, and though increase in numbers has been attended by a vast increase in all forms of athletics, yet the principle of this strange interference with University sports continues in the new "Athletic Committee" of nine, on which there are only three undergraduates, the remaining two-thirds being graduates and Dons. In the hands of this committee are placed all arrangements for the contests with Yale or other universities; with them rests the final and indispensable confirmation even of a captain whom a team have elected for themselves. One result is a quantity of preliminary correspondence which is far too like the prelude to a modern prize fight. I have no doubt that reluctance to begin relations with an epistolary war of words has often caused Oxford and Cambridge undergraduate captains to seek refuge in silence from the multitudinous queries of an American athletic committee more than half composed of Dons.

But the tyrannous way in which these young Republicans are governed is not the only thing which fills an inquiring English visitor with surprise. He regrets to discover that the spirit of competition is not nearly such a keenly living thing as he remembers it at home. It is replaced by a fatal lust for scoring victories and making "records." I will show what I mean by a quotation from one of their own prophets, one of the best sportsmen America has ever sent over here to write the result of his experience for his compatriots' instruction. Mr. Caspar Whitney remarks with surprise on the frequency with which our University football teams continue to play matches after the most important fixtures on their card is over. This, he writes, "differs materially from our own system, and is not so good, since it makes a series of anti-climaxes, where there is nothing to gain and everything to lose." Mr. Whitney has evidently yet to learn that English athletic contests are not arranged solely from the spectacular point of view. It is obvious that he cares more for victory in a certain match than for any enjoyment of the sport itself. But his admirable book seems to have done some good already. For soon after its publication there were signs that "college politics" were losing some of their severity. Early last spring (in 1897) a meeting between Harvard, Yale, and Cornell was arranged without any difficulty; and Columbia, Cornell, and Pennsylvania agreed to race as well. But this was only after a period of disputing which had almost resulted in the death of college athletics altogether. It seemed to have been entirely forgotten that victory or defeat were alike far less important than the fact of racing or playing one team against another, whatever the results.

I cannot but think that one reason for this diminution in the competitive spirit is to be found in the constitution of American Universities. For these abodes of learning are "one and indivisible." There are no separate colleges, apparently no centres round which that keen individual rivalry can cluster which is so well known at Oxford and Cambridge. Consequently there is no struggle twice a year for the headship of the river, no competitions for a college cup, no body of separately organised boat clubs from which ready-trained oars can be selected for the University crew. A far more fatal result is that an American undergraduate cannot get one-fiftieth of the racing or of the competition in any form of sport that his more fortunate English rival may enjoy. By the efforts of Mr Rudolph Lehmann—to whose book I, like every one interested in these matters, am already an acknowledged debtor—an attempt has been made to widen the somewhat sterile rivalry of the various "classes," or years, into a longer series of competitions; and with excellent results.

But there is one thing that even Mr. Lehmann cannot do; he cannot change the climate. Though he can encourage sport during October and November, which were hitherto left useless, he cannot thaw the rivers that are icebound from December to March, nor can he mitigate the torrid heat from July to September. This is one reason, though not the chief one, why the American's opportunities compare so unfavourably with the list already given of an English undergraduate's chances, even in one sport alone. For in January a Yale or Harvard man is already sent to the training table for his University crew, already begins regular exercise, and learns the slow heart-breaking labour of rowing in a tank on a machine. Varying the monotony by no racing whatsoever, the coach keeps his men at this until the eight appears on the water early in March. Their great and only race comes off in June. No wonder they are worked up to a pitch of nervous excitement that is often as pitiful as it is unnecessary. That they last through it at all is an uncommon testimony to their physique and pluck. Until the mere division of the whole body of students according to their age of residence is given up, until they race at least once in sculls and pairs, and fours (all of which are apparently unknown), and more than once in eights, I cannot think that even their splendid physical development and their undoubted courage will ever get a proper opportunity for successful display on this side of the Atlantic.

Because I have said a good deal about one form of sport, it must not be imagined that Americans have not as many opportunities for different games as we have. But I have taken the management and the conditions of rowing as typical of all the rest; for all other forms of sport are managed and carried on in the same way. Their football I have already described elsewhere in these volumes, and the results of American specialisation need not be further alluded to. Cricket they soon found too slow for the quick and nervous temperament which their climate has produced. Baseball was invented in its stead and developed on the lines I have already suggested. Athletic sports, in their specialised sense, Americans attacked with their usual vigour, and the number of "records" they have already created show that the results they prefer have not been long in rewarding them for their perseverance. But Mr. Whitney may again be taken as a witness of his companions' over-energy. "Have we not been carrying our preparation too far in all branches of our college sports?" he asks; "We make too much of a business of our sport. Let us invest it with a little more of the recreative feature." If Americans took this advice we might perhaps see an American Henley; whereas, at present, a sight equivalent to Leander racing Thames, or New College winning the Grand Challenge, is out of the question in America; while the spectacle of a University team playing an outside club like Yorkshire or Richmond, is as impossible in America as it would be for them to see Yale or Harvard playing the State of Connecticut at baseball. But clearly something must be done if they are either to have more competition on their own side of the water, or to arrange international meetings upon ours. They must understand the real meaning of an "undergraduate," and of a "member of a University," when it comes to athletic meetings; and they must think of some more "recreative" methods of preliminary training when it comes to a race upon the water. In these two sports are the only two opportunities for a real international contest, because the element of "rules" enters into them the least, and it is only a question of moving a boat through the water, or getting first to the finish by superior speed over the cinder path. Baseball and cricket are out of court, football even more so. And I can imagine that the present time (June, 1898) is a favourable one for arranging a rowing fixture in the near future; because recent events must have confirmed Americans in their opinion that we are all wrong, and that they will only have to come over here to win.

In the University race, which was decided while these lines were being written, the Cornell crew, coached entirely on the American plan, came in a long way ahead. The Yale eight, which used a mixture of the American and English systems, was second. Harvard, coached by Mr. Lehmann on solely English principles, was last. This, I say, may suggest to them an international meeting in the near future. But on this side we are more used to neglecting the actual result and considering the mere rowing; and I believe that Mr. Lehmann's work has been more valuable because its fruits are yet unseen. He may not have had time to teach Harvard how to win a race, but he has planted (in the soil where another Cambridge man, two centuries ago, set the first seed) the spirit of English competition and the details of English training, which cannot fail to do good in the end. Over here, it is our Universities who keep up the highest standard of amateur sport in all its branches. They do that by competing with every good amateur club in every possible form of sport, and by encouraging within their own borders a system of generous rivalry that is of the highest value to themselves and to the nation. Harvard, Yale, Cornell, and Pennslyvania have still got to learn what all this means. Their energy, in work and play, is far greater than our own;

their thirst for victory and records is far keener; but in time they will discover that there are even better things than these.

THEODORE ANDREA COOK.

It is worth noting that the American Universities have adopted one game practically unknown in England, namely, Pelota (*q. v.*). The game, largely played in the Spanish States of South America, has been adopted, and somewhat modified, by the students, under the name of Basket Ball.

VETERINARY WORK—HORSE—None of the domesticated animals associated with man in the pursuit of sport is so liable to disease or so much exposed to injury as the horse. His speed and strength, and the manner in which he is employed, render him especially disposed to accidents, often of the most serious description; while the very artificial life to which he is subjected in order that he may be in the fittest condition to perform the functions imposed on him, predispose him to diseases of various kinds, which demand careful and generally immediate attention. We shall here refer briefly to some

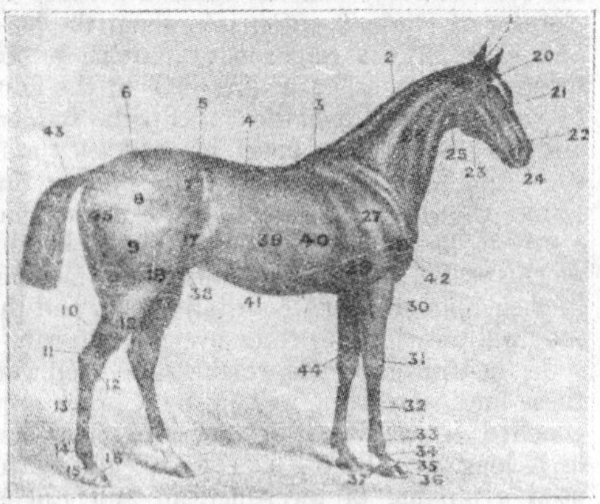

EXTERIOR OF THE HORSE.

1, Poll; 2, Crest; 3, Withers; 4, Back; 5, Loins; 6, Croup; 7, Angle of Hip or Haunch; 8, Quarter; 9, Thigh; 10, Leg (wrongly named the Thigh); 11, Point of Hock; 12, Hock; 13, Hind Shank, Cannon or Metatarsal bone; 14, Hind Fetlock; 15, Hind Pastern; 16, Hind Coronet; 17, Flank; 18, Stifle, properly the knee; 19, Gaskin; 20, Forehead; 21, Face; 22, Nose; 23, Lower Jaw or Jowl; 24, Upper Lip; 25, Throat; 26, Neck; 27, Shoulder; 28, Point of Shoulder; 29, Elbow; 30, Fore-arm; 31, Knee (properly the Wrist or Carpus); 32, Fore Shank, Cannon or Metacarpal bone; 33, Fore Fetlock; 34, Fore Pastern; 35, Fore Coronet; 36, Fore Hoof; 37, Heel; 38, Sheath; 39, Body; 40, Chest; 41, Belly or Abdomen; 42, Breast or Counter; 43, Dock or Tail; 44, Chestnut; 45, Point of Hip or Buttock.

of these diseases and accidents with which the horseman may have to deal before he can obtain professional assistance, and show him how to render first aid to the suffering animal, whether in or out of the stable.

Accidents — Wounds — The horse is particularly exposed to wounds, from the simple cut to the wide lacerated tear. According to their character and mode of production, they are usually described as "incised," "punctured," "lacerated," and "contused." The *incised*, or clean-cut wound, is generally the simplest and that most readily dealt with, though much of the success attending its treatment will depend upon its situation and the textures which are divided. In the treatment of all wounds, cleanliness is of the utmost importance in order to secure rapid and favourable union of the cut surface. Therefore the first thing to be done is to cleanse it from dirt and foreign matters, and if there is much bleeding this may be checked by the application of cold or hot water. If the wound is not large and the part can be bandaged, then the edges should be brought together as evenly as possible, and the bandage applied. It is well to place a piece of fine tow or lint (asepticised) over the wound before the bandage is put on. When the wound is extensive and the skin hangs in a flap, an attempt should be made to fix it by means of stitches of silk thread, or pins passed through the edges of the wound and across it, and thread twine or fine tow twisted round them, from heads to points, in figure of 8 fashion. In some cases, strips of cloth covered with glue may be applied across the wound to keep its sides together after the hair has been clipped or shaved off, and the wound itself covered with antiseptic lint.

In all cases, whenever possible, wounds should be treated with dry antiseptic dressings, and of these the best are probably chinosol and boric acid, each of which may be mixed, if need be, with a certain proportion of starch powder. The exclusion of the air from wounds is, when possible, always to be aimed at, and this can be effected most readily and the healing process best promoted by such dressings.

Rest of the parts is also essential to rapid healing of wounds, and this can be secured in various ways, but chiefly by means of bandaging, which also aids in maintaining apposition of the borders of the wound and the dressings applied to it; but care must be taken that the bandage is evenly applied, and that it will not impede the circulation to an inconvenient extent. To wounds of the lower part of the limbs these remarks more particularly apply; in this region, after obtaining apposition of the edges of the wound, dry dressing and careful bandaging are all important.

Punctured wounds, such as stabs from nails, sharp stakes, splinters of wood, pointed weapons, &c., are often the most dangerous to the animal, as they are also generally the most troublesome to deal with. Having ascertained that no portion of the substance which caused the wound remains therein, and having cleansed it as well as can be done, it should be dressed as in the case of a simple wound. Often, however, severe pain and great swelling occur soon after the punctured wound has been inflicted, and then it may be necessary to poultice or foment the part with warm water, and, after washing out the opening by means of a syringe, to get rid of putrid matter, to inject a solution of chinosol to destroy putrefactive germs. But unless constitutional symptoms become manifest, and there are indications that the wound is not doing well, it is the best course to keep to the dry dressings and interfere as little as possible with the injury.

Punctured wounds of the horse's feet produced either in shoeing, picking up stray nails on the roads, &c., are often followed by very serious consequences if not immediately attended to. The lameness soon becomes very great, and the animal evidently experiences intense pain. Sometimes much care is necessary in discovering the cause of this suffering. Nails picked up on the road are usually inserted alongside the frog, where they may be buried so deeply as to injure the flexor tendon of the foot and open the sheath through which it plays over the navicular bone. When, therefore, a horse falls suddenly lame in travelling on the road, the first thing to do is to lift the foot, and, if a stone is not found wedged between the shoe and the sole, to examine carefully the spaces on each side and in the middle of the frog. If a nail or other sharp body is found there, it should be removed before the horse is allowed to go further, and as soon as convenient the foot should be immersed for half an hour, or even an hour, in a bucket of warm water. Then it may be necessary to remove the horn from around the wound and dress this with Stockholm tar smeared on a pledget of tow, the dressing being retained by one or two pieces of thin wood or hoop-iron placed over it, their ends being pushed beneath the shoe. The horse should be kept as quietly as possible in a stall for a few days until it is presumed the wound has perfectly healed, and there is no longer danger of complications. If, however, the lameness and distress, instead of gradually subsiding, increase, it will be advisable to resort to warm water fomentations several times a day, to feed the horse on a light, laxative diet, and, if there is great pain in movement and in getting the heels to the ground, a shoe considerably raised at the end of the branches should be put on, as this will considerably relieve the weight-strain on the injured parts. Should the serious symptoms continue, the services of an expert had better be obtained.

If nothing be discovered elsewhere to account for the lameness, then the shoeing may be suspected, and faulty driving of the nails most probably will be found acting as the cause. Fortunately there is no difficulty in putting this suspicion to the test. The horse will have been recently shod, or will have had fresh nails driven into the shoe of the lame foot, and this, if the nail or nails have been driven into or too close to the living parts, will be higher in temperature than the other feet. Lift the foot and squeeze firmly and steadily around it, between the wall and sole, by means of a pair of pincers; when the injured part is compressed, the animal will demonstrate this by wincing considerably. The same manifestation will be made if the foot is placed on the ground and tapped around the neighbourhood of the nails with a hammer or the head of a hunting-crop, the opposite foot being held up meanwhile. The shoe must be taken off and the injury sought out by paring down towards the nail-holes, when, if matter has formed, this will escape on the puncture being opened; if this stage has not yet arrived, the exalted sensitiveness shown in paring and the evident traces of puncture will testify to the cause of lameness, which should be much diminished by relieving the pressure on the part in this way. Immersing the foot in hot water for half an hour, or keeping it in a poultice of mixed bran and linseed for twelve hours, should tend to abolish the pain. Then the cavity made in searching for the injury may be filled up with Stockholm tar (melted by moderate heat) and a piece of tow, and the shoe replaced, omitting, however, to insert nails at or very near to the puncture. When the foot has been nail-bound and the nail or nails press too much on the sensitive parts, which is sometimes even more troublesome than puncture, the same treatment must be adopted. It should here be remarked that long continued fomenting or poulticing of the horse's foot is nearly, if not always, to be avoided, as after the urgent pain has been relieved its employment is not only unnecessary, but, as a rule, detrimental. Antiseptics, and cleanliness and rest are the mainstays of a cure.

Thorns often inflict troublesome punctured wounds, especially when they are lodged in the joints or in the sheaths of tendons. Hunters are more particularly exposed to these punctures, which sometimes cause considerable lameness when the thorns remain *in situ*. The first business is, of course, to discover the thorns and remove them. Their presence is revealed by the sudden symptoms of pain which the horse exhibits when the hand is passed over them, and they not infrequently produce swelling of the part. The finger nails or a pair of forceps can be employed to remove them—in their entirety, if possible—but sometimes they are so deeply buried that a careful examination has to be made of the skin, and the hair clipped or shaved off before anything can be attempted for their removal. Softening the skin by means of warm fomentations or poultices will facilitate the operation and also lessen the pain and inflammation.

Contused and lacerated wounds are often more troublesome than, and quite as serious in results as, incised and punctured wounds, inasmuch as not only are tissues cut, but they are also bruised and torn, and very often have foreign substances imbedded in them. Their gravity, as in the case of other wounds, depends very much upon their situation, extent, and the amount of bruising or laceration of tissues. A bruise is merely a form of contused wound in which the skin is intact, but the parts beneath it are more or less injured. This form frequently occurs from forcible contact with a blunt object, such as a stake, or pole, or a kick from another horse on the fleshy parts. There may be considerable pain and swelling, the latter being usually soft and containing fluid. To relieve the pain and diminish the swelling, the part should be bathed with hot water or with lotions that produce cold. It is not advisable to lance the swelling, so as to allow the contained fluid to escape, until it is seen whether the inflammation continues. If it does, then it may be surmised that matter has formed, and this must be drained away by making a very small incision through the skin at the most dependent part of the swelling. Contused and lacerated wounds occur most frequently on the limbs, through horses falling or stumbling, and the fore-legs are most exposed to such injuries.

"**Broken knees**" is the term commonly applied to injuries of this kind occurring to the front of the carpal, or, as they are wrongly designated, "knee" joints. The damage may be nothing more than a slight graze, merely abrading and bruising the skin, or it may pass through varying grades of injury to the most extensive and serious laceration, the knee joint itself being opened. When the skin is merely grazed, little more requires to be done than carefully and gently to remove any dirt and grit from it and bathe with warm water, afterwards dressing with a little chinosol ointment. If there be swelling and stiffness of the joint, the fomentation must be continued until these disappear. When the skin is cut and bleeding, the same treatment is to be adopted; but if the wound is clean it may be dressed with boric or chinosol powder and covered with a piece of lint and a bandage. If the wound is rather extensive and transverse, the horse should not be permitted to lie down until the healing process is well advanced. In some cases, after the wound has been well cleansed, it may be dressed with tincture of myrrh, and then a piece of lint on which Canada balsam has been spread laid over it, and over this a bandage may be placed. This dressing will often remain on the knees until the wound is healed.

When the wound is ragged and contused, and the tendons passing over it are probably lacerated, so that there is great danger of one or more of the joint capsules being opened, then all the skill and care of the expert will be required to repair the injury and preserve the horse's usefulness; therefore he should be called in early. In the meantime something may be done by the amateur. After the wound has been freed from grit and all foreign matter by gentle washing with warm water, it should be dried with lint; then a wide piece of the same should be covered with a layer of the boric acid or chinosol and starch powder, and placed on the wound, this dressing being retained by a bandage. The leg should be made immovable by means of a starch bandage wrapped round it from above the knee down to the fetlock, and, as the horse must not be suffered to lie down until the wound is healed —which may occupy some weeks—he should be supported in the standing position by means of a sling. The wound will require to be dressed in the course of a few days, and to permit of this being done without taking off the starch bandage, a hole may be made in this by a pair of sharp-pointed scissors immediately over the seat of injury. When the knee has been dressed, the dressing can be kept in place by an ordinary bandage. The treatment of irritative fever and other unfavourable symptoms ought to be left to the veterinary attendant. It must be remembered that poulticing and fomenting such wounds is most injurious, and that the best results are derived from the dry antiseptic treatment. A tendency to fever must be combated by laxative diet in the shape of mashes, and by small quantities of nitrate of potass in the water given to drink. The temperature of the feet of the other limbs must be watched after a few days, and especially of the opposite foot, as congestion and inflammation sometimes attack them, owing to the strain imposed on them from the continued standing. This, however, is not so likely to occur when the horse is slung, as the legs are then relieved of much of the weight of the body.

Wounds of other joints, such as the hock and fetlock, are to be treated in a similar manner, as are also those of sheaths of tendons. Dry antiseptic dressings, moderately firm bandaging, immobility of the limb, and keeping the horse quiet until the injury has been quite repaired, are the chief points to be remembered.

A sometimes severe and troublesome form of contused wound is that known as "over-reach." This is usually produced in galloping, especially on heavy ground, and in jumping; it occurs most frequently in the hunting field and on the steeplechase course. The parts injured are the back of the leg or heels of the fore feet, and the damage is inflicted by the toe of the shoes of the hind feet. The extent of damage varies from mere laceration of skin to exposure of the posterior surface of the back tendon, or even tearing of the tendon itself or of the lateral cartilages of the foot at the heels, and sometimes involves the coronary frog-band at this part. When an accident of this kind happens in the field, all dirt should be removed by washing, and a temporary bandage—such as that afforded by a handkerchief—applied until the injury can be properly attended to. Mention of a temporary bandage calls to mind the great benefit that is often derived from a linen bandage, a piece of lint, and a few pins wherewith to close skin wounds; these can be easily carried by the horseman, as they are light and occupy little space, and may be of great service in an emergency, and even in the case of an accident to man. When the "over-reach" can be properly dressed, it should be again well cleansed, and it may be necessary to remove, by means of sharp scissors, any shreds of tissue hanging from the wound. This should then be dressed with chinosol or boracic acid powder, a piece of lint placed over it and a bandage evenly applied around the leg. When the heel is the seat of injury and there is evidence of much bruising, it is often advantageous to thin the hoof immediately below it, in order to relieve the tension from subsequent swelling of the bruised tissues. The wound should be dressed with the dry antiseptic powder every second or third day, and no washing, fomentation, or poulticing ought to be allowed. The horse should be rested and have light diet. With regard to the prevention of this accident, it is to be remarked that the injury is inflicted by the back lower edge of the toe of the hind shoe, and that the hind shoes of all horses that have to jump or gallop should be straight across at this part—"square-toed shoes," which should also be convex on the ground surface and have a clip at each side. The hoof may be allowed to project slightly beyond the shoe at the toe, but it ought to be well rounded.

Another kind of contused wound is that produced at the top of one foot by the opposite foot, or the foot of another horse, treading on it, and known as a "tread." The wound may be slight or severe, its character not being always ascertainable at first, so that it should not be neglected even when apparently trivial. If the wound is lacerated and there are loose shreds, these must be removed by sharp scissors. Then the part must be freed from dirt, washed clean, and dressed with antiseptic powder in the manner already described, keeping the part always dry. If the portion of hoof immediately in contact with the wound becames detached, it should be cut away by the shoer's knife.

A very serious form of lacerated wound is that which is sometimes met with in the hunting field, when a horse becomes "staked," *i.e.*, has the wall of the abdomen or chest or the muscles inside the thigh torn by a stake while jumping. It is usually the lower part of the belly which suffers from staking, and the tear is not infrequently so wide and deep that the abdominal cavity is opened, so that the intestines escape therefrom and may descend even to the ground. When the muscles only are wounded, all that can be done is to cleanse the wound and cover it up with handkerchiefs, bandages, or anything of the kind conveniently to hand, until it can be properly attended to. Wounds of the abdomen with protrusion of the intestines, though formidable looking, are not always hopeless if the bowel is not torn or severely bruised. As a temporary measure at the time of the accident, the intestine should be returned to the abdominal cavity if possible, the manipulation in effecting this being very carefully conducted; then a long bandage should be made by tying several handkerchiefs together; this is placed on the wound and tied over the back, being supported with the thong of a whip. If the intestines cannot be returned without the risk of injuring them, they had better be let alone and kept suspended in the bandage until an operation can be conveniently undertaken. The horse can generally be walked for some distance after being bandaged. The operation consists in throwing down the horse gently, taking great care of the intestines, placing the animal on his back, after having administered chloroform to him, returning the bowel, and passing sutures, or, better, a steel pin or pins through the lips of the wound and passing tow round the ends of them in figure of 8 fashion. The wound should be treated antiseptically during and after the operation. A wide bandage encircling the body should include the wound. The diet ought to be light and laxative.

Hæmorrhage—The most serious accompaniment of wounds of all kinds is hæmorrhage, and this cannot always be easily checked or controlled, especially when the blood proceeds from arteries. This is known by the bright red hue of the blood and by its flowing in pulsating jets, whereas blood from the veins is of a purplish colour and comes away in an even flow. Pressure is the most ready means of stopping bleeding, though if this be mere oozing of the blood in small quantity, cold or somewhat hot water will answer the purpose. If the bleeding occurs in the limb, a handkerchief dipped in cold water and applied to the part, being kept there by another handkerchief tied over it and around the leg, may succeed in checking the flow, if it does not altogether suppress it. When the bleeding proceeds from a deep narrow wound, it may be checked for a short time, until other measures can be taken, by passing the finger down into the opening and making pressure on the injured blood vessel; or a handkerchief may be thrust deeply and firmly into it, so as to stanch the flow. Should these measures prove unsuccessful, the garrot tourniquet can be adopted. This is readily made by folding a handkerchief in the longest direction, tying it quite loosely around the limb, between the wound and the body, and then tightening it to the required extent, *i.e.*, until the bleeding stops, by means of a hunting-crop or a stick passed through this loop and twisted round. If the horse has to travel any distance, which should not be far, with this tourniquet in position, the hunting-crop or stick may be tied to the leg by means of another handkerchief round one end. If a pad, made by a handkerchief folded into a lump or by a round smooth stone, is placed over the large artery of the limb and included in the tourniquet, the latter need not be so severely twisted. At any rate the tourniquet is a very temporary arrangement, and must not be kept on the limb any longer than is necessary to obtain expert assistance in order to tie the bleeding vessel.

It is astonishing how in these emergencies a little knowledge, self-possession and common sense will avert serious, if not fatal, consequences.

Contusions—Contusions are frequent in the horse, and are caused in a variety of ways. One kind has been alluded to. When the skin is not broken, applications of cold water or astringent lotions are the most convenient, and generally the most effective treatment. What is termed "sore back" is usually a contusion of the skin produced by severe and unequal pressure of the saddle in some particular part of the back. The saddle may have been badly constructed or fitted, the stuffing lumpy, the lining hard and dirty, the weight on the back long continued or unsteady, or the saddle removed too soon after a long journey, especially in hot weather. In some cases sore back is doubtless produced by the manner in which the saddle is put on—placing it back and then pulling it forward against the hair into its proper seat, instead of putting it on forwards and then moving it backwards in the direction of the hair. Prevention, it need scarcely be said, is most important, for a sore back may imply inability to carry the rider, or even the saddle for some days. When there is danger of sore back from long continued pressure, it is an excellent plan, when the rider dismounts, to leave the saddle on the back for some time, to allow the skin to become cool and the blood circulation in it to regain its normal condition; if the weight has been great and the girths are somewhat loose, it is even advisable to tighten these to some degree after the rider has left the saddle. If, unfortunately, the skin becomes tender and puffy, applications of cold water, lead lotion, or common salt dissolved in water must be resorted to at once. If the skin is abraded, then astringent lotion is needed; and there is nothing more effective nor handier than dressing the part with ordinary writing ink, as the iron and gallic acid in it are eminently astringent. It is a good plan, when the weather is hot and the journeys long, to sponge over the back with a solution of alum, oak bark, or sulphate of iron, in order to render the skin hard and less sensitive and vascular. If the journey must be prolonged and the horse ridden, then the part of the saddle that impinges on the bruised place must be eased by removing the stuffing from it.

Fractures—Of all the domesticated animals the horse is the most exposed to fractures of the bones. This exceptional liability might be predicted when the nature of the services he is compelled to render is taken into account. And of all the bones of the body the most frequently broken are those of the limbs, especially those below the knee and hock.

Fractures are usually divided into five kinds:—(1) *simple*, (2) *compound*, (3) *comminuted*, (4) *compound comminuted*, (5) *impacted*.

The *simple* fracture is that in which the bone is broken into two pieces, but the skin remains whole; in the *compound* fracture the bone is broken, and there is a wound in the soft tissues and the skin covering the fracture through which the ends of the bones may protrude. In the *comminuted* fracture the bone is broken up into a number of pieces; and in the *compound comminuted* fracture, in addition to this break up of the bone, an external wound exists which leads to it or through which the splinters may project; while in the *impacted* fracture one end of the broken bone is wedged into the other end. In the horse, fractured bones are always serious, but especially when those of the limbs are concerned. This is not because broken bones are less ready to become united in the horse than in other animals, indeed, fractured bones are more rapidly repaired in favourable cases in this animal than they perhaps are in mankind; but it is because of the difficulty in keeping the parts sufficiently at rest to ensure continued apposition of the fractured portions and no interruption of the healing process. This is particularly the case in the limb bones, which have to sustain weight; a favourable position of the animal cannot be obtained, the only one usually secured being the standing one, with the weight of the body of the horse sustained more or less by a sling passed under it and suspended by ropes to beams or poles.

Fractures of the limb bones and the vertebræ are generally looked upon as incurable, and the animal is accordingly destroyed. Fractures of the vertebræ may unhesitatingly be pronounced as hopeless when they are diagnosed, and the horse should be mercifully slaughtered. The same conclusion unfortunately has to be arrived at in nearly all cases of compound, comminuted, and impacted fractures, especially of the leg bones; for even under the most favourable conditions, when the broken pieces of bone can be brought into their proper place and kept there until firmly united and the wound healed, the horse may remain a cripple afterwards, and be of little or no use except for breeding purposes, if a stallion or a mare. The difficulty of maintaining the broken bones in place, the complications which are likely to occur during the treatment, and the expense incurred, no less than the great uncertainty of even an imperfect cure, all militate against keeping the animal alive. But every case of fracture must not be condemned as hopeless, as is too often done in those of the leg bones, for simple, and even compound, fractures have been successfully treated, and the horses have subsequently performed good service. Much depends on the situation and nature of the fracture, as well as on the health and temper of the horse, and also on the skill of the expert and the patience and humanity of the owner.

Fractures generally occur out of doors, though they sometimes happen in the stable, and are produced by kicks from other horses, by falls in jumping, by pulling up short while galloping, by forcible impact of hard bodies against the bones, &c. A fracture may occur without any marked symptoms except, perhaps, the evidence of pain on manipulating the parts, and lameness if the limb bones are involved. Much will depend upon the situation and the character of the injury. When the bone is not concealed too deeply by thick masses of muscle, crepitation, or grating on each other of the broken pieces, may be felt, and even heard, on moving the limb; when there is displacement, the limb may be shortened, more or less pendulous, and capable of being moved in directions which it could not be made to do were there no fracture. In other cases the existence of fracture is at once apparent without manipulation being necessary, as when the angle of the haunch is broken and displaced—an accident not very uncommon, and usually brought about by this part being struck against the side of a door in entering or leaving a stable or loose-box. Of course, if the fracture is compound or comminuted, or both combined, the diagnosis is generally rendered easier. Sometimes, when the bone is only cracked, there may be lameness for a day or two and nothing serious suspected—the animal may even be exercised or worked, when all at once displacement occurs and then the leg is really broken. Such cases are far from unusual; the fracture generally occurs in the hind limb, the leg bone (tibia), between the stifle and hock, often erroneously designated the thigh bone, being nearly always the one that offers this peculiarity. The cause of fracture here is nearly always a kick from another horse, the injury being inflicted inside the leg a short distance above the hock, where the bone is only covered by the skin. There may be great lameness immediately after the kick, but this soon passes off, and then there is nothing more evident than the wound in the skin until, a few days afterwards, the horse is found in the morning with a broken leg and has to be destroyed. The explanation for this somewhat extraordinary occurrence lies in the fact that the bone—which is one of great solidity and strength—is cracked or starred into perhaps a number of pieces, but there is no displacement of these; this is prevented by the dense resisting membrane covering the bone (the periosteum), until the exudation that is thrown out preparatory to cementing the fractured surfaces separates these from each other and the containing membrane so far that the horse, in lying down or getting up, throws so much strain upon the leg that complete separation takes plack, and the animal is found with the limb dangling in so peculiar a manner that the experienced eye can at once perceive what has happened.

In troop stables this accident most frequently occurs, though it also happens in the field; and so apprehensive was I of complete fracture ensuing that, for many years, when a horse received a kick on this part, I immediately had him put in a sling and kept as quiet as possible until I could assure myself either that no fracture had taken place or that there had been one, and that union was so far accomplished that there was no reason to fear displacement; though the horse was usually kept in the sling until he could be safely allowed to lie down. The evidence that there had been fracture was found in the great majority of cases, and consisted in the presence of a hard enlargement (callus) where the blow had been given.

As has been mentioned, and for the reasons adduced, many cases of fracture in the horse are not considered suitable for treatment; among these there are often cases which would, if occurring in man, be undertaken with every prospect of a good recovery. Therefore it is that treatment for fracture in the horse is seldom attempted, and especially when the bones are those of the limbs, even when the fracture is of the simple kind. So that, in arriving at a decision as to whether the attempt should be made, several considerations must be kept in view, among which are the nature and situation of the fracture, the value of the animal, the conveniences for and the probable cost of treatment, whether he is likely to be quite free from lameness or other infirmity which will diminish his usefulness afterwards, and whether if he, if a stallion (or she, if a mare) may not be useful at the stud should the cure not be complete.

Fracture of the vertebræ, whether of the neck, body, or loins, is, it may be said, always fatal. Death may be instantaneous, as when the neck vertebræ are fractured near the head, or death may not ensue for some days when the back is broken. There is generally no difficulty in diagnosing "broken back," an accident which occurs more frequently in the field than in the stable. The horse is down and cannot rise, for he has no power over his hind limbs, though this inability might also be due to a bad sprain of the muscles or ligaments of the loins. But in broken back, in addition to immobility of the hind extremities, there is also loss of sensation in them; so that when they are pinched or pricked with a pin the horse does not show any sign of pain, which he would do if the back were merely sprained. As broken back is incurable, the animal should be killed to obviate needless suffering.

With regard to killing horses which have met with very serious accidents, the means are not always at hand for doing so, and it not infrequently happens that a considerable time must elapse before a knacker, a gun, or a pistol can be procured when the mishap has occurred in the field; and even when a firearm and ammunition have been obtained, it is not every one who knows how to shoot a horse dead instantaneously. The brain must be perforated if this is to be effected, and the best part of the head to aim at is the middle of the forehead, about three inches above the line of the eyes, where there is usually a curl in the hair. The firearm should be held close to the head, and the bullet or shot directed towards the top of the neck, so as to reach the base of the brain—death is then instantaneous. But shooting cannot always be carried out, and some other plan must be resorted to. If a blacksmith's forge is near, a sledge hammer and a pointed punch may be borrowed, and the latter instrumen tdriven deeply into the brain, at the spot and in the direction indicated above, by a smart blow from the hammer. Death is then as prompt as by shooting, if the operation is properly performed. Or the carotid artery may be exposed by making an incision with a pocket knife in the side of the neck about midway between the head and chest, in the furrow immediately above the windpipe, and pushing the forefinger inwards until it meets the artery, which is distinguished by its strong pulsations; the vessel is then drawn to the surface by the finger being hooked round it, and a slit an inch or two long made in its wall. On allowing the vessel to go back the blood gushes out in a full stream, and death—almost painless—rapidly ensues. But this sanguinary business is not pleasant to witness, and I have on several occasions, when driven to my wit's end to find a ready way to kill a horse, when there was nothing with which to do it except a knife, thrown off my belt and tunic, rolled up my shirt sleeve, and introduced my hand, armed with an open pocketknife, well into the rectum, where, turning the point of the blade upwards and pushing it towards the loins, I made a strong cut across, and in this way divided the posterior aorta or one of its divergent branches. The horse was dead in a few seconds without a drop of blood escaping externally, and without anybody being cognisant as to how death was caused.

When fractures of the limbs occur on the road or in the field, and it is decided not to destroy the animals on the spot, but to give them a chance for their lives, great care must be taken, when moving them to some suitable habitation, that the injury is not made greater by the movement. To prevent a simple from becoming a compound fracture, the broken bone should be "set" as perfectly as may be possible under the circumstances—*i.e.*, the broken portions brought into their natural position, and kept there by any simple means until better can be devised. A bandage or handkerchief may be tied round it, and, if thought necessary, splints of wood cut from a paling, or stout branches of trees or twigs sufficiently long to extend some distance above and below the fracture, may be employed; hunting-crops sometimes answer very well in an emergency. Some soft material, such as reeds, grass, hay, or moss, should be laid around the limb on the bandage, so as to make the surface as level and even as possible; on this the splints are to be placed, inside and outside the limb, and their ends kept fixed by handkerchiefs tied around them.

When this has been done, an attempt must be made to get the horse to his stable or some other convenient shelter where he can remain until he is well. If a horse-ambulance cart can be procured, this difficulty is at once solved; but such a useful conveyance is rarely available in the country, and not always even in towns. Therefore the animal must travel on his own legs, only three of which can be used for this purpose. If the damaged limb is a fore one, with time and patience a considerable distance may be travelled, but frequent short halts are needed. When it is a hind limb that is disabled, progression is much more difficult, and a longer time and more frequent rests are required to travel the same distance. In these cases travelling is quicker and the crippled horse is much relieved if a portion of his weight can be borne on a narrow plank placed beneath his chest, each end of which is carried by one or two men; or each end of a sack may be tied securely to a stout piece of wood, and on this the chest may rest, while men at the sides of the horse partly carry him by means of the sticks.

Arrived at his destination, the horse must be slung, and in default of the proper gear a very useful sling may be made by nailing, or strongly sewing, each end of an ordinary sack to a short pole five or six feet long. This sling is placed beneath the body, and secured at the ends of the poles by ropes passed over beams in the roof. The shafts of a cart or wagon, firmly propped up, have sometimes been successfully employed to sling a horse. It must be remembered that the lame horse should not be lifted off his feet by the sling; this should just be in contact with his chest when he is fully standing up, so that when he seeks to rest he simply bends his knees and hocks and allows his weight to fall on the sling. The greatest care should be taken that everything is sufficiently strong to sustain the weight, as great damage is often done when the sling suddenly gives way while the horse rests on it.

The proper bandaging of the fracture can now be carried out, and this demands some skill. The temporary bandage and splints having been removed, a more careful examination of the limb may be made, but the broken bone should be handled as little as possible, if the parts are in their proper place. If there is no external wound, a thick layer of cotton-wool may be placed around the damaged part of the limb, and over that a linen bandage, evenly wrapped and moderately tight. Then a starch bandage may be placed upon this, and, if need be, splints of wood or iron, the object being completely to immobilise the limb. To allay the pain, lead lotion and laudanum may be poured between the skin and the upper part of the inner bandage, and if the inflammation runs high, cold water may be applied by a sponge or a hose frequently during the day.

This treatment is more particularly applicable to fractures of the leg bones, but it must be remarked that little can be done in the way of "setting" such bones as the arm bone, the humerus or bone between the shoulder blade and bone of the fore-arm; nor yet the thigh bone or femur (that between the hip joint and stifle), as these are too much surrounded by masses of muscle. Even the bone of the fore-arm, the radius, is difficult to set and fix, especially when the fracture is oblique; and the leg bone of the hind limb, the tibia (extending from the stifle to the hock), is still more troublesome, the broken ends of the bone being very rarely brought together and kept so, if they are displaced. The same may be said of fracture of the bones of the pelvis, one of which, the ilium, is much exposed to this accident, especially at its anterior part, the point of the quarter or hip. This part, as has already been mentioned, is very liable to fracture when horses are passing through doorways, and when a considerable piece has been knocked off and displaced the animals are said to be "down in the hip." For such cases scarcely anything more can be done than to apply warm water fomentations to the part, sling the horse, and keep him as quiet as possible. Fracture of the hip joint generally occurs through a fall in the stall or on a hard road, and is not always easily diagnosed. It may be regarded as incurable.

The bones of the face are sometimes fractured by kicks from other horses, and displacement is usually the result. If this displacement gives the horse an unsightly appearance, or interferes with the breathing, the depressed bone or bones can be raised by an operative procedure that can best be carried out by the surgeon. In these cases there is often profuse hæmorrhage from one or both nostrils, to check which plugging cannot be resorted to, as in man, because the horse breathes only through his nostrils; so that little more can be done than apply cold water to the face and inject it up the nose.

The shank bones—large metacarpal or large metatarsal bones—if not much splintered, and provided the fractured ends can be brought together and kept so, may, in many cases, be successfully repaired, if properly set and bandaged. The pastern bones are often fractured, more particularly the smaller or lower one; the accident generally occurs in jumping at a fast pace or in pulling up sharp when galloping; it may also happen in slipping on ice or soft ground. The bone may be merely split vertically or obliquely, or it may be broken up into a number of pieces. Diagnosis is usually easy; there is great lameness and intense pain, especially when handling the damaged pastern, and, if the fracture is comminuted, the unusual mobility of the part, together with the crepitus, or grating of the fragments on each other, should leave no doubt as to what has happened. When the bone is merely split, the only evidence is the lameness, pain on handling the part, and probably some swelling. Recovery from split and fractured pasterns is not by any means rare, and if the horse is a valuable one, and the bone not much broken and displaced, an attempt at cure may be made with a reasonable hope of success. The treatment has already been suggested.

The foot bone—os pedis—is sometimes fractured, especially that of the fore-foot, and in a similar manner to the bones of the pasterns. Unfortunately, owing to its being completely buried within the hoof, the existence of this accident can only be inferred from the intense lameness and the great heat of the foot, and the absence of signs of fracture elsewhere in the limb. The treatment is simple enough, and consists chiefly in keeping the horse quiet in the sling, and resorting to continuous irrigation of the foot with cold water.

Dislocations.—The dislocation of bones which enter into the formation of joints is not a very common occurrence, though one may be surprised that, considering the great strain often imposed on many of the joints, especially those of the limbs and back, it is not more frequent. The most common form of dislocation is that of the stifle or patella, which usually happens in young or debilitated animals, and is due almost entirely to weakness or relaxation of the ligaments that attach the patella to the front of the thigh and leg bones. This dislocation is often only partial, and therefore not so serious, for it can generally be rectified without any manipulation. So persistent is it in some horses that at every few steps the animal takes when in motion the patella slips off to the outside of the joint, momentarily checking the extension of the leg, and slips on again as readily, this reduction being often accompanied by a dull clicking sound. Such partial dislocation may occur with both patellæ at the same time. Complete dislocation is usually witnessed in older horses, and is more serious, as the patella has not a tendency to return to its place without manual assistance.

The signs of dislocation of the patella are very marked and, to the experienced horseman, unmistakable, but those who see a case for the first time are inclined to look upon it as a very grave condition—nothing less than a broken leg in one case which I was called upon to see. The limb is rigidly fixed and thrust backward, the fetlock being bent forward until the front of the hoof nearly touches the ground, and no effort of the animal can bring it forward; so that in walking the leg is dragged after the body in the same rigid fashion, none of its joints being moved. The animal does not give evidence of suffering from pain, unless compelled to walk quickly, which is very difficult and fatiguing.

In the simpler form of patellar dislocation, if the bone does not return to its place spontaneously, drawing the leg forward and at the same time pushing the bone from the outside forward and inward, will make it resume its normal position with a smart jerking noise. To cure this relaxed condition of the stifle ligaments (which usually disappears with age), the animal should be kept tied up in a stall for a week or so, and the stifle blistered in front and on each side.

When the dislocation is more complete, reduction is not so easy. In order to draw the hind leg sufficiently forward, a rope must be passed round the pastern and brought towards the shoulder or placed around the neck; this rope on being drawn steadily, will carry the leg in advance, until the stifle joint is sufficiently straightened to allow of the patella being restored to its natural position by pushing it from behind forwards. This manœuvre rarely fails, at least it has always been successful with me; but if the attempt does not succeed, which is just possible with horses that have large muscular development, then, in order to induce muscular relaxation, the animal should be thrown down and chloroform administered. When reduction has been effected—and this ought not to be delayed if the joint is inflamed and painful—cooling lotions should be applied, after which it may be advisable to resort to blistering, and allow two or three weeks' rest.

Dislocations of the shoulder-joint, fetlock, and pastern joints, have been recorded, but these are too serious for the amateur to deal with unless he can reduce them easily without doing any damage. The smaller joints he may be able to put right by getting the dislocated bones in place and keeping the limb bandaged until the expert arrives. Some of these dislocations have made a good recovery. The vertebræ of the neck are sometimes partially dislocated through falls in the hunting field, but more particularly from being "cast" in the stable. The dislocation is outward, to the right or left side, and several of the bones may be involved. The neck is curved to one side, and this gives the horse a curious appearance. To straighten the neck again is nearly always a serious task, and takes a considerable time, if some days have elapsed before treatment is adopted. A splint apparatus or cradle has to be placed on the neck, and pressure applied on the convex side. This pressure must be exercised continuously, and gradually increased until the neck is straight; but the cradle must be worn some time afterwards until the ligaments have gained their normal condition.

The Detection of Lameness in Horses.—Among the many things which the intelligent horseman ought to know is, not only when a horse is in good health and condition or when it is sick or unfit for work, but also when it is lame and, if possible, where it is lame, as well as the cause of the lameness. This is indeed expecting a great deal from him, and in truth there are not many amateur horsemen who are privileged to possess this knowledge to such an extent as to meet every requirement; but the more he knows the more likely is he to keep his horses in health, to avoid being imposed upon or misleading others, and to be in a position to apply the stitch in time when anything is amiss and expert assistance not immediately available. These remarks are more particularly applicable to cases of lameness, as the ability to distinguish unrhythmical from rhythmical movement of the limbs is often of great moment to those who employ horses, and, in only a less degree, is the faculty of being able to fix upon the ailing leg or legs, and to detect the seat and cause of imperfect movement.

It is more important for the rider to know when a horse is lame than to be absolutely certain as to the part affected or the cause, for an expert can generally be trusted to discover this; whereas, if an animal suddenly becomes cripple and continues to be worked without this being perceived, great, and sometimes even irreparable, mischief may be the result.

Lameness has been defined as the manifestation, in the act of progression, and by one or more of the limbs, of pain or weakness, inability or impediment in movement. Though pain is usually a cause of lameness, yet a horse may manifest irregular or halting movement of the limbs during motion without experiencing pain. There may be stiffness of a joint or malformation of a limb impeding movement, and yet no evidence present of any pain being suffered. For instance, the nervous affection of the limbs popularly known as "stringhalt" is a kind of lameness, and yet there is no sign that it is in any way productive of pain. It is most important to remember this, as very often people who are not acquainted with horses or their diseases, imagine that an animal must be suffering if they see it limp or move unevenly, and very often unfortunate drivers or owners of horses are unjustly punished for cruelty to them because of this mistake—some deformity of a limb preventing its being used as freely as the other legs, but causing no more pain than a club-foot or a stiff knee does in man.

Lameness may be only temporary, and be due to local causes, without disease being present. A wound, or bruise of the leg or foot, or even a stone lodged between the shoe and sole or about the frog, may induce limping; or lameness may be permanent from chronic disease, or the effect of such disease. Even weakness of muscle may cause lameness in one or more limbs, and the opposite of this condition, such as cramp of the muscles, will produce the same result, as will also partial or complete dislocation of a joint—that of the stifle, for example—in which there is complete inability to draw the hind leg forward.

In some cases lameness is so marked that the veriest tiro can scarcely fail to notice it, especially if only one limb is involved, and to determine in which leg it is. In other instances, however, it is so slight that it may escape casual observation, and even among experts it may chance to be of such a peculiar or trifling character that there will not only be a diversity of opinion as to the limb affected, but whether the horse is at all lame. Therefore it is that a horse will be passed as sound by some experts, and pronounced lame by others, though these again may differ not only as to the seat of lameness, but even as to the lame leg.

Skill in the detection of lameness would almost appear to be a special faculty in some people. Doubtless long experience and close observation among lame horses will tend to render this detection easier and more certain, but there are people whom no amount of practice will thoroughly teach, and whose eyesight and hearing do not enable them to detect if a horse is lame or on which leg it limps. Many even of those who have successfully passed through the veterinary schools have had their professional reputation seriously marred in the early days of their career through failing to detect lameness, or mistaking the limb, the location of the ailment, or the cause. Other men, again, are quick at detecting lameness, and not only in deciding on the lame leg, but in fixing upon the part where the cause of the lameness exists; some of these men can do this in certain cases before the horse has moved many yards.

Of course nothing but practice and careful observation can ensure the acquirement of this knowledge, but a few simple directions may render it easier of attainment.

Lameness is generally detected when the horse is in movement, this being either walking or trotting, or both, though it is generally necessary to make the animal trot in every case, unless the lameness is so marked, or progression causes so much pain, that the faster pace can be dispensed with.

But even when the horse is at rest the existence of lameness may in some cases be suspected from the attitude of the animal and the position of the limb or limbs. One or more of these, if pain is present in them, may be placed forward, backward or outward, and they may be extended or flexed. Indeed, to those who understand the anatomy of the limbs and the physiology of movement, the attitude of the horse and the position of the legs when at rest are in many cases of great diagnostic value. For it is to be observed that a limb in which there is pain is "rested"—that is, relieved from the animal's weight—as much as possible, and the manner in which this relief is effected is an indication not only as to the limb involved, but also, in numerous instances, of the seat of pain or infirmity.

For example, when a horse is experiencing pain in a fore or hind foot, the limb is usually extended forward. If it is in the back part of the fore foot, this "pointing," as it is termed, will be accompanied by raising of the heels from the ground, the symptom so characteristic in cases of corn and navicular diseases; but if the pain is in the front part of the foot, then the heels are placed on the ground more firmly than usual and the toe is relieved as much as possible, this attitude being very characteristic of laminitis. Lameness from injury or disease in the knee or its vicinity is generally marked by the horse standing with that joint bent forward, but when the elbow is the cause of lameness the knees will also be bent in the same direction, but the fore arm is carried forward and the foot backward. When the shoulder is the seat of pain the knee and foot are generally in the same position as in elbow lameness, but the entire limb droops in a very significant manner.

When the pain in a limb is severe, there is frequent, if not incessant movement of it; it is continually being raised from and gently placed on the ground, and if it be a fore limb the litter may be pawed back by it, while the animal's countenance and other signs will betray the agony experienced. Should the lameness be in a hind limb, there are similar indications of great value, and here "knuckling over" of the fetlock is more marked in many of the lamenesses of the hind than of the fore leg. In the majority of these cases the lame leg is advanced, and especially if the pain is below the hock; if the foot is rested on the toe, it generally indicates pain in the back part of the limb, tendons, ligaments or heels, while a bent hock is usually seen in disease or injury of that joint. Pain in the hip is manifested by an apparent shortening and resting of the entire limb; stifle trouble is indicated by a peculiar straightening of the leg, which can be drawn backward, but cannot so readily be carried forward. When the pain is in both hind feet, the attitude is very noteworthy; these are brought forward under the body, and they are lifted alternately in an evidently uncomfortable manner, the movement being often accompanied by groaning, hurried breathing, perspiration, and other signs of suffering, while the fore legs are carried back in order to sustain a greater share of weight-bearing. In some cases of this description it has been observed that the pain in the hind feet prevents urination being properly performed. The animal cannot extend itself as it must do in that act, though it may raise the tail and make efforts to carry the hind legs back, but the horse quickly resumes its former attitude with a groan, and agonisingly raises the feet in a spasmodic manner. This inability to extend has not infrequently led the attendants to imagine that the urinary organs were at fault.

The position the lame horse assumes when stationary is that in which the infirm or injured parts find most relief, and this indication is of the greatest service in arriving at a knowledge of the cause when the cripple limb has been detected. Sometimes it is necessary slightly to move, or attempt to move, the horse in order to accentuate the evidence as to the degree and nature of the ailment. In laminitis, for instance, though the attitude is very striking and characteristic when the animal is not disturbed, it is more particularly significant when an attempt is made to make him move a step backward or forward. If the inflammation is at all severe, it is almost impossible to compel the horse to lift the feet from the ground; the body may sway to and fro, but the feet remain fixed as if rooted in the earth, the weight being thrown altogether on the heels, where the inflammation is not so severe.

It is the same with some other forms of lameness, the attitude in the stable often furnishing a valuable guide in ascertaining the leg that is at fault, and even the nature of the damage. It is therefore very necessary to see the horse when at rest in the stable, and the attitude should be observed for a few minutes, and the horse then moved backward and forward, as well as sideways in the stall. For it is to be remarked that horses affected with certain infirmities of the limbs will exhibit symptoms of lameness in the stable which they quickly lose when exercised out of doors; but when they return and stand still again for a short time, they limp even more than before. Of course the converse is also true of other kinds of lameness, which may appear to be absent when the horse is in the stable, but become very apparent during movement.

An examination of the limb by eye and hand after movement will in all probability confirm and complete the information acquired by observing the horse during progression. It must be stated, however, that a knowledge of the anatomy of the limbs is of great value in the diagnosis of lameness. It is always advisable to have slight cases of lameness, about which there is any doubt, tested at a trot upon hard ground; a horse which will then show inequality in movement may go apparently sound on a soft surface.

A lame horse in walking or trotting always endeavours to avoid increasing the pain by throwing as little weight as possible on the affected limb. Therefore, if a fore leg is amiss, when the foot comes to the ground the head is thrown upwards; if it be a hind leg, the quarter of that side is raised when the weight falls on it. It is wrong to say that a horse "drops" on the lame leg. Lamenesses are best detected when standing behind or before the animals in motion; in front of them if the fore limbs are to be observed, behind them if the hind ones are to be scrutinised. Then, having ascertained the lame leg, careful observation of the manner in which the leg is moved, the observer standing on that side, will give an idea as to the region where the cause of lameness is located, and a manual examination will generally complete the diagnosis.

We will now briefly take notice of the accidents and diseases which occasion lameness, in addition to those already mentioned incidentally when dealing with wounds and fractures.

Splints are sometimes a cause of lameness, though not so often as is supposed. They are usually looked for on the front limbs (they are very rarely seen on the hind), between the knee and the fetlock and on the inner side of the leg, so that in standing in front of a horse, if a splint is present and of a considerable size, it is at once evident. In exceptional cases, chiefly those in which there is malposition of the limb—the elbow inclining inwards and the toe of the hoof outwards—the splint is observed on the outside of the leg. Splint is really a bony tumour, nearly always formed between the shank bone and the small bone attached to it on the outside and inside—the so-called "splint bone"—which generally unites them immovably together, whereas in early life these bones are only held together by a kind of ligamentous substance. When the horse is worked on hard ground and shod with iron shoes, and especially if he carries weight on his back, the splint bone, from its position on the inner side of the leg and closer relationship to the knee bones, has to bear a larger share of the weight and concussion than the outer one. The ligamentous connection with the shank bone is strained, inflammation is set up in this, and in the end bony matter is thrown out between the two bones, and often to a considerable amount on the shank bone in addition, constituting the tumour. People possessed of the evolution craze have attempted to explain this pathological process as a natural tendency towards unification of the three bones—quite a normal transition. But it is forgotten that splint usually appears only on one side of the limb—that which is most under the body, and therefore has to sustain most weight; that it occurs, it might be said, always on the fore limbs—those which sustain most weight—and is indeed exceedingly rare on the hind limbs; and that every horse does not have splints, those which are unshod and employed on soft ground rarely having them.

When the inflammation is only slight it causes little lameness, but in proportion to its severity the movement of the limb is impaired and the lameness increased. At first there may be no perceptible enlargement to account for the great lameness, but generally, in a short time, a gradually increasing and rather hard swelling is perceived, and this is hot and painful on manipulation. These signs, and the fact that young horses are most liable to splints, as well as the knowledge that the lameness is least noticeable at a walking pace and most marked in trotting, especially on hard ground, and that it increases in intensity as movement is continued, are distinctive. The severity of the lameness nearly always depends upon the situation, not so much on the size of the tumour, and upon the extent of bone implicated. When once fully formed, if the tumour does not interfere with the movement of the knee or with ligaments or tendons, the lameness disappears and there is no further trouble. But in exceptional cases splints are a source of inconvenience, even if they do not cause pain and interfere with the horse's action.

The treatment for splint must largely depend upon whether it causes lameness, and also whether, from its size, it is likely to prove an eyesore. If it is small and does not make the horse lame, there is little need to meddle with it; and if it is recent, all that requires to be done is to take off the shoes and allow exercise on soft ground, keeping the animal standing while in the stable on soft bedding, such as moss litter. If the lameness is very marked and it is desired to check the inflammation, thereby preventing the tumour from growing, acetate of lead lotion applied to the part by means of two or three folds of lint tied round it and kept constantly moist, will prepare the inflamed part for the application of a blister. After a few days of the lead lotion, a small portion of biniodide of mercury ointment should be rubbed into the skin of the affected part; the blister may be repeated two or three times, at intervals of about a week. This is as much as the amateur can venture to do, for though in extreme cases it may be advisable to cut into the swelling and so divide the dense membrane covering it, thereby relieving the tension, yet the operation is almost too delicate for an unskilled person.

An inflammation of the shank or cannon bones of the fore legs, rarely the hind ones, similar to that of splints, and also occurring in young horses, especially those in hard training for racing, has not unfrequently to be combated energetically if chronic lameness and deformity are to be avoided. This condition, commonly known as "sore shins," is usually ascribed to the concussion and strain to which the immature tissues of the limbs are subjected. It is generally witnessed in two or three year old race horses, mostly the former, and, unlike splints, the inflammation occurs on the front of the bones, nearly always towards the middle or the lower end of the shank. The symptoms are at first slight lameness and hesitation in extending the limbs when moving on hard ground; then the action becomes that of a cripple, and walking even induces pain. If galloping is continued when this stage has been reached, serious consequences will ensue. A very perceptible swelling appears on the front of the leg, as if the animal had received a blow there, and this is hot and very painful on pressure, while the attitude betrays uneasiness and suffering; this is still more indicated by constitutional disturbance, such as diminished appetite, fever, dejected countenance, &c. In extreme cases, when treatment has not been undertaken in time, these symptoms increase in intensity, the swelling will increase and, if not relieved by lancing, the bone involved may perish, the soft textures slough, and the patient eventually die. In many of those animals which recover, the bone remains enlarged where it was inflamed, and gives the limb a more or less deformed appearance.

In the early stage a speedy cure can generally be effected by appropriate treatment. The training should be suspended for a few days, and the animal allowed rest. The leg should be enveloped in lint covered by a calico bandage, and this must be kept constantly wet by lead lotion, with which has been mixed a little laudanum to lessen the pain. After two days, when the inflammation has been somewhat subdued, the part may be painted over with compound tincture of iodine, repeated every second or third day until the skin is slightly blistered; or, if the swelling is more considerable, the application of biniodide of mercury ointment instead will act more promptly and effectively as a blister. The diet should be soft food. If the case has been neglected and the swelling is great, deep scarification or incision will be necessary to relieve the pain and preserving the bone from serious alteration, but this had better be done by an expert. Such cases require a long rest and exercising gently on soft ground before training can be recommenced, and this should only be gradual.

Ringbone is an analogous condition to splint and sore shins, though it is, with regard to its consequences, a more serious cause of lameness than these. It is due to inflammation on the surface of the large or small pastern bones, and though it may appear on either hind or front pasterns, the former are probably most frequently the seat of it; exceedingly rarely the foot bone is affected, the membrane covering it—periosteum—being mainly involved. There is swelling, considerable lameness, and pain on pressure of the enlargement, which may be on any part of the bones, but is generally on the front or sides. The lameness is likely to remain permanently after the inflammation subsides, as the deposit of bone that almost inevitably results is immediately beneath the expansion of tendons and ligaments, and interferes with them. Sometimes the enlargement is so considerable as to catch the eye at once, while in other cases it requires a nice sense of touch to detect it. The horse has a tendency to travel more on the heels of the affected limb than is customary, and there is not much difference in the degree of lameness on soft or hard ground. In the treatment, the animal must be rested as much as possible, cold applications being continuously made to the inflamed part, after which there should be repeated blistering with biniodide of mercury ointment; in bad cases it may be necessary to have recourse to the actual cautery.

Spavin, the name commonly given to a diseased condition of the hock, is frequent in horses, and is generally marked by the presence of a bony tumour on the inner side of the front of that joint. It is due to much the same cause as splint and ringbone, the predisposition to it being a hock defective in shape. There is nearly always lameness, but the degree of this will depend not only upon the size of the tumour, but also upon the manner in which the implicated bones are affected; the lameness is nearly always permanent, and the horse usually travels more on the toe of the affected limb than when there is no spavin. When the disease is commencing, in order to ensure a rapid and satisfactory cure the joint should be relieved from weight and movement as much as may be possible, and this is best obtained by placing the animal in a sling and blistering the inside of the hock repeatedly, the stall being laid with moss litter. A long rest must be allowed, and, when the horse is put to work, this should at first be light. When spavin is very pronounced, so that the horse goes lame and treatment is of no avail, he can be much relieved in travelling by raising the heels of the shoe.

Lameness from **navicular disease** is less frequent, perhaps, than it was half a century ago, thanks to a better knowledge of the horse's foot and how it should be managed, especially in the matter of shoeing. The causes of this troublesome malady are somewhat numerous. It may appear suddenly or gradually—suddenly when it is the effect of an accident, such as sprain of the perforans tendon where it passes over the navicular bone; or gradually when due to mismanagement of the fore feet, in which alone it is seen. The symptoms are resting the affected foot when the horse is at rest, which is done by advancing the foot and raising the heel, and "pointing," as in this way the tendon is relieved from strain. The step is short and the toe comes sooner to the ground than the heel, hence the toe of the shoe is most worn; the temperature of the affected foot is increased, and in the stable the litter is often pawed away from before and raised behind the foot to give it a better resting place. Little can be done to cure the disease, though certain measures may palliate it and keep the horse serviceable. The foot should be kept cool, the toe of the hoof shortened as much as can be done with safety, and the frog allowed to come into contact with the ground, or, if this cannot be contrived, an artificial frog of india-rubber may be placed over it.

Lameness from **congestion of the laminæ** of the feet is not infrequently a result of over-exertion in travelling, especially on hard ground in warm weather; it may also come from long continued standing in the stable or on board ship, and in some cases it may be a sequel of disease. There is intense lameness, and the horse can scarcely move the fore feet, which usually suffer most. The tendency is to rest on the heels. The temperature of the feet is increased and there may be fever present, with impaired appetite. Gentle exercise and cold applications to the hoofs will frequently dispel the symptoms in a short time. It is judicious treatment, after a long or a fast journey in the saddle during hot weather, to walk the horse about for some time after the rider has dismounted, so as to allow the circulation in the laminæ to acquire its normal condition.

Laminitis is the stage beyond congestion of the laminæ, and is much more serious, for here we have inflammation of these delicate and highly sensitive structures. The pain is much more intense, and movement is more distressing; there is fever and loss of appetite; the pastern arteries throb, and the agony is so intense that the body is often covered with perspiration. If the horse is standing, he will not attempt to lie down, and if recumbent he makes no effort to get up, but lies and groans, with the fore limbs thrust out in front of him. If the horse is standing, he must be put in a sling or compelled to lie down, so that the feet may be relieved by taking the weight off them; then cold water swabs must be wrapped round them, or cold bran poultices applied. Morphia should be injected under the skin to diminish the pain, and the diet must be laxative and sparingly given until the inflammation subsides. Then gentle exercise in a loose-box or on soft ground may be permitted for a short time, and gradually increased until all danger of a relapse has disappeared.

It should be noted that in all cases of disease or accident in which the animal is compelled to lie for some days on the hard ground, or on hard litter such as wheat straw, there is danger of severe bruises to the prominent parts of the body, and these "bed-sores" have sometimes worse results than the disease or accident itself. To prevent or retard their appearance, the horse should rest on a thick bed of some soft material, such as dried moss, moss litter, or old but dry oat straw which has already served as bedding.

Corns are often a cause of lameness, especially when shoeing is not carefully attended to. What is termed a "corn" in a horse's foot is really a bruise of the sensitive sole, this bruise being the result of undue pressure, usually made by the shoe. The ordinary situation of the bruise is the angle formed by the wall and bar of the inside heel of the fore foot; corns may be said to be unknown in the hind feet. In some cases the lameness is considerable, and the bruise may run on to suppuration if neglected. The signs are those which are induced by pain in the back part of the foot, and tapping with a hammer upon the wall of the hoof in that situation will at once reveal the cause. Removal of the shoe is necessary, and paring away some of the horn at the bruised part—which will be bloodstained—is also required in order to discover the extent of the injury. If this is slight, nothing more may be necessary than lowering the wall at the heel so that it will not touch the shoe when this is nailed on, and, still further to ensure this, it is advisable to leave out the nail nearest the damaged heel. When the bruise is more severe, the pain and inflammation will be lessened by immersing the foot in a bucket of warm water for an hour, or in a poultice for twelve hours. After this the shoe is to be put on and the bruised part smeared with Stockholm tar, care being taken that the shoe does not touch the heel when the horse's weight is on it.

In some cases of chronic corn much benefit is derived from the horse wearing a shoe with the part chopped off that would rest on the bruised heel.

Thrush is an unhealthy condition of the horny frog, brought about by the shoer paring it, by standing on foul litter, or by the frog not coming into contact with the ground, and sometimes it is an accompaniment of navicular disease. The horn is softened and ragged, and usually there is a very offensive discharge from the cleft in the middle of the frog. The treatment is simple. Clean out the frog well, remove all shreds of horn, dress the cleft and other parts with calomel, covering this by pledgets of fine tow pushed firmly into the recesses, and keep the horse on dry clean litter. In a day or two remove the tow and insert other pledgets smeared with Stockholm tar. After a few of these dressings the morbid condition disappears.

Sandcrack is not very common among light horses, but it is occasionally met with, and when it is suddenly produced generally causes severe lameness. It is a vertical split in the wall of the hoof extending, when it causes lameness, to the sensitive tissue within, from which blood sometimes escapes. In the fore foot the split is generally on the inside, rarely at the toe or outside; in the hind foot it is nearly always in front. It is usually produced during severe exertion, as when jumping, and commences at the top of the wall of the hoof. When the lameness is considerable, the foot should be kept in a bucket of warm water to soften the horn and reduce the pain. This may have to be frequently repeated. When the lameness has gone, and if the horn is sufficiently thick, a fine horse-shoe nail may be driven through the edge of the crack and the ends brought together by pliers so as to form a clamp to hold the sides of the fissure together; or the hoof may be firmly bound round with many strands of fine tar twine. A little Stockholm tar may be rubbed into the coronet, above the crack, in order to stimulate the growth of sound strong horn. The shoe should not be allowed to rest on the part of the hoof corresponding to the crack. "**Seedy-toe,**" another disease of the foot, is sometimes accompanied by lameness. It is a separation between the wall of the hoof and the horny laminæ on its inner surface, and this separation may be only to a very limited extent, or it may involve a large portion of the wall, and extend from the lower border to near the coronet. There is little or nothing to denote its existence until the shoe is taken off, when the cavity is readily seen. This contains some loose crumbling horn, to which the disease probably owes its name. The cause is usually severe pressure on the wall of the hoof, produced by the shoer driving the clip of the shoe too close against it, and, as the clip is in front of the fore shoe, so we find the separation there. The hind feet are largely exempt from this defect. To make a radical cure, it is the best course to take away all the separated wall as far as the sound hoof, carefully removing all the discoloured horn beneath and cutting out all cracks and fissures in it. The gap left in the hoof can be filled up with gutta percha or covered with pitch. The shoe must not have a clip at the toe, but one on each side if necessary; the coronet should be stimulated to increased secretion by rubbing a little Stockholm tar into it at intervals of a few days.

The secretion of hoof horn is sometimes so very defective in quantity and quality that the shoer has great difficulty in attaching the shoes. This may arise from mismanagement of the feet, and especially to the mutilation the hoofs undergo when being shod, such as over paring the sole and frog and rasping the front of the wall, or rubbing oil and certain compositions on this part; or it may be due to natural weakness. The face of the wall should not be rasped, and the sole and frog never ought to have more than the loose portions removed from them, while nothing but water should be applied to the wall by means of a sponge. To promote a healthy secretion of hoof wall, the coronet should have an application of Stockholm tar at intervals of a few days.

Sprains—Muscles, tendons, and ligaments are all liable to sprain, those of the limbs of the horse—especially the fore ones—being particularly exposed to damage done by sudden and severe extension. In fast galloping and in jumping such accidents are most common, and in many cases the results are extremely serious, so far as the future soundness and usefulness of the horse are concerned. Sprain of tendons and ligaments is more frequent than that of muscles; the position of some of these, their function, and their texture, predispose to this accident, as do faulty conformation and weakness of structure, owing to lack of tone. The injury may be merely over-extension of the fibres, or these may be ruptured; the number involved may be very many, or only a comparatively small number. Sprain of muscle is indicated by lameness or stiffness, with pain on pressure, and sometimes swelling. The muscles of the limbs, especially those of the shoulder and hip, suffer most frequently from this injury. Fomentations with warm water and rest will be found the best treatment. It may be necessary in some cases to put the horse in a sling in order to secure rest.

It must be remarked that in the case of sprains of all kinds, as indeed in the matter of lameness generally, rest is an indispensable requisite in treatment, and nothing can be more injurious than to compel horses to take exercise until lameness has disappeared; as not only does this, in the majority of instances, cause a relapse, but it often converts a curable case into an incurable one, or an acute case into a chronic one. It is not at all unusual to hear of lame horses being turned out to exercise or to graze in order that they may become sound. Of course, when the limbs are injured it is most difficult, if not impossible, to secure that absolute rest which can so readily be obtained in man, but everything should be done to make it as perfect as circumstances will permit.

Sprains of the shoulder and hip-joints, as well as of the muscles and ligaments in their vicinity, are not so frequent as of the tendons and ligaments below these, and are indicated by inability to extend the limb, and pain on manipulation. Fomentations with warm water, rest, and the application of a blister over the part if the lameness does not subside in the course of a few weeks, are the measures to be adopted.

Sprain of the loins occurs in jumping, backing, pulling up suddenly in a fast pace, over-exertion in draught, getting cast in the stall, &c. If the horse can move, there is generally much difficulty in bringing the hind legs forward, with stiffness in the back—and especially in turning round—a straddling gait, in which the hind quarters sway more or less from side to side. If the horse lies down, he is often unable to rise without assistance, and not unfrequently he cannot extend himself to micturate; there is nearly always pain on pressure over the loins. In severe cases, the horse is down and cannot get up, though the hind legs are warm and can be moved about, and sensation in them is perfect. This will differentiate sprain of the loins from broken back. Warm water fomentations to this part for several hours a day, with rubbing in of stimulating liniment in the intervals, sloppy diet, and slinging are about all that can be done by the amateur.

Sprains of the knee and hock are to be treated by fomentations with warm water, succeeded after a few days by lead lotion or tincture of arnica, applied by means of swabs round the joint. A frequent cause of lameness, especially in light horses, is a sprain of an important ligament at the back of the hock, producing a convex swelling more or less marked, and known as "curb." Sudden severe exertion, such as jumping, bucking, the hind legs slipping forwards, &c., are the immediate exciting causes, but in very many instances the defective shape of the hock predisposes to the sprain. At first, in many cases, there may be considerable lameness with swelling of the part; in other cases the lameness is not very perceptible, though the curb may be distinctly observed. Even when the lameness does pass off, it is rare indeed for the swelling to subside. The treatment is limited to wrapping round the part fine tow or lint, and applying a bandage firmly over this, pouring in at the top, and frequently, tincture of arnica lotion, or one composed of sal ammoniac and nitre in the proportion of two ounces of each to a pint of water. The horse should be kept tied up in a stall. When the inflammation and lameness have subsided, the swelling should be frequently painted over with tincture of iodine or, better, a small portion of biniodide of mercury ointment may be rubbed in at intervals of a week. This may be continued when the horse is at work.

In speaking of curb, mention may here be made of what is called "capped hock," which is usually due to contusion, but may in some instances arise from sprain; in the latter the swelling is on each side of the joint of the hock, in the former it is immediately on this part, and projecting backward. Unless the injury or sprain is very severe, the lameness at first is but slightly, if at all, noticeable, though there may be swelling, heat, and pain. If this is the case, a cooling lotion should be applied—such as an ounce each of arnica and Goulard's extract in a pint of water, and by means of lint maintained by a bandage; if the lameness is marked, a high-heeled shoe will relieve it. In the course of a few days a stimulant may be used on the part, such as the tincture of iodine or the biniodide of mercury ointment. If the enlargement becomes chronic it is most difficult to reduce it. It has been recommended to plaster it over, while the horse is in the stable, with pipeclay or whiting mixed into a paste with vinegar, and this is to be rubbed off when the animal goes out to work.

Sprain of the back tendons occurs in either the fore or hind limbs, and is due to a sudden and severe effort. These tendons are below and behind the knee and hock, and are two in number, one in front of the other—the posterior is the flexor of the pastern, the other, in front of it, is the flexor of the foot. It is rare that both are sprained, the one in front being most frequently involved in the accident, when the swelling is most marked at the inside and outside. If the posterior one is sprained, the swelling is noticeable immediately behind, and forms a convexity. There is swelling, heat, and pain on handling the part, and lameness commensurate with the degree of injury. The limb at the seat of sprain should be thickly enveloped in tow, cotton wool, or lint, and bandaged firmly, then the arnica and Goulard's extract is poured in between the padding and the skin, which is to be kept continually moist with it. Or, if the weather is not cold, water may be applied by means of a hose from the water tap. A high-heeled shoe should be put on the foot if the horse is afraid to place his weight on the limb; indeed, in all cases this kind of shoe expedites recovery, but it should not be kept on longer than a fortnight. Instead of employing the lotion or cold water, it has been recommended to pad the sprained part firmly by first wrapping a moderately tight bandage round it, then on top of this at each side, a thick pledget of cotton wool evenly laid on, and another long bandage tightly wound over all. The bandages must be removed morning and evening and re-applied, the leg being gently rubbed each time they are taken off, and bent up and down. When the pain and lameness have disappeared, and thickening of the tendon remains, it will be advisable to blister it, perhaps repeatedly, with biniodide of mercury or cantharides ointment. Sprain of the check ligament below the knee, or of the suspensory ligament, is indicated by similar symptoms to sprain of the back tendon, the horse manifesting signs of pain on pressure of these parts. The treatment must be the same as first indicated, though it has usually to be longer continued.

Diseases—Only a few of the many diseases the horse is liable to can be noticed here, and these must be those which the amateur can deal with, or at any rate palliate, until the arrival of the veterinary surgeon.

Congestion of the Lungs—None of the domesticated animals is more liable to congestion of the lungs than the horse. This is doubtless due in some degree to his anatomical structure, but more to the nature of his work and the management to which he is subjected, and also in many cases to the nature of his surroundings. Congestion of the lungs may be an accompaniment or sequel of other diseases, or occur by itself, when it usually appears in the acute form, or "pulmonary apoplexy," as it is termed. This may be induced by sudden severe exertion when the horse is not in condition, or it may be brought on by long continued severe work when not in good training—as in the hunting field; it may also be caused by exposure to cold, and especially to cold winds and wet. The symptoms are very marked; the breathing is extremely hurried and laboured, the nostrils are widely dilated, the head is carried low, and the countenance is anxious and haggard; the body is often covered with cold perspiration, the legs are stretched out and are cold—the flanks heave tumultuously, there is tremor of the muscles, and, if the congestion has been induced by over-exertion, the heart can be heard beating violently. When the congestion is extreme, in many cases blood flows from the nostrils, and if this is foamy it is an indication that the blood is effused into the lungs. If not speedily relieved the horse will succumb to suffocation; so that treatment must be prompt. The horse should not be moved or disturbed, if possible, and, if he is wearing harness, this ought to be removed. An abundance of fresh air must be allowed; if the horse is in the field his face must be turned to the wind, and if in the stable his head ought to be brought to the door; the legs and body are to be well rubbed and clothed; before the limbs are bandaged they may be rubbed with stimulating liniment. Brandy or whiskey should be given in large doses (four to six ounces) and frequently at first—say every two hours for two or three doses, in a pint or two of water, warm if possible, or in oatmeal gruel. Tincture of arnica in doses of one or two ounces has been recommended. If there is thirst, tepid water or warm oatmeal gruel can be given. In very urgent cases the horse's life may be saved by abstracting a quantity of blood—from four to six quarts—from the jugular vein, but this operation requires some skill. When the animal is able to eat, the diet for some days should be restricted and of a kind that is readily digested; quietness is necessary, and the body and legs must be kept warm.

Inflammation of the Lungs—This is often a sequel of congestion of the lungs, though it may also follow catarrh, bronchitis, &c., or occur spontaneously. It differs in symptoms from congestion by the presence of fever—otherwise the symptoms, if perhaps less urgent at first, are somewhat similar. The horse is dull and prostrate, though he may wander about the loose box, but seldom lies down. The surface of the body and the legs are often cold, though the mouth is hot and dry, and the lining membrane of the eyes and nostrils is of a dark red colour; a short painful cough is emitted from time to time, and when the disease is advanced there is not unfrequently a rusty coloured discharge from the nostrils. In some cases the inflammation is complicated with pleurisy.

With regard to treatment, this is somewhat the same as for congestion, so far as keeping the body warm, fresh air, and diet are concerned. Every four hours there should be given, in a quart of thin gruel or tepid water, tincture of aconite six minims, nitric ether one ounce, solution of acetate of ammonia four ounces. But, if there is much weakness, for this draught may be substituted six ounces of brandy or whiskey three or four times a day. The food is often refused, so it should be made as enticing as possible; it may consist of sloppy mashes of bran or boiled linseed, with oatmeal gruel, a small quantity of picked hay, green forage, and sliced carrots, &c. Cold or tepid water is to be given to drink, with an ounce of nitrate of potass dissolved in a bucket of it. Litter should be thinly spread on the floor of the stall or box, so that it may not get entangled among the feet, and great attention should be paid to the admission of fresh air without draughts. When recovery has begun and only debility remains, a more generous diet can safely be allowed, and with it a tonic—such as finely powdered sulphate of iron in one or two drachm doses daily, mixed up in a little mash, morning and evening.

Bronchitis—This is an inflammation of the membrane lining the air-passages entering the lungs, and is usually due to colds. It nearly always begins with shivering and dulness, and some degree of fever, as well as loud, hard, and very frequent cough, accompanied by quicker breathing than in health. A discharge from the nostrils is generally present. The cough increases in frequency and severity, and causes exhaustion and loss of appetite; consequently debility soon sets in, and death not infrequently ensues from the air cells of the lungs becoming filled up with effusion. When the fever gradually subsides and the cough becomes softer and less frequent, the discharge from the nostrils ceasing and the appetite returning, amendment is taking place. When bronchitis occurs in cold weather, which is usually the case, the horse should be kept in a well-ventilated loose box, the body well clothed, and the legs enveloped in woollen bandages after being firmly hand rubbed. The throat should be well rubbed with stimulating liniment—such as compound camphor liniment, which may also be applied to the sides of the chest; or a woollen blanket may be wrapped round the chest, and hot water poured on the outside of it for an hour or two at a time, after which the blanket is to be taken off, the skin well dried, and the liniment rubbed into it. The horse should also be made to inhale the vapour of hot water from a bucket on which some hay has been spread; into this water a quantity of oil of turpentine or carbolic acid may be poured. A draught composed of camphor one drachm, solution of acetate of ammonia two ounces, and nitric ether one ounce, all mixed up in a pint of tepid water, should be given two or three times a day. The diet to be as for inflammation of the lungs.

Colds—Catarrh is very common among horses kept in hot, badly-ventilated stables, or exposed to variable weather, especially cold and wet. An attack usually begins with sneezing and slight fever, perhaps shivering; the legs are also cold, and the horse is dull and listless. Then cough becomes frequent, there is discharge from the eyes and nostrils, and soreness of throat is shown by more or less difficulty in swallowing, and swelling of the glands about the jaws. The breathing is but little disturbed, and the horse gets up and lies down. With judicious treatment of a simple kind the symptoms subside in a week or ten days, and complete restoration to health is generally the result. Good nursing is nearly all that is required in the way of treatment. A comfortable, well aired stable, clothing for the body and legs, sloppy mashes, with carrots, a little good hay, and water into which small quantities of nitre have been introduced, are about all that is needed until convalescence sets in. If the cough is troublesome, the upper part of the throat may be rubbed with camphor liniment, and the head held over the vapour of hot water in a bucket, to which oil of turpentine has been added.

Exhaustion—When this is due to over-exertion of any kind—as in the hunting field—the symptoms are not unlike those of acute congestion of the lungs. While going, the horse becomes unsteady in his pace and soon begins to stagger; the breathing is hurried and distressed and often accompanied by sighing, the eyes show extreme anxiety, the ears and tail are drooping, the body is covered with cold perspiration, and the head is carried low and heavily. If the pace is continued, the horse will quickly fall and lie in a semi-comatose state until he slowly rallies, if he does not speedily die. No horseman would knowingly or willingly push his horse to this dangerous stage of exhaustion, and there must be few indeed who could not perceive when it was being approached and take action accordingly. The horse must be relieved from saddle, bridle or other harness, and allowed to stand at liberty with his face to the wind. If brandy or other spirit is at hand, six ounces in water should be carefully poured down his throat, if he can swallow it all at once; if not, then it must be given by one or two mouthfuls at a time. When he has somewhat rallied, a little cold water or some tepid gruel may be offered him, and then his legs and body can be well rubbed.

Fits and Fainting—Horses are sometimes attacked with epilepsy, usually while at work, and as the attack is sudden and generally without warning, it is not without its inconveniences and dangers if the animal is being ridden or driven. Harness horses appear to be most liable to these attacks, though they are sometimes witnessed in riding horses. In some cases the attack is begun by a few rapid shakes of the head, then the horse staggers, may give a slight scream, and, running forward, falls unconscious. The limbs and lips are moved convulsively, the jaws are champed, and the eyes rotate in their sockets. After lying for a short time, consciousness is regained, though the horse may be unable to rise immediately. He looks stupefied, bewildered, depressed, and is an hour or two before he resumes his normal condition. But little can be done in such cases in the way of treatment with any prospect of cure. When the premonitory symptoms—such as shaking of the head—are observed, the horse ought to be pulled up and held by the head to prevent his falling, and this timely succour may avert the more severe phases of the attack. Should he fall, efforts must be made to prevent him doing damage to himself by keeping his head down and throwing a rope or rein round his legs. Two or three ounces of alcohol in water will be beneficial when the attack has passed off.

Horses sometimes, though rarely, faint. They fall to the ground suddenly and are unconscious, but they lie perfectly still and do not struggle as in epilepsy. The girths and throat strap should be loosened, and, if the horse is wearing a collar, this ought to be shifted up the neck. Cold water may be applied to the head and passed into the mouth by means of a sponge or handkerchief; when the horse can drink, water should be offered, and a dose of alcohol—four to six ounces—administered in a quart of water or gruel.

Sunstroke or Heat Apoplexy—Horses soon experience exhaustion when undergoing exertion in a high, moist temperature, and especially in the direct rays of the sun. Even when away from the sun's rays and standing quiet, great exhaustion, and even death, may occur in a very hot climate.

The animal suddenly becomes distressed, breathes heavily and quickly, ceases to travel or to notice surroundings, and, if not urged on, lies down, when he may become more or less unconscious, struggle with his fore limbs and make attempts to rise, or he may remain quite tranquil. In a severe case, the temperature of the body is increased and the breathing more rapid, and the muscles are in a state of tremor, with perspiration covering the skin. In these cases death often ensues in a few hours. Treatment, to be of any avail, must be prompt. If the horse is out of doors and there is any shade procurable, he ought to be moved to it, and all equipment removed from him; cold water should be dashed over his head and body, and the air agitated above him by means of a waving blanket, board, or sheet; hand-rub the legs. If there is struggling, the leg should be tied, and when the horse is able to swallow, a dose of alcohol and water may be given. Careful dieting must be observed for a few days after recovery, and the horse should not be exposed to a high temperature until he is well and strong.

Colic—Colic is not an infrequent disease where stable management, and especially feeding and watering, are not properly attended to. Bad or improper food, giving water immediately after grain, exposure to cold draughts of air, particularly on the legs, drinking a large quantity of water during cold weather, or at any time if the horse is exhausted, are the chief causes of colic. The symptoms are well marked. The horse is very restless and violent in his movements; he strikes at his belly with the hind feet, stamps and paws, often throws himself down and rolls and looks back at his flank. There are lulls in these manifestations, during which the horse appears to be nothing amiss and may commence to eat, until another attack comes on. If the pain is due to spasm of the bowels, the abdomen is not altered in dimensions, but if flatulence is the cause—and this is generally the case in crib-biters and wind-suckers—then it will be much distended. As spasmodic colic is the most painful form, the horse is more violent during the paroxysms, but these are longer continued in flatulent colic, and the horse lies down more carefully. Colic is usually readily and speedily amenable to treatment. The horse must be prevented from throwing himself down, and four to six ounces of whiskey or brandy administered in a quart of warm water, or, better still, if at hand, two or three ounces of laudanum; much benefit is also conferred by rubbing the surface of the abdomen firmly with wisps of hay or straw, or fomenting it with hot water. It is generally advisable to give a dose of purgative medicine—such as from four to six drachms of aloes dissolved in a pint of warm water; and an enema of warm water will aid in relieving the intestines. In flatulent colic, the addition of an ounce each of ammonia and oil of turpentine to the laudanum will be most useful.

Inflammation of the Bowels—This most painful and rapidly fatal disease may be ascribed to several causes, among them being colic, poisonous substances, exposure to cold, exhaustion, drinking much cold water when fatigued, &c. The earlier symptoms are those of colic, though to the expert there appear others which differentiate it from that disease; the horse lies down with greater care, the pain is continuous, and its severity is indicated by the animal's expression; the pulse and respiration are hurried, groaning is frequent, and the skin is wet with perspiration. All these symptoms become aggravated, and if not soon relieved the horse dies. To assuage the pain, large doses of opium powder mixed in tepid water—beginning with one drachm and followed at short intervals by half-drachm doses—should be administered; blankets steeped in hot water must be applied to the abdomen for an hour at a time, stimulating liniment being used in the intervals. Enemas of warm water may be administered twice or thrice, but in small quantity. For this disease the veterinary surgeon should be sent for as soon as possible.

Rheumatism—Some horses are very subject to attacks of rheumatism about the joints, sheaths of tendons, muscles, &c., and they may be acute or chronic. Exposure to cold winds and wet weather will induce them, and they sometimes accompany such diseases as influenza. In the acute cases there is often a considerable degree of fever, and the disease localises itself in one or more parts of the body, *e.g.*, in the stifle, hock, knee, sheaths of tendons; there is generally swelling and great lameness, with pain on handling the parts, and sometimes the disease will suddenly leave one situation to appear in another. With regard to treatment, the horse must be kept warm and comfortable, fed on sloppy food, and given oatmeal gruel in which bicarbonate of potass in ounce doses has been dissolved. If the fever runs high, salicylate of sodium in two-drachm doses should be given in a pint of water or gruel three times a day. The inflamed parts may be fomented with warm water and bathed with tincture of arnica or laudanum; when the inflammation is subsiding, they should be frequently rubbed with soap liniment, or one composed of Coutt's acetic acid, whiskey, and oil of turpentine, two ounces of each, with the white of one egg beaten up in them. The skin should be well brushed, and the liniment then firmly rubbed in.

Surfeit—This term is popularly applied to several affections of the skin, but more especially to one which appears as an eruption of small, hard lumps in different parts of the body, accompanied by itching and symptoms of indigestion. It is usually transient, and disappears in a few days. Care should be taken with regard to the diet, and a mild laxative may be given—such as an ounce of sulphur in a small mash, or a pint of linseed oil; an ounce of nitrate or carbonate of potass should be given in the drinking water once a day.

Eczema is a term also sometimes applied to surfeit and to some other diseases of the skin, but it is usually employed to describe a condition in which there is an eruption on one or more parts—back, sides, shoulders, neck and root of tail—of minute vesicles or blisters that burst, when scabs or scales form in their place, and the hair falls off. There is considerable itching, which causes the horse to rub or gnaw the affected part. It generally appears in summer, and in some horses recurs year after year. It is not contagious, and is very troublesome to get rid of, as it must be ascribed in the majority of cases to constitutional causes. In treating the affection, attention must be paid to the diet, which ought to be of a laxative kind. Arsenic has been given in three-grain doses in a little mash every morning and continued for some months with advantage, with a mild dose of physic once a week, and the following lotion has been applied to the skin: bicarbonate of soda one ounce, oxide of zinc two ounces, and lime-water eight ounces; to be thoroughly mixed. For chronic cases, boracic acid ointment, to every ounce of which a few drops of creosote have been added, may be well rubbed into the part night and morning.

Mud Fever—This odd designation has been given to an inflammation of the skin which is usually seen in winter among horses whose limbs or bodies are liable to be spattered with very cold mud or that of an acrid kind. It is most frequently seen in hunters whose stable management is not carefully attended to, and is easily prevented by abstaining from clipping the hair off the legs, and not washing them when the horse returns to his stable, unless they can be thoroughly dried and kept warm. As much as possible of the mud should be removed by a wisp, and when the skin is dry the remainder must be brushed out. If the legs must be washed to free them from dirt, this should be done with cold water in a place sheltered from the wind; then they ought to be dried, well hand-rubbed, and covered with flannel bandages. When the skin is inflamed and painful, it should be dressed with Goulard's extract of lead, one ounce to the pint of water or to four ounces of olive oil; oxide of zinc ointment answers the same purpose—as does also a liniment composed of Goulard's extract five ounces, eucalyptus oil and laudanum of each one ounce, and olive oil five ounces; or another liniment made up of acetate of lead one ounce, olive oil one pint, water one pint, to be well rubbed up together. Either of these may be applied once or twice a day, and continued for some time after the inflammation has gone, if the horse has to go out in cold wet weather. If fever is present, a mild laxative will prove beneficial, as will also half an ounce of bicarbonate of potass in a small mash morning and evening.

Cracked Heels—The skin behind the pasterns is very liable to become inflamed from the same causes as produce mud fever, the inflammation in both being erythema; but in the heels it often runs on to ulceration in the form of cracks or fissures; consequently there is great pain and lameness, the horse walking on his toes in a very cramped manner. Not only will mud and dirt cause cracked heels in cold weather, but fine, peaty sand will do the same, especially if there is wet. Even washing the heels and not drying them well will often excite inflammation of the skin. Clipping the hair off, no doubt, predisposes to it. To cure the ailment, the skin should be well cleansed, and if there are cracks it will be advantageous to apply a linseed meal or bran poultice to free them from dirt and allay the pain. Afterwards use either of the applications prescribed for mud fever. If the skin is not cracked, the zinc ointment answers well, and if there is a discharge from it, powdered oxide of zinc rubbed gently into it will be beneficial. When cured, it is advisable to smear over the skin with an ointment composed of equal parts of lard and beeswax to protect it from the weather and dirt, for some time.

Warts—These are sometimes, from their situation, troublesome, and often cause inconvenience when they are in the way of the harness. They grow only from the skin, but their mode of growth varies, and this influences the measures to be adopted for their extirpation. Those with a narrow pedicle may be removed by tying a silk thread tightly round that part, or snipping them off by knife or scissors; others can be pulled off by the thumb and first finger nails, while those with a wide base have to be dealt with by the very careful application of arsenic, after making the surface slightly raw; sometimes the application of strong acetic acid or a solution of chromic acid will destroy them.

Itching Tail—Some horses are disposed to rub their tail on every opportunity, and to such an extent as to break the hair and even make the skin raw. In some cases this is due to eczema at the root of the tail; in other cases there may be some irritation underneath, or when nothing can be discovered there may exist a morbid sensation in the skin of the tail which impels the horse to rub it so continuously and energetically.

The cause should be ascertained, and a remedy then applied. If the itching is due to irritation of the skin, one of the dressings recommended for eczema may be tried; if it is owing to small worms about the anus or the rectum, these can be removed by injections of a solution of common salt or an infusion of quassia chips. When the rubbing is persistent, the root of the tail should be covered by a leather or cloth guard fastened to a crupper, and beneath the tail by tapes.

Ringworm—This is an unusual disease among well-kept horses, and is always due to contagion, the spores of the fungus which occasion it being derived directly from affected horses, or through the medium of clothing, brushes, harness, &c., which have been in contact with them. At first there are minute elevations on the skin which can be felt with the finger, and soon the hairs at these spots break, leaving a bare place that extends more or less rapidly, and generally in a circular manner. In this way the whole of the skin will be soon invaded by the parasite, and the horse then presents an unpleasant appearance. There is slight inflammation in some parts of the denuded patches, with a raw surface, but the horses do not seem to suffer much, if any, inconvenience. Precautions must be taken with a view to prevent the disease extending to other horses, and all brushes, combs, &c., should be well washed in a strong solution of chinosol; blankets should also be steeped in this solution. The horse must be dressed with an effective parasiticide—the best I have found to be chinosol ointment; it is not only a potent destroyer of the fungus, but, being non-poisonous to the horse, it can be freely applied over the entire body if need be; it should be well rubbed in, and left on the skin for two or three days before it is washed off.

Mange—This is caused by a minute insect of which there are three kinds, but the most common, and certainly the most troublesome, is the one that infests the whole surface of the body and burrows into the skin. It causes an intense itching from which there is no respite; consequently the infected horse has not a minute's rest, but rubs and gnaws himself day and night. The hair is shed where the insects burrow, and there are minute raw places that are sometimes covered with crusts. In the course of time, from the incessant irritation, the horse suffers in health and becomes emaciated, while the skin is gathered up in wrinkles and is raw and scaly. As the disease is very contagious and can be communicated even to men, efforts should be made to prevent its extension and to cure it as soon as possible. All implements and clothing must be thoroughly cleansed, as well as the stall or stable and fittings; the litter used by the infected horse or horses ought to be put in the manure pit. The horses should be dressed over the entire body with chinosol ointment after they have been well washed with soft soap and warm water and dried; if the coat is long, it should be clipped off. If the ointment cannot be procured, or is deemed too expensive, the following makes a good and a cheap dressing: powdered sulphur eight ounces, oil of tar one ounce, common oil one quart. These should be well mixed, allowed to simmer at a gentle heat, and frequently stirred. When being applied to the skin, the dressing should again be kept stirred. After two or three days another application should be made, and in two days more a complete cure may be relied on and the dressing washed off.

DOGS—As might be anticipated, the dog is very much less liable to disease, and is far more exempted from injury than the horse; and the sporting dog lives a healthier life than the over-domesticated creature that is pampered and limited in its movements to a short stroll beyond the drawing-room. So that when given good food and kept clean, the dog used for sport is comparatively free from serious disorders, though perhaps he incurs some risks that are inseparable from the work he is called upon to perform.

Wounds—These are not, as a rule, so serious in the dog as they generally are in the horse, because the intelligence of the former greatly assists in ensuring the position and quietude essential to the repair of injuries. The different kinds of wounds described as occurring in the horse are met with in the dog, and it is sometimes quite astonishing to find this animal recover rapidly, often without any assistance, from the gravest incised and lacerated wounds, which would be considered almost beyond repair in the larger animal. Perhaps the commonest wounds are those from the bites of other dogs,[1] and as these are punctured they are more troublesome to deal with than some of the other kinds; moreover, they may be inflicted by rabid dogs or by those with foul mouths and teeth, which may lead to dangerous disease. With ordinary wounds very little, if any, treatment is needed, beyond keeping them clean, and this the dog's tongue will generally accomplish if the part is within reach. If any dressing is required it should be of a non-poisonous kind, such as solution of chinosol. Simple wounds can be painted over with collodion, friar's balsam, or solution of gutta percha, or an ointment of oxide of zinc, iodoform, or boracic may be employed; but, when they are applied, the dog should wear a muzzle to prevent him licking them off, unless a bandage will answer the purpose. He must also be kept well muzzled when large wounds are in process of healing, as at a certain stage there is so much irritation that he would otherwise do great mischief to himself by tearing the part with his teeth. Large gaping wounds may be closed by stitches in the manner described for the horse, though it is to be

[1] Quarrelsome and savage dogs are dangerous not only to others, but to mankind, and it is well therefore to know how to act in releasing oneself from the fangs of such an animal, rescuing a helpless dog that is being worried by him, or in separating fighting dogs. I will here quote what I wrote on this subject some years ago in my work on *Rabies and Hydrophobia*:—"The only safe place to seize a dog is at the back of the neck, behind the head; there the skin is sufficiently loose to afford a good hold, while the hands and arms cannot be touched by the animal's teeth so long as the grasp is maintained. . . . . Blows will not prevent dogs biting and holding on, indeed they will generally make them more furious. . . . . The simplest, safest, and by far the most effectual plan of rescuing one's self, or defending other persons or dogs from some infuriated or mad animal's fangs, is *choking him*. If the animal wears a collar this is easily done, as one has only to seize it firmly at the back and pull it tightly against the throat in front; the knee, the foot, or the other hand will usefully aid in the operation by pressing strongly against the back of the neck. The dog should by no means be released immediately he lets go his hold, but ought to be still further choked until he is harmless for the time, when means may be had recourse to for securing him properly. When there is no collar on the neck, a strong handkerchief or piece of cord tied round it and pulled in the same manner, or twisted with a stick, is a ready appliance. . . . . It requires strong arms and a little coolness and tact."

observed that sutures rapidly ulcerate out in the dog. This may be obviated to some extent, however, by not bringing the sides of the wound too close together, so as to allow for the subsequent swelling, and the stitches themselves must not be very near the margin. In many cases the sides of the wound can be kept in apposition by glue or pitch plasters, or by bandages if the wound will permit. The wounds of dogs, if beyond reach of the tongue, and if the weather happens to be warm, are likely to become infested with maggots when not kept clean. These can be got rid of by washing the wound with solution of chinosol.

Fractures—Broken bones are very frequent in dogs, as they are much exposed to external violence; but fortunately, owing to their comparatively small size and their intelligence, they may be easily handled, and the fractures can therefore be satisfactorily examined, set and fixed in the best position for repair, the animals themselves aiding in this by remaining patient and tranquil. Besides, repair is usually rapid, and constitutional disturbance rarely takes place.

Fractures of the *skull* are always serious. If the bones are depressed, so as to make pressure on the brain, they must be raised, and removed if necessary. The *lower jaw* is sometimes broken, but unless there is much displacement, little more is needed than taking away any splinters or loose teeth. *Broken ribs* are extremely rare, as these bones have long cartilages and are very elastic; when this accident does occur, a wide bandage fastened tightly round the chest, and quiet, are all that is necessary. Fracture of the *bones of the shoulder blade* is dealt with by applying a pitch plaster to the skin over it, making it firmer by splints of pasteboard, while a starch bandage passed round the neck and fore-arm in a figure of 8 manner, and then round the body two or three times, keeps the shoulder immovable. The arm bone (humerus) and thigh bone (femur) are often broken, and until it is convenient to fix them properly, the leg should be firmly bound up with a handkerchief to prevent displacement. When all is ready, the broken bone is "set," by bringing the fractured ends together and keeping them in place by means of bandages and splints. If there is a wound extending to the fracture, it should not be covered by the retaining apparatus; and if there is swelling, before reducing the fracture it is well to get rid of it by warm water fomentations. When bandaging, allowance must also be made for subsequent swelling, as the circulation in the part may be seriously hindered if the bandage is too tight. The splints may be of wood, cardboard, stiff leather, sheepskin, or gutta percha; there is often advantage in having them of some material that will become pliable when steeped in warm water, as then they can be made to fit better; otherwise they are liable to cause bruises or ulceration. Various substances are employed to stiffen the bandages and support the splints, and keep them in place; these substances are usually solution of gum, pitch, starch, or plaster of Paris. The pitch is melted and applied at a moderate heat; it is smeared over the skin or the bandage, as is also the gum; the starch is dissolved in laundry fashion, the bandage soaked in it, and then rolled round the limb. The plaster of Paris bandage is generally preferred, and is prepared by spreading the gypsum in a dry condition over the extended bandage, rolling this up, and then steeping it in water. The limb having been enveloped in a dry cotton bandage, that with the plaster in it is put on evenly above it; when it becomes dry it forms a rigid case, so that no splints are required. When pitch is employed, it may be spread on basil leather, and pieces of this having been stuck on the skin inside and outside the limb, a long splint is placed outside, and held there by a bandage or broad tape. The entire limb may be kept immovable by a bandage encircling it and the body.

Fractures of the other bones of the limbs are to be treated in a similar manner. Detached splinters of bone, if projecting through a wound, are to be removed by means of forceps, and the wound is itself to be dressed with chinosol. After a limb is set, there is often so much irritation that the dog shows a disposition to tear off the bandages; a muzzle should therefore be worn for some days. The splints and bandages should not be removed in less than a month. A dose of cathartic medicine is beneficial.

Dislocations—Dislocations readily take place in the limbs of dogs, especially if young, and are in some cases complicated with fracture. There should be no difficulty in discovering them, the lameness and distortion being significant, while the absence of crepitation distinguishes them from fractures. After reduction, which is effected by extension and judicious manipulation, the limb must be bandaged as in the case of fractures, and kept immovable for as long a time.

Diseases and Accidents to the Feet—Foot lameness in the dog is due to a variety of causes, and in order to discover these, a careful examination of the toes and pad is necessary. In addition to the lameness, the animal favours the limb in every way and frequently licks it. There is also pain on manipulation. Thorns, pins, and other sharp foreign bodies are a frequent cause; these should be sought for, removed, and the foot immersed in hot water or poulticed. When the foot is bruised or crushed, the same treatment will generally suffice. The pad is liable to over-wear from long travelling on hard, broken ground, and sometimes the pain is so great that the animal has difficulty in moving; in some cases there may be actual inflammation and ulceration of the skin, with accompanying fever. This accident occurs more especially in sporting dogs which are not in condition when suddenly put to hard work; they may also be due to frost-bite. When the feet are merely tender, resting them for a few days and bathing with milk and water, or solution of alum or sulphate of zinc, and wrapping them up in a piece of cloth, will set them right. In the more severe cases, fomentations with hot water and poultices will subdue the pain; the poultices must be protected with a bandage or a laced boot made of cloth or soft leather, and the dog should wear a muzzle. In two or three days, astringent lotions—such as solution of alum or sulphate of zinc—may be applied. If an abscess forms, it must be opened and the resulting wound dressed with chinosol or iodoform. A long rest will be necessary to ensure recovery, and the dog may have to wear a boot for a considerable time afterwards. In such cases, a good but temporary protection to the skin is afforded by painting it with a solution of gutta percha. An eczematous condition of the skin between the toes is at times observed, redness, vesicles and moisture being the chief symptoms; in these cases a similar eruption is generally noticed elsewhere. Powdering the inflamed skin with chinosol, oxide of zinc, or iodoform once or twice a day and keeping the feet dry, is the local treatment to be adopted, and it may be necessary to supplement this by the administration, morning and night, of a few drops (4 to 10) of Fowler's solution of arsenic, given in milk or broth.

In *mange* the parasites sometimes burrow in the skin around the root of the toe nails, and cause much irritation, ulceration, and eventual loosening of the claws. This condition is usually troublesome to get rid of, and it may be needful to extract the claws before a radical cure can be effected. Chinosol ointment may be tried before this operation is adopted; it is certainly most useful after it. An ulcer is occasionally found beneath the claw, from which there is a slight discharge. This is caused by dirt, or the sand used on kennel floors, finding entrance between the skin and claw; there is soreness and swelling around the horn. In many cases the claw must be extracted; then the toe is poulticed for a day or two, and afterwards dressed with tincture of calendula or myrrh.

Over-grown Claws are more frequently seen in house than in sporting dogs, owing to their receiving insufficient exercise out of doors. The claw grows to such a length that it curls backward and inward until it enters the pad, and causes ulceration and intense pain. The claw must be shortened by wire nippers, pruning scissors, or a small triangular saw—though this last is not to be recommended. The foot is then to be poulticed, and the wound afterwards dressed for a few days with chinosol lotion, to be succeeded by solution of gutta percha.

Not infrequently parasites of different kinds—among them harvest mites—lodge between the toes, and cause the dog such great annoyance that he bites the skin severely. An examination will reveal the presence of these insects, and dressings with chinosol ointment will kill them.

Ticks—Sporting dogs are occasionally troubled with ticks on the surface of their body, which give rise to restlessness and local irritation. A good dressing with chinosol lotion or ointment will cause them to disappear, though they may also be removed by the fingers, or with scissors or forceps. Washing the dog in warm water to which a small quantity of chinosol or ammonia has been added will allay the irritation.

Burns and Scalds—These accidents are not very frequent with dogs. A very good application is the famous carron oil, which is a mixture of lime water and linseed oil in equal parts. Cotton wool is to be dipped in this and applied to the injured parts. A solution of picric acid—made by dissolving the acid in water until no more can be taken up—painted over the burnt place, which is then to be powdered with starch or wheat flour, is sometimes recommended, as is also bathing the part with a solution of baking soda, and afterwards dusting it with chalk, flour, starch, or kaolin.

Diseases of the Skin—These are comparatively few, but two or three of them are rather common.

Eczema—This is a special form of inflammation of the skin, largely due to constitutional causes, and is extremely difficult to get rid of in the great majority of cases. The skin is inflamed, more or less destitute of hair, and has a crop of vesicles on its surface or a moist discharge on its surface. Only a small portion may be affected, or the greater part of the body may be involved. There is not much itching. When local, if the disease is only slight, oxide of zinc powder may be dusted on the part, or kaolin if it is very moist; should the surface be raw, chrysophanic ointment ought to be applied once or twice a day, the kaolin or zinc powder being put on afterwards. When the disease is very extensive there is a tendency to rub the skin, and the dog should therefore wear a muzzle, or a broad collar round his neck. External treatment must be supplemented by internal medication. Fowler's solution of arsenic is usually prescribed in doses of from three to twenty drops twice daily; the smaller quantity is given at the commencement, the dose being gradually increased up to the maximum, but for small dogs this should not exceed ten or twelve drops; it may be given in the food. As there is generally some debility, this medicament is often combined with tonics, and the following is a good formula:

Citrate of iron	2 drachms
Acetate of potash	3 drachms
Fowler's solution of arsenic	1½ drachms
Infusion of calumba	8 ounces.

One teaspoonful increasing up to one tablespoonful is to be given twice a day. This mixture should be continued for a considerable period—several months—though it is recommended that an interval of a week should be allowed between each quantity. It may also be necessary to give cod liver oil or malt extract. The food should be chiefly meat, and the dog ought to have abundant exercise.

Mange—There are two forms of this disease in the dog, in one of which the insect lives on or in the surface of the skin (*Sarcoptic scabies*), and is easily destroyed. The parasite multiplies rapidly and soon spreads over the body, causing great irritation and congestion of the skin, with continuous itching. Consequently the dog is always scratching and biting itself, making the skin sore; while the parasite, burrowing into the substance of this, causes the formation of vesicles or pustules, which break, discharge, and form small scabs. Various remedies have been prescribed, but chinosol ointment I have found as good as any. Some of the others are as follows: balsam of Peru, one part dissolved in alcohol four parts; or sublimed sulphur and whale oil, of each sixteen parts, well mixed with one part each of mercurial ointment and oil of tar; or one ounce each of oil of tar and sulphur well mixed in a pint of common oil; or lime and sulphur eight ounces, water three and a half pints, to be boiled until there is only one quart left; or oil of tar, powdered sulphur, powdered oxide of zinc, of each one drachm, glycerine two drachms, lanolin one and a half ounces. Whatever application is selected, it is advisable first to wash the dog thoroughly with soft soap and warm water; if the coat is long, it must be removed, and the dressing should be applied at least once again in two or three days, when the skin may be again washed. As the dog, in scratching itself, is likely to carry some of the parasites to the root of its claws, particular care should be observed in washing and dressing the toes, as well as every part of the skin elsewhere. The affected dog should be kept isolated from all others, and everything with which it has been in contact must be destroyed or thoroughly cleansed. It may be necessary to attend to the general health by giving tonic and laxative medicine, as well as good food and shelter.

The other form of the disease is known as "follicular mange," because the peculiar parasite that causes it is lodged deeply in the hair follicles of the skin; and therefore, though it is less contagious than sarcoptic mange, it is far more intractable to deal with. It usually commences in patches about the head, but soon extends to the body, and is most noticeable about the loins, sides, belly, and legs, to which it gives a very disagreeable appearance, as there is much suppuration, as well as a foul odour. At first the hair falls off in patches, upon which red spots appear; from these comes serum, then pus and blood, which form scabs, among which are cracks and other sores. The dog soon becomes unwell and appears to suffer considerably, though the itching is not so intense as in the other form, so that the animal, instead of scratching, rather shakes himself; but this may be from the pain, as he objects to have the affected parts handled, whereas, in sarcoptic mange, pleasure is manifested when the skin is rubbed. After a time, emaciation and debility are very marked, and the dog becomes such a loathsome object that he is usually destroyed before he succumbs to the effects of the malady. Treatment has often been unsuccessful, but this was probably because it has not been properly conducted, or was adopted when the disease was too far advanced. The hair should be removed as close to the skin as possible, and the treatment adopted may follow that recommended for ordinary mange. A solution of chinosol (1 to 100 or 150 of water) has proved effective. Another dressing is creosote and liquor potassae of half an ounce each, barley water eight ounces. Both of these dressings should be applied frequently, after the skin has been well cleaned by scrubbing with soda and hot water. Another dressing is olive oil fourteen parts, well shaken up with one part of creosote, and two parts of strong liquor potassae added; this is to be applied every third or fourth day to all the affected parts, the dog having been washed a few hours before each dressing. As a rule the treatment has to be continued for a considerable period, during which the dog's strength must be maintained by good food, to which small doses of sulphur should be occasionally added. For bedding, red-pine shavings should be employed, in preference to anything else, and they ought to be renewed at least twice a week, the soiled shavings being burned. Precautions should be taken against the disease extending to other dogs.

Lice, fleas, and other vermin of this kind, are got rid of by cleanliness of surroundings, washing the animals with soap and warm water, and dressing the skin with any of the simpler mange applications, especially chinosol solution.

Ringworm in two forms affects the dog, though rarely; both are due to a vegetable parasite. The ordinary form presents itself in circular and always increasing patches of baldness, in which are seen broken hairs and greyish scales or crusts. There is not much irritation of the skin, though the patches are reddened, and the dog does not appear to be seriously inconvenienced. Washing with soap and water, and painting over the places with tincture of iodine, or dressing with chinosol ointment or lotion, will readily effect a cure. The other form, known as "honeycomb ringworm," has yellow crusts of a cup shape, which join each other to constitute comparatively large masses possessing a peculiar smell. These crusts usually show themselves first on or about the head. In treating the disease, all the hair and crusts must be got rid of, the skin thoroughly washed, and dressed with one of the mange applications, glacial acetic acid, or solution of corrosive sublimate.

Canker of the Ear—The skin lining the ear is not infrequently the seat of inflammation or ulceration, accompanied by a foul-smelling discharge; there is generally much pain and irritation, as the dog usually carries the head to one side, is constantly shaking it, and shows great dread and agony when the ear is handled. Sometimes there is bleeding from the ear, and when treatment is long deferred large granulations (proud flesh) spring up and obliterate the passage leading to the internal ear; deafness is the consequence. This is commonly known as internal canker, and is most frequently witnessed in long-eared dogs, and especially in those which are liable to be wet—such as water dogs; though it is sometimes seen in over-fed dogs which do not get sufficient exercise, and particularly if their ears are allowed to become very dirty, or if soapy water is allowed to remain in them. For the earlier stage, washing out the ears and thoroughly drying them, then dressing with chinosol lotion, or with one made by adding ten grains sulphate of zinc to an ounce of water, or two drachms liquid acetate of lead to eight ounces of water, are very serviceable. When there is much discharge and ulceration, chinosol or iodoform powder should be dusted into the ear after using the lotion. Calamine ointment makes a good dressing. It is most essential, in endeavouring to effect a cure, to prevent the dog flapping the ears, and this may be best secured by causing the animal to wear a cap fastened round the head. I have always preferred a fine net, such as ladies wear their hair in, as it keeps the ears confined without heating them.

External canker is merely an injury to the outside of the ear or a slight eruption that soon becomes ulceration; it is usually towards the tip of the ear, and is most frequent in long-eared dogs. Either of the above lotions, or a weak solution of corrosive sublimate, should be applied frequently and the head-net worn. Sometimes a soft painful swelling appears suddenly inside the ears of certain dogs, and the pain causes them to keep continually shaking the head, which makes the swelling still larger. It is produced by injury, and the tumour contains blood, a portion of which may be in the form of a clot. An opening or long slit should be made in the lowest or most dependent part, so that all the contents will drain away, and, to keep the wound open, the edges may be touched with caustic, or a piece of lint inserted for a short time. The interior should be dressed with chinosol lotion, and the dog made to wear the head-net until the part is healed.

General Diseases.

Distemper—The most serious, as it is the most common disease to which dogs are exposed, is that known as "distemper," which, attacking all varieties, is most fatal to well-bred, delicate dogs, and especially to puppies. It is a most infectious and contagious fever, being due to a microbe, and can be communicated not only by actual contact of healthy with diseased dogs, but by means of almost every conceivable medium—even through the air for a certain distance. It is maintained and spread solely by the microbe, and cannot be spontaneously developed; though bad or improper food and insanitary conditions may favour its reception and extension. Some persons believe that every dog should have it, and dogs are often exposed to the contagion purposely, in order that they may acquire it and so have done with it. This is a great mistake, as there is no necessity whatever for a dog to have such a dangerous and damaging disease; on the contrary, everything should be done to avert it. There is no doubt, however, that if a dog gets the disease and recovers, he generally enjoys immunity from another attack, as is the case in several other specific fevers; but this rule does not always hold good, for I have known of dogs being infected twice. The malady would appear to be special to the canine species, as I am not aware of its having been conveyed to any others. It is such a serious disease, and is so often fatal or followed by grave *sequelæ*, as well as accompanied in many cases with troublesome complications, that on an outbreak the advice of an expert should be obtained. The symptoms are generally those of catarrh; in from one to two weeks after exposure to infection, there is discharge from the nose and eyes, which are inflamed; shivering, sneezing, and cough; fever, listlessness, and depression, with the loss of appetite and much thirst—sometimes there is vomiting. The animal seeks warmth, and does not care to move. There is a tendency to constipation, though in young dogs there is often diarrhœa, the fæces being streaked with blood. The loss of condition is rapid, and extreme debility soon becomes manifest, especially if diarrhœa with ulceration of the bowels sets in. The nervous system only too frequently participates in the disorder, and this is shown by the occurrence of epileptic fits and convulsions or paralysis. In the course of the disease, in very many cases, the front of the eye (cornea) undergoes ulceration. There is often a pustular skin eruption. The complications are bronchitis, pneumonia, or liver disorder. The disease runs its course in two or three weeks, and little can be done to shorten this period; the chief thing to be observed is to nurse and maintain the strength of the patient most carefully. Cleanliness must be attended to, and at the same time the dog must be kept warm and comfortable; the diet should be meat broth or beef tea, egg, or finely chopped raw meat, and if it is not taken voluntarily, the animal must be fed with it. Small quantities of brandy must be given at short intervals; or three to five grain doses of quinine in a tablespoonful of port wine. The nose and eyes are to be kept clean by gently sponging them with warm water and milk; for the eyes, two or three drops of a lotion of sulphate of zinc may be dropped into them after cleaning them.

When recovery is taking place, from twenty to forty drops of tincture of gentian may be given three or four times a day.

But, as may be readily understood, prevention of distemper is all-important, and it is to be remembered that it is one of those scourges which can be completely extirpated by preventive measures. These are: keeping the diseased, or those which have been in contact with them, rigidly isolated until all danger of communicating the infection has passed away; disinfecting or destroying everything which has been in actual contact with or in proximity to the diseased, and not allowing people who have been with them to go near healthy dogs. The greatest cleanliness possible should be strictly observed. As dog shows are largely instrumental in extending the malady, every care should be taken to prevent infected dogs gaining admission to these, and sanitary measures likely to be efficacious in averting infection ought to be scrupulously adopted.

Rheumatism is not infrequent among dogs, especially sporting ones, and is due to exposure to cold and damp, particularly in their dwellings. It is most prevalent during the winter and spring. It may be acute or chronic—most frequently the latter, and though the joints may be involved, it is generally the muscles which are the seat of inflammation.

In the acute form there are all the signs of fever, with those of pain in the affected part. Should this be in the loins, constituting "lumbago," there is stiffness in the hind extremities, and often the animal walks as if partially paralysed, though he is averse from movement; the back is arched, and so painful on manipulation that the creature whines or screams; while the abdomen feels hot and is tender on pressure. Constipation is a constant symptom. When the muscles of the shoulders are affected—"kennel lameness" or "chest founder"—the pain is as great on movement or in handling, while the lameness is of course limited to the fore limbs. When the joints are affected, they are swollen, painful, and hot. In chronic rheumatism there is no fever, but the joints are enlarged and make a clicking sound on movement; the animal is stiff, and often whines and howls, especially at night.

Dogs affected with rheumatism should be kept dry, warm, and comfortable. In acute rheumatism a dose of purgative medicine must be administered, and the bowels afterwards kept rather relaxed. Warm water fomentations of the affected part, and, after well drying it, rubbing in a liniment made up of equal parts of belladonna, camphor, and capsicum liniments, or the acetic acid liniment prescribed for rheumatism in the horse, night and morning, will allay the pain and stiffness. When the fever runs high, the following mixture has been recommended in doses of a teaspoonful to a tablespoonful, according to the size of the dog, every six hours: salicylate of soda four drachms, tincture of colchicum three drachms, acetate of potass two drachms, bicarbonate of soda one drachm, water six ounces. In chronic rheumatism the above liniments may be employed, and in the food may be given from three to eight drops of Fowler's solution of arsenic daily for one or two weeks at a time. Careful attention must be paid to the diet.

Catarrh—This differs from distemper in being non-infectious, unaccompanied by prostration and high fever, and usually in rapid recovery under suitable treatment. There is sneezing, a watery discharge from the eyes and nose, with dulness, and perhaps slight cough. The body should be kept comfortable and dry; the food nourishing, and small doses of any stimulant—such as brandy or whisky, a tea- to a table-spoonful—two or three times a day.

Sore Throat. Laryngitis—These disorders are sometimes noted in dogs, and are denoted by a hard or soft cough, which is very persistent; difficulty in swallowing, with extended head, and pain on manipulation of the throat. When acute, there is generally some fever. The animal should be kept warm in a moist atmosphere, the throat fomented with warm water, or rubbed with camphorated or other stimulating liniment, and covered with cotton wool and flannel. As swallowing is difficult, an electuary, composed of one drachm of chlorate of potass rubbed up in an ounce of honey, a little of which is to be placed frequently on the tongue, is useful in allaying the irritation.

Bronchitis—This may be the result of neglected catarrh, a complication of distemper, or it may occur independently of other diseases. It is sometimes caused by parasites. If acute, there is frequent cough, which may be dry or moist; fever, loss of appetite, attempts as if to vomit, rattling in the throat, quickened breathing, pulse increased in frequency, and debility. The dog should be kept warm in an equable temperature, with plenty of fresh air; the food must be good and easily digested, with small doses of stimulants frequently. Warm linseed-meal poultices should also be applied to the chest, and the vapour of hot water, to which a small quantity of eucalyptus oil has been added, inhaled. Doses of laxative medicine should be given at intervals.

Chronic Bronchitis is often seen in old dogs, and especially those which have been over-fed and under-exercised. It much resembles asthma in man, and is generally accompanied or preceded by indigestion. The chief symptom is a harassing cough, that comes on in paroxysms, and the breathlessness is so distressing that the animal looks as if about to succumb. However, after coughing for some time, a frothy mucus is expectorated and relief follows. Exertion develops these attacks. Little can be done in the way of cure, except in diet, which should be given in small quantities and frequently, and laxative medicine occasionally. Tonics, in the form of arsenious acid and quinine, are sometimes advantageous.

Inflammation of the Lungs—This is very often a sequel or accompaniment of bronchitis, and demands similar treatment; but as it is a very serious disease, and demands special skill in order to bring about restoration to health, a veterinary surgeon should be called in to undertake this task. The same may be said with regard to **pleurisy**, which nearly always complicates pneumonia.

Jaundice is sometimes a complication of other disorders, but in all cases the liver is disordered in its functions, or may itself be the seat of disease. The skin and eyes and mouth are tinged yellow, as is the urine; there are signs of sickness, and constipation is noted. After a time there is wasting and general unhealthiness; the right side of the body and the belly are enlarged, and the breathing becomes affected. If the liver itself is diseased, a warm linseed meal poultice may be applied over it. A half grain opium and calomel pill should be given, together with a dose of castor oil, to be followed by dilute nitro-hydrochloric acid in ten to fifteen drop doses every three or four hours. The diet should be light, and plenty of exercise is often beneficial.

Rabies—Until this formidable disease is finally eradicated, every one possessing dogs should know its early symptoms, so as to be on their guard against it. Usually the earliest signs are changes in manner and habit. The dog is ill-tempered and aggressive, particularly towards other dogs; he seeks retirement, or wanders away from home; his appetite is depraved, and he has a tendency to gnaw wood-work and swallow all kinds of foreign matter; he snaps at imaginary objects, and there is a peculiar alteration in his voice when he barks or howls; he has no dread of water, though he may be unable to swallow it; at a certain stage of the disease, in some cases, the muscles of the lower jaw become paralysed and the mouth remains open, while the eyes appear to squint; saliva often dribbles from the mouth; the gait is slouching. In countries in which the disease exists, and especially when it is prevalent, any change in the usual habits or manners of the dog as above described, should at once excite suspicion, and cause the animal to be at least carefully secured until his condition can be assuredly determined.

Worms—Dogs are perhaps more infested with worms than any other of the domestic animals, a circumstance due to their habits. The bowel worms are of two kinds —tape and round worms. The tape worms are flat, as their name implies, and they are in segments or joints, each of which can have an independent existence and propagate, as it contains male and female generative organs; these segments are cast off at a certain stage of development, and expelled from the body of the dog, to be taken up by some other creature and become a parasite in it. There are several kinds of tape worm, but their description would be of little value to the amateur. They are all more or less injurious to the animal infested with them, and though in all cases the signs of injury may not be equally apparent, yet it is desirable in every instance of such infestation to destroy these parasites as soon as they are detected. They, in the majority of cases, cause general unthriftiness, depraved appetite, bowel derangement, indigestion, convulsions, and in young dogs they retard growth. Perhaps the best remedy for all tapeworms is areca nut in doses of from half a drachm to two drachms, according to the size of the dog. Or half a drachm of this powder and the same quantity of liquid extract of male fern in combination, mixed in an ounce of milk, makes an effective dose. After this has been given, a dose of purgative medicine—castor oil is safe and convenient—should be administered. The fluid male fern can be given alone, and it is to be had in capsules, which are convenient for administration. Oil of turpentine, in doses of from one to three drachms mixed with three or four times the quantity of oil or milk, is a handy and prompt remedy.

Round worms are not so injurious as tapeworms, but they often cause much annoyance; in puppies they frequently give rise to convulsions and death. Santonine, in doses of from two to ten grains, mixed up in a full dose of castor oil, generally causes their expulsion. The oil of turpentine, as above, is also useful in this direction. Tonic medicine—the best of which is, perhaps, powdered sulphate of iron in two to four grain doses given in milk twice a day for four or five days—should be given afterwards.

Poisoning—Dogs are frequently poisoned accidentally or maliciously, and if remedies are at hand, death may be averted.

Strychnine is frequently the poison from which they suffer, and if the dose has been large, death from general convulsions, in the form of intense cramp, is not long delayed. If sulphate of zinc is at hand, a dose of from ten to thirty grains may be given as an emetic in a wine-glassful of water if the poison has been quite recently swallowed. When the spasms have set in, the dog should be kept partially under the influence of chloroform, which is administered by inhalation, a small quantity at a time being placed on cotton wool, which is held close to the dog's nose; the dog is placed on his chest and held in that position. The treatment must be continued until the spasms have subsided; then extract of belladonna—eight to ten grains in solution—can be administered by the mouth. Hydrocyanic acid, in minute doses—ten drops in water—may be given occasionally.

Apomorphin administered hypodermically, in one-eighth of a grain dose, has also been given to induce immediate vomiting, followed by the inhalation of half a drachm of nitrate of amyl at short intervals; this was succeeded by two draughts of chloral hydrate in solution, ten grains in each draught, an hour elapsing before each dose. Recovery has resulted from this treatment.

Carbolic acid is sometimes a cause of poisoning, either when absorbed through the skin or taken in by the mouth. It produces great depression, heart failure, and convulsions. Its presence is indicated by its odour. Stimulants and douching with cold water until the convulsions cease, have been recommended.

Arsenic, antimony, corrosive sublimate, and other mineral poisons, are sometimes taken by or given to dogs, and if the quantity is sufficiently large they induce severe vomiting, diarrhœa, and inflammation of the bowels, with blood-tinged fæces. Until the nature of the poison can be ascertained a suitable antidote cannot be given; but, in the meantime, some relief may be afforded by giving the poisoned animals plenty of milk or white of egg, or both combined. An emetic of sulphate of zinc may be given immediately after the poison is taken, if that opportunity be afforded. For arsenic the best antidote is freshly prepared peroxide of iron. For antimony, strong boiled tea infusion has been recommended, the dose being a small cupful.

G. FLEMING.

WAPITI (*Cervus canadensis*)—The wapiti is the lordliest of all the true deer; and among all the beasts of the chase there is none more stately or more beautiful, and none which yields a finer trophy to the hunter. It is essentially a gigantic Scotch stag, or, rather, the stag and the wapiti are the extreme forms of several races of the red deer type, which succeed one another in tolerably regular gradation as we pass from west to east through temperate portions of Europe, Asia, and North America.

Habitat—The white hunters throughout its range invariably call the wapiti "elk," because this was the name given to it by the settlers, who first encountered it near the Atlantic coast a couple of centuries ago. Formerly no game animal of North America, except the common or white-tailed deer, was so widely distributed as the wapiti; for though its habitat was, generally speaking, the same as that of the bison, it extended further west and further east. It abounded throughout the Alleghany ranges in the middle of the eighteenth century, and was very plentiful between them and the Mississippi as late as the Revolutionary War. Like other large game, however, it vanished with

WAPITI.

Av. height at shoulder, 60 in. Av. horn meas. 52 in. Max. horn meas. 73 in. (right), 64 in. (left).

melancholy rapidity before the oncoming of the rifle-bearing settler.

By the beginning of the present century it had become practically extinct in most regions east of the Mississippi, except in some spots just south of the Great Lakes and in a small stretch of the Pennsylvania mountains, where the last individuals lingered until after the close of the Civil War. During the first half of the present century, wapiti abounded on the great plains; and all the earlier explorers bore witness to the abundance of the great herds, though they were not found in such incredible myriads as were the bison. Being conspicuous animals, which could often be run down with a good horse, they were killed off much sooner than deer or antelope. Like the bison, they were practically exterminated from the plains early in the eighties, excepting in an isolated tract here and there. They are now limited to the wooded mountains of the Rockies and the Cascades, where they are in places still very abundant. Indeed, there are parts of western Wyoming, Montana, Colorado, and Washington where they are almost as plentiful as ever.

Characteristics—The wapiti is highly polygamous, and during the rut the master bulls gather great harems about them, and do fierce battle with one another, while the weaker bulls are driven off by themselves. At this time the bulls are comparatively easy to approach, because they are very noisy, incessantly challenging one another by night and day. Settlers and hunters usually speak of their challenge as "whistling," but this is a very inadequate description. The challenge consists of several notes, first rising and then falling. Heard near by, especially amid unattractive surroundings, it is not particularly impressive, varying in tone from a squeal to a roar, and ending with grunts; but at a little distance it is one of the most musical sounds in nature, sounding like some beautiful wind instrument. Nothing makes the heart of a hunter leap and thrill like the challenge of a wapiti bull, as it comes pealing down under the great archways of the mountain pines through the still, frosty, fall weather; all the more if it be at night, under the full moon, and if there is light snow on the ground.

Methods of Pursuit—Doubtless the most exciting way to follow the wapiti was on horseback in the old days. Then the mounted hunter pursued him either with dogs or without, and in the latter case trusted to get alongside and kill him with a revolver-shot. The great size of the quarry was such that only the largest and most powerful dogs could in any way interfere with its flight.

Nowadays, however, wapiti must be generally killed by still-hunting, and the rifle has of need supplanted horse and hound. To me, still-hunting the wapiti has always been amongst the most attractive of sports. It cannot be said to be as difficult as the chase of the big horn, and it is free from the almost intolerable fatigue attendant upon clambering over mountain-tops after the white goat; but there is plenty of exercise about it if one hunts faithfully. Usually the scenery is very grand, for the wapiti are found scattered through the glade-broken forests which clothe the rolling mountain sides, and they have a habit of occasionally standing and even lying on bare, jutting look-out points on the edges of cliffs, from which one can see, as far as the eye can reach, nothing but vast stretches of lake-dotted, wooded wilderness. Often when I have killed a wapiti bull early in the morning, or at least with plenty of daylight ahead, so that there was no hurry about reaching camp, I have sat down by the dressed carcase, and literally for hours have gazed across deep valleys and at giant mountains, whose wild and savage beauty was unmarred by the least trace of man; then, with the tongue at my belt, I would start off to camp, timing myself so as to get there just as dusk came on and the blaze of the pitchy pine stumps shot upward through the darkness.

In the old days I not infrequently killed wapiti near my ranch on the Little Missouri. Even when I first went there, however, in the early eighties, wapiti had become scarce, while the black-tail deer still swarmed. I do not think I ever got a wapiti in one day's hunt from the ranch house. We always went with a wagon to some likely spot and began the hunt early the following morning. At the ranch house we depended for our fresh meat exclusively on our rifles; and on these occasions I was usually hunting for the table. I never got a wapiti head of any size on the Little Missouri.

My chief hunting after wapiti has been done in north-western Wyoming and western Montana, and there I got many splendid trophies. The largest head I ever killed had antlers fifty-six inches in length, and this is well above the ordinary size; nevertheless, in wholly exceptional cases they grow eight or ten inches and even a foot longer. Nothing can exceed the splendid massive symmetry of such a head.

On a trip in the mountains after elk it is usual to go with a pack train, for the country is too rough for wagons, and yet not so utterly impracticable as to forbid the use of horses, which is often the case in the haunts of sheep, goat, and caribou. With a pack train many comforts can be carried along, such as tents, and an ample supply of bedding, and of small luxuries for the table. In consequence it is far pleasanter, especially on a long trip, to have a pack train, for although any good hunter will always rough it as much as is necessary to get the game, still it is a pleasant thing to be comfortable when the chance offers. In fine weather a man can lie out in the open with impunity, and indeed I personally much prefer it to lying in a tent; but in the rain a man who has to lie out in the open is sure to have a rather dismal time. In the plains country, long-continued rains are rare, and, with a stout tarpaulin in which to wrap the bedding, a man can afford to disregard the chances of bad weather; but sometimes in the mountains it will rain every day for a considerable time, and then the discomfort of coming back to camp at night to pass a wretched hour standing up in a downpour, or couching under a leaking brush lean-to, with the certainty of damp blankets for the night, takes away a good deal of the fun of hunting. On the other hand, with a comfortable tent, a great deal of the fun of the hunting trip is after nightfall. To come back from a long all-day's walk, thoroughly tired, yet not so done up as to be unable to appreciate rest and a hot supper, to sit around the blazing pine logs after the meal of elk venison, grouse, trout, and flap-jacks, and to turn into one's warm sleeping bag as the ice begins to skim the water in the buckets, make up, in the aggregate, as much real comfort as often comes to any man.

From the point where one meets the pack train it is now usually several days' journey into good elk country, for the skin- and meat-hunters butcher all game, the haunts of which are accessible from railroads. Once on the hunting grounds, it is easy to determine what are the chances for elk. If they are at all numerous, their trails will be seen everywhere, making well-beaten paths through the forests, while the edges of the streams and marshy hollows will be trodden up by the great round foot-prints, like those of two-year-old cattle. If it is during the rut, bulls are certain to be heard challenging one another. Later in the season, when there is apt to be snow on the ground, the trails are of course more distinct than ever.

In fairly wild country, there is less need in the case of wapiti than in the case of deer for being abroad early in the day. Although fond of taking siestas, they feed irregularly throughout the day; and during the rut the bulls are rarely still for any length of time, either by night or by day. In wild weather the herds are particularly active, although they are also then rather more difficult to get at, seeming to be more on the alert than when the weather is still and warm.

In hunting wapiti, some use can be made of glasses, but not nearly as much as in the case of sheep or goats, for there is too much forest. If it is rutting time, the bull can usually be placed by the sound of his challenge; otherwise his tracks must be diligently searched for, or else the hunter simply works his way cautiously through and across likely places until he comes upon some sign of his quarry. It is always necessary to go across or up wind, the nose of the wapiti being very sharp; but his eyesight is not particularly good—hardly as good as that of a deer, and not to be compared to that of a prong buck or mountain sheep. In very wild places wapiti bulls, especially during the rut, are so bold and self-confident that it is easy to stalk and kill them; but where they have been much hunted they become as wary as a deer, and it is then only their superior size, and the greater eagerness with which hunters follow them, that places them at a disadvantage in the struggle for life when compared with their smaller kinsfolk. Owing to its bulk, the wapiti is much more easily seen, and the hunter will of course follow it under circumstances in which he would abandon the chase of a deer, because the trophy is so much more valuable. Moreover, the wapiti lives in ground that favours the still hunter. The moose and the white-tail deer dwell in forests so dense that the difficulty of approaching them is very great; for it is almost impossible for any white man not to make some noise in slipping through the bushes and over the dead sticks and dried leaves. The sheep and goat are protected by the inaccessible nature of the lofty cliffs in which they delight. But the wapiti, like the black-tail deer, is not a beast of the high crags, nor, by preference, of the dense woods. The ground in which he delights is the broken rolling hill country, where groves and glades alternate, just as the black-tail loves the open hillsides, riven by gorges clad with ash and cedar. In consequence the wapiti and black-tail can be readily seen at quite a distance; whereas the moose and white-tail live in cover where it is hard to catch a glimpse of anything thirty yards off; and, moreover, when once seen, the wapiti and black-tail can generally be stalked without much difficulty, for there is always cover on rough hillsides and among patches of scattered timber. Under like conditions, however, I do not think that there is very much difference in point of wariness and keenness of sense among these four different beasts. Undoubtedly the moose and the white-tail are a little more clever, and the white-tail especially is the most cunning of all; but those wapiti and black-tail which do haunt the deep woods are nearly as hard to get at as their two slier relatives; at any rate, the difference is not great enough to warrant the hunter in taking liberties. Of course, in places which hunters have not yet penetrated—and there are a very few such in out-of-the-way mountain regions even nowadays—all four beasts are absurdly tame; but they never show the stupid self-confidence of the white goat.

Though the wapiti is so large and powerful, it is not a very tough beast, and succumbs to a bullet as readily as a deer or antelope. In shooting it I have usually carried a 45·75 or 45·90 Winchester; but the new small calibre smokeless powder cartridges, using a bullet with the nose of naked lead, will probably become more and more in use among the hunters who follow them.

The flesh of the wapiti is to my taste more delicious than that of almost any other wild game; though it must be eaten hot, as the fat tends to form tallow as soon as cool. The wapiti is easily domesticated, at least to the extent of being hardy and breeding well when kept in parks; but as soon as the bulls lose the dread of man which they have when wild, they become very dangerous in the rutting season.

There are several aberrant forms of wapiti, including one that dwells in the great Tule swamps of California. There is also an entirely distinct species with its centre of abundance in the Olympic mountains of Washington and in Vancouver Island. This species, which Dr. Hart Merriam has recently done the present writer the honour of naming after him (*Cervus roosevelti*), is larger than the common form, with the head in winter black instead of dark brown; and the antlers have a straight beam, ending in a cluster of erect points instead of the long terminal prong with backward sweep, so characteristic of the ordinary form. The ordinary wapiti in the north reaches west to the Rocky Mountains. There then comes a great space where no wapiti are found at all until the coast ranges of the Pacific are reached, and the recently described species appears. From the days of Lewis and Clark these wapiti of the Pacific coast have been known, but they have always been confounded with the ordinary form, from which they are as distinct as is the Columbia black-tail deer from the ordinary black-tail or mule deer of the Rockies and the great plains.

THEODORE ROOSEVELT.

WART HOG—This animal (*Phacochœrus æthiopicus*), the *Vlakte vark* (pig of the plains) of the Cape Dutch, *Nkulubu* of the Matabele, *Kolobe* of the Bechuanas, is the most familiar of the wild boars known to the African Continent. It has a wide distribution, and, in slightly varying forms, is found from North-east Africa to the Cape Colony. The northern wart hog (*Phacochœrus œliani*), which is classed by naturalists as a separate species, differs but slightly from the *Vlakte vark* of South Africa.

A full grown wart hog stands at the shoulder from 27 to 30 inches. In colour the animal is of a darkish-brown, inclining somewhat more to drab in the northern species. The top of the head and the upper parts of the neck, back, and shoulders are covered with long, stiff bristles, those on the top of the head radiating a good deal. The wild ferocious-looking head is disproportionately large and the muzzle very broad. The tusks are remarkably large and thick; they stand out wide from the jaw, curving upwards, and are often of surprising length. Fifteen or sixteen inches is about the limit of the great upper tushes of the South African wart hog; but Mr. Rowland Ward, in his *Records of Great Game*, makes mention of a pair, procured by Captain Berners, R.N., from Annesley Bay, Abyssinia, which reach the extraordinary measurements of 27 and 26 inches respectively. The most remarkable feature of this wild hog, from which, of course, it takes its name, lies in the great fleshy warts or wens which protrude from the face. Of these, the upper and larger grow outside each eye, while the lower pair are found between the eye and mouth, not ar above the upper tushes.

The flesh of the wart hog, when the animal is fat and in fair condition, is very good eating, and forms a by no means despicable addition to the hunter's larder. As a general rule, it may be said that this wild pig is not so formidable an opponent as his relative of India; yet, when pursued by dogs, he often inflicts severe wounds; he has been occasionally known to attack horse and man, and more than one South African hunting pony has been badly ripped by his tremendous tusks. The fashion of spearing wild boar, pursued with such zest in India, has never come into general vogue in Africa, although in Somaliland one or two Indian sportsmen have tried their hog spears on these animals, and the legations protect wild pig for sticking around Tangier. The reason for this is, probably, that the wart hog is neither so common nor so easily found as the boar of India, and that he has a habit of running to ground when pursued. When a wart hog goes to earth, which he usually does in the hole of a Cape ant-eater (*aard-vark*), he twists suddenly

WART HOG.
Av. height at shoulder, 28 *in.*

round and backs in stern foremost. He can be bolted, after allowing a short interval, by two or three men jumping lustily together upon the ground above.

In former days it would seem that the wart hog was more commonly found feeding upon open plains than is now the case. He is now more often found in the vicinity of well bushed country. The hunter in the wilder parts of the interior, however, even at the present day, often gets a fair shot at this pig with the rifle. The wart hog can go very fast for a few hundred yards, but a pack of strong, rough dogs, or a mounted man, can pretty easily run into him. With good and plucky dogs, who understand their work, this animal affords very excellent sport, and can be killed by a man on foot armed with a long knife or an assegai. Systematic boar hunting is, however, seldom resorted to in South Africa, and the wart hog is only slain occasionally by hunters in the veldt in pursuit of other and nobler game. When alarmed or excited, the wart hog bolts with his family as hard as he can lay legs to the ground, his tail held stiffly erect, with the tassel hanging curiously over. If he can find thick bush handy, he seeks shelter there, and if very hard pressed, will, as shown above, go to ground in the nearest earth or hole known to him. When set up at bay, he will attack dogs fiercely and inflict severe wounds, and the hunter on foot should approach with caution. More often than not a rifle bullet puts an end to his defence. If any of the dogs are badly ripped, a stitch or two and a washing of weak carbolic and water will usually set matters right, but occasionally an over-plucky or incautious hound is killed outright by the wart hog's formidable weapons of defence.

The tushes and head of a well-grown wart hog form a very remarkable trophy. It may be noted that the sow of this species carries fine tusks, only a little inferior in size to those of the boar. The appearance of the wart hog is hideous and ferocious-looking, but, save when molested or driven to bay, the animal is quite inoffensive. It is shy in its habits and has excellent powers of scent, and, if the hunter attempts a stalk, it is necessary to take every advantage of the wind.

H. A. BRYDEN.

WHALING—This is a sport that few amateurs have shared, and it therefore became necessary for me to take some of the information given here from professional fishermen. It is a maxim among true sportsmen never to take the life of an animal without making proper provision for saving those parts that are useful for food or other purposes, and all vessels employed for this fishing ought to be supplied with tanks or barrels to hold any oil that may be got, and, if it be Arctic whaling, some salt is required for bear, seal skins, &c.

There are several species of whales, some of which are much more dangerous to catch than others, and the grounds these different species frequent cover a large area of the ocean.

The pursuit of the Greenland whale (which supplies the best whalebone) would probably be found the most interesting from a sporting point of view, for, even if the voyage proved unsuccessful, there is just the chance of some sport at seals, walrus, bears, reindeer, narnwhale, sometimes white whales, and by extreme good luck one might get a musk ox.

Habitat—Sport in the Arctics almost entirely depends on the position of the ice, which varies considerably every year, and, like the big game in Africa, Arctic game and fish of all kinds have become very scarce, and retire further every year to more inaccessible places.

The Greenland whale, called "black fish" by the Scotch fishermen, and "bowhead" by the Americans, is found in the ice, and never goes far from the pack. The fishing grounds of this species are roughly, Behring Straits, Baffin's Bay, and North Greenland, but of late years I believe very few fish have been got in North Greenland.

Equipment—The vessels for this work are steamers strongly fortified and protected for ice navigation, carrying from six to eight whale boats, with a crew sufficiently strong to man the boats. They are also provided with plenty of sail power, for, when once among fish, the screw is stopped. The boats used by our Scotch fishermen are from 26 to 30 feet long, and about 5 feet 9 inch beam, with a depth of from 28 to 30 inches.

They have very little keel, and are built with a slight curve from the centre of the keel to the stem and stern posts, which rake outwards so as to allow the boat to turn easily and follow the motions of the whale. Their bows are protected from ice by a sheet of copper or zinc.

The gun, bollard heads, &c., are fitted as described in the "Sharks" article, Vol. ii. p. 235.

The usual complement of **line** for each boat is five lines, of 120 fathoms each, of from 2½ to 3 inches soft laid Europe or tarred rope, made especially for the purpose. The lines are coiled down in a box, placed in the centre of the boat and in the stern sheets.

The boat is steered with a long oar, and the oars are so arranged by a grommet and a thole pin, that when let go they remain attached to the boat.

The **crew** is usually made up of harpooner, boat-steerer, line-manager, and three seamen.

The American whale boats are from 28 to 29 feet long, with a beam of from 6 feet 2 inches to 6 feet 5 inches, and are made with a centre board. Their lines are 300 fathoms of very soft laid Manila rope, and their bollard head is right aft. As a rule, the American fishermen do not use gun harpoons, but are very successful with rockets and bomb lances, which explode in the fish and often kill her on the spot. If any sportsman wishes to try this fishing, probably his best course would be either to purchase a steam whaler, or hire one for the season ready equipped with a suitable crew. As he is only fishing for sport, a crew sufficient to man four or five boats would be strong enough.

A fair-sized vessel for the purpose might possibly, with economy, be built for from £10,000 to £12,000.

There are some keen sportsmen who cannot afford such a large outlay, and, if they do not mind roughing it a little, it is quite possible to arrange for a berth on board one of the regular whalers, and, if they happen on a lucky year, they might have some good sport.

This fishing is a great lottery, for even when it was in full swing a ship would sometimes have two bad seasons in succession. A few small vessels still winter, I am told, at certain points in Baffin's Bay or the neighbourhood, and employ Esquimaux to make up their crews.

The whaling is done from the shore. The expense of hiring one of these vessels would probably be far less than the hire of a steam whaler for the season, but an Arctic winter would have to be faced. If any sportsman contemplates taking up whaling as a sport, probably his best course would be to try the bottlenose whales for one season before embarking in the expense of a steam whaler. They take line rapidly, and I have seen them occupy four or five boats for several hours before they were killed. These fish are found from Iceland to Jan Mayen, and about Bear Island to the south of Spitzbergen. They do not go into the ice.

A small vessel, either a schooner or a brig, with an experienced crew, could probably be hired at Peterhead or Dundee. I am sure Messrs. Robert Kidd and Co., of Peterhead, would render every assistance for this purpose.

Should this fail, another course would be to hire one of the Norwegian schooners, crew, equipment, &c., which could probably be done through the British Consul at Christiania.

We now come to a group of whales which seem to frequent more temperate waters—viz.: Right whale, Pacific right whale, sperm whale, humpback whale, Californian grey whale, sulphur bottom whale, fin-back whale.

The vessels mostly in use in these waters are sailing barques and schooners, but there are also shore stations along the American coast and elsewhere, where at times a good many fish of some of these species have been taken.

The Californian grey whale, although by no means the largest, is said to be the most dangerous, and it appears usual to fire a gun rocket into the fish, so as to disable her seriously before the harpoon is driven in. The same tactics are carried out with the sulphur bottom and fin-back. If the sportsman wishes to try one of these species of whales, his best course would be to engage a suitable vessel and crew in America.

Most of these whales require different tactics for their capture, and it is extremely doubtful whether a crew in this country could be got together with sufficient experience for this class of whaling. Probably with the assistance of four or five American harpooners something might be done, but under these circumstances it is nearly certain that American whale boats would be required.

There is still another class of whaling practised round the north coasts of Norway. The whales are of four species, and are too wild and strong to be captured in the ordinary way, so small steamers from 80 to 90 feet long are employed. In the bow is placed a very powerful harpoon gun. The harpoon has a neat arrangement attached to it by which, when the strain comes on the closed barbs, they open, and explode a powerful shell, which frequently kills at once.

The line used for this fishing is about 500 fathoms of 5-inch rope, with a foregore of thirty fathoms of 4½-inch rope.

There does not seem to be anything like the sport attached to this fishing that there is in the capture of the other whales, but if any one wishes to try it, the best course would be to communicate with the Consul at Tronso and endeavour to come to some arrangement with one of the companies, which own these steamers and have boiling stations on the coast to dispose of the blubber.

A good deal of practical information can be obtained from the following:—*Fisheries of the United States*, George Browne Goode. (Mr. Goode's book is the best authority I have come across, as he deals with every class of whaling, and has a map of the whaling grounds.) *An Account of the Arctic Regions*, 1820, W. Scoresby, Jun. *Journal of a Voyage to the Northern Whale Fishery*, W. Scoresby, Jun. *Whaling Cruise to Baffin's Bay*, Albert Hastings Markham. *Old Whaling Days*, 1895, Captain William Barron. *Whaling*, in sea-fishing volume of Badminton Library.

H. W. GORE-BOOTH.

WHIPPET RACING—Since in many parts of England this sport is practically unknown, it may be as well to explain that the whippet is a dog specially bred and trained for speed, to be run against others of its kind. Certainly no dog approaches it in fleetness for its size, as a course of 200 yards is covered by the whippet in about 13 seconds. The breed was originally a cross between the Italian greyhound and fox-terrier, but probably no first cross between the two would result in the type that is now termed a whippet, so the breed may reasonably be said to have separated itself from the parent stock on both sides. A true whippet should weigh from 12 to 20 pounds. Most of its points should be those of the greyhound, but the terrier blood should show through in a shorter head, slightly stouter build, and stronger coat.

The course for whippeting should be laid down in cinders and well rolled while wet, but it must never be allowed to get hard on the top, for that is sure to result in sore feet or other lameness. It should be 220 yards in length, and about 10 yards wide. This allows 1½ yards for each dog, as the usual number to start in a heat is six. The course is then divided lengthways by boards or strips of canvas about 18 inches high, supported on pegs, and for some 30 yards from the start the course is marked across from side to side with parallel creases one yard apart, every fifth having the number of yards from "scratch" clearly marked at the side. At 200 yards from scratch is the winning post, and 15 yards beyond that is the "overmark." The judge's box should be sunk in a pit some three feet below the level of the course, to admit of a good view of the finish. The whole should be railed round at a convenient distance for onlookers, and there should be a tent with scales for weighing in at the start, and a telegraph board at either end. The competitors in each heat are given distinguishing colours, which are worn round the dog's neck, and the winning colours are posted on the board in the order of finishing, as the heats are run off. At well-attended meetings, the number of heats is large, and smart management will keep an almost incessant stream of dogs racing up the course. Whippets are handicapped according to weight and previous performances, and the name of the dog, colour, owner, and handicap is entered on the race-card in the following manner:—

HEAT FIVE.

			lbs.	st.
—	R.	Mr. Robinson's f. d. Peter	$19\frac{3}{4}$	19
1	W.	Mr. Wardell's b. w. d. Old Father .	$20\frac{1}{2}$	20
7	B.	Mr. Hide's b. w. d. Doge	17	26
12	Y.	Mr. White's bl. w. d. Blue Funk . .	16	31
14	G.	Mr. Noble's b. w. b. Thoughtless Beauty	$13\frac{3}{4}$	33
21	Bk.	Mr. Rice's b. b. Hannah	12	40

By this it will be seen that Mr. Robinson's fawn dog with the red ribbon starts at scratch, though his handicap is 19 yards, and the others start at distances reduced in proportion from their respective handicaps. Generally speaking, bitches are faster than dogs and are more severely handicapped in consequence. A fifteen-pound dog, for instance, gets 4 yards advantage over a bitch of the same weight.

The dogs are weighed in at the start of the racing and should remain inside the enclosure so long as they are left in the handicap. The clerk of the scales allows 4 ounces over the weight at which the dog is entered to run, and under some circumstances as much as 8 ounces, with 6 ounces extra in the final heat. After weighing in, the dog is taken to its handicap mark by the slipper. On the crack of the pistol the slippers simultaneously throw the dogs into their stride, and they race up the course to a white cloth which is waved before them by their respective "runners up." These runners have preceded the dogs up the course, and the signal to start must not be given before they have all passed the winning post, and the race cannot be declared fair if they have not all passed the over-mark at the moment at which the first dog breasts the tape.

Such, broadly speaking, are the rules of the course, and when a meeting is well-managed and anything is known of the various competing dogs, a good deal of amusment may be got out of the game little creatures. At the same time the element of sport cannot be said to be so prominent as the medium that is afforded for betting.

Training—There is considerable variety of opinion upon the subject of training. Some consider that a whippet requires a month or six weeks preparation before he can be expected to render a good account of himself in a handicap. It is understood, of course, that from early youth he has been encouraged to worry a cloth at all odd moments, and it is surprising how soon he will take to what is born in the blood, for it has been mysteriously ordained that the lure for a whippet should be a cloth held by the "runner." However, his physical training is another matter, and, taking into consideration the delicacy of the animal, it is often a difficult one. First, it should be ascertained that the dog is in good health, and then he should be put upon a diet of wholesome plain food:—biscuit or bread soaked in broth with an occasional boiled onion or parsnip is the staple diet. Sometimes a new laid egg mixed with the food is advisable if the dog has been rather over-exercised.

LITTLE JOE.

For exercise, walking smartly about five miles a day with an occasional gallop is sufficient, for the dog will do considerably more than this if taken over a country with some grass. As the day of the race approaches, he is put upon the best mutton diet, and beaten eggs if necessary. The trainer of "Little Joe," a dog that is tolerably well known in the neighbourhood of London, has kindly put a few notes on the subject at the disposal of the writer. He gives a course of three weeks only, and proceeds as follows:—

First week.—Dose with castor oil, and, if it should not seem necessary to follow this up with areca nut, feed twice a day on brown bread soaked in tea or mutton broth, and weigh the dog at the end of the week.

Second week.—Feed with brown bread soaked in beef-tea with a small piece of meat twice a day. Exercise for two miles morning and evening. Rub well, keep the feet clean, and weigh every morning.

Third week.—Feed with four ounces of grilled beef night and morning, with a teaspoonful of linseed tea on a piece of toast. For exercise, a walk of a mile and a half in the morning, a short turn at mid-day, and a run on the grass in the evening. The last three mornings before the race an egg should be given with the food, and a small piece of boiled fish at night. On the day of the race, about three ounces of beef-tea and toast should be given in the morning, and a piece of lean roast beef or mutton after the first and second heat. "Little Joe's" trainer adds that kindness is essential in training a whippet, and that a bath once a week in summer is necessary.

Whippeting is still in its infancy, and has so far been almost exclusively practised by the mill-hands and miners in the manufacturing districts of Yorkshire and Lancashire. It is also said to be popular in Holland, but if dog-lovers among the English country gentry were to see the possibilities of the sport for a summer amusement, it would probably alter its character considerably. In a county like Surrey, for instance, where many people of moderate means live within easy distance of one another, a whippet meeting would form a very pleasant change from the monotony of the stereotyped garden party, for races can readily be run over turf, though of course a cinder track is preferable. Then the training of the dogs is an interesting occupation, and when out of training a whippet is a delightful companion, having most of a terrier's intelligence coupled with a greyhound's grace. His worst proclivities are a greed for carrion and all sorts of refuse, with a wonderful capacity for catching cold. The first of these makes a box muzzle almost a necessity while in training, and the second a Jæger coat with the owner's initials in the corner. Amongst the North Country miners, whatever may be the state of the family exchequer, the whippet is never denied his mutton. Perhaps this is not so much due to sporting instincts as to the chance of winning a large handicap—for it is no exaggeration to say that in many such cases the whippet is the chief bread-winner of the family.

An attempt was made a few years ago to popularise whippeting in the eyes of polite society, and a handicap was arranged in connection with the show of the Ladies' Kennel Association at Ranelagh. But from one cause or another the handicap resulted in failure. This was not the fault of the dogs, which were as smart a lot as could have well been brought together; but the management was bad, and the onlookers were in want of explanations which no one could be found to give them. Moreover, since whippets were then kept only by the rougher element and the owners were present, the better-dressed habitués of Ranelagh seemed a little shy of the sport. This was not unnatural, for it must be admitted that as at present practised it is crude and unpolished.

In the opinion of the writer a decently-trained whippet should race up the course to the whistle of its runner, and so avoid the ridiculous spectacle afforded by a troup of ungainly "runners" cantering up the course shouting and gesticulating to their respective dogs.

The slipping, too, would be a much more workmanlike performance if the dogs were despatched from boxes opened simultaneously by a wire under the control of the starter. This leads on to another point, namely, the size of the dogs. In order to make this system of starting at all possible, it would be necessary to limit the weight of competing dogs, so that boxes of a uniform size could be used, not too large, to be easily lifted about between the heats. This would all tend to result in prettier racing and better sport, for at present whippets range from nine to thirty pounds, and a heat may often present anything but a level lot of competitors. Moreover, with the present mode of starting, it is possible for a slipper to hold his dog if he wishes to avoid showing his true form. The rules are the making of a game, and so far whippeting has been a duller game than need be, for want of more stringent rules.

F. I. THOMAS.

WIGEON—A species of wild duck (*Mareca penelope*), best known in the British Islands as a visitor during the winter months, when it is extremely common on most parts of the coast. Indeed, it may be doubted whether any other wildfowl, except perhaps the Brent goose, is ever seen in such flocks as those of wigeon, which resort hither in the cold weather.

Intermediate in size between the common wild duck and the teal, few birds present a handsomer appearance than the cock wigeon, thus described by Professor Newton:—"The greater part of the bill blue, forehead cream colour, head and neck chestnut, passing into pinkish grey below, and above into lavender grey, which last, produced by the transverse undulations of fine black and white lines, extends over the back and upper surface of the wings, except some of the coverts, which are conspicuously white, and shows itself again on the flanks. The wings are further ornamented by a glossy green speculum between two black bars; the tail is pointed and dark; the rest of the lower parts is white. The female has the inconspicuous coloration characteristic of her sex among most of the fresh-water ducks." Although a good many pairs may be found nesting in the north of Scotland and fewer in Ireland, the greater number retire to breed in Lapland and countries further to the eastward. Small flocks begin to arrive on the east coast about the middle of October, increasing in numbers till the middle of November, by which date there are as many probably as will be seen during the winter. They leave us about the end of February or beginning of March, although on the larger inland pools of fresh water, where they are but little disturbed, a few may linger on until April.

During the winter they afford almost unlimited sport to the wildfowler, both ashore and afloat, the greatest number being killed by the punt-shooters on such parts of the coast as afford shallow water over mud flats on which the favourite weed *Zostera marina* grows abundantly.

The haunts and habits of the wigeon have been well described by many writers, amongst whom may be named Colonel Peter Hawker, William Thompson of Belfast, Folkard, Abel Chapman and Sir R. Payne Gallwey, to whose works the reader may be referred.

A large flock of wigeon is termed by wildfowl shooters a "company"; a smaller number they term a "bunch." A company of wigeon, when first collecting, may be heard at an immense distance by the whistling of the drakes and purring noise of the ducks; but, when they are quietly settled and busy at feed, the only sound heard arises from the motion of their bills, which is similar to that of tame ducks.

It is a wonderful sight to observe a large company of wigeon congregating on a mud flat, the area of which is gradually becoming reduced by a flowing tide. "As the mud begins to disappear" (to quote the words of Colonel Hawker), "they will concentrate themselves on the last uncovered spot, where, as soon as the water begins to whiten the mud, thousands may be seen, literally wedged among one another, whence they are so unwilling to fly that they will seldom stir until the water actually sets them afloat." Then is the time for the wildfowler to work up to them in his punt, in which he will lie down and push or paddle towards them until near enough to get a shot. In this way an enormous number of wigeon are killed every winter on the coast.

An Irish wildfowler, Captain Kinsey Dover, shooting in Mulroy and Sheephaven Bays, in the north-west, killed in one winter 671 fowl, of which 518 were wigeon. The following year he secured 594, of which 386 were wigeon, and the next season the bag was 642, amongst them 408 wigeon. The number of duck and mallard killed by him in these three seasons amounted to 59, 55, and 46 respectively; teal 41, 55, and 70, the remainder being pochard, scaup, and divers.

WIGEON.

Those who do not own a gunning punt, nor care for this particular phase of wildfowling, may sometimes enjoy excellent sport by shooting wigeon from the shore at flight time. The *modus operandi* is thus described by Sir R. Payne Gallwey in his excellent book, *The Fowler in Ireland.* "Place yourself and dog," he says, "behind a bank, looking in the direction in which the fowl will appear when making inland. You must choose a position over which you know they cross in the morning flight. They will return the same way and face you if posted right. Should the wind be against them, they will travel low over the land, just topping the banks and hills. If the wind is favourable, they skim along with extended wings, high, and often out of reach. In calm weather they are up in the sky, and can oftener be heard than seen."

It is well never to fire at fowl coming towards you; they should be taken sideways overhead, or, better still, when they have just passed. By shooting thus the shot will not glance off nor encounter the dense mass of down and feather presented by an approaching bird.

In bright and early morn the flight is late and uncertain. The fowl will then straggle in at all hours up to 10 o'clock, when they usually decide to visit the flats or swim above them until their food is exposed. At dawn their movements are reversed. On fine, still mornings the main body quit their haunts before it is daylight; others following later. After a boisterous night they rest on the flats, or float over them longer than usual. They are loth to face the storm, and afford a good chance to the early flighter as they fly to sea, and doubly so if forced to fly against the wind.

For flight shooting a good retriever or Irish water spaniel is indispensable, for by his aid much valuable time will be saved in recovering wounded birds and picking up the slain.

Seeing that so good an authority on wild-fowling as Folkard spells "wigeon" with a "d"—widgeon—and many writers of the present day follow his example, it may be well to state here the grounds of objection to such a practice. Etymologists are agreed that "pigeon" comes through the French from the Latin word *pipio*. In the same way "wigeon" comes from *vipio*. The old French form is *vingeon* and *vigeon*; in Anjou *digeon*, male, and *digeonne*, female. Professor Skeat has shown that the spelling *wigeon* is to be found as early as 1570, and that the insertion of the "d" in the word has no more etymological significance than has the same letter in "judge," from the French *juge*. Hence there can be no doubt that if we spell "pigeon" without a "d" we must spell "wigeon" by the same analogy.

J. E. Harting.

WILD BIRDS' PROTECTION—It is inevitable that wild creatures should suffer from the encroachment of a civilised and rapidly increasing population upon their haunts, and the avifauna of the British Isles has already lost some interesting species for ever. The great auk, the black tern, the avocet, the black-tailed godwit, the bittern, the great bustard and Savi's warbler must be reckoned extinct as breeding species; the first-named has ceased to exist anywhere; the rest are known to us only as vagrant individuals, almost invariably shot as soon as their presence is detected, to be added to some private collection or local museum. Other species, once very plentiful, have been reduced to the verge of extermination, partly by the drainage of their native swamps, partly by that rigour of game preservation which has caused all birds of prey to be entered in the black list, and, lastly, in the case of the ruff and reeve, by the diligence with which they have been persecuted at all seasons because of their edible qualities. In only one instance has the attempt to re-establish a lost species been rewarded with success, that, namely, of the capercaillie in Scottish woods.

In one respect, Great Britain has shown itself more hospitable to its native birds than has almost any other European land. It has never become the fashion with us to shoot or capture many species of small birds which are eagerly sought for on the continent for the table: and the destruction of birds of prey in this country in the process of game preservation has tended to maintain an abundant stock of song birds. So general has been the destruction of small birds in parts of Europe, notably in France, parts of Germany and Italy, that agriculture and horticulture have suffered seriously owing to the consequent increase of injurious insects and land molluscs. In 1895 the French Government invited all European Governments to send delegates to an International Congress, to consider the question of concerted action for the purpose of protecting birds useful to agriculture. M. Méline, the late Prime Minister of France, acted as President of the Conference, at which every European State, except Turkey, and some of the Danubian Principalities, was represented, Mr. Howard Saunders and the writer of this article having been appointed delegates by Her Majesty's Government. The proceedings were exceedingly earnest and harmonious, and resulted in a series of very strong recommendations. It was gratifying to the British delegates to know that the principles of these recommendations (except as regards prohibition of the importation of birds killed in other countries) have already practically been carried into force in this country by the Wild Birds' Protection Acts of 1880, 1894, and 1896.

These Acts certainly provide sufficient means for the preservation of rare or otherwise desirable birds, if their provisions can be carried into effect. This is left in large measure to the discretion of County Councils and other local bodies, which have shown a gratifying degree of activity in adopting the optional powers entrusted to them, and already, during the few years the Acts have been in force, a notable increase in some species has taken effect in some localities and an extension of the breeding range of others, such as pochards, tufted duck, and great crested grebes.

Authorities are divided in opinion as to the usefulness of prohibiting the taking of eggs of certain birds, owing to variability in the eggs of different individuals of the same species, and a close resemblance of the eggs of some species to those of others. But all agree that advantage may safely be taken of the power given in the Act of 1894 to prohibit all egg-taking whatsoever within limited and strictly defined areas, frequented by birds which it is desirable to protect. It is clear, however, that the Acts must remain a dead letter in those places where landowners and other residents do not bestir themselves to see that they are enforced.

The following abstract shows the extent to which the legislature has interfered to protect birds other than game. It is unfortunate that, although the Act extends to Ireland, the police in that country have received instructions not to enforce them.

I. Summary of the Acts.

Wild Birds' Protection (Principal) Act, 1880 (43 & 44, Vict. c. 35).

(1) Shooting or snaring all wild birds during a particular period (*close time*) is prohibited, and in the case of certain wild birds, named in the Schedule, special and fuller protection is granted.

(2) Offering for sale, after March 15th, any wild bird recently killed or taken, is prohibited.

(3) Provision is made for the extension or variation of the close time.

Wild Birds' Protection Act, 1881 (44 & 45, Vict. c. 51).

(1) Amends the law as to the offering for sale in respect of wild birds killed abroad.

(2) Adds the lark to the Schedule.

Wild Birds' Protection Act, 1894 (57 & 58, Vict. c. 24).

(1) Enables orders to be made, on the application of County Councils, to prohibit the taking or destroying of the *eggs* of certain wild birds, and of the eggs of any wild bird in particular breeding areas.

(2) Enables orders to be made to add further species of wild birds to the Schedule.

Wild Birds' Protection Act, 1896 (59 & 60, Vict. c. 56).

(1) Enables orders to be made to prohibit the taking or killing of any wild bird beyond the breeding period (or close time), and orders prohibiting the taking, &c., of all wild birds, in particular places, during the period to which the Act of 1880 does not extend.

(2) Enables application to be made by the Council of a County borough to prohibit the taking of eggs, and to add birds to the Schedule.

(3) Gives power to forfeit traps, nets, snares, decoy birds, &c., on conviction, in addition to any penalty, under any of these Acts.

These four Acts are to be read as one, and may be quoted as the Wild Birds' Protection Acts, 1880—1896.

II. Protection of Wild Birds.

Offences—*Any Wild Bird*—During the close time :—

(*a*) Any person (other than the owner or occupiers of any land or his authorised agent on such land) is guilty of an offence who shall knowingly and wilfully shoot, or attempt to shoot, *any* wild bird ;

(*b*) Or who shall use any boat for the purpose of shooting, or causing to be shot, *any* wild bird ;

(*c*) Or who shall use any lime, trap, snare, net, or other instrument, for the purpose of taking *any* wild bird ;

(*d*) Or who shall, after March 15th, offer or expose for sale, or have in his possession or control, any wild bird recently killed or taken.

Penalties—Upon conviction, the offender shall for a first offence be reprimanded and discharged upon payment of costs : for every subsequent offence, forfeit, and pay, in addition to costs, a sum not exceeding five shillings for each bird, and, in addition to this penalty, the trap, net, snare, or decoy bird used by such person may be forfeited.

Offences—*Scheduled Wild Birds*—During close time, or the further period which may be fixed under the Act of 1896, it is an *offence* for *any* person, including the owner or occupier of land and his agent, to commit any of the acts enumerated in respect of "any wild bird," and such person, upon conviction, is liable to the following punishment :—

Penalties—For every such bird in respect of which an offence has been committed, a fine not exceeding £1 may be imposed. In addition, the trap, net, snare, or decoy bird used by such person may be forfeited. Both as regards "any wild bird" and "scheduled birds," for refusal to give name and address, or giving false name and address to any person asking for such name and address, a penalty not exceeding ten shillings may be imposed.

These paragraphs apply to England, Wales, Scotland, and Ireland,[1] but in the case of Ireland, there is not the further power to confiscate the nets, snares, &c.

The penalties are to be recovered under the Summary Jurisdiction Acts, and all informations must be laid within six months.

Offering for Sale, &c..—A person shall not be liable to be convicted, however, if he satisfies the court, either—

(1) That, if in a place to which the Act extends, the killing or taking was lawful at the time when and by the person by whom it was taken or killed ;

(2) That the wild bird was killed in some place to which the Act does not extend (see Sec. 1, Act 1881).

A special Act was passed in 1888 with reference to the Sandgrouse (51 & 52, Vict. c. 55), under which any person who shall kill, wound, or take or expose, or offer for sale any Sandgrouse, killed or taken in the United Kingdom, shall be liable, on conviction, to a penalty of £1 for every bird.

III. "Scheduled Birds."

The original list of about one hundred birds appears in the Schedule to the Act of 1880, but power has been given under the Act of 1894 for orders to be made so that other birds may have the special protection "as if such species were included in the Schedule to the Act."

By the Act of 1881, the lark was added to the Schedule. In a supplement to this pamphlet a list is given of all the birds named in the Schedule, and those which have as yet, in any county, or part of a county, been added to the Schedule.

IV. Close Time.

By the Act of 1880 the close time for scheduled birds was fixed as between March 1st and August 1st in each year. Power, however, was granted to vary the close time locally, and this varies in different districts between the maximum of February 1st to October 1st, and the minimum (Essex) March 15th to August 1st.

Under the Act of 1896 the following further period has been granted for Middlesex, viz., October 1st to February 1st, for forty-seven birds, many of whom are migrants. This in effect gives protection to these birds all the year round.

V. Protection of Eggs.

Applications may be made by County Councils to the Secretary of State for an order to prohibit—

[1] The island of St. Kilda is exempted from the provisions of the Act of 1880.

(1) The taking or destroying of wild birds' eggs in any specified place or places;

(2) The taking or destroying the eggs of any specified kind of wild bird within a county, or county borough, or any specified place.

It is incumbent on the Council applying to specify—

(*a*) The limits of the place or places, or otherwise;

(*b*) The particular species of wild birds to which the prohibit is to apply; and

(*c*) The reason on account of which the application is made.

Offences and Penalties—Any person who shall take or destroy or incite any other person to take or destroy the eggs of any wild bird protected under an order shall, on conviction, forfeit and pay for every egg so taken or destroyed a sum not exceeding £1.

Under the Game Act (1831, 1 & 2, W. IV., c. 32), any person not having the right of killing the game upon the land nor having permission from the person having such right, who shall wilfully take out of the nest, or destroy in the nest upon such land, the eggs of any bird of game, or of any swan, wild duck, teal, or wigeon, *or* shall have in his possession any such eggs, shall be liable, on conviction, to a fine of five shillings and the costs of the conviction.

Under the Poaching Prevention Act (1862, 25 & 26, Vict. c. 114), the *eggs* of pheasants, partridges, black and moor game are treated as game.

VI. Breeding Areas.

Orders may be issued by the Secretary of State on the application of a County Council, defining specified areas within which the taking or destroying the eggs of *any* wild bird is prohibited. Various areas have been thus protected, such as Holy Island in Northumberland, part of the Island of Sheppey in Kent, and the Broads' district in Norfolk.

VII. Jurisdiction, and how to enforce the Acts and Orders.

The first point to remember, is that *any* person may take up the duty of preventing disobedience to the Acts and Orders, and help in obtaining convictions for any offences.

It is itself an additional offence to refuse to give the name and address, or to give a false name or address, to *any* person asking for this information.

Any person may also apply for a summons against an offender, and himself prosecute. If particulars are given to the Police, to a Secretary of the Society for the Protection of Birds, or to an officer of the Society for the Prevention of Cruelty to Animals, every assistance in their power will be given. In the cases of the taking of eggs of particular birds, it is expected that difficulties about identification will sometimes arise, and that expert evidence may be necessary.

A summons should be taken out for each offence against each person to be charged, and it is advisable to apply for two summonses where more than one bird or egg has been taken, &c.

All offences under these Acts are to be prosecuted in the manner provided by the Summary Jurisdiction Acts.

Where any offence is committed in or upon any waters forming the boundary between two counties, districts of Quarter Sessions or Petty Sessions, such offence may be prosecuted before any justices of the peace or sheriff in either of such counties.

All offences which shall be committed within the jurisdiction of the Admiralty,[1] shall be dealt with as if they had been committed upon any land in the United Kingdom, and tried in any county or place in the United Kingdom in which the offender shall be apprehended or be in custody, or be summoned, in all respects as if such offence had been actually committed in that county or place. Any information or conviction for any such offence may be averred to have been committed "on the high seas." In Scotland, any offence committed on the sea coast or beyond the ordinary jurisdiction of any sheriff, justice, or justice of the peace, shall be held to have been committed in any county abutting on such sea coast or adjoining such sea, and may be tried and punished accordingly.

IX. How to obtain an Order.

It is advisable first to interest some one or more of the Councillors in the question; to write to the Chairman, or petition the Council. The proposal will probably be referred to a committee to draw up a report as to the form of application and the reasons to be assigned. The opinion of an ornithologist should be sought, as it will be of great assistance.

The Home Secretary has sent circular letters on the subject to all the County Councils in England, and the orders which have been asked for have, as a rule, been granted. The application should deal with the following matters:—

(1) The extension of the close time.

(2) The addition of birds to the Schedule of the Act, 1880.

(3) The protection of the eggs of certain birds in the whole County or County Borough, or a specified area therein.

(4) The special reservation of any parts of a County or Borough as a breeding area, prohibiting therein the taking of the eggs of all birds or of certain named birds.

(5) A further period for the protection of particular kinds of birds which may in effect secure for them protection during the whole year.

The application for an Order may be made by any County Council in England, Wales, or Scotland, and, under the Act of 1896, the Council of a County Borough (except in Ireland) has now the power to apply for an Order.

X. How to make the Orders known.

The duty of making known the Orders is thrown upon the Council, who, in every year, are directed to give public notice of any Order during the three weeks preceding the commencement of the period of the year during which the Order operates—

(1) By advertising in the local papers.

(2) By fixing notices of the Order in conspicuous spots.

Copies of the Order should be sent to the county constabulary, police, coastguard stations, parish councils, and all elementary and secondary schools in the County. Private persons can help by inquiring if this has been done, and also by themselves obtaining copies of the Order from the Clerk to the Council; by distributing them and posting copies on their own land. In some cases, as in the County of Middlesex, the notice which has been issued contains engravings of some of the birds named in the Order. In Chester an excellent memorandum has been issued by the County Council giving full particulars.

It is very important that the existence of any extension of close time should be well advertised in the district affected, and the Protection Orders well placarded, so that "prevention" may have its full effect, and avoid, to a great extent, the necessity of prosecutions.

The Orders are published for England, Scotland, and Ireland, in *The London*, *The Edinburgh*, and *The Dublin Gazettes*, respectively, and all the Orders are to be obtained in separate form at the Queen's Printers.

This notice of what has been done to protect British wild birds would be incomplete without

[1] The Admiralty jurisdiction is "the high seas," and "the high seas" commence below low-water mark when the tide is out, or, in the case of rivers in the United Kingdom, outside an imaginary line drawn from the one point of land to the other, between which the river-tide flows.

some reference to the useful work done by the Society for the Protection of Birds, under the presidency of the Duchess of Portland. The committee of this Society have shown great discretion in avoiding ultra-humanitarianism, and great activity in the diffusion of knowledge and attraction of intelligent sympathy by means of lectures, pamphlets, leaflets, &c. The indefatigable secretary is Mrs. Lemon, Hill Crest, Redhill, Surrey, from whom the rules can be obtained.

HERBERT MAXWELL.

WOLF-COURSING—The wolf has always been recognised as the inveterate foe of man, and especially of domestic beasts; moreover, his fur is quite valuable. Wherever he is found, therefore, men wage merciless war upon him with guns, traps, and poison. He is very wary and cunning, however, and is well able to take care of his skin, so that every means must be taken to outwit him and every ally enlisted against him. Accordingly, from the earliest times, man in chasing the wolf has made use of the wolf's close kinsman and hated foe, the dog.

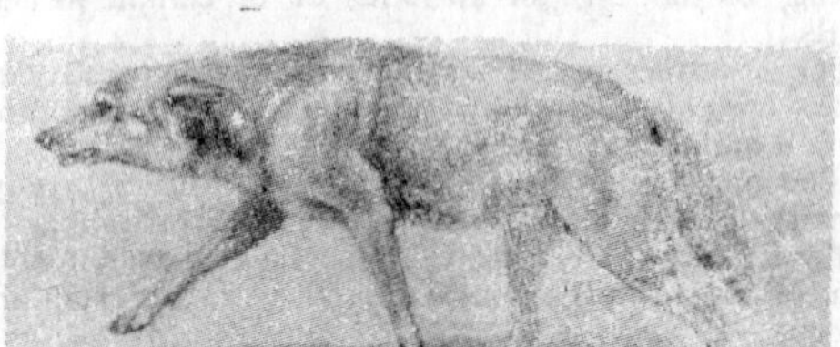

COYOTE.

Most domestic dogs loathe and fear the wolf more than any other beast; and a hungry wolf will snap up one of them as readily as he will snap up a sheep. Only a few breeds can be brought to face the wolf, and these must be specially trained. The huge shaggy dogs used in different pastoral countries to guard the sheep or cattle often have to encounter wolves. The big smooth-haired dogs, certain varieties of which were especially trained in the Middle Ages to assist in the death-grapple with dangerous beasts of the chase, can also be used against wolves. Hounds proper will only run a wolf if specially trained, and they are too weak to assail him singly or in small parties; but for centuries the great sportsmen of Continental Europe have hunted the wolf with specially trained packs, and a few of these are still kept up and trained for this purpose. But the true dog to use in the chase of the wolf is what was anciently called the "long dog," the gaze-hound, now called the greyhound. The Irish wolf-dog was simply a giant, rough-haired greyhound, and the quaint old sporting books of three centuries back show how frequently powerful greyhounds were used to overtake and tackle wolves, which the ordinary track-hounds had roused from their lairs.

The ordinary greyhound used for the chase of the hare is too light for rough work against dangerous prey, and in most countries the few remaining wolves have retired into wooded and rocky fastnesses where greyhounds are of no use; but where wolves are found on great open plains, like those of Russia and Siberia, and parts of western North America, greyhounds are specially adapted for their chase. At present there is a good deal of wolf-coursing done both in America and in Russia, though the conditions of the sport are widely different in the two places; for in Russia it is regarded as a sport pure and simple, to be followed only by a few of the great nobles; while in America, aside from an occasional army officer or ranchman, it is followed as a business by men who wish to exterminate the wolves, either for the bounty or to protect the cattle heads. Moreover, as in America the settlements continually increase, the wolves continually decrease, and the sport is so much more evanescent that it has never had the opportunity to assume any fixity of type.

In both places special types of dog have been bred for the purpose. In Russia these are the so-called borzois, or long-haired greyhounds, a type which has been in existence for centuries. In America a few men, during the last thirty or forty years, have bred big greyhounds, both smooth- and rough-coated, producing a type which shows signs of reversion to the old Irish wolfhound; dogs weighing something like 100 pounds, of remarkable power and of reckless and savage temper. The professional hunters, however, draft into their packs any animal which can run fast and fight hard, and their so-called greyhounds are often of mongrel breed.

In Russia the sport is a science. The princes and great landowners who take part in it have their hunting equipages perfected to the smallest detail. Not only do they follow wolves in the open, but they capture them and let them out before the dogs, as hares are let out at ordinary coursing matches. The huntsman follows his hounds on horseback. Two, three, or four dogs usually run together, and they are not expected to kill the wolf, but merely to hold him; and as soon as possible after he is thrown the huntsman leaps to the ground, forces the short handle of his riding-whip between the beast's jaws, and then binds them tightly together with the long thong. Great skill and coolness is needed, both on the part of dogs and men. The borzois can readily overtake and master partly-grown wolves, but a full-grown dog-wolf, in good trim, will usually gallop away from them, and will outfight any reasonable number. A good many borzois have been imported into America, but when tried against our wolves they have not, as a rule, done as well as the best home-bred dogs.

In America, the only place where I have had a chance to take part in the sport, it is of course conducted in a much more rough-and-ready manner. For fifty years the officers of the United States army on the great plains have used greyhounds to chase jackrabbits, foxes, coyotes, and occasionally antelopes. Now and then those dogs which had been entered on coyotes were used against the big wolves; but it was only during the last few decades that the sport became at all common. There are now, however, a good many men who follow it in Montana, Wyoming, and here and there in Colorado and western North Dakota. There is a pack near my ranch on the Little Missouri which has a record of several hundred wolves to its credit. The owner is a professional wolfer, and his dogs represent every kind of pure blood and half-blood greyhound; but they are a wicked, hard-biting crew, and as they are usually hunted eight or ten together, they will, unlike the borzois, tear even the biggest wolf literally to pieces, without assistance from the hunter. Numerous casualties of course occur in the pack, for a wolf is a desperate fighter, and the sound and sight of the worry is fairly blood-curdling. The Sun River, in Western Montana, was at one time a famous place for its wolfhounds, and there was another celebrated pack near Fort Benton; but it is eight years since I was in either neighbourhood, and time marches fast in the Far West. My own experiences have usually been with scratch packs, to which I have occasionally contributed a dog or two myself. Ordinarily these packs contained nothing but greyhounds, either smooth- or rough-coated, but in one of them there were two huge fighting dogs of mixed ancestry, which could not keep up with the greyhounds, but did most of the killing when their lighter-footed friends had succeeded in stopping the quarry. The greyhounds with which we usually hunted had not been specially trained to the work, and were not bred for the purpose, having simply served an apprenticeship as coyote hunters. In consequence they were not capable of killing the wolf without assistance. They usually stopped him by snapping at his hams, and would then form a ring through which he could not break; or if he did break they would overhaul him shortly, and once more bring him to a standstill. The hunters either shot him or roped him.

I doubt if the sport, even when carried on in a more legitimate manner, could afford more fun than these helter-skelter skurries over the plains gave us. We generally started for the hunting-grounds very early, riding across the country in a widely spread line of dogs and men, and if we put up a wolf we simply went at him as hard as we knew how. Young wolves, or those that had not attained their full strength, were readily overtaken, and the pack would handle a small she-wolf quite readily. A big dog-wolf, or even a full-grown and powerful bitch-wolf, offered an altogether different problem. Frequently we came upon them after they had gorged themselves on a colt or calf. Under such conditions, if the dogs had a good start, they ran into the wolf and held him; but if a big wolf in good running trim was able to keep ahead of them for half a mile or so, his superior strength and endurance told, and he gradually drew away.

Of course the packs composed of nothing but specially trained and specially bred greyhounds of great size and power made a better showing. Under favourable circumstances three or four of these dogs readily overtook and killed the largest wolf, rushing in together and invariably seizing by the throat. The risk to the pack was so great, however, and dogs were so frequently killed or crippled in the worry, that the hunter always endeavoured to keep as close as possible, and on his arrival he put an immediate end to the contest by a knife-thrust. In running, the dogs usually had an advantage, because they were so apt to find the wolf near a carcase from which it had just made a hearty meal; and, moreover, the dogs, when possible, were taken on a wagon to the field of their exploits. Their dashing courage and ferocious fighting capacity were marvellous, and in this respect I was never able to see much difference between the smooth-haired and the wire-haired, or Scotch deer-hound, types, while the smooth-haired were generally faster.

THEODORE ROOSEVELT.

WOLF SHOOTING IN RUSSIA — In Russia the wolf is every one's enemy, and it is therefore the business of every man to kill him whenever and wherever met, so long as his killing can be brought about without much danger. There are many ways of doing this, for the wolf is not a dangerous animal when single, or in twos and threes, or even in a company of four or five. It is only when, half starved and frantic with hunger, he assembles in tens and scores to ravage the country, that he may be a source of real peril to human beings, and this—in spite of many excellent and exciting tales of wolf-packs and pursued human beings—is a matter of very rare occurrence, since wolves are not so numerous that a pack of a hundred or so can easily get together for the purpose of hunting human beings.

In the south of Russia wolves are hunted with dogs of a special breed. Men on horseback follow the hunt, and the quarry is not, as a rule, pulled down by the hounds, but shot by the guns of the mounted sportsmen. In the north of Russia wolves are not hunted with dogs, their destruction being brought about, as a rule. in one of three ways; either by battue, by decoy, or by a peculiar method of discovering and killing them, which may be described as the pig-squeaking method.

To consider the first of these three ways of ridding the country of a pest, it may be said that a wolf may be started, unexpectedly, at any hare battue in autumn, for until the snow comes, to give unfailing evidence of his presence, he may of course appear anywhere. For this reason, when battue shooting, it is as well to have a slug cartridge handy for his benefit, should he, as he occasionally does, suddenly show himself among the hares and the black-game. While upon this subject it may be further suggested that a ball cartridge, in another pocket, is not amiss on such occasions, for

RUSSIAN WOLF.

during the autumn battues around St. Petersburg it has happened before now that a bear has suddenly darted out and away in response to the yells of the beaters.

But a real wolf battue is quite a different affair. This has been carefully prepared for, it may be for a month beforehand. Carcases of horses or cows have been laid down for the purpose of attracting any wolves that happened to be wandering in the neighbourhood; but wolves are no longer very numerous, and perhaps two or three weeks may have passed without the odour, which is strong enough to sicken a human being at a quarter-mile range, having reached the nostrils of a single wanderer. But suppose the wolves have scented the feast and have arrived in force, four or five of them. After they have supped off the malodorous carcase once or twice, they should, if need be, be coaxed to remain about the place, by new decoys placed close to the original spot. The keeper has his eye upon the party, and while they lie surfeited and sleepy with the carrion provided for them, he first sends a telegram (if he is in civilised regions), or a messenger, summoning his employers from St. Petersburg; then he noiselessly rings the wolves by walking round upon his snow shoes until he has completed a circle into which the wolf-tracks have entered, but out of which none have re-issued; he engages his friends and relatives at the village—to the number of fifty or more—as beaters; and surrounds the overfed slumberers with a cordon of silent and most alert and anxious peasants, each of whom has a personal animosity against the common enemy, perhaps only hereditary, but possibly justified by the actual loss of lamb or dog or sucking-pig. Afterwards, when the sportsmen have come down, and these peasants and their wives have suddenly, at a signal, raised pandemonium in the silent forest by a simultaneous uproar of yelling and cursing, those surfeited wolves will have to run the gauntlet and one or two of them are sure to breathe out their savage lives upon the snow. Soon every foot will have a kick at the victim and every tongue will curse him from generation to generation, as he lies bleeding and mangled, the most unpopular thing that lives—for a Russian peasant community.

Or, again, the sportsman who has paid for the carcases laid down to attract the wolves, may have elected to make no battue for his wolves, but to take up his position within the branches of some tree overlooking, at easy range, the spot where lies the garbage of which the wolves have already partaken once or more, and will partake again to-night.

The keeper who has brought him to the place, if he is wise, will leave him there and walk away again. Wolves (and bears also) are suspicious folk, and have been known to retire on discovering that the scent indicated the arrival of a human being but not his departure, arguing that he must therefore be present somewhere. The shooter must come early and stay among the branches until it is light enough to shoot, and this will be some little while; he is therefore recommended to dress very warmly and to bring with him such creature comforts as the circumstances would suggest. Another word to the wise: do not fall asleep among the boughs, and snore; for if you do this thing, not a wolf, worthy the name, will come near you. Moreover, fix yourself in so secure a position that even though you fell asleep you would not fall out of the tree; for, whether the wolves were there or no, this would be an uncomfortable thing to do. Bears may be shot from ambush, over a kill, as well as wolves; and it has happened occasionally that both bear and wolves have visited the food during the same night. In such a case the bear will, as a rule, give way to the wolves if these are more than two or three, retiring in terror and with moans and roars of rage, and very likely pursued by his foes into the branches of some adjacent tree, from which he will watch his rival's enjoyment of the food with the most dismal utterings of his displeasure, in groanings and scoldings which are quite piteous to hear.

The third recognised method of obtaining a wolf-skin—or at least of endeavouring to achieve that distinction—is original and entertaining, and may perhaps be considered the most "sporting" way of the three. We will now suppose that the English sportsman has penetrated into some out-of-the-way Russian village, during winter, *en route*, perhaps, by sledge for some outlying destination such as Olonetz, the headquarters of the bears, and that he is obliged to pass the night there. There are wolves about, he is told; perhaps he has observed their tracks, but there is no time to lay down a carcase and wait about for days until it shall have attracted the animals so that he can sit in ambush with good hope of a shot; a battue is also impossible, because there is no Ochotnik, or village sportsman, in the place capable of organising such a thing, with any chance of success, against so acute a beast as a wolf. The animal must be approached with scientific skill and much caution, and surrounded at the right moment and in a proper manner, or he will slip out of the ring and stand grinning and looking on at the beat from a quarter of a mile away, on the *outside* of the ring, as the writer has seen him do before this. But though neither ambush nor battue is practicable, the sportsman need not despair. Let him inquire in the village for a young pig, one with good lungs, and a sack, and, having obtained both, let him put the pig in the bag. There are some who advocoate the cutting of a small hole for the pig's tail to emerge from the sack, with a view to pinching, in order that the little creature's squeaks may be, as it were, "turned on" when required; but it will be found that sufficient squealing will be done without special inducements. Having secured his pig and his sack, the sportsman must engage a sledge and horse, with a man to hold the reins. The moon must not be too bright, neither must the night be too dark, as the enterprising sportsman takes his seat, slug-loaded gun in hand, in the sledge, and drives softly and slowly into the loneliest road that will bring him into mid forest. A dense wood with cover on both sides and a good smooth sledge track, running like a white ribbon through it, will best suit his purpose. The sledge must have no bells, there must be as little urging of the horse as possible, no coughing or sneezing, and above all no conversation of any kind. The only sound permissible is the squealing of the pig, and the more of this, the better. Wolves—if within a mile or so—will hear it and come, and since the sledge is constantly moving, the area within which a wolf may happen to be prowling and to hear the call, is constantly widening. There are many chances against the sportsman: the wolves may never come within earshot; or, if they do, and respond to the invitation, an unlucky cough or a Russian expectoration (never withheld for long by the true Muscovite), may turn them aside before they have come within shooting distance of the sledge, even if seen; and again, they may approach quite close and follow the sledge or even accompany it, some twenty or thirty yards away among the thick cover to right or left, and yet never be seen at all. Nevertheless luck is not always on the wolf's side. It may be that the sportsman is a lucky person or the wolf the reverse, and in that event a delightful thing may occur. The shooter is sitting or reclining in his luxurious seat—there is nothing more luxurious to recline in than the bottom of a village sledge well padded with hay; he is half asleep, in spite of the pig's constant and frantic vocal efforts, which have never ceased for a moment, and which first enraged him almost beyond endurance, but at length gradually lulled him to slumber. His eyes occasionally sleepily glance at the trees to right and left; the forest has been a very dense one, but is gradually thinning out, and revealing here and there a little space of open which the moonlight illuminates in a weird manner. Suddenly he starts up, wide awake, and grasps his gun tighter—it has half subsided into the bottom of the sledge: he has seen something. The driver is fast asleep, holding the reins perfunctorily in his lap; the horse is walking in his sleep, Russian horses generally are. Another moment and the moonlight reveals first one gaunt, grey, cantering form and then a second, leaping from cover to cover, accompanying the sledge, thirty yards away. Up goes the trusty weapon; there is a bang and instantly a second, the horse wakes up and dashes forthwith into a confused, oblique gallop which lands the sledge and its occupants against a pine tree and thence into the deep snow; our sportsman is on his legs in a moment, and rushing into the wood to ascertain the effect of his shots. When, at last, the vituperating driver has caught and turned his startled steed and brought the sledge back to the scene of its disaster, he finds, maybe, our shooter—supposing him to be a fair shot—standing over the body of one wolf and preparing to administer the *coup de grace* to its snarling, wounded companion.

FRED WHISHAW.

WOODCOCK — The general characters which distinguish the different species of woodcock from the true snipes have been already pointed out in the article SNIPE, and need not be recapitulated. The European woodcock (*Scolopax rusticula*), and the American woodcock (*Philohela minor*), are the two best known representatives of their kind, for they are both widely distributed, and both are much sought after by sportsmen of every country which they frequent or visit. Indeed, it may be doubted whether any game bird affords more thoroughly enjoyable sport than a woodcock, or leads the shooter into wilder or more picturesque haunts.

Licence for Shooting—It may be well to note, by the way, that although neither woodcock nor snipe come within the definition of "game," as laid down by the principal English Game Act (1 & 2 Will. 4, cap. 32), a game licence is nevertheless required for shooting them (23 & 24 Vict. cap. 90), and this applies also to quail and landrail. (*See* LICENCES.)

Result of Protection—Since the passing of the Wild Birds' Protection Act in 1880, many more woodcocks have remained to nest in the British Islands than used formerly to be the case. At one time the discovery of a woodcock's nest was so rare an occurrence that it was deemed worthy of record in journals devoted to sport and natural history; at the present day, there is perhaps hardly a county in the United Kingdom in which at least a few pairs do not remain to breed; and this not merely in the north, but in many of the southern counties. In Sussex, for example, Mr. Monk, of Lewes, ascertained a few years ago, from statistics carefully collected from the owners of game coverts and their keepers, that not less than 200 nests might be found in the eastern division alone. In view of this fact it will be readily perceived how difficult, if not impossible, it is to determine whether a so-called "early woodcock" is really a fresh arrival from across the North Sea, or has been here, perhaps bred here, during the previous summer.

Migration—It is of course well known that the great majority of woodcocks which are met with in the British Islands during the autumn and winter are visitors from the continent. In Northumberland these birds have been observed to arrive in the greatest numbers in hazy weather with little wind, and that blowing from the north-east. In Norfolk it has been remarked that the nocturnal migrations of the woodcock are influenced rather by the wind than the moon, and they have been found quite abundant on that coast after a dark night, with the wind from the north or the north-east. In Yorkshire and Lincolnshire some of the largest flights have been known to arrive about October 10th or 12th with a strong east wind, fog, and drizzling rain. At Spurn Point sixty have been shot in one morning after a fresh north-east wind during the previous night with drizzling rain, and at Skegness forty-three were shot in the same day under similar conditions of wind and weather. In Cornwall the first flights generally arrive about the second week in October, and with the wind at any point from south to east. In one year, however, a continuance of north-east winds to the end of October, with a waning moon, brought a large flight of woodcocks to the Land's End district. One gun there killed fifty-four in a week, and another thirty-nine in a day.

The Annual Reports published by a Committee of the British Association appointed to collect information in regard to the migration of birds from the keepers of the lighthouses and lightships, furnish some curious and interesting statistics concerning the arrival of woodcocks in autumn, and establish the following facts. Their migration takes place chiefly at night. Birds which strike the lanterns of the lighthouses are generally picked up between midnight and daybreak. When a large number come over together, as they often do, they fly with the wind; but, as an exception, single birds have been seen to arrive with the wind against them. During the autumn migration comparatively few are observed at stations on the west coast of Scotland, while during the spring migration few are seen on the east coast, and this applies to England as well as to Scotland.

Condition on Arrival, and Weight—It is generally supposed that woodcocks on their arrival here are lean and out of condition, but this is not always the case. Sir R. Payne Gallwey states that out of hundreds which he examined during the exceptionally long and severe winter of 1880–81, only a dozen were small and poor birds; and at the end of the frost he picked out three birds, each of which weighed exactly 16 ozs., a fourth weighing 18¼ ozs. These must have been exceptionally fine birds, for the average weight of a woodcock may be set down at 12 ozs. or thereabouts.

Sexes and Alleged Races—It has not been ascertained whether the sexes travel apart, as is known to be the case with certain small passerine birds; but some persons maintain there are two distinct races of woodcock, one large and light-coloured, the other small and dark, which keep apart and arrive independently. At Kilnsea, near the Spurn, it is said that a south-east wind always brings large grey or light-coloured woodcocks, and a north wind small and red-coloured birds, and this is reported from other parts of the coast. (See *Fifth Report on Migration*, 1887, p. 51, note.) According to Professor Newton, however (*Dict. Birds*, p. 1042, footnote), those who have taken much trouble about the matter are unanimous in declaring against the existence of two "species" or even "races." In other words, the difference observable in size and colour is due to individual variation and age, and not to specific distinctness.

It has often been asserted that the sexes of the woodcock may be distinguished by the appearance of the first primary, in which, it is said, the outer web is of a uniform colour in the female, and has white or buffy-white zig-zag markings on a darker ground in the male.

Woodcock.

This, however, is a fallacy. We have seen the first primary of a woodcock which had the markings referred to for half its length only, the remaining half being quite uniform in colour. Thus no dependence can be placed on this character, which varies not with sex, but with age; nor can any constant character be pointed out as an invariable indication of sex.

White and Pied Varieties—Occasionally the variation of colour is carried to excess, and woodcocks are met with having more or less white about their plumage, giving them a pied appearance, while more rarely an albino or nearly pure white specimen is shot and preserved as a curiosity. See an article on "White Woodcocks," by the present writer, in *The Field* of November 20, 1897.

Good Bags—In his excellent work on the *Birds of Norfolk*, the late Mr. Stevenson has given some interesting details of woodcock shooting in that county, mentioning some notable bags which have been made in certain favoured coverts; and allusion has been already made to the sport which these birds sometimes afford in Cornwall and the Scilly Isles. But of all places in the United Kingdom for this kind of shooting, none is comparable to certain localities in the west and south-west of Ireland. Kerry, Sligo, and Mayo are noted counties for woodcock. In Mayo ten to thirty couple is a fair day's sport for a party of six guns, but forty couple have been killed in a day in one of Lord Sligo's woods. At Lissadel, in co. Sligo, 150 couple were killed in three days by a party of eight guns; and at the same place on another occasion 338 cocks were bagged in six days by seven guns. In co. Kerry, the year Lord Elcho resided at Muckross, Killarney, the party, averaging five guns, shot in ten days 840 cocks, and during that winter (1863–64) 1,250 were killed on the estate. On Lord Ardilaun's estate at Ashford, co. Galway, the woodcock shooting is famous. There, on a January day, five guns have bagged 106 birds, and six guns 350 cocks in a week. On the two best days of this week there were killed respectively 117 and 115 birds. In January 1880 six guns shot 365 cocks in four days, killing on one day 165, and on another 82 birds.

WOODCOCK.

According to Sir R. Payne Gallwey, from whose work, *The Fowler in Ireland*, these figures are quoted, from 300 to 400 cocks is a good yearly average on a favoured estate in Ireland, but in exceptionally good seasons even this number has been exceeded.

J. E. HARTING.

WRESTLING—In Great Britain, wrestling, although much practised in days gone by in Cumberland and Westmorland, Lancashire, Devon and Cornwall, and in some parts of Ireland, cannot in any sense be considered a national pastime, or one that is cultivated so generally throughout the land as the sister science, boxing. There exists, however, so strong an affinity between wrestling and boxing that the one may be considered a useful and natural adjunct to the other. But, in order to make the pastime generally popular, it is the opinion of many that a style on the "catch hold" principle should be generally adopted as the recognised English method. At the present time we are lost in the maze of a variety of systems, to wit—Græco-Roman, Cumberland and Westmorland, Lancashire (catch as catch can), Cornish and Devon, Scottish, Irish, German, Swiss, Japanese, Indian, &c. Without doubt the Græco-Roman fashion of wrestling is productive of some excitement when witnessed by the uninitiated; but apart from that it may be asked, "What useful purpose does it serve?" As the struggle proper does not commence until both the competitors are on all fours on the ground, it is useless in a hand to hand encounter, where fair play is insisted upon. To have to throw an opponent down, and afterwards mangle him while in a helpless position, is somewhat inconsistent with the feeling which prevents a man striking an adversary when he is down. The following are the Græco-Roman rules.

(1) The wrestlers are only allowed to take hold from the head, and not lower than the waist.

(2) Tripping and taking hold of legs are strictly forbidden.

(3) The wrestling is with open hands, and the wrestlers are not allowed to strike, scratch, or to clasp hands.

Clasping hands means that the wrestlers shall not clasp one of their hands within the other, nor interlace their fingers, but they are permitted to grasp their own wrists to tighten their hold round their opponent's body or otherwise.

(4) The wrestlers must have their hair cut short, also their finger nails, and they must wrestle either barefooted or with socks.

(5) If one of the wrestlers fall on his knee, shoulder or side, they have to start again.

(6) If the wrestlers roll over each other, the one whose shoulders shall touch the carpet first is deemed the conquered.

(7) To be conquered it is necessary that both shoulders of the fallen shall touch the ground at the same time, so as to be fairly seen by the judges and the public.

The most surprising thing is that tripping should be prohibited. Tripping is the very essence of the art of wrestling; without the chips and other manœuvres peculiar to the science of English wrestling, there remains very little beyond weight and strength to battle with.

Some two or three years ago, when Paul Pons, the gigantic Frenchman, and the equally brawny Memisch of Turkey, met in a real contest, Græco-fashion, on the Canterbury stage, the men both got down on the carpet early in the struggle and sat on the floor for two hours and fifty-five minutes, neither daring to get on his feet, and a draw had to be declared, no fall being recorded. This so-called system, dignified by the high sounding Græco-Roman title, was foisted upon the British public in 1870, when the French giants, Le Boeuf and Dubois, contended with the Cumbrian champions, William Jameson and Richard Wright, at the Agricultural Hall. Both parties scored in their own style, but the Frenchmen eventually won the match through the doubtful issue of a toss up for choice of styles in the concluding bout, the Frenchmen, who won the toss, naturally choosing their own method. The two systems are so dissimilar that the merits of the men were never fairly tested. Yet, though Jameson and Wright failed to hold their own under Gallic rules, it was evident at the time that a little tuition and practice would have enabled the Cumbrians to compete successfully with their rivals. The English and French champions subsequently visited most of the principal wrestling towns in the North, but the game was generally looked on with disfavour except in a few of the leading wrestling resorts in Lancashire, where a style of wrestling nearly akin to the Græco-Roman fashion prevails. This, instead of being the art of standing up against an adversary, is simply the art of getting down in a certain position, so as to avoid being thrown a fair back fall. Tripping is the very backbone of the science of wrestling, and a system that does not teach a man to retain his perpendicular in the face of attack is of very little service, either as an athletic exercise, or as a means of self-defence. Ground wrestling on all fours, which includes throttling, is dog fighting pure and simple, and can only have been invented with the view of bringing an ancient and useful pastime into disrepute. When Greece took a leading position in the promotion of wrestling and other athletic exercise, ground wrestling is scarcely hinted at. In the celebrated contest, for instance, between Ajax and Ulysses, we are told that the champions endeavoured to "keep on their legs," and when Ulysses plied the outside stroke, supplemented by the back heel, and fell on the top of his opponent, the contest was over and the populace satisfied.

Cumberland and Westmorland Rules—On taking hold with the arms round the body, the right arm underneath and the left above, the wrestlers stand chest to chest, each placing his chin on his opponent's shoulder and grasping him round the body, each placing his left arm above the right of his antagonist.

When both men have got hold, and are fairly on their guard, the play commences, and, with the exception of kicking, they are allowed to use every legitimate means of throwing each other.

If either party breaks his hold, that is, loses his grip, though not on the ground, and the other still retains his hold, the one so leaving loose shall be the loser.

If either man touches the ground, with one knee only or any other part of his body, though he may still retain his hold, he shall not be allowed to recover himself, but shall be deemed the loser.

If both fall to the ground, the man who is first down, or falls under the other, shall be the loser, but if they fall side by side, or otherwise, so that the umpires cannot decide which was first on the ground, it shall be what is technically called a "dog-fall," and shall be wrestled over again.

The Cumberland and Westmorland Hold—In securing a grip, the best way is to make of the hands a couple of hooks, by placing all the fingers of one hand into the other hand held in the same way, so that the back of the right hand shall press on an antagonist's back. Laying hold of one wrist with one hand, or clasping hands, are fruitless methods, as the former shortens the arms, and the latter gives an insecure grip which is easily broken. Having obtained a good hold, make play at once while the grip is retained, and always keep the right arm well up in order to prevent an adversary from getting too low a hold.

The back heel—The back heel is without doubt the father of all wrestling chips; in fact, every man, boy and child in the universe naturally resorts to the back heel in the emergency of a hand-to-hand struggle. When a wrestler gets a leg behind his opponent's heel on the outside, it is termed back-heeling. Always back heel with the left leg and as near the ground as possible. Those learning wrestling in the Cumberland and Westmorland style—indeed, in any other style where tripping is recognised—should commence their study of the art by getting proficient in the back heel, which is also a saving measure, for when a wrestler is in danger of being lifted from off his feet or swung round, the insertion of the back heel often brings about the downfall of an antagonist. Again, when a wrestler feels he is being back heeled, he should slacken his hold and lean forward; if he once allows himself to be pushed back, over he must go. Finally, the back heel should not be taken out when once inserted, especially against a long legged man, who is always a dangerous opponent.

The outside stroke (left leg)—This is George Steadman's, the champion of England's, favourite chip. The best way of using it is to twist your antagonist suddenly to the left, at the same time striking him with the left foot against the outside of his right ankle, as near the ground as possible. This, with the assistance of the arms, is generally effective.

The hank—The hank, when manipulated by an expert wrestler, becomes one of the hardest and most dangerous falls of all. It is a very insidious chip, and brought about by turning your left side to your opponent, then click him and lean, or rather fall, backwards; but be mindful that the click is secure, and the result will be that the leverage supplied by the inside click will bring about the downfall of your antagonist. The only way to elude the hank is to lean forward and endeavour to obtain an improved hold. The hank is one of the most uncomfortable falls imaginable, as the wrestlers usually reach the ground glued together like a couple of planks. If the man who falls uppermost is sometimes thoroughly shaken, how, may it be asked, does the underneath individual fare?

The inside click—Face your opponent squarely and jerk him towards you, when he will naturally step forward with one leg. He will try to steady himself by hanging back, which assists the expert inside clicker, who dashes in the chip, adding to it all the weight at his command. To click an opponent's right leg on the inside with your left, or his left with your right, or to use the cross click, that is, to click his right with your right or his left with your left, seems easy on paper, but the manœuvre requires an enormous amount of practice, and few men excel in the movement.

The crossbuttock—The crossbuttock with the left leg is the best. Turn your left side to your antagonist, and rapidly cross both his legs with your left leg, at the same time twist your man forward with all the force at your command.

The buttock—Few know the difference between the crossbuttock and the buttock. In the buttock, which is the finest of all wrestling chips, the legs are not used, and therefore great strength and quickness of action are necessary. It is accomplished by turning the left side quickly round, getting your back under your opponent's stomach and throwing him bodily over. It is an unsafe chip and, although very attractive-looking in exhibition wrestling, is seldom resorted to in genuine contests. Buttocking is little known beyond the confines of Cumberland and Westmorland, as no other style of wrestling is suitable for its display.

The hype—After securing a tight grip, step forward with the left leg, lift your opponent, and carry him to the left about a quarter of a circle, taking care the while that both his feet are free of the ground; at the same time strike the inside of his left leg with your right knee, which, if properly done, will land him plump on his back. This is the right leg hype. The left leg hype is used in the same way, only the left leg is used as the aggressive weapon. It is accounted the utmost folly for a short man to attempt to hype a wrestler much taller than himself. A short man, say of 5 feet 6 inches, cannot lift a 6 feet grenadier high enough from the ground to hype him.

The swinging hype—The swinging hype differs in no great degree from the hype itself, except that it is necessary for the wrestler to swing his man after lifting him, and previous to applying the hype.

The outside click—When you find yourself being lifted, click your antagonist with your left leg, as in the back heel. Light weight men cannot attach too much importance to this chip, as it often happens that the click on the outside is the only defence they can make against superior weight and strength. Click smartly and low down, for in that consists the efficiency of the chip.

The breast stroke—This seems a simple move, but it is difficult to meet, and has baffled some of the best wrestlers in England. There is nothing particularly clever about the manœuvre. The assailant, however, requires great development of chest in order to accomplish it successfully. Grasp your opponent firmly round the body, twist him suddenly to one side and then to the other with a rapid jerk. As the legs are not brought into play, the fallen one often cannot realise by what he has been thrown.

The foregoing are the principal chips used by the best Cumberland and Westmorland wrestlers of the present day. Wrestling, however, can only be learned by continual practice commenced at an early age, as it is very seldom that a man attains any proficiency who commenced to study the exercise when out of his teens.

The Lancashire style (catch as catch can)—The Lancashire fashion is considered by its exponents to be much in front of all other recognised systems. It is certainly the roughest of the three English methods, as unlimited action is allowed, which includes struggling on the ground, catching hold of legs, and other tactics. Throttling and breaking arms are forbidden, but these are sometimes indulged in when the Lancastrian "birse" is up. A man on his hands and knees must not be choked by being pulled upwards by his opponent, but either party may break fingers or arms, so long as the referee is satisfied that such took place solely in the struggle for the mastery, and not through any desire to act unfairly. The Lancashire system is closely allied to the French or Græco-Roman style, the only material difference being that the French method forbids tripping, and catching hold of legs, whereas both are allowed under Lancashire rules. The principal chips associated with catch as catch can wrestling are the double Nelson, the half Nelson, the heave, the Lancashire lock, the flying mare and the three-quarter Nelson. The double Nelson is now barred at most wrestling gatherings, on account of the danger attending its accomplishment. It is brought about by getting behind an antagonist and placing both arms under his; the assailant then clasps his hands behind the neck of his opponent, and bends his head downwards in such a manner that his breast-bone will give way if he does not previously measure his length on the ground. Two shoulders down constitutes a fall.

The hold—Generally speaking, Lancashire wrestlers assume a half-stooping position at the commencement of an encounter, and either seize each other by the wrists or get into head holds, when, after much wriggling, they fall struggling to the ground. Here the real contest begins, the point aimed at being to bring the opponent on to his back with both shoulders at the same time, which constitutes a fair back fall.

The half Nelson and heave—In the **half Nelson**, grasp your opponent by the right wrist with your left hand, place your right hand under his arm while you seize him by the neck, and press his head forwards: then quit his right hand and clasp him round the waist underneath with your left arm and you will easily heave him over on all four points. The **heave** is a useful chip. Place your right arm round your opponent's right shoulder and reach over to his left loin, at the same time slip the left arm under him so as to get hold of his left elbow; a complete somersault is often the result. One way to stop the heave is to cross click your man and then ply the crossbuttock.

The Lancashire lock—The lock is simply that each wrestler grasps the other by the thigh when both struggle to get on all fours, the half Nelson usually then coming into play. If you catch your opponent by the thigh, and get underneath his body before he is down, you can lift him bodily up shoulder high and dash him down with considerable violence if so minded. This is called the Lancashire ham and leg.

The three-quarter Nelson—Probably the three-quarter Nelson is the most useful of Lancashire chips. In the first place, grasp your antagonist round the neck with both hands, without allowing him to get a similar hold, and then you have him in a good position for the buttock or crossbuttock, which no other form of catch hold wrestling supplies. The flying mare will be dealt with under the Cornwall and Devon style.

The Cornwall and Devon style—In the emergency of an unexpected attack, the West Country method, as it is often called, would probably serve a man better than either the Cumberland and Westmorland or Lancashire systems, provided fair play were observed on both sides. The champions hailing from the west wrestle in strong linen loose jackets reaching to the hips and tied by linen strings in front. Catch hold above the waist is the rule or by any portion of the jacket. There are two great drawbacks connected with this style of wrestling. First, the wrestler must be attired in his jacket ere he can display any of his best points, and, second, their definition of a fall, viz., three points down, two shoulders and one hip or two hips and one shoulder, is always productive of endless wrangling amongst the partisans of the contending parties, a circumstance that has probably tended to wipe the practice of this exercise almost out of existence. A man must be thrown flat on his back before any portion of his body touches the earth ere a decision can be given againt him. Kicking, which was a speciality of the Devonians, is now abolished and the two styles amalgamated. The jacket is the great factor in these contests, and some astonishing throws are often brought off when a proper grip has been secured by a powerful and expert wrestler. It is usual to grasp the jacket by the bottom corners, or, by slipping one arm under the garment and seizing the opponent's collar, a telling hold can be obtained. The wrestlers are forbidden to take hold of the two corners of an opponent's jacket for the purpose of strangling him, and they must not grasp by the drawers, handkerchief or belt. The flying mare, the inside lock forward and inside lock backward, which are the best throws in this style of wrestling, may be briefly described. First, however, comes :—

The hold—The best position to assume before taking hold is to stand with the feet a trifle apart and the knees slightly bent, so as to be ready for either attack or defence. Ground wrestling is forbidden, and a man must be thrown very decisively before a verdict can be recorded against him. A cunning wrestler, when he finds himself going down, very adroitly makes for the ground, face downwards, in order that he shall not be landed on his back. Consequently a match in this style often lasts several days.

The flying mare—Seize your opponent's left wrist with your right hand, then quick as thought turn your back upon him, at the same time grasp his left elbow with your left hand and swing him over your back, as in the buttock, with a sudden jerk. The best method of preventing this is, directly your adversary gets in front of you, to click him from behind, at the same time clasping him round the body with your right arm. By this means you may get in the front position, when the half-buttock should come into operation and your antagonist will, as a rule, be thrown on his face.

Scotch Wrestling—A new system has recently been adopted at some of the tournaments held across the Border, which is simply Cumberland and Westmorland and catch hold wrestling combined. The wrestlers commence operations in the North Country style, with the arms round the body, and the hands grasped in the ancient back hold fashion. The tussle which ensues frequently lands one or other of the competitors flat on his back, which ends the contest before the struggling on the ground has a look in. If, however, a fair back fall with two shoulders down does not result, the bout is continued on the ground. Scotsmen, as a rule, do not excel in wrestling, probably from want of practice and the necessary tuition. The only time a Scot ever took the first prize at Carlisle was in 1812, when James Scott of Canonbie, Dumfriesshire, threw all comers.

In Ireland the national style of wrestling is the collar and elbow method. Take hold of an opponent's collar with one hand and his elbow with the other. First point down, as in Cumberland and Westmorland, constitutes a fall. German wrestling is a mixture of Lancashire and Græco-Roman and therefore calls for no comment.

Turkish wrestling is principally carried out in catch as catch can style. No kicking is allowed, and the throw must lay the vanquished man upon his back, so that both shoulder blades touch the ground at the same time.

The Swiss wrestle in stout drawers and shirt, and the champions are girded with a stout belt, for the purpose of affording a good hold, but they are allowed to catch either by the belt, shirt or drawers, or by all at one and the same time. There is no ground wrestling; first man down loses in Switzerland.

WALTER ARMSTRONG.

WRESTLING — INDIAN — The Indian differs *in toto* from the English wrestling. There is more art and less of brute force in it. The experts say that a man has to learn some four hundred tricks or *Penches*, before he can be considered a *Pulwan*, or expert wrestler; and I fear even a clever English wrestler, unacquainted with the Indian mode, would run a great risk of coming off second best in an encounter at first. It is just possible that before he could close with his antagonist, he might find himself on his back. The sport is most popular. Great crowds collect round the arena, in which noted performers of the art—as well known to fame in India as were Sayers, Mace, Heenan and other pugilists in Great Britain and Ireland—are about to try a fall. Whilst the wrestlers are silent, the audience often gets wild with excitement. This is bad enough amongst the solemn Indians, but with the excitable Burmese, the excitement reaches blood heat, and the men and women bet their last rupee on their favourite.

A wrestling match in India strikes a European spectator as being decidedly slow. There is, apparently, too much patient waiting, manœuvring and watching for an adversary's blunder. A Cornish or a Cumberland wrestler would accuse his fellow-athlete of Hindostan of too much and too prolonged inaction. But the initiated appreciate the skill that is being exhibited even when the two opponents are, to all appearance, motionless as the sculptured statues they closely resemble, and he knows that the chances are in favour of many trials of that skill rather than of strength, and many changes of fortune before the contest is ended by one of the combatants being laid on his back so that both shoulders at once touch the ground. There is no calling of time; from the moment the two opponents enter the arena, and until that fair and square back throw, the struggle must proceed without pause.

Often there is considerable delay in getting to that grip which in English wrestling is speedily determined, if—as is the case in some countries—it be not arranged by agreement at the start.

The Indian wrestler has to be wary in his approaches to embrace his opponent, for he knows of *penches*, deftly dealt, jerks of his thumb and elbow by which he may be thrown before he holds his adversary at all, and therefore he indulges in much fencing at a respectful distance, and breaks the silence by slapping his biceps and his thighs with hollowed palms as he stalks round the other, looking for an opening, or hoping to find his opponent off his guard for a second. Nude, save for a scanty cloth round his loins, he is, when not too obese, a graceful object as he creeps lithely and cautiously round the ring.

At last the two get hold of each other, and the struggle commences. Now it looks as if one is about to be thrown, and the spectators expect to see him deposited on the broad of his back. Finding he cannot keep his foothold facing his adversary, he turns a somersault, using the body of his antagonist as a fulcrum; his legs go over the other's shoulders and he alights on the ground firm on his legs behind the other's back, and possibly with an advantage that imperils in his turn the stability of his opponent.

If one finds himself hard pressed and on the point of being thrown upon his back, he anticipates this by throwing himself down with his back uppermost and face downwards, clings to the ground while his opponent sits athwart his loins, and applies all his knowledge and strength with a view to reversing the position of his foe. So they remain awhile, the one in vain exhausting himself, the other husbanding his strength and recovering his wind for a favourable moment. The crowd look on breathlessly, wondering which will win. There is a sudden change, the uppermost man has been incautious, and he who was below and all but vanquished apparently, has thrown aside his opponent, has risen from the ground and, with a dexterous *penche*, has the other stretched beneath him, perhaps with shoulders that touch the ground, and so ends the conflict.

These wrestlers are always in training, and practise with the Indian clubs when not engaged in swallowing *Dahie* (clotted milk) or struggling in the arena itself.

F. T. Pollok.

YACHTING—Yachting in general, and yacht racing in particular, are not, and never can be, popular in the sense and to the degree that horse racing, cricket, football, and many other sports and pastimes are popular. Circumstances do not permit of it. A yacht race is, except perhaps on the Clyde, inaccessible to the multitude. The elements of excitement derived from betting are absent, as are also all the ordinary adjuncts of a holiday outing. Moreover, the rules and science of the game are so technical as to be appreciable only to those more or less initiated. It is a sport in which the people cannot largely participate, and consequently it cannot claim to be national in the sense of being universally popular. But in another sense it is *par excellence* the national sport of the United Kingdom. It is indigenous. It is the outcome of intense love of the sea—the modern expression of those roving characteristics which drove the long-ships of our Scandinavian ancestors from Norwegian Fiords and Icelandic bays along the Western sea-board of Europe, and far up the waters of the Mediterranean Sea. It is the peaceful complement of warlike naval power, the exhibition and satisfaction in a pastime of those qualities which, under sterner circumstances, made us mistress of the seas. And it satisfies the craving for independence so strongly implanted in our race, for in these modern times where can liberty of action be sought so well as upon the boundless ocean, where no notices of trespass can be found, and where every man is free?

And yachting is national in other senses. It started, or at any rate it grew to large dimensions, under the stimulus of laudable and patriotic ambition to increase the efficiency of our naval forces at a time when we were very keenly alive to the fact that national existence depends upon supremacy at sea. That mission is fulfilled; but yachting is still of national importance from a strictly practical and commercial point of view.

According to Lloyd's register, the yachts owned and built in the United Kingdom amounted in 1898 to 898 steam yachts, with a tonnage of 95,015, and to 3,206 sailing yachts, having a tonnage of 60,739, making a total of 4,104 vessels with a tonnage amounting to 155,754. But many yachts are built in this country and owned abroad; and according to the same authority the total number of yachts built in the United Kingdom and now upon the register, amount to 4,603, with a tonnage of 214,533. The total number of yachts in the world is 6,747, with a tonnage of 265,568. The United Kingdom thus owns, roughly speaking, $\frac{3}{5}$, and has constructed $\frac{4}{5}$ of the tonnage of the world. Putting the average cost of steamers, racers, and cruisers at £50 per ton, the capital sunk in our own pleasure fleet, exclusive of vessels built for foreign owners, amounts to no less a sum than £7,787,700, and assuming that two-thirds of the total number are put into commission for the summer months, and that up-keep amounts to £10 per ton, the annual expenditure upon the fleet will be, in round numbers, something over £1,000,000.

To calculate the number of hands engaged either as seamen or in the yards would be a difficult task. The number of seamen employed on a yacht is, of course, not proportionate to tonnage, a small racing yacht requiring many more hands than ordinary cruisers of a much larger size; but estimating the number at the ratio of one hand to every ten tons, it is not too much to say that some ten or eleven thousand of the smartest seamen that this or any other country can produce, depend largely for their living upon our pleasure fleet. Many of the hands working in shipbuilding yards are not exclusively occupied in building or repairing yachts, and it is impossible, therefore, to arrive at an accurate calculation of the total number of men whose livelihood depends on the pastime of yachting. But if yacht designing and building, spar making, sail making, block making, rope making, upholstering, the manufacture of metal frames and plates and sheathing, and the making and fitting of the multifarious objects required in a yacht, be taken into consideration, there can be no doubt that many thousands of families on shore owe their employment to our national love for the sea, and that yachting contributes not a little to the maintenance of a race of seamen upon whose skill and courage the country has relied in the past, and will have to rely again.

To trace yachting from the beginning is a difficult task, but it appears to have originated in a well defined desire to supplement the naval power of the country. Our pleasure fleet being subject to conditions similar to those which have so profoundly affected both our ships of war and our mercantile marine, great changes have taken place in it since the early years of the present century. Steam has almost completely superseded sail as the motive power of large yachts, and, among sailing vessels, the tendency is to multiply in numbers and to diminish in size. As the direction in which a pastime such as yachting develops is dictated by the temper and bent of national feeling, the change from long years of war to long years of peace profoundly modified the character, aims, and objects of yachting. Racing has become of absorbing interest now, whereas formerly yachtsmen devoted themselves almost exclusively to cruising in company and performing evolutions under an admiral or commodore, after the fashion of a fleet of ships of war. Though these formal cruises and manœuvres, and the lavish expenditure of gunpowder in vogue half a century ago, appear somewhat ridiculous to us now, their object was sound and laudable and their meaning is clear enough.

Though occasional matches are mentioned as early as 1661, there can be no doubt that yachting developed into an important pastime under the stimulus of patriotism. Largely for that purpose clubs were formed, pre-eminent among which on account of numbers, wealth, and enterprise was the Royal Yacht Club, now known as the Royal Yacht Squadron. Fleet evolutions, signalling, chasing imaginary foes, and all the incidents of naval war,—to excel in these was the ambition of yachtsmen; moreover, the fact that we were constantly at war, and that privateering was universal, must have tended to encourage armament and cruising in company.

Early in the century our yachts were essentially sea-going cruisers, and the ambition of their owners was to emulate the performances of the smaller frigates, brigs, and despatch vessels of the Navy. The extent to which yachts copied men-of-war may be gathered from a description in *Bell's Life* of August 12th, 1827, of the Duke of Buckingham's yacht. She is described as carrying 12 brass guns, 18- and 12-pounders, and a full complement of seamen and marines, with a chaplain and doctor. This vessel was a brig, and probably of the same class as the 10-gun brigs of the Navy, of which there were such a number in the service. Discipline was kept up on these private vessels with a degree of strictness equal to that maintained in the Navy, and was enforced by similar means. The *Hampshire Telegraph* of August 5th, 1826, gives the following account of the discipline maintained by Lord Yarborough:—"The 'Falcon' yacht, Lord Yarborough," it states, "is manned by 54 choice hands who are governed in every respect as on board a man-of-war. The honest tars were so well convinced of the impossibility of being properly managed without a due sense of the 'cat o' nine tails' that they voluntarily consented to its lawful application on board, and ere the 'Falcon' left Plymouth Sound last week, all hands cordially signed a paper setting forth the usefulness of a sound flogging in cases of extremity and their perfect willingness to undergo the experiment whenever deemed necessary for the preservation of good order." It was no uncommon thing for yachts of this class to obtain leave to join the squadrons of his Majesty's fleet. For instance, we learn from the *Morning Herald* of August 3rd, 1809, that Sir William Curtis, an alderman of London, wrote a pressing request to Mr. Percival for permission to sail with the fleet. Mr. Percival answered that as a friend he did not like to refuse Sir William Curtis, but as Chancellor of the Exchequer he could not write upon the subject to the Admiralty unless the worthy alderman would consent to put his vessel under their orders, which condition Sir William Curtis readily accepted.

Discipline was perhaps harder to maintain among owners than among crews, but goodwill and a hearty desire to co-operate towards making the manœuvres a success seem to have been fairly effective.

That muddles were occasionally made is shown by an account in the *Sporting Magazine* of October, 1831. It is there narrated that the squadron, consisting of 33 sail, weighed for Cherbourg in two lines, Lord Yarborough in the "Falcon" leading the weather, and Lord Belfast with his flag flying on board the "Harlequin" the leeward line. In consequence of the fleet being at Spithead and the wind nearly right through the Needles, they went out by St. Helens. Soon after getting round St. Helens the wind freshened considerably, and a great many of the smaller ships were obliged to shift jibs and reef. About 3 o'clock, the wind still freshening, some yachts with ladies on board made a signal for permission to anchor, and the commodore replied "Anchor when you please and where most convenient." Of course this signal was in reply to those yachts which had asked permission to anchor, but unluckily it was understood by a great many to be a general order, and the consequence was that almost all bore up and ran in under the land, leaving their noble commodore and a few others to face the anticipated gale. The consequence was the dispersion of the squadron, to the great mortification of their commodore, who doubtless would willingly have brought many of the captains to a court martial, had it been in his power to do so.

Lord Yarborough took a leading part in promoting manœuvres, and we learn from the *Hampshire Advertiser and Royal Yacht Club Gazette*, which paper is a mine of information on nautical matters of the day, that his lordship, availing himself of the offer of Mr. Markham to lend his yacht, as a tender to the "Falcon," struck his broad pennant on board his own yacht and hoisted it in Mr. Markham's schooner. He then proceeded with the fleet to sea, where he exercised them in a variety of evolutions.

Though racing among yachts was not neglected, speed was looked at from a naval point of view. Owners sought to demonstrate the advantages of certain improved models and types by building yachts identical with king's ships in all respects of tonnage, armament, crews and stores. They raced them against picked specimens of men-of-war; and naval constructors were glad to avail themselves of the information thus derived.

Men like Lord Yarborough and the Duke of Portland took their yachts to sea with the Royal Fleet, as these two gentlemen did with the "Falcon" and "Pantaloon" in 1831.

The purpose with which these yachts accompanied the fleets was clearly not simply for pleasure, but to demonstrate to the authorities the advances which private enterprise had made in the science of ship-building.

In an interesting article on the utility of yacht clubs in a number of the *Sporting Magazine* of the year 1832, it is explained that naval constructors were so bound by hard and fast rules, and the Merchant Service by tonnage regulation, that the only means the dockyard designers had of getting new ideas was when they happened to catch a fast privateer. "But at length," it adds, "a Society has sprung up, abounding in resources, enjoying more than princely wealth, independent of power, unshackled by the mercenary views of interest, and marshalling in its lists half the rank and talent in the country. Its aim was to associate pleasure with profit, and to establish on a patriotic basis a national and splendid festival worthy of the brightest age of England, but there was another and more direct object to which it tended—the improvement of the art of construction. The Naval administration foresaw this consequence and were not backward in promoting the welfare of the Society, which it is unnecessary to say was the Royal Yacht Club. How bright has been the result! Every year has brought additional improvements, and every day has pointed out some new field of experiments, and even while I write the Navy has acknowledged its inability to compete with one of the newest models." On July 13th and 17th, as we learn from the same source, an interesting match took place, by order of the Admiralty, in the presence of Sir Thomas Foley, the commander-in-chief at Portsmouth, between the "Emerald," the fastest cutter in the Navy, and the "Paddy from Cork," the property of Mr. James C. Beamish, a member of the Water Club of Cork Harbour. The "Paddy from Cork" beat the "Emerald" on every point of sailing, in running, reaching and beating to windward, in smooth water and in a sea way. She was so far superior to the naval cutter that it was deemed useless to prolong the contest to a third day.

That the Admiralty recognised the value of the service rendered by private owners is shown by the fact that in 1832 Mr. Fincham, Superintendent of the School of Naval Architecture in the dockyard of Portsmouth, measured up the following yachts:—Lord Yarborough's "Falcon," Mr. Thorold's "Coquette," Lord Anglesey's "Pearl," and Lord Grantham's "Nautilus"; and reports that "from having the elements of a variety of vessels, and their ascertained sailing qualities, conclusions may be drawn which will greatly conduce to the improvement and adjustment of vessels. The excellency of many of the vessels belonging to the Royal Yacht Club, and the improvements which are frequently made in the construction of new vessels added to the list, render the operations of this distinguished club highly interesting and important."

"The advantages to be derived from yacht sailing to the general improvement of naval architecture, are principally in the forms, as particularly adapted to fast sailing, which under the favourable circumstances the yachts are placed in by not having those weights which men-of-war necessarily have on board, they are so well calculated to promote."

"When vessels of this description are found to possess superior qualities by ascertaining the principles, it may be determined whether they may be, or may not be, adapted to ships of war, either directly or by some modification."

The most remarkable instance of a direct private experiment in naval architecture, for public purposes, is to be found in the case of the "Water Witch," built by Lord Belfast in 1833. Lord Belfast, taking the given length of the most despised class of vessels in his Majesty's Navy, the 10-gun brigs, commonly known as "bathing machines," declared that he could construct a brig that would outsail any vessel in the Royal Navy, and be superior to any vessel of her class for purposes of war. To work his lordship went and produced the celebrated "Water Witch," built for him by Joseph White, of East Cowes. Every possible attention was paid to constructing and perfecting her exactly as a man-of-war brig. She was built with the same heavy scantling; and with all her proper complement of guns and crew, stores, provisions, water and other weights on board, she started under Captain George Pechell and joined the experimental squadron at sea.

The task she had before her was formidable, as the fleet contained four new ships built on the most approved principles.

The trials were brought off near Cork, and we learn that the "Water Witch" beat the whole squadron in a way hardly to be credited.

In a trial of 6½ hours in a fine breeze she weathered on "Castor" ½ mile, on "Prince of Wales" 2½ miles, and on "Donegal" and "Nimrod" 3¾. We learn also that she beat "Vernon," "Snake," "Pantaloon," and "Serpent" on other occasions.

Sir P. Malcolm, who commanded the squadron, reported of her that she was perfect of her class, carrying her guns higher out of the water than the "Trinculo," 18-gun brig, with complete storage for crew, stores, water and provisions. *Bell's Life* attributes her success to her finer entry.

Thus it will be seen that the object and ambition of yacht owners was to set an example to the Royal Navy in construction, and to vie with it in the skill and seamanship necessary to manœuvre fleets of sailing ships in company. But as the memory of war became less and less distinct, the character of yachting gradually changed, and manœuvring and formal cruising died out by degrees. The last occasion on which the R.Y.S. executed any nautical manœuvre was in 1887 when, on the occasion of her Majesty's Jubilee, they sailed past Osborne in two columns, steam and sail, finishing up with a signal from the commodore—"Steam full speed ahead."

As steam gradually superseded sail in the Navy, it became more and more difficult for private owners to render much assistance to the Board of Admiralty, and it is practically impossible for them to do so now.

No private gentlemen are possessed of wealth sufficient to enable them to experiment in line-of-battle ships, or ships of the cruiser type, while the discomforts of life on board torpedo boats and "destroyers" are such as to deter any sane man from building one for his own use.

Occasionally a vessel, built for private owners, has been utilised for some special warlike purpose, such as, for instance, the "Candace," now "Fire Queen," built by Messrs. Ramage and Fergusson for the late Mr. John Lysaght, which is now serving in her Majesty's Navy as a despatch boat, and the "Giralda," designed and built by the Fairfield Shipbuilding and Engineering Company for Mr. McCalmont, which has recently passed into the service of Spain. From the designs of Mr. G. L. Watson have come the "Mayflower," built by the Clyde Bank Engineering Company for the late Mr. Goelet, and the "Hermione," built by Messrs. Fleming and Fergusson, both of which vessels have been added to the navy of the United States. But, in spite of these few examples to the contrary, it is to the last degree improbable that yachtsmen will in the future be able to render that practical assistance to the Navy that they certainly did in the past. Fortunately, however, their services are no longer necessary. The advantage of great speed in the numerous mail steamships of our mercantile marine stimulates private firms and companies to carry out experiments in naval architecture and marine engineering analogous to those which in the early days of the century were mainly conducted by yacht owners. Naval constructors can, and it is to be hoped do, study the results of private enterprise exhibited in the wonderful ships turned out from building yards on the Tyne, the Clyde, the Thames and Belfast Lough.

The origin and development of yacht clubs is so intimately connected with the origin and development of yachting that no review of that pastime would be complete without some notice of the clubs.

As the pastime of pleasure sailing became popular, and as men joined in cruising in company, in performing combined evolutions, and occasionally in racing, some organisation among them became necessary. Yachting created clubs, and clubs encouraged yachting.

Owing to the dearth of records, it seems impossible to do more than guess at the earlier or regattas were passed, formed the germ of a society which gradually developed into a club.

The most ancient club of which we have any authentic record is the Water Club of Cork Harbour. The origin of this club is lost in obscurity, but in the year 1720 it was established on a permanent basis, and its regulations were set down in writing, forming quaint and curious regulations which throw an amusing light on the manners and customs of our forefathers.

These rules are, like so much of the statute law of England, only declaratory of a common law, which existed long previously. This is

FLEET OF WATER CLUB IN CORK HARBOUR—MANŒUVRING.
(*From a painting in the possession of the Cork Yacht Club.*)

events which led to the formation of clubs. A few of those now in existence can claim lineal descent from ancient institutions, but the greater portion of the numerous clubs which now occupy almost every available yachting centre round our coasts, are of comparatively modern date.

Where yachts were gathered together it was inevitable that matches between them should take place, and as these occasional private matches developed into regular open regattas, some sort of organised authority for the regulation of the sport became essential

A short cruise or the performance of combined nautical manœuvres, followed by a dinner, after which resolutions for the regulation of manœuvres

clearly established by the rules themselves, particularly by Rule 3, which runs as follows:—"Resolved that no admiral presume to bring more than two dozen of wine to his treat, for it has always been deemed a breach of the ancient rules and constitutions of the club, except when my Lords the Judges are invited." From this it is quite clear that even in the year 1720 there were "ancient rules and constitutions."

The club appears to have consisted of an admiral, elected annually, twenty-four captains, and a chaplain, added to which there was an official known as the Knight of the Island, the island in question being Haulbowline Island. The objects of the club seem to have been to carry out a formal cruise at every spring tide, from April to September; and to dine together after the cruise, it being a rule of the club that each captain should entertain in succession. The fleet was ordered to rendezvous on club days between Spithead and Spike Island, at a quarter ebb. Any boat not in sight when the admiral was abreast of Spike Island forfeited a "British half-crown" for gunpowder for the fleet. Gunpowder seems to have been in great requisition, and elaborate rules existed as to signalling by guns and saluting the admiral.

Whether the club possessed a club-house of its own at this early date, or whether its meetings were held in some convenient tavern, it is difficult to determine. References are made to the "Castle" at Haulbowline, and it would be very interesting to know what building was referred to, and whether it constituted a club-house. Such would seem to be the case, for it is laid down in the rules that it was the duty of the Knight of the Island, under severe penalties, to see that no unauthorised person entered the club-room, that the secretary had the rules of the club affixed to some proper place in the club-room at Haulbowline Island, and that on club days the flag—consisting of a Union with a green centre charged with the Irish harp in gold—should be hoisted on the Castle at Haulbowline.

The fortnightly cruise must have afforded a gay, and to our ideas a quaint, sight in the beautiful harbour of the Cove of Cork, when the fleet, decorated with huge ensigns and streamers, and manned by petticoated and pig-tailed seamen, worked up to their rendezvous at Spithead, and let go their anchors. The admiral, who had been pacing his deck with as much importance as if he commanded a squadron of ships of the line, gives the word to hoist his foresail half-up, and at the appointed signal the others heave short and get their anchors apeak, all except perhaps one belated ship, which is struggling round the far side of Haulbowline Island. In a moment the admiral's foresail is hauled right up, while the hills reverberate with the sound of his gun, and the fleet weighs anchor. They glide in stately, and probably somewhat slow procession round Spike Island, led by the admiral, who doubtless notes the absentee, and subsequently extracts from him that "British" half-crown provided for in the rules.

Passing through the entrance of the harbour, the admiral proceeds to manœuvre his fleet, to the great gratification of the host of spectators, and after summoning first one captain and then another to receive his directions by a profuse expenditure of gunpowder, he hoists Dutch colours and fires two guns. This is the signal for a general chase after an imaginary enemy, a chase which continues till he hauls down his flag and fires another gun. The fleet re-assembles and once more falls into line in its appointed order. Back again through the Narrows and up to their anchorage they proceed in line, and the captains, having anchored in position and made up everything for the night, foregather at the club room to enjoy the hospitality of the host of the day.

This manœuvring and chasing of an imaginary foe sounds somewhat trivial in our modern ears; but when it is considered that the nation at this period was usually at war, and that yachts of those days bore a very close resemblance to the smaller class of king's ships and might do useful work, the origin and significance of the custom becomes clear. A fleet of steam yachts, analogous to our destroyers, might do worse under similar circumstances than learn to manœuvre together.

Quaint club rules existed apparently for the purpose of checking extravagance in their convivial meetings. It was ordered that no admiral should bring more than two dishes of meat for the entertainment of the club, or more than two dozen of wine to his treat. From 1720 to 1735 no restriction seems to have been put on the amount of wine consumed, and over the events which led to a change in this practice sympathetic history draws a veil. But in 1735 appears a rule that no member shall drink more than one bottle of wine, unless it be a "peremptory." What a "peremptory" was is not explained, but perhaps Rule 14, which says: "*Resolved* that such members of the club or others as shall talk of sailing after dinner be fined a bumper," may throw some light on the subject.

Peremptories were probably not infrequent or unpopular. Every member of the club being peremptorily obliged to drink the bumper inflicted as a fine for talking shop, it is hard to believe that when a number of enthusiastic yachtsmen sat down to dine after cruising all day, that they were not peremptorily obliged to drink a very large number of bumpers, to the inevitable and perhaps not unpremeditated infringements of the one bottle rule.

The club took cognisance also of the dress of its members, and in the rules dated 1720 it is ordered that no long-tail wigs, large sleeves or ruffles be worn by any member at the club.

In 1817 the club settled upon a uniform, and admitted ladies to the privileges of the club. The records of July 9th contain the following resolutions:—

"*Resolved* that the members of the club shall dress in the following uniform: plain blue cloth coat lined with buff, yellow buttons engraved Cork Harbour Water Club, buff waistcoat and breeches."

"*Resolved* that the wives and daughters of the members be also considered members of the club, and entitled to wear the uniform except the breeches."

The Water Club continued upon these lines

until the year 1765, at which time it appears to have almost died out, and from 1765 until 1806 the records concerning it are scanty. The reasons are not far to seek. Great Britain was passing through a troublous period, taxation was heavy, and the pressure of hard times and consequent necessity for retrenchment was felt by people of all classes, and especially in Ireland. Moreover, during the prolonged naval war, the press gang was continuously at work, and as the crews of yachts were not exempt from service, a yacht owner was liable to find himself stripped of his best men at any moment.

Under these circumstances it is not strange that yachting should have languished for a time.

After the victory at Trafalgar had relieved the strain on our naval forces, and at the same time had increased the national enthusiasm for all things nautical, we find a great impulse given to the formation of yacht clubs, and in 1806 the Cork Water Club was revived, mainly owing to the energetic action of the Marquis of Thomond, Lord Kinsale and Mr. Smith Barry.

About 1821 the club appears again to have fallen into decay, but continued to exist under the name of the Little Monkstown Club. This lasted for a few years, till in 1828 the remaining members of the Cork Water Club and the Little Monkstown Club amalgamated under the title of the "Cork Yacht Club," and took over the property of the old Cork Water Club, among which are the very curious club records alluded to, and a set of very valuable paintings, which now adorn the walls of the club, and which are exceedingly instructive as showing the type of yacht prevalent at that time.

In 1831 the club received a Royal Warrant entitling it to call itself Royal, and it now numbers 284 ordinary members, 315 honorary members, and 52 yachts sail under its flag.

Next to the Cork Water Club the Royal Thames Club can boast of the longest history. It dates from 1775, when the pleasure yachts on the Thames joined together and called themselves the "Duke of Cumberland's Fleet." The commencement does not appear to have been of a very glorious nature, as their races, which were sailed from London Bridge to Putney and back, were held in connection with the fêtes at Vauxhall and for prizes given by the proprietors of the gardens.

With the exception of a few years, the Cumberland Fleet held races regularly from 1775 until the coronation of George IV. in 1821, when the fleet was renamed "His Majesty's Coronation Sailing Society." Apparently the change was not altogether a success, as the result of a protest in connection with a race held in July of the same year was that eight of the captains called a meeting and formed "The Thames Yacht Club." They started with forty members, which included most of the old members of the Cumberland Fleet, and they attained such importance as quite to overshadow his Majesty's Coronation Sailing Society, which dwindled away and was finally dissolved in 1831.

In 1827 the Duke of Clarence joined the Thames Yacht Club, and on his accession to the throne in 1830 granted it the title of Royal. The first below-bridge match was sailed in 1823, and the last above-bridge match in 1840. The Royal Thames is one of the most successful clubs in existence, and numbers 827 members, with 355 yachts.

Next in point of age to the Royal Thames is a small Irish club called the "Loch Erne" Yacht Club, which still exists, with its headquarters at Belturbet.

The Solent, with an area of about 80 square miles, including Southampton Water, forms the most perfect stretch of water for yachting purposes in these islands, and yachtsmen were not slow in availing themselves of its natural advantages.

At the beginning of the century it was the custom for large numbers of the fashionable world to assemble at Cowes for a period of some weeks, many of them arriving in their own yachts. The fact of so many yachts being gathered together led inevitably to racing, and accordingly we find that in 1804 fifteen yachts competed on the 18th August for certain prizes given by Mr. George Henry Rose. The *Hampshire Courier* for the year 1810 gives lists of "fashionables" arriving at Cowes from July 16th until the end of October, and frequent mention is made of yacht races taking place off Cowes.

The first indication of a dinner, that invariable precursor of a club, is on September 18th, 1813, when it is recorded that after a match for pilot boats, at which a number of yachts were present, a select party of gentlemen dined together at the Marine Hotel at West Cowes.

On September 2nd, 1814, yacht races, which are referred to as the annual regatta, took place and were followed by a dinner at Aldred's Hotel, East Cowes, and in 1815 the *Hampshire Telegraph* alludes to "many members of the Yacht Club," thus showing that the gentlemen who had been in the habit of arranging the regatta and dining together afterwards, had practically banded themselves into some sort of club.

The Yacht Club was formally constituted at a meeting held on June 1st, 1815, at the Thatched House in St. James's Street, London. The chair was taken by Lord Grantham, and it was resolved that the club be called "The Yacht Club." The actual phraseology of the minutes is worth noticing, as showing that in this case, as in the case of the Water Club of Cork, an organisation in the nature of a club had previously existed, for we find it in the minutes that "At a meeting of the members of the Yacht

A Gale of Wind.

Club it was resolved," and again "That the following are regarded members of the Club," and here followed forty-two names, these being no doubt the names of the gentlemen who had been in the habit of attending the annual dinners at Cowes.

It was at the same meeting settled that the qualification for membership of the club should be the ownership of a vessel not under ten tons, that ten members should ballot for the election of any new member, and that two black balls should exclude; that the entrance fee should be two guineas, to pay for two copies of the signal book, and that the flag of the club should be white, with a union in the corner.

On August 24th, the first annual meeting of the Yacht Club was held at Cowes to elect members and transact other business. It was at the same meeting decided that yachts should fly a plain white burgee, and that officers of the navy should be eligible as honorary members. The first of such honorary members elected was Sir Thomas Hardy.

The club seems to have prospered, for on September 15th, 1817, the Prince Regent expressed his wish to join, and in 1818 the Dukes of Clarence and Gloucester also became members. It was about this time that the club became much exercised as to the pattern of their uniform buttons, a controversy which raged at intervals for many years.

In 1820 the King was graciously pleased to give the club permission to use the term "Royal." The club was henceforward called the "Royal Yacht Club," and in June, 1821, its colours were changed to a red ensign and a plain red burgee.

It was agreed in 1822 that the members should meet on the first and third Monday in each month at Cowes, for a cruise under the commodore. Long and elaborate sailing regulations are set forth, some of which profess to be made for the comfort of ladies, who, it is interesting to note, were by this time participating in the sport.

In 1824 the club appears to have been rising in importance. It obtained considerable assistance from Government in negotiating with foreign countries for the remission of various port and tonnage dues, and the first step towards a club-house was taken in securing a coffee room in the Marine Hotel.

On August 22nd of the same year, seventeen yachts of the Royal Yacht Club, under Commodore Lord Yarborough, sailed for Cherbourg on the annual cruise. They encountered a thick fog which necessitated their anchoring off Lymington for the night, but though the fog lasted during the following day, they got under weigh, and when at last the fog lifted, found themselves within two miles of Cherbourg. The commodore hoisted the signal to anchor as convenient, and sent ashore a list of the yachts to the French Admiral, with the information that it was the squadron of the Royal Yacht Club on pleasure bent, and asking leave to salute. Leave was granted, whereupon the ships saluted with seventeen guns, to which the admiral replied. After three days of high festivity in the French port, the squadron sailed for Guernsey, and thence home.

The leading position of the Royal Yacht Club at this time is indicated by the fact that in 1825 the Plymouth Regatta Committee appealed to the Yacht Club to decide a protest of Mr. Wills's "Arrow" against Mr. Godfrey Webster's "Scorpion."

In this year, on September 13th, the general meeting of the club was held at the new club-house, West Cowes.

In 1826 qualification for membership was raised to the possession of yachts of 30 tons.

In 1829 the Admiralty granted to the Yacht Club the right to wear the St. George's ensign, and as a consequence a white burgee with a red cross and a yellow crown in the centre, as worn at present, was adopted.

In 1833 the King expressed his desire that the club should henceforth be known as "The Royal Yacht Squadron" of which his Majesty was graciously pleased to consider himself the head, at the same time presenting a cup, value 100 guineas, to be sailed for annually. On her accession to the throne, her present Majesty was pleased to become a patroness of the Squadron, and to present a cup for competition at the annual regatta.

Other Queen's cups are, by her Majesty's good pleasure, handed over, for competition annually, to the various principal yacht clubs in turn.

The Squadron was, at this date, using a house on the Marine Parade at Cowes, now known as the Gloucester Hotel, as their club-house, and continued to do so until 1857, when their lease expired. Cowes Castle becoming vacant about the same time, by the death of the Marquis of Anglesey, who had occupied it as Governor of the Isle of Wight, the Commissioners of Woods and Forests granted a lease of it to the Squadron.

In 1865 the Prince of Wales was elected a member, and in 1882, on the death of Lord Wilton, was appointed commodore, an office which he has held from that time to the present day.

The subject of classification of yachts for racing purposes has been before the Squadron on many occasions. The first attempt was made in 1829, when yachts were divided into five classes as follows:—Yachts above 140 tons constituted the first class, and started scratch Those between 140 and 100 formed the second class, and received a start of half a mile. The third class consisted of vessels between 100 and 75, receiving a mile and a quarter; the fourth class of those between 75 and 55, receiving two miles and a quarter, the fifth class of those between 55 and 40, and receiving four miles; while vessels under 40 received seven miles, all calculations being made for a forty mile course.

In 1867 the Royal Yacht Squadron resolved "that it is desirable that a general Sailing Committee be appointed to consist of members of the different Yacht Clubs, with power to draw up general rules of yacht racing, and to act as a Court of Reference," and from this resolution the present Yacht Racing Association may be said to spring.

In 1824 the Royal Northern Yacht Club was established, with two branches under separate management, one in Scotland, on the Clyde, and one in Ireland, on Belfast Loch; but this plan was not found to answer well, and each division was constituted a separate club. The Irish club dissolved in 1838.

Belfast Lough, however, was not destined to remain without a yacht club, and the Royal Ulster Yacht Club, which was started in 1866, is now a very flourishing institution. The Marquis of Dufferin and Ava is the commodore, and commands a fleet of 110 ships, with an aggregate tonnage of 6,020 tons.

The Royal Western of England Yacht Club was (under the name of the "Port of Plymouth Royal Clarence Regatta Club") started at Plymouth in 1827, but in 1833 its title was altered to that of "The Royal Western Yacht Club." H.R.H. the Duke of Sussex, was patron, and H.R.H. the Duchess of Kent patroness, while eight Devonshire worthies were appointed presidents, of whom one, Sir Thomas Dyke Acland, of Killerton Park, died in this year (1898). In 1835 there were 43 yachts on the register. The number of yachts now belonging to the club is something over 100, and its membership is very large.

The Royal London was founded in 1838, under the title of "The Arundel Yacht Club," but changed its name in 1845, in which year it was granted by the Corporation of the City of London the right to use the City arms on its flag.

It is peculiar in possessing two club-houses, one in London, the other in Cowes. It numbers 700 members, with 265 yachts.

The races held by this club were originally sailed above London Bridge, but, after a time, a course from Erith round the Nore and back was substituted.

The Royal London was the first club to institute flying starts instead of starts from an anchor, a principle which has since been universally adopted.

The Royal Clyde is the largest club in the kingdom, and, I think, in the world. The number of members is 1,036, owning 322 yachts, of 15,468 tons. It was founded in 1856, and received the prefix "Royal" in 1871.

The Royal Harwich is one of the most important clubs on the eastern coast. In 1870 the commodore, Mr. Ashbury, raced his schooner "Cambria," against the American Schooner "Dauntless" across the Atlantic, beating the "Dauntless" by two hours. The club numbers about 350 members, with over 200 yachts.

Corinthian Yacht clubs are numerous about our coasts. Their principal function is the encouragement of amateur seamanship, and they have taken a very active part in promoting sport.

In the early days of Corinthian clubs, of which the Orwell Corinthian Yacht Club, established in 1830, was the first, it was the rule that the whole crew should consist of amateurs. This rule has been greatly relaxed, mainly owing to the increasing size of ships, which has made the employment of a certain number of paid hands advisable, if not essential. The number of hands to be so employed is, however, still regulated by the rules of each particular club, and no paid hand under any circumstances is allowed to touch the helm. Corinthian clubs are much to be commended. Every owner of a small or moderate-sized yacht should aspire to steer and sail her himself, for in that lies the great delight of yacht racing. Where it is a rule of the club that amateurs are to steer, crews cannot grumble, which they may be inclined to do if the owner steers against professionals, for in yacht racing, as in all other arts, amateurs that come quite up to professionals are few in number; yet owners should always steer in all races, and if a man with a natural aptitude begins young, and works his way up from the small classes to, say, 40-raters, few, if any, professionals will be able to give him points.

The Royal Corinthian Club hails from Erith, on the Thames, where it has a very comfortable club-house, and a yard for laying up small vessels. There are 324 yachts on the club's list.

One of the oldest and most successful of Corinthian clubs is the Mudhook, which has its headquarters at Hunter's Quay on the Clyde. Its membership is limited to 40, "and ane forbye," and 27 yachts constitute its fleet.

The Portsmouth Corinthian was started in 1880, and at its fourth meeting made the rule "that no person shall be considered an amateur who has been at any time engaged in the navigation or sailing of a yacht for pay." But this definition has subsequently been altered to the following:—"An amateur is a gentleman who has never received pay for sailing in a fore and aft vessel, officers of the Royal Navy and Mercantile Marine excepted," and this definition is now universally accepted.

In 1880 the race, held by the Portsmouth Corinthian for service boats of her Majesty's ships stationed at Portsmouth, was remarkable from the fact that the "Wren" was steered to victory by Miss Foley, the daughter of the admiral commanding. Her good example has been largely followed, and many ladies owning yachts in the small classes now steer their own boats.

The Clyde Corinthian Club, at Hunter's Quay, was started in 1846. Like the Portsmouth Corinthian, it admits ladies to its membership, and the club rolls now show over thirty ladies, many of whom own their own vessels.

The Royal Plymouth Corinthian was founded in 1877, and numbers 260 members, with over 100 yachts.

Kingstown Harbour is the headquarters of the Royal Irish, Royal St. George, and Royal Alfred: the last is a Corinthian club. It was founded in 1857, and has been very active during the whole of its career. It started originally as a model yacht club, and has gradually developed. In 1864 the club took the name of the Prince Alfred Yacht Club, and in 1866, when the Duke of Edinburgh became its patron, and presented a cup to be sailed for, the club changed its name to The Royal Alfred. It was in this year also that the annual matches from Kingstown to Holyhead were established.

The club has no club-house, and one of its rules is, that all money received shall be devoted to the Prize Fund and Racing Expenses, the result being that for a minimum subscription a maximum amount of sport is provided.

The Minima Yacht Club was originally formed in 1889, and its chief station is at Hamble, on Southampton Water. Branches of the club have been established at Dartmouth, Southend, Surbiton, Sandersfoot, and Weymouth. As its name implies, it devotes itself to promoting racing among the smallest classes of yachts, and it is rapidly acquiring great popularity. The total number of members now attached to the club is 560, a very large portion of whom race their own ships.

The Castle, with its diminutive club-house on Calshot Spitt, has the advantage of possessing the best site in the United Kingdom. It holds races about once a week during the season for the small classes, but gives prizes for vessels up to and including twenty rating at its annual regatta.

Distinct in character from all the clubs hitherto mentioned are the Ocean Yacht Squadron and the Cruising Club. The former is international, but members fly a distinctive burgee, consisting of a red cross on a white ground charged with a blue wavy stripe and a golden crown and anchor.

It consists of thirteen members owning yachts, but the tonnage is, as might be expected, relatively very large.

The Cruising Club is, as its name implies, devoted principally to the encouragement of cruising in foreign parts and in home waters. It aims at the dissemination of local knowledge, and to its list of membership a valuable index is appended, specifying the waters, whether lake or river, sea or ocean, known to individual members. Mr. Arthur Underhill, Q.C., is commodore, and the club numbers 180 members, owning 105 yachts and 60 boats.

It is, of course, impossible to allude to all the yacht and boat sailing clubs established about our coasts, or even to mention the names of the most flourishing among them. A few have been selected, not on account of their importance, but as being typical and exemplifying the various stages of development and various uses to which yacht clubs are put. On the shores of the Solent alone sixteen yacht and boat sailing clubs are located, and races are held on nearly every week-day from early in May till the close of September. The yacht clubs and sailing clubs of the United Kingdom number altogether 120, to 43 of which the prefix "Royal" has been accorded.

Owing to causes already mentioned, yachting has long ceased to be of practical value as auxiliary to the Navy, and has become more and more a pastime or sport; but even in modern times it is rather difficult to confine it within the limits of sport, pure and simple, for many voyages have been, and probably will be, undertaken in the cause of science, adventure, exploration, and travel. Eliminating these functions of yachting, and looking at the matter as a pastime or sport, it divides itself naturally into two great branches, racing and cruising. I will take them in the order not necessarily of merit, but of convenience, and will treat of racing first.

The first yacht race of which any mention can be found was sailed on the Thames on October 1st, 1661, between Charles II. and his brother the Duke of York. The match was for 100 guineas, and the course was from Greenwich to Gravesend and back. The king won.

The next recorded instance consists of a race which took place in the Bristol Channel under the auspices of the Bristol Sailing Society—a society concerning the origin, history, and fate of which I can find no information. The race is thus described in the *Sporting Magazine* of July 21st, 1796:—

"This morning the following boats took their station in King Road, to contend for the premiums given by the Bristol Sailing Society, viz., 'Severn,' 'Despatch,' 'Antelope,' 'Dolphin,' 'Experiment,' 'Hope,' 'Frolic,' 'Fancy,' 'Industry,' and 'Chausen,' a Dutch boat.

"About eight o'clock they started, but the wind blew so strong from the westward all day, and the swell was so great, that only four boats out of the ten could keep the sea; the rest were obliged to run into different places for security. The other four sailed round the Holmes. The 'Antelope' was the first boat that returned; about two minutes after her the 'Dolphin' came in, the 'Hope' third, and the 'Experiment' fourth, when the first received their respective prize cups, and the latter a telescope. No accident happened the whole day of any consequence, notwithstanding the high wind and rough sea they had to encounter in a race of fifty miles, allowing for traverse sailing."

Of course, vessels have raced from time immemorial, and will always do so. To get there first is, commercially, of great advantage, and wherever vessels sail together, emulation in the matter of speed is certain to arise. But of racing pure and simple, premeditated racing, without any ulterior purposes of gain, the above mentioned matches in the Bristol Channel and the Thames are the first instances on record.

For a long period racing consisted of matches between vessels used for ordinary cruising purposes, and it was not until comparatively modern times that racing developed into a distinct branch of yachting, and that vessels were designed primarily and principally for the purpose of racing. Racing is conducted subject to certain rules of the road and rules of measurement, which will be alluded to later on. Up to 1875 these rules and regulations existed in a somewhat chaotic condition, and were not reduced to uniformity and to accuracy of definition until the creation of the Yacht Racing Association in that year. The object of rating, or measurement rules, is to define for racing purposes the size and capacity of yachts, and to bring them as far as possible into distinct and homogeneous classes.

Obviously the interest of racing is enormously enhanced if all the competitors start on even terms, and consequently if the vessel first across the line wins; but it has been found impossible to insist upon absolute uniformity in rating, especially among big vessels. The cost of building and racing vessels like "Britannia" or "Satanita" is very large. Vessels of that description will always be few in number, and the men who can afford to build them will not be —and cannot be expected to be—tied down to particular classes; they suit their own convenience and their own ideas as to size; and in such cases yachts are brought together—or, to be accurate, an attempt is made to bring them together—by a time allowance, something in the nature of weight for age in horse racing—so many seconds a mile per ton being allowed to them. But in the case of smaller yachts, the object of clubs and of the Yacht Racing Association has been, and always ought to be, to confine vessels as far as possible to distinct classes, in which all the competitors are of one and the same

YACHTS OF THE CORK WATER CLUB.
From a painting by Peter Monamy (1749).

rating. Rating rules endeavour to provide for the development of the most speedy type of vessel, subject to certain conditions affecting safety, seaworthiness, and comfort. The object of the rule is to restrict the designer: the object of the designer is to get the better of the rule.

Various rating rules have been in force in the United Kingdom, and types have evolved according to the different formulæ from time to time adopted. There are four principles upon one or more of which any and every rating rule must be founded. First, tax motive power,—that is sail, and leave the designer a perfectly free hand in respect of displacement, that is to say weight, and of form. Secondly, tax displacement, and put no restrictions upon form or motive power. Thirdly, tax dimensions, and leave displacement and motive power alone. Fourthly, tax both dimensions and motive power. The last principle has been adopted with various modifications, since the introduction of the Length and Sail Area Rule.

The first two propositions possess the merit of simplicity. To tax sail area alone as the measure of size for racing purposes, and to ordain that vessels carrying a certain number of square feet of canvas should be classed as of so many tons, would be an easy and simple method of classification, and it would seem at first sight as though in the course of time the most perfect type of hull must by such a rule be evolved. Designers being restricted in a certain class to a given number of square feet of sail area, would gradually discover the form of body which would be most easily moved by the power derived by the wind acting upon that area of canvas; and very likely such a result would be arrived at through the operation of the law of the survival of the fittest. But evolution would be attended by considerable loss of life, quite incompatible with ordinary ideas of legitimate sport. Displacement and natural stability, that is, stability deduced from breadth, would be reduced and reduced, until vessels became dangerously over-canvassed and over-sparred.

The tendency of such a rule would be to reduce displacement, strength and stability to a minimum. Of course other considerations would act as a check. Racing yachts from 20 tons upwards have to voyage round our stormy coasts from the Thames to the Clyde, from the Clyde to Ireland, back to the Solent, and down the west coast to Falmouth, in the routine of a regatta season; they must be capable of making passages in any ordinary weather, and sometimes in very extraordinary weather, and they must have sufficient stability to stand up to their canvas under average conditions of wind. But the check would be insufficient: men become very reckless in racing. It is an historical fact that the Largs Club on the Clyde made it a rule that the hands sailing in their class of open lug sail boats should wear cork jackets, as capsizes were not infrequent. But they had to discontinue the rule, as it was found that the men filled their jackets with shot instead of cork, in order that by sitting up to windward, and acting as shifting ballast, they might give their boats an advantage when sailing on a wind.

It would not do, therefore, to rely upon the self-preservative instincts to prevent vessels from being built unduly weak, or becoming dangerously over-canvassed and over-sparred. The converse rule of taxing displacement, or taxing displacement and dimensions, and leaving motive power that is, sail area—free, would obviously produce precisely similar effects, and for similar reasons it is objectionable. Hence it follows that framers of rating rules have been driven to adopt the last alternative, and to tax both dimensions and sail. Naval scientists have never been able to propound a definite and satisfactory rule as to the true basis for measurement of tonnage, or rating of yachts in competitive sailing. The various formulæ from time to time employed are purely empirical. They are not, and probably cannot be, based on any simple principle, but are of the nature of a compromise, consisting of the taxation of motive power, and of one or more of the principal dimensions; and they have been altered and modified from time to time to meet the various objectionable characteristics in the type of vessel produced under them.

How far they have been successful is a matter for argument, but one thing is quite certain, they are all exceedingly imperfect, and it still remains for some genius to hit upon an ideal rating rule.

Without going deeply into the mysteries of yacht designing it is evident that the gradual pressure brought to bear by designers upon the weak points of the rules of measurement in their efforts to reach perfection in speed has been the primary cause of the principal changes in the construction and form of racing craft during the past twenty years. As the weak points in the several methods of measuring "tonnage" or "rating" are detected or supposed to be detected by the critics, an inevitable cry for some change in the rating rule follows, and the alteration, when made, has invariably brought about a considerable change in the form of the racing yacht.

But it must not be supposed that the change has always been for the better, or that the desire for change was evinced by yacht owners and practical men.

During the present century the measurement rules have undergone fundamental alteration, and new rules have come into force, in the years 1854, 1881, 1887, and 1896. Prior to the year 1854 several methods were adopted for finding the tonnage The original system of measurement was to multiply length, breadth and depth of hold and divide the result by 96—the figure 96 being chosen because it produced a result approximate to the tons burthen the vessel could carry. 94 was subsequently substituted for 96. This method, which was used for ascertaining (for purposes of assessment) the registered tonnage of all British vessels, was subsequently altered to the present system of assessment upon the actual cubic contents of the vessel. Lloyd's, while recognising registered tonnage for calculating the weight of outfit necessary for yachts built under their survey, determined the scantling by a numeral ascertained by adding together breadth, depth, and girth, and multiplying the sum by length. As regards yachts, the first change consisted of the introduction of what is known as builder's measurement, in the place of the before mentioned rule. Builder's measurement, or as it is sometimes called old measurement, is usually signified by the symbols (BM) or (OM) and is found as follows: (length $- \frac{3}{5}$ breadth) × breadth × $\frac{1}{2}$ breadth divided by 94 = tonnage. This method is still used by builders in finding the tonnage of yachts.

In the year 1854 "Thames" measurement with the following formula (length − breadth) × breadth × $\frac{1}{2}$ breadth divided by 94 = tonnage was introduced. The length was measured from the fore part of the stem to the after part of the stern post in a straight line along the deck.

In taking measurements for scantling the committee of Lloyd's Register make a proviso as to yachts of peculiar construction, so that they may vary the points from which the measurements are taken to meet the necessity of the case in such vessels. This gives the committee a free hand to keep to the true meaning of the law and demand scantlings proportionate to the size of the vessel classed, whatever her shape or style, and for this reason the "tonnage cheater" before the vigilant eye of Lloyd's Register is reduced to a nonentity.

"CORSAIR," "METEOR," "AILSA," "ISOLDE," "SATANITA."

The measurement of yachts for racing, however, is the branch of the subject which has more interest for the majority of yachtsmen of the present day, and this leads us to look to the era of Builder's and Thames measurements and to find why these methods eventually came to be deserted.

The true value of sail area as a natural factor in the measurement of yachts for racing was not realised by the experts until a later date, but apart from this point, in which all rules that did not tax the "driving power" were equally weak, the Thames measurement was considered unsatisfactory, inasmuch as it encouraged the development of yachts of too small beam in proportion to their length.

For many years during which the rule had been in force this tendency was slow in its development because designers had not learned to adopt the use of outside ballast, and consequently had to rely upon beam for stability. Prior to the year 1870, no yacht had been built with more than ten per cent of her ballast on the keel. In 1871 "Peg Woffington," of eight tons, carried all her ballast in the shape of an iron keel. During the next few years experiments were made in the smaller yachts with outside lead ballast, which proved so successful that lead keels bolted on outside were fitted to larger craft, and the advantage of decreasing breadth and making good the loss of stability, without increasing displacement, by lowering the centre of gravity was proved.

The method of measuring the length between stem and stern post was also found to be unsatisfactory, as it produced long immersed counters; and one of the first moves of the Yacht Racing Association, which had been founded in 1875, and had adopted the "Thames" rule as its code of measurement, was to alter the mode of finding length in favour of the present method of measurement, namely on the load water line. This alteration was made in 1879, and two years later, in 1881, the formula for finding the tonnage was altered to

$$\frac{(\text{Length} \times \text{Breadth})^2 \times \text{Breadth}}{1730}$$

This rule, known as the 1730 rule, which was in force until the year 1886, saw the sport at its height amongst the classes of 40 tons and upwards, of 20 tons, 10 tons, 5 tons, and 3 tons; but curiously enough, its effect was exactly the reverse of the intention of its authors. It was meant to increase the proportion of beam to length; it succeeded in decreasing it. In each successive year yachts in all classes became longer, narrower and deeper, and in the classes below ten tons the "plank-on-edge" craze was at its worst.

Yachts of composite construction became general under this rule, the increasing weight of lead keel that year by year the craft were called upon to carry popularising the use of steel frames and the heavy internal T iron keels or foundation plates.

However, the doom of the narrow type was effectually sealed for large and small yachts alike in 1886, when the Yacht Racing Association went in to the matter of the measurement rule, and in an exhaustive report, arrived at after consultation with many eminent yacht designers, decided that the tonnage rule, which had been in force since 1881, was unsatisfactory, and recommended another.

The change was a new departure, and consisted in linking hull and sails together by the following formula

$$\frac{\text{Length} \times \text{Sail area in square feet}}{6000}$$

The idea was by no means a new one, having been under consideration in this country in 1880, and adopted by the Americans in 1882. In fact, it may be said that British yachtsmen proved to have been six years behind the times in adopting their own formula. Be that as it may, the Yacht Racing Association set to work and revised the "Classes" as follows:—

The new 60 rating and above in place of 40-tonners and above.
,, 40-raters for 20-tonners.
,, 20-raters for 10-tonners.
,, 10-raters for 5-tonners.
,, 5-raters for 3-tonners.

And after some discussion a sixth class was admitted for $2\frac{1}{2}$ raters.

In 1887 this style of measurement came into force, and continued law until 1895.

It is evident from the records of yacht racing, that from the date of the framing of the length and sail area rule the pastime in all its branches attained a popularity far beyond the expectations of its most ardent supporters, and as far as can be gathered from records and correspondence, yacht owners, after six years' experience of this code of measurement, were for the most part satisfied with the type of craft which the rule had developed.

Nevertheless, builders and designers, supported by the inevitable crowd of "theorists," whose pockets were literally bulging with rating rules of every conceivable kind and character, the accumulation of a six years' peace, were ready to declare war against the length and sail area code of measurement.

Their chief argument against the rule was that it tended, especially in the classes of 40 rating and under, to the production of vessels with small under water body, and poor internal accommodation unfit for any purpose but racing. No immediate action was taken until August 1894, when the subject was brought before the Council of the Yacht Racing Association at Ryde.

After nine months' consideration, a conference of the Yacht Racing Association Council and certain experts and designers brought forth the present rule, and recommended that the formula be altered to

$$\frac{\text{Length} \times \cdot 75 \text{ Girth} \times \cdot 5 \sqrt{\text{Sail area}}}{2} = \text{Linear rating.}$$

and that the new rating lengths be arranged as follows, to correspond with the former class ratings:—

Linear Rating.	Old Rating.
18 feet.	$\frac{1}{2}$ rating.
24 ,,	1 ,,
30 ,,	$2\frac{1}{2}$,,
36 ,,	5 ,,
42 ,,	10 ,,
52 ,,	20 ,,
65 ,,	40 ,,

The rule was finally passed by the members

of the Yacht Racing Association in July 1895, and came into force in the season of 1896, with a subsequent provision that no change should be made for another three years.

It will be seen at a glance that the principal point in which linear rating formula differs from the preceding rule is in the introduction of a girth measurement. This measurement is taken round the skin of the vessel from water line to water line, technically round the vertical cross section, at a distance 0·6 from the point where the stem cuts the water. If the draught forward of this point, not including the girth of a bulb, if any, exceeds the draught at this station, twice any such excess is to be added to the girth.

Centre-boards or plates, whether fitted with bulbs, or ballasted, or otherwise, are measured as fixed keels.

It was feared by some that the practical difficulties in the way of measuring girth would tend to make the sport unpopular, but such does not appear to be the case, for practically no decrease either in the number of yachts built or of matches sailed has taken place. The advisability of adopting a different code of measurement for large and small classes was considered but was wisely abandoned, in the hope that at some future time an international rule might be adopted for yacht measurement, under which yachts of any country might compete in any waters without serious disadvantage.

The Council of the Yacht Racing Association have expressed themselves as thoroughly satisfied with the working of the present rule.

It is difficult to see why, unless it be on the ground that the rule has made very little change in the form of racing yachts.

Certainly the type promises to remain much the same as that adopted in the later stages of the length and sail area rule, which may be regarded as the most successful method yet formulated for ascertaining the rating of racing yachts.

All matters relating to rules for determining rating, to measurement and the granting of certificates, to the rules of the road to be observed during races, and to many other details connected with racing, are under the control of a body styled the Yacht Racing Association.

This association was formed in the year 1875 by Count—now Prince—Batthyany, the Marquis of Exeter, Sir George Leach, and Mr. Dixon Kemp, and originally consisted of the owners of racing yachts of and above 10 tons measurement, and "such other gentlemen as the committee might elect." The functions of the Association have been the framing and forming the various rules of measurement of tonnage and rating, the arrangement of the sailing rules of yacht racing and the settlement of such protests and questions of dispute as may be referred to them by sailing committees by desire of the parties interested or otherwise. The rules of the Association, however, provide that the decisions of sailing committees shall be final unless they think fit to bring the matters under discussion before the Council for their decision. At the present time the Yacht Racing Association, under the Presidency of the Prince of Wales, and Vice-Presidency of the Earl of Dunraven and Sir George Leach, consists of a Council of 24, and about 150 members, almost entirely composed of yacht owners and members of the leading Yacht Clubs, and 28 Club delegates.

The Association decrees that a Certificate of Measurement of Rating shall be held by every yacht starting in a match, which certificate states in detail the various measurements of hull and sail area necessary to determine the rating of the vessel. These measurements are taken by the Association's own official measurers at all the principal yachting centres. Mixed races between vessels of different rigs are discouraged by the Yacht Racing Association, which aims at dividing yachts as far as is possible into separate and distinct classes according to the rating.

Provision is made in the rules that racing craft shall use no shifting ballast of any kind; that every yacht if exceeding 60 feet rating and not exceeding 80 feet shall carry, when racing, a boat not less than 10 feet in length by 3 feet 6 inches beam, and, if exceeding 80 feet rating, a boat of not less than 12 feet in length by 3 feet 6 inches beam, with oars lashed and ready for immediate use; and that all yachts exceeding 42 feet rating shall be fitted below deck with the ordinary fittings of a yacht, including two transverse bulk heads of wood. The greater part of the work of the Yacht Racing Association Council consists in hearing and adjudicating upon protests referred to them by sailing committees, which is nearly always done in the not improbable case that the decision of the committee is considered unsatisfactory by one of the parties interested.

The position that the Yacht Racing Association holds in yacht racing is to some extent similar to that which the Jockey Club occupies in respect to the turf, but most unfortunately its powers are not so complete. Its relation, for instance, to the increasing number of local classes, and "one design" classes both in the Solent, Clyde, Irish waters, and round the coast generally, is at present somewhat ambiguous, and it exercises but little effective control over the eccentricities of ignorant or foolhardy sea jockeys.

It may be interesting to consider the creation of a racing yacht, under, for instance, the present rule.

A person of sporting instincts and seafaring proclivities determines to build a racing yacht of a certain class or rating, and consults a designer.

The first question to be decided is what is to be the strong point of the proposed ship, is she to be a fine weather boat, a hard weather boat, or an all-round boat? If designed to sail exceedingly fast in light breezes, she certainly will not excel in strong breezes; if sailing fast in hard winds is to be her principal merit, she cannot be expected to obtain phenomenal speed in light airs; if intended to be equally good in all weathers, super-excellence will be sacrificed to general utility. Unfortunately neither intuition nor meteorological science are very reliable guides in forecasting weather, and a man building a light weather boat may find himself very much out of it during a windy summer, while a stormy petrel may bitterly bewail the prevalence of light winds during an unusually fine season. But, as a matter of fact, the difficulty of choice is generally solved by a desire to beat some particular yacht. Some crack among the forties or twenties may have kept pride of place for two or three seasons, and the ambition of the prospective owner will be to beat that particular vessel, and ambition will therefore dictate instructions to the designer.

"VALKYRIE."

Yacht designing is a most maddening, complicated, and beautiful art. A successful racing vessel consists of a bundle of compromises, most perfectly balanced, and adjusted into a symmetrical and harmonious whole; and without going deeply into the subject, some account of the conflicting principles which the perplexed designer has to reconcile is necessary in order to understand the nature of his art.

Those principles in hydrostatics which show that a body floating in water displaces a volume of water exactly equal in weight to the weight of the body, and adapts itself as regards depth and line of flotation according to its peculiarities of form and the situation of its centre of gravity, have become so generally understood as to render any detailed reference to them unnecessary. They form, however, the foundation upon which a designer has to work. With probably a wealth of experience, and numerous actual examples in the shape of previous successful productions to fall back upon, it is not necessary that a designer should begin to scheme out the elements of any new creation purely on the lines of abstract science. Nevertheless, in yacht designing, more than in any other branch of marine architecture, careful regard to scientific principles, tempered by practical experience, is essential. That science alone cannot be relied upon is proved by the tentative methods adopted, and the slow degrees whereby approximate perfection is arrived at, under any new rating rule. A wise designer, therefore, will—especially if restricted by a rating formula of which he has not had much experience—proceed on scientific principles, but also on the system of "trial and error." Whatever plan or combination of plans be adopted, the essential properties and characteristics of the proposed vessel have to be schemed out mentally, and tentatively figured down, before the graphic process of giving actual form to the vessel is proceeded with.

A short, but for the purpose sufficiently accurate, statement of some of the principles affecting a floating body will help to the better understanding of the nature of the problems which the yacht designer has to solve.

A vessel, floating upright and at rest in still water, will fulfil two conditions: first, as already stated, she will displace a weight of water equal to her own weight: and secondly, her centre of gravity will lie in one and the same vertical line with the centre of gravity of the volume of water displaced, or, as it is called, with the centre of buoyancy. The whole weight of the vessel may be supposed to be concentrated at her centre of gravity, and to act vertically downwards, and the resultant pressure of the surrounding water may in the same way be said to act vertically upwards through the centre of buoyancy.

When a ship is inclined from the upright position through any cause extraneous to herself, for instance, through the pressure of wind on the sails, the downward and upward forces of weight and buoyancy respectively act through their respective centres in two separate but parallel vertical lines, and form what is technically known as a "couple." The horizontal distance between the vertical lines varies with the inclination, and is called the "arm" of the couple. This arm measures the leverage with which the weight and the buoyancy of the vessel tend either to force her back into an upright position or to incline her to a still greater angle.. The former effect is the result of what is known as a "righting" couple; the latter, as an "upsetting" couple.

From a consideration of these facts it will be seen that the centre of gravity in every properly-designed vessel must be in such a position as to be below the point of intersection of a line passing through the centre of buoyancy, as shifted out when the ship is inclined, and the vertical plane of the ship, which point of intersection is called the meta-centre. The combined effect of both forces in this case is to rotate the vessel upwards towards the upright position; in other words, they form a righting couple.

In the opposite case, where the centre of gravity—either initially through top-heaviness, or as the result of a shifting of weight on board —falls to the other side of the vertical line, acting upwards through the centre of buoyancy when the vessel is inclined, the effect is to rotate the vessel in the direction of her inclination, and eventually to capsize her: that is to say, the forces form an upsetting couple.

When neither of these results positively follows, but the inclination from the upright is simply maintained, as in the case of a yacht under wind propulsion, the force of gravity, plus that due to wind pressure, is balanced by the force of buoyancy, and the stability of the vessel may be considered satisfactory.

The curve of stability of a vessel consists of a curve traced along the extremities of the lengths of the righting and upsetting arms at stated angles of inclination, set off from a base line, the former being set off above and the latter below the line. Or sometimes, and perhaps more conveniently, the curve set off, instead of being a curve of "arms," represents a curve of "moments," that is to say of the lengths of the arms multiplied into the displacement.

The centre of buoyancy is determined with almost absolute accuracy from the displacement caluclation, into which, in an article of this nature, it is unnecessary to go.

The centre of gravity can be found by calculation, after the size, scantling, and position of the various materials forming the vessels have been ascertained and fixed, by first finding the position of the centre of gravity of each of the component parts, and from this deducting the common centre of gravity of the whole vessel, including spars, rig, and equipment. As, however, this process cannot be entered upon, except very roughly, until the form, scantling, and position of all the various parts have been fixed, and as the calculation is in any case laborious and liable to error, it is usual to arrive at the position of the centre of gravity, approximately, from data derived from calculations of similar vessels previously built, or from results obtained, purely experimentally, by inclining existing vessels to various angles.

Another term essentially concerned with stability, is the "meta-centre," mentioned above. The meta-centre is the point where the new line of upward support, when the vessel is inclined at a small angle, intersects the original line when she was upright. The point can be determined from the displacement calculations.

"Meta-centric" height, that is, the distance or interval between the meta-centre and the centre of gravity, is an important measure of the stability of vessels, and in all cases where the type is not much out of the common, meta-centric stability is the only measure which it is necessary to take into account. The value that meta-centric height should possess varies with the type of vessel, but only to a small extent, unless the types vary very largely. In six yachts whose stability was carefully investigated by Mr. Dixon-Kemp, the meta-centric height ranged from 3 feet in "Kriemhilda," and 3 feet 6 inches in "Miranda" to 4 feet in the "Rose of Devon." In the case, however, of very broad shallow-bodied yachts, the corresponding heights may be as much as 8 or 10 feet.

For preliminary purposes, a fair approximation may be made of the volume of displacement appertaining to a suitable form of hull of given dimensions by assessing it as a percentage of the capacity given by the products of the three principal dimensions. This percentage is known as the "block co efficient." Or an approximation may be arrived at by assessing the relation between the volume of displacement and that of a prism, having for its base the immersed mid-ship cross section of the vessel, and for its length her proposed length on the load-water-line. This percentage is called the "prismatic co-efficient."

By either of these means a fairly accurate estimate can be obtained of the displacement which will be the product of any proposed dimensions, and conversely from this result a more definite determination can be made as to what the precise dimensions should be.

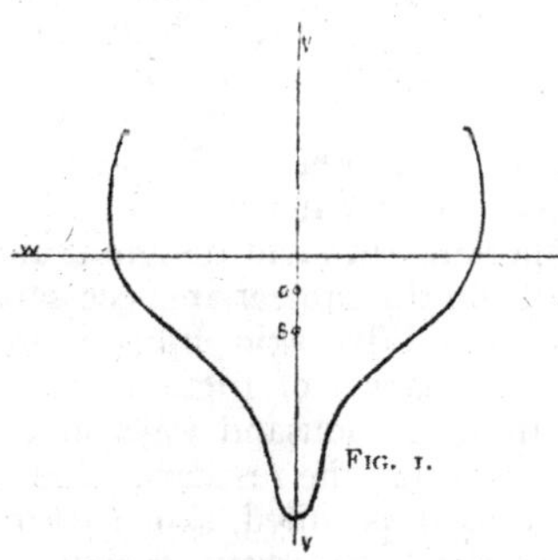

Fig. 1 represents a vessel upright, with her centre of gravity in a normal position. G is the centre of gravity, B the centre of buoyancy. WL the water-line. VV the vertical line passing through the centre of gravity.

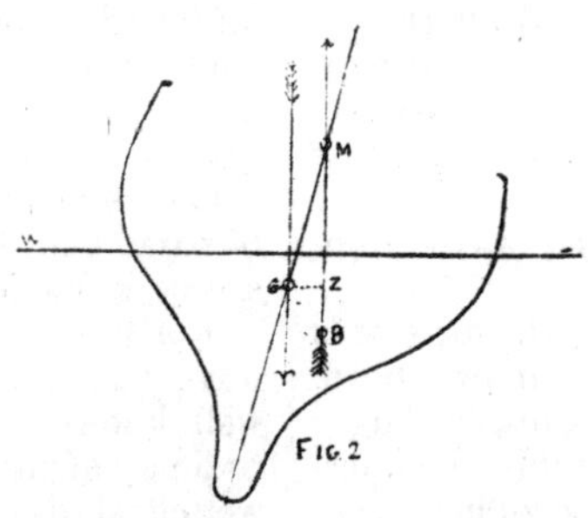

Fig. 2 represents a vessel inclined, the centre of gravity being properly placed at G. B is the centre of buoyancy shifted out by the inclination of the vessel. M is the meta-centre. GZ is the couple, and it is a righting couple, as the force of buoyancy acting perpendicularly upwards through Z rotates the vessel towards an upright position.

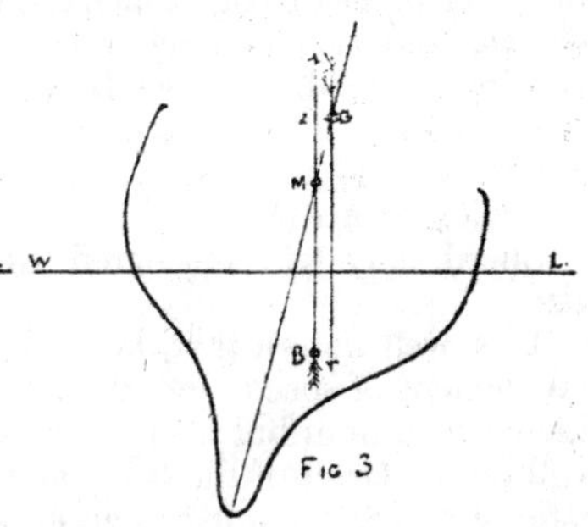

Fig. 3 represents a vessel inclined, whose centre of gravity is improperly placed in reference to the centre of buoyancy. In this case the arm, ZG, forms an upsetting couple, as the force of buoyancy, acting perpendicularly upwards through Z, tends to capsize the vessel.

The conventional centre of effort, that is, the centre of the effect of the propulsive power of the wind upon the sails, must also be considered. This is arrived at by simple triangulation applied first to each of the sails, and from those various centres of effort the centre of effort for the whole of the sails can be deduced. The true effective centre of effort and also the effective amount of lateral resistance, differ no doubt considerably from results theoretically derived; but by means of these preliminary calculations a designer gets a rough but fairly accurate idea as to the dimensions, displacement, stability, and sail area possible under the rating formula to which he is confined.

A designer in selecting an example need not confine himself to a vessel of the same size as that which he is shaping out in his brain. A basis of comparison has been established between the actual ship and her model, and equally therefore between big and little ships of the same shape. This measure, which is known as "Froude's Law of Comparisons," may be roughly stated to consist in this, that the equivalent speed of a ship and of its small scale duplicate or model, are proportional as the square roots of their lengths: for instance, if a vessel 100 feet long is represented by a model 4 feet long, the speed of the ship would be five times the speed of the model, and at these equivalent speeds all the phenomena which the ship would exhibit in the water would be fairly represented by the phenomena observed in the case of the model. Though this law requires special qualifications, for various obvious reasons, in respect of sailing vessels, yet it is no doubt fairly accurate, and Mr. G. L. Watson has put it on record that relying on this law, and judging from his experience in small boats, he carried out the design of his first large racing vessel, the "Vanduara," with confidence and with success.

Acting within the constitutional limits of these general laws, the object of a designer is to obtain the greatest possible speed out of a vessel of a given size; in other words, his problem is to find the maximum motive power, that is to say, the greatest sail-carrying capacity, relatively to resistance. This sounds fairly simple. But "size" is, in a ship, an indefinite and undeterminable quality, and "size," so far as the designer of a racing yacht is concerned, is "rating"—a certain ratio arrived at empirically in reference to certain dimensions, and frequently modified and changed; resistance is of various kinds, and is due principally to wave-making and to skin-friction; sail-carrying power is not a constant quality, but varies directly in reference to wind force; other qualities also besides speed pure and simple must be considered, such as lateral resistance, which mainly determines the weatherly qualities of a yacht; and, moreover, all the above-mentioned factors in determining design are affected by the condition of the element through which the body has to be driven, and vary in magnitude and effects according to whether the sea be rough or smooth. The solution of the apparently simple problem becomes, under these circumstances a most complicated matter.

Speed may be considered first apart from size.

It is well known that, in sailing boats, size is an element of speed, and that, given two boats identical in lines but of different sizes, the larger will be the faster of the two; and this characteristic of "size," regarded as an element in speediness, is not easy to eliminate in any definite way. Thus, in considering two yachts of different design, it may be very difficult to say which is the larger boat of the two, or how much larger she is, or to determine to what extent the extra speed of the faster boat of the pair is due to superiority in design, or to superiority in size. Nevertheless, if too close a definition of statement is not insisted upon, it is possible to study the features of design which make for speed, without introducing the question of size, and it is desirable to do so, because size cannot be considered apart from rules of measurement, and from what may be termed the *artificial* influences which these rules have upon design.

If, for the present, the quality of "closewindedness" which, though of great importance, may be best considered separately, be ignored, the secret of speed in a sailing boat may be said to lie in obtaining the maximum of sail-carrying power relatively to resistance. It may be objected that, in sailing in very light winds, at any rate, the question is one not of sail-carrying power, but of actual sail spread, which is a very different thing. But *ceteris paribus*, in virtue of certain practical reasons which are not far to seek, the actual potential sail spread which it pays to give a boat bears a fairly fixed proportion to sail-carrying power; and, therefore, the propulsive force, whether the wind be light or strong, may be regarded as approximately measured by sail-carrying power, in other words, by "stability." Hence, in judging of the wisdom of any contemplated modification of design such as, for instance, increase of beam, draught, or displacement, the question to be asked, on general principles, is whether the consequent increase in stability is worth the increase in resistance. On the other hand, if the contemplated change were of a nature to decrease resistance, the question would be whether the decrease in resistance outvalued the loss of stability.

The features of design principally conducive to resistance are large wetted surface; unfairness of lines; big displacement. But before entering upon these topics, a few words on resistance are advisable.

To go at length into the laws affecting solids in fluids would far transcend the limits of an article of this kind, and those who require information on that interesting subject must study the exhaustive experiments and conclusions of Mr. Froude, Professor Macquorn Rankine, Mr. Scott Russell, and others. But, as the results of the resistance of water upon vessels is of paramount importance in yacht designing and sailing, a few words on the subject are necessary.

Resistance is caused by skin friction and wave making. The effects of friction are so well known to all in a thousand ways in the ordinary affairs of life, that the resistance due to wetted surface, or, as it is called, skin friction, needs no explanation. But wave making is a factor with which seafaring people alone have any experience, and some explanation of the phenomenon is therefore desirable.

A body, a ship, for instance, travelling through a fluid such as the sea, imparts to the particles of fluid the motion requisite to enable them to get out of the way in front, and to fall into their places again behind. This change from a condition of quiescence to one of motion involves the creation of a system of local excesses and defects of pressure in the fluid, which system moves with the moving body. The surface of the sea being covered by atmosphere exercising uniform pressure, this moving system of excesses and defects of pressure must be satisfied by elevations and depressions resembling waves; and such waves, if really natural, or, as it is called "free" waves, would travel at a speed determined by the length of the waves from crest to crest. But the quasi waves here referred to are not natural waves, but are artificial, being created by the body moving through the water. If the speed of that body is much less than the speed proper to a natural wave of the same length as the artificial wave, the latter will acquire no natural wave life; it will consist merely of an undulation which moves with the body, but which does not spread into the surrounding water, nor throw out any train of waves. Very little power is required to maintain such an undulation; in other words, the undulation produces very little effect in diminishing speed. But if the speed of the body coincides with the speed proper to a natural wave of the length of the artificial wave, the latter will acquire natural wave life and all the properties of a living wave to the fullest extent. It becomes accentuated; it propagates a train of waves extending sideways and backwards, according to the natural properties of waves, and covers more and more water with waves. The resistance which causes the formation of a wave system of this character requires a great expenditure of force to overcome it, or, in other words, the action of such a wave is to greatly diminish speed.

A natural free wave system, originated in the disturbance caused by a ship moving through the water, takes the shape of a series of crests and hollows ranged in a certain plan relatively to the line of progression. This series consists of low but massive transverse or athwart-ship waves, and of echelon, or diverging waves, forming steep ridges. The different component parts of this system are not always all equally well developed, because their development depends upon the degree in which the various parts of the system harmonise with the conformation of the undulations satisfying the pressure. Those parts only which harmonise with the undulations obtain life and become active.

In practice it will be found that at the bow of a vessel sailing at quite a moderate rate of speed, a portion of undulation exists, sufficiently small and steep to fit in with a similar portion of the diverging wave, with the result of giving birth to a lot of little live echelon waves, trailing away from the stem and bow. The resistance to which these waves are due does not consume much power A similar state of things occurs at the stern, where even at moderate speeds a series of little live transverse waves are formed, which require greater power to overcome. But on the whole, these bow and stern wave formations at low and moderate speeds, have not much effect in reducing speed. The real trouble commences when the speed of the vessel through the water is sufficient to lengthen out the distance between the crests of the transverse waves to about the same length as that of the vessel. Then the pressure undulation and the artificial wave system fit exactly, from end to end of the boat, and a strong live natural wave system is produced.

A great and fully formed transverse wave is thrown off from or hangs on to the counter, followed by a series of equally well-developed waves. Wave making is then at its maximum. The resistance causing this form and degree of wave making is enormous; in other words, speed is most seriously interfered with. So great is the resistance that as a matter of fact it may be said to put an end to any further development of speed, for in practice it is found that as soon as a vessel throws out this well-defined complete wave, at about right angles from her counter, she has attained her maximum speed, and no amount of pressure will make her go any faster. The only way to increase her speed would be to reduce the wave making characteristics of her hull. That problem involves very deep and complicated questions, and the most that can be laid down shortly and broadly is, first, that a boat relying on depth for displacement will, length for length, suffer more from wave making than a boat relying on breadth for displacement. For one thing, in a broad shallow vessel the trough of the undulation amidships materially lessens the immersed section of the vessel amidships, and consequently mitigates the pressure disturbance in which the wave originates. Secondly, such a form of entry as will throw the displaced particles of water upwards and outwards, and more especially such a form of run as will permit the displaced particles of water to close in upwards and easily, will delay the formation and mitigate the severity of the fatal counter wave.

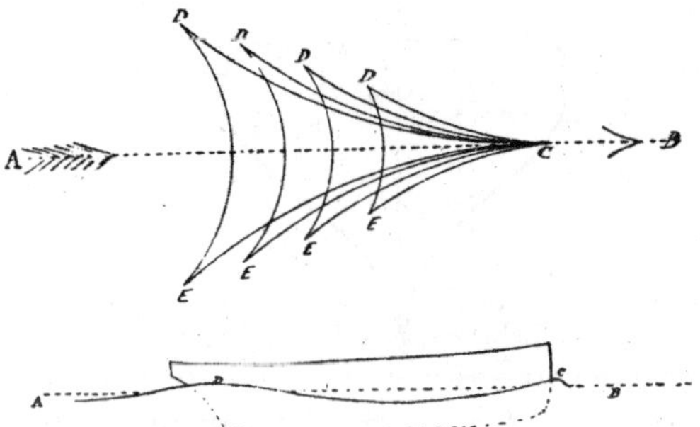

A B is the mean level of the water.
C is the wave thrown up by the bow.
D is the first transverse wave.
If the distance *C D* is the natural distance due to two waves travelling at the same pace as the boat, then these waves become natural waves and give birth to an enormous succession of transverse waves which consume a tremendous amount of energy to overcome or rather create. When this state of things occurs, a vessel may be said to have attained her limit of speed, as any addition to her driving power will be expended in increasing the size of her transverse waves.

Skin friction—that is, the friction of the water upon the immersed surface of the boat, is the most important cause of resistance up to a certain rate of speed proportionate to the size, or rather, principally, to the length dimension of the vessel. After that proportionate rate of speed has been attained, skin friction ceases to operate as the chief form of resistance, and "wave-making" takes its place. Hence, other things being equal, a large bodied boat will be faster in light winds than a vessel designed on a hollow midship section. Midship section A has obviously less wetted surface than midship section B, and a vessel built on A will be faster in light winds and slower in strong winds than a vessel built on B. To lessen skin friction a smooth immersed surface is most desirable. Black varnish applied to perfectly smooth wood makes a good surface; but it has this great disadvantage, that it fouls quickly, and a vessel so coated must be docked or laid ashore and scrubbed every few days. "Valkyrie III" was coated with black varnish. Her opponent "Defender" was built up to the aluminium topsides of a manganese bronze polished to the

A

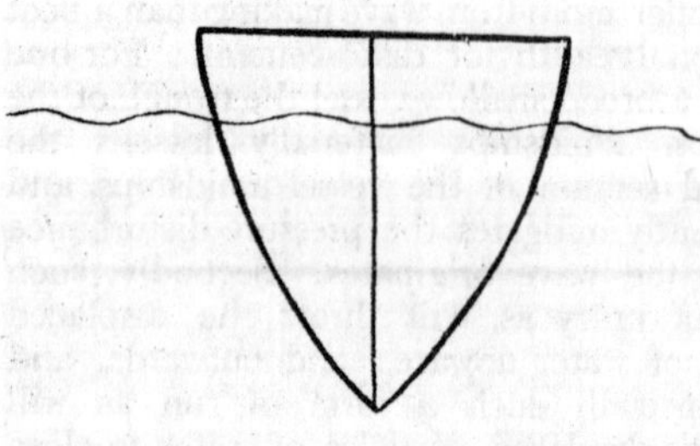

B

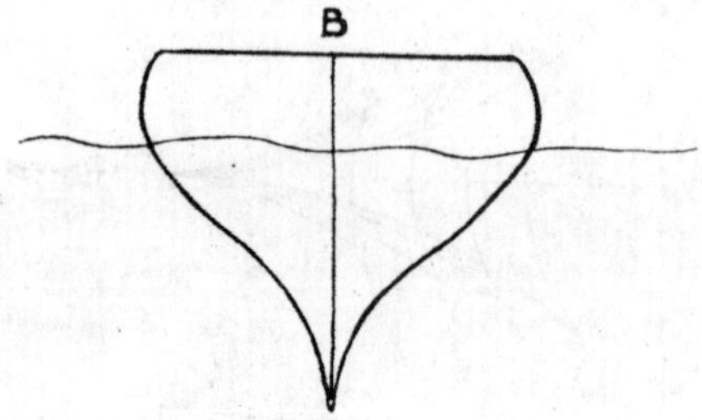

smoothness of a mirror. Cold drawn copper sheathing is the material generally used among us on wooden skinned yachts of any size.

Unfair lines, abrupt curves and thick ends—especially of the after body, are also important features as producing resistance, principally at low rates of speed.

Conformably to the principles already considered, largeness of displacement, especially when associated with small length, is important mainly at high speeds, as for instance when sailing off the wind in a good breeze. It is conducive to resistance in proportion to the degree to which displacement is taken in the form of depth of underwater body, because displacement at a low level specially conduces to the formation of the end to end wave which boats create when hard driven. In fact, boats with very large and deep underwater bodies may be almost said to have a hard and fast limit of speed dependent on their length, beyond which no conceivable power can possibly drive them. This resistance-creating function of displacement is much less marked in its effects if the same displacement is associated with greater beam, and is therefore spread more widely over the surface of the water. So much for design in relation to resistance.

The features of design principally conducive to stability, are—

Breadth of beam; which—with a certain laxity of expression—may be said to measure the width of the base on which the vessel stands. Its efficacy is, of course, largely increased if a heavy crew can be utilized as live, shifting ballast.

Lowness of weight; which measures the leverage with which the weight acts to keep the vessel upright.

Quantity of weight at low level; which measures the amount of weight acting at that leverage.

If these several expedients for obtaining stability be considered in connection with the elements of resistance which they involve, the following points may be noted—

Increase of beam must generally increase wetted surface, and consequently resistance from skin friction, especially at low speed; but the loss through increased resistance is not proportionate to the gain due to increased stability. The limit to the advantage which can be thus gained by increase of beam arises apparently out of the following circumstances. Beyond a certain point, unless the increased beam is accompanied by a considerable increased displacement, and thereby of resistance at high speeds, the stability it gives extends to a very limited angle of heel, and, apart from the risk of an actual capsize, the boat will sail very badly in squally and unsettled weather unless under-canvassed for the average strength of the wind. In rough water increased beam means greater resistance owing to the greater effect of the waves upon a broader boat, and from this cause a boat of large beam and small displacement will probably sail very badly in rough water, especially if the wind be light. These conditions are aggravated by the larger spars necessary to utilise the extra stability given by increased beam. Stability derived entirely from beam, in other words unballasted boats, reached the height of perfection or absurdity—as the case may be considered—in the productions of Mr. Linton Hope, who, with his ½-raters, swept the Thames and Solent. They were wonderfully speedy little crafts in any weather, but they were capsizable, and did capsize; and their existence was perhaps wisely terminated by a decree of the Yacht Racing Association, that no certificate should be granted to boats weighing less than 17 cwt.

Lowering of weight, so far as feasible without altering the external shape of the hull, is, of course, pure gain. Hence, anything that can be done, by good design and workmanship, or by structural contrivances, to reduce top weight, whether of spars or hull, consistently with adequate strength, must tell in favour of speed.

With this object in view, vessels like "Audrey" are built with a double skin of thin planking, the inner planks being laid diagonally, and the outer planks longitudinally, which is, strength for strength, lighter than a single skin of thicker planking; the top sides of the "Defender" were made of aluminium; the booms of big cutters are of built steel tubes instead of solid wood, and the centre cores of topmasts have been bored out. So also structural contrivances may work wonders in the way of increase of speed if, by altering the disposition of the weights, they enable the shape of hull to be so altered as to give increased stability for the same resistance, or lessened resistance for the same stability. All the principal changes which the closing half century has witnessed in the designs of racing yachts are, in the main, traceable to developments of this kind. The first step lay in substituting iron for stone, and then lead for iron ballast; the second, in putting the lead on the keel; the third, in forming the outside lead into an isolated fin, projecting deeply below the hull proper; the fourth, and last, in carrying the lead in a cigar-shaped bulb, at the lower end of a deep metal blade or plate. In some of these steps, and notably the last, owing partly to the difficulty of giving sufficient strength to the plate, the change has been rather in the direction of obtaining the same stability by using less lead at a longer leverage, and so lessening displacement and resistance than in that of obtaining greater stability; but the effect has been equally to obtain greater speed by increasing stability relatively to resistance.

An absolute increase in the quantity of weight carried at a low level, in other words, of ballast, may, to some extent, be effected without increasing displacement by greater compactness of hull, or by any other characteristic tending to diminish structural weight. But otherwise it can be procured only by increasing the total weight of the vessel, and, for smooth water work, larger displacement generally results in a loss of speed, except in light airs and turning to windward. Nevertheless, up to a certain point, in rough water, especially combined with light winds, weight appears actually advantageous even apart from the extra stability it gives. The heavier vessel carries her way better through the seas.

The several foregoing considerations point to the conclusion that the type of cross-section most favourable to success in racing will depend very largely on the nature of the courses sailed over, and of the average conditions of wind and sea prevailing. The prevalence of reaching courses and sailing down wind, of smooth water, and steady moderate breezes, will tend to encourage light weights and dependence largely on natural stability, that is, stability derived from beam; while rough water and much turning to windward will encourage heavier weights and more artificial stability, that is, stability derived from ballast. For normal average conditions, and barring the effect of measurement rules, the plate and bulb type, in some form, is the most efficient, and seems almost certain to hold its own.

So far attention has been concentrated on considerations influencing the choice of type of cross section, rather than of general proportions or of "lines," properly so called, meaning by "lines" the longitudinal sections of the hull, whether in horizontal, vertical, or diagonal planes.

The lines, in this sense, are governed mainly by desire to fulfil two principal requirements. In the first place a certain degree of sharpness and gentleness of taper of the afterbody is essential in order to allow the displaced water to close in behind, and to avoid the serious resistance that arises from eddy or "drag" behind the vessel. So necessary is a fine afterbody that in boats of very large displacement in relation to length, or, to speak more strictly, of very large ratio of displacement to cube of length, such as the normal cutter yacht of half a century ago, an afterbody fulfilling this requirement absorbed more than half the length of the boat, thus making a bluff entrance a necessity. This seems to be the *rationale* of the "cod's head and mackerel's tail" precept of those days.

Presuming this first requirement to be fulfilled, and presuming also that all sharp corners or abrupt unfairness of surface are avoided, the remaining requirement concerns the shaping, not primarily of the outline of any of the actual lines, whether "water-lines" or other, but of what is known as the "curve of cross section areas," or "curve of displacement."

In order to make the best use of available length in minimising resistance due to wave-making, it is essential that this curve should pretty closely resemble a curve of versed sines or "wave-line"; but the very finely tapered terminations of the curve must be somewhat blunted in order to make the most of the length. This being the real nature of the requirement to be fulfilled, it follows that the precise character to be given to the "water-lines," or horizontal sections, must largely depend on the character of the vertical longitudinal sections, or "sheer profiles," and "buttock lines." Thus, in a vessel with a deep forefoot and straight keel, the surface water-line almost inevitably approximates to the "wave curve," showing considerable hollow, and the fuller and more U-shaped are the bow cross sections, the more pronounced will the hollow be. On the other hand, in boats with no forefoot at all, like modern yachts, a concave water-line, or, indeed, anything except a convex one, would necessarily give too little area of cross section in the forward part of the forebody. The clue, therefore, to the apparently inconsistent changes which have at various periods taken place in the character of the water-line, must be looked for mainly in the developments which have taken place in the profile. These, again, evidently hinge, to a great extent, upon developments in the shape of cross section. Thus the cutting away of the forefoot and all "deadwood" is consistent with and has fostered the fin, or plate and bulb, types of construction, though in recently built boats the feature has doubtless been accentuated by the influence of measurement rules.

The question of proportionate length is the only one in the first rank of importance which has not been touched upon, and this cannot be fully considered apart from the effect of "size" and the influence of measurement rules. But it is worth while noticing, that besides the tax on length, which has hitherto entered into every measurement rule, there are certain natural considerations of importance, which tend to impose an early limit on development in the direction of increased length. Length, besides increasing the area of wetted surface, is a most potent factor in weight of hull. If an imaginary design of given type be taken, and length be increased without increasing displacement, the result must be diminished ballast which, with diminished cross-section dimensions, will give very greatly diminished sail-carrying power; and, with the consequent rapid decrease in the proportion of sail area to wetted surface, the limit of advantage of length, for racing purposes, will be very quickly reached, so long as there is a reasonable proportion of light weather sailing and windward work to be reckoned with. Increase of length may, in fact, be properly regarded rather as an instrument to enable a fuller form of cross-section and relatively heavier displacement to be used without too serious a sacrifice of speed off the wind. In other words, speaking broadly, a certain displacement requires a certain length to enable the available driving force to be utilised with the greatest advantage in propelling a boat off the wind in fresh breezes; if greater length than this is given, the slight further gain obtainable under those conditions of wind and sailing will be too dearly purchased at the cost of greater loss in light winds, and in turning to windward. The allowance of length which a given displacement thus requires will be increased, indeed, by developments in structure and design which tend to increase driving power relatively to resistance, in the manner already considered, and thereby raise the standard of attainable speed. But, apart from development of this kind, there is not likely to be any marked increase in length, except as the necessary concomitant of an increase in displacement.

Beating to windward is the crucial test of excellence in a fore and aft vessel, and the quality of close-windedness as affected by shape must be considered. It does not, indeed, follow that the closest-winded boat will be always the fastest, even to windward; but a certain high degree of close-windedness is certainly essential to first-rate performance to windward.

Close-windedness is of course favoured by high lateral resistance, but, strictly speaking, it depends not so much on lateral resistance simply, as on the ratio of lateral to fore and aft resistance; and it may, therefore, be favoured by decrease of the latter as much as by increase of the former. This is an important point to bear in mind, especially since decrease of fore and aft resistance, if secured without forfeiting sail-carrying power, means increased speed through the water also.

The lateral resistance of a vessel's hull acts as a lee-board and prevents her from being driven sideways or to leeward by the force of the wind.

In boats of the extreme "plank on edge" type, the entire area of the immersed profile must count at something approaching its full value, by way of leeboard. In those of the extreme modern fin, or plate-and-bulb type, on the contrary, almost the entire leeboard duty may be presumed to devolve on the plate or fin and rudder. In craft of an intermediate type, theory can do little to assess the leeboard effectiveness of different positions of the immersed profile.

The requirement of effective lateral resistance, for promoting close-windedness, though one of great importance, does not seem greatly to modify the problem of best design for speed, as already considered, because the depth of keel requisite for good sail-carrying power will generally in itself provide a fairly adequate leeboard. But it is clear that the general tendency of importing leeboard considerations into the problem must be to attach somewhat greater value to depth of keel than considerations of sail-carrying power relatively to resistance would alone warrant.

In theory the lateral resistance of immersed profile ought not to be affected by the shape of sections, and is not, I believe, considered to be affected by the majority of designers; but in practice, according to my experience, the lee-board action due to a given number of square feet of plate and bulb is superior to the leeboard effect of the same number of square feet of immersed surface of an old-fashioned keel boat. But when all is said and done the quality of close-windedness is still mysterious and difficult to trace. The productions of some designers are always more weatherly than those of other designers, and the reason why is impossible to detect. The shape of forward cross-section has much to do with it, as has also the securing of perfect balance of sail plan, and the proper relations of the centres of gravity, lateral resistance and effort. The effect of wind on sails in beating to windward will be dealt with later on, and we may now turn to the consideration of speed as affected by size, and the influence of measurement rules upon design.

Imagine two yachts, the one a precise model of the other in every respect, but on a smaller scale; and suppose that they are both sailing in smooth water, with all sail set, on the same point of sailing, with sails similarly trimmed, and heeling at the same angle. A very simple calculation will then prove that in order for this condition of things to obtain, the wind speed in the case of the smaller yacht must be less than the wind speed in the case of the larger yacht, in the ratio of the square root of their respective linear dimensions. As an example, if the smaller one is one-half the size by linear measurement of the other, the ratio of the wind speeds must be $\frac{1}{\sqrt{2}}$ or 0·707; and under these circumstances, the speed of the smaller yacht through the water will be less than that of the larger, in the same ratio.

Subject to certain minor qualifications, this theoretical proposition furnishes a sound and nearly exhaustive exposition of the principle of the influence of size upon the speed of sailing yachts. It is important to notice this, because it is sometimes urged that the true factor of speed is not size generally, but length simply, because the length measures what is sometimes called the "finality speed," that is the speed at which resistance commences to mount up so fast as to impose a nearly hard and fast limit to attainable speed. But as has been already pointed out, increase of length does not always afford a royal road to increase of speed, because beyond a certain point it involves, *ceteris paribus*, such a sacrifice of sail-carrying power that the critical point of "finality speed" will not be reached at all. In fact it comes to this: that when the best has been done that can be done by selecting the best type and proportions, the most efficient way of getting more speed is by a simple increase of scale, in other words by increase in all dimensions proportionally.

That mere bigness, apart from difference in shape or proportions, is a factor of speed, has of course long been practically understood, and as soon as yacht-racing came to be systematically pursued it was found necessary to adopt some system of classification or allowance for size. There would have been no difficulty about this if the circumstances were such as to constrain all yachts to be built on substantially identical models, since in that case any single easily measured leading dimension would have sufficiently served as a measure of size for penalising purposes. But as plenty of opportunity for variation of shape and proportions existed, such a mode of measurement must necessarily tend to dwarf the particular dimension which is measured, relatively to the others. And in the same way, however elaborate a measurement rule may be made, however many dimensions may be taxed, and however carefully the several taxations may be adjusted, the rule must inevitably influence design, by furnishing the designer with an additional aim, namely that of getting the biggest boat for a given measurement. And thus, side by side with what may be called genuine speed qualities, and in some degree to their detriment, others which can be best described as measurement-cheating qualities will always be found.

On this principle it would be easy to trace the conspicuous developments of design in racing yachts, during modern times, to the changes which have been made from time to time in the measurement rules. Nevertheless it would be a great mistake to attribute them wholly to the direct and immediate effect of these rules. As has been already noticed, the most conspicuous developments in hull design seem directly attributable to the introduction of novel structural contrivances in the matter of ballasting and to the realization by designers of the importance of the resistance due to surface friction; but, on the other hand, it is only reasonable to attribute the structural contrivances to the pressure put upon the designer by the various rating rules. These rules may therefore be regarded as at any rate the indirect and ultimate causes of the several developments of type and form.

The three tonnage rules which were successively in force from the earliest days of systematic racing till 1886, did not, except in the case of a change in method of length measurement, differ very seriously in adjustment of taxation between the two measurements, length and beam, which alone they took into account. Under all of them alike, beam was heavily taxed and the endeavour of the designer was to secure the requisite sail-carrying power with the minimum beam. The developments in mode of ballasting were all in favour of this object, and when the whole of the ballast came to be placed on the keel, yachts attained the phenomenal proportions of six beams to length.

The introduction, in 1887, of the tax on sail area, was nearly equivalent, so far as hull design was concerned, to a tax on sail-carrying power, irrespective of the cross-section dimensions whereby that sail-carrying power was obtained; and the substitution of this for the tax upon beam alone quickly led to transverse expansion and vertical shrinkage of the body of the boat; and this produced the fin type in order to secure economy in wetted surface. At the same time, the desire to lessen length, which was the only hull dimension subject to direct taxation, made economy of displacement a prime necessity; and directly led to the development of the bulb keel as an instrument for obtaining the requisite sail-carrying power from a smaller weight of ballast.

Reference has already been made to the alterations in water-lines which have resulted from developments in ballasting, and to modifications in the character of cross-sections and the concomitant changes in profile. It only remains to notice that the convexity of bow waterline which is a necessary concomitant of cutting away the forefoot and of extreme rake of stem—if indeed an up-to-date racing yacht can be said to have any stem—has probably been accentuated by the desire to make the greatest use of overhang in order to increase the effective length when sailing, as much as possible beyond the length as measured for taxation with the vessel upright and at rest. The shallow character of section favoured by the bulb keel type lends itself especially to this object, and so well has it been accomplished, especially in the smaller classes, that a boat measuring say 25 feet on the load water-line when upright will, when heeling over to a moderate breeze, lengthen out to say 30 feet. The additional immersion at the ends, due to the creation of waves, adds also to this result.

Of the effect of the change of rule made in 1895, it is as yet premature to speak. It may be noticed, however, that, as draught, as indirectly measured by girth, is now taxed as well as beam, in principle the change consists mainly of a partial restoration of taxation of extreme cross-section dimensions which contribute tc sail-carrying power, in place of the mere taxation of the sail-carrying power obtained. The particular mode of measuring the girth, viz., all round the hollow of the section, is of course an additional hit at the bulb keel type, and at hollowness and leanness of section generally. At the same time, the relaxation of the tax on actual total area of sail-spread has already arrested, and to some extent reversed, the undesirable tendency towards the concentration of the whole sail spread into the mainsail.

The results so far are salutary, and the new rule would seem to answer fairly well in vessels of some size. In the small classes it certainly has not deterred building; but it has transformed the five-raters from nice wholesome *boats*, moderately canvased with two or three working sails, into horrid little toy *ships* with topsails and jibtopsails and all the paraphernalia of a "yacht."

Having thus sketched out the principal theories under which a designer works, it will be well briefly to consider the means whereby he proceeds to give tangible effect to the owner's ideas of what he wants, and concrete form to his own conceptions of the best means whereby those ideas can be embodied.

Two broadly distinctive methods of procedure may be followed: first, a small scale model may be shaped out according to rough general outlines, approximately answering to the form of the mid-ship section, principal dimensions, displacement, and rating required; which lines may be modified by the designer as the work of shaping proceeds. From this model, when thoroughly perfected and approved of, the "offsets"—which are necessary to lay off the lines of the vessel full size—may be taken, and drawn in chalk, properly faired, on the floor of the mould loft. This method, though it is still adopted to some extent, may be regarded rather in the light of a relic of former times, when hewing and fashioning to the eye was all-important, and was, on the whole, the most effective agency in the work of designing. But in these modern days, when our insight into the laws governing the movement of solids through water, the effect of wind on sails and the results of the various forces acting upon a vessel under sail is much keener than it was heretofore, geometrical rule and scientific accuracy of calculation count for more than eye, and the preparation of a design has become the product of the drawing office rather than of the model-maker's bench.

Nevertheless, the practice of first pleasing the eye by means of a model, which can be licked into shape with the gouge and the spoke-shave in hand rather than the pencil and the measuring scale, has still some votaries, and it must be admitted that in old times designers, relying upon the eye and practical experience, turned out remarkably fast and successful vessels. The superiority of scientific drafting to eye lies principally in this, that whereas the old-time designers made frequent mistakes, such accidents are very rare now, and a first-class designer can be relied upon to turn out a first-class article.

The second and more approved method is to scheme out and draft the form of the vessel on paper, to the scale of say quarter or half inch per foot, and to construct a half model from this draft, carefully faired.

But the best system of all consists, as is usually the case, in a compromise. Lines of the proposed vessel should be carefully drafted and faired on paper, then a half model should be made in wood, or, as I personally think better, in modelling clay, or wax from those lines. This half model should be worked over and perfected by eye, and finally the lines should be taken from the model, transferred to paper, and again accurately faired.

The lines can be taken off the model by shaping moulds of cardboard or thin wood to fit accurately to the model at stated and equidistant intervals; and by other methods known to designers. From the sections thus taken, the water and other lines can be arrived at, and the whole plan faired—that is, drawn to natural curves by means of thin wooden battens.

Lastly, a wooden model should be made, not so much on account of its conveying to the owner, designer or builder, a more realistic impression of the actual vessel than the plan of lines, but because it is almost indispensable as an aid to the draughtsman in arranging the framework and the plating and planking of the hull structure, and in measuring off the quantities of material to be ordered.

The draft plan exhibits by a series of curves and straight lines, the contour of the vessel's hull on three distinct planes: the "sheer plan," or longitudinal elevation, showing the lines of length from stem to stern, that is to say, the sheer-line, water-lines, line of keel, and the lines of height from keel to gunwale, namely frame stations and stem and stern; the "half breadth" plan, which shows the lines of length and breadth, namely the gunwale or deck margin line and the water-lines from stem to stern; the "body plan," which shows all lines of breadth, such as water-lines, and line of deck, and all lines of height, such as frame stations.

Water-lines, it will be observed, have an important place in all three planes on the draft plan. Upon them and upon the frame stations chiefly devolves the function of exhibiting the hull form. On the half-breadth plan, the water-lines appear much in the same way as, for example, the lines of angle bars forming the deck margin in a large ship present themselves to an observer looking down on the skeleton of the vessel from an elevation. On the body plan, the frame stations appear just as the actual framework of the vessel would, when erected, present itself to any one looking at it end on.

"VALKYRIE."

Other lines appearing on the draft plan, not so essential for exhibiting the hull form as the others, but of the greatest importance as means towards securing accuracy and fairness of the water-lines and frame stations, are buttock and bow-lines, and diagonals. The former represent the intersection with the contour of the hull surface of imaginary vertical planes parallel with the centre plane of the vessel fore and aft. On the half-breadth plan and body plan they appear as straight lines, and on the longitudinal elevation as curved lines. They convey a fair impression both of the after end and counter of the vessel, and of the contour of the forward end and bow. The diagonals represent the intersection with the hull surface of imaginary planes, which are arranged to be as nearly perpendicular to that surface as possible where curvature is greatest; hence they are most valuable checks upon the fairness of the hull, and are perhaps the most important of all lines in designing sailing ships.

From the drawing office delineation of the hull form, thus generally described, and after every means has been taken to secure fairness, off-set measurements are made, and from the sheet containing them the lines are laid off full size on the floor of the loft. In this full size delineation small inaccuracies, unavoidable in minute measurements from the small scale drawing, are eliminated, and, in the process of fairing by means of long wooden battens, a careful designer will find additional scope for the exercise of his skill and taste.

It is on the floor of the loft that some of our best designers impart a finish and character to their conceptions which are barely possible on the small scale draft plan.

From the sections so drawn, life-size on the floor of the loft, wooden moulds are, according to the custom of some designers, accurately cut, and these moulds are subsequently placed in their proper position upon the keelson of the vessel, and along this temporary skeleton long wooden battens are fastened from stem to stern. The designer can then judge by eye of the fairness of his lines. If they bulge out too much in one place, however infinitesimally, the frame mould must be proportionately reduced: if the slightest undue hollow is anywhere perceived, the batten must be wedged out, and the mould altered accordingly.

So far the outline given applies generally to yachts of any type or size, except the very smallest. Further operations are complicated and differentiated according to whether the vessel is to be built of iron, steel, or other metal, or of wood, or is to be composite, that is, composed of steel frames and a wooden skin. The question as to what style of construction shall be adopted will necessarily be determined at a very early stage of the undertaking. Up to a certain size, say, roughly speaking, 40 tons, wood is the lightest and cheapest form of construction. Beyond that size, composite or steel is cheaper and lighter.

Large sailing yachts, vessels of, say, 150 tons or upwards, intended for cruising, are not infrequently constructed of steel, iron, or of some alloy of which those metals form the major constituent; and steam yachts are almost invariably built of those materials. But though steel, some of the bronze alloys, and alloys containing aluminium, have been used for the construction of racing vessels even of the largest size, they are generally built on the composite principle.

Each system has its advantages and disadvantages. Construction in wood is the best for small vessels; but for a large vessel it is not to be recommended, as it takes longer and is more costly, and, moreover, the vessel will weigh heavier than if built on any other system. Steel, metal, or composite is lighter and cheaper for good sized vessels, and both systems possess the additional advantage, that under them considerable space is gained in the interior for cabin accommodation, owing to the small size of iron or steel frames as compared with frames made of wood. In a composite yacht of, say, 300 tons, a gain of possibly one foot in breadth would be due to this feature, while in vessels plated with steel alone, the difference between the steel plate of ¼-inch thickness and a wooden plank of 3 inches, is also available for increasing internal breadth.

The principal disadvantages of steel and metal consist in the rapid variations of temperature due to a metal shell, and to the liability of the latter to become foul and to corrode.

Composite yachts not only possess the advantage of roomier and more comfortable interiors, but the wooden planking can be sheathed with copper, which is the best material that can be used under water as far as fouling and corroding are concerned. In large vessels, which may have to be docked to be cleaned, this is a matter of the greatest importance; in small boats, which can be easily beached, it does not so much matter, and, in point of fact, small racing vessels are never coppered.

To follow out the growth of a vessel from inception to completion in greater detail than this would transcend the limits of a formidable book. Suffice it to add that the vessel is coppered with sheets of cold drawn metal most carefully adjusted, the deck furniture is fixed, cabin fittings, tanks, and all internal fitments are put in, and she is launched into the element in which, let us hope, she is destined to have an honourable career. The mast is stepped and stayed, the other spars are put in their places, all the running gear is rove, sails are bent, and she is ready for a trial trip.

The launch is a moment of some anxiety, not owing to the probability of accident, for that is an occurrence of exceeding rarity, but because as soon as she is in the water and her weights are on board, the accuracy of her designer's calculations is put to the test. Her designed load-water-line length is marked on the stem and on the stern post, and if no error in calculating the weights has been made, she will float exactly as designed. It may be that she will be a little too much down by the head or by the stern; in that event weight must be shifted fore and aft of the centre of gravity. Possibly she will not come down to her marks, and lead ballast may have to be added. Or she may float below her marks, and it becomes necessary to reduce the amount of lead ballast. These are simple operations, but they may involve serious consequences. If the ship floats too high or too low in the water, the designer has obviously miscalculated his weights. His curve of stability must be erroneous, and, to put it shortly, he has made a somewhat serious mistake. But so accurately is everything calculated out, with such marvellous precision is the exact weight of every particle of wood and metal, hemp and cotton estimated, and its effect upon the centres of gravity and stability determined beforehand, that mistakes are excessively rare, and the vessel is generally found to float within some fractions of an inch of her designed marks.

Before proceeding further with a racing vessel's career, sail making must be considered. This is a beautiful art, and well-cut, perfectly fitting sails are as necessary—if not more necessary—to success in racing, as perfection in design, in construction, and in balance of hull.

The materials used in sail-making are flax, cotton, and ramie fibre. Flax is never used for racing sails, though on account of its greater pliability and the comparative ease with which sails made of it can be handled, it forms the best cloth for cruising purposes. But for racing, cotton cloth is far superior, and the best possible canvas is made of long-fibred American sea island cotton; but the expense involved in its use is enormous. The quantity is very limited, and as the fibre is nearly twice as long as that of ordinary cotton, and of a beautiful silky character, it is used largely for lace-making, for which purpose the yarn fetches 21*s.* per pound. The market price of Sea Island cotton is three times as much as that of the best Egyptian. Sail-cloth made of the former costs double as much as that made of the latter, and the cost of a mainsail is about half as much again. As the best Egyptian cotton is scarcely inferior, it is generally employed.

The advantage of cotton over flax consists in this: cotton cloth has a closer texture than flax cloth, and consequently presents a smoother surface to the wind; the wind does not escape through it so easily as through flax cloth, but it does escape more easily off it, and its effort is therefore expended with less friction. The best sail cloth is a beautiful material, and is made chiefly of Egyptian cotton.

Though cotton has been grown in Egypt from time immemorial, it was as an ornamental plant; and it is only during the present century that it has become an important article of export. The value of a long stapled variety from Dongola and Senaar, growing in the garden of Maké Bey in Cairo, was observed by a Frenchman, and being brought under the notice of the Pasha, its cultivation was undertaken with such success that "Maké" cotton became an important production.

Cotton seed was also introduced from Isle de Bourbon and under instructions from Mehemet Ali its cultivation was carried on so energetically, that in 1824—5 the yield amounted to 9,464 tons. The civil war in America, and consequent cotton famine in England, greatly stimulated the cultivation of the plant in Egypt, and in 1892 the production amounted to about 220,000 tons. The cotton is of a superior quality, and best Egyptian fetches nearly double the price of American cotton, with the exception of that known as "Sea Island Cotton." This Sea Island cotton is grown on some small islands off the coast of Florida. It is very long in the fibre, and of unequalled quality, but the supply is small, and the price practically prohibitive.

The cotton yarn is all spun in Manchester, and the cloth woven by the well-known firm of R. Hayward and Co., whose ancestors started the trade 100 years ago. Their business is now managed by Mr. Edward Taylor, whose forefathers made sail cloth at Coker 200 years ago from flax grown in the west of England; hence the name "Coker" sail cloth, which is a trade mark to this day. They continued in the trade from generation to generation until 1878, when the present Mr. Taylor became associated with the firm of Hayward and Co., and under his able superintendence, sail-cloth making has become a fine art.

Ramie fibre is no new discovery. It was known to the Egyptians, and has been found in mummy cases. It is obtained from a tropical or semi-tropical plant, which grows wild in great profusion, and is very easily cultivated.

Although the fibre has many good qualities, it has not up to the present, or at any rate not till quite recently, been able to compare favourably with cotton for various reasons, the chief of which is, that whereas cotton can be put straight from the field on to the spinning machine, ramie fibre has to be separated, or de-gummed, from the bark of the stalk on which it is found. This operation is costly, and until very recently it could not be accomplished without damaging the fibre. The latter difficulty has been overcome by the "Gomess" process, but the former objection of cost still remains in operation.

Another objection to ramie cloth is that, although the fibre is long, and very strong as compared with cotton, and is of a fine silky texture, the small loose fibres work up during the process of weaving, with the consequence that the surface of ramie cloth is more thickly covered with small hairy fibres than is the case with cotton cloth, and it consequently creates more wind friction than the latter material. Ramie fibre is, however, likely to come into use. A composite cloth is now made, composed of cotton warp and ramie weft threads, and inasmuch as the cotton warps cover up the ramie weft, the difficulty of wind friction has been overcome, and a cloth stronger than cotton, equally smooth, and consequently very suitable for the mainsails of big cutters, is the result.

The "Defender," the yacht that defended the American Cup under the challenge of "Valkyrie III.," had a ramie mainsail and topsail, but the mainsail was not used during the race, and has not, I think, ever been seen in public. Report said that the "Defender" Syndicate bought up all the ramie fibre on the British market, took it to Belfast, had it spun into yarn there, and carried it over to the United States, where it was woven into cloth.

"Bona," the Duc d'Abruzzi's cutter, had a ramie mainsail which stood to its work very well, but has this year been fitted with an Egyptian cotton sail; and "Flavia," a 36-feet rater, has all her sails made from ramie cloth. But though these experiments have been made, and have, I believe, given satisfaction, ramie does not appear likely to supersede cotton.

Although a great advance in sail-making has taken place during the last half century, the substitution of steam for sails has naturally stifled the scientific development of the art. Demand is small in the yachting world, and only one firm has given the very difficult subject of cutting sails the attention it deserves. Scientific men have not been encouraged to invest much time upon it, and what is known on the whole subject of the propulsion of boats by means of sails has been slowly and gradually learned by practical experience and by rule of thumb. Tradition says that the Dutch originally instructed the English in the art of fore and aft sail-making when Holland was in her zenith some two centuries ago; with the result that, the English proving apt scholars, the mainsails of the London smacks and coasters, Revenue cutters, and last, but not least, of the large privateers, some of them of 400 tons burden, which scoured the seas during the latter part of the last and the early part of the present century, were fairly cut, and were probably almost as perfect as the loose hand-spun and hand-woven cloth of those days permitted. Early in the present century, machine-spun yarn superseded hand-spun threads, to the great benefit of sail-making, for, although hand-spun yarn is preferable for ropes till this day, such is not the case in respect of yarn for sail cloth.

About thirty years later, weaving machinery was introduced and gradually took the place of the old hand looms, and the make of sail cloth was thereby very much improved. In this, as in other trades, the employment of expensive machinery brought about the gradual extinction of small men, and nowadays the yacht sail cloth business is practically confined to four firms in the south of England. Up to recent times, loose-footed sails were used; they were cut with a considerable hollow in them and flax was exclusively employed in their manufacture. It was not until the form and body of yachts had been greatly improved that the value of flat sails and the superiority of cotton over flax was demonstrated. Flax was good enough for the full-bottomed, iron ballasted yachts of early days, as was shown when flat sails were tried and proved to be of no advantage whatever. Then came the year 1851, and the revolution in yacht designing caused by the success of the "America." Great importance was attached to her flat cotton sails, and it was thought that her close windedness was due to that cause alone. Such, however, was not really the case; her fine performance was due principally to her beautiful model, fine lines and small displacement, factors which ensure that a vessel possessing them will hold a better wind than a full-bottomed beamy boat of large displacement. The "America's" sails undoubtedly suited her model, but they did not suit the British yachts of that day equally well, as was very soon discovered by experiment. Flat sails did little to increase their speed, and until improved models were introduced the advantages of flat sails were not made apparent. Cotton sail cloth was introduced about this time, but although tried for a year or two it was found useless in making full-bottomed boats go any faster, and it was abandoned.

"BRITANNIA."

The object of the sail-maker is to obtain a material possessing great strength, little elasticity, uniformity of stretch, close texture, and a smooth surface, from which the wind frees itself with the least possible friction. Sail cloth makers and sail makers busied themselves for years in pursuing these requirements, and progressed faster than did designers and builders of yachts, for it was not until the advent of the "Alarm," "Gloriana," "Flying Cloud," "Galatea," and "Shark," that laced-footed and flat mainsails came into use. The year 1863 saw a lot of famous schooners, among them the "Aline," "Albertine," "Egeria," "Pantomime," and "Witchcraft," all vastly improved in model, and therefore capable of standing their sheets being pulled in; and once a yacht will allow of that, flat sails can be used with great advantage. Flat sails accordingly became the rule and not the exception; but flax cloth was still used, for the yachting world was not yet educated up to cotton. In 1868 appeared the beautiful 400-ton schooner "Sappho," from America, canvased with cotton. She was a lovely model, but had neither power nor ballast to stand up to her cloth, and she made a sorry show in a race round the Isle of Wight against such boats as the "Cambria," "Aline," "Oimara," and "Condor." Completely remodelled and rebuilt in 1870 by Bob Fish, one of the smartest men in America at designing and sailing boats, she sailed three matches against the "Cambria." As "Sappho" measured 400 tons, and "Cambria" only 200 tons, and as no time allowance was given, the former had naturally by far the best of it. She won easily, and her success set the fashion in cotton cloth.

The following year Mr. Ashbury built the "Livonia." She was canvased with cotton, and the sails did well. But the boat was not a great success, and in consequence cotton cloth again dropped out of use for some years, and was not tried again till the year 1887, when the "Thistle" had all her sails made of that material. East India cotton was, however, used instead of Egyptian, and the cloth did not come up to expectation. The next boats to use cotton were "Yarana," "Valkyrie," "Deerhound," and "Iverna," and all the succeeding racing yachts, including "Britannia," "Satanita," "Calluna," "Valkyrie II." and "III." were canvased with cotton cloth.

The mainsails of "Valkyrie II." and "III." were both made of Sea Island cotton, but the latter was also given a white Egyptian cotton sail, which was used for the Cup races, as it was considered a better sail than the one made of Sea Island cotton.

It is no compliment, but a universally recognised truism, to say that the best sails in the world are made by Messrs. Lapthorn and Ratseys.

"VALKYRIE II."

George R. Ratsey, born in 1769, served his apprenticeship at East Cowes, and in 1790 set up on his own account in that town. In those days hundreds of merchant ships called at Cowes for orders, and Mr. Ratsey's business was principally concerned with them.

But he also made sails for His Majesty's Navy, as in those stirring times, when fleets were constantly fitting out at Portsmouth, a good deal of sail-making was given out to private firms. He made the sails for the "Waterwitch" brig, owned by Lord Belfast, to which allusion has already been made.

Mr. Ratsey subsequently retired in favour of his son, and the Cowes business was carried on very successfully by him until the year 1880, when he retired, and his sons entered into partnership with Mr. Edwin Lapthorn.

James Lapthorn served his apprenticeship at Kingsbridge, near Salcombe, and then went to London, where he managed a large sail-making business. In 1825 he migrated to Gosport, and started sailmaking on his own account, and in the course of time was joined by his two sons, James and Edwin, who carried on the business most successfully for many years. James Lapthorn died in 1868, and his son James in 1869, and the business was conducted subsequently by his surviving son, Edwin, until he entered into partnership, as already mentioned, with Messrs. Ratsey in 1880.

The firm of Lapthorn and Ratseys carry on business at Cowes, Gosport, Gourock, and Southampton, and there can be no doubt that the combination of talent and experience derived by this amalgamation has been very beneficial to the art of sail-making.

Under these circumstances, immense strides have been made in the art of sail-cutting of late years, and the difficulty in setting sails properly and keeping them in their places has been proportionately decreased. Five and twenty years ago racing yachts were started from an anchor, with all their sails down, and it was a very difficult business, especially if there was any weight of wind, to set properly the canvas of a 100-ton cutter in those days. In fact, with much wind the mainsail could never be got to set all day. Hemp stays and gear were also stretching all the time, and even if the sails were properly set at starting, a pull here and there was constantly required to keep them in their place. Nowadays, with perfectly cut sails, and with wire gear and rigging, which practically has no stretch, a sailing master's difficulties in respect to setting his canvas are much diminished. The sail-maker always sends printed instructions with the sails, and the skipper has not very much more to do than to carry them out. Some care, of course, must be taken with a new mainsail, although it is not nearly so easily damaged as is generally supposed. Popular opinion is that a sail may be spoilt irretrievably if it gets wet, or if it is reefed before it has become thoroughly stretched. It is certainly better to avoid reefing it if possible before it is stretched into shape, but far from wetting spoiling a sail, I believe it does it good, provided of course that it gets thoroughly dry afterwards.

The difference between a well-cut and a badly-cut sail, though plain enough in practice, is due to such small and almost imperceptible causes, that it is not easy to account for the fact that one firm have succeeded in acquiring a practically complete monopoly of sail-making for racing yachts, especially as the superiority of their productions is not due to any patent process, or secret of trade. Excellence led up to monopoly, and monopoly has conduced to excellence.

Severe competition would inevitably have produced depreciation of quality in the material used, and the primary consideration in sail-making is that the sail-cloth shall be A 1; it is no more possible to make a good fitting sail from inferior stuff, than it is to make a good fitting pair of trousers out of shoddy. There are many small points in sail-making, individually of apparently but small importance, that go to make a good sail, and it is the combination of all these small items that ensures the success of the whole. If all sails were square sails, the difficulties in the way of sail-making would be comparatively small, and an ordinary skilled mechanic would be able to turn out as good work as any one else. But in respect of fore and aft sails, the case is very different. The cloths of such sails are all more or less cut on the gore, and one of the chief arts in cutting the gore is to allow for its stretching, so as to counteract the stretch of the sail, and thereby prevent the sail getting out of shape.

Another very important point to be considered in sail-making is the relative stretch of the cloth and the rope. This must be exactly calculated, allowed for, and adjusted, for if the rope is too tight, the sail will be baggy, and on the other hand if it is too slack, the cloth will be stretched out of shape or burst.

The constant and undivided attention of intelligent and talented men for some three generations directed to these and similar practical matters connected with sail-making, together with the fact that, owing to absence of competition, nothing but the very best material has been employed by them, no doubt explains the fact that, as is universally admitted, the work of no sail-maker in any country can compare with that turned out by Messrs. Ratseys and Lapthorn.

The following plan illustrates the most approved and up-to-date method of cutting the cloths of sails. Jibs, foresails, and topsails certainly stand much better cut according to this method, owing to the fact that, the after-leeches and foots being cut square with the cloth, the stretch is reduced to a minimum. Mr. Herreshoff has gone in rather largely for horizontal cloths, but apart from the fact that they are very unsightly, no advantage appears to be gained, and the old-fashioned method of cutting a mainsail holds its own to this day.

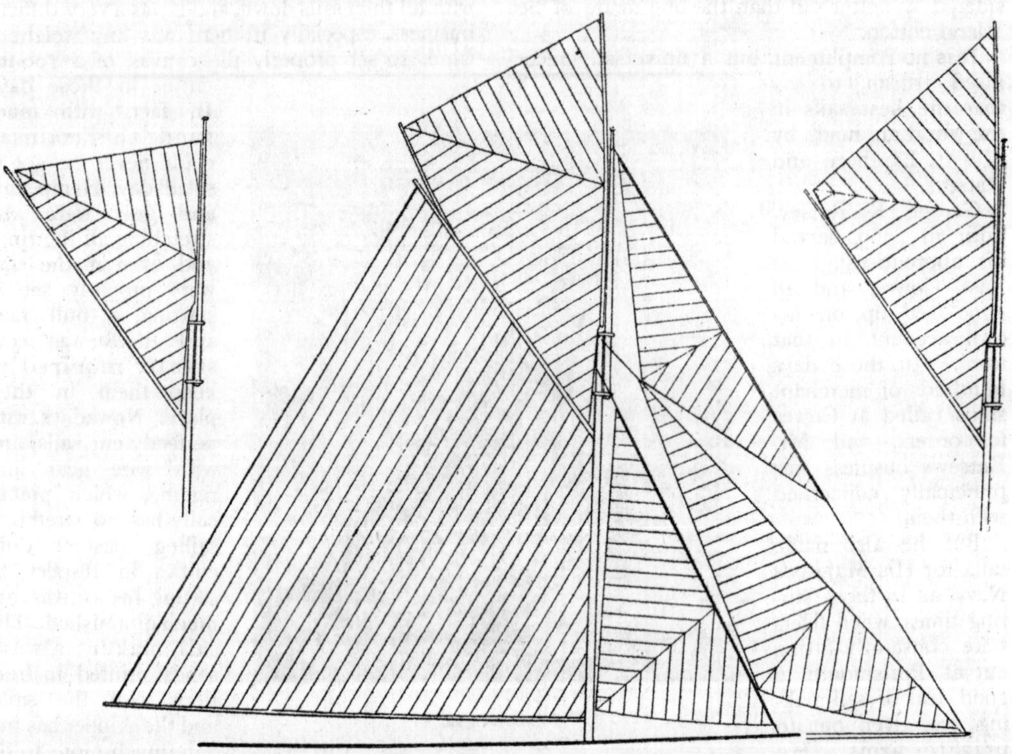

DIAGRAM SHOWING THE WAY CLOTHS ARE PUT INTO SAILS.

The propulsion of boats to windward and the trimming of sails is a most interesting subject.

History does not record the name of the astonished boat or ship sailor who first discovered that by trimming the yard of his square sail, and hauling in a little of his sheet, he could manage, by going about, gradually to work his way dead against the wind; but there can be no doubt that the first steps towards beating to windward were made by accident, and that from sailing before the wind it was found out little by little that it was possible to work gradually against it. Though all that we know about windward sailing has been originally derived from practical experience, the theory and science is well worthy of consideration.

But before discussing why a vessel can be propelled almost against the wind, by the wind acting on her sails, the difference between true and apparent wind must be understood. The true wind is of course the direction of the wind as it strikes a stationary object; apparent wind is the direction of the wind as it strikes the sails, as it is indicated by the vane at the masthead of a ship in motion, and it is constantly changing according to the velocity of the motion of the ship.

As a craft close-hauled moves forward maintaining a certain angle between the plane of the sail and the direction of the *true* wind, she obviously draws the wind ahead, and lessens the angle between the plane of the sail and the direction of the *apparent* wind, in a degree dependent on her speed. Hence it is that under equal conditions of wind and of weatherly qualities, a boat progressing at the rate of five miles an hour will hold a better wind; that is to say, will sail closer to the true wind than one moving at the rate of ten miles an hour. The difference in the angles between the true and the apparent wind will be much less in the former than in the latter case.

It is this difference between the true and the apparent wind, and not, as is generally supposed, the action of tide under the lee bow, that makes a boat hold so good a wind when sailing against a foul tide. Imagine a cutter close-hauled going at the rate of five miles an hour through the water, stem on against a five mile an hour current; she will be stationary as far as the wind is concerned. She will feel the true wind, because the ship being stationary the true and apparent winds will coincide, and she will point, say, within three points of the wind.

Suppose the tide to turn, and to run with the same velocity in the opposite direction. The craft will then be travelling at the rate of ten miles an hour in reference to the wind, and the apparent wind which she feels will be drawn about two points ahead; in other words, the ship will break off two points, and will point within five instead of three points of the true direction of the wind.

In treating of the action of wind on sails in propelling a boat to windward, the apparent wind only has to be considered. The effect of air in motion upon a sail set at any angle to its direction, is to create an excess of pressure upon the side of the sail exposed to the wind and a diminution of pressure on the other side, and the result is a force acting at right angles to the plane of the sail. If, therefore, in the case of a ship, a sail were in the same plane as the keel, the force of the wind would be exerted in a direction forming an angle of 90 degrees with the keel, and, independently of shape, would drive the vessel in the same direction, that is to say, sideways. But sails are always trimmed at some angle, exceeding, say, 10 degrees to the line of keel; and, therefore, the force of the wind is exerted upon the body to be moved at an angle of less than 90 degrees, and that body will have a tendency to move forward. As an example, a truck on rails, equally free to move forwards or backwards, will, with the sail properly trimmed, move forward within about four points or 45 degrees of the wind. A sail being fixed on a body equally free to move in any direction, the body will move in the same line as the direction of the wind-force; in other words, at right angles to the plane of the sail. If the body is not equally free to move in all directions, the direction of motion will be correspondingly modified towards the line of least resistance. In the case of a ship, the line of least resistance is a prolongation of the line of the keel forward. If the resistance fore and aft be equal, and the wind is right aft, it will blow a vessel straight forward; if the wind is right ahead, it will blow her straight backward. If the wind strike the vessel at any angle sufficiently large to fill the sails, the course of the vessel will be in a corresponding angle determined by the relative proportions of fore and aft to lateral resistance.

So much for the effect of wind on a ship, on the assumption that the force of wind upon the hull, spars, and rigging, the friction of wind on the canvas, and the effect of curvature of the sail, are eliminated. But taking these factors into consideration, the result for a vessel sailing close hauled is that the various forces of the wind may be reduced to one resultant force acting in a direction nearly perpendicular to the plane of the sail; the angle between the direction of this single effective force and the apparent wind will be somewhat greater than a right angle.

But a vessel is not moving freely in the water; she is affected by fore and aft and lateral resistance, and the effect of the latter is much greater than the effect of the former. These resistances are also reducible to one resultant force, the direction of which forms an angle of something more than 90 degrees with the path of the vessel through the water. These two forces, the one forming an angle of over 90 degrees with the direction of the apparent wind, and the other forming an angle of over 90 degrees with the direction of the path of the ship through the water, are the only two external forces acting upon the craft; consequently, assuming that the vessel is travelling steadily, they must be equal and opposite, their directions being in the same straight line. Hence it follows that the angle between the direction of the apparent wind and the path of the ship through the water, or her course made good, is equal to the sum of the excesses over 90 degrees of the angles formed by the two forces above mentioned.

Why, then, do vessels go to windward as well as they do? is a fair question to ask. Suppose, as an ideal condition, that a vessel has no fore and aft resistance, and has complete lateral resistance; assume, further, that there are no spars, rigging, or hull above water to hold wind, that the sail is a perfectly flat plane, and that the frictional value of the wind on the surface of the canvas is nil. In such a case the excesses of the angles under consideration over 90 degrees will be infinitesimal, and the ship would go nearly head to wind. It follows, therefore, that the close-windedness of a vessel depends mainly upon the relative proportion of lateral to fore and aft resistance, upon the effect of windage upon hull, spars, and rigging, upon the friction of wind upon the surface of the sail, and upon the curvature of the sail.

A smooth surface is very important, hence the superiority of Egyptian cotton over flax as a material for racing canvas. A flat sail is also important, but as elsewhere explained, a certain form of hull is a condition precedent to getting full value from a flat sail. Both these conditions help a vessel to windward, and other factors come under consideration which produce the same happy result.

Wind, which may be considered as a fluid, striking a sail must escape somehow, and naturally does escape in the easiest possible direction. In the case of a square-rigged vessel with the wind right aft, the wind may be said to escape in all directions; the only distinct effect produced, beyond propulsion, is the creation of a cushion of air, which is by some thought to interfere with the effect of the wind upon the canvas. It is to mitigate this supposed diminution of force that holes are cut in square sails, to allow the spent wind to escape through the canvas.

In the case of fore and aft rigged vessels, if the wind strikes the sail perpendicularly to its surface, it may also be assumed to escape equally in all directions. But under nearly all circumstances sails are trimmed at such an angle to the keel, that the wind strikes them obliquely. The case of a cutter or other fore and aft vessel with the wind abaft the beam, need not be considered; the effect is practically entirely propulsive, and in the line of the ship's keel: she makes no leeway.

We are dealing with vessels close-hauled, and in that case the wind, striking the sails obliquely from before the beam, flies off the sail abaft the beam, with the exception of a certain quantity which escapes round the luff, or leading edge of the sail. If the sail can be imagined in a vacuum, the wind would escape in this manner without interference; but as a fact, the wind flowing from a sail meets a mass of atmosphere moving past the sail in a different direction, and is thereby deflected from its natural course. To enter into a discussion on the exact effect of this deflection would be beyond the scope of this article; it is sufficient to point out that this opposing force drives a vessel to windward.

Another assistance to a vessel turning to windward consists in this: one effect of wind upon a sail is to create a diminution of pressure at the back of the sail. The extent and scientific results of this diminution cannot be given, but the practical effect is to draw the vessel up to windward. Sailormen have by experience discovered that the luff of a mainsail should not be extravagantly taut: a slight slackness, they say, makes a "little draught in the sail." It does something of the kind, for it utilises some of the wind which would otherwise flow round the leading edge or luff of the sail. It is no doubt partly due to this cause that a London barge is able to turn to windward under a huge staysail, bulging out in an immense curve. The barge holds a good wind, and the sail keeps full. The bargee does not know why, and he would not sail his craft any better if he did.

Turning to windward is so important a matter in yachting, and especially in yacht-racing, that a diagram illustrating the above-mentioned theories may be useful.

These theories are, it must be admitted, somewhat obscure; and, as the effect of wind on sails, and of water on ships, have not been reduced to an exact science, they are no doubt open to criticism. Be that as it may, their application leads up to a very practical and interesting subject, namely, the angle at which a racing vessel will lie to the *true* wind and also to the *apparent* wind, and the latter needs more careful consideration than the former in calculating the angles for the leads of the head sheets. A smart racing yacht will work within 8 points (90°) of the true wind, that is to say, within 4 points (45°) on each tack; but in reality she sails within 1½ or 2 points of the apparent wind, for owing to the speed of the vessel the wind is brought 2 or 2½ points more ahead on each tack, and consequently the vessel's head breaks off 2 or 2½ points. Were it not for this fact, boats would go to windward nearly as fast as to leeward, and, excepting in calms, steam would have little or no advantage over sail. It is the speed of the vessel which causes the difference between the true and apparent winds, and the faster a vessel is going, the flatter will her sheets need to be drawn in, and the worse wind she will appear to hold. In the case of ice boats, which travel with fearful velocity, the apparent wind is always nearly ahead, no matter in what direction the true wind is blowing, and the sails must be trimmed nearly in the

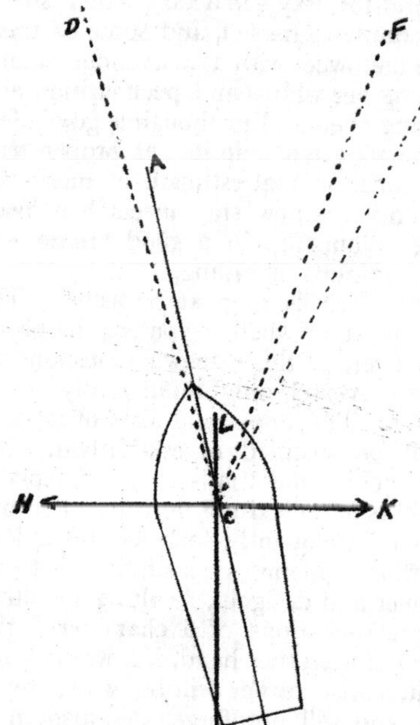

This diagram represents a ship closehauled on the starboard tack. *A B* is the direction of the keel; *L M* the plane of the sails, represented for the sake of illustration by a straight line; *E C* the direction of the true wind: *F C* the apparent direction of the wind on board, it being brought more ahead by the forward movement of the ship. Although the lateral resistance, particularly in a deep-keeled vessel, is enormous relatively to the fore and aft resistance, still, it is not sufficiently great to prevent a certain amount of lee-way. Let *C D* represent the line of progression made good, the lee-way is the angle *A C D*. Now let *C H* represent the resultant effective force of the wind, made up of its action on sails, masts, rigging, hull, &c.; and let *C K* be the resultant of the resistance of the water to the lateral and fore and aft movement of the vessel. The angle *F C H* must be greater than a right angle, and the flatter the sails can be set the less the angle need be, or, in other words, the closer the ship will sail to the wind. Also, the angle *K C D* must be greater than a right angle; but, if the fore and aft resistance could be done away with it would become a right angle.

Now, if the ship is moving steadily along, as *C K* and *C H* are the only two forces acting upon her, they must necessarily be equal and opposite. The sum of the two angles *F C H* and *D C K* exceeds two right angles by the angle *D C F*, which is the angle between the direction of the apparent wind and the real path of the ship. Supposing the fore and aft resistance to become nil, the angle *K C D* becomes a right angle; and (neglecting the frictional force of the wind and its effect upon the masts, rigging, &c.) theoretically, with perfectly flat sails by making the angle *F C H*, a fractional amount greater than a right angle, the ship might sail nearly in the wind's eye, because the lee-way would be hardly appreciable and the angle *A C E* would be made infinitely small.

Practically, in modern racing yachts, the angle *E C D* is found to be about 40°.

fore and aft line of the boat. An Atlantic liner with anything like a moderate wind on the quarter, will also bring the apparent wind nearly ahead, and, if she sets a sail, the sheet will need to be hauled flat in. For the same reason the big cutters, when turning to windward, require to carry their main booms almost amidships in anything like smooth water. Under these circumstances it may seem strange that they get to windward as fast as they do. It is their great speed through the water, and the fact that they make little or no leeway which enables them to do so. It is not because they hold a higher wind than other vessels. A big cutter does not point so high as a 1-rater, she requires a larger arc to work in, and if a boat is ever built capable of sailing 15 knots on a wind, she will not work within less than 10 points; but her speed through the water and the total absence of leeway will get her to the weather mark far ahead of a slower antagonist sailing closer to the true wind. A London barge turning up the river on a flood tide with a hay-stack half way up the mast, will hold a good wind, but she will move very slowly through the water. The bargee would probably say that his ship went better to windward loaded in that way than she would if light, and would add that the hay-stack did it, especially the leeside of the hay-stack. Very likely he is right and has arrived at perfectly accurate conclusions purely empirically.

It is the apparent wind which has to be considered in calculating the proper angles for the leads of the head sheets. It is most important that a vessel's sails should be trimmed at proper angles, and at equal angles. The leads for the fore and jib sheets of a large cutter are generally drawn at an angle of from $7\frac{1}{2}$ to 8 degrees to the line of the keel, and those of small vessels at from 9 to $9\frac{1}{2}$ degrees, the difference in angle being due to the relative difference in speed. The main sheets of big cutters are, as before mentioned, brought in almost amidships, but as the angle of the gaff is considerably broader than that of the boom, the mean angle of the mainsail is about the same as that of the headsails. In the case of small boats, in order to obtain equality of angles, main sheets are not brought in nearly so flat.

A great deal has been said lately about the advantage of having holes in sails, in order to let the wind out. The idea seems a strange one, but it is by no means new. The Japanese, for instance, have always laced their sails together with about a 4-inch opening between the cloths so as to allow of the escape of the spent wind Experience proves that the wind becomes banked up in front of a mainsail with the sheet out, a spinaker, or any square sail; and that there is nothing like the weight of wind in the sails that there appears to be. All yachtsmen know that it is the first filling out of a spinaker that tries the gear, and that afterwards it settles down quietly. Doubtless the decrease of wind pressure, owing to increase in speed of the vessel, is a partial cause of this; but it is also due to the fact that the sails are then backed by large air cushions of spent wind, and it is the pressure of the following breeze on that air cushion which drives the vessel along. Any landsman may demonstrate the same fact by standing on a lee shore under a high cliff, and even at some distance from it, during a heavy gale of wind and then mounting to the summit of the cliff He will find almost a calm at the bottom, and a gale fit to blow him off his legs at the top. It is the air cushion which produced the effect, and were it not for this the launch of boats from off a steep lee shore would be impossible. It is the force of the sea, not the force of the wind, which drives a lifeboat back and washes her broadside to the beach; the strength of the gale is not felt until she gets some distance from the shore. Holes in the canvas of square-rigged vessels may therefore be beneficial by allowing the dead wind to escape, and enabling the living wind to exert more direct force on the sails; but holes would be useless and worse than useless in fore and aft vessels on almost every point of sailing. Spinakers are practically the only sails to which the principle could be properly applied, but as we are slow to adopt new, or to revert to old ideas, and as neither the scientific mind nor the practical mariner has arrived at a definite conclusion on the subject, holey spinakers are not likely to come into fashion.

And now having briefly glanced behind the veil of mystery surrounding designing, construction, and sail-making, let us return to the consideration of the yacht—launched, sparred, canvased, ready for sea. Though a good designer may safely be trusted to make his calculations so accurately as to ensure that the vessel's flotation line, stability, centres of effort, gravity, and lateral resistance, are all as he intended them to be, no human ingenuity, science, or experience, will ensure her sailing up to her proper form at once.

A racing yacht is a marvellous product of the human brain, but, like all such products, imperfect; and its imperfections can be reduced to the lowest possible minimum only by the anxious care, study, and experience, of those who have to sail her. I have never known the scientific designer to be of much use in screwing a vessel up to her best form. Ships are very human, and rather feminine; they act like intelligent, but slightly unreasoning creatures. They do all kinds of odd things, and do not seem to know themselves why they do them, and it is very difficult to find out. They have their own individual peculiarities of disposition; one vessel will like her mast stayed as rigid as an iron bar, while another won't sail at all with the runner too taut. In some cases the boom can be carried almost amidships on a wind; in others the sheets must be eased a wee bit. In getting a new vessel perfectly fit some little alterations in ballast will almost certainly be required; a bit of weight may have to be shifted fore or aft to make her comfortable on her helm, and it may be found desirable to stay the masthead a bit aft or forward as the case may be to make the balance perfect.

All this requires a great deal of attention. An experienced skipper can tell by the feel of the vessel and the way she acts whether she is going comfortably to herself, and some of these skippers are endowed with a marvellous faculty for discovering her whims and peculiarities, and for humouring them. But though a good deal can be done to get a ship in her proper trim during trial trips, no real estimate of merit can be formed until the new ship meets her rivals with racing colours up in a good breeze and under fair conditions of sailing.

The first match is a great occasion. The momentous question whether you are the proud owner of a flyer, or the somewhat despondent possessor of a vessel only indifferently good, will be tested. The hopes and fears of anxious months will be justified or established. But even though achievement falls short of expectation, the yachtsman need not despair. The first match is not infrequently followed by a long and somewhat gloomy consultation between owner, skipper and designer, resulting in alterations and modifications of a character highly beneficial. On the other hand, if a winning flag is the result, a wise owner will be wary, shy of experiment, and will not forget the wisdom of the adage "let well alone." The first few races will suffice to get your vessel into the best possible trim. The proper position for every ounce of movable weight and the exact way she likes her masts to be stayed, and her sails trimmed will have been ascertained. But to keep her invariably to her best form surpasses the wit of man. So delicately balanced are all the factors and forces involved, that differences too slight to be perceptible produce most appalling results. Ships act like sentient creatures, they are subject to moods and fancies, and are liable to fits of temper, good and bad. Sometimes the vessel will not sail; the helmsman knows at once that something is wrong, he feels it, the vessel seems half asleep, drowsy, irresponsive, and the fact is soon made disgustingly evident by comparison with your competitors in the race. What is the matter? Nobody knows and nobody can find out. Everything—weights, stays, sheets—are exactly as usual, and all hands become reduced to a frame of mind that finds a natural though perhaps immoral relief in language of a strictly un-parliamentary character. And then, after straining patience to breaking point, the fickle jade wakes up, sails like a witch, and does her best to atone for past misdeeds. And the reason of all these vagaries is beyond human ingenuity to discover. Of course some minute change in the angles of the sails, in the position of the crew, in the tautness of the weather runner, has made all the difference in the world, a difference, that is to say, imperceptible in cruising or pleasure sailing, but very noticeable when it comes to racing against vessels with an average difference of speed of perhaps only a few seconds in a twenty-mile course. These perturbations of perfection, however annoying they may be at times, undoubtedly constitute one of the many charms of racing. You have got a very beautiful machine, but you can never feel that you are utilising it to the utmost of its capacity. You may sail the same boat, season after season, and yet every day there is much to be observed if you have eyes to see, and much to be learned if you have brains to note, and something to be done if you have ingenuity to act. Possibilities of improvements are ever present, and hence the interest in your vessel never flags, nor does the pastime of racing ever pall.

The rules to be observed in yacht-racing are, with one or two exceptions, identical with the ordinary Board of Trade rules of the road at sea. The principal regulations may be summed up as follows :—

Yachts having the wind free must keep clear of yachts close-hauled; yachts on the port tack must give way to yachts on the starboard tack; an overtaking yacht must keep clear of the overtaken yacht. A yacht may luff as much as she pleases to prevent another yacht passing her to windward, but she may not bear down off her course to prevent a yacht passing her to leeward. If in rounding any mark in a race, or any obstruction, an inside yacht has an overlap, the outside yacht or yachts must give her sufficient room. A yacht is considered to be overtaking until she has passed clear of the other; and overlapping means that when the leading vessel's helm is altered to round a mark the following vessel has not a free choice and cannot pass outside the leader without touching her. Then

"VALKYRIE" COMING THROUGH "NAVAHOE'S" LEE.

there are various regulations as to anchoring, sounding, &c., &c., all with the object of carrying out the principle that vessels may be propelled by sails only.

In former days yachts were started from an anchor, but about thirty-five years ago the Royal London Yacht Club substituted flying starts. This system has been universally adopted, and vessels are now always started under way.

Good judgment and knowledge of weather are most valuable qualities in a racing skipper, for shortening or making sail is practically out of the question during an ordinary race. It is possible to set a topsail or take in a topsail, or to substitute one topsail for another, and of course it is a simple matter if all competitors act in the same way, but usually the gain accruing from shifting sail is not commensurate with the detriment owing to the loss of time incurred through doing so. Staysails, jib topsails, spinakers, can of course be set, taken in, or shifted at will with no more harm than is caused by the men running about:—a matter, however, which should not be overlooked, for shaking a vessel interferes, especially in light weather, very seriously with her speed; but reefing is generally out of the question during a race; and as a rule it may be said that whatever canvas you start under must be carried or dragged along somehow to the finish. It is very necessary, therefore, that the canvas set should be adapted, not only to the strength of the wind at the time the race is started, but also in view of what the weather, wind and sea is likely to be during the match.

The start is effected across an imaginary line. The usual custom is to moor a small boat bearing a big flag at a distance of some hundreds of yards from the shore, or from the Committee boat. The starting line consists of the projection of a line formed by the alignment of two objects on shore, such as two posts, or a post and a church steeple, or factory chimney; and the competing vessels must cross it between the shore and flag boat, or between the Committee boat and flag boat as the case may be. At five minutes before the time appointed for the start, a gun is fired and the Blue Peter hoisted, and the yachts are then in the starter's hands and subject to all the rules of the Yacht Racing Association. At the exact moment of the start a second gun is fired, the Blue Peter is hauled down and the race begins. During the interval of five minutes elapsing between the two guns, the object of all helmsmen is to manœuvre so as to get into the best possible position,—which position is determined by the direction of the wind and tide, and to cross the line, if possible, exactly at gun fire. If a yacht crosses too soon by the fraction of a second, she must go back and recross the line, her number on the card will be displayed from shore or from the Committee vessel, and some suitable sound signal given to attract her attention. To re-cross the line is a manœuvre which in nine cases out of ten reduces the chance of winning to the lowest possible ebb. It is well to get under way and jill the ship about some time before the first gun fire, so that all things may be in their proper places and all panic and confusion avoided at the last moment. The ship should be placed in a good position for seeing the gun; some one is told off to watch for the puff of smoke with his finger on a stop watch; he will catch the flash of the gun on the instant, start the stop watch and call out the time to the helmsman as it elapses:—"One minute gone," "two minutes gone," "half time," "two minutes to go," "a minute and a half to go," "one minute to go," "forty seconds, thirty seconds," and so on. This is not quite so easy as it sounds, for the man taking the time must be ready to answer instantaneously, and above all things correctly, the helmsman's agonised inquiry, "How much to go?" and all the time the men are tumbling about over each other, booms are flying about his head, sails are shaking and slatting, collisions appear, to say the least of it, probable, and a good deal of shouting and confusion prevails. "No panic," should be the skipper's motto. All his business, good easy man, is to know instantaneously what he ought to do, and decide instantaneously what he is going to do in reference to his own and every other vessel in the race; to work his boat into a weather berth somehow or other; and so to estimate his speed and so to manœuvre his vessel as to bring her bowsprit end within a few yards or feet of the line when the second gun fires. Try to imagine, say, eight 20-raters manœuvring in a confined space not infrequently obstructed by shipping, each vessel struggling to get into a weather berth and to be on the line to the moment, the whole eight striving to occupy a position just big enough for one, twisting and turning about, shaving each other by hairsbreadths; and some idea of the difficulty of a start may be formed. A racing skipper should have eyes all over his head, his brain must work like lightning, and his action must be equally swift. He must meet every emergency as it occurs, automatically obeying the racing rules without thought, and he must be a marvellous judge of pace. When it is remembered that, in class racing and when vessels are pretty evenly matched, a good start means winning and a bad start means losing the race, it is not surprising that first-rate racing skippers are few in number, or that their hair turns grey early in life.

Some men make very elaborate plans for starting. It is a good thing, no doubt, for the helmsman to set definitely in his mind what he wants to do and intends to do if he can, but as probably everybody else desires to do precisely the same thing, plans require frequent modification. A good rule is, I think, to come down to the line with plenty of way on. The advantages derived from the commanding position of a weather berth are enormous and obvious, but if to get into and keep that position you have to waggle your ship about, or shoot her up into the wind to deaden her speed, and eventually cross the line with but little way on, a rival coming down fast may shoot by you to leeward, and even pretty close to leeward, and take your pride of place before your ship gets on her legs. Of course no two starts are alike. Some may be in a flat calm, when you drift over the line stern first, others in light airs with vessels jostling each other and no harm done; others in plenty of wind, when a mistake may mean collision, big breakages, and perhaps dangers to life and limb. One day a start will be down wind, on another the wind may be blowing right up, or it may be a reaching wind. Infinite variety is the law and constitutes one of the many charms of racing upon the sea.

Courses vary in every locality according to the necessities of the case. They are marked out by light-ships or buoys, or, if such natural marks are not available, by flag boats moored. Usually the race is twice round the course, and the distance to be sailed is generally 8 miles for ½ raters, 12 for 1 raters, 15 for 2½-, and 17 or 18 for 5 raters, 25 or 30 for twenties, 40 miles for 40 raters, and 50 miles for larger yachts. Occasionally races are three times round a short course, as for instance at Torquay, and Channel races are from point to point, as in the races from the Nore to Dover, or Southend to Harwich.

The interest attaching to a race is so obvious to the initiated, so incomprehensible to those ignorant of the sport, that any attempt at description is but labour lost. It seems but a dull affair to those who do not understand the game. Half a dozen yachts start to sail over a certain distance, one of them is faster than the others and must therefore win, such is a very general conception of a yacht race; but it is far from true, for skill in handling a racing yacht on the sea is a more important factor in determining victory than skill in riding a race-horse on the turf; and the element of chance plays a most important part, especially in light summer weather. The movements of the clouds, the surface of the water, all the signs of the weather are carefully scanned, and every little catspaw taken advantage of, but in spite of the utmost watchfulness flukes are of common occurrence, the last is often first and the first last, and until the gun is fired no race is safe. Moreover, an inferior vessel by getting a good start, or otherwise obtaining a commanding position may, and very frequently does, beat a superior boat under perfectly fair and equal conditions of weather. On a reach or turning to windward, it is obviously difficult for a vessel behind or to leeward to get by an opponent, even though she is the faster of the two. She cannot pass to windward, for to do so she must get into the leading vessel's wash, and that will stop her, and the leading boat may luff as she pleases in order not to be passed, and does luff, and will luff till both vessels are head to wind. These luffing matches between two noted rivals not infrequently result in putting them both behind slower boats. To pass to leeward, an overtaking vessel must keep a long way to leeward, otherwise, even if sailing two feet to the other's one, she will stop as soon as she gets under the lee of her opponent's sails, and it must be borne in mind that the canvas of a yacht of any size affects the wind for a long distance. While the leading slower boat is sailing along the chord of an arc straight for the mark, the faster overtaking vessel has to describe the arc, and may not get to the mark in time to cut her adversary out. In turning to windward a boat once in a weather berth must be very badly handled or very inferior to allow herself to be passed. Your opponent may work up to you, but he cannot get through your lee, and once you are planted on his weather bow it is very difficult for him to get to windward of you. In cross tacking you will stay upon his weather bow as he passes, and though he tacks at once you will give him a terrible shake up. Of course every dodge will be tried. In approaching you, and not being quite able to pass ahead of you, she will keep a good full and pass just under your stern, and still keeping a good full may scramble out clear, and certainly will do so if you are a moment too late in staying. A series of short tacks in rapid succession may be tried, and if your opponent boat is quicker in stays, or carries her way better than yours, she will reduce you to a standstill and so wriggle out clear. She may try a false tack, pretend to stay, but put her helm up and fill again on the original tack, and if you are not watching her closely and do not follow her quickly enough, she will scrape clear of the lee of your sails, feel the true wind, and it is all up with you. A hundred dodges may be resorted to, but for all that it is extremely difficult for one boat to get by another boat to windward unless she is very much the faster and more weatherly vessel of the two. Running dead before the wind is the most disastrous situation for a leading yacht; she can do nothing to impede the vessel behind her, but the latter can do something to stop her. By sailing dead in the wake of the leader, the sails of the pursuing vessel intercept some of the wind, and the vessel herself will be drawn ahead by the moving water in the wake.

Running with spinakers set is the most trying point of sailing. Two vessels may sail for miles and miles abreast of each other—the spinaker boom of the one almost touching the main boom of the other, and sometimes one will draw ahead a few yards owing to some little extra flaw of wind, and will then fall back again, and the other will temporarily draw ahead, and the helmsman can do nothing except try to hold his ship straight with no object to guide him, crouched in a constrained attitude, craning his neck to try and see under the spinaker, often with a blazing sun on the back of his neck, and, if running by the lee, in abject terror of a sudden jibe. With the breeze falling toward evening, as is often the case in fine weather, the leading boat on a run home is at a great disadvantage. She may sail into a calm and see the rest of the fleet coming up with a nice little breeze, and passing her; and, paradoxical as it may sound, the same untoward event may overtake her when, towards the close of a calm day, a breeze springs up. The hindmost yachts will feel it first, and by the time it reaches the despairing leader, the whole fleet may have sailed by. The tide also, in places where it runs strong, as in the Solent, wins and loses many races. You may be leading by half a mile in a very light breeze, and, on rounding a mark, be brought almost to a standstill by meeting a foul tide, and before you have proceeded half a dozen yards the others are on top of you, and practically the race begins all over again. On the other hand, you may have a very slight lead of a vessel overhauling you, but by scraping round a mark a few fathoms ahead, you may get into a fair tide, and be a mile away before your adversary rounds.

Great is the uncertainty of racing, an uncertainty that adds infinite variety and charm to the sport; and though in the long run superiority will tell, and the best boat will show the longest string of flags at the season's close, if you have a decent boat you need never despair, and may make a gallant show also when you sail home to lay up.

It is scarcely necessary to say that a smart crew is essential to success. The men must be young and active, intelligent, courageous, and possessed of endurance and of the peculiar quality that enables a man to skip about on a tumbling slippery surface, sloping like the roof of a house, without falling off. Quickness is necessary, for your chance of cutting out an opponent at a mark, or holding or passing him at any time during a race, depends upon the rapidity with which every operation is carried out. To get a spinaker set or to shift stay-sails a few seconds quicker than anybody else may give you the race. Courage is necessary, especially to work aloft when a vessel is hard driven in a nasty sea; and endurance, for to race perhaps twelve days in a fortnight, and be wet to the skin most of the time, takes a good deal out of a man.

Some races are doubtless uninteresting. But little fun is to be found in drifting round a course on very calm days. On such occasions vessels get strung out, flukes are the rule, and some lucky air of wind will probably lift some fortunate boat into a position which makes her victory certain; but such days are infrequent in our climate. The vast majority of races are sailed with plenty of wind, and sometimes a good bit to spare; and the interest and excitement of a race under such circumstances are intense. The attention can never flag; every moment is full of possibilities, and brain and nerve are kept on a constant strain. To give an adequate conception of the excitement of a closely contested race is impossible, but the closeness may be gathered from the fact that in class racing over courses of 20 miles victory or defeat frequently hangs upon a question of a few feet.

When vessels of different rating race in common, time allowance is used to bring them together.

For the convenience of yachtsmen the Yacht Racing Association has arranged the time allowance between yachts of various sizes in a time table or scale, on reference to which the allowance that one yacht has to concede to another may be easily reckoned.

At the same time it must be observed that no time allowance will bring a very big vessel back to the level of a very little one. In light winds, lofty canvas feels an air that would not touch the lower sails of a small vessel, and in strong winds power will prevail. Where the difference of rating is great, the big ship is, bar accident, bound to win; on the other hand, where the difference of rating is but small, the advantage —if any—rests with the smaller vessel of the two. To be given a few seconds of time is a good thing. It may frequently mean having just enough in hand to enable you to win without passing your antagonist, and in many cases you may be able to get close to her, and to keep there, though to pass her would, for reasons already explained, be impossible.

Where vessels of various rating sail together, they all start at the same moment, and the time allowance is given at the end of the race. It is an anxious moment for the owner of the first one in, watching, stop-watch in hand, to see if he has succeeded in giving the time, and for the owner of the second vessel to see if she has succeeded in saving her time. How slowly the time goes in the first case, how rapidly in the other!

On the whole, the present tendency of time allowance to check size is a wise and salutary one. Huge racing cutters are magnificent vessels, and it is a splendid sight to see them race, but they are too big. They are unhandy and unsafe, and the expense involved in their upkeep is well nigh prohibitive. Moreover, great size is destructive of the niceties of the game; skill and talent find more profitable employment in yachts of moderate dimensions.

Of late years handicap races have come much

into fashion. It is a reversion towards racing in its origin, when cruisers were occasionally matched against each other. It is difficult to handicap yachts even with the moderate success that attends handicapping in horse racing—which is not saying very much—for the simple reason that many most important conditions are unknown to the handicapper in the former, and are, or ought to be, known to him in the latter case. Yacht A. may be ten minutes better than yacht B. in light winds, and ten minutes worse in strong winds; and who shall foretell the weather? The element of uncertainty, therefore, attains to large proportions in handicaps, and for that and various other reasons the interest attaching to them can never equal that involved in legitimate racing. In that case, every ounce you can get out of your vessel by the expenditure of money and the sweat of your brain tells in your favour; while in handicaps the inducement to furnish your ship with new canvas and gear, and to string her up to the last point of perfection, is but small. Still, handicaps afford a great deal of amusement to men who cannot afford, or do not care to own, vessels intended for racing, and practically for nothing else. It opens up a field of utility for old racing vessels, and vessels which have not come up to expectations; and for these reasons it should not be by any means discouraged.

Before leaving yacht racing, some description of the various types evolved and of notable examples of those types is necessary to complete the subject.

As may be gathered from the foregoing pages, the modern racing yacht, and the sport of yacht racing, may be said to have originated within the Victorian Era, for, prior to 1837, square canvas was largely used, and, in the fore and aft rig, designers did not get far beyond the form of the old revenue cutter in their efforts to attain the beau ideal of a speedy craft; moreover, class racing was unknown. The fast boats used for smuggling purposes in those days were usually cutter rigged, and in the latter half of the last century the Government began to build vessels of a similar type known as revenue cutters to suppress the "free-traders."

Mr. C. White, of Broadstairs, constructed some of the fastest of these vessels. He does not seem to have been particular for whom he built, for a smuggler and a revenue cutter were often laid down side by side in his yard, and the legend goes that if the former promised to turn out the flier of the pair she was at once bought by the Government at a premium. This Mr. C. White had a son who settled at Cowes early in the present century, and who was the father of Mr. Joseph White, afterwards famed as the builder of the cutter "Louisa," and the brigs "Daring" and "Waterwitch" in the years 1830 and 1832.

The racing constantly taking place between smugglers and revenue cutters, and the desire on either side to attain to the highest possible rate of speed, caused great interest to be taken in the lines of the vessels, and certainly did much to stimulate yacht racing. The revenue cutters of 1780 to 1800 were large craft, many being over 200 tons; but later on, from 1815 to 1825, smaller vessels of 80 to 120 or 150 tons, of the type that is familiar to us in many of Clarkson Stanfield's pictures, and more especially in his illustrations of Captain Marryat's works, became the fashion.

Charnock's *History of Marine Architecture* says that in 1802 there were fifty-eight cutters in the service. Amongst the largest of these were:—

	Length.	Breadth	Depth.	Tons.	How acquired.
Kite	77·5	27·1	10·5	218	Bought in 1778.
Flying Fish	75	25·9	10·5	190	,, ,,
Busy	75	25·9	10·5	190	Bought at Folkestone.
Pigmy......	80·3	26·1	13·2	201	,, ,, ,,
Alert	78·9	25·2	11·5	205	Built in 1779.
Mutine ...	79·9	26·1	10·1	215	Taken from the French.
Pilote	78·5	26·1	10·2	218	,, ,, ,,
Ranger ...	80·30	26·1	—	201	Bought.
Seaflower..	72·5	26	10·7	203	,,
Lapwing ...	47·8	21·1	8·1	82	Bought of C. White, of Broadstairs, 1764.

The superiority of the fore and aft rig in weatherly qualities, handiness and speed, being demonstrated by these service cutters as well as by the smugglers and privateers, it became fashionable also in the pleasure fleet; and though topsail schooners and brigs occasionally competed in matches, the cutter, or fore and aft schooner, became the favourite rig for racing.

Trials of speed between the yachts of that period could not, however, have been very satisfactory. Vessels of different tonnage were raced one against the other, and as no time allowance of any kind was granted the biggest craft generally came in first, especially in anything of a breeze.

The Royal Yacht Squadron, which had been established in the year 1815, did much to improve the pastime in British waters, though at first its efforts were attended with only moderate success. For some years the club languished, and according to the *Nautical Magazine* for the year 1836, it was reported to be about to close its doors. Both the Commodore and Vice-Commodore had sold their yachts, the Duke of Norfolk had offered his yacht "Arundel" for sale, and the secretary had given notice to Mr. Goodwin, the proprietor of the Club House, that the club intended to vacate the premises as soon as the lease was out. However, a decade later the sport had become far more popular and the Royal Yacht Squadron had revived. In the year 1844, its list contained no less than 100 yachts, whilst some dozen Royal Yacht Clubs had been established round the coast, comprising a fleet of about 400 yachts in all. All the biggest vessels were owned by members of the Squadron, the largest in that year being:—

Yacht.	Rig.	Tons.	Owner.
Brilliant	Bark	393	Mr. G. H. Ackers.
Mischief........	Schooner..	221	Sir H. Hawley, Bart.
Kestrel	Yawl	202	The Earl of Yarborough.
Jeannette	Schooner..	186	The Earl of Egmont.
Alarm........	Cutter......	193	Mr. Joseph Weld.

Previous to this date, the last-named gentleman, who was a most enthusiastic yachtsman and yacht designer, had built the famous old cutter "Arrow." She may be taken as a sample of the most approved form of the type known as the "cod head and mackerel tail," a barrel-bottomed craft with short bluff bows and long fine run. The "Arrow" was 61 feet 9 inches long, by 18 feet 5 inches beam, and 8 feet 8 inches depth of hold. Yachts in those days were ballasted with pig iron, iron ore, or even stones, outside ballast being unknown. A crusade was initiated against this type of craft by Mr. T. Assheton Smith, Mr. William Simons, and Mr. Scott Russell, but their endeavours to introduce a fine entrance and hollow bow in the place of the old bluff nose did not find much favour until the visit of the American schooner "America" to our shores.

Mr. Assheton Smith was actually the first to introduce the hollow bow in his yacht the "Menai" of 163 tons, built in the early years of the century, but as she did nothing remarkable in the way of sailing she failed to dispossess the old type.

Mr. John Scott Russell's wave line theory found another exponent in the "Mosquito" cutter, built in 1848 on the Thames by Mr. Mare of Blackwall. She was 59 feet long by 15 feet 4 inches beam, the greatest beam being 4 feet 6 inches abaft the centre of the load water-line length.

The "Mosquito" was built of iron, and yachtsmen probably paid more attention to this than to her designer's departure in form, and did not credit the speed she possessed to her long hollow bow.

Scotland must take credit for the most striking departure of the period; in 1850, Mr. William Simons, a Renfrew shipbuilder, turned out "Tiara," whose dimensions were—

Length on L.W.L.	38 ft. 6 ins.
,, over all..................	45 ft.
Beam extreme	10 ft.
Draught extreme	7 ft. 3 ins.
Draught forward	4 ft.

"Tiara" was therefore a much narrower vessel than her contemporaries, and, in addition to having a fine long bow and clean fair after body, she was a long way before her time in the matter of a shallow draft of water forward. The Royal Clyde Yacht Club possesses a very interesting model of her.

But little impression, however, was made upon the old form of hull until the arrival of the "America" in 1851. It is a matter of history how the new clipper took English yachtsmen by surprise, and an hour's trial with her did more to open the eyes of yachtsmen than several years' preaching from Mr. Scott Russell and from the designers of "Menai," "Mosquito," and "Tiara."

It may be interesting to recall how the cup, which was presented by the Royal Yacht Squadron for a race round the Isle of Wight with no time allowance, was won in 1851.

The following were the starters, and it will be seen that they were not a particularly level lot in the matter of tonnage and rig:—

Yacht.	Tons O.M.	Rig.	Owner.
Beatrice	161	Schooner..	Sir W. P. Carew,
Volante	48	Cutter	Mr. J. L. Craigie.
Arrow	84	,, ...	Mr. T. Chamberlayne.
Wyvern	205	Schooner...	Duke of Marlborough.
Ione........	75	Cutter	Mr. Almond Hill.
Constance	218	Schooner...	Marquis of Conyngham.
Gipsy Queen..	160	,, ...	Sir H. P. Hoghton.
Alarm	193	Cutter	Mr. Joseph Weld.
Mona	82	,, ...	Lord Alfred Paget.
Brilliant	393	Bark........	Mr. G. H. Ackers.
America	208	Schooner..	Mr. J. C. Stevens.
Bacchante	80	Cutter	Mr. B. H. Jones.
Freak	60	,, ...	Mr. Wm. Curling.
Eclipse	50	,, ...	Mr. H. S. Fearon.
Aurora	47	,, ...	Mr. Marchant Thomas.

The race was started to the eastward, and the yachts went out by Bembridge Ledge, with the wind from west-south-west. Working past Bonchurch to Ventnor, "Volante," "Freak," and "Arrow" were all ahead of "America," but "Arrow" got ashore, the "Alarm" went to tow her off, and later on "Freak" fouled "Volante" and knocked the bowsprit out of her, so that the leading British yachts were altogether in a bad way. There was a light wind, and they had to beat to the westward down to the Needles. "America," who was not doing much good in short tacking with the small cutters, made a long cast off, and with a slice of luck fetched the Needles some six or seven miles ahead of "Aurora" and "Freak."

On going through the Needles, "America" had a fair wind, but meeting the ebb tide in a light breeze she made but little headway boring against it, whilst the ebb was fetching "Aurora" down the back of the island to the Needles hand over fist. By the time the tide eased, the stern division had just got round the Needles point and consequently were the first to feel the young flood when it set in. Although this brought them up pretty close, "America" kept ahead, and finished at 8.30 P.M., eighteen minutes ahead of the 47-ton cutter, "Aurora."

Although "America's" victory afforded no decisive test of merit, on account of the weather prevailing and the disablement of her principal opponents, there is no doubt that the schooner, designed and built by George Steers, the son of a Devonshire shipwright who had settled in New York, was a great improvement on any vessel previously constructed in this country.

Her design combined the peculiarities of "Tiara" and "Mosquito," and in addition she had the advantage of a suit of canvas the like of which even the old salts, who were ready enough to condemn her lines, admitted had never been seen in Cowes roads.

These elements were the secret of her success; indeed, as that veteran yachtsman, the late Marquis of Anglesey, said when he saw her for the first time, "If she is right, we are all wrong."

In 1852 and 1853 scores of yachts were hauled up in the yards to have the old bow cut away and the new American type of bow built on to them. The schooner for the first time became the most popular rig in our waters, and Mr. Joseph Weld had his cutter "Alarm" brought up to date by being lengthened by the bow and converted into a schooner. The "Alarm" is often quoted as being a craft of much renown, but if her performances from the year 1830, when she first came out as a cutter, to 1869, when she finished her racing career, be analysed, they will not strike the yachtsman of to-day as being in any way remarkable. In the 39 years she was fitted out she only raced 38 times and won 21 prizes, which nowadays is but an ordinary performance for a racing yacht in a single season. Mr. Weld, her original owner, whom we have already mentioned as the builder of the old "Arrow" in 1823, was one of the most distinguished yachtsmen of the time; he also built three cutters, "Julia" in 1820, of 60 tons, "Lulworth," of 130 tons, in 1827; and "Lulworth II," of 80 tons, in 1856. Mr. Weld really built the second "Lulworth" because his big "Alarm" overpowered all antagonists, and could find nothing to race against; he was most successful, for the little "Lulworth" won a wonderful reputation for soaking out to windward of the big schooners and cutters of those days.

In 1858 Mr. Weld had "Alarm" out again, and in the month of August of that year, when her Majesty and the Prince Consort visited Cherbourg, took part in a remarkable match across the Channel, which was sailed under the auspices of the Royal Yacht Squadron. This race is specially interesting to the modern school of yachtsmen, who know little and care less about the doings of these old time craft, because the Royal Yacht Squadron decided to rate the vessels by sail area, and arranged for a time allowance scale of $\frac{3}{4}$ of a second per square foot. Eleven yachts started, six schooners, four cutters and a yawl.

"Zara," schooner, was the largest in tonnage, measuring 312 tons and having 8,677 square feet sail area; but "Alarm" set the most sail, having 8,891 square feet of canvas to her 248 tons (she had been increased when she was lengthened and turned into a schooner from 193 to 248 tons).

The distance, 65 miles, was done by "Alarm" at an average speed of about 12 knots per hour, so it may be imagined that the old vessel was driven hard. It is recorded that there was a fresh wind a little forward of the beam, and the large craft carried whole mainsails and housed topmasts, while the small vessels were all reefed down. The prize went to "Ursuline" yawl of 112 tons, and 4,115 feet sail area, who, with her snug canvas, was 41 minutes astern of "Alarm," but was in receipt of 48½ minutes' time allowance.

The result was the cause of much discussion, and for the future "sail area" races were regarded with dissatisfaction, although as a face the race was undoubtedly one of the most satisfactory matches on record.

In 1859 and 1860 a controversy raged over the tonnage rules and time allowances almost as heated as that which has disturbed the rest of yachtsmen in the last decade; however, the clubs, unmindful of the sail area rating in the Cherbourg race, reverted to the old method of handicapping on merits as a way out of the difficulty.

From this time forth yacht racing began to flourish. In 1863, 113 races were sailed; and in 1870 the number had risen to 168. It was during this period that schooner racing came to its height. The most successful schooners were "Aline," built in 1860 by Camper and Nicholson, of Gosport; "Pantomime," by Ratsey, of Cowes, a straight stemmed craft which for some years was a noted vessel, and in 1873 won 19 prizes in 25 starts; "Egeria," by Wanhill, in 1865; and subsequently Mr. Ashbury's famous "Cambria," which defeated the American craft "Dauntless." "Cetonia" was built by Ratsey in 1873, "Sea Bell" in 1874, and "Miranda," owned by Sir G. Lampson, by Harvey of Wivenhoe in 1877. This was about the last great year of schooner racing, and "Miranda" had the name of being the fastest and most weatherly schooner ever built. She rather frightened away the rest of the class, which dwindled down to very small dimensions in the early eighties. "Miranda," however, often joined in the hunt with the cutters and yawls, and proved herself as good as the best of them. In eight consecutive seasons she started in 144 matches and won 95 prizes, valued at £5,010. Her career in America, where she afterwards went, was equally successful, for she completely outsailed the centre-board schooners in anything like a rough water trial.

Racing amongst the big 100-ton cutters, including the fliers "Kriemhilda," "Oimara" and "Cythera," was popular in the seventies, whilst some grand matches were sailed in the big yawl class led by "Florinda," "Surf," "Gertrude," "Condor," and others. In 1875, "Vol-au-vent," designed by Ratsey, came out and carried off the palm in the big cutter class. She had the name of being a very fast vessel in light weather, and gave the schooners a rare dressing round the courses inside the Isle of Wight. In 1876, "Neva," a comparatively small cutter of 60 tons, built two years previously, had a wonderful season, and saved her time on many occasions off "Vol-au-vent," "Cuckoo," "Arrow," and the other cracks of that year.

The new yawl had an extremely rockered keel and long immersed counter. Her fore foot was completely cut away and she was the first yawl built with a clipper stem. A notable feature in "Jullanar's" design was her raking midship section, that is to say, the greatest beam of each succeeding water-line was further forward, or, as the old salts say, the vessel was slightly "club-footed"; thus the entrance and run of the yacht were harmonically blended. "Jullanar" proved herself to be a marvellous vessel in thrashing to windward in a hard wind and heavy sea, but in light breezes the balance was in favour of "Florinda."

The season of 1878 was chiefly notable for the advent of "Formosa" in the big cutter class. She was an extremely beautiful vessel

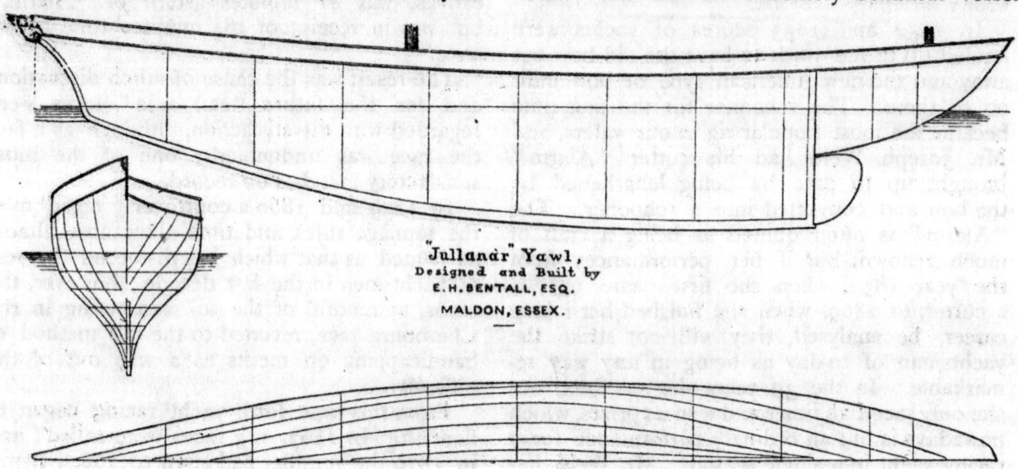

Length on load line, 99ft.; Greatest breadth, 16ft. 10in.; Greatest draught, 13ft. 9in.

From *Yacht Architecture* (1885), by kind permission of Messrs. Dixon Kemp and Horace Cox.

"Neva" and "Vol-au-vent" had the winnings of the big cutter class pretty much to themselves, and "Florinda," a yawl which came out in 1873, for the fourth year in succession headed the yawl class, winning altogether 21 firsts and 23 seconds in 64 starts. "Florinda" was almost without a rival until 1877, when Mr. Macleay bought the famous "Jullanar," designed and built by Mr. Bentall, of Maldon, on the Blackwater. "Jullanar" was an entirely new departure in yacht building, and a comparison between her and her famous opponent "Florinda" may be interesting.

	"Florinda."	"Jullanar."
Length of load water-line ...	85·9	99
Breadth ...	19·4	16·10
Draught 5 ft. from stem ...	7·3	2·9
Draught extreme ...	11·9	13·8
Mean draught ...	10	9·4
Displacement in tons ...	150	158
Area of midship section ...	106 sq. ft.	106 sq. ft.
Ballast...	54 tons	79 tons
Area of lower sail ...	5,257	4,988

above water, though below she was hardly as perfect in form. Be that as it may, however, she was too much for "Vol-au-vent" and the other new cutters, and, curiously enough, her principal adversary during the next two seasons, in which she was in the zenith of her fame, was the venerable old cutter "Arrow," built some sixty years before, but entirely reconstructed by her owner, Mr. Tankerville Chamberlayne, with the exception of her midship-section. Year by year during this period, longer, narrower, and more powerful vessels were gradually coming into fashion. Designers began to learn the value of outside ballast in the shape of heavy lead keels. Experience had taught them the eccentricities of the Tonnage Rule, and it was found that they could turn out a craft of 90 tons more powerful than vessels of the older type which measured over 100, and "Formosa," which had been bought by the Prince of Wales, was completely overpowered and outclassed by "Vanduara," designed by Mr. G. L. Watson, and built of steel, in the year 1880, and

"Samœna," designed by Mr. Richardson, her most formidable rival.

It is worthy of note, too, that correspondingly successful innovations in type were made in the forty class about this time. "Annasona" and "Sleuth-Hound,"—built off the same scrieve from lines by Mr. Fife—and "May," a Watson boat, came out in 1881. "Annasona" was the crack of the three, winning fourteen matches to her sister ship's six, and "May" also was superior to the latter.

"Samœna" and "Vanduara" again had things pretty much their own way in 1882, when "Erycina," another 90-ton cutter by Fife, was built, but did not come up to expectations. "Silver Star," designed by Richardson, joined the forty class, but was not in it with "Annasona."

1883 saw one of Mr. G. L. Watson's masterpieces, "Marjorie," of 68 tons, joining in the fray, and also a new yawl "Wendur," 124 tons, by the same designer; "Tara" a 40-ton cutter designed by Mr. Beavor Webb, a vessel of abnormally heavy displacement, raced through the season against the old cracks in the 40 class, but her qualities were not properly brought out until her second season.

In 1884 Mr. Richardson designed "Irex" for Mr. J. Jameson, and "Genesta" was built from lines by Mr. Beavor Webb for Sir Richard Sutton, Bart. "Genesta" in her second season went to America to compete for the Cup, and "Irex" had a very successful racing career in home waters. She was a remarkable vessel, surviving the strain of class racing for four successive seasons without having her wings clipped, and racing for six seasons before being put down into the Handicap class, a fate which overtook most of the first class cutters in a much shorter time.

"Irex," "Genesta" and "Marjorie" were the finest vessels built of the old narrow type, and the latter was the most weatherly narrow cutter ever produced; but really very little improvement in yacht architecture could be claimed for them over the yachts of ten years previously, beyond the introduction of outside lead ballast, the extension of the buttock lines, which gave them a more sightly appearance, and the rounding off of the fore foot, after the example set by "Jullanar," which lessened skin friction and made them quicker in stays. The success of the yachts, as racers, was accounted for by the fact that they were longer and, as has been said, narrower and more powerful vessels, with greater sail spread than their predecessors. The climax was reached in 1885, when "Irex" was the top of the big cutter class, by "Galatea." She was the longest and most heavy displacement vessel in proportion to her Y.R.A. tonnage that had ever been built, and it was anticipated that she would create an epoch in the annals of yacht building, in fact, be a second "Jullanar." However, surprise and disappointment were general when the new steel cutter turned out an unqualified failure. The "Galatea" had rather a light draught for her proportion of length to beam, her draught being only ·9 of her greatest beam and her proportion of length to beam was 5·8. Most of her rivals went up to 1·16 for proportion of draught to beam, and this may in some measure account for the dismal failure which resulted. She was a cumbrous vessel and greatly oversparred. We have only to look at the result of the 1885 season's racing to get a clear idea of the "Galatea's" qualities.

"Irex"	19 first prizes.
"Marjorie"	13 ,, ,,
"Marguerite"	4 ,, ,,
"Galatea"	2 second prizes.

In 1885 and 1886 the long narrow flat-sided type had reached its height in all classes, and the exaggerated plank-on-edge overcrowded with sail was becoming unpopular. Hardly any class racers were built during these seasons, and matters had come to such a pass that the proverbial "something" had to be done. The "something" consisted of the institution of what were then known as the A., B. and C. classes, with the object of bringing together a large number of unclassed racers. In the B. and C. classes a limit was put on the sail area allowed to the vessels, and, although this new idea worked well and resulted in many sporting matches, and even to a considerable increase in the number of matches sailed during the last year, it sadly deteriorated first-class yacht racing. A natural tendency manifested itself to clip the wings of A. class yachts so as to get them into the B. class, and to cut down B. yachts so as to make them eligible for the C class. Under these circumstances it was generally felt that the time had arrived for a new rule of measurement to be devised, and the Length and Sail Area Rule, propounded by Mr. Dixon Kemp, was introduced in the year 1887 by the Yacht Racing Association. The first big vessel built under the new rule was the "Thistle" from the lines of Mr. G. L. Watson. Though built under the rule she was also intended to compete for the "America" cup, to which match the rule did not apply, and as her designer was so to speak serving two masters he was probably somewhat hampered in turning out the best possible exponent of his views. However, Mr. Watson took advantage of the new rule to give his cup challenger a considerable increase of beam as compared with the proportions obtaining under the previous rule. The "Thistle" was 85 feet L.W.L. against "Irex's" 83·54 feet and had 20·30 feet beam against "Irex's" 14·99. "Thistle's" performances against "Irex" in 1887 were in every respect creditable to her designers, for the pair met thirteen times and the new cutter won eleven matches to "Irex's" two. The following year "Thistle" was an absentee and old "Irex" had her sail area reduced, which, although it spoiled her chances in light winds, was rather an advantage to her in a blow of jib header strength; and, as this was the kind of weather in which the old narrow type of ship stood the best chance of winning a prize, she was probably rather improved.

The new first-class cutters consisted of "Petronilla" and "Yarana," and the one addition to the forty class was "Mohawk." "Yarana" was designed by Mr. G. L. Watson and must be taken as his first venture purely under the Length and Sail area rating rule. She was a composite built vessel of 60 rating, and was built by Messrs. D. and W. Henderson of Glasgow, as was also the "Thistle": she had a clipper stem, and a neat elongated counter. Her dimensions were: 66 feet L.W.L., beam 14·8 feet, and draught of water about 13 feet. Her chief successes were in light and moderate breezes and in her first season with "Irex" and "Petronilla" as her opponents she won 24 first prizes out of 38 starts. "Irex" did very well against her in strong winds, and eventually won 11 firsts out of 31 starts, and yachtsmen will have a vivid recollection of the way the sole survivor of the old 1730 tonnage rule went when driven hard, and especially of the match round the Isle of Wight, when she did the course in 4 hours 50 minutes and 41 seconds, a record which remains unbeaten to the present day.

"VALKYRIE I."

Of "Petronilla's" racing career but little good can be said. She was not a success, winning only five first prizes out of twenty-eight starts, and in three out of these five wins she had not to meet "Yarana" as an opponent. She won at the Royal Cinque Ports Regatta at Dover, and at the Royal Southern Regatta at Southampton; but at that time the "Yarana" was round on the Clyde, sailing against "Irex," and "Petronilla's" opponents were reduced to the 40-raters "Neptune," "May," and "Mohawk."

She beat "Yarana" for the first and practically the only time at Falmouth on July 23rd. She made a very good start, and in a fresh wind succeeded in keeping ahead of "Yarana" and taking the prize, but had to content herself with a view of "Yarana's" taffrail for the rest of the season.

Her most creditable performance took place at Plymouth, in an amateur helmsmen's race, sailed in a whole gale of wind. "Petronilla," "Yarana," "May," "Neptune," and "Mohawk," started all under close-reefed mainsails, and with topmasts housed, in weather under which no sailing committee ought to have started a race. The sea was too heavy to put out mark boats—even the large trawlers which are there generally used for that purpose, and the vessels were ordered to go round the buoys off Rame Head and the Mewstone. They had to stay round one and jibe round the other, and considering that these buoys are placed to keep vessels off the rocks, and that the sea was breaking nearly out to them, it was nothing short of scandalous to send vessels round such a course.

All the yachts, with the exception of "Yarana" and "Petronilla," gave up, after making a few terrific dives, soon after they got outside the breakwater. "Yarana" worked out to the weather mark, the Rame Head buoy, and then gave up, and "Petronilla" alone completed the first round and came in with two out of three shrouds burst on her starboard side. The committee proposed to sail the race over again, and on "Petronilla's" refusing to agree, ordered her to complete the race and go round the course twice again; however, they thought better of this, and relieving her from the necessity of going round again, gave her the prize.

The best that can be claimed for "Mohawk" in the forty class is that she was about on a par with the old 40-tonner "May" and the cruiser "Neptune," which had been converted into the 40-raters.

In 1889 Lord Dunraven brought out "Valkyrie I," a cutter of 77 rating designed by

Mr. G. L. Watson; and the late Captain Nottage had a new forty "Deerhound" built from lines by the same designer. The last named completely extinguished "Mohawk," but "Valkyrie" and "Yarana" were pretty evenly matched.

The balance was in favour of Lord Dunraven's cutter whenever there was a fresh wind, but in light airs "Yarana" was generally the winner. "Irex," although in her sixth season, and despite the change of rule, was not quite outclassed, for on her day, a strong wind and a reaching course, she not unfrequently got the winning gun. "Yarana" won 15 firsts in 39 starts, "Valkyrie," 14 firsts in 34 starts, and "Irex," 8 firsts in 33 starts.

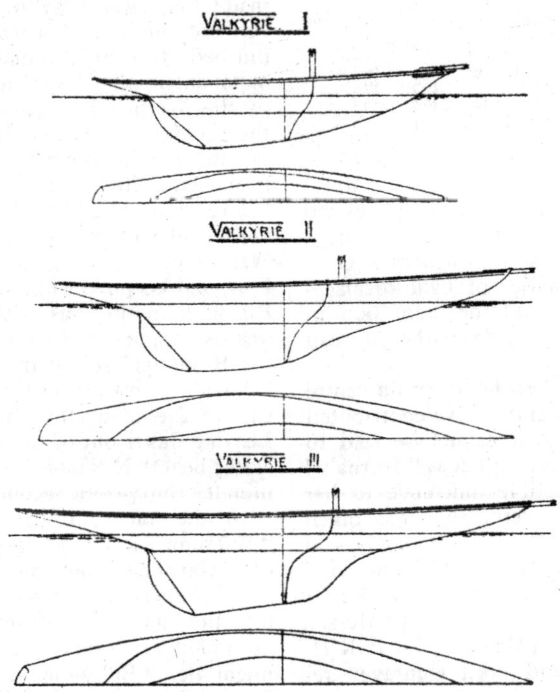

Mr. Jameson sold the "Irex" the following season, and she dropped out of first class racing; in her place he built "Iverna" from lines by Mr. A. Richardson, who had also designed "Irex," and in the same season (1890) "Thistle" was fitted out again. "Thistle" had not raced in British waters since her first season, 1887, when she gave "Irex" such a dressing and consequently had not met either "Valkyrie," or "Yarana."

"Iverna" rated 118 and "Thistle" 121, so that they were much larger and more powerful vessels than "Valkyrie I" and "Yarana." The last-named won ten first prizes during the season, chiefly by her wonderful qualities in light winds, but "Valkyrie" was between two fires, for "Yarana" could beat her in very light weather, and in strong winds she was overpowered by the big ships, and she only won three first prizes during the season.

The results of the matches between "Iverna" and "Thistle" were somewhat curious. The Richardson boat was at first fitted with a centre board, but she did not seem to relish this feature, for out of the first eighteen occasions on which she met "Thistle" the latter beat her no less than sixteen times. The plate was then removed, when she immediately began to turn the tables on "Thistle," and won fifteen out of the next sixteen races they sailed together.

In the forty class in the same year three new boats came out, "Creole," designed by Watson, "Castanet" by J. M. Soper, and "White Slave" by Fife; the last was rigged as a lugger and, it is unnecessary to say, proved a complete failure. "Castanet" and "Deerhound" were about on a par in fresh winds, whilst the former was best in light weather; "Creole" turned out the crack and, like most of the Watson boats, her best point was sailing on a wind.

In the seasons of 1891 and 1892 no new first-class cutters were built. In 1891 "Thistle" was an absentee, "Yarana" changed hands and was re-christened "Maid Marion," and was not given a racing fit out. "Iverna" won fifteen first prizes and "Valkyrie I" eleven, each starting twenty-seven times, and the latter followed up her successes by going out to the Mediterranean in the spring of 1892, and winning eight firsts out of nine starts, sailing against "Deerhound," "Castanet" and "Blue Rock." "Valkyrie" was bought by the Archduke Carl Stephan of Austria, and "Thistle" by the German Emperor, who renamed it "Meteor." In 1892 the latter was tuned up to concert pitch for another set to with "Iverna," but the balance remained slightly in favour of the latter, although the pair were very well matched. "Iverna" won thirteen matches and "Meteor" ten, whilst once on the Clyde in a fresh wind they sailed a dead heat.

Although nothing was done in the years 1891 and 1892 in the big class, a great advance had been made in the second class (the forty raters), "Reverie," "Thalia," "Varuna," "Corsair" and "Queen Mab" had been built and they showed a gradual improvement on the first type of cutter built under the Length and Sail area rule. With increased beam and the continual cutting away of the fore foot and raking of the stern post, the natural sequence was an increase of overhang fore and aft; and the necessity of utilising the overhang by reducing the angle made at the stem and stern between the water-line and the overhang led up to long counters, and the modern "pram" bow. The vessels built in 1892 and 1893 all showed this development, and, especially in 1893, the fore foot was cut away to such an extent that a hollow profile to the longitudinal vertical section was introduced. The second class is perhaps the best in which to observe the changes in dimensions and type, as new craft have been built to it in each consecutive year since the year 1888, and a table of the dimensions of some of the principal vessels is appended :—

Date	1888	1889	1890	1891	1892	1892	1893	1895
Designer	Clayton	Watson	Watson	Fife	Watson	Watson	Fife	Fife
Yacht	Mohawk	Deerhound	Creole	Thalia	Varuna	Queen Mab	Lais	Isolde
L. W. L.	61·23	58·85	59·5	59·14	59	59	60	60·02
Beam	14·5	13·5	13·2	13·9	14·7	16·7	17	17·05
Depth	9·5	11·6	12	12·6	13·4	10·9	—	—
Displacement	58·8	58	58	57	55	54·8	—	—

The splendid performances of "Queen Mab" in 1892, when she won twenty-four first prizes and thirty-six prizes out of forty-six starts from a powerful class of forties, gave designers a great insight into the possibilities of light displacement, and the advantages of the pram bow in skimming over the seas in bad weather instead of charging through them.

"Queen Mab" was at first fitted with a centre board, but it does not seem to have contributed to her success. Though it cannot be said to have had the effect of stopping her as "Iverna's" did, it made no perceptible difference to her weatherly qualities, and eventually it was taken out. In 'Queen Mab" Mr. Watson may be said to have scored heavily, for she was the forerunner in form of his famous pair of first-class cutters, built the following year by Messrs. D. and W. Henderson, of Glasgow, for H.R.H. the Prince of Wales and Lord Dunraven respectively.

The season of 1893 was especially remarkable for its splendid series of matches sailed by the first class yachts represented by "Britannia," "Valkyrie II," "Satanita," and "Calluna." The deep fin keel was fully developed in these vessels, and, although the old-school yachtsmen proclaimed that the craft shared every element in construction and design that a yacht ought not to own, it can be truly said that the boats were faster and more capable in heavy weather and open sea, and enormously superior in moderate and light winds to the yachts of any previous generation.

Excepting in a hard reaching breeze "Satanita" could not hold a candle to either "Britannia" or "Valkyrie II," and as "Calluna" was also comparatively a failure, the honours fell mainly to the Watson pair.

In the twenty-one matches in which these two vessels met, "Valkyrie II" led home twelve times, and "Britannia" nine times, and as far as can be judged by that trial, the former was a trifle the faster of the two.

To lend additional interest to one of the best seasons on record, the American yacht "Navahoe" came over towards the end of July, and was got ready to try the mettle of the British yachts.

Her first match was on July 31st at Cowes, when "Britannia," "Valkyrie II," "Satanita," "Calluna," and "Iverna" were ready to try conclusions with the Herreshoff yacht in a fresh breeze, for the Royal London Yacht Club's prize.

Such a flutter of excitement had not been seen in Cowes Roads since the "America" made her *début* forty-two years before, and it was not diminished when the American cutter finished the first round, leading her five opponents. She kept ahead as they ran down to the Warner Lightship, and rounded it for the second time, when the real windward trial of the match commenced. The breeze had freshened a little, and was blowing steadier than before, and "Valkyrie II" and "Britannia" fairly collared the "Navahoe," the Prince of Wales's cutter taking the lead off the Horse Fort, and keeping it until she sailed into Cowes Roads, a meritorious winner. "Valkyrie II" was second, and "Navahoe" in third place.

"Britannia" repeated her success by beating "Navahoe" every time they met excepting in the case of the match for the Brenton Reef Cup. Leaving flukes out of the question, the Prince's cutter beat "Navahoe" on an average by five minutes thirty-eight seconds.

In the race for the Brenton Reef Cup "Britannia" finished fifty-seven seconds ahead of "Navahoe," but as she started fifty-five seconds ahead and by an arrangement made before the match the difference at starting was to be added or deducted at the finish, as the case might be, "Britannia" had a balance in her favour of two seconds only. "Navahoe" protested that, the boat-mark having been moved from its original place, the finishing line was not the same as the starting line, and that she had to sail over more water to reach it. This she claimed made a difference to her of several seconds, and after hearing the evidence, the Royal Yacht Squadron, who were responsible for the alteration of the position of the mark, awarded the match to "Navahoe." The match, it may be mentioned, finished at night, and the captain of the mark-boat had shifted out of the fair way.

The visit of another American yacht, the "Vigilant," to our shores in 1894 added greatly to the interest of yacht-racing. Her meeting with "Britannia" was looked forward to with much excitement, and the result affords a notable example of the uncertainty of racing. On public form "Valkyrie II" was somewhat better than "Britannia," the former having beaten the latter twelve times in twenty-one matches, as already mentioned. "Vigilant" was built to defend the America Cup, challenged for by "Valkyrie II," and defeated the latter in New York Bay; and "Britannia" somewhat easily defeated "Vigilant" in British waters. Either "Britannia" must have enormously improved with age, or "Valkyrie II" or "Vigilant" did not sail up to their true form on strange waters. The season was a very good one, but was, however, marred by an unfortunate accident on the Clyde. While manœuvring for the start at Hunter's Quay, "Satanita" ran down and sank "Valkyrie II," and was herself seriously disabled.

"Britannia" beat "Vigilant" eleven times, including a series of seven successive victories; and "Vigilant" beat "Britannia" five times, including the private match at Cowes on August 3rd. The result of this race, however, was not altogether satisfactory as, shortly after the start, when standing in towards the mainland, the yachts having started to the westward, "Vigilant" hailed "Britannia" for water and, owing to some misunderstanding, did not put about herself, and the error gave her a considerable advantage.

The most notable feature in the year 1895 was the production of the two large racing cutters, "Ailsa" and "Valkyrie III." The first-named, designed by Mr. W. Fife, jun., made a brilliant display in the Mediterranean, but subsequently was not so successful in home waters, whilst the third "Valkyrie," was from Mr. G. L. Watson's board.

The *début* of "Valkyrie III" on the Clyde left her practically an unknown quantity, as she only raced three times before she went across the Atlantic to contest for the America Cup.

"Britannia" won thirty-eight first prizes during the whole year, out of fifty starts, and £3,039 in money, against "Ailsa's" twelve first prizes out of forty-one starts and £2,362, so Britannia was again the champion cutter of the year. However, Mr. Watson had not matters entirely to himself, for in the second-class (the forties) there were two additions, "Isolde," by Mr. W. Fife, jun., and "Caress," by Mr. Watson. The Fife boat proved by far the better all-round performer of the pair, winning thirty-one first prizes to "Caress's" seven.

In 1896 Mr. Watson designed a new "Meteor," for the German Emperor, in the place of his old "Meteor," *née* "Thistle." The last named, having been re-christened for the third time, is now known as "Comet." The new cutter was built at Messrs. Henderson's, on the Clyde, the cradle of most of the crack racing yachts of later years. She was the first big cutter built under the present rule, which came into force in the season of 1896, and Mr. Watson may be credited with having turned out a magnificent and in every respect a highly successful vessel, a repetition, in fact, of his success with "Yarana" under the previous rule eight years before.

"Meteor" had some rivals worthy of her steel, as "Ailsa" was showing improved form, and even had a better record at the end of the season than "Britannia." The result of the season's racing was briefly as follows:—

	Starts.	First.	Other Prizes.	Total.	Value.
Ailsa.............. ..	60	21	13	34	£2,020
Meteor..............	22	13	4	17	1,465
Britannia...........	58	14	10	24	1,562

About this time it became evident that the dimensions reached by the big cutters were becoming too great for safety, comfort and the general prospects of first-class cutter racing; and the Yacht Racing Association, with the object of discouraging the building of yachts over ninety rating, made an alteration, already described, in the time allowances under the new Linear Rating Rule, in the direction of slightly penalising yachts above that rating.

Mr. G. L. Watson's production of 1897 was "Bona," of 82 rating, built for the Duke d'Abruzzi, and with the advantage of the alteration in the time scale, she had a lion's chance with "Meteor."

There can be no doubt that the new cutter is a more handy-sized craft for match sailing than "Meteor" or "Valkyrie III." She is a beautiful vessel, and her record of sixteen first prizes out of twenty-six starts against "Meteor's" thirteen out of twenty-nine showed her to be in every respect equal to her predecessors. "Britannia's" record for 1897, including her racing in the Mediterranean, was ten first prizes in twenty starts.

Considering that "Britannia" was not pre-eminent when she first came out, and that her record in 1897, her fifth season, was much on an average with that of her other seasons, an almost unique performance in yacht racing, it would not appear that the Length and Sail area rule was inadequate for the development of the nearest possible approach to perfection in racing vessels.

"Aurora," designed by Mr. F. E. Soper, was the only other first-class cutter built in 1897. She was not a success.

The following is a table of the dimensions of some of the first-class cutters mentioned above.

	Year.	Length.	Breadth	Draught approximate.	Length over all.	Sail area.
Valkyrie I.	1889	69·6	15·10	13·3½	94	6,026
Satanita ...	1893	87	24·7	16·5	131	9,923
Britannia ...	1893	87	23 6	15·6	121	10,328
Valkyrie II.	1893	85	22·4	16 6	117	10,271
Calluna	1893	82	24 3	15	—	10,303
Vigilant ...	1894	86	23	13	128	12,330
Valkyrie III.	1895	88·85	26	19·8	129	13,900
Meteor	1896	89	24·28	18	124	12,326
Bona	1897	75·8	18·1	14·1	105	7,597

"Valkyrie III," when she raced for the America Cup, had a main boom of 105 feet. That of the "Vigilant" measured 97 feet 6 inches. The "Meteor's" boom was 96 feet 6 inches in length, whilst the "Bona's" spar is of far more handy dimensions, being only 78 feet long.

It may be concluded, therefore, from this review, that prior to the advent of the "America," a short full bow and long fine after body was in vogue. From the time that famous schooner came to our shores the system was partially reversed, and a long fine bow and comparatively short run was introduced. Yachts then gradually became longer, narrower, and deeper, relying less and less on beam, and more and more on lead for stability, until the year 1887, when craft were again given more beam in proportion to their length.

The cutting away of all dead wood to avoid skin friction led to the development of a hollow longitudinal vertical section forward, and this caused the forward transverse sections to become shallow and spread out. The natural development from this was the "spoon" or "pram" bow.

The craving to obtain speed by reducing the proportion of displacement to sail carrying capacity, resulted in a shallow body and deep keel, which further developed into the short-deep fin keel in the shape of a shark's fin in the small yachts, and the longer fin in larger craft, and subsequently to the fairly general use of the plate and bulb keel in vessels up to about 30 tons B.M.

It is interesting to note that a modern yacht's entrance is not unlike the old "wave line" concave bow with all the fore foot cut away; and that the "America" lengthened by the stern, her buttock lines eased, and her deadwood entirely cut away would bear a strong resemblance to "Valkyries II and III" and "Britannia."

Whether modern vessels are more speedy than old time craft, and, if so, to what extent, it is very difficult to say. Enormous improvements have been made in sail cloth and in the cutting of sails, in the scientific staying of masts, in the substitution of steel wire for hemp ropes, in the manufacture of gear of all kinds, and especially in the adoption of methods of construction which have tended to greatly reduce weight. Discounting all these advantages and judging by recorded races, it would seem that flyers of fifty years ago sailed off the wind about as fast as the modern clippers; but the present-day racer sailing *over* the water, rather than punching through it as in days of yore, attains a far higher rate of speed close hauled than was possible for its predecessors and is possessed of qualities of weatherliness and handiness that formerly were quite unknown.

Many scientific men have tried to prove their theories regarding the "shape of the solid of least resistance," but no hard and fast mechanical or geometrical system of yacht designing has yet been discovered, and affairs remain to-day much as they did more than two and twenty years ago when Mr. G. L. Watson declared that "A good boat is simply a happy compromise in which Beam and Depth have the good taste not to come too prominently to the front in order that Length may give her speed; while Length returns their courtesy by not pushing herself into undue prominence and thereby sacrificing Power."

The twenties, though in all essentials miniature big ships, are yet sufficiently distinct to require separate treatment.

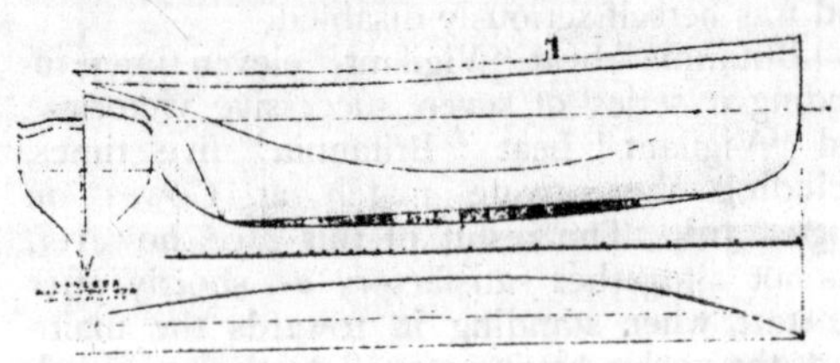

From *Yacht Architecture* (1885), by kind permission of Messrs. Dixon Kemp and Horace Cox.

The "Vanessa," built by the late Mr. Dan Hatcher in 1873, was one of the most remarkable 20-tonners ever launched in this country, not only on account of her successful career, which lasted from the year she came out until 1879, but also owing to a superiority in construction and design which was really many years in advance of her time.

It is difficult to describe "Vanessa's" beauties in words, for, unlike "Jullanar," "Clara," "Queen Mab," or other epoch making vessels in their several classes, there was nothing extreme about her; suffice it to say that her lines were blended in a series of beautiful curves and that the pith of her design was introduced into the successful twenties of later years.

When "Vanessa" was eventually out-classed it was by the introduction of really larger boats into the class. Designers worked on the weak point of the Thames and 1730 tonnage rules which, by their severe tax on beam, admitted vessels into the twenty ton class of but a few inches less beam than "Vanessa," but with several feet more length. The absence of any tax on sail area allowed of huge sail spreads, to carry which greatly increased displacement became necessary, and was supplied to such an extent that some of the later twenties were at least one-third larger in displacement than "Vanessa," and she may fairly be credited with competing successfully against larger craft which, in name only, were of the same tonnage. The same may be said of "Audrey" during the last two seasons as an instance of history repeating itself. No improvements on "Vanessa's" lines were made whilst the Thames tonnage rule was in force, and scarcely any under the

1730 rule which followed it. In 1874 she had "Sunshine," "Quickstep," "Fleetwing," and "Lizzie" against her. None of them could make much of a show with Dan Hatcher's beauty, and it was not until 1876 that a new boat came out that could do anything with her. The "Challenge," when she made her *début* in that year, became top of her class, but it is doubtful whether she was as good a boat as "Vanessa" in her best days.

1878 was another splendid season for twenties. "Maia," designed by Mr. C. P. Clayton, a steel built yacht, "Moira" and "Irene," iron boats, designed and built by Messrs. A. and J. Inglis, and "Frederica" came out in this year, as did also "Maggie," a 15-tonner from Hatcher's board, which raced with the twenties for several seasons; but in spite of these new antagonists, "Vanessa," in new hands, sailed by George Cranfield, won no less than twenty-four first prizes. "Challenge" was not competing in home waters this season; she had gone to France, where she swept the boards.

In 1879 "Sayonara" was built at Reid's, in Glasgow. She was a nice little composite cutter, and her principal opponents were "Louise," built at Payne's, Southampton, and the redoubtable "Vanessa." Both the new cracks were defeated by "Freda," designed by Mr. J. Beavor Webb for Sir Thomas Freke. She speedily went to the top of her class, and practically held her position for three successive years.

The introduction of the 1730 tonnage rule in 1881, which failed so signally in its intention to put a stop to increased length in proportion to beam, saw only three new 20-tonners built—namely, "Lenore," designed by Mr. W. Fife, jun., and built at the Fairlie yard in 1882, "Amathea," designed by Mr. A. Richardson, and built by G. Inman and Son, of Lymington, and "Clara," designed by W. Fife, and built at the Culzean Yard in 1884.

In 1883 "Lenore" and "Amathea" had some sporting matches round the coast. In this season "Lenore" won ten matches out of thirteen starts against "Freda," but the latter generally beat "Amathea" when they met. The most striking development of the 20-ton class, however, was "Clara." She was the last of the narrow vessels built under the 1730 rule, and in the eleven years that had elapsed between the births of the Thames Measurement crack, "Vanessa," and "Clara," it is interesting to note the remarkable alterations that had taken place in the size and type of vessel, in spite of the effort made in 1881 to bring about an increase of beam in proportion to length. "Vanessa's" dimensions were 47 feet in length on the water-line, and 9 feet 10 inches beam, and she carried 2,600 square feet of sail. "Clara" was 53 feet on the water-line, had 9 feet beam, and 3,500 square feet of sail area. Under the length and sail area rule, which came into operation in 1887, "Vanessa" would be 20 rating, but "Clara" would be 31 rating. There was little virtue in this style of development, which simply meant carrying the plank on edge type to excess, and increasing the cost of the vessel. "Clara" won seventeen matches the first year she came out, and in the following year, 1885, it was looked upon as hopeless to enter any existing twenty tonner in a race against her. It was not a very tempting task to build a still more slender plank on edge to try to lower her colours, and there was practically no racing. "Clara" was sold to go to America, and the twenty ton class became temporarily extinct. "Clara" had a very successful career in American waters, and with Mr. Wheeler's old 15-tonner, "Maggie," designed by Dan Hatcher, and "Madge," and later on the 40 rater, "Queen Mab," both designed by G. L. Watson, made among American yachtsmen a revolution similar to that made among British yachtsmen by the schooner "America" many years before.

The twenty class was not revived until 1888, when "Vreda," designed by Mr. G. L. Watson, came out. She was the first 20 rater built under the Length and Sail area rule, and in displacement, length, breadth, and sail spread very closely resembled "Vanessa" as she was in 1873. "Vreda" had an easy task to gain her laurels, as she was only called upon to tackle the two old narrow ten tonners, "Melissa" and "Marguerite," which had become 20 raters under the new rule.

It is rather curious that under the Length and Sail area rule of 1887, old beamy twenty tonners built under the Thames measurement, such as "Vanessa," "Quickstep," or "Sunshine," worked out as 20 raters, and the extremely narrow 10-tonners, such as "Queen Mab," "Marguerite," and "Melissa," which were built towards the end of the era of the 1730 rule, which came into force in 1881, also worked out to be of 20 rating.

The next year, 1889, saw several new boats, "Dragon I," built for Mr. F. C. Hill, from designs by Mr. W. Fife, jun., "Mimosa" and "Windward," and the first-named was regarded as the best. "Chiquita" and "Siola" from Mr. Payne's board came out in 1890, whilst Mr. G. L. Watson turned out "Velzie," and Mr. C. P. Clayton designed the "Ghost." "Velzie" and "Ghost" had less beam, and slightly heavier displacement than their rivals, but as far as sailing powers went there was not much difference between the lot. A decided improvement, however, was made by Mr. W. Fife, jun., in 1891, when he turned out "Dragon II" for Mr. F. C. Hill. She won twenty-seven first prizes out of thirty-two starts, and as might be expected, took the heart out of racing in the following year.

1893, however, saw a tremendous revival.

"Deirdré," designed by Mr. G. L. Watson and built by Reid for Lord Dunraven, the third of Mr. F. C. Hill's notable series of "Dragons," designed by Mr. Fife, jun.; "Maladetta," a semi-cruiser, designed by her owner, Mr. McGildowey, "Zinita," by Mr. Fife, jun., and "Vigorna," by Mr. Charles Nicholson, formed a splendid class. "Dragon" was the most successful, though "Deirdré" ran her very close; neither of them, however, went to the Clyde to meet "Zinita," which was unbeaten in her own waters. "Vigorna" was the first bulb keeled boat with a pram bow and a very shallow body, and turned out a complete failure.

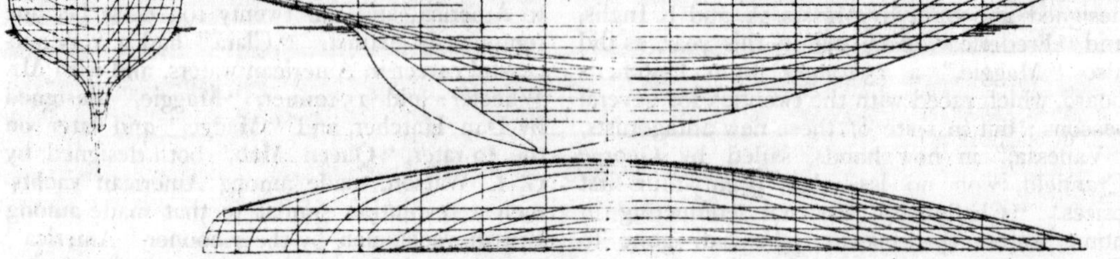

PLAN OF "ZINITA."

The following season Mr. Fife, who may fairly claim to have turned out more successful twenties than any other designer, scored a great success with "Luna," built for Mr. F. B. Jameson, and she came out top after an eventful season's racing. The twenty class was in this season admitted into the Solent classes, which meant sailing in Solent waters from May 26th until the end of August—some fifty matches, with amateur helmsmen upon every occasion. As a result the twenties enjoyed a thoroughly sporting season, but the class was found to be a rather severe tax on the Solent Clubs in the matter of prize money. Five new boats were built in the Solent, in addition to "Luna," which hailed from her designer's own yard on the Clyde, so with "Dragon III" and "Deirdré," and the still practically untried "Zinita," which, by the way, was much more heavily fitted below than the rest of the class, there was no lack of interest in the racing. The famous twenties which raced in 1894, besides "Luna," which won twenty-one first prizes out of fifty starts, were "Inyoni," designed by Mr. Charles Nicholson for Lord Dudley, a very short beamy boat, with fin keel and large sail spread, which attained quite phenomenal speed in light weather; "Deirdré," "Dragon III" and "Zinita," built the previous year, "Thelma," a centreboard cutter, designed by Mr. Fife; "Asphodel," designed by Mr. J. L. Watson, and owned by H.R.H. the late Prince Henry of Battenberg; Prince Batthyany's "Stephanie," designed by Mr. Clayton and finally, towards the end of the season, "Audrey," designed by Lord Dunraven.

Numerous changes of ownership occurred during the seasons of 1893 and 1894. Mr. Hill sold "Dragon III" to Lord Dunraven, who subsequently sold her to Lord Brassey, and "Deirdré" was purchased by Lord Lonsdale.

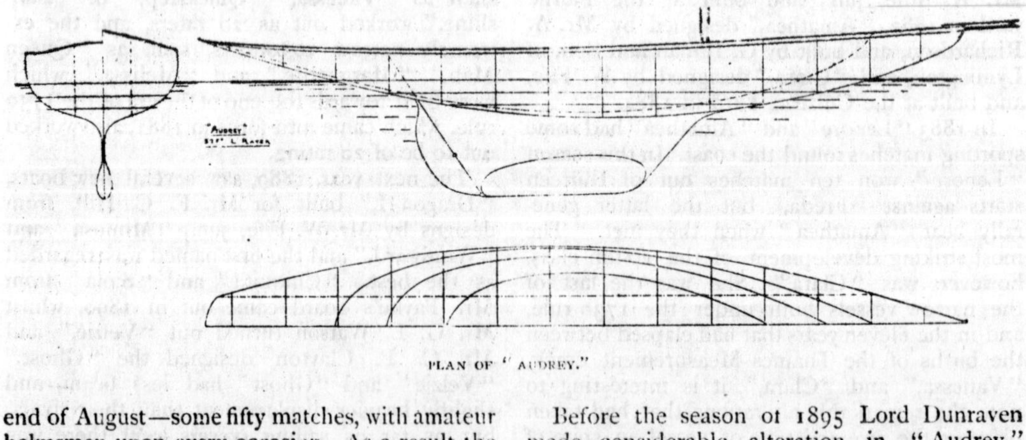

PLAN OF "AUDREY."

Before the season of 1895 Lord Dunraven made considerable alteration in "Audrey." She was a round bodied boat with a wooden fin and bulb; the wooden fin was removed and a metal one fixed in its place, and the body of the yacht having been found too deep it was reduced about 6 inches by the transverse sections being taken in from the water-line downwards. The hull of the vessel was thus made shallower and flatter in the floor by practically almost rebuilding her, though the original idea of design was retained.

To complement the reduction of draught of body, the buttock lines were drawn out and the boat given a slightly longer snout. She was greatly improved and turned out to be the only boat fit to tackle the Herreshoff fliers "Niagara" and "Isolde," which came over in 1895.

The peculiar characteristics of the American pair, which were said to be built from the same design, were the exaggerated overhanging pram bows, the full, almost boxy, quarters, and counters sawn off at the end. Where the plate keel met the body of the vessel, the angle was neatly filled in by two flanged plates, transforming the sections of the vessel into curves. The spars, gear, and canvas, and the scantling of these American boats were of the lightest and yet the most serviceable description. The hull was a mere shell sub-divided by lath and canvas bulkheads. "Niagara" was the best of the pair and displayed remarkable sailing powers, for although "Audrey" could tackle her in a nice whole sail breeze and was equal to her in a fresh wind, in really hard weather the American could generally turn tables on Lord Dunraven's cutter.

"AUDREY."

"Eucharis," launched at Fairlie from lines by Mr. W. Fife, jun., was the only new twenty built in 1895, and she turned out to be a very moderate vessel. She was a plate and bulb boat of the extreme type, but although she twice beat "Niagara" on the Clyde, she could do very little except on a reaching course

As to the result of the season's racing, "Niagara" won 25 firsts out of 46 starts, "Audrey" 16 first prizes out of 32 starts, and "Inyoni," still the crack in light weather, 15 firsts in 40 starts. It must be mentioned, however, that on leaving the South "Niagara" lost the competition of her formidable opponents "Audrey" and "Inyoni." On the Clyde, the Mersey, and at Torbay she met only "Eucharis," "Zinita," and "Mimosa," and eleven of her first prizes were practically walks over.

The first year of the Linear Rating or Girth rule saw the return to a rather more roomy type of boat, for "Penitent" and "The Saint," designed by Mr. A. E. Payne and Mr. W. Fife, jun., respectively, were somewhat deeper in the body than the bulb keelers of the previous season. "Penitent," indeed, was a keel boat not unlike an elongated "Dragon II," or "Luna" with fuller bow sections, whilst "The Saint" was a wooden fin keel boat, a kind of compromise between the "Penitent" type and the pure plate and bulb.

"Samphire," a plate and bulb boat designed and built by Mr. Chas. Sibbick, also made her appearance in the Mediterranean.

"Audrey," "Niagara," and "Isolde" were all brought out to do battle with the new cutters, all being in pretty much the same trim as 1895.

The year 1896, by reason of the trial of the different types, proved a most interesting season's racing, and the excellent performance of "Audrey" and "Niagara" with the new cutters speaks well for the value of the bulb keel type, for, looking at the dimensions of the boats, it will be seen that the newer craft had a decided advantage over them.

Yacht.	Built	Designer.	Length.	Breadth	Sail area.
Audrey	1895	Lord Dunraven	44·33	13·15	2,699
Penitent	1896	Payne	47·9	12·52	3,076
The Saint ...	1896	Fife	46·84	12·20	2,975
Niagara	1895	Herreshoff	44·45	12·13	2,726

"The Saint" turned out the most successful prize winner. Out of a total of 57 matches sailed during the season she started 42 times and won 20 first prizes; "Niagara" started 43 times, winning 12; "Penitent" 50 times, winning 15 firsts; and "Audrey" won 7 firsts out of 28 starts. One of "Niagara's" wins, that by which she won outright the Challenge Cup presented to the Castle Yacht Club by Lord Dunraven can hardly be estimated as a victory. "Audrey" handsomely defeated "Niagara," but lost the cup on a protest of the latter, on a technicality, namely, that "Audrey's" entry was not made according to the letter of the rule.

"The Saint," after her successful season in British waters, took her departure for Germany where an unfortunate accident befell her. Whilst in tow of a tug the hawser parted and the yacht drifted on the rocks and became a total wreck.

The new cutters were a compromise between an ordinary keel yacht and one of the fin keeled type, with rather deeper body than "The Saint"; in fact, their midship sections were not unlike "Dragon III," Mr. Fife's design of 1893; but they had the extreme rake of stern post, immense overhang and pram bows which were the developments of four seasons' competition in yacht designing.

"Penitent" was sold by her original owner,

"Penitent."

Last season, 1897, saw two additions to the 52 foot class, both built at Fairlie from Mr. Fife's design, namely, "Morning Star" for Mr. Andrew Coates and "Senga" for Mr. F. A. Dubs.

They were about a foot longer on the L.W.L. than the same designer's creation of the previous season, being 47 feet 6 inches against "The Saint's" 46 feet 6 inches; their beam was identical with that of the latter vessel, and their sail area slightly larger.

Mr. C. D. Rose, to Mr. W. P. Burton, but she was not brought out until the Solent racing began in August. "Audrey," Lord Dunraven's cutter, now in her fourth season, or third since she was rebuilt, was tuned up in a wonderful fashion. Her owner had the angle of her plate and bilge padded to reduce her girth, which, under the present rule, allowed her nearly 100 feet additional sail area, though even then, with 2,780 square feet she had nearly 300 feet less sail area than "Penitent." The effect of the alterations to "Audrey" was most satisfactory, for the old boat was quite as good as her rivals; the season's racing may be briefly summed up as follows:—

"Penitent," the keel boat, which was much better handled than in 1896, was most successful beating to windward in light and moderate weather; "Audrey," the plate and bulb boat, was the best in a breeze, especially in rough water; and "Morning Star," the semi-fin keeled cutter, proved a perfect flier in light weather.

It is safe to conclude that for all round sailing there was very little to choose between the trio, "Penitent" winning 9 firsts out of 16 starts, "Audrey" winning 10 firsts out of 37 starts, and "Morning Star" 17 firsts out of 37 starts whilst sailing in class races. A curious instance of the difference that sometimes occurs in the capabilities of yachts, although built to the same lines, may be found in "Senga," a cutter which, although a sister ship to the successful "Morning Star," was comparatively a failure, the case being one of "Niagara" and "Isolde," and "Annasona" and "Sleuth Hound" over again.

Looking at the annals of the twenty class during the last quarter of a century, although many changes have occurred in the shape of the yachts, the dimensions of the craft have kept tolerably level.

The length of a twenty has usually been from 45 feet 6 inches to 48 feet, and the sail area from 2,600 to 2,900 square feet.

"Clara" was the only wide departure from the rule; but "Audrey" and "Inyoni" have gone below the average in the matter of length, and "Penitent" exceeded the usual limit of sail area.

The beam of the 20-tonners in "Vanessa's" days was about 10 feet; in the time of "Freda," "Amathea," "Lenore," and "Clara," it fell gradually as low as 9 feet in the last-named vessel. In the early 20 raters, from 1888 to 1890, it was about the same as in old "Vanessa's" time, whilst latterly the beam has increased to from 12 to 13 feet.

With regard to the speed of the craft, there is no doubt that a modern 52-footer would complete the same course in less time than a yacht of "Clara's" type in any weather. The only possible chance for the narrow boat would be on a reaching course. The advantage of the bulb keel and pram bow combined is very evident in "Audrey," which, after three hard seasons' racing, could still hold her own with the boats built with deeper sections, such as the framers of the present rule anticipated it would produce, and her performances speak well for the prospects of bulb keel craft during the next three seasons during which the rule will be in force.

The dimensions and form of the latest 52 foot Linear raters differ but little from those of the boats built last year. The Fife boat "Viera" is very similar to "Morning Star," and Payne's "Eldred" to "Penitent." It is too early to comment on their performance, but they do not appear to show much improvement on "Penitent" or "Senga."

Appended is a table showing the dimensions of some of the principal twenties constructed during the last 25 years:—

Date.	Rule Built under.	Yacht.	Length on load water line.	Beam.	Sail area.	Measurement.
1873	Thames	Vanessa ...	47	9·9	2,600	20-tonner
1884	1,740	Clara	53	9	3,500	"
1888	Length & Sail area	Vreda	45·4	10·1	2,641	20-rater.
1889	"	Dragon I..	45·5	10·3	2,632	"
1890	"	Velzie	46	10·1	2,641	"
1891	"	Zinita	46·2	13·01	2,554[1]	"
1895	"	Audrey ...	44·33	13·15	2,699	"
1897	Present rule	Audrey (altered)	44·03	13·15	2,780	52 ft. lin. rater.
1896	"	Penitent...	47·9	12·52	3,076	"
1897	"	Morning Star	47·74	12·15	2,929	"

1 "Zinita" now carries 2,838 feet of sail under the present rule to make her 52 feet linear rating.

Before dealing with the small classes in their present high state of perfection, it is necessary to glance briefly into the annals of small yacht racing as it existed in the "seventies," for if the past history and origin of the modern "rater" with its comparatively shallow body, bulb or fin keel, and hull so lightly yet skilfully and strongly put together that it is a masterpiece of the cabinetmaker's, rather than of the shipwright's, art, be disregarded, it would be impossible to recognise in her the logical outcome of the old time miniature racing cutter.

The five ton class, under the old Rule of Thames measurement, first came into existence on the lower reaches of the Thames, where the crack boats were the "Arrow," built by Stone of Erith in 1870, and four years later the "Virago" from the hands of the same builder.

In 1876 all the existing five tonners were eclipsed by the "Freda," which was designed by Mr. Beavor Webb, and built by the late Dan Hatcher for Sir Thomas Freke, and she may be said to have been the most successful boat of her size built under the Thames tonnage rule. During her first season she won fifteen matches out of seventeen starts; and in September of the same year her owner issued a challenge in the *Field* to sail any boat of her size belonging to the Clyde or Ireland, for £100 a side. The challenge was accepted by Mr. F. Lawson, owner of the Fairlie built "Camellia," and Mr. J. Lawrence, who owned the Watson designed "Vril"; and it was arranged that "Freda" should sail three races with each boat at Holyhead in May of the following year. The races resulted in a decisive victory for the English craft, which thus vindicated her right to the title of champion 5-tonner.

The "Thames" tonnage rule was found to tax beam rather severely, and in view of this Mr. Beavor Webb made "Freda" somewhat longer, narrower and deeper-draughted than her predecessors. She carried her lead lower, and consequently had more sail-carrying power. These advantages, coupled with the fact that she had exceptionally pretty lines for a boat built two and twenty years ago, ensured her success.

In 1880 came a change of Rule and the $\frac{(L+B)^2 \times B}{1730}$ measurement was introduced in the place of the Thames Rule with the hope of relieving what was considered an excessive tax on beam. However, in this respect the rule proved a failure, and the 5-tonners went on growing longer, narrower and heavier with a corresponding increase in sail plan and in weight of spars and gear. They became exceedingly costly craft into the bargain.

After the rule had been working a few years, builders began to turn out yachts which were of 5 tons measurement by dimensions, but displaced as much as 8, 10 or even 12 tons, instead of 5 tons as was the original intention.

When the 1730 rule was found to have the effect of increasing the cost of 5-tonners to a very considerable extent, a 3-ton class sprang into existence. These soon became boats of a very extreme type, long, narrow, deep, and very wet in a sea. The Clyde was the original home of this class, but they spread round the English coast, and in 1882 several of them were to be found on the Thames. The most noted of these little crafts that year were the "Snarley Yow" and "Mascotte" on the Thames and a Devonport built boat called the "Chittywee," designed by Mr. J. Ash, which was the best boat of the year. The masterpiece of the 3-ton fleet was fated, however, to come from the hands of that promising young designer, Mr. W. E. Paton, who lost his life in the wreck of the "Oona," off the East coast of Ireland, just when he had succeeded in making a name for himself, and in his creation, the "Currytush," was found a boat which was destined to prove the most successful 3-tonner in Southern waters. So successful indeed was the "Currytush" that no boat could be found to compete against her, and as any hope of building a craft to rival her appeared to mean going to great expense only to produce something still longer and narrower, small boat sailers fought shy of the task. As a result she was left alone in her glory, having practically extinguished the 3-ton class in the South.

On the Clyde, however, there was still a sporting class of narrow 3-tonners which kept up a series of matches for some years after the class had lost its popularity in the South: the best of these were "Ariel," "Cora," "Coila," "Rona," and "Daisy." The class may be fairly said to have died hard, for up to the year 1887 they still kept up races among themselves under the 1730 rule after it had been abolished and the Length and Sail area had become law.

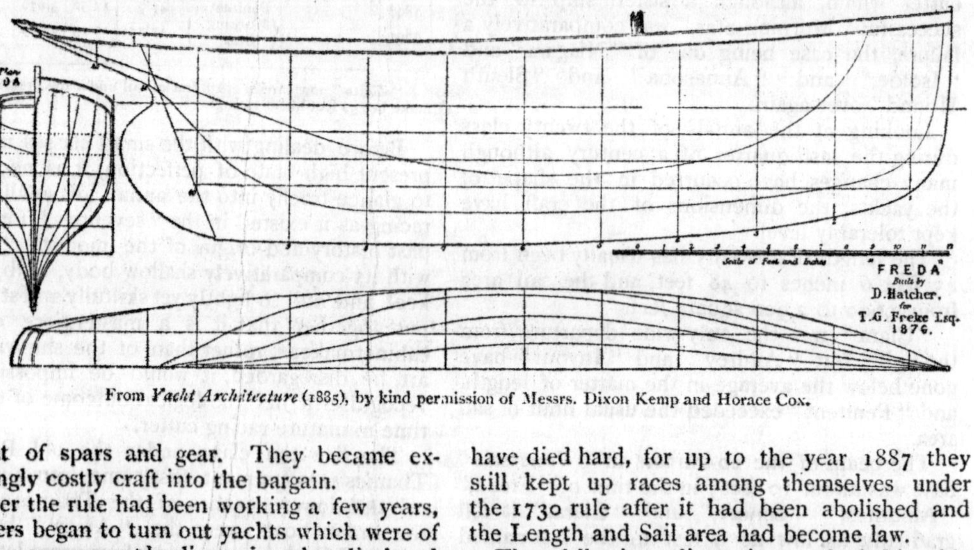

From *Yacht Architecture* (1885), by kind permission of Messrs. Dixon Kemp and Horace Cox.

The following dimensions of fashionable small racing craft in the years 1885–6 will be looked at with astonishment by many modern yachtsmen.

Name.	Length.	Beam.	Draught	Displacement.	Sail area.	Tonnage.
	Feet.	Feet.	Feet.	Tons.		
Oona	34	5·5	8	12·5	1,750	5
Cocker	32	5·95	5·75	8·2	1,528	5
Jenny Wren	34	5·45	7·5	11·4	1,645	5
Currytush....	28·5	4·7	6	—	1,060	3
Eclipse	30	10	7·7½	13·6	2,280	33 feet Itchen Ferry Boat.
Keepsake ...	30	9·8	7	13·7	—	30
Verena	25	9	6·8	8·6	1,750	25

The overhanging stem was introduced into some of these little vessels, but owing to the narrowness of the water-lines forward it is obvious that but small advantage was gained by

In Falmouth Harbour.

it. Another freak of construction, which first saw light in the days of the "plank-on-edge" type, but which did not become popular for many years after, was the hollow in the forward longitudinal vertical section, or what is colloquially termed the bow profile. All the crack "threes" and "fives" had their fore foot severely cut away, but we believe Mr. R. E. Froude, who designed and sailed the famous 5 tonner "Jenny Wren," was the pioneer in this respect. She, at any rate, was the first craft of the type of any note, although some yachtsmen will doubtless remember Mr. Bentall's long wall sided 10 tonner "Evolution," which carried her lead in a cigar-shaped bulb bolted on to a boiler-plate and had a profile not unlike some of the modern raters. "Evolution" was as big a failure as his great yawl "Jullanar" was a success. The dimensions of the "Evolution" were :-

Length on load line	51 ft.
Beam	6·5 ft.
Draught	10 ft.

She was built in 1881.

Apart from the Y.R.A. classes, various local types flourished round the coast. These boats, in nearly every instance, sailed under a pure length measurement and, broadly speaking, played a far less important part in the evolution of the modern "Rater" than the small tonnage rule classes, though they formed a capital school for amateur talent.

Many an amateur now-a-days—aye, and many a paid hand too—out of a "Solent Class" rater would be very much at sea in one of the Itchen Ferry 30 footers as they existed in their palmy days, with gigantic sail spread and a spinaker boom longer than the ship over all.

The Itchen Ferry boats, which sailed under a simple length on the load-water-line rule, were classified as follows : 30 feet, 25 feet, 21 feet, and 13 feet. The craft of course originated from the straight stemmed and square sterned Itchen Ferry fishing boats, which were fitted with iron keels and inside iron ballast. From these handy fisher craft, the keen competition of racing developed in a few years yachts of about three beams to their L.W.L. length, instead of three and a half, much fuller midship sections, and heavy lead keels coupled with greatly increased draught, whilst the sail spread was also carried to great excess.

These beamy length class boats had really very little to recommend them, and adverse criticism was general. They were unhandy and, in a seaway, jumped like porpoises; whilst the narrow tonnage rule yachts, on the other hand, though terribly wet, had the virtue of being fairly fast craft in a heavy sea, and in their time were regarded as wondrous weatherly vessels; in fact British yachtsmen a dozen years since were loth to believe that the plank-on-edge was not the beau ideal of a racing craft in the diminutive as well as in the large classes.

In much the same manner as "Currytush" had extinguished the three tonners, the 30 footers, "Eclipse" and "Curtsy," both designed by Mr. C. P. Clayton, settled the 30-foot length class, and "Bird of Freedom," designed by Feltham of Portsmouth, and "Verena," a similar boat, carried off most of the prizes in the 21-foot class. In 1886, the last year of the "1730" rule, small yacht racing was not in a flourishing condition anywhere ; it was at its lowest ebb on the Solent, where the introduction of the Length and Sail area rule was hailed as a welcome change.

A crucial test of light versus heavy displacement, and beam versus depth, came about in August of the year 1887, and yachtsmen got an inkling of the potentialities of light displacement with plenty of beam under the new Length and Sail area measurement rule.

At the regatta of the Royal Irish Yacht Club at Kingstown, a remarkable trial took place between "Mischief," a Lough Erne boat, owned by Lieut. H. Gartside Tipping, and the crack Scotch five-tonner, "Doris"; the latter being Mr. G. L. Watson's happiest venture under the old narrow style. She was owned and sailed with an almost unbeaten record by Mr. Bryce Allan. The Lough Erne boat was a mere skimming dish ; she had been originally fitted with a centre board, but the centre plate had given place to a fixed lead fin of about five tons weight, so that she was practically a forerunner of the modern type. Both boats measured 10 rating under the Length and Sail area rule.

"Mischief's" career had been somewhat eventful prior to her *début* in open waters at Kingstown. She had been carried across country from Lough Erne to the coast on a truck, and then sailed across to Birkenhead to have the before-mentioned keel fitted, and thence back to Kingstown to try her luck in the Bay. Her owner being anxious not to miss the trial with the Scotch champion, had not time to get her caulked, and she could hardly be kept afloat during the passage, as she leaked like a sieve. Old salts ridiculed the idea of this half walnut-shell attempting to lower "Doris's" colours, and her owner, on asking for his sailing instructions, was chaffingly told that if he followed "Doris," provided he could keep her slender taffrail in sight, he could not go wrong.

Great was the astonishment, however, when in a grand breeze, with reefed mainsails, "Mischief" completely out-sailed "Doris" on every point ; it was emphatically an open-water trial, too, and there were some tearing squalls in the second round. Col. E. Saunderson, M.P., was at the helm of the Lough Erne boat, which won by seven minutes over a fourteen mile course.

In a light weather trial on the following day

"Mischief," this time steered by her owner, was again the victor, and her performance was considered even more remarkable than on the previous day, for the boat could only set lower canvas to keep her within the rating, whilst "Doris" had the advantage of jackyarder and jib topsail, and was driven for all she was worth.

Though "Doris" had her revenge at Kingstown in the Royal Alfred Regatta, when she got the best of the skimming dish going to windward, the result of the matches gave designers such an insight into what could be done with light displacement craft when well handled, that it is fair to regard Lieut. Gartside Tipping's plucky venture as one of the most important events in the annals of modern yacht racing.

The same summer of 1887 saw the commencement of what have since come to be called the "Solent classes," though the term is not altogether appropriate as, of course, the smaller Y.R.A. classes compete under identical conditions at other yachting centres.

The $2\frac{1}{2}$-rating class sprung first into existence, and the first boats built to it were "Madcap," owned by Miss Mabel Cox, and "Thalassa," by Col. J. T. Bucknill, R.E.; they were only 21 feet on L.W.L., and set 690 square feet of sail—very small craft compared with the later competitors in the $2\frac{1}{2}$ rating class; they had the first year of "Solent class" racing pretty much to themselves.

The following season was a fairly quiet one, as the new classes had scarcely become organised; in fact the duty of keeping small class racing alive devolved entirely upon the $2\frac{1}{2}$ raters. Several new boats, such as Mr. T. W. Waller's "Lady Nan," "Chipmunk," owned by Mr. S. C. Watson, "Fairy," Captain J. W. Hughes, a 1·9 rater, "Ada," Mr. Manning, and "Tottie," a Thames 21-footer, a very deep narrow craft, which rated about 1·8, and was brought round from the river by Mr. Simpson, after having made a great reputation amongst boats of her own type in Sea Reach: these with "Madcap" and "Thalassa" kept up the class.

The 10-raters of 1888 were an equally scratch lot, consisting of "Dis," a smart clipper stemmed craft, designed by Mr. J. M. Soper; "Lollypop," of 6·5 rating, a straight stemmed cutter with her mast rather far forward, a short boat in comparison to her sail area; the old narrow five-tonner "Jenny Wren," designed by Mr. R. E. Froude, and sometimes the ancient square-sterned Itchen ferry boat, "Dolly Varden." "Dis" fairly eclipsed all comers, and carried off twenty-five first prizes out of twenty eight starts; but she occasionally met her match, and it was something of a surprise to see "Dolly Varden," which at that time was about fifteen years old, tuned up to racing trim and given a new lease of life by the change of rule, leading "Dis," round the course and getting the winning gun, as she did on one occasion at the Royal Southampton Club.

The summer of 1889 was a season of good whole sail breezes and the chief interest in the Solent amongst the small classes lay in the meeting of "Decima," a new 10 rater, designed by Mr. A. E. Payne, with "Dis," the champion of the previous year, and subsequently in her matches with the Clyde favourite "Yvonne." "Decima" had a nearly plumb stem, and was a deeper vessel than "Dis," and carried rather more canvas in her mainsail; both were about 36 feet on the water-line, and carried about 1660 square feet of canvas. The new cutter gave "Dis" a pretty good dressing, and could beat her soundly by the wind in a breeze, and her battles with the Clyde boats "Yvonne" and "Doris" caused immense excitement in the Solent at the time.

"Decima" beat "Yvonne" five times out of eight starts and "Doris" eleven times out of fourteen starts. So keen was the interest in the racing between the first-named pair, that an enthusiastic compiler of statistics went so far as to ascertain that in the three races in which "Yvonne" beat "Decima," they sailed one hundred miles, and "Yvonne" beat "Decima" 5·94 seconds per mile, and in the five races won by the latter they sailed 163 miles, and "Decima" beat "Yvonne" 9·68 seconds per mile. The 10-rating class in the South came to an end in 1890, and to this day has never been revived.

The $2\frac{1}{2}$-raters had a capital season in 1889, and a new boat named "Humming Bird," designed by Mr. A. E. Payne for Capt. Hughes, came out and won 25 first prizes out of 38 starts. She was one of the first fin-keeled craft with straight stem and square stern.

The "Fives," which first came to light in 1890 and have become increasingly popular ever since, have more than taken the place of their bigger sisters, the 10-raters.

The 5-raters which opened the ball were "Glycera," Mr. P. Perceval; "Alwida," Lord Dunraven; and the old straight-stemmed "Lollypop," Mr. W. P. Burton, all designed by Mr. A. E. Payne, and a centre-board boat "Archie" from the board of Mr. G. L. Watson.

They sailed upwards of 40 matches, and as a result "Alwida" and "Glycera" were very much on a par, though the latter had 19 firsts to "Alwida's" 14; "Lollypop" and "Archie" had 9 and 8 first prizes respectively.

The same season was a first-rate one for the $2\frac{1}{2}$-raters. "The Babe" and "Cock-a-Whoop," Payne boats, and "Dolphin," designed by Mr. C. P. Clayton, were the best of the fleet. Mr. Arthur Payne, with his numerous additions to the Solent fleet during the years 1890, 1891, 1892, set the pattern of the modern small rater, and by his originality may fairly claim in these years to have done more than any other designer in the development of the type. Nearly all the racing craft became deep draught fin-keel boats, with what is known as a sawn-off counter, the overhang aft finishing about where it ceased to touch the water when the vessel was heeled over, with the very sensible object of getting rid of all superfluous weight. The innovation was certainly unsightly, but a boat like "The Babe" was much superior on every point of sailing to

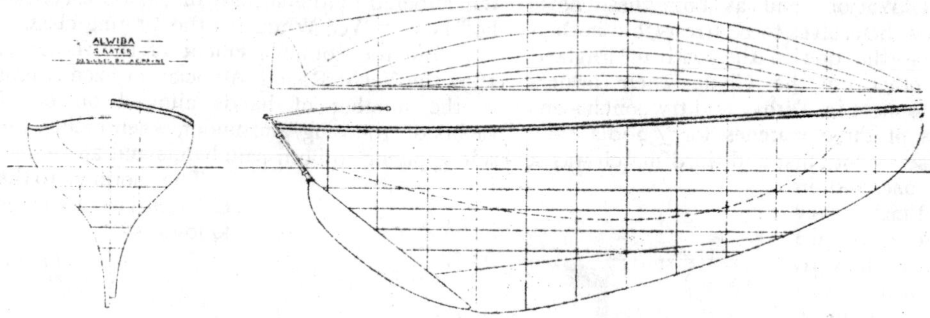

the old type of craft built under the Thames and 1730 Tonnage rules. The characteristics of the new boats were extreme quickness in stays, handiness and power of thrashing to windward in broken water. Changes were made in the rig as well as in the design of racing craft, and by the season of 1891 almost all boats had adopted the standing lug in place of the gaff mainsail.

There being no tax on beam under the Length and Sail Area form of measurement, the boats were treated to a liberal amount of it. Five years' experience of the rule made it manifest that by reducing displacement as much as

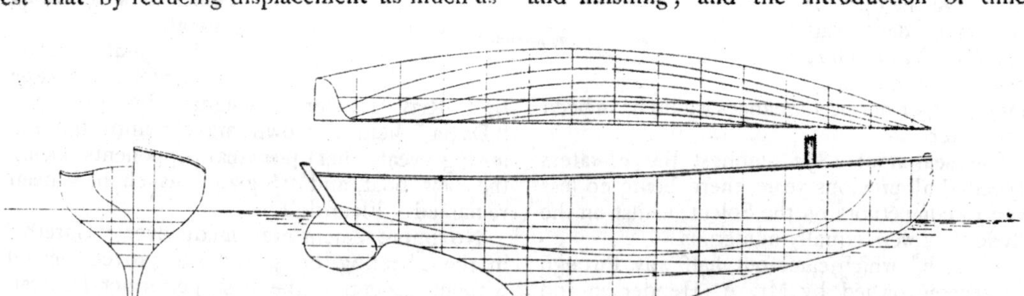

possible, and sail area slightly, and proportionately increasing the load water-line, a faster type could be produced.

Hence it will be found that nearly all the 2½-raters produced in 1891 and 1892 measured 28 feet in length on the water line, whereas 25 was the average in the previous season, and only 21 in the opening year; whilst 33 feet was found to be about the most suitable length for a 5-rater.

Mrs. Schenley's "Windfall," designed by Mr. A. E. Payne, proved the best of the 5-raters in 1891, whilst "Savourna," owned by Mr. P. Perceval, from the board of the same designer, was a good second. "Iernia," a Fife boat, owned by Mr. H. R. Langrishe, and "Quinque," designed by her owner, Col. J. T. Bucknill, were less successful.

In the 2½-rating class "The Babe" still held the sway, winning no less than 36 first prizes out of 45 starts, although several new boats competed with her. Her record was an excellent one, and small boat sailers will have a vivid recollection of the masterly manner in which she was handled by her owner.

This season was the first year of the 1½-rating classes, but mixed races were often indulged in, Y.R.A. time allowance being given between the classes.

This method of sailing was not satisfactory, as the excitement of small boat racing, more than in any phase of yacht racing, lies in the close work when rounding marks, cross tacking and finishing; and the introduction of time allowance naturally spoiled the fun of the game; it was consequently decided to keep the classes entirely separate in the future.

Perhaps the best ½-raters built in this season were "Dee Dee," designed by Mr. A. E. Payne, and "Coquette," from lines by Mr. Chas. Nicholson, whilst "Unit" in the 1-rating class from the board of Mr. G. F. Flemmich, was a handy little craft.

The following year, 1892, "Cyane," owned by Lord Dunraven, and "Squall," both Payne boats, came out in the 5-rating class, but were fairly eclipsed by another new craft, built for Mr. Langrishe and sold by him to Lord Dudley, the "Dacia," which was far and away the best boat in the South, and one of the most even performers that Mr. C. E. Nicholson, her designer and builder, ever produced. Her success was phenomenal; indeed, the only 5-rater which could be compared with "Dacia" in 1892 was the Scotch boat "Natica," designed by Mr. G. L. Watson, and as both these boats had proved themselves to be irresistible in their own waters—the one in the south of England and the other on the Clyde—their owners arranged to meet in Torbay and try conclusions in a series of three matches for £200 a side. The course in the first and third match was a triangular one, and in the second match they had a dead to leeward and dead to windward trial. "Dacia" won the first race in a summer breeze by 30 seconds. The second match fell to "Natica," who ghosted along in the lightest of airs in a remarkable manner and won comfortably. In the concluding match "Dacia" led from start to finish, coming home with a lead of 1 minute 5 seconds, but she was disqualified for a slight foul. On neither of the three days did "Dacia" get that amount of wind which suited her, or her performances would have been still better.

2½-RATER.

The season of 1892 amongst the 2½-raters exceeded all previous years, there being no less than 14 competitors on the Solent, whilst on the Clyde they were equally numerous.

"Gareth," which came out half way through the season, owned by Mr. A. Henderson and designed by Mr. Charles Nicholson, was the crack in fresh winds on the Solent, and "Faugh-a-Ballagh" and "Polynia," both Payne boats, were the best in light weather. In Scotch waters "Wenonah," designed and built by Herreshoff in America, came over and showed a marked superiority over the local fleet. This year the 1-raters had their first notable season. "Doushka," by Payne, and two boats, "Mahatma" and "Kitten," built at a newly started yard in Cowes, made a creditable display; the first-named was from Mr. G. F. Flemmich's design.

If these were not the first they were, at any rate, the first racing boats of any note built at a yard, the name of which was destined to become a household word in connection with small yacht racing. The success of Mr. Chas. Sibbick's designs in yachts up to 5-rating and the immense number of craft that have been turned out from the Cowes yard is truly remarkable, and during the last seven years Sibbick's raters have made a name far beyond the Solent. The season of 1892 will also be remembered by the success of the little Herreshoff boat, "Wee Winn," in the ½-rating class.

Before the commencement of the season of 1893 the Yacht Racing Association fixed a limit to the number of hands allowed on board yachts of 10-rating and under, when racing, the rule applying to both paid hands and amateurs.

The allotment to the different classes was as follows:—

Class.	Number of persons allowed on board.
½ Rating	2 persons.
1 ,,	3 ,,
2½ ,,	5 ,,
5 ,,	7 ,,
10 ,,	9 ,,

The motive of the new regulation was to put a stop to "live ballast," for in some of the light displacement 1-raters and ½-raters the practice of crowding five or six passengers on the weather gunwale whenever there was a fresh wind seemed to be becoming general.

The 5-rating class was reinforced in 1893 by "Red Lancer," designed by Fife, but "Dacia" held her own bravely until the following year, her principal opponents being the new boat, and "Squall," which had been re-named "Fleur-de-Lys."

No improvement was made over "Gareth" in the 2½-rating class, and she proved herself without exception the best performer in fresh winds ever built under the Length and Sail area rule; indeed, in a strong head wind and lumpy sea it is probable that, to this day, Mr. Nicholson's production of 1892 is equal to any of the more modern boats. She is a remarkable instance of what may be done with a well-balanced plate-and-bulb craft.

Although "Gareth" was the best boat of the year, "Meneen," a Herreshoff production, made a great name as a light weather flier, and created quite as much sensation as did the Herreshoff ½-rater, "Wee Winn," in the previous season.

On the Clyde an interesting class of 2½-raters

continued in fashion, but "Wenonah," the American crack, still held the sway.

The Herreshoff boats about this period played an important part in British waters, for Miss Sutton's "Morwena" more than held her own against the Solent fleet of 1-raters, of which the Payne designed "Sacharissa," and the Sibbick designed "Tartar" were the most conspicuous. The little American fliers were very light displacement craft, and their success to a great extent precipitated the introduction of the "pram" bow in our waters, as this was a prominent feature in all the Herreshoff designs.

The 5-rating class in 1894 was strengthened by several additions. They consisted of a new "Fleur de Lys," designed by Mr. Fife, the first "Fleur de Lys" having been turned into a cruiser, and her name changed to "Dragon Fly," "Delanagh," designed by Mr. G. L. Watson, and "Flat Fish." built at Messrs. Fay's Yard, Southampton, from lines by Mr. F. E. Soper. The last-named was a remarkable production, being an absolute exponent of the skimming dish type; her floor was as flat as a hat, and she carried an abnormally deep plate and bulb, she had great beam, her L.W.L. length not exceeding three times her breadth.

The initial stability of such a craft was enormous. In hard winds she sailed merrily along on practically an even keel, and consequently the strain on hull and gear was so great that by the end of the season the vessel was badly buckled. When in a hard wind she could get through a match without a carry away, she was all of five minutes better than any of her rivals, but mishaps were so frequent with her that the Fife boat "Fleur de Lys," which was very fast on a reach though an indifferent performer to windward, had the best string of flags at the close of the season.

In the 2½ class "Gareth" and "Meneen" easily defeated all newcomers, the former winning in heavy weather and the latter in light breezes. The 1-raters became too numerous to enumerate; Mr. Arthur Payne's creation "Red Rover" was the most weatherly of the fleet, while some of the host of Sibbick raters were fastest on a reach. The old saying that over the Solent courses "'tis the reaching that wins the matches" proved very true.

In the season of 1895 the number of starters in the Solent matches in all classes, except the 5-rating class, continued to increase, and it is not too much to say that the season must be regarded as one of the most remarkable in the history of the sport.

The doings of the 5-raters are soon recorded; "Fleur de Lys" went out to the Mediterranean, where she found a new owner, and did not return to take part in the English racing; "Delanagh" followed suit; Mrs. Schenley sold the remarkable "Flat Fish," and under her new flag the yacht took very little part in class racing

Two new craft were built for the Solent—namely, "Norman," for Captain J. Orr Ewing, from Mr. Charles Sibbick's board, and "Sea Shell," from lines by Mr. G. L. Watson, for Captain J. A. Orr Ewing; on the Clyde, "Almida," designed by Mr. W. Fife, jun., proved a great success.

"Norman" completely outsailed "Sea Shell," and secured a perfectly wonderful record, winning fifty-one first prizes out of fifty-six starts; however, she had very little opposition, for she only met "Flat Fish" five times in the whole season.

The first two of these trials were sailed in hard winds. "Flat Fish" won the first match by three minutes, and the Sibbick boat the second trial by the same margin; on the second occasion, there was less wind and rather more close hauled work, which seemed to favour "Norman." The three remaining races were in light weather, and "Flat Fish" was completely outclassed. It was unfortunate that "Norman" never met the Clyde five, "Almida," as a contest between the pair would have proved instructive.

"Norman" was the last and the most famous 5-rater built before the advent of the present rating rule. She was essentially a skimming dish, being 30 feet on the L.W.L. by 10 feet 9 inches beam, and 50 feet over all, whilst her depth from deck to keelson was only 3 feet 6 inches. She was rigged, like most of the raters of the time, with standing lug, single head sail, and no bowsprit.

In the 2½- and 1-rating classes it is curious to note that British designers, having made a study of light displacement craft, turned out some boats that could completely outsail the representatives from Mr. Herreshoff's board "Vaquero" 2½-rater, and "Lagopa," 1-rater, that were shipped across the Atlantic to compete in Solent waters. The Sibbick 2½-rater "Lorette," which, as an all-round performer, was about on a par with "Gareth," and Mr. Nicholson's 1895 production "Corolla," met "Vaquero," the Herreshoff boat, five times, defeated her on four occasions, and was some distance ahead when she took the ground during the fifth match.

H.R.H. the Duke of York owned the Sibbick built 1-rater "White Rose" during this season, which recalls the fact that a royal Prince had not been seen at the tiller of a small racing boat since the days of the Cowes Una boats, from 1880 to 1886, when the Prince of Wales used to sail his smart little "Belle Lurette," against the Marquis of Stafford's craft "The Unknown," and Viscount Dursley's "Merry Duchess." "White Rose" has now found a quiet repose on the placid surface of Virginia Water.

Great has been the increase of racing during the years under review, and old-time yachtsmen will wonder when they realise the fact that whereas in 1876, in the palmy days of the

Thames Measurement rule, some 400 matches were sailed by the forty-tonners, twenty-tonners, fifteen-tonners, ten-tonners, and five-tonners, in 1885, under the "1730" rule, nearly 600 matches took place, and in 1895 no less than 1,700 matches were sailed under the Length and Sail area rule. This great increase was mainly due to the development of the small classes.

By this time the process of evolution from the old-fashioned keel miniature yacht of the eighties had been completed. With the exception of a few centreboard craft, the entire fleet of Solent raters had adopted the fixed plate and lead bulb system of ballasting, an improvement and modification of arrangement which, as has already been mentioned, was for the first time fitted to the ten-tonner "Evolution" by Mr. Bentall, some fifteen years before. It seems passing strange that after such a phenomenally successful season as that of 1895, the Y.R.A. should bring in a change of measurement; but nevertheless such is the fact, and the present Linear Rating rule was introduced in the face of a strong current of adverse criticism from small yacht owners.

Sporting instincts proved, however, too strong for pride or prejudice and shoals of yachts were built in 1896 to the new Y.R.A. classes of 36 feet Linear Rating and under. Though undoubtedly the new rating Rule was unpopular with the majority of owners, the pastime in the Solent did not in any way suffer from its introduction. Exciting and crowded starts and beam and beam matches were still innumerable, but, as is often the case with the commencement of a new era of measurement, the opening season was not remarkable for any great change in construction or design. The first productions under the new rule showed a very slight increase in displacement, a decrease in draught, and a considerable increase in sail area; whilst the body form of the boats, though it still kept to the plate and bulb in most cases, showed a tendency towards a deepening of the midship section, and pinching in of the beam, while the overhang and "pram" bow form continued to become exaggerated.

'WESTRA.'

The season opened in the 36 foot class with four new boats from the Albert yard, all from Mr. C. Sibbick's design; these were "Heartsease" for Mr. C. L. Orr-Ewing, M.P., "Ermin," Mr. C. A. Tonge, "Silvia," Mr. A. H. E. Wood, and "Westra," Mr. J. C. Connell; they averaged about 31 feet on the L.W.L. with 9 feet 6 inches beam, and 5 feet 9 inches draught, and carried 1250 to 1300 square feet of canvas. Two additions came from Messrs. Camper and Nicholson's at Gosport, but neither were of much account. Mr. Fife had one new boat "Fern," and Mr. Arthur Payne produced "Emerald"; whilst Mr. C. P. Clayton made a bold move and built a heavy displacement boat with an O.G. section. The result of the racing was that "Westra" and "Heartsease" were the pick of the fleet, whilst "Emerald" had too heavy a bulb, and Mr. Clayton's boat, "Edie," had overdone it in the way of displacement. "Westra" and "Emerald" were the best performers in hard winds, but the balance was considerably in favour of the former, and "Norman," of 1895 fame, had a good look in when it blew very hard.

In rig the boats, with the exception of "Westra" and "Fern," which still kept to the lug sail, reverted to the style of the old 5-tonners, for they all set cutters' canvas with jack yarders and jib headers, though of course bowsprits were more stumpy and spinaker booms of a more handy length than in former days.

"Heartsease's" record of 26 firsts out of 50 starts; and "Westra's" 24 firsts out of 34 starts constituted the best performances of the year; and, as both these boats were the lightest in displacement craft of the whole fleet, things did not look very promising for the resurrection of the V-sectioned type anticipated by the framers of the new rule.

The 30 footers had a good season and Mr. Sibbick turned out the best boat in the fleet in "Lora" for Mr. A. C. Connell and she was sailed to perfection by her owner. The other 30 foot boats, built during the season of 1896, were "Tatters," for Mr. H. Welch Thornton, "Florence" for the Marchese di

Serramazzana at the Cowes yard, "Valeria I" for Lord Albemarle at Messrs. Summers and Payne's, and "Memsahib" at Gosport from Mr. C. Nicholson's design.

The entire fleet of 30 footers were plate and bulb boats, and their average dimensions were—

L.W.L.	26 ft.
Beam	7 ft. 6 ins.
Draught	4 ft. 6 ins. to 5 ft.

All were lug rigged, with bowsprits, with the exception of "Valeria," which set a gaff mainsail.

As the honours in the 36 and 30 foot classes rested with the Albert yard, Cowes, so success in the 24 foot class went to Messrs. Summers and Payne, who without doubt have in "Speedwell" produced the best 24 footer built up to the present time. The "Speedwell" bears a strong resemblance to the American 20-rater "Niagara" in miniature, and like that vessel her best point of sailing is at close hauled work in a breeze.

She had, in 1896, a serious rival in the Sibbick boat, "Bodagh"; "Bodagh's" best point of sailing was on a reach, and when she came by the wind she was clean out of it with "Speedwell," and though, owing to the fact that reaching winds are prevalent in the Solent, "Bodagh's" record was slightly the best, there can be no doubt that "Speedwell" was the better boat. "Bodagh" beat "Speedwell" 21 times and "Speedwell" was victorious over "Bodagh" on 16 occasions.

An incident is worth recording that occurred at Ryde in the season of 1896 when Miss Hughes sailed Miss Cox's "Speedwell" over the course in a hard wind, only one boat of the whole fleet of fourteen 24 footers having temerity enough to turn out against her. This was practically a repetition of the same bold show which occurred a year or two before, when Miss Sutton sailed over the same course in the Herreshoff boat "Morwena" on a day when many owners felt safer and drier on the broader decks of Ryde Pier Head.

The season of 1897 was a remarkable one amongst the 36 foot and 30 foot classes from a sporting point of view, though it proved a still greater surprise to the backers of the Linear Rating than the result of the first season had done. Instead of establishing the advantages of heavier displacement the experience of 1897 makes for the contrary conclusion, for an 1896 boat which had her displacement reduced finished the season with the longest string of flags in the class. This occurred in the case of the Payne designed cutter "Emerald," which had some lead removed from her bulb and was thereby greatly improved. Indeed she and the 1896 Sibbick lugger, "Westra," which had no alteration made to her hull, were undoubtedly the best pair of the season of 1897.

Captain J. Orr-Ewing had a new keel boat "Hermes" built, and "Diamond," nearly a sister ship to her, was launched for Mr. A. H. E. Wood. Both were designed by Mr. Sibbick and they were very fast boats in light weather, but as luck would have it fresh and strong breezes predominated in jubilee year, and the new craft made very moderate records. A third keel boat, "Forella," was built by W. Fife for Mr. Evelyn Parker, but they appeared unable to ascertain her proper trim, for she did little until the latter part of the season. When her balance was eventually found she proved a fair boat, but scarcely up to the form of "Emerald" or "Westra." The most that can be said for these additions to the fleet is that they were fine handsome cutters, but it is a question if their performances were satisfactory enough to warrant a belief in the merits of greater displacement keel boats.

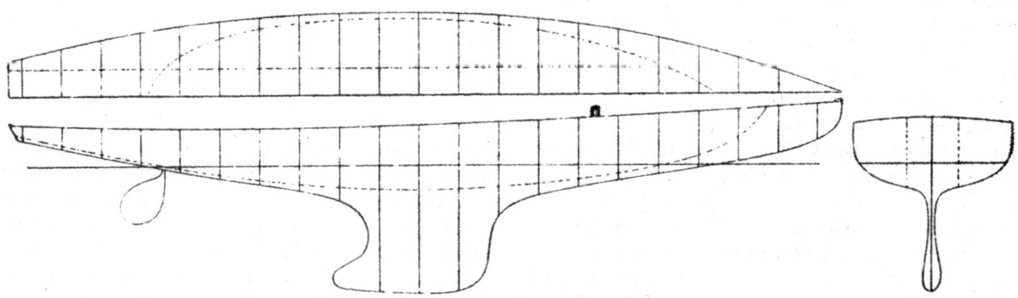

24-FOOT LINEAR RATER.

The cutter rig being introduced into the 30 foot class was the only innovation last year so far as they were concerned.

"Carol," a fin-keel boat built at Nicholson's, "Gwendolin," a plate and bulb boat with fairly deep body by Sibbick, the 1896 "Lora" and another new Sibbick boat, "Tattoo," may be fairly said to have divided the honours between them.

A change has been introduced during the present year by the Yacht Racing Association, which will beneficially affect the 18 foot class by stamping out the unsafe and capsizable, though undoubtedly swift, type of diminutive racing machine, which has been so prevalent during the last three or four seasons in Solent waters and elsewhere. This kind of boat has, in fact, become almost universal on rivers, such as the Thames, where the "Sorceress," 1-rater designed by Mr. Linton Hope, was sailed during the season of 1894 with phenomenal success. She was the first of a series of the same type from the board of the same designer, who proved the ability of the unballasted rater to take prizes by sweeping the Solent with the ½-raters "Lotus" in 1895, and "Kismet" in the following year. The American Sneak boat or Devil's Coffin may be said to be a facsimile of this type of craft, minus the long elegant stern of the rater.

The Association, with a view to putting an end to the antics of these fliers, has effectually eliminated them from the Register with a sweep of the pen by decreeing that no certificate of rating shall be granted to any yacht weighing less than 15 cwt. without crew.

What is known as the "one boat one design" class has become very popular of late. The creation of this class in the Solent was due to the initiative of Major the Hon. C. Colville and Lieut.-Colonel Bucknill in the summer of 1895, the object being to encourage sport in racing in small crafts, and, as an important means of so doing, to diminish the expense incidental to it.

These yachts are charming little vessels; they are excellent sea boats, fast, and have, for their size, very fair accommodation. This consists of a forecastle large enough for the two paid hands which are allowed, and a nice little cabin. They are decked all over, but have a well or cockpit large enough to accommodate half a dozen. No limit is placed upon the number of amateurs that may sail in races, but only two paid hands are allowed. The wages of the paid hands are limited to a fixed amount, as is also their racing money.

As the name "one boat one design" signifies, all these little craft are built from one and the same model. No alteration in lead keel or hull or sail plan is allowed, neither can any alteration be made in the cockpit without the consent of the captain of the class; but in staying the mast, and in all matters of that kind, owners have a perfectly free hand.

Up to the end of the season of 1896, three lower sails only were allowed; but since that date small topsails containing about forty square feet of canvas have been permitted. The lead keel weighs 2·65 tons, and is in all cases weighed in the presence of the captain of the class or of his deputy. Each boat has to carry 200 pounds weight of ground tackle, and the stores and fittings common to all boats of the class.

The racing is very close and very keen; and for 16 to 18 boats to start together is a common occurrence. Though in a class containing this number of boats, even though they are as far as is humanly possible identical, one or two are almost certain to show some slight superiority over the others, still they are so nearly alike that success depends upon skill in handling and skilful pilotage, perhaps more than in any other kind of racing.

The one design class, therefore, acts as a very wholesome stimulus to seamanship of all kinds, and affords most excellent sport. It does not, of course, develop yacht designing to any great extent; for as all the boats are alike, speed is a matter of comparative indifference.

Sailing cruisers, especially those which are devoted largely to racing, require only a few words of description. Everything that has been stated in reference to racing vessels applies, with certain modifications, to them; for there is no essential difference in form, structure, canvassing, or ballasting, between a racer and a cruiser. It is difficult to find a better sea boat than a racing vessel properly ballasted, sparred, and canvassed. The only variation in structure between the ideal racer and the ideal cruiser is that the former would probably be given more beam than is desirable for the latter. Racing vessels generally sail in smooth, or comparatively smooth, water, where initial natural stability derived from beam is advantageous. But when a ship has to be sailed over a heavy sea, the action of waves upon beam, as previously explained, comes into operation, and beam should, for sea-going purposes, be slightly reduced. In other respects, modification in detail is all that is necessary to transform a racer into a cruiser.

The enormous stability imparted to racers by heavy lead keels at great depth tells against them in a sea way: it causes their movements to be very rapid and violent; they plunge heavily, are very hard upon their gear, and particularly disagreeable to most human stomachs. A vessel to be easy in a sea way must not aspire to extraordinary speed; her ballast must not be too low; in fact, the less outside ballast she carries the better. Her stability and righting angle will be, of course, comparatively small, and she must be sparred and canvassed accordingly. That a tender ship is an easy ship is an ancient and true assertion.

It is frequently argued that the superiority in dryness, ease, and comfort in a sea way which vessels with the centre of gravity rather high possess, as compared with vessels having their centre of gravity very low, depends not at all on the relative amount and position of their ballast, but entirely upon the fact that the lightly ballasted ship carrying proportionately small sail goes relatively slower through the water; on the other hand, it is asserted that, in really heavy weather, a racing vessel or fast cruiser would have to be slowed down to such an extent that a smack or trawler, for instance, would sail as fast and be much safer and more comfortable. There is some truth in both these arguments.

There are no bulwarks on racing vessels; they would hold too much wind. A ledge of from 1 inch to 6 inches in height, just sufficient for a man to rest his foot against, is sufficient for their purposes. But bulwarks are a mere matter of super-structure; they can be added to a vessel at any time, and conduce to comfort but not to safety. Good free board is desirable, but high bulwarks will not keep out heavy water; and if a green sea does come on board, the sooner it gets off again the better. With no bulwarks it runs off directly, while with high bulwarks tons and tons of water will be kept on deck for a considerable time.

A combination of superior racing and cruising qualities in one vessel is impossible of attainment, and owners, if they desire satisfaction, should make up their minds which of the two they want. If they desire to race, speed is the prime necessity, and seaworthiness and comfort must be subordinated. If they purpose to go cruising, whether round our coasts or about the ocean, then ease at sea and comfort should be the first consideration, and speed must take second place. In this respect the alteration to the rating rule made in 1896 was a mistake. It aimed at producing a larger bodied type of vessel. Many complaints were made in many quarters about the want of accommodation in racing yachts, and the difficulty of getting any price for them after they had had their day. Well grounded complaints no doubt but, to satisfy them, speed has been sacrificed. Nobody wants to live in a 1-rater or even in a 5-rater. The 20-raters of the old rule, though quite habitable, were from lack of head room, not comfortable; but I don't think many owners wished to utilise them as houseboats. They used them for racing and lived in other vessels, or on shore. The accommodation in 40's was fairly good, though of course not so good as if they had been bigger and deeper in the body; and moreover the amount of waste space in the overhang fore and aft is immense. Above that size, accommodation and head room was ample under the old rule. Judging by the 52 footers and 65 footers built under the new rule, which correspond with the 20's and 40's built under the old rule, it is true a few inches of head room have been gained, but it is a question if there has been a corresponding gain in speed. No exact standard of comparison of size between vessels exists or can be found, and it is impossible therefore to prove that a yacht constructed under one rule is so much larger or smaller than one built under another rule; and as speed is in reference to size, their relative speeds cannot be definitely measured. But judging by the principal factors involved, the old rule seems to have been superior to the new. The modern 20 is longer—and length is the principal dimension affecting speed—she is heavier, carries more canvas, bigger spars, costs more, and requires more hands than the old 20. She may justly be reckoned to be considerably the larger vessel of the two, but her gain in speed is but small and certainly is not in proportion to her increase in size.

It is difficult, if not impossible, to express in terms the differentiation between a racer and a cruiser. The best definition of a *bona fide* cruiser would probably be, a vessel which habitually makes passages and voyages under her proper working sails. None of the thorough-bred, and but few, if any, of the half-bred, or cruiser-racing yachts, would dream of making a voyage to the Mediterranean, or a passage round to the Clyde, under their mainsail: they would start under trysails, with their mainsail stowed, and boom secured; and rightly so, for if caught in bad weather and a big sea with mainsail set, the consequences would probably be very seriously disastrous. On the other hand a real cruiser sails always under her working sails, and resorts to a trysail only in the extremity of bad weather. The huge sail, and long and heavy boom of a first-class racing cutter would be unmanageable, and would "take charge" in a blow, while the small sail and light boom—all in board—of a cruiser, could under similar circumstances be easily handled and reefed, or lowered and secured. But for racing no definition is possible, and sailing Committees must be left to their own judgment to decide whether a yacht is or is not eligible to sail in cruising races. All such races are sailed in what is called "cruising trim," that is to say, under certain restrictions as to sail and crew, jackyard topsails and extra hands being forbidden, and the ship must also carry her boats on board, and her anchors at the bow.

To turn from cruiser racing to cruising proper. Ocean cruising has become very popular among yachtsmen during the last half century. As long ago as between the years 1854 and 1863 yachts both under sail and steam, made voyages to Iceland, Spitzbergen, North and South America, the West India Islands, the coast of Africa, and round the Horn to Australia.

The voyage of the schooner "Foam" to Iceland, embodied by Lord Dufferin in his most delightful book *Letters from High Latitudes*, will be familiar to all. The love of the sea seems to have been deeply ingrained in the nature of that distinguished man; for during his long and brilliant diplomatic career he has never ceased to indulge in his favourite form of yachting, single-handed cruising, whenever the opportunity served, doubtless much to the astonishment of his *confrères* and other personages in foreign parts, who probably looked upon sailing about alone in a little vessel as one of the most curious forms of relaxation which even a "mad Englishman" could indulge in. Lord Dufferin's little yawl, the "Lady Hermione," with her owner at the helm, is a familiar object to all yachtsmen who frequent the Solent waters, and long may she continue to be so.

The successful voyage round the Horn to Australia of the little schooner "Chance," of 72 tons y.m., owned by Mr. William Walker, is a good instance of the excellence of the construction of vessels of the pleasure navy, as well as the skill of yachtsmen as navigators. She sailed from Cowes on 13th January, 1861, and arrived at Sydney on the 3rd of June, having behaved admirably in all sorts of weather during a voyage of 141 days.

In the sixties, cruising became more general, and a run from Cowes to Gibraltar and up the Mediterranean, or a cruise to the Baltic and other northern waters, were events of nearly as common occurrence as they are at the present day.

In the year 1864, "Themis," a schooner of about 150 tons T.M., owned, commanded, and navigated by Mr. Thomas Hanham, made a round voyage to Madeira, Teneriffe, Rio Janeiro, the River Plate, round the Horn to Valparaiso, Callao, and Vancouver's Island, thence to the South Sea Islands, New Zealand, Australia, and the China Seas, and eventually home by the Cape of Good Hope.

Deep sea yachtsmen of the present day, who generally make voyages of this character in a 1500 ton steamer, or in the comparative luxury of such craft as Lord Brassey's 500 ton auxiliary, "Sunbeam," would regard Mr. Hanham's feat of thirty-four years ago as a remarkable one in the history of pleasure navigation. In these days of large vessels, the voyages made in former days by quite small craft seem very remarkable, and the discomfort which they must have entailed to owners and passengers would be hardly compatible with our ideas of pleasure in these modern and more luxurious times.

Mr. Knight's voyages to the coasts of South America, and up the rivers Parana and Paraguay, in the "Falcon," and to the desert island of Trinidada in the "Alerte," are well known, as they have been graphically described by him in two most interesting books, *The Cruise of the Falcon* and *The Cruise of the Alerte*. They are remarkable chiefly on account of the small size of the vessels, and for the fact that his crews were composed almost entirely of amateurs, and that many of those amateurs had never been to sea before. The "Falcon" was of only 18 tons register and 30 tons Thames measurement, and the ship's company consisted of Mr. Knight, who was owner, captain, and navigator, three amateurs, and one paid hand to do the cooking and cleaning up.

The "Alerte's" cruise was in search of a hidden treasure in the island of Trinidad, off the coast of Brazil, and it is scarcely necessary to say that though the island was found the treasure was not. But both his voyages were most interesting and instructive, and demonstrated the capacity of small vessels to keep the sea, and of amateurs, if properly commanded, to work them.

Two very notable voyages made by small yachts were those of the "Vivid" and "Alert." The "Vivid" was built in 1859 by Fife of Fairlie on the Clyde, for Mr. Ternan, an Irish gentleman. She was originally known as the "Scourge," and raced successfully in Dublin Bay in the year in which she was built, and was looked upon as a smart racing cutter. She was of 25 tons y.m. and 16 tons register. She afterwards became the property of Mr. Sidney Bert, who changed her name to the "Vivid." Her new owner took her out to Sydney in 1864, making a voyage of 16,000 miles in 130 days.

The "Alert," of 56 tons T.M., was built by Ratsey of Cowes, and was bought by Mr. William Walker, the owner of the schooner "Chance," already alluded to, and was sent out by him to Australia. She made an excellent voyage of 108 days from England to Sydney, including 5 days' detention at the Cape.

Another small vessel, the "Spray," of 33 tons Thames measurement and 20 tons register, made a voyage from Cowes to Hobart Town, under the command of Capt. Wylie. Previous to this, a still smaller cutter, of only 22 tons T.M., the "Teazer," had made voyages out to the West Indies and back; and the performances of quite a little boat, the "Pet," of only 8 tons T.M., which went out on a cruise to the Baltic and back, may be enumerated among the records of long cruises and passages undertaken by quite small sailing craft as proving that size is by no means necessary for safety, though very essential to comfort in deep sea sailing.

Probably the longest voyage ever undertaken by a yacht under sail alone was that of the schooner "Nyanza," of 218 tons y.m She sailed on July 1st, 1887, for a cruise in the Pacific, with her owner, Capt. Dewar, and his wife on board, and was, I think, the first sailing yacht to reach the Pacific through Magellan's Straits. She cruised among the Sandwich Islands and on to Japan, but was wrecked in October, 1890, near the Caroline Islands, all hands being fortunately saved. Her cruise, though it had a disastrous ending, was remarkable. She sailed 42,784 nautical miles, and averaged 104 miles a day.

Few yachtsmen have had greater experience of yachts and of cruising in vessels of every description, than Lord Brassey, who has recounted his experience in craft ranging from 8 up to 552 tons. He has made voyages to Norway and Holland, has on twelve occasions been through the Straits up the Mediterranean, has four times circumnavigated Great Britain, has been once round the world in the "Sunbeam," and has made voyages to India, the Straits Settlements, Borneo, Australia, and the West Indies. His yacht, the "Sunbeam," is one of the most successful auxiliary vessels ever built, and is equally handy under sail or steam. This type of vessel has of course been considerably improved since the days when the "Sunbeam" was built, by the introduction of steel as a material of construction, by new engineering inventions giving greater speed with less consumption of coal, and at the same time compactness of engine space, and by improvements in cabin accommodation of all kinds. An auxiliary craft of from, say, 300 to 500 tons, is probably on the whole the most luxurious and comfortable type of vessel for making long ocean voyages, and to gather some idea of the proportion of the distances traversed under steam or sail by ships of this kind, the log of the auxiliary yacht "Golden Fleece," of 261 tons y.m., owned by Mr. Ralli, may be referred to. She made a voyage round the world of 33,020 miles in the years 1886 and 1887, sailing 14,143 miles, and doing 18,877 miles under steam.

Of the large fleet of sailing vessels on commission in British and foreign waters, but a small proportion have at any period of their existence come into the category of racing vessels. By far the larger number are of the *bona fide* cruiser type, and although more attention is now given to speed than was the case in the early days of the Victorian era, when it was asserted by an old writer that with the advent of the famous "America" the first blow was struck at the healthy rule that the perfection of a gentleman's yacht should be a vessel combining speed with accommodation, most cruisers of the present day seem to fulfil the precepts of that old adage pretty well.

Of course the general form and type of racing vessels in fashion at different periods has influenced the form and type of cruising yachts. Prior to the arrival of the "America," short, bluff-bowed, narrow-sterned cruisers were in vogue; afterwards, the long, narrow, wall-sided type came into fashion, while in recent years yachts built exclusively for cruising have been given more beam, and in form of midship section and of hull generally, approximate to the shape and type of modern racing vessels.

This subject of cruising is a very wide one, but in yachts of, say, from 5 to 100 tons, there is not much to be said as to any distinctive difference between the type of vessel used for racing and for cruising. But pleasure craft used for cruising attain to the proportions of 2,000 tons. In the case of vessels over about 400 tons, steam power has for the last 35 years or so been used almost exclusively, though in some cases it has been adopted as auxiliary to sail power. The tendency, however, is to go into steam. A man builds a large auxiliary cruiser, and finds that though sail is very useful in making long ocean voyages, it is of comparatively little service to him when cruising about at home, or making short voyages, say up the Mediterranean or to Norway. He becomes dissatisfied with the speed of his vessel under sail, and gradually reduces his masts, till for sail-carrying purposes they disappear, and increases his steam power. Though steaming can never be so interesting as sailing, steam has numerous advantages in these busy days, and we may make up our minds that steam is destined to supersede sails in large yachts.

The huge vessels of from 1000 to 1500 and even 2000 tons built during the last few years are, for all practical purposes, steamers pure and simple. Several steam yachts were launched in the fifties, and in 1858 an iron vessel of 148 tons, a very big yacht for those days, was built. In 1859 the "Ceres," of 301 tons, then considered one of the finest steam yachts ever launched, was built for the late Duke of St. Albans. In 1864 the "Eothen," and in 1868 the "Cornelia," both iron vessels, were built for Mr. Ashbury and Lord Londonderry respectively, and in 1874 the "Sunbeam," a composite vessel and the first yacht exceeding 500 tons measurement was constructed for Lord Brassey.

Iron, though occasionally used in the construction of sailing vessels, may be said to have come into fashion at the same time that steam power was introduced. During the last twelve or fifteen years it has been superseded by steel, and since the introduction of that material steam yachts have largely increased, both in number and tonnage. In the year 1886, 907 steam yachts were in commission in European waters, as compared with 1436 in the year 1897, and during the same period the total tonnage of yachts has increased from 86,407 to practically double that amount, namely, 172,559 tons. is curious to note the relative development of sail and steam during those years. In the year 1886, 2,942 sailing yachts were commissioned, having a total tonnage of 80,936 tons. At the present time 5,311 sailing yachts are afloat, with a total tonnage of 93,009 tons. That is to say while the number of steam yachts built during the last twelve years has increased by 60 per cent., their tonnage has increased 100 per cent., and during the same period the number of sailing craft has increased 80 per cent. but their tonnage shows an increase of 15 per cent. only. These figures demonstrate the number of large steam yachts that have been constructed during the last decade, and also the very large number of small sailing vessels which have been built, both for racing and cruising purposes.

With regard to the actual number of cruisers afloat: in the year 1886 there were only 23 steam yachts of over five hundred tons measurement in commission. Of these the largest vessel of British build was the "Amy," of 812 tons, built by Messrs. D. and W. Henderson, and designed by Mr. G. L. Watson. Notable for their size among the others was the "Bretagne," built for a French owner in America, the "Nourmahal," of 939 tons, and the "Namouna," of 740 tons, built in America from the design of a British naval architect, Mr. Sinclair Bryne.

During the present season (1898) no less than 71 steam yachts of over five hundred tons are in commission; 14 of these are over 1000 tons, and Mr. Vanderbilt's yacht, the "Valiant," exceeds 2000 tons. She is the largest yacht afloat, and measures 2184 tons y.m.; her length is 331 feet over all, and 293 feet on the load water-line, and she has 39 feet beam, and 29·3 feet depth. She is brig-rigged, carries 700 tons of coal, can average 14 knots, and can attain a speed of 17 knots under forced draught. She was built and engined by Messrs. Laird and Co., of Birkenhead, from the design of Mr. Sinclair Bryne.

A big steamer is the luxurious plaything of the few, while a trip in a 10 or 15 tonner affords amusement to the many, and it is probable that the Corinthian who skippers his own little craft has by far the greater share of pleasure and amusement.

All round the coasts are to be found plenty of yachtsmen who enjoy making passages in dirty weather in their little 5, 10, or 15 tonners; but, perhaps, if in search of the amateur capable of handling his own vessel in all weathers, and ready and able to bear a hand aloft or forward with equal readiness, the estuary of the Thames would be the best place to look. There on almost any day may be found scores of small craft, turning down Sea Reach in workmanlike fashion, flying the gold wreath and crown on blue ground, whose owners, when the ties of the Stock Exchange or Lloyd's or other business permits, are only too anxious to undertake more than a mere Saturday to Monday cruise.

In these expeditions paid hands are often voted more trouble than they are worth: amateurs do most of the work, if not all; and when a paid hand or two are shipped it is merely for the convenience of having someone to "cook and wash up."

It is of course impossible to particularise or describe cruises of this kind, but as an instance of what may be done in small vessels cruising in home waters, a glance at the log of the "Sonata," a 15 tonner in the year 1882, may suffice. She sailed from Brightlingsea on July 2nd, and made her first run of 506 miles to Inverness without putting into port. She then passed through the Caledonian Canal, visited the ports of the beautiful Firth of Clyde, Rothesay and Lamlash, in which latter place she was detained about four days by a violent gale of wind. She then sailed to Carlingford Lough, and from there to Kingstown. From Kingstown they made a run of 278 miles to Plymouth, where they stayed a day or two, and then made a passage of 281 miles to Brightlingsea, so completing the round trip in thirty days.

The ship's company consisted of the owner and two friends and two paid hands. The ship was entirely navigated by her owner, and he made all his ports without the assistance of a pilot. This may be looked upon as a good but fair sample of cruising in small yachts.

It is scarcely necessary to observe that in such a sport as yachting the amount of enjoyment derived depends a good deal upon the possession of some practical knowledge and technical skill. In a sailing craft something is occurring all the time and a man who commands his own vessel, or who understands all that is going on, will not find many idle hours pressing heavily on his brain. The pleasures incidental to command and exercise of responsibility are great, and moreover, to be a mere passenger on one's own ship, subject to the convenience and caprices of the skipper, is somewhat ignominious, and an owner will find many advantages in being able to form and express his own opinion. Seamanship, the handling of a vessel, is of course a highly technical art, and though there are and always have been, and I trust always will be, many amateurs who in seamanship are unsurpassable, their number must be comparatively few, for by natural aptitude and long experience only can a very high degree of excellence be attained. But long apprenticeship to the sea is not necessary to enable a man of average intelligence to acquire sufficient knowledge to get his own vessel under weigh, to bring her up, and to handle her under ordinary circumstances, and to judge of the weather for himself and be able to decide what the vessel can or cannot do.

The services of a professional sailing master cannot usually, at any rate in a vessel of any size, be dispensed with; and his advice should be taken. But in a very few years a yacht owner ought to be able to handle his own ship fairly well, and to be in a position to assert his authority as owner. He will then no longer feel diffident, abashed by his own servant; he will understand the reason for everything that is done, and will be constantly acquiring knowledge.

For cruising in home waters he ought to understand the use of charts and the lead, and should acquire some knowledge of plane and transverse sailing, and of tides, so as to be able to find his own way about. If he aspires to longer voyages, he should learn the practical rudiments, at any rate, of navigation, and the use of the sextant, and should understand compass deviation. He ought to be able to find his position at sea by the ordinary simple means, and to ascertain his compass error.

Should he take the trouble to pass the Board of Trade examination and get a master mariner's certificate of competency, he will not regret it. His sailing master and crew sign on to him, he is really master of his own ship, a position which in foreign ports and distant lands affords many advantages. Yacht skippers are as a rule excellent men, who understand their position and do not presume upon it, but they are human, and the position of an owner in a foreign port under a recalcitrant skipper, who is quite aware that his services cannot be dispensed with, is not a happy one. Moreover, nautical astronomy, and magnetism, are rather fascinating subjects, and their study may fill up agreeably many leisure hours, both on sea and on land.

Yet to all, whether instructed or not, the sea, if it appeals to them at all, exercises a fascination which cannot be described. Something of the "mystery of the sea" permeates their being. Yachtsmen are generally enthusiastic lovers of their favourite pastime, and no wonder, for in all its phases it conveys infinite delight and infinite charm. If a yachtsman is scientifically inclined, he can interest himself in nautical astronomy, in the scientific principles involved in the staying of masts and trimming of sails, and in everything connected with the action of wind on sails, and the action and effects of solids and fluids.

If he spends his leisure days in cruising about the Channel, in the shallow waters of the North Sea, or among the harbours and fiords of the beautiful Western sea-board of both islands, his favourite pursuit leads him to lovely scenery, affords him constant interest in the working of his own ship, and in watching the doings of merchantmen and fishing fleets, and of those who make their living upon the sea. It offers him excellent sport in the way of fishing, and it compels him to fresh breezes, and a natural, wholesome life. If he has time and money to go for long voyages, he sees the wonders of the great deep, and can visit all the most interesting parts of the world with the greatest comfort in his own home. And if he take delight in racing, he will find a sport most exciting, most interesting, and physically and morally healthy and clean.

DUNRAVEN.

[*The Editors beg to express their hearty thanks to the following gentlemen, who have assisted them in the illustrations of the Yachting article:—Mr. Horace Cox, Mr. W. J. Fife, Mr. Dixon Kemp, Mr. A. E. Payne, and Mr. G. L. Watson.*]

SAILING RULES, 1898.

1. All Races, and all Yachts sailing therein, shall be under the direction of the Flag Officers or Sailing Committee of the Club under whose auspices the Races are being sailed. All matters shall be subject to their approval and control; and all doubts, questions, and disputes which may arise shall be subject to their decision. Their decisions shall be based upon these Rules so far as they will apply, but as no rules can be devised capable of meeting every incident and accident of sailing, the Sailing Committee should keep in view the ordinary customs of the sea, and discourage all attempts to win a Race by other means than fair sailing and superior speed and skill. The decisions of the Sailing Committee shall be final, unless they think fit, on the application of the parties interested, or otherwise, to refer the questions at issue for the decision of the Council of the Yacht Racing Association, whose decision shall be final. Any such reference, if made on the application of any party interested, must be accompanied by a fee of £5 in the case of yachts exceeding 36 ft. rating, and of £3 for yachts not exceeding 36 ft. rating, payable by the party or parties on whose application the reference is made, and such fees shall go to the funds of the Yacht Racing Association in the event of the appeal not being sustained. It shall be the duty of the Sailing Committee whose decision is appealed against to forward to the Secretary of the Yacht Racing Association a statement of the case put before them, and their decision thereon accompanied by the fee. In the event of a protest involving the re-measurement of a yacht, the fees and expenses of such re-measurement shall be paid by the unsuccessful party to the protest, and in the case of a re-measurement demanded by an official measurer, acting under the authority of the Council, such expenses and fees shall be paid by the Y.R.A. if the certificate is upheld. No member of the Sailing Committee or Council shall take part in the discussion or decision upon any disputed question in which he is directly interested. The Sailing Committee, or any Officer appointed to take charge for the day, shall award the prizes, subject to Rule 29. If any Yacht be disqualified, the next in order shall be awarded the prize.

2. The Sailing Committee, or officer in charge for the day, shall have power to postpone any Race, should unfavourable weather render such a course desirable. Letter N of the commercial code hoisted over the flag denoting the race shall be the signal that a race has been postponed.

3. The rating of every Yacht entered to sail in a race shall be ascertained by adding together length (L), beam (B), 0·75 of girth (G), and 0·5 of the square root of the sail area (SA), and dividing the sum by two according to the following formula:—

$$\frac{L+B+0{\cdot}75\,G+0{\cdot}5\,\sqrt{SA}}{2}=\text{Rating.}$$

In all ratings, figures in the second place of decimals below 0·05 shall be disregarded, and those of 0·05 and upwards shall count as 0·1. The length shall be taken between the outer edges of the Official marks of the Y.R.A. as placed by the owner at the bow and stern of the Yacht, this length to represent the extreme length for immersion, provided always that if any part of the stem or stern-post or other part of the vessel below the marks for length project beyond the length taken as mentioned, such projection or projections shall, for the purposes of the rule, be added to the length taken as stated; and pieces of any form cut out of the stem, stern-post, or fair-line of the ridge of the counter, with the intention of shortening the length, shall not be allowed for in measurement of length, if at or immediately below the marks for the length, nor above if within six inches of the water level. The breadth shall be taken from outside to outside of the planking, in the broadest part of the Yacht, and no allowance shall be made for wales, doubling planks, or mouldings of any kind. The girth shall be taken from L.W.L. to L.W.L. under the keel at a station 0·6 of the distance between the outer edges of the length marks from the fore-end. The girth shall be measured along the actual outline of the vertical cross section at that station at right angles to the L.W.L. If the draught forward at that station (not including the girth of a bulb, if any) exceeds the draught at that station, twice such excess to be added to G. In taking these measurements all hollows in the fore and aft under-water profile of the vessel to be treated as filled up straight. Centre-boards or plates, whether ballasted or fitted with bulbs, or otherwise, to be measured as fixed keels. Owners shall mark the length for rating of their Yachts on both sides at the bow and stern in such manner as the Council may direct, with the Official marks supplied by the Y.R.A., which marks shall at all times represent the extreme length for immersion when the yacht is lying in smooth water in her usual racing trim, including racing crew on board at and about the mid overall length. Owners shall mark the points for measuring the girth as follows: by fixing three metal discs of suitable size on each side of the yacht, not less than 2 in. or more than 6 in. above the load water-line level, and parallel thereto, and not less than 3 ft., or more than 6 ft., from end to end, and so that the centre-mark of the three coincides with the distance 0·6 from the fore edges of the bow marks; and the owner shall also place a disc coinciding with this centre mark (perpendicular to the load water-line level), under the rail or covering board, and another on the side of the keel perpendicular to the load water-line level. The distances between the load water-line level and the horizontal marks to be measured when the yacht is afloat in smooth water, with crew on board according to the rule, and deducted from the girth as obtained from centre mark to centre mark.

MEASUREMENT OF SAILS.—*Mainsail*—A. Measured from the top of the boom (under the pin for outhaul shackle on traveller, or clew side, when hauled chock out) to the gaff under the pin of the sheave of the topsail sheet, provided the peak cringle of the mainsail does not extend beyond the pin: in the case of the yacht having no top-sail, or of the peak cringle extending beyond the pin of the top-sail sheet sheave then the measurement to be taken to the pink lacing-hole. B. Perpendicular to A, measured to underside of gaff close in to the mast. C. Measured from top of boom over the pin of the sheave for outhaul or end of clew slide to underside of gaff close in to the mast. D. Perpendicular to C, measured in to the mast, in a line with a top of the boom, or to tack cringle of mainsail, if below top of boom. *Yard Topsail*—E.—Measured from upper side of gaff close in to the mast to pin of sheave for topsail sheet, or to lacing-hole in jackyard. F.—Perpendicular to E, measured to lacing-hole in yard. G.—From lacing-hole to lacing-hole in yard. H.—Perpendicular to G, measured to pin of sheave for topsail-sheet in gaff; or to lacing-hole in jackyard. *Jib Header*—K.—Measured from top of gaff close in to mast to pin of halyard-sheave in topmast. L.—Perpendicular to K, measured to pin of topsail-sheet sheave in gaff; or to lacing-hole in jackyard. *Head-Sails*—I.—The perpendicular I to be measured from the deck at the foreside of the mast to where the line of the luff of the foremost head-sail when extended cuts such perpendicular; in case a schooner has no fore-topmast, but a main topmast and a main spinaker, the perpendicular for the fore-triangle shall be measured from the deck to where the line of luff of such spinaker when extended cuts the main topmast. J.—To be measured from the foreside of the mast to where the line of the luff of the foremost head-sail when extended cuts the bowsprit, other spar hull, &c., as the case may be. In all cases if the distance from the centre fore and aft line of the mast to the outer end of spinaker boom (when shipped in its place and square to the keel) exceeds the distance from the foreside of the mast to the bowsprit end (where cut by the line of the luff of the foremost head-sail), the excess shall be added to the base of the triangle formed by the head-sails; and the area of the head-sail to be computed accordingly. In the case of a yacht having no head-sail, but carrying a spinaker, the area for head-sail shall be computed from the length of spinaker boom and the height from deck to where the line of the luff of the spinaker when extended cuts the mast. The length of head-stick or head-yard to spinaker shall not exceed one-twentieth the length of spinaker boom. Foot yards not allowed on spinakers. In the case of a yacht carrying a square sail or square topsail, or raffee (together or separately) the actual area of the same shall be computed; and if such area exceed the area of the fore-triangle, the excess shall be used in the total area for determining the rating. *Foresail of Schooners*—A. Measured from foreside of mainmast (in a line with main boom goose-neck) to gaff under the pin of topsail-sheet sheave. B. Perpendicular to A, measured to underside of gaff close in to the mast. C. Measured from foreside of mainmast (in a line with main boom goose-neck) to gaff close in to the mast. D. Perpendicular to C, measured in to the mast in a line with the top of the fore boom or tack cringle.

CALCULATION OF SAIL AREAS.—*Area of Mainsail*—To find the area of the mainsail—Multiply A by B and C by D, and add the two products together and divide by 2. *Area of Yard Topsail*—To find the area of yard topsail—Multiply E by F and G by H, and add the two products together and divide by 2. *Area of Jib Header*—To find the area of jib header—Multiply K by L and divide the product by 2. *Area of Head-Sails*—To find the area of head-sails, jib topsail or spinaker—Multiply I by J and divide by 2. *Area of Pole Mast Head-Sails*—To find the area of head-sail, for pole mast—Multiply I by J and divide by 2. *Area of Schooner's and Yawl's Sails*—The area of a schooner's sail or a yawl's sail would similarly be found; in the case of a yawl having a lug mizen the lacing-holes in the yard would be taken as the upper boundaries. *Areas of Lug-Sails and Head-Sails*—In the case of a lug-sail, standing lug-sail, or balance lug-sail being carried, the actual area of the same shall be computed; and if head-sail be also carried, the measurements for computing the area of the same shall be taken from foreside of mast, &c., in accordance with the method provided in the rule for head-sails. *Area bound by Curved Edges of Sails*—The area bound by the round in the foot, head, luff, or leach of a sail, if at any time extended by battens or otherwise beyond the line between the points for measurement, shall be computed as follows: Multiply the base E by two-thirds of the perpendicular P. In cases of disputed measurement of sail area, or if the necessary measurements cannot be obtained from the sail-maker, the sails can be measured in the manner following:—Take the length of boom from mast to pin of sheave for outhaul, and length of gaff from mast to pin of topsail-sheet sheave or lacing-hole as the case may require; then hoist the sail with the tack fast and set the peak and luff up taut, and let go the topping lifts so that the weight of the boom comes on the leach of the sail. With a line and tape measure the leach and luff and the diagonal, C. For the head-sail measure the height, I, and the distance, J, as provided for in the section dealing with head-sail. For topsail the sail would be hoisted and marked in a line with the gaff; then lowered and the other dimensions taken. From the measurements so taken a sail plan would be made and the areas calculated as described. In all calculations whether relating to length, sail area, or rating any fraction beyond the second place of decimals shall be disregarded. As soon as a yacht has been measured by the Official Measurer, a certificate of rating of the Yacht Racing Association shall be granted to her owner, unless from any peculiarity in the construction of the yacht, or other cause, the measurer shall be of opinion that the rule will not rate the yacht fairly; in which case he shall report the circumstances to the Council, who, after due inquiry, shall award such certificate of rating as they may consider equitable. The certificate of rating of the Yacht Racing Association shall cease to be valid as defining the yacht's rating for racing if any dimension measured for rating is found to exceed the measurement stated in the certificate. If it should arise from any cause whatever that one or both of the official marks of the Y.R.A., as placed by the owner at the bow and stern, fall within the length immersed when the yacht is lying in smooth water in her usual racing trim, with racing crew on board, at and about the mid overall length, or if any alteration be made so as to increase the beam or girth, or the length of any spar or spars, or the sail area, as respectively measured for rating, or if any mark denoting the yacht's length or girth is moved from its position, or if it should come to the knowledge of the owner or his representative that any dimension measured for rating exceeds the measurement stated in the certificate, the certificate becomes irregular; and the owner or his representative must give notice of such irregularity and the grounds thereof, in writing, signed by him and addressed and sent by registered post to the Secretary of the Yacht Racing Association, before the yacht is again started in any match, in order that the yacht, or her spars, or sails, may, if necessary, be re-measured, and a new certificate issued. It is especially incumbent on the owner, or his representative, to ascertain from time to time by inspection of the length marks, whether the immersion of the yacht has from any cause whatever become such as to render the certificate irregular. Yachts which have been raced previously to 1896, and which are over the new classes of linear rating (corresponding with the classes they competed in under the old rating rule) shall be allowed to compete in such new classes by allowing time on the excess rating, providing no alteration has been made in their hulls and no increase made in their load water-line length as defined by the Y.R.A. marks, and no increase made in their sail area since 1895. A duly regular certificate of rating of the Yacht Racing Association shall be held by every yacht starting in a match, unless the Sailing Committee give special permission in writing, before the start, that the yacht may compete without it; but in the event of any dispute as to the rating of a yacht so exempted or otherwise, she or her sails shall be measured by the Official Measurer before she can be entitled to a prize. No certificate of rating shall be granted to any yacht of less than 15 cwt. displacement without crew. If an infringement of any of the foregoing provisions in respect of the regularity of the certificate of a yacht should in the opinion of the Council be proved against any yacht, such yacht shall be liable to be disqualified by the Council from starting in any match sailed under Y.R.A. Rules for the remainder of the current year, or such period as the Council may elect, reckoning from the date at which her certificate is proved to have become invalid. Should the certificate under which a yacht has sailed in any match or matches be proved to have been incorrect, solely by reason of any error of measurement or calculation on the part of the Y.R.A. measurer, the Council may, after inquiry, assign such correction to the certificate as they may deem proper, and should the rating so corrected exceed the rating according to the incorrect certificate, the yacht shall concede in every such match sailed the scale of time allowance for such excess up to the limit rating of her class and double the scale allowance above that limit. Every owner sailing under Y.R.A. Rules shall permit all reasonable inspection by an official measurer and shall afford such measurer all reasonable facility to carry out such inspection in regard to measurements, marks, and such other matters within the scope of the measurer's duty.

4. In time for Rating Races, time shall be allowed on arrival for differences in rating, according to the annexed time scales, in proportion to the length of course. In all cases where time has to be allowed for difference of rating, it shall be computed by the rating and tenths of a unit of the rating in accordance with the time scales. Should it be necessary during a race to shorten the course, the signal flag denoting the race hoisted under the White Peter, or in case of fog or darkness two guns fired, shall show that the race is to finish with the round about to be completed, or at such mark as the Sailing Committee or officer of the day may appoint, and the time allowance shall be reduced in proportion.

5. Entries shall be made with the Secretary at least forty-eight hours previous to noon of the day appointed for starting each race. In case of a Sunday intervening, twenty-four hours shall be added. Entries may be made by telegram, and it shall be deemed sufficient that the same shall have been despatched before noon of the day on which the entries close, subject to the provision as to Sundays, but such entries by telegram must be confirmed on a duly executed form of entry and forwarded simultaneously with the telegram. A Sailing Committee may, if they consider it expedient, refuse any entry. Form of entry to be signed by the owner, or his representative, previous to the race:—

"Please to enter the Yacht for the Race at on the . Her distinguishing Flag is ; her rig is ; and her rating, in accordance with Y.R.A. Rule 3, is . And I agree to obey and be bound by the Sailing Rules of the Yacht Racing Association.

"Signed this day of ."

A yacht which did not start in the original race shall not be allowed to compete in a re-sailed race, and a yacht which has, in the opinion of the Sailing Committee, committed a breach of the rules in the original race shall not be allowed to compete in a re-sailed race, but no new entries shall be received under any circumstances whatever for a postponed race.

6. Each yacht entered for a race must be the *bona fide* property of the person or persons in whose name or names she is entered, who must be a member or members of a recognised Yacht Club. A Yacht Club shall not be considered a recognised Yacht Club within the meaning of this rule unless it shall have been proposed and accepted as such by the Council of the Yacht Racing Association, who shall have the power of cancelling such recognition should they deem it expedient so to do. A yacht, whilst let on hire, shall not be allowed to compete under these rules.

7. No owner shall be allowed to enter more than one yacht in a race, except in cases in which a prize is given for each rig, when one yacht of each rig may be entered, nor shall he be entitled to enter the same yacht under different rigs for any race. If a yacht is entered for two or more races which are to be sailed at the same time, the owner, before starting the yacht, shall (in writing or by showing in the rigging the signal flag denoting the race) declare to the Sailing Committee in which of the races the yacht will compete; but this section of the rule shall not apply to postponed or re-sailed races. An owner shall not steer any other yacht than his own in a race wherein his own yacht or yachts compete.

8. When a prize has been offered for competition any yacht duly

entered shall be entitled to sail over the course (subject, however, to Rule 2), and be entitled to a prize of not less than half the value of the first prize.

9. In the case of a yacht fitted with a centre board or plate, or other form of shifting keel, manual power only shall be employed in working it.

10. Every yacht sailing in a race shall have on board a member of a recognised Yacht Club, who, before the prize is awarded, shall sign a declaration that the yacht has strictly conformed to all the sailing regulations, as follows :—

"I, , a Member of the Yacht Club, do hereby declare that I was on board and in charge of the yacht while sailing in the race this day, and that all the Sailing Rules and Regulations were obeyed during that race."

(Signed) ....

Date............................

11. Each yacht must carry, at her main topmast head, a rectangular distinguishing flag, of a suitable size, which must not be hauled down unless she gives up the race. If the topmast be lowered on deck or carried away, the flag must be rehoisted in a conspicuous place, as soon as possible.

12. Every yacht entered for a race shall, at the time of entry, or as soon after as possible, be supplied with written or printed instructions as to the conditions of the race, the course to be sailed, marks, &c. Nothing shall be considered as a mark in the course unless specially named as such in these instructions. Each yacht shall be given a number with the sailing directions, and should any yacht cross the line before the signal for the start has been made, her distinguishing numeral shall be exhibited as soon as conveniently may be as a recall, and kept displayed until the said yacht shall have either returned and recrossed the line to the satisfaction of the Sailing Committee, or have given up the race. The numbers to be in white on a black ground, and the figures not less than 2 ft. 6 in. in height.

13. There shall be no restrictions as to sails, or the manner of setting and working them; but manual power only may be used for hoisting and working them.

14. In yachts above 42 ft. rating there shall be no limit as to the number of paid hands, and no restrictions as to the number of friends. In yachts of 42 ft. rating and under, the total number of persons on board during a match shall not exceed the number set forth in the following table :—

	Persons.
Not exceeding 18-ft. rating	2
Exceeding 18-ft. and not exceeding 24-ft. rating . . .	3
Exceeding 24-ft. and not exceeding 33-ft. rating . . .	5
Exceeding 30-ft. and not exceeding 36-ft. rating . . .	7
Exceeding 36-ft. and not exceeding 42-ft. rating . . .	9

If an owner of a yacht elects to have such yacht measured for rating length with a smaller number of persons on board than set forth in the foregoing table, such number shall be stated on the certificate of rating, and shall not be exceeded in any race sailed under the certificate. No paid hands shall join or leave a yacht after the first gun has been fired, or the Blue Peter hoisted, except in case of accident or injury to any person on board. There shall be no restriction as to friends working.

15. All yachts exceeding a rating of 42 ft. shall be fitted below deck with the ordinary fittings of a yacht, including two transverse bulkheads of wood. The following shall apply to all yachts: their platforms shall be kept down, and bulkheads standing. No water shall be started from or taken into the tanks after the signal to start has been made. No more than the usual anchors and chains shall be carried during a race, which must not be used as shifting ballast, or for altering the trim of the yacht. No bags of shot shall be on board, and all ballast shall be properly stowed under the platform or in lockers, and no ballast or other dead weight (a centre plate or board excepted). shall be shifted or trimmed in any way whatever during a race. No ballast or other dead weight shall be shifted, shipped or unshipped so as to increase the length of immersion beyond the marks at the bow and stern, placed by the owners to define the rating length, after a yacht has been entered for a race. No ballast shall be shipped, unshipped, or shifted after 9 P.M. of the day previous to the race. A race re-sailed shall be regarded as a new race so far as the 9 P.M. condition is concerned.

16. Every yacht exceeding a rating of 60 ft. and under a rating of 80 ft. shall carry a boat on deck not less than 10 ft. in length and 3 ft. 6 in. beam, and every yacht rated at 80 ft. and over, one of not less than 12 ft. in length, and 3 ft. 6 in. beam, with oars lashed in them, ready for immediate use. Each yacht shall carry at least one lifebuoy on deck ready for use.

17. The yachts shall start from moorings, anchors, or under way, as directed by the Sailing Committee. Fifteen minutes before the time of starting one of the following flags of the Commercial Code shall be hoisted as a preparative flag for the yachts of each successive race; in case of a start from anchors or moorings, to take up their stations for the start with head-sails down, or all sails down, as the Sailing Committee may direct; or, in case the start be a flying one, to approach the starting line, viz. :—

B of Commercial Code for the yachts of the 1st race.
C———————————————— 2nd ,,
D———————————————— 3rd ,,
F———————————————— 4th ,,

and so on. Five minutes before the start the preparative flag shall be lowered, a Blue Peter hoisted, and a gun fired; after which the yachts in the race shall be amenable to the rules. At the expiration of five minutes *exactly* the Blue Peter shall be hauled down and a second gun fired as a signal to start. If the start is to be made from anchors or moorings, lots shall be drawn for stations, and springs shall be allowed on the same bridle or anchor chain or warp as the bowfasts, but are not to be carried to a buoy, pier, other vessel, or fixed object. If any yacht lets go or parts her bridle before the signal to start, or if she drags any moorings or anchor to which she is made fast for the purpose of starting, she shall be liable to be disqualified, unless such parting or dragging be explained to the satisfaction of the Committee, or unless she has returned, after the signal to start, within the line of starting buoys so as not to obtain any advantage by the accident. In a flying start, if any yacht, or any part of her hull, spars, or other equipment be on or across the line before the signal to start is made, she must return and recross the line; a yacht so returning, or one working into position from the wrong side of the line after the signal to start has been made, must keep clear of all competing yachts. Should the gun miss fire, the lowering of the Blue Peter shall be the signal to start. A yacht shall have completed a race as soon as any part of the hull or spars be on or across the winning line.

18. When two yachts are approaching one another, so as to involve risk of collision, one of them shall keep out of the way of the other as follows, viz. :—A yacht which is running free shall keep out of the way of a yacht which is close-hauled. A yacht which is close-hauled on the port tack shall keep out of the way of a yacht which is close-hauled on the starboard tack. When both are running free with the wind on different sides, the yacht which has the wind on the port side shall keep out of the way of the other. When both are running free with the wind on the same side, the yacht which is to windward shall keep out of the way of the yacht which is to leeward. A yacht which has the wind aft shall keep out of the way of the other yacht.

19. When rounding any buoy or vessel used to mark out the course, if two yachts are not clear of each other at the time the leading yacht is close to, and actually rounding the mark, the outside yacht must give the other room to pass clear of it, whether it be the lee or weather yacht which is in danger of fouling the mark. No yacht shall be considered clear of another yacht unless so much ahead as to give a free choice to the other on which side she will pass. An overtaking yacht shall not, however, be justified in attempting to establish an overlap, and thus force a passage between the leading yacht and the mark after the latter yacht has altered her helm for the purpose of rounding.

20. When passing a pier, shoal, rock, vessel, or other obstruction to sea room, should yachts not be clear of each other, the outside yacht or yachts must give room to the yacht in danger of fouling such obstruction, whether she be the weather or the leeward yacht; provided always that an overlap has been established before an obstruction is actually reached.

21. A yacht overtaking any other shall keep out of the way of the overtaken yacht; and a yacht may luff as she pleases to prevent another yacht passing to windward, but must never bear away out of her course to hinder the other passing to leeward—the lee side to be considered that on which the leading yacht of the two carries her main boom. The overtaking vessel, if to leeward, must not luff until she has drawn clear ahead of the yacht she has overtaken.

22. If two yachts are standing towards a shore or shoal, or towards any buoy, boat or vessel, and the yacht to leeward is likely to run aground, or foul of such buoy, boat or vessel (a mark vessel excepted), and is not able to tack without coming into collision with the yacht to windward, the latter shall at once tack on being hailed to do so by the owner of the leeward yacht, or the person acting as the owner's representative, who shall be bound to see that the leeward yacht tacks at the same time.

23. Any yacht running on shore, or foul of a buoy, vessel, or other obstruction, may use her own anchors, boats, warps, &c., to get off, but may not receive any assistance except from the crew of the vessel fouled. Any anchor, boat, or warp used must be taken on board again before she continues the race.

24. Each yacht must go fairly round the course; and must not touch any buoy, boat, or vessel used to mark it out, but shall not be disqualified if wrongfully compelled to do so by another yacht. Any yacht causing a mark vessel to in any way shift her position to avoid being fouled by such yacht, shall be disqualified. If a yacht, in consequence of her neglect of any of these rules, shall foul another yacht, or compel other yachts to foul, she shall forfeit all claim to the prize, and shall pay all damages as provided by Rule 32.

25. No towing, sweeping, poling, or pushing, or any mode of propulsion except sails, shall be allowed except for the purpose set forth in Rule 23.

26. A yacht may anchor during a race, but must weigh her anchor again, and not slip. No yacht shall during a race make fast to any buoy, stage, pier, or other object, or send an anchor out in a boat, except for the purpose of Rule 23.

27. No other means of sounding than the lead and line allowed.

28. All yachts sailing in a race at night shall observe the Board of Trade rule as to the carrying of lights.

29. In case of a man falling overboard from a competing yacht, all other yachts in a position to do so shall use their utmost endeavours to render assistance; and if it should appear that any yacht was thereby prevented winning the race, the Committee shall have power to order it to be re-sailed between any yacht or yachts so prevented and the actual winner.

30. Should the owner of any yacht, or the person acting as the owner's representative, consider there is fair ground of complaint against another for foul sailing, or any violation of these rules, such owner or the owner's representative must, if it arise during the race, signify the same on first passing the Committee vessel, by showing an ensign conspicuously in the main rigging. The protest shall be made in writing, and under such regulations (if any) as the Sailing Committee may have determined, within two hours of the arrival of the protesting yacht, unless such arrival shall be after 9 o'clock P.M. and before 8 o'clock A.M., in which case the time shall be extended to 10 o'clock A.M., and the protest shall be heard by the Sailing Committee and decided, after such

inquiries as they may consider necessary. A protest made in writing shall not be withdrawn. Should it come to the knowledge of the Sailing Committee, or should they have reasonable grounds for supposing that a competitor in a race has in any way infringed these rules, they shall make due inquiries, and if an infringement or breach of the rules be proved, they shall disqualify the yacht accordingly.

31. Should any flag vessel or other mark be removed from its proper position, either by accident or design, the race shall be re-sailed, or not, at the discretion of the Sailing Committee.

32. Any yacht disobeying or infringing any of these rules, which shall apply to all yachts whether sailing in the same or different races, shall be disqualified from receiving any prize she would otherwise have won, and her owner shall be liable for all damages arising therefrom, not exceeding in amount and subject to the same limitations as provided by the Merchant Shipping Act of 1894. A breach of these rules shall be considered "improper navigation" within the meaning and for the purposes of that Act. Should a flagrant breach or infringement of any of these rules be proved against the owner of a yacht, or against the owner's representative or amateur helmsman, such owner, his representative, or amateur helmsman may be disqualified by the Council, for any time the Council may think fit, from sailing the yacht in any race held under the rules of the Yacht Racing Association; and should a flagrant breach of these rules be proved against any sailing master he may be disqualified by the Council, for such time as the Council may think fit, from sailing in any race held under the rules of the Yacht Racing Association.

33. When yachts are ordered to sail in cruising trim, the following rules are to be strictly observed:—1. No doors, tables, cabin skylights, or other cabin or deck-fittings (davits excepted) shall be removed from their places before or during the race. 2. No sails or other gear shall be put into the main cabin in yachts exceeding a rating of 73 ft. 3. Anchors and chains suitable to the size of the yacht shall be carried, one at the cathead (or in yachts rated at 73 ft. and under, at the usual place on the bow), which anchor shall not be unshackled from the chain before or during the race. 4. Every yacht exceeding a rating of 60 ft. and under a rating of 80 ft. shall carry a boat on deck not less than 10 ft. in length and 3 ft. 6 in. beam—a yacht rated at 80 ft. and over, her usual cutter and dinghy. 5. No extra hands, except a pilot, beyond the regular crew of the yacht shall be allowed.

APPENDIX.

The Yacht Racing Association further recommend for the consideration of Sailing Committees:—1st. That as mixed races are no satisfactory test of the relative speed of yachts, the different rigs should, whenever practicable, be kept separate; but when mixed races are unavoidable, the following rule shall be observed:—The rating of schooners and yawls to be reckoned for time allowance as follows, viz., schooners at 0·85, and yawls at 0·92 of their actual rating; provided that in case of a yawl her mainsail does not exceed 0·37 of her total sail area, and that her mizen is not less than 0·06 of her total sail area. In the case of a pole-masted yawl, her mainsail shall not exceed 0·46 of her total sail area, and her mizen shall not be less than 0·075 of her total sail area. In schooners the foreside of the mainmast shall at the deck be not farther forward than the middle of the rating length. Ketches and luggers shall be reckoned for time allowance at 0·85 of their rating; provided that in a ketch the distance between the masts does not exceed half the rating length of the yacht, and that the smaller sail is carried aft. In the case of a lugger, to be entitled to the rig allowance, the yacht must have two or more masts, and the after, or the middle mast, at the deck must not be forward of the middle of the rating length, and in the case of a two-masted lugger, if the area of the after lug be less than half the area of the main lug, she will be rated as a yawl. In calculating the deduction for difference of rig, the rating by certificate to the exact fraction must be used. The time allowances to be calculated from each yacht's reduced rating; but schooners, ketches, luggers and yawls shall not be allowed to qualify to enter by their reduced rating in a class race. 2nd. In races for mixed rigs, the time allowances between yachts of the same rig must be calculated on each yacht's reduced rating. 3rd. That flying starts should be adopted when practicable, but no time should be allowed for delay in starting. 4th. That, as weatherliness is a quality which it is especially desirable to test in yacht racing, the courses should, wherever possible, be so laid out as to include a large proportion of windward work. 5th. That any limit to the time for concluding a race should be avoided as far as possible. 6th. That the classification of yachts should, when practicable, be as follows:—

For yachts whose rating, by Rule 3,
does not exceed . . . . 18 ft.
Above 18 ft. and not exceeding 24 ft.
,, 24 ft. ,, ,, 30 ft.
,, 30 ft. ,, ,, 36 ft.
,, 36 ft. ,, ,, 42 ft.
,, 42 ft. ,, ,, 52 ft.
,, 52 ft. ,, ,, 65 ft.
,, 79 ft.

7th. That as distance is an important element in the calculation of time allowance, the marks and flag boats should be placed so as to mark as accurately as possible the length of the course, for which time is allowed. 8th. That in heavy weather it should be arranged, if practicable, for yachts to stay instead of gybe round marks. 9th. That Sailing Committees should be particularly careful to provide ample room between the points marking the starting line. 10th. That where, owing to the distance of the yachts from the signal station, or the crowded state of the roadstead, or from other reasons, it is difficult for the competing yachts to see their recall numbers, some suitable sound signal shall be given to call the attention of the competitors to the fact that a recall number is being displayed.

LIST OF RECOGNISED YACHT CLUBS.

Royal Albert Yacht Club.
Royal Alfred Yacht Club.
Royal Anglesey Yacht Club.
Royal Bombay Yacht Club.
Bangor (Ireland) Corinthian Sailing Club.
Royal Barrow Yacht Club.
Bembridge Sailing Club.
Bristol Channel Yacht Club.
Cambridge University Cruising Club.
Castle (Calshot) Yacht Club.
Royal Channel Islands Yacht Club.
Cheshire Yacht Club.
Royal Cinque Ports Yacht Club.
Royal Clyde Yacht Club.
Clyde Corinthian Yacht Club.
Royal Corinthian Yacht Club.
Royal Cork Yacht Club.
Royal Cornwall Yacht Club.
Cruising Yacht Club.
Cultra Yacht Club.
Dart Boat Sailing Club.
Royal Dart Yacht Club.
Royal Dee Yacht Club.
Royal Dorset Yacht Club.
Dublin Bay Sailing Club.
Royal Eastern Yacht Club.
Royal Engineers Yacht Club.
Exe Yacht Club.
Royal Forth Yacht Club.
Fowey Yacht Club.
Royal Harwich Yacht Club.
Royal Highland Yacht Club.
Hythe (Southampton) Yacht Club.
Royal Irish Yacht Club.
Island Sailing Club.
Isle of Purbeck Yacht Club.
Royal Jamaica Yacht Club.
Royal Largs Yacht Club.
London Sailing Club.
Royal London Yacht Club.
Lough Derg Yacht Club.
Lough Erne Yacht Club.
Lytham Yacht Club.
Minima Yacht Club.
Medway Yacht Club.
Royal Mersey Yacht Club.
Mudhook Yacht Club.
Royal Munster Yacht Club.
New Brighton Sailing Club.
New Thames Yacht Club.
Norfolk and Suffolk Yacht Club.
Royal Northern Yacht Club.
Royal Nova Scotia Yacht Club.
Orwell Corinthian Yacht Club.
Penarth Yacht Club.
Royal Plymouth Corinthian Yacht Club.
Poole Yacht Club.
Royal Portsmouth Corinthian Yacht Club.
Royal St. George's Yacht Club.
Salcombe Sailing Club.
Seaview Yacht Club.
Solent Yacht Club.
Royal Southampton Yacht Club.
Royal Southern Yacht Club.
Southampton Corinthian Yacht Club.
Southport Corinthian Yacht Club.
Royal South-Western Yacht Club.
Start Bay Yacht Club.
Royal Tay Yacht Club.
Teignmouth Corinthian Sailing Club.
Royal Temple Yacht Club.
Royal Thames Yacht Club.
Torbay Sailing Club.
Royal Torbay Yacht Club.
Torquay Corinthian Sailing Club.
Royal Ulster Yacht Club.
Royal Victoria Yacht Club.
Royal Welsh Yacht Club
West Lancashire Yacht Club.
West of Scotland Yacht Club.
Royal Western (of England) Yacht Club.
Royal Western (of Scotland) Yacht Club.
Royal Windermere Yacht Club.
Royal Yacht Squadron.
Yare Sailing Club.
Royal Yorkshire Yacht Club.

N.B.—For the purposes of General Rule 3, and of 6 and 10 of the Sailing Rules, all yacht clubs of the United Kingdom which hold Admiralty warrants are recognised; and such other clubs (including those of the British Colonies) as may apply for recognition and be accepted by the Council under the second paragraph of Rule 6. The recognition of a yacht club does not necessarily, nor of itself, qualify a member of that club as an amateur.

TIME ALLOWANCES.

In preparing the new Time Scale to come into operation with the new linear rating rule of 1896, the following equivalents between the ratings for the classes under the length and sail area rule and the new linear rating rule, were, on the recommendation of the yacht designers, adopted:—

Ratings under length and sail area rule.	Equivalents under linear rating rule.
0·5	18 ft.
1·0	24 ft.
2·5	30 ft.
5	36 ft.
10	42 ft.
20	52 ft.
40	65 ft.

85 rating, under the length and sail area rule, has also been taken as equivalent to 80 ft. rating under the new rule. The time allowances from 24 ft. to 80 ft. rating correspond nearly with those of the previous scale, but small alterations have been introduced to make the figures accord with a true curve, plotted with the vertical scale of seconds double the horizontal scale of feet. Above 80 ft. rating the time allowances accord with a tangent to the time scale curve from that point, increasing by 1·3 seconds per foot of rating. This principle has been followed with the object of increasing the time allowances to be given by yachts of the larger ratings. In like manner, the time allowances for ratings under 24 ft. accord with a tangent to the curve from that point. The allowance a yacht has to make to any smaller yacht is obtained by multiplying the difference between the times set against their respective ratings in the time tables, by the length of the course in knots. For example, the time a yacht of 70 ft. rating has to allow a yacht of 65 ft. rating, over a 50 knot course, is as follows:—

70 ft. . . . 199·20
65 ft. . . . 190·45

8·75
50

60)437·50

7·17·5 seconds.

When a fraction of a second equals or exceeds 0·5 it is to be counted as a second, but fractions less than 0·5 are to be disregarded. In the case illustrated above, the time allowance is, therefore, 7 minutes and 18 seconds. If one of the yachts is above and the other below 24 ft. rating, the time allowances in the two tables found, from their respective ratings, added together, and multiplied by the length of the course, will give the time the larger allows the smaller yacht.

At a general meeting of the Y.R.A. held on the 12th November, 1896, the time scale above 90 rating was altered as follows:—The tangential or constant difference of 1·3 seconds per foot previously mentioned, was increased by a cumulative addition of 10 per cent. or 0·13 for each foot, and the table has been altered accordingly.

AMERICAN YACHTING—**Historical**—The birth of American yachting, truly so called, may be said to have taken place in the cabin of the little schooner "Gimcrack," on the 30th of July, 1844, when the New York Yacht Club was organised. Doubtless there were pleasure craft worthy of the name of yachts before this time, but with hardly an exception they have left neither history nor legend behind them, and the consideration of the subject must, therefore, begin at this point.

A number of gentlemen, representing most of the pleasure craft of any size owned in American waters, came together in the cabin of the "Gimcrack" by request of her owner, Mr. J. C. Stevens, to organise the club, whose history has been to a great extent the record of American yachting. The second yacht club in the United States was the Southern, of New Orleans, but this organisation never had more than a local interest, as its fleet was composed entirely of small open boats. Then followed the Neptune Yacht Club of the Highlands, which was organised in 1850, with headquarters on the Shrewsbury River, New Jersey, but, like its Southern sister, it was known only in its immediate vicinity. Next in order comes the Carolina, of Wilmington, North Carolina, in 1854; but it was not until 1857, when the Brooklyn Yacht Club was founded, that the New York Yacht Club had a rival.

The New York Yacht Club held its first regatta July 16th, 1845, and its rating for time allowance was 45 seconds per ton, Custom House measurement. The course was entirely an inside one in New York Bay, the outer mark being the South-west Spit Buoy. This was not only the first yacht regatta under the auspices of the Club, but the first recorded in America. Schooners and sloops were classed together, and the only dimension given was the tonnage, as follows:—Schooners: "Cygnet," 45 tons, W. Edgar; "Sybil," 42 tons, C. B. Miller; "Spray," 37 tons, H. Wilkes; "La Coquille," 27 tons, John C. Jay; "Minna," 30 tons, J. Waterbury; "Gimcrack," Com. J. C. Stevens. Sloops: "Newburgh," 33 tons, H. Robinson; "Adder," 17 tons, J. Rogers; "Lancet," 20 tons, G. B. Rollins. The "Cygnet" won.

With some exceptions, there cannot be stated from any data now extant the exact type of these boats, but some were keel and some, probably, centreboard craft. No light sails were then used, except, possibly, a maintopsail. Spinakers, balloon jib topsails, and even fore- and jib-topsails were unknown.

With a few words more about the clubs, it will be noticed how the type of the "La Coquille" and the "Cygnet," the comparatively blunt, low, and "mackerel stern," developed into the "wave-form" and the "fin-keel."

The general public interest in regattas was far greater then than it is to-day. The stores, exchanges, and banks were closed, and a general holiday prevailed. The shores of Bay Ridge, Staten Island, and that part of New Jersey from which a glimpse of the course could be obtained, were lined with people in holiday attire eager to catch the first view of the leader. As the number of clubs increased, however, and yachts

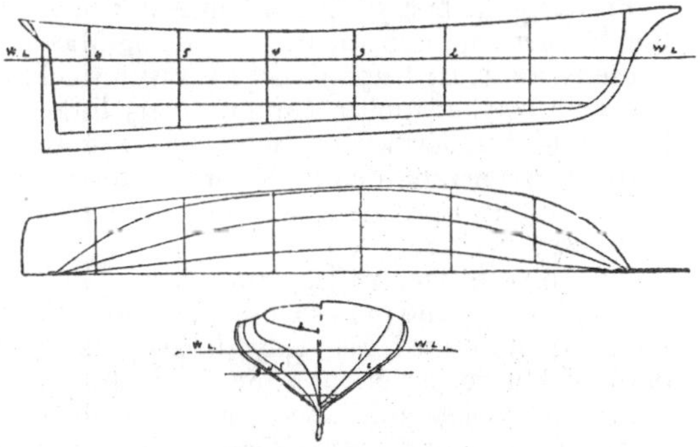

"CYGNET."

were seen in every bay and harbour, the interest, except in international contests, was confined to the yacht owners and their friends.

In 1858 the Jersey City Yacht Club was organised; seven years later the first New England Club, the Boston, was founded. This was after the close of the Civil War, in 1865; but there is not space to enumerate all the clubs, which rapidly multiplied until nearly every town on the seaboard of ten thousand inhabitants possessed its club signal and its house. Indeed, this statement need not be confined to the seaboard, for all the large places on the great lakes and many on the smaller ones had their yacht clubs. As early as 1867 the Golden Gate Yacht Club of San Francisco, California, was founded; so "the western slope" was only two years behind New England in opening its first home for the owners of pleasure craft. Among the later group of clubs in New York Bay or along the shores of Long Island Sound must be mentioned the Atlantic, founded in 1866, the Seawanhaka Corinthian in 1871, and the Larchmont in 1880—all organisations which are second only to the New York Yacht Club; in fact, it is highly probable that there is a larger number of expert sailors, who habitually sail and command their own vessels, in these last-named clubs than in the older organisation. This is particularly true of the Seawanhaka Club. Although New

England was somewhat late in the field, Boston is to-day more of a yachting centre than even New York, although she lacks Long Island Sound. Among her prominent clubs are the "Eastern" (founded in 1870), the "Beverly," the "Bunker Hill," the "Corinthian of Marblehead," and, in other New England towns, the "Hull," "New Haven," "Portland," Norwalk, "Riverside," Stamford, and many more.

Among other clubs which have permanent homes on the various harbours of the Sound, are the New Rochelle, Corinthian Fleet, Sea Cliff, Hempstead Harbour, Riverside, Indian Harbour, and Huguenot. Most of these clubs, outside of those previously spoken of, are composed of comparatively small boats, and have but little place in the history or development of yachting, except, perhaps, locally.

Probably the first yacht built in America was the "Jefferson," constructed at Salem, Massachusetts, 1801, for Capt. George Crowninshield, and built by Christopher Turner. Very little is known of her beyond the fact that she was twenty-two tons burden; she was afterwards converted into a privateer, and took some prizes in the war of 1812.

Fifteen years later "Cleopatra's Barge" made her appearance, and was so much admired that many people visited her daily during the later days of her construction. She was brigantine-rigged and looked much more like a small war vessel of that period (1816) than a gentleman's pleasure-craft. Like her predecessor, she was built at Salem for the same owner, and was 83 feet on the water line and 91·41 tons, a keel boat drawing 11 feet of water. There was little yachting in America, however, until the years immediately preceding the formation of the New York Yacht Club, when there was a sufficient number of yachts in existence to form a nucleus for the young enterprise to work with. The first cruise of the squadron took place when the Club was just four days old, and was called by the Secretary, John C. Jay, in his minutes, "An expedition to Newport." They stopped at Huntington and New Haven, rendezvousing at White Stone

Now appeared upon the field the first famous American yacht designer, George Steers. In 1839, when he was but fourteen years old, he built a sail-boat 17 feet long, called the "Martin Van Buren," which was considered a marvel of speed. In 1841 Steers constructed for Mr. (afterwards Com.) J. C. Stevens a sloop 30 feet long, which proved a successful craft.

The "Cygnet," a keel schooner built for Mr. Edgar, 45 tons, was launched in 1842, designed by the same hand, and was probably the best yacht of her kind produced in the country previous to the existence of the New York Yacht Club; but it was not until 1846, when Commodore Stevens, with Steers's help, constructed the "Maria," that the famous designer's name became noted beyond all others of his time. This celebrated sloop was 110 feet over all, 97 feet on load water-line, 26·6 feet beam, 5·2 feet draught, displacement 145 tons, sail area 5,850 square feet. For some time the "Maria"

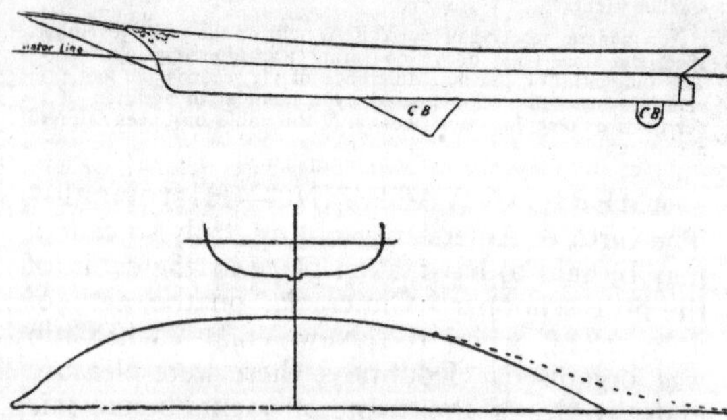

"MARIA."

was considered a marvel of perfection, although she was once beaten in a severe blow by a schooner. She was a centreboard, as her light draught would imply. Her first race was sailed October 6th, 1841, which was also the first Corinthian race in the country, the boats being handled exclusively by amateurs.

In 1847 Steers built for James Waterbury, Esq., the scarcely less noted "Una," originally a sloop, but since altered into a schooner. This later production was much smaller than the "Maria," being only 54 tons. The "Una" is still in existence, and is to-day a fine-looking boat, which speaks well for the "Steers" construction. Most of the vessels of this designer became historic in the yachting world, and all of them were more than ordinarily fast for that time.

The second great period of American yachting was ushered in by the advent of the famous "America," Steers's greatest triumph. She was built for Com. J. C. Stevens, owner of the "Maria," and was a keel schooner of 170 tons. The career of this vessel in foreign waters is so

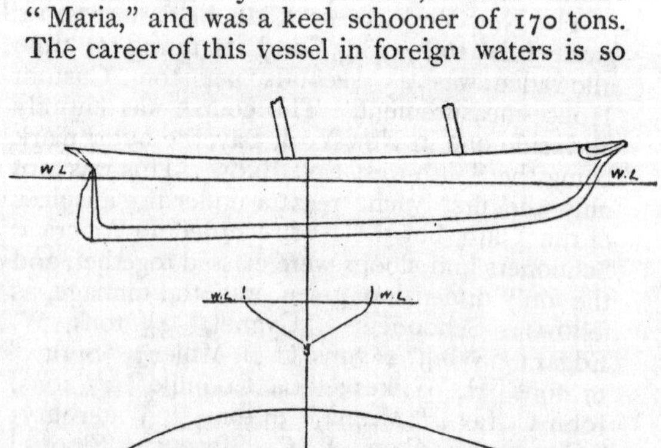

"AMERICA."

well known as to need only a passing mention here. It may be well, however, to give her full dimensions. She was 94 feet on deck, 84 feet L.W.L., 82 feet keel, 22·6 beam, 11·6 draught, mainmast 81 feet, foremast 79·6, maintopmast 33·6, main boom 58 feet, main gaff 28 feet, fore gaff 24 feet, bowsprit outboard 17 feet.

In this enterprise were associated with Commodore Stevens his friends, Hamilton Weeks, George L. Schuyler, James Hamilton, and J. B. Finlay. The "America" sailed for Europe early in July, 1851, and arrived at Havre twenty-one days later, in which port she was put in racing condition, and as soon as in trim sailed for Cowes, the headquarters of British yachting. The great race for the cup, now known as the "America's," was sailed August 22nd, 1851, the course being around the Isle of Wight. The American schooner finished at 8 h. 37 m., while the first yacht of the Royal Squadron crossed the line at 8 h. 55 m. This time-record, however, is hardly fair to the "America," as her nearest opponent, the cutter "Aurora," was some miles astern until near the finish, when a lucky "fluke," so common in yachting, made her a fair second; the thirteen remaining vessels, however, were hopelessly beaten. While in English waters, the "America" was easily successful in a match sailed with the schooner "Titania." Before speaking of other yachts it should be noted that the "America" was the first yacht that ever crossed the Atlantic in either direction. Like the "Una," she is still in existence, and in her modern rig is still rated as one of the fast sailers. During the season of 1897 this grand old schooner, in a cracking breeze and rigged in modern style, beat the swift and scarcely less famous Burgess schooner "Puritan" (formerly the cup defending sloop).

The next yacht worthy of mention is the centreboard sloop "Sylvie," 101 tons, drawing only $4\frac{1}{2}$ feet of water with her board up. She was owned by Louis Depau, Esq., and, like the "America," raced in English waters; but she was not successful. She had, however, the honour of being the first sloop-yacht to cross the Atlantic.

About the year 1854 balloon-sails and club and sprit-topsails came into use on racing yachts, though not such large ones as we see to-day. In this year appeared the famous and, for years, invincible sloop "Julia," owned by James Waterbury, Esq., former owner of the "Una." This new craft was also designed by Steers. Her dimensions were 80 tons, Custom House measurement; for some years she was the pride of the yachting world, and considered the best of the Steers's boats, with perhaps the exception of the ever famous "America." The "Julia" is still, like the "America," in existence, but is now the schooner "Nirvana"; she never was successful as a racer since her change of rig. The "Julia" was the last vessel of note modelled by Steers, as he died soon after at an early age.

In the next period in the yachting history of the country there was a dearth of great designers. Plenty of yachts were built, but they were not much better that those which preceded them. Although it was not until the days of Burgess that anything superior was designed, there was a gradual evolution in the construction of yachts which produced many good results. The Civil War for a short period turned men's thoughts in other directions and possibly delayed for a time advance in the sport. The schooner "Magic" was designed by R. J. Loper in 1857, and was afterwards famous for leading the New York Yacht Club fleet in winning the America's cup race of 1870, against the English schooner "Cambria," the owner of which, Mr. Ashbury, had offered the challenge. The "Magic" was 97·17 tons, and was always considered a good rather than a remarkable boat, until she won her fame in the race above alluded to. In 1865, or during the war, the "Henrietta," owned by James Gordon Bennett and designed by William Tooker, made her first appearance. She was a schooner of 230 tons, and was one of the famous three vessels participating in the celebrated ocean race in December, 1866.

The well known schooners, "Idler," "Palmer," "Fleetwing," and "Vesta," all came off the ways during 1865. This was the beginning of what

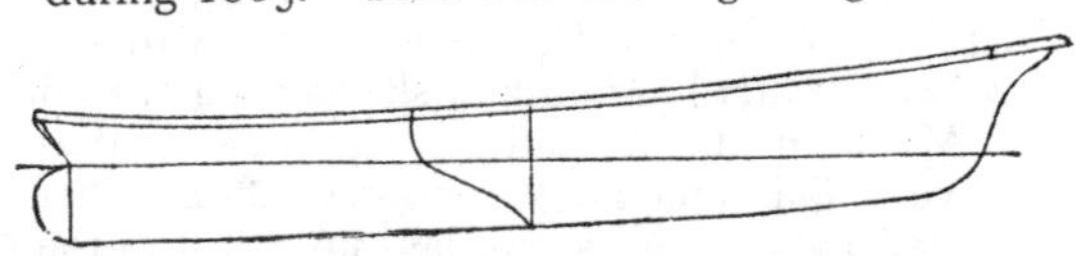

"MAGIC."

might be called the schooner epoch, which lasted from 1865 until about 1885. This statement does not imply that the schooner was not a popular craft before, or that she disappeared from American waters at a later period, but simply that the schooner "craze" or "fad" reached its zenith during this epoch. Earlier than this many were satisfied with sloops of moderate size, and later the former owner of the sea-going schooner became possessed of the more luxurious but less picturesque steam yacht, that is, if he did not aspire to become a "single stick" cup defender.

J. W. Herreshoff, father of the famous designer of the "Gloriana," first attracted the attention of yacht owners in 1861 by the appearance of the little sloop "Qui Vive," but it was not until many years later that he became celebrated as the "blind builder."

The year 1866 is famous in yachting annals for the great ocean race between the keel schooners "Henrietta" and "Fleetwing" and the centreboard schooner "Vesta." This race was probably for the largest purse ever known in the history of yachting—90,000 dollars—and the season selected was the most tempestuous of the year. The start was made December 11th, 1866. The yachts were owned as follows:—"Henrietta," James Gordon Bennett; "Fleetwing," Franklin and George A. Osgood; and "Vesta," Pierre Lorillard. The thermometer stood at 11° Fahrenheit when the yachts were towed down New York Bay and let go from the tug outside of Sandy Hook. They set every stitch of canvas, including a square sail, despite the severe winter gale.

The "Henrietta" won, having sailed 3,106 miles (or to the light-house on the west end of the Isle of Wight) in thirteen days, twenty-one hours, and fifty-five minutes. This was the first yacht-race across the Atlantic, and was one of the most courageous events in yachting history.

In 1867 the famous schooner "Sappho" first appeared, but was not very successful that season. She was built by the Poillons in Brooklyn, and they had great expectations as to

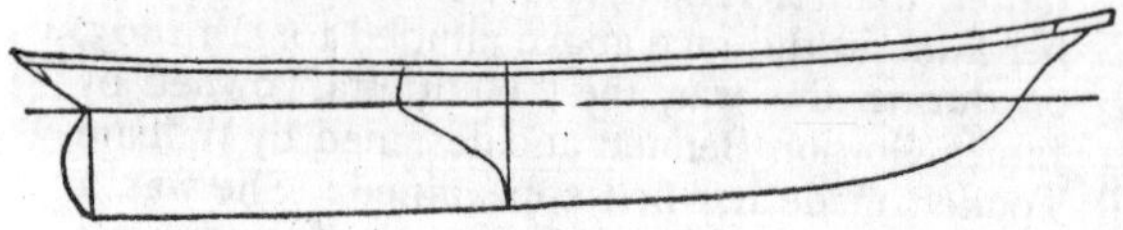

"SAPPHO."

her speed; but it was not until after she was hipped out that she became the fastest thing then afloat. Some little time before the "Sappho's" appearance, the "Dauntless" came out. At first, as "L'Hirondelle," she was owned by Mr. Bradford; from him she was purchased by Mr. Bennett, who had her name changed as above. This famous old schooner, after all her triumphs as a racer, is now laid up to rot in the Connecticut River.

In 1870, as before mentioned, Mr. James Ashbury challenged for the America's Cup with the schooner "Cambria," and after much correspondence with the representatives of the New York Yacht Club a race was arranged. The New York Yacht Club course was settled on, namely, from Owl's Head around the Sandy Hook Light-ship and return. Mr. Ashbury desired to have a single vessel pitted against his schooner, but as the "America" had sailed the fleet of the Royal Squadron in English waters, the Committee decided that the "Cambria" should also sail against the New York Squadron in these waters. Shortly before the "Cambria" sailed for America, Mr. Bennett, who was abroad at the time with the "Dauntless," challenged Mr. Ashbury to sail an ocean race across the Atlantic. Mr. Ashbury immediately accepted, and on July 4th they started from England. At about one o'clock on July 27th the first one sighted proved to be the "Cambria," and she shortly afterwards passed the Sandy Hook Light-ship and rounded the point of Sandy Hook, beating the "Dauntless" by just one hour and seventeen minutes—a very close race considering the distance. August 8th was the day selected for the America's Cup Race, and a great fleet assembled, namely, the keel schooners "America," "Fleetwing," "Dauntless," "Restless," "Rambler," "Alarm," and "Tarolinta," and the centreboards "Tidal Wave," "Silvie," "Madge," "Phantom," "Madeline," "Idler," "Magic," "Jessie," "Halcyon," "Widgeon," "Calypso," "Josephine," "Eva," "Fleur de Lis," "Alice," and "Palmer." Yachts at that time started from their anchor, and the "Cambria" was given the weather position; but just before the time for giving the starting signal the wind changed, and placed her dead to leeward of all her rivals, which was extremely unfortunate for her. The "Magic" was the first to get her anchor, and was well on her course before many had weighed at all. The "America" was noticeably slow, and was the last to get away. The "Cambria" was beautifully handled, and, despite her unfortunate position, soon took a good place. The "Magic" never lost her lead, and finished at 3 h. 33 m. 54 sec. The times of a few of the leaders were: "Idler," second, 3 h. 37 m. 23 sec.; "Silvie," 3 h. 55 m. 12 sec.; "America," 3 h. 47 m. 54 sec.; "Dauntless," 3 h. 35 m. 28 sec.; "Madge," 3 h. 55 m. 7 sec.; "Phantom," 3 h. 55 m. 5 sec.; "Alice," 4 h. 18 m. 27½ sec.; "Halcyon," 4 h. 3 m. 8 sec.; "Cambria," 4 h. 0 m. 57 sec.; the corrected time of the same vessels were: "Magic," 3 h. 58 m. 26·2 sec.; "Idler," 4 h. 9 m. 51 sec; "Silvie," 4 h. 23 m. 45·3 sec.; "America," 4 h. 23 m. 51 sec.; "Dauntless," 4 h. 29 m. 19½ sec.; "Madge," 4 h. 29 m. 57·1 sec.; "Phantom," 4 h. 30 m. 44·5 sec.; "Alice," 4 h. 34 m. 15 sec.; "Halcyon," 4 h. 0 m. 35·9 sec.; "Cambria," 4 h. 37 m. 38·9 sec.

The visiting schooner joined the fleet of the New York Yacht Club on its annual cruise, and sailed a number of races during that period, winning her full share.

Even as late as 1871 there was but little yachting outside of the New York Yacht Club, though the Brooklyn, Eastern, and Atlantic Clubs were beginning to force themselves into notice, with boats of a much smaller size. The Brooklyn, for instance, at this time had but two schooners enrolled—the flagship "Madeline" and the "Fleur de Lis"—though the Club was second only to the New York. A few years later, however (1873), the Boston had thirteen schooners, twenty-five sloops, and two steamers; but the Brooklyn had already begun to decline, and the Boston was more nearly approached in this year by the Atlantic than by any of the smaller clubs.

Of the sloops of this time, the "Fannie" and "Gracie" were undoubtedly in the lead of the large ones, though the "Vision" and "Meta" were close rivals. The "Meta" was afterwards changed into a schooner, but was not improved by the alteration.

During the annual cruise of the New York Yacht Club, that organisation was again challenged for the America's Cup by Mr. Ashbury with his new schooner "Livonia." After much correspondence it was decided that the "Livonia" should not sail the entire New York Fleet, but that the Cup Committee should select four vessels, any one of which they could name to sail the "Livonia" on the morning of the race. The agreement also stated that there should be a series of seven races, four of which must be won by the representative boats of the New York Yacht Club or by the challenger, in order to retain or obtain the cup. The four boats selected by the Committee of the New York Yacht Club were the schooners "Dauntless," J. G. Bennett; "Sappho," W. P. Douglas; "Palmer," Rutherford Stuyvesant; and "Columbia," Franklin Osgood. October 16th was named as the day for the first race, and the "Columbia" (centreboard) was the schooner chosen to meet the "Livonia." The wind was light and from the north-west, and the time of finish was: "Columbia," 4 h. 57 m. 32 sec.; "Livonia," 5 h. 23 m. 0 sec.

The second race, October 18th, was in a very strong breeze outside the Light-ship, and the "Columbia" again sailed, winning by ten minutes andthirty-three seconds, Mr. Ashbury protesting that the "Columbia" rounded the outer mark in the wrong way; the protest was over-ruled by Committee.

The third race, October 19th, was over the New York Yacht Club course. The "Dauntless" meeting with an accident and the "Sappho" and "Palmer" not being on hand, the "Columbia" was again named (per force). The "Columbia" broke down, and the English yacht won by 15 m. 10 sec.

For the fourth race the "Sappho" was named, and beat the "Livonia" 30 m. 21 sec. over ocean course.

In the fifth race the "Sappho" again beat the "Livonia" on New York Yacht Club, inside course, 28 m. 27 sec. This ended the series, the American yachts "Columbia" and "Sappho" having won two races each. The "Livonia"

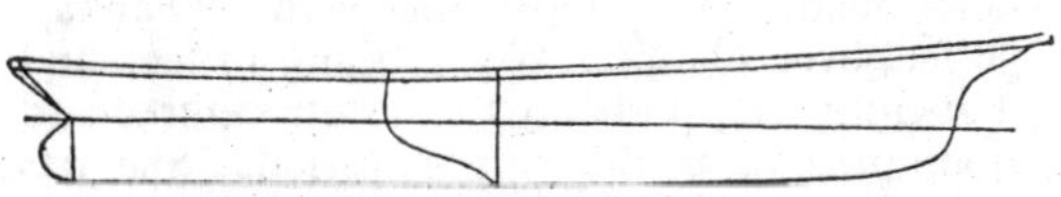

"COLUMBIA."

sailed a match with the "Dauntless" before the close of the season, which the latter yacht won by 10 m. 31 sec.

The next two or three years were not very eventful in yachting. The usual number of races were sailed, but no vessels of any historic interest appeared. The "Sappho" was, probably, still the fastest schooner in the waters of the United States, though the "Comet," owned by Mr. W. H. Langley, and the "Estelle," owned by Commodore Smith, were attracting some notice. The large schooners "Dreadnaught" and "Resolute" were magnificent vessels, though not especially successful as racers.

On June 9th, 1875, was launched the unfortunate "Mohawk," built by Mr. Joseph Van Dusen for Mr. Garner. She was probably the largest centreboard pleasure vessel afloat, being 121 feet on water line, 30 feet 4 inches beam, and 9 feet 4 inches depth of hold. In the autumn of this year the "Mohawk" sailed several races, and did not attract attention for her speedy qualities. In this year also the famous sloop "Arrow," built and designed by David Kirby for Mr. D. C. Edgar, first made her appearance, beating the "Fannie," "Gracie," and "Vision" with ease. The "Arrow" has been laid up a long time at Cold Spring, L. I., and is so dilapidated and apparently decayed that she looks as though she would never stretch her canvas again. The "Arrow," although she joined the New York Yacht Club cruise in 1875, did very little racing until the following year, when she won all the annuals in which she started, and also the special Centennial Regatta. The schooner prizes of this famous race were awarded to the "Dreadnaught" and "Peerless" in their respective classes. This race was also celebrated for the first appearance in these waters of the catamaran ("Amaryllis"). She was designed and built by Herreshoff, then coming into prominence. She distanced the entire fleet, but was ruled out by the Committee. Strange to say, this type of craft has never become very popular, though undoubtedly the fastest of all sailing vessels. In this year Mr. John Hyslop designed and launched, for his own private use, the first true wave-form boat (in this country, at all events), the trim little "Petrel." She was a keel craft, and, for her size, was very successful, being only 32 feet over all.

Towards the close of July, 1876, an accident occurred which gave the most severe blow that yachting has ever suffered in this country. The schooner "Mohawk" lying at anchor off Staten Island, with all sails set, was struck by a hard squall and capsized. The owner, Mr. Garner, his wife, and several other ladies lost their lives. How much the schooner's model had to do with this accident, it is impossible to say; but it seems strange that a vessel of her size should have turned over before her spars were carried away.

1876 was also the year in which another America's Cup challenge was received and the race sailed. This time, however, the challenge came, not from England, but from Canada. Major Charles Gifford, Vice-Commodore of the Royal Canadian Yacht Club, was the challenger, with his schooner "Countess of Dufferin," and the New York Yacht Club selected Commodore Voorhis's schooner "Madeline" to be its representative. After the usual large amount of correspondence, the first race was set for August 11th, the victory to be decided by the best two out of three races. The result of the first race over the New York Yacht Club inside course was 9 m. 58 sec. in favour of the "Madeline"; the race of the following day, over an ocean course from Sandy Hook 20 miles to

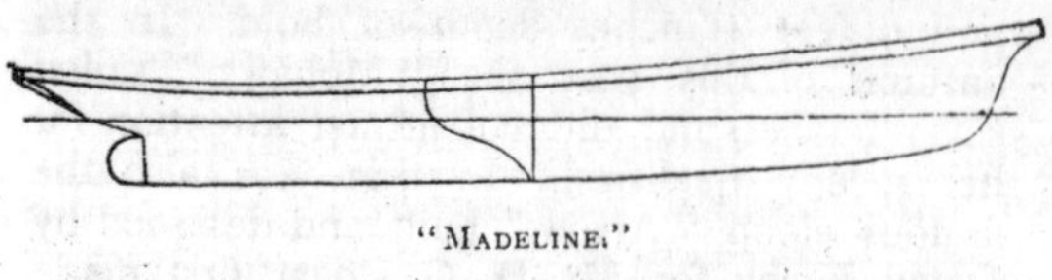

"MADELINE."

windward and return, was also in the "Madeline's" favour by even a greater margin, 27 m. 14 sec. This decided the contest. The "Madeline" was modelled and built by David Kirby (designer of the famous "Arrow") in 1868, and rigged as a sloop. She was afterwards altered into a schooner and lengthened, in which rig she gained her reputation for speed.

The years 1877 and 1878 were not eventful in the yachting world. The usual number of boats were, of course, constructed, and the usual races were sailed without any special interest. This year there was built the first genuine English cutter in this country by John F. Munn, for Robert Center, Esq. She was 40 feet on water line, 12 feet beam, 6 feet 10 inches deep, and carried outside lead. This may be considered the start of what is known as the "cutter craze," and that class of vessel soon became as common in our waters as the old "skimming dish" sloop had been, and its effect has certainly been most beneficial in the modifying of the less seaworthy type.

The year 1879 was noteworthy for an ocean race by four small sloops in the month of October. The course was from Sandy Hook to Cape May Light-ship and return, all the vessels being of the centreboard type. They were the "Mischief," J. B. Buck, 67 feet 5 inches over

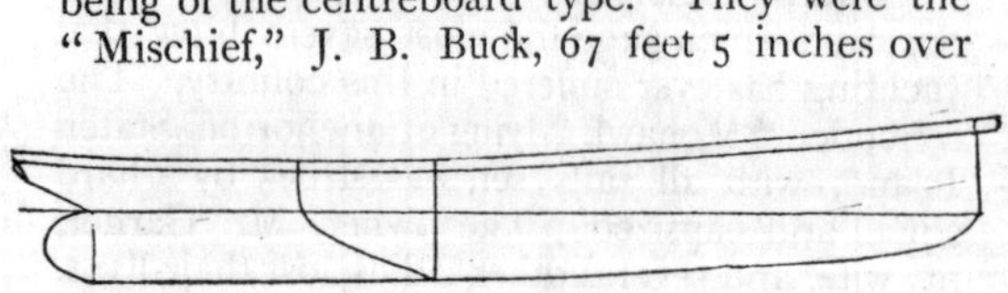

"MISCHIEF."

all, 67 feet L.W.L., 19 feet 10 inches beam, 7 feet 9 inches depth; "Regina," W. W. W. Stewart, 50 feet 8 inches over all, 47 feet 3 inches water-line, 16 feet 3 inches beam, 5 feet 6 inches depth; "Wave," Dr. J. G. Barron, 41 feet 8 inches over all, 38 feet 7 inches water-line, 14 feet 8 inches beam, 4 feet 3 inches depth; "Blanche," 41 feet over all, 38 feet 6 inches water-line, 14 feet 6 inches beam, 4 feet 4 inches depth. It is hardly necessary to say the "Mischief" won, but it may be of more interest to learn that all returned in safety, which is somewhat surprising.

In March, 1881, another challenge for the America's Cup was sent from Canada, and this time by a big "single sticker," the "Atlanta," from the Bay of Quinte Yacht Club. She was designed by Captain Cuthbert, the designer of the Canadian schooner which had raced the "Madeline" in 1876. The New York Yacht Club immediately sent an order to David Kirby to build an "improved" "Arrow"—that sloop herself being no longer in the Club. This boat (the "Pocahontas") was built, but proved a total failure in the trial races with the "Gracie," "Mischief," and "Hildegarde." The "Arrow" would have easily defeated any of the sloops named above. The "Atlanta" arriving late in the season, the first race did not come off until November 9th. The "Mischief" having been successful in the trials, was selected to defend the cup. Dimensions of "Atlanta"—centreboard sloop 70 feet over all, 54 feet L.W.L., 19 feet beam, 6 feet 10 inches depth of hold, draught 5 feet 6 inches. The result of the first race at the finish was:

	Elapsed time.		
	h.	m.	sec.
"Mischief"	4	17	9
"Atlanta"	4	48	24½

This race was over the inside course of the New York Yacht Club, and was sailed in a heavy breeze. The next day's race was from the point of Sandy Hook, 20 miles to sea and return, and was won by the "Mischief" by over thirty-eight minutes.

This same year there came to the United States from Scotland the little cutter "Madge," 46 feet 1 inch over all; "at home she was rated as a 10-tonner." She raced with such yachts as the "Schemer" and "Wave," and the famous Boston sloop "Shadow," beating them, to the surprise of American yachtsmen, for they then considered them their best boats.

Between 1882 and 1885, in which year the next cup challenge was sent from Sir Richard Sutton, owner of the "Genesta," the following boats made their appearance: the "Fanita," 50 feet over all, 44 L.W.L., beam 17 feet, and draught 5 feet, probably the fastest centreboard sloop previous to the Burgess period. She was modelled by Philip Ellsworth for J. G. Prague, Esq. Then came the schooner "Grayling," designed by the same hand for Com. L. A. Fish, and the "Fortuna" of Boston for Com. Henry S. Hovey, of the Eastern Yacht Club, designed by Mr. A. Cary Smith.

These gentlemen were probably the best American designers of yachts between the death of Steers and the advent of Burgess. Ellsworth was responsible for the celebrated schooners "Grayling," "Montauk," and "Comet," and the scarcely less famous sloops "Fanita," "Elephant," "Crocodile," "Sasqua," "Arab," and "Atlantic" (the last not much of a success), while A. Cary Smith produced among others the cup defender "Mischief," and the schooners "Prospero," "Harbinger," and "Fortuna"; his "Vindex" was also celebrated in her day. The "Montauk" had the honour of making the best time over the New York Yacht Club course; the "Grayling" won the noted race around Long Island and two of the famous Goelet Cup contests. The "Goelet Cups," so called, were prizes annually presented for a number of years by the late Ogden Goelet, Esq., and were to be sailed for at Newport during the cruise of the New York Yacht Club. The "Fanita" won the match race around Long Island with the "Ulida," beating that cutter four hours and eleven minutes.

Great preparations were made by the New York Yacht Club to meet the "Genesta" in the America's Cup Race of 1885. Two new boats were built and appeared at the trial races, one, the "Priscilla," designed by A. Cary Smith for James Gordon Bennett, and the other the "Puritan," designed by Edward Burgess. The "Puritan" proved herself the superior, and was selected to meet the English cutter. The first

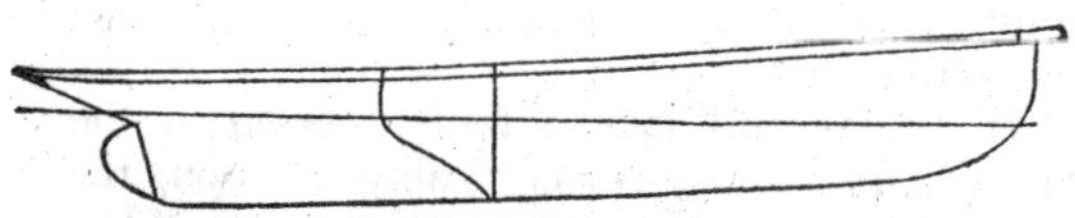

"PURITAN."

race was sailed September 14th over the inside course. Several attempts had been made before this over the ocean course, but they had been failures owing to lack of wind, except on one occasion when a foul had occurred. The result of this first (completed) race was in the "Puritan's" favour by 16 m. 47 sec. The second race was sailed on September 16th in a gale of wind, and resulted in favour of the "Puritan" by the small margin of 1 m. ·38 sec. This settled the race for the America's Cup, but the English cutter won that autumn the Brenton's Reef and Cape May Challenge Cups. The schooner "Dauntless" and not the sloop "Puritan," however, was her opponent. She did have one good race outside Sandy Hook, that fall, with some of the best American yachts of the older style, and she beat the "Gracie" by over 29 m.

The "Puritan's" dimensions were: Length over all, 93 feet; L.W.L., 81 feet 1 inch; beam, 22 feet 7 inches; draught, 8 feet 10 inches; sail area, 7,370 square feet.

The following year, 1886, Lieut. Henn brought over the "Galatea," another English cutter, to race for the much-coveted cup, and the New York Yacht Club had another boat of the famous Boston designer's to meet her. Ellsworth had also designed for a syndicate of the Atlantic Yacht Club the sloop "Atlantic," but she was defeated by the new Burgess boat "Mayflower," as were the "Puritan" and "Priscilla" in the trial races. The "Mayflower" was somewhat larger than the American champion of the year before, being 100 feet over all; L.W.L., $85\frac{1}{2}$ feet; beam, $23\frac{1}{2}$ feet; draught, $9\frac{3}{4}$ feet; sail area, 8,500 square feet. The "Galatea" was probably not so good a yacht as the "Genesta,"

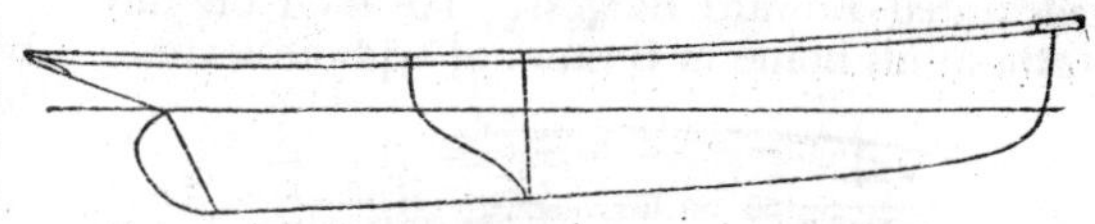

"MAYFLOWER."

and, as the "Mayflower" was better than the "Puritan," the races were not very exciting. The first race was September 7th, 1886, and the "Mayflower" won over the inside course by 12 m. 2 sec. The outside race, called for September 9th, was a failure, both yachts running into a fog; but the decisive race was sailed on the eleventh of the month, and the "Mayflower" won by 29 m. 48 sec.

The following year Vice-Commodore James Bell, of the Royal Clyde Yacht Club, challenged for the same cup, and another new Burgess sloop, the "Volunteer," built for Gen. Paine, was selected to meet her. Again, the size was slightly increased, the "Volunteer's" dimensions being 106 feet over all, 85 feet L.W.L., 23 feet beam, 10 feet draught. The "Thistle's" length over all was 108 feet 5 inches; L.W.L., 89·46; beam, 20·3; depth of hold, 14·3.

The first race was sailed September 27th over the inside course, and "Volunteer" won by 19 m. $23\frac{3}{4}$ sec. The outside race was not sailed until September 30th, when, in a good breeze, the "Volunteer" won by 11 m. 48 sec.

The year 1888 was principally noted for the popularity of the Burgess "40-footers," a class of yachts that sailed many races during that

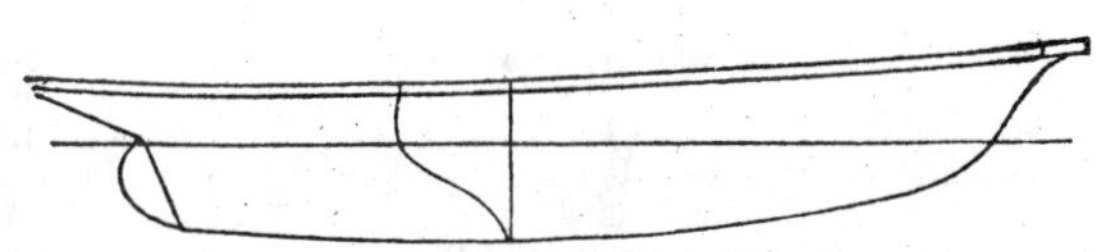

"VOLUNTEER."

season and the next. The most successful of these were the "Papoose," "Banshee," "Chispa," "Tomahawk," "Nymph," "Choctaw," and "Gossoon." There may be added also the Gardiner yacht "Lyris"; but it is doubtful if any of these equalled, as they certainly did not excel, the famous Fife cutter "Minerva." Probably the "Gossoon" came nearest to her.

There was much talk of a challenge for the cup in 1889, but nothing came of it. There was, however, some very pretty racing this year (outside of the forties) among the large sloops (70-footers), three new ones of merit having appeared—the "Shamrock," J. R. Maxwell, Esq.; the "Titania," C. O. Iselin, Esq.; and the "Katrina," Messrs. E. S. and H. D. Auchincloss. These yachts were so closely matched that the honours were nearly even.

In 1891 occurred the greatest blow to the advancement of yacht designing since the death of George Steers. This was the death of the celebrated Edward Burgess. He died on July 11th, at his home in Boston, of typhoid fever.

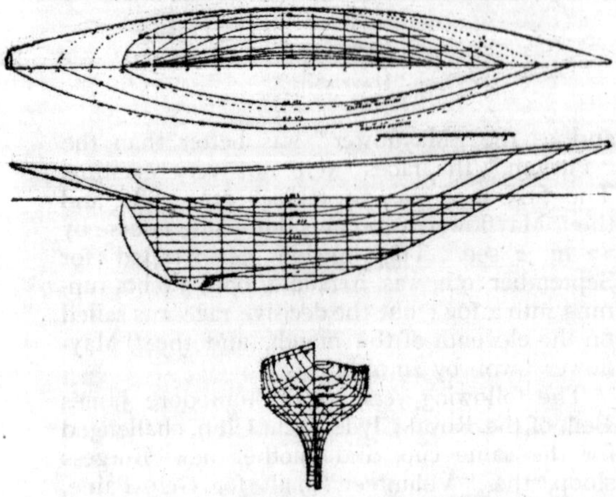

Design of a 46-foot Yacht similar to "Gloriana."

The 46-footers, which in popularity took the place of the forties, appeared this year (1891), and Herreshoff brought out the "Gloriana," the most speedy boat of the season. She was not

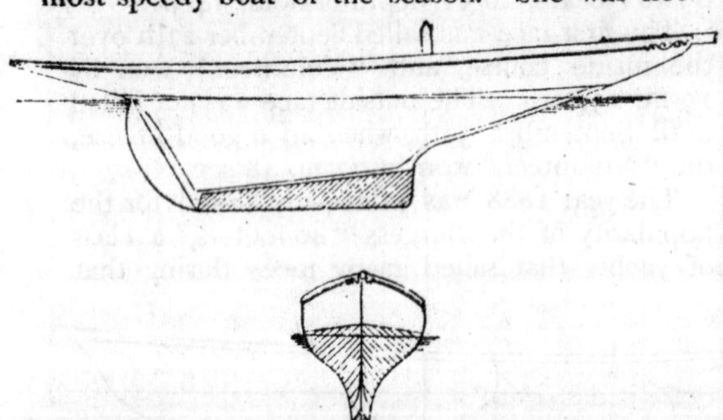

Outline similar to "Wasp."

defeated until a year later by the "Wasp," a production of the same designer.

In 1893 came another challenge for the cup from Lord Dunraven, owner of the "Valkyrie II." Several yachts were built to meet her—the "Jubilee," "Pilgrim," "Colonia," and

"Vigilant."

"Vigilant." The last, a Herreshoff production, was successful in the trial races, and was selected to defend the cup. Her dimensions were: Length over all, 130 feet; water-line, 85 feet; beam, 26 feet; and 14 feet draught. All the races were to be outside (best three in five). Without noting the races that were failures for want of wind, the results were:—

October 7th. First race, "Vigilant," won by 5 m. 48 sec., race sailed in moderate wind.

October 9th. Second race, "Vigilant," won by 10 m. 35 sec., over a triangular course in a heavy breeze.

October 13th. Third race, "Vigilant," won by 40 sec. in half a gale.

During this year the "Navahoe," another of Herreshoff's designs, owned by Royal Phelps Carroll, Esq., had been in British waters racing, but she had not been particularly successful, though she brought home the Brenton Reef Cup, won by the "Genesta."

In 1895 another challenge for the America's Cup came from Lord Dunraven, owner of another "Valkyrie," known as "Valkyrie III." There was but one boat constructed to meet her, the "Defender," designed by Herreshoff for a syndicate of well-known yachtsmen.

The first race was sailed on September 7th, and was won by "Defender," by 8 m. 49 sec., corrected time.

In the second race a foul occurred at the start; and, although the "Valkyrie" won, the race was awarded by the committee to "Defender."

In the third race "Valkyrie" crossed the line under lower sails only, and declined to go over the course. The race was necessarily awarded to "Defender."

As these races, the second and third, were decided upon technicalities, and not upon the sailing of the yachts, the reader desiring to pursue this matter further is referred to the printed report of the Cup Committee of the New York Yacht Club.

In 1895 a series of races was sailed on the lakes between the 51-foot Canadian cutter "Canada" and the United States cutter "Vancedor" for an international cup, which was won by the "Canada."

In conclusion, among the crack yachts of this year (1897) may be mentioned the schooners "Colonia" (formerly sloop), "Emerald," "Amorita," and "Quisetta"; and the sloops "Wasp," "Syce," and "Norota."

Sailing in Small Boats—Small boat sailing and racing started in the United States in the "skimming dish," "sand-bag" type of boats, and has now developed into the fin-keel. Among the boats of the first-mentioned type that won celebrity may be named the "Sousie S.," "Maud," "William T. Lee," W. F. David's, "Mary Emma," "Pluck and Luck," "Cruiser," "Fairy," and the Boston cat-boat "Fancy." These ranged from 15 to 30 feet over all, and were rigged both as sloops (jib and mainsail) and as cat-boats at different times. This change was easily accomplished by shifting the mast of the sloop forward to a step in the extreme bow, and taking off the bowsprit. Of late years the "sand-bagger" has become unpopular from its propensity to capsize in every ordinary squall when not properly handled.

In 1890 and 1891, 25-foot water-line keel and fin-keel sloops were built, with all outside lead, and were certainly a safer if not a more comfortable style of craft. Among the better known

"SMUGGLER."

of these were the "Smuggler," "Needle," and "Nameless," and later the "Pixie," and they sailed in many fine races.

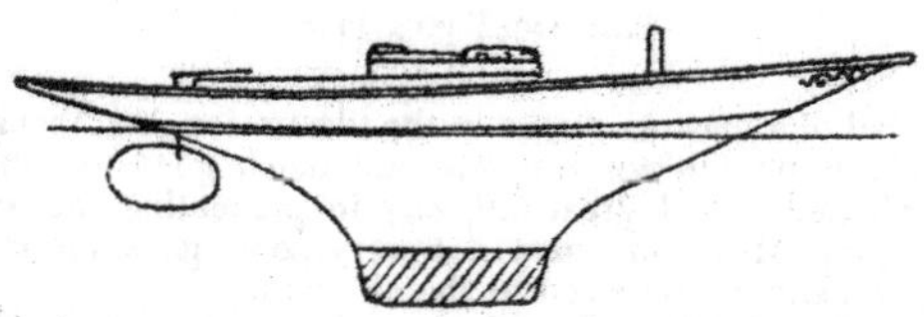

"PIXIE."

In 1893 and 1894 the so-called "half-raters" appeared, and have since formed an interesting class. They were small boats of about 15-foot water-line, and of all shapes imaginable, including even the scow.

In 1895 the Seawanhaka-Corinthian Yacht Club offered an international challenge cup for this class, which was won in a series of races by the "Ethelwyn" against the English boat "Spruce II"; but the following year (1896) the "Glencairn," a Canadian boat, succeeded in winning it from the "El Heire." And again, in 1897, the Seawanhaka-Corinthian boat "Momo," having challenged the Canadian, was defeated in two out of three well-contested races on Lake St. Louis, Canada, by the "Glencairn II."

In 1894 and 1895 a number of 30-foot fin-keel boats made their appearance, and formed a most interesting racing class, which had many important additions in the two following seasons. Among the most prominent were the "Vacquero," "May," "Raccoon," "Carolina," and "Musme."

In conclusion may be mentioned the 36-footers, including the "Acuspla," "Dragoon," and "Vorant II," which have sailed many good races; during the season of 1897 the "Surprise" and "Anoatok" were added to the class.

American Steam Yachting—It always has seemed to sailors and racing men that steam yachting was an agreeable and luxurious method of transportation and sight-seeing rather than a sport. Be this as it may, the steam yacht has long been popular in the United States, and the waters are filled with every kind of steam craft, from the 20-foot launch to the ocean-going steamer. Of late years the steam launch has almost entirely disappeared from American waters, to give place to the naphtha launch, and it looks now as though this craft in turn would be superseded, at no distant date, by the electric motor; but for larger craft steam still holds its sway. Some of these steam yachts, in smooth water, have attained an almost incredible speed, the maximum being over 30 knots an hour. Among these flyers are the "Vamoose," "Norwood," "Now Then," "Rob Roy," "Stiletto," and the little "Half Moon."

A race between the "Vamoose" and the "Norwood" was much talked of but never took place. Several steam-yacht races have occurred, but no records were broken. Of the larger ocean-going steam yachts, some are most graceful in appearance and costly in their appointments. The best known of these are the "Atlanta," "Corsair," "Utowana," "Electra," "Orienta," "Golden Rod," "Mai," "Sapphire," "Golden Fleece," "Alicia," "Conqueror," "Narada," "Valiant," and "Sovereign." Then there are the "auxiliary" schooners, which have a limited amount of steam power to enable them to keep off a lee shore in a gale or to make headway in a calm. Of these the "Intrepid" and "Sultana" are good representatives. The Herreshoffs have been great designers of steam as well as sailing yachts, and probably rank as high in one class as in the other. In steam navigation, since more depends upon the mechanical contrivance than upon the model of the boat itself, there is less attention given to the design of the hull, and much more to that of the engine.

In conclusion it must be regretted by true sportsmen that the steam yacht's popularity is increasing with many of the best American yachtsmen, who, a few years ago, were racing in their beautiful sloops and schooners.

CHAS. PRYER,

Ex.-Com. New Rochelle Yacht Club, and Corinthian Fleet of New Rochelle.

ICE YACHTING—The opportunities of ice-boating in England are so few and far between that it takes a long time to find out from our own experience the best form of boat, with the proper proportion of sail, length, beam, weight, &c., suitable for the thin ice we get on our lakes. I made my first attempt at an ice-boat in 1877, but not until 1895 did I arrive at anything I could thoroughly recommend. February of 1895 afforded a splendid opportunity of trying experiments and making improvements, as Windermere was frozen over, and the ice lasted a fortnight without any snow, and became 9 inches thick. On ice like this, American ice-boats would do very well, but they would be too heavy for the average ice we get in England, as I believe they are more than twice the weight of mine. Weight can easily be added by ballast if the ice is strong enough to carry it, and will be found of great advantage in beating to windward. The boat I have had for the last sixteen years weighs 6 cwt. 28 lbs. complete, but I am building one which will weigh 9½ cwt.; this will be found quite heavy enough.

Ice-Boating on the Lakes—The English Lakes naturally afford the most room and the best ice for sailing in this country, and as they do not all freeze at once, snow and bad ice can generally be avoided by removing the boat from one lake to another. Esthwaite Water is generally the first to bear, for it is shallow, but there are dangerous places in it and often a great deal of air in the ice. There is a shallow ridge running right across the lake diagonally, so shallow that a man can nearly wade across, and, curiously enough, the ice over this ridge is never as thick as the rest. When Esthwaite is spoilt by snow, Windermere is generally on a fair way for bearing, but only in parts. Windermere is never frozen over completely, there being always large cracks right across it which never seem to freeze, and a mile or a mile and a half is the most one can ever expect to get on a straight run. The ferry track is always kept open, and there is nearly always a large piece of open water between Belle Grange and Millerground. Even in 1895 there was a crack about 9 feet wide over which it was impossible to skate or sail in this part. Rydal Lake is very much shut in by the hills and very small, being little more than a mile long.

(It is necessary to have permission from the lords of the manors of both Esthwaite and Rydal before one can sail on them, as no boats are allowed on the water.)

I will not dwell long on my first attempt at building an ice-boat, as it was a very rude machine, made in a day and a night, and consisted of a simple cross of yellow pine planks with upright pieces to strengthen them, a small lugsail, and two ordinary wooden skates screwed under the ends of the cross beam. I steered with the skates on my feet, one on the ice on either side.

The first time I tried it was on Esthwaite in a gale of wind from the south-east against which one could hardly skate. This was a grand opportunity of trying its speed over a measured mile, and a friend of mine skated ahead to take the time at the finish. I had great difficulty in shaping my course, as the boat would broach to, but at last, after several false starts, I managed to get her straight before the wind, and flew down the lake, keeping my feet as straight as I could on the ice. I had only one passenger on this occasion, an old salt who had been accustomed to nothing but full rigged ships, and he clung to the mast all the time with both his arms and all his might. I had taken the precaution to tie the end of the main sheet round my wrist so that I should not part company with the ship in any case.

All went well till about half way, when the skate on my right foot came in contact with something on the ice and I was flung overboard in a trice. It was lucky I had taken the precaution to tie the main sheet round my wrist, as by it I hauled myself hand over hand up to the boat, and was very soon on board again, finishing the mile in exactly three minutes.

The next thing was to stop, but as the old man was far too terrified to let go the mast and lower the sail, I knew there were only two courses open, either to be dashed to pieces on the rocks, or to make as easy a capsize of it as possible. I chose the latter; and having hailed the old man with a "Now then, look out," rounded to, and over she went.

I have a very indistinct recollection where the old man went to, though when we brought up he was still on the ice, and I should think the boat must have gone at least 70 yards on the mast head, with our runner up in the air, before it stopped, not many yards from some very ugly rocks.

I was so disgusted at the inefficiency of this boat that I at once set to work to make a new one, stronger, wider, longer, and with more sail; with bevelled steel runners and steel rudder. I improved this boat from time to time by increasing the beam from 12 to 14 feet, by putting three short runners on each side instead of one long one, by placing the mast further forward, and by and by adding a jib, so that it is now exactly like the drawing and a fairly good machine. In 1895 I did a measured mile in it, with five people on board, in 2 minutes 15 seconds, and later with the same number on board, ⅜ of a mile in 36 seconds, or 38½ miles an hour.

In the hard winter of 1880, I tried a new ice-boat with a triangular sail supported by three light sheer legs,

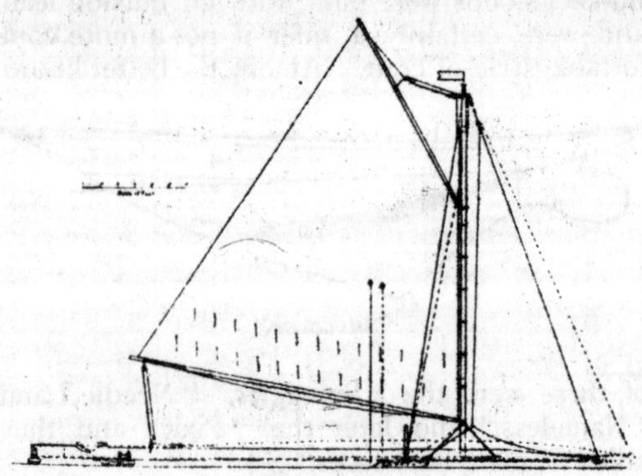

SAIL AND SHEER PLAN.

instead of a mast as shown in the illustration, but, though very fast off the wind, it was not much good to windward, and I had great difficulty in preventing the sail swinging about in stays. I very soon gave up this experiment and returned to the old plan.

On March 9th, 1886, I had a splendid breeze on Esthwaite from south-east, but though the ice was strong it was full of melted snow, white and very rough. The boat nearly flew, and we had a splendid sail, but in the evening, when it was beginning to get dark, we happened to come across a rotten piece of ice about 2½ inches thick, exactly over the shallow ridge previously mentioned. The lee runner made a perfectly straight cut through the ice about 30 yards long, and quietly settled down to leeward in the water. I was very soon up to my neck, and a lady sitting in front of me fell over to one side and afterwards told me that her foot touched the bottom. I could hardly believe this, for we were very nearly in the middle of the lake, but afterwards we found it was actually the fact. I think there were four of us on board, and we succeeded in climbing to the bows, which were up in the air, and eventually got on to strong ice and reached the shore.

We left the boat just as it was for the night, with the sail up, and the next day I went with a cart load of planks and ladders and got her out of the hole. The water was just about 3 feet deep at the stern and the stern was resting on the bottom.

Construction of Ice-Boat—The chief things to be considered in constructing an ice-boat are lightness, strength, and simplicity, with as little surface to meet the wind ahead as possible. I hope my drawings are sufficiently plain to show my method of arriving at this without much explanation, but the runners and rudder must be gone into at some length, as they are very important parts of the boat.

Frame—The main body of the boat is a long trough of 1 inch yellow pine hung under a bent T iron beam by a ¾ inch bolt, as shown in the plan, and the cross platform is also 1 inch yellow pine bolted to it.

There is a strengthening piece about 12 feet long and and 1¾ inch thick, laid in the bottom of the trough, to prevent the mast driving the bottom out. The sides of the trough are screwed into this and the cross platform is bolted through it, thus giving great additional strength. Over this is a triangular block of wood, as shown in the cross section, through which the ¾ inch bolt goes which keeps the trough from twisting over and keeps the iron beam upright at the same time.

The bent beam is ⊢ iron 2 inches × 2 inches and ½ inch thick, and the thick lines in all three plans represent the edges of the flanges.

The wood of the cross platform is cut away to allow the horizontal flange to rest on the tops of the runners, and the lower flange is notched on to the runners so that the side is dead on them. The three runners on each side are the steel runners have to be prised out of the ice in the morning unless a piece of wood has been put underneath them for the night.

Runners—The steel runners, six in number, are parallel to each other and side by side, as shown in the plan. I am not at all sure that three on each side are better than two, but I am sure two are better than one;

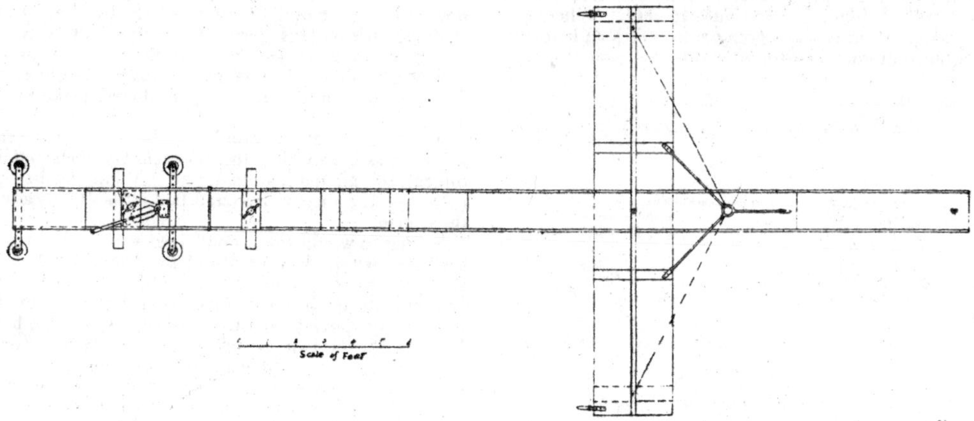

Body Plan.

bolted through blocks of elm 32 inches × 5¾ inches × 1¾ inches, and then there are two ⅝ inch rods 14 feet long, about 2 feet apart, which go right across the boat under the cross platform and through all the runners and elm blocks. These are tightened with nuts that the bridge may not drive the runners outward, thus binding the whole together.

The end of one of these rods is shown in the section of the outside runner, but not in the other plans, as it would only confuse them. The blocks of elm are bolted through the horizontal flange of the iron beam, one of the bolts on each side being used for the rigging. I have always screwed the steel runners to the blocks of elm with common screws, but think bolting them together right through would be better.

The mast is held in an ordinary tripod, and the shrouds and forestay, which are $\frac{5}{16}$ inch iron rods, are tightened up with nuts, but perhaps right and left handed screw lanyards would be better. Wire rope would not do so

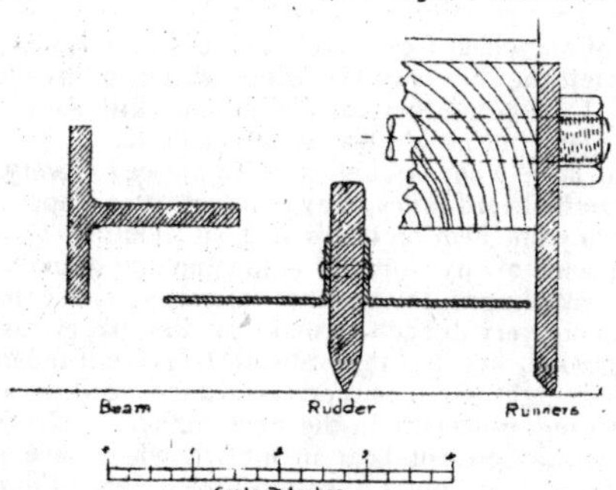

Beam, Rudder, &c.

well for an ice boat, for it would stretch under the great strain.

The stern is carried by two beams resting on four glass bull's eyes, 8 inches in diameter and 1⅛ inches thick, clipped to blocks of wood with felt in between the wood and glass to prevent any sudden shock breaking the glass. I think I have broken only one in the many years I have had them. They are flat underneath, like curling stones, and run beautifully on ice, and, glass being a bad conductor of heat, they do not stick much after stopping; however, I tried three with very good results. They cannot get into a crack unless the crack is a foot wide, and they have lateral resistance equal to one long runner touching the ice four feet, with the turning capacity of one, touching the ice only a foot and a half.

The camber and bevel of the runners should be very carefully studied, as it makes all the difference in the sailing to windward. The most effective runners to windward I have tried are cambered $\frac{1}{16}$ of an inch in a foot and a half, which is practically their touching length when sailing, and the ends are rounded up in a fair curve from this. The bevel, which is of course outwards, is about 45 degrees; the outer edge is slightly bevelled back in a round form, as shown in the plan. I have tried runners perfectly sharp like chisels, but they simply chip the ice right away and let the boat drift to leeward.

The round form makes for itself a hollow bed in the ice, which does not chip so easily, and prevents leeway. This rounded edge goes the whole length of the runner, so that the sharp edge is perfectly straight fore and aft. It is very necessary that the runners should oscillate fore and aft, so as to accommodate themselves to rough ice; but with the iron beam resting in the middle on the flattest part of the runners, the oscillation will be found quite sufficient. I should like to have made the three runners on each side oscillate independently of each other, but it would add more weight and complicate the construction.

Rudder—The rudder is somewhat in the form of a wood chopper with the handle turned up, and goes through a fan-shaped hole in the bottom of the trough. It is held at the fore end by a bolt in a close-fitting hinge, turning in two plates as shown in the plan, so that it is in a universal joint, and the rudder can be moved from side to side or up and down at pleasure. Going free, its own weight is generally sufficient to steer the boat; but, when beating to windward, it is often necessary to put one's entire weight on it; not to turn the boat, but to hinder it from turning too quickly and to keep it steady. The blade of the rudder is about ⅜ inch thick and sharpens in the form of a V. It is necessary to have a horizontal plate on each side of it that the cut ice may not fill the end of the trough, and cover one's clothes.

There is a hook under the board just over the tiller in which to set it when not wanted, which is handy when it is necessary to push the boat round quickly.

Sails—The sails I tried this year had a total area of 307·27 square feet, 241·71 in the mainsail, 105·56 in the jib. The combined centre of effort is just about 2 feet aft of the centre of the runner, but I am going to try it further forward in the new boat, as the head sail will be two feet longer on the foot, the mast being in the same place.

This will balance the sails, practically, on the side runners, and the boat will hardly want any weather helm, which will, I think, be an improvement. When you lose control of an ice-boat going at 40 miles an hour and it begins to fly round two or three times without stopping,

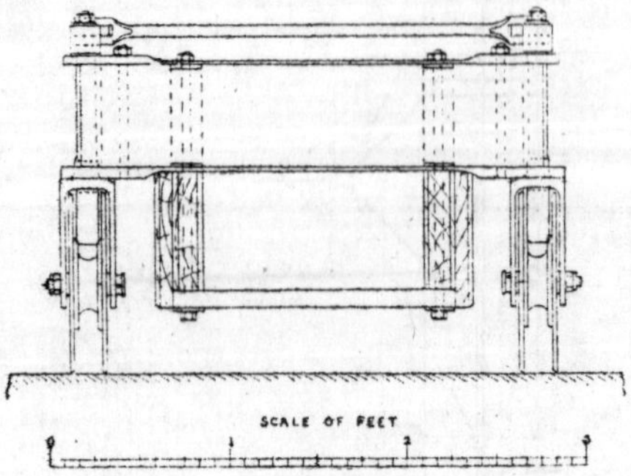

RUDDER (BACK).

the result is truly appalling, and I wish to prevent this by putting the centre of effort further forward; besides, I do not see any advantage in giving her so much weather helm, as it only stops her. The sails should be of fairly strong stuff, and I prefer a loose-footed mainsail to a laced one, as, in the latter, it is so difficult to reef without tearing out the reef points. With a laced

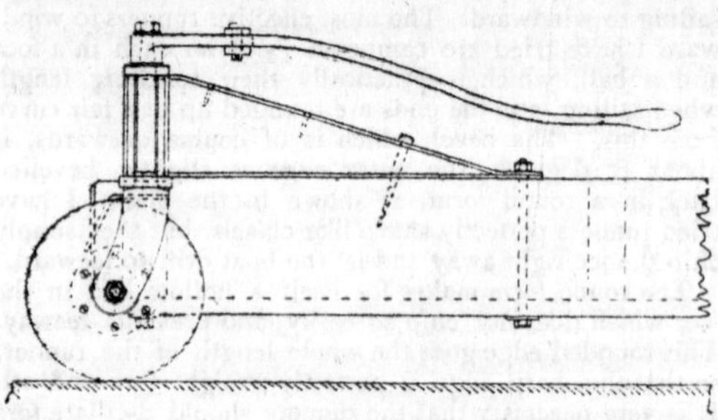

RUDDER (SIDE).

mainsail I once tore three sets of reef points clean out one after the other, and had to go home for a fresh sail.

In the winter of 1895 I tried a jib with sheets, but next time I shall try a staysail with hanks on an iron forestay, and a toggle running on a fixed iron horse. It is necessary to shift the top block strip forward on the boom with each reef taken in, so as not to break the boom.

The idea of an ice-boat sailing faster than the wind has often been ridiculed, but I will try to prove in a very simple way that it is possible to sail three times faster than the wind.

Take a metal plate with two grooves in it, running at right angles to each other, get two dies fitting these grooves, one in each, both bevelled to 45 degrees, and press one bevelled edge against the other. It will be found that they will both travel at exactly the same speed; but, if you bevel one at 15 degrees and the other at 75 degrees, it will be found that the one bevelled at 75 will have to travel three times faster than the one bevelled at 15, with the same process.

If the sail is let out to 45 degrees, it is impossible, under any circumstances, to go any faster than the wind; but if the sail is pulled in to 75 degrees the effect will be just the same as with the dies, and the boat will go three times faster than the wind. This, of course, is owing to the resistance not increasing in proportion to the wind pressure, as in an ordinary boat, and this is why ice-boats always sail best with their sheets close hauled.

Handling the Sails—The best point for sailing on ice is with the wind dead abeam and the sheet well in, not quite as close as *on* a wind, but very nearly. Although the wind is abeam, the burgee will fly at about 45 degrees, and, as there is no ripple on the ice to show any change of wind, it takes a remarkably clever man both at the mainsheet and at the tiller to make the best of it.

There is a certain point, combined with a certain angle of sail, at which the boat simply flies, but it is difficult to find and maintain, and I think the best plan is to keep the sheet well in and find it by slightly altering the course.

Sailing to windward, a good boat with good sails will easily go within four points of the wind, but I do not think any advantage will be gained by trying to go closer. In going about, the chief difficulty is to prevent the boat doing it too quickly, and the less tiller given the better. In a good wind, two seconds will see the boat full on the other tack and off. In beating to windward, it is necessary for everyone to keep as flat as possible, and a man standing on the weather runner, though often necessary, is a great detriment to speed.

No matter how strong the wind, the sail is always hanging straight up and down, and the main sheet trails on the ice, in fact it is difficult to keep it from getting foul of the rudder.

There is apparently not a breath of air, and a pipe can be lit with the greatest ease. Running before the wind is quite the slowest point in ice sailing, which will be thoroughly appreciated when you begin to luff and pull in the main sheet.

Going at a high speed it is necessary to be very careful, in any case never going anywhere where there is not at least a hundred yards room to turn in, and always keeping a perfectly steady hand on the tiller. Several times I have tried to turn too quickly, with the result that the boat has spun round two or three times without stopping, and the passengers have been flung in all directions. She sometimes goes round in a very ugly way, too, taking side jumps, and at each jump chiselling hollow basins out of the ice. When this manœuvre takes place the rudder becomes quite useless, simply filling the air with cut ice. It is very difficult to hang on, and at the same time to put all one's weight on the tiller; but I have a place just in front of me which I can catch hold of in a moment, and I never left the ship once last winter except of my own free will. I am afraid this was not the case with some of the passengers, but no one was seriously hurt.

The noise when sailing at a high speed is very great, and can be heard miles away; in fact, it is impossible to make any one hear on board without shouting, and I am afraid some of my words of command and opinions have been made known to those not intended to hear them.

It is not very difficult to make an ice-boat go fast in a strong wind, but it is very difficult to make it move at all in a very light wind, as there is always a certain amount of sticking, especially in the steel runners. However, I can keep my present boat in motion when once started with an ordinary piece of cotton thread, when there is no wind.

The grooves left in the ice are very slight, and do not interfere with skaters in the least. Sailing to windward, when they are deepest, they are not much more than $\frac{1}{16}$ inch deep and $\frac{1}{8}$ inch wide. It is very easy to calculate from these grooves exactly how close the boat can go to the wind, by measuring the angle formed in going about.

An ice-boat is stopped in exactly the same way as an ordinary boat, by rounding up head to wind. After it is stopped, the sheets should be considerably eased off, especially the jib, as a change of wind might start it again; and, if it did, there is no knowing when it would stop or what mischief it might do.

There is very little tendency to go astern, but to prevent the possibility of this I have two little spikes, like marline-spikes on hinges, as shown in the drawing, one on each side, just aft of the runners. These either trail on the ice when going ahead, or can be turned up. It is safer to let them trail, as they do no harm, and immediately dig in the ice when she wishes to go astern.

Boat designs.—I have ticked in on the drawings the side view of the new boat built this winter; also the end view and cross section at the beam. It will be seen that it is 2 feet shorter at the stern and 2 feet longer at the bows than the old one, thus keeping the weight further forward, which is very desirable, and giving room for a larger head sail. It will also be seen from both plans that the trough is deeper and wider, giving the passengers room to sit inside it instead of on the top, and there are comfortable back rests and handles outside to hold on by, screwed on to the sides. The extra depth gives additional strength, which is needed, as the old boat was too weak at the mast, and gave way towards the end of last winter. All the trough in front of the mast is closed in and made watertight, and I think part of the stern will be too. The cross section shows the extra beam and higher bridge, also an iron span in place of the triangular wooden block, which catches a good deal of wind.

I give separate drawings of the new wheel rudder, so as not to confuse the plan.

This rudder is only just finished, and as I have not had an opportunity of trying it yet cannot guarantee its efficiency. It is composed of four circular steel plates, bevelled as shown in the drawing, mounted in the form of castors, and running on ball bearings. The man steering sits *in* the trough, forward of the tiller in this case, instead of *on* the trough aft of the tiller, as the old type. This should be much more comfortable, and keep the weight further forward at the same time. When the weight is far aft the tendency to fly round is very much increased.

There will be no glass bull's-eyes required, as the weight will rest entirely on the wheels, which run with very little friction.

When a rudder cuts the ice, as in the old plan, there is always friction, but these wheels will crush it rather than cut it, and the only friction will be in the ball bearings. However, it remains to be proved how it will act, and whether it will steer the boat.

The boat is unfortunately rather heavy, and with three pieces of wood, the cross beam, and two triangular pieces weighs 128 lbs.

The new mast is stronger than the old one, being $4\frac{1}{8}$ inches thick at the tripod, and 4 inches at the hounds. The boom is also stronger, being $3\frac{1}{4}$ inches thick at the thickest part.

I have done away with the after legs of the tripod, and put two $\frac{3}{8}$ inch rods, shown by ticked lines, in their place; also two extra shrouds, shown in the same way.

The centre of effort will now be only 1 foot 4 inches aft of the centre of the runners, instead of 2 feet, which will give her very little weather helm. The total area will be 327·31 square feet. The main sheet horse will be a foot further forward, to give the steersman more room.

HERBERT CROSSLEY.

ICE-YACHTING IN AMERICA.—This fascinating and exhilarating winter sport has at the present time reached a very high degree of perfection, and for pleasure sailing and racing is, one may say, practically confined to the frozen rivers and lakes of the United States and to some localities in Canada where the conditions favour it, as at Toronto and Kingston. It began to take definite shape some fifty years ago on the Hudson, where in 1861 the first regular club was organised and christened the Poughkeepsie Ice Yacht Club, to be followed, as the sport developed, by the formation of similar clubs from Sandy Hook on the Atlantic to the lakes in Minnesota, half-way across the continent.

Good ice-boating requires certain climatic conditions that are rarely combined over a large area of country. During the winter months in a very cold climate there is of course plenty of ice, but as it is usually covered with snow, more or less deep, that stays all winter, ice-boating is then out of the question. The best climate, therefore, seems to be one where there is during the winter months cold enough to make six or eight inches of clear ice to start with; and then, after snow has covered this, frequent thaws or rains soak up and melt the snow, followed by a quick frost. That portion of the Hudson River Valley from Newburg to Hyde Park seems to fill best the conditions outlined above for the necessary development of the sport. Here, too, will be found the leading clubs and the fastest yachts. The distance on the river between the points named is about twenty-three miles. Including the Orange Lake Club, a sturdy organisation on the lake but a short distance back from the Hudson, there are five clubs. The Orange Lake Club claims ten yachts, the largest of which is a cat-rigged craft of 800 square feet, sail area.

The southmost club on the Hudson is the Carthage Club, possessing a fleet of twenty-six yachts, mostly of the jib and mainsail type, though some are cat-rigged and two are lateen. Of the latter, one is an uncommonly fast yacht. The largest yacht in the Carthage Club is of jib and mainsail rig, and spreads 950 square feet of canvas to the winter breezes. The remainder of the fleet will average about 400 square feet, sail area.

The New Hamburgh Ice Yacht Club, one of the older organisations, has twenty-three yachts enrolled, ranging from 900 to 250 square feet, sail area.

The Hudson River Ice Yacht Club, of Hyde Park, New York, which, without injustice to any of the others, may be styled the leading club of the United States, possesses a fleet of forty-one yachts of all types, the favourite one, however, and by far the most numerous, is the jib and mainsail. The yachts range in size from 800 square feet of sail area down to 200. Outside of the Hudson River some of the leading clubs are as follows:—The North Shrewsbury, at Red Bank, New Jersey, with some fourteen yachts averaging about 452 square feet, and one large boat of 800 square feet. At Lakes Minnetouka and Pepin in Minnesota, and at Toronto and Kingston, Canada, are many fine yachts and clubs, and it is to be hoped that some of the newer and younger devotees of the sport will try conclusions on the Hudson for the championship of America.

All the clubs mentioned are progressive and active associations, controlled by the usual officers—such as commodore, vice-commodore, treasurer, and secretary, along with a regatta or sailing committee, whose duty it is to take charge of the racing.

The ground work in the construction of an ice-yacht is rather simple, and consists of two pieces, one called the centre timber running fore and aft, on which is stepped the mast, the forward part constituting the bowsprit and the after part carrying the box and the rudder-post. The dimensions vary from about 28 feet to 50 feet in length, and from 4 to 6 inches in thickness, and from 8 to 15 inches in greatest depth. The other piece is called the runner-plank, a broad stout plank with some crown to it, from 12 to 17 inches wide, and from 3 to 7 inches thick in the middle, and from 14 to 28 feet long, tapered in thickness towards the ends to which the runners are attached, working in chocks. The centre timber rests on the runner-plank to which it is secured by a gammon iron. Stays leading from the ends are secured and set up to turn-buckles on the runner-plank. The mast is secured by shrouds leading on each side to the runner plank and by a fore-stay leading to the outer end of the centre timber. The early yachts of the Hudson River fleet were constructed a good deal on the lumber-box order. They were heavy, hard riding and hard-headed too, jib and mainsail rig, with the mast in line with the runner-plank and not some distance forward, as prevails at present. They carried short gaffs, long booms, moderate hoist of mainsail and big unwieldy jibs with jib booms.

This stepping the mast over the runner-plank, gave the boats a bad balance. That is, it brought the centre of effort, as well as the weight, too far aft; consequently the tendency in beating to windward was to luff, and this had to be avoided by keeping the boat's head off, and the weight of the mast being too far aft also brought additional pressure on the rudder. All this unnecessary friction caused a proportionate loss in speed, especially to windward.

This type of yacht reached its greatest development in the "Icicle," the largest ice-yacht ever constructed. She was built in 1869, and was improved and enlarged until she measured 68 feet 11 inches long, with sail-driving area of 1070 square feet. She was unquestionably the fastest in 1879 of any of the yachts on the river. It was not long, however, before an improved type of rig and construction made its appearance, and this was accomplished by stepping the mast about 3½ feet further forward or ahead of the runner-plank. This necessitated shortening the jib, making it more of a balance sail than before. Main booms, too, were cut off and gaffs lengthened, bringing the sail more inboard, and thus placing the centre of effort in a much more proper relation to the centre of resistance. Side rails and cockpits gave way to wire guys with adjustable turn-buckles, and small elliptical boxes for the helmsmen.

The essential elements that all these yachts possess in common are: lightness, combining great strength of construction; a runner-plank that has considerable elasticity or spring to it, the effect of which is not only to make the boat more comfortable to the user, but I think also, in connection with the long runners, hung well back and rockered towards their forward ends, a great factor in attaining speed, as the impacts or blows resulting from inequalities of the ice are distributed easily and more slowly to the swiftly moving mass of the boat taken as a whole.

To explain: Take one of the large yachts; her weight would be at least 3000 lbs., including everything. Move this body, say, at the rate of 40 miles an hour, or $58\frac{6}{10}$ feet per second; a hard, frozen hummock of snow or ice is encountered; now if the plank is rigidly trussed and the runners straight or without rocker, the blow must be a severe one, and the shock to the other parts of the yacht much more severe, entailing heavier construction in all its parts, hence increased friction and a loss in speed. Whilst, on the other hand, with a properly-proportioned flexible runner-plank, and an easy, gradual rocker to the runners, the yacht so equipped will glide up the obstruction, and shooting ahead clear of the ice, drop down with very little perceptible jar, though the runner-plank may have been deflected, as I have often witnessed, 6 or 7 inches vertically from its normal arched position.

The angle or bevel of the runners is somewhat a matter of fancy, many of the fastest yachts having two sets of runners, the one with a sharp or acute V-shaped cutting edge for very hard ice, and the other pair of a more obtuse angle, just a trifle over 90°. The material used for runners is generally a hard cast-iron V-shaped shoe bolted to an upper part of well-seasoned oak. These are attached by a pin through a metal bushing in the runners to the chocks, which are in turn bolted securely and braced by knees to the runner-plank. The material used for these planks and also for the body of the yacht is either basswood or butternut. Ash is used for runner-planks when they are required to be very large or support considerable weight. The greatest care and attention are bestowed upon the sails, their quality, and the way they fit. Yachts of a few years ago spread very heavy canvas in comparison with the size of the sail. This has, I think, been found an error, and much lighter sails are now used. No doubt further improvement in this direction is desirable.

In the selection of material for a first class yacht, great pains are taken to get only the very best growth of timber, which is usually picked out on the stump and taken to the nearest mill to be properly sawed out. The finest crucible-steel wire should be used for shrouds, stays, and fore and aft side guys. Turn-buckles should be hand-forged. As windage plays an important part in the speed of ice-yachts, care is taken to reduce it as much as possible, and to that end masts and spars are as short and light as is consistent with properly setting the sails and the requirements of safety. All woodwork has the highest cabinet finish. The cost of a yacht such as I have described, and about 48 feet long, complete in every respect, would be about $900.

Before closing it may be well to consider the wonderful and phenomenal speed attained by these interesting productions for winter sport and amusement.

Absolutely reliable data beyond the championship races are few and far between, for it is seldom a course over which other races take place is accurately measured. The distances for the pennant contests are known by marks on the shore which have been placed there permanently by surveys, and in placing the buoys or turning-marks on the ice the greatest pains are taken to have them accurately established. In order to examine this matter of speed, I have made a table of the races for the Challenge Pennant, showing all the particulars, especially the distances between the marks, and therefore the lengths of the courses sailed, and I believe these distances to be substantially as stated. The course on February 5, 1892, was surveyed, and also measured by a registering wheel. I have also plotted on paper the approximate distances an ice-yacht would actually sail in covering the various courses. These results are tabulated on the sailing card. In working this out the river was laid off as half a mile wide, which is about the average width where the races take place, and as most of these were sailed with a wind blowing or drawing nearly straight up or down the course, which also is always up and down the river, the calculated distances sailed should not deviate to any great extent from the real distances. At any rate the plan adopted has seemed to the writer the best way of arriving at anything like the truth.

The fastest time made in any of the races for the pennant was that of "Jack Frost," February 9, 1893. The 20-mile course was sailed in 0 h. 49 m. 30 s., or at the rate of a mile in 2 m. 28 s. for that distance, but the calculated distance the yacht sailed was 31·38 miles, and this means a mile in 1 m. 34 s. The slowest rate occurred February 18, 1885, when it took "Northern Light" 1 h. 8 m. 42 s. to sail the 20-mile course. This, it will be seen, is at the rate of a mile in 3 m. 26 s., but in reality 2 m. 11 s., as the calculated distance sailed was 31·36 miles.

The average rate of speed for these races is 1 m. 55 s. per calculated mile; and, as I believe a yacht in actual practice will sail over rather than under the calculated distances, it is safe to assume that the speed of an ice-yacht with a strong, steady breeze, over a true course to windward and return, is faster than this rate of a mile in 1 m. 55 s. The narrowness of the river forces the boat to tack or alter its course frequently when sailing either to windward or off the wind, which not only increases the time, but also the distance over a given course. One point must always be borne in mind, and that is, that an ice-yacht invariably sails close-hauled, that is, with her sails trimmed flat in, whether in beating to windward or driving off before the wind. This is easy to comprehend when going to windward, for here a boat on ice sails the same as one in the water, but off the wind or sailing free it is another matter. It can be readily understood that in this case if sheets were started and sails were allowed to go off, so as to be at or nearly a right angle to the wind, the yacht would not advance to leeward quite as fast as the wind, as some force must be expended in overcoming friction; hence it is that in sailing before the wind the sails are trimmed close aboard, so that the course of the yacht to reach a given point to leeward the fastest angle would be 150° or 13⅓ points from the wind, when the advance to leeward would be one and a half times that of the wind itself.

A. ROGERS.

YAK—The Yak or Grunting Ox (*Poëphagus grunniens*, Linnæus), is found in its wild state on the highlands of Tibet, north of the Himalayas, not further west than Yarkund and Cashgar, and certainly as far east as Lassa, and probably much further. The bulls and cows herd separately, except in the rutting season, in October and November. During the rest of the year the bulls wander considerably and are found in herds of ten and twelve, long distances away from the cows. The largest specimen of a wild bull yak, shot by the writer in 1859, on the northern slopes of the Himalayas, north of Kumaon, measures as follows :—

	ft.	in.
Circumference of neck	4	2
Circumference of horn at base	1	6
Length of skull (stuffed) from the nose to the occipital ridge	2	5½
Width between the orbits	1	4
Length of each horn measured along the curve	3	0
Length from the nose to the root of the tail	10	10½
Do. to the extremity of the tail	13	11½
Height at withers	5	10
Girth behind the shoulders	10	1
Do. round belly	9	8
Length of tail	3	1
Circumference of fore foot	1	9¾
Do. do. hind foot	1	7

I shot another wild bull yak in the same year, of much the same size. One of these is set up entire in the Leeds Museum; the other (the head only) is at Elkington Hall, near Louth, Lincolnshire. This also was set up entire, but unfortunately moths got in to the skin, and the head only has been preserved—a very fine specimen. Both of these were shot in July, the very worst season of the year for preserving the skins.

The yak is one of the very few animals existing both in a wild and domesticated state; and as the former is not much known, a brief description is desirable. The general colour of its summer coat is a deep and rich brown, palest on the withers, where it is slightly freckled with grey, and becomes a darker brown in every direction as it recedes from this. The hair of the forehead is rather long, curly, and dark brown, the hairs tipped with grey, producing a grizzled appearance, which increases towards the nostrils, while the hair becomes short and close; above the centre of the nostrils is a patch of white, which colour also pervades the lips, and slightly the chin. The muffle, or naked space between the nostrils, is contracted to less than an inch in breadth on the lip. On the ears, cheeks, lower jaws, and upper portion of the throat, the hair is rather long and black; between the horns, and behind the occipital ridge, it is divergent and grizzled. The legs are very dark brown; the fore legs, from the shoulders nearly to the knees, are covered with long black silky waved hair, as is very nearly the whole length of each flank, and a line rising obliquely across the buttocks, where the colour of the long hair changes to a brown hue. This long pendulous hair, which constitutes one of the chief characteristics of the species, attains its greatest length on the groin and tail. The tail at its origin is clothed with short adpressed hair, which rapidly increases in length, and forms a huge black whisk, completely hiding the remainder of the caudal extremity. Along the ridge of the neck is a dark brown streak, reaching nearly to the withers, which are free from any medial line; but the lumbar region is traversed by a pale central streak, which becomes dark brown as it approaches the tail. From the hip a blackish line passes diagonally across the loins; this is composed of slightly longer hair than that on the upper part of the body, the whole of which is short and close. In winter the long hair of the flanks probably extends much higher.

The horns are black, very strong, compact

YAK.
Av. ht. at shoulder, 66 in. Max. single horn meas. 36 in.

and roundish, diverging outwards at the base, and slightly forwards, then bending backwards with a bold curve, the tips converging towards each other. The hoofs are solid, compact, and black.

The grey hairs about the nostrils are found only in wild, not in domestic examples.

The wild yak is known by the people of Kumaon and Gurhwal as "*bunchour.*"

My principal object in visiting Hoondes[1] and Tibet in 1853, was to get one or two wild yaks, at that time looked upon as almost fabulous animals. None, so far as I was aware, had ever been seen by an Englishman until 1852, when one was seen and shot by Mr. Beckett (a sportsman from Almorah) in Hoondes, just across the passes leading into that country from Almorah. The spoils (head and skin) were brought into Almorah in great triumph, and the event was very much talked about. In 1853 several were shot. I shot six (all bulls), five of them very near the place where Mr.

[1] That part of Chinese Tartary north of the district of Kumaon and Gurhwal, and of part of Nepal.

Beckett shot his. A party who went to the Mausurobur lake, about eighty miles to the east of where I was, shot three; and Wilson, the great Himalayan sportsman, shot one or two in Roopshu, 300 or 400 miles to the north-west of where I was, near the great Chumereri lake; and many have since been shot.

The yaks (tame and wild) are, like all other animals in Tibet, provided with the fleece of "pushum" wool, as a protection against the severe cold. This "pushum" is a great article of trade; it is manufactured into cloth. The yak "pushum" is very much coarser than the goat "pushum," and is not so valuable. The wild yaks are found in certain localities in different parts of Hoondes and Tibet; the bulls herd separate from the cows, and wander a good deal; while the cows, from what I learn, chiefly remain about the same place, in of course the very wildest places, where man scarcely ever goes. I never saw any cows, so I cannot speak from personal experience; but the party who went to the Mausurobur lake in 1853 appear to have seen an immense number of them—several herds of 100 and upwards.

The high mountains to the north of the "Milum" and "Neetee" passes from Almorah to Hoondes, where I shot all my wild yaks in 1853 (and '59, '60 and '61; since 1861 they appear to have deserted these hills, for I did not see or hear of any in after years when I visited that country), are visited by the wild bulls only, between April and September. Cows are never seen there. Some of these mountains rise as high as 24,000 feet above the sea. In 1853, I saw altogether fourteen yaks—nine one day in one herd, three another, and two another day—all bulls. They were in the most retired places: and I am told, and I think it true, that whenever they see a man, at whatever distance, off they pack, and do not stop anywhere within fifteen miles or so. I was led to believe they were very sagacious, but I found them easy enough to stalk, and stupid unwieldy animals after they were hit. I was also told they were very savage; and on my first meeting them (nine of them), and when by a judicious stalk I got within an easy distance, I certainly expected an adventure, but I was disappointed with all except one, which charged me, but which I knocked over with a bullet through his head when within ten yards of me. I got three out of this herd of nine. They were, when I first saw them, lying down at an elevation of about 18,000 feet, on the snow.

All the other yaks which I saw were very nearly at as high an elevation. They seem to go down to grass about sunset, feed all night, and are up again at this enormous elevation by a little after sunrise. I am talking of the months of July and August. Doubtless in the winter months they go as low as they can; the lowest valleys in this country are about 14,000 feet above the sea. I have seen their traces very numerous as high as 19,000 feet, and in the valleys as low as 15,000 feet. Those at the latter elevation were always old traces, doubtless of April, May and June, before the passes were open, and before a single man had arrived in the country.

E. Smyth.

ZEBRA—The zebras form a well-marked and distinctive group of equine species, found only in the continent of Africa. They are to be met with from the highlands of Abyssinia and Gallaland to the mountains of Cape Colony; some of them, as the true or mountain zebra, affecting only the wilder and more inaccessible sierras; others, as the well-known Burchell's zebra, frequenting by preference open plains or level thinly-bushed country. There are now only three species to be found in Africa, viz., (1) the true or mountain zebra (*Equus zebra*); (2) Grèvy's zebra (*Equus grèvyi*); (3) Burchell's zebra (*Equus burchelli*). Until about thirty years ago, a fourth and very well-known species, the quagga (*Equus quagga*), was to be found in Cape Colony and the Orange Free State. This handsome and very interesting animal has, however, been completely exterminated, and has now—probably for some twenty years or more—become extinct. The zebras were formerly found in immense numbers in various parts of Africa. They are still abundant in the more remote and less explored regions; but, as they are pretty easily shot, as their skins have some commercial value, and as they are a favourite food of natives, they are much hunted and, during the present century, have been subjected to a great deal of persecution. The quagga has vanished; the mountain zebra is becoming more and more rare, and it seems scarcely probable that, under present conditions, the remaining two species can resist the fate of extinction for more than a few score of years.

The True or Mountain Zebra (*Equus zebra*), familiar to the Hottentots as the *daow*, and to the Boers as the *wilde paard* (wild horse), has been known to Europeans ever since the first colonising of the Cape by the Dutch in the middle of the seventeenth century. It is peculiarly a mountain dweller, and has always had a singularly restricted habitat in Southern Africa. Formerly it seems to have been common upon every mountain range, from Great Namaqualand in the west to Swaziland in the east; but at the present day, thanks to incessant and senseless persecution, it is now much scarcer, and is only found in small troops of from five to a dozen or fifteen in certain mountains of Cape Colony (where it is as far as possible preserved), and here and there along the Drakensberg and Lebombo mountains towards Swaziland. In Cape Colony it

Zebra.

may still be found in the Sneeuwberg, Great Winterhoek, Zwartberg, Tandtjesberg, and one or two other ranges, where it maintains its existence in the wildest and most remote parts of the mountains. The mountain zebra stands from 12 to 12½ hands in height, and, from its strong, sturdy, and compact build, is wonderfully adapted for getting about the difficult mountain country which it so peculiarly adorns. The legs are short and beautifully clean, the hoofs small, well-shaped, and hard as flints; the ears are long—much longer than those of the Burchell's zebra and quagga—and give to the animal a more asinine look than either of these two congeners. The body colouring is a clear, silvery white, and the markings of black, or very dark brown, extend to every part of the body except the stomach. The legs are perfectly and beautifully banded in black and white, right down to the hoofs. The head—except the ears, which are black and white—is finely and evenly marked in bright brown instead of black, and the muzzle is of a rich tan colour. The tail is shorter, thinner, and more ass-like in character than that of the Burchell's zebra. The stripings of the mountain zebra differ markedly from those in the other species, and especially from those of the quagga and Burchell's zebra. A glance at a good modern natural history—such, for instance, as the *Royal*—will at once indicate the peculiar variations in the markings of this very interesting equine group. In its own mountain habitat the true zebra is a shy, solitude-loving beast, and, from the inaccessibility of its habitat and the ease with which it traverses the steep rocky sierras, is nowadays not very easily stalked. As a matter of fact, although to some extent preserved, it may be looked upon as a fast-vanishing species, and ought now never to be shot at. The mountain zebra is of a fierce, intractable temper, using its hoofs and teeth freely, and, unless taken very young, is practically untamable. In the old days at the Cape, when these animals were abundant, the Boers captured some numbers of the young, which were exported to Mauritius and there driven in their equipages by the French colonists. Upon the flat the mountain zebra has no very astonishing pace, and can be ridden into by a good horse. Its usual habitat is amid ranges of from 2,000 to 7,000 feet in altitude.

Grèvy's Zebra was, until the year 1882, practically unknown to Europeans. In that year a living specimen was sent by Menelek, King of Shoa—now King of Abyssinia—to M. Grèvy, the President of the French Republic. For a short period the animal survived in the Jardin des Plantes, where it attracted much notice. Grèvy's zebra, as it is now called, was thought at first to be merely a variety of the Cape mountain zebra. Since 1882, however, many travellers and hunters have penetrated into Somaliland and Gallaland, where this zebra has been found in large numbers, and a close examination of the skins procured has established the fact that the new zebra is a clear and distinct species. The animal is considerably larger than the true or mountain zebra, and exceeds in stature every other member of the group, adult specimens measuring as much as 14 hands at the withers. The body colour of this handsome zebra is of a clear white—as with the true zebra—but the black or chocolate-brown markings are much finer, thinner, and more numerously distributed. They are, in fact, pretty even in width all over the body. The ears are enormously large, exceeding in size even those of the mountain zebra.

Grèvy's zebra is found principally in Gallaland and in that part of Somaliland bordering upon the Galla country. Its habitat is described by Captain Swayne, who has made many sporting expeditions into Somaliland and the adjacent regions, as "low plateaux covered with scattered or thick thorn-bush, and tall, feathery 'durr' grass, with red gravelly soil, and rocks cropping up now and then." They are found in herds of a dozen, and when first encountered, were extremely tame and easily shot. In places they are often seen in large numbers. As they become more persecuted, it seems probable that they will gradually betake themselves to the higher mountain ranges.

Burchell's Zebra (*Equus burchelli*)—This, the Bonte quagga (pied quagga) of the Boers, often called, erroneously, the quagga, may be termed the zebra of the plains, and is quite the commonest, as it is the handsomest, of its group in all Africa. Its range was much wider and less restricted than was the case with the other striped *equidæ*, and, until comparatively recent times, it was found, in suitable country, roaming in immense herds from the Orange River to Northern Equatorial Africa. Even at the present day, after an extraordinary amount of persecution, it may be found pretty plentifully from the Pungwe River, Rhodesia, and Ngamiland in Southern Africa right away to the north of the equator. This zebra is best known to Europeans, and the various zoological gardens of this country and the continent are seldom without specimens. Sixty years ago it was found by Cornwallis Harris in the Transvaal and South Bechuanaland in "immense herds," but, thanks to wanton and incessant slaughter, the traveller in South Africa encounters it nowadays, first in Khama's country, Ngamiland, and Matabeleland. Its habitat is by preference open plains or rolling, thinly bushed country. Quite recently in Benguela, Portuguese West Africa, Mr. G. W. Penrice, an English hunter, has, however, found this zebra inhabiting absolutely hilly country. It is found in places abundantly in Central and East Central Africa, as far as Uganda and even beyond. In Northern and

North Western Africa the zebra seems to have been always unknown. Burchell's zebra stands about 13 hands at the shoulder. Its body-colouring varies from pale sienna to white. The black or deep chocolate stripings are quite differently arranged from those of the mountain and Grèvy's zebra. The head is light and elegant, and the small ears are more equine than asinine. The thick, upstanding mane is somewhat fuller than is the mountain zebra's, and comes down well over the forehead. The tail is white, and more flowing than that of the mountain zebra. In some localities the leg stripings of this zebra extend nearly to the hoofs, in others little beyond the shoulders or forearms. In specimens in which the leg stripings are fuller and more numerous, some naturalists have distinguished the animal as Chapman's variety of Burchell's zebra, and have dignified it by the scientific name—*Equus chapmani*. It is extremely doubtful, however, whether this can be looked upon as a good variety. Burchell's zebra is one of the softest and most easily slain of all the game animals of Africa, and a single bullet will usually suffice to turn the animal out of the troop, when it may be easily finished off. With a broken leg, the Burchell's zebra is—unlike the antelope and deer families—rendered at once quite helpless. Its paces in flat, open country are very good, and unless the hunter is exceedingly well mounted, a troop of these zebras will often gallop right away from him. The flesh is sweet and unpalatable to Europeans, and the fat very yellow; nearly all natives are, however, extremely fond of zebra meat. Of all animals, the lion is, perhaps, fondest of the zebra, and large numbers of Burchell's and Grèvy's zebras are slain annually by these carnivora, lying in wait near the drinking places. Zebras cannot resist thirst as can many of the antelopes, and usually drink each night or at very early morning. Of late years a good many of the young of Burchell's zebras have been captured alive by Dutch hunters. Some numbers of these were broken to harness and tried in Transvaal mail coaches and carts. It was found, however, after careful trial, that they were unable to stand the wear and tear of prolonged and heavy coach work so well as horses and mules, and the experiment has since been abandoned. Mr. Walter Rothschild has used four of these animals in a coach for light work in London and Hertfordshire with some success, and the animals appear to lend themselves to domestication more easily than any others of the various species of this group.

The Quagga (*Equus quagga*), which takes its name from the Hottentot word *quacha*—derived from the peculiar neigh or cry of the animal—was formerly extremely abundant in the Cape Colony, and, it is believed, parts of Griqualand West and the Orange Free State. Its habitat was curiously restricted, and it seldom or never seems to have wandered beyond these limits. So lately as the time of Cornwallis Harris (1837) the animal is described by that great naturalist and sportsman as inhabiting the plains of the country now known as the Orange Free State in "immense herds," and even in Gordon Cumming's time (1843–1850) it was quite common on the northern karroos of the Cape Colony. Its downfall was wrought entirely by the skin-hunting Boers, and its final extinction seems to have taken place somewhere between 1865 and 1870 in Cape Colony, and possibly a little later in the Orange Free State.

The quagga was invariably a denizen of wide, open plains, where it roamed in herds, numbering in the aggregate tens and hundreds of thousands. Upon the march, these animals usually moved in single file, in long lines; when grazing the animals scattered over the veld; and when really alarmed they fled together in dense troops. In height the quagga stood about 13 to 13½ hands—about that of the Burchell's zebra. It was, however, of more robust build than that zebra, while in colour and marking it differed widely from all others of this group. The upper body-colouring was pale rufous-brown, darker upon the face and neck, and the dark-brown stripings usually extended from the head only as far as the middle of the barrel, or, more often, a trifle behind the shoulder. The stomach and legs were pure white. A dark dorsal line ran from the mane to the tail. The ears and tail were more equine than asinine; the tail was white and flowing; the muzzle black; the crest high and arched; the mane full, upstanding, and marked in brown and white. Altogether, the quagga was an extremely handsome creature, which but for the senseless and short-sighted slaughter of the Dutch farmers, never ought to have become extinct in South Africa. In pace the quagga seems to have been slightly inferior to the Burchell's zebra, and the animal was usually to be ridden into by a light, well-mounted hunter. The species seems, under the exterminating rifles of the Boers, to have faded gradually from existence, and attention was first called to its actual extinction by the present writer in an article in the *Field* in 1888. Most unfortunately, the Natural History Museum only possesses an old and extremely poor stuffed specimen of this unique and now extinct animal. Specimens seem to be equally scarce in other museums of Europe.

H. A. BRYDEN.

GENERAL INDEX

GENERAL INDEX

Signed articles are printed in small capitals.

INDEX OF AUTHORS

NOTE

VOL. I.

Page ix. Author of Bustard, *for* "Abel Chapman" *read* "Lieut.-Col. L. H. Irby."
,, 31. *Omit* "August" *add* "November."
,, 33. *Omit* "Aspiuoparia Morar."
,, 160. *For* "S. H. Whithead" *read* "S. H. Whitbread."
,, 302. "Nick Sight" block inverted in error.
,, 476. Author of Gooral, *for* "A. F. Mackenzie" *read* "Donald Macintyre."

VOL. II.

Page 364. *For* "Dr. Holland" *read* "Mr. Wills."
,, 435. The illustration is of the Caucasian Túr.
,, 470. The illustrations to the Tobogganing article are kindly lent by Mr. T. A. Cook, from his *Notes on Tobogganing at St. Moritz*, published by Messrs. Rivington.

APPENDIX

TO

THE ENCYCLOPÆDIA OF SPORT

THE object of this Appendix is to bring the matters dealt with in it and the *Encyclopædia* as far as possible up to date. The chief care has been to make clear the alterations in the Rules governing their respective sports, not so much in those cases where verbal alterations have been made simply to defeat those whose chief object seems to be to twist a rule altogether away from its obvious meaning, as to make plain those alterations which involve something new and important. In some cases where no rules had been given they have been supplied.

September, 1900.

APPENDIX

AMERICA CUP.

	Yacht.	Rig.	Owner.	No. of Victories.
1899.	*Columbia* (winner).	cutter	Messrs. C. C. Iselin and J. P. Morgan	3
	Shamrock	cutter	Sir T. Lipton	0

ARCHERY.

Shooting Regulations.

1.—The Grand Annual Meeting will consist of three days shooting: the first two for the principal prizes; the third for prizes subscribed for handicap sweepstakes based upon the shooting of the two previous days.

2.—The Judges will be appointed by the Committee.

3.—The Ladies will shoot each day the National Round, viz.: four dozen arrows at 60 yards; two dozen arrows at 50 yards. The gentlemen, the National York Round, viz.: six dozen arrows at 100 yards; four dozen arrows at 80 yards; and two dozen arrows at 60 yards. Three arrows to be shot at each end.

4.—The Targets will be placed farther apart than the specified distances, but at the proper distances marks will be fixed, from which alone the Archers are to shoot.

5.—The bugle will sound the assembly at 10.45 a.m., and will again sound for the commencement of the shooting at 100 yards at 11 *precisely;* after the 100 yards shooting, time will be allowed for luncheon; at 2.15 p.m. the assembly will again be sounded, and at 2.30 *precisely* the bugle will sound for the Ladies to commence the shooting at 60 yards and the Gentlemen at 80 yards. The judges will appoint the time for the commencement of the shooting at 50 yards and 60 yards as they shall see fit. The bugle will sound accordingly. The judges shall also make what arrangements they shall see fit should anything occur to interfere with the shooting.

6.—The Targets will measure four feet in diameter, and the centre of the gold shall be four feet from the ground.

7.—The Captains will be placed—No. 3 at each Target, to take charge of the Targets and to score, assisted by No. 4.

8.—Any Lady making three golds at one end shall be entitled to receive 1*s.* from every other Lady competitor, and any Gentleman making three golds at one end, 1*s.* from every other Gentleman competitor.

9.—Any Archer having won one or more of the Grand National Medals, and, at subsequent meetings of the G.N.A.S., not wearing one (at least), shall pay a fine of 10*s.* each day that he appears without wearing and showing one such Medal, and the same with respect to the Brooches.

10.—Every Archer's arrows must be clearly and distinctively marked with his or her name or initials, so that the owner may have no difficulty in claiming them or the Captain in distinguishing them. Archers must not draw their arrows from the target till the Captain has called on them to declare their hits, and has scored them. If an arrow be drawn by its owner before it is scored, it shall not be allowed to count or to be measured as a gold.

11.—If from any cause an Archer is not prepared to shoot before all have shot, such Archer shall lose the benefit of that end.

12.—Gentlemen will not be allowed to smoke at the Ladies' Targets, and it is particularly requested that no person will divert the attention of the Archers shooting by talking; and, while the Archers are in the act of shooting, no one (except the Archers) will be allowed to stand in front of the *white line* behind the Targets. As soon as the Archers have all shot and advanced to the opposite Targets, all spectators must follow them and remain in front of the Targets to which they are going, until the arrows are picked up, when they must immediately take up their position again at the *white line* behind the Targets.

13.—No persons, except competitors whilst shooting, will be allowed in front of the Targets.

14.—The value of the rings on the Target shall be:—Gold, 9; red, 7; blue, 5; black, 3; white, 1. If an arrow touch two colours it shall be scored as in that of the higher value. Should any dispute arise as to whether an arrow touch the higher colour, the matter shall be decided by the Captain of the Target, subject to an appeal to the judge

15.—No Archer shall take more than one prize (the Challenge Prizes excepted). In the case of ties for any of the prizes, if two or more have an equal score, the prize for score shall be adjudged to the one who has the greatest number of hits. If two or more have an equal number of hits, the prize for hits shall be adjudged to the one who has the greatest score. In the event of the occurrence of ties which cannot be decided as above, the names of those interested shall be retained for further consideration. If any have an individual claim upon a subsequent prize, the name shall be struck out, the money pooled with that of the previous tie or ties, and divided amongst all those having an individual or collective claim to the prizes under consideration, a decoration being given to each person. The decoration for any individual prize shall be allotted to each person interested.

16.—The Champion Prizes shall be awarded to the Archers gaining the greatest number of points, provided that those for gross hits or gross score be included; any points won by other Archers shall be re-distributed amongst those gaining the points for gross hits and gross scores.

The points are:—

Ladies.		Gentlemen.	
Gross hits	2	Gross hits	2
Gross score	2	Gross score	2
Hits at 60 yards	1	Hits at 100 yards	1
Score at 60 yards	1	Score at 100 yards	1
Hits at 50 yards	1	Hits at 80 yards	1
Score at 50 yards	1	Score at 80 yards	1
		Hits at 60 yards	1
		Score at 60 yards	1
Total	8	Total	10

Should there be a tie between two or more Archers, the prize shall be awarded to the Archer having the greatest gross score.

17.—If, owing to the state of the weather, the full number of arrows are not shot on the first two days, the deficient number shall, if possible, be shot on the third day. No prizes will be awarded unless one complete round is shot. And if the double round be incomplete, the Gross Score and Challenge Prizes shall be awarded on the one round only that has been completed.

18.—No shooting will be allowed in the field during the three days, except when competing for the prizes.

19.—It shall be the duty of the Committee to take cognizance of all Matters whatsoever concerning the good order and fellowship of the Meeting, and also, if they think proper, to impose a fine of 2*s.* 6*d.* for any infringement of these rules, or for any offensive or improper conduct; and if the Committee shall be of opinion that the case is deserving of more serious notice, or if any fine imposed by them be not paid, the person so offending shall be disqualified from winning a prize, and from shooting again at the National Meetings.

20.—Any Archer moving forward before all have shot their arrows, and the signal is given to advance, shall be liable to be fined 2*s.* 6*d.*

21.—If any doubt or dispute shall arise on any point connected with the shooting, the matter shall be referred to the judges, whose decision shall be final.

County Challenge Cup.

1.—This cup will be competed for by Gentlemen only, in teams not exceeding six in number, at the Grand National Archery Meeting every year.

2.—Each Archer competing must have resided for at least twelve months previous to the Meeting in the county he represents. A temporary absence will not disqualify.

3.—The entrance fee for each county will be 6*s.*

4.—Each Archer taking part in this contest must enter as a competitor for the Grand National Archery Meeting.

5.—The nominations must be made in writing, and the entrance fees paid to the Hon. Sec. of the G.N.A.S. not later than the evening before the Meeting.

6.—The York Round will be shot, and the Cup awarded to the team making the highest aggregate score on the first two days' shooting (subject to shooting regulation 17).

7.—The Archer making the highest score in the winning team will be entitled to hold the Cup for the year; the Cup to be returned to the Hon. Sec. of the G.N.A.S. on or before July 1st in the following year.

The same rules apply to the Ladies' County Challenge Prize, with the following exceptions, viz.:—The National Round will be shot instead of the York Round (Rule 6 and Rule 7); there will be six Challenge Prizes, so that each lady will retain one for the following year.

Medals for County Competition.

1.—The G.N.A.S. will provide annually Bronze Medals, to be competed for by residents in the different counties.

2.—One Medal will be provided for Ladies and one for Gentlemen, the necessary subscription being 12*s.* 6*d.* for each medal.

a. A county can enter for either or both.

3.—The Medals to be competed for at such time and place as a Local Committee shall select.

N.B.—The Competition may take place at a Meeting within the county, or at a match between two or more counties, or at the Public Meeting in the district of the competing county, *i.e.*, Leamington for the Midland Counties, Crystal Palace for the Metropolitan, Grand Western for the Western Counties, Grand Northern for the Northern Counties.

4.—The Ladies must shoot the National and the Gentlemen the York Rounds, and the Medal will be awarded to the maker of the greatest gross score.

Sh uld the Local Committee appoint a two days' Meeting, the double round will count.

5.—Each Archer competing must have resided at least twelve months in the county to be eligible to win the Medal. A temporary absence will not disqualify.

6.—The entries must be made, and the subscription paid, before the date of the Grand National Archery Meeting each year.

7.—The Meetings must be regulated by the Grand National Society's Rules.

8.—Should any Archer win the Medal more than once, a bar will be given instead of the Medal.

LAWS AND RECOMMENDATIONS OF THE A.A.A.

(I.) Laws.

For Athletic Meetings and Competitions.

Law I.—Definition of an Amateur now reads, "An amateur is one who has never competed for a money prize, or monetary consideration, or for any declared wager or staked bet; who has never engaged in, or taught any athletic exercise as a means of pecuniary gain; and who has never taken part in any competition with any one who is not an amateur."

For the "exceptions to this law" the following alterations have been passed :—

(*a*) That amateur athletes . . . . by competing with or against professionals in cricket matches or in ordinary club football matches for which no prizes are given . . . .

(*d*) That the "Championship of the Army" Races be exempt from the effect of this rule.

(*e*) and (*f*) disappear, (*g*) appears as (*e*), and for (*h*) the following is substituted :—

(*f*) That a competitor in athletic competitions (other than A.A.A. Championships or bona fide International, Inter-Club, Inter-Team, Inter-College, or Inter-School contests), who asks for or receives travelling expenses ceases to be an amateur. No Club, Society, or Managing Body promoting an athletic competition shall, either directly or indirectly, pay or offer a monetary consideration to, or the travelling expenses of, any competitor in such competition. Clubs, Colleges, or Schools shall be answerable for any payments made by them, and if called upon to do so shall produce full details of the same and accounts to the A.A.A. (North, South, or Midlands) Committee.

Law VI. is a new rule: "That a fee of 5*s.* be lodged with all objections to the value of prizes, to be retained if the objection be considered frivolous."

Law VII. is old Rule VI. with three N.B.'s attached; the first and third of which are respectively sections (*e*) and (*f*) of the old Law I., the second is new, and provides that "All clubs holding open handicap races shall employ an official handicapper."

Law VIII. is old Law VII.

Law IX. is old Law VIII. and old Law IX. conjoined, with the addition of "and shall exhibit their certificates of registration or permit on the day of the meeting in a conspicuous place in the competitor's dressing room."

Law XI. is a new one; that "All entries shall be made to the secretary of the sports, and entries made to the handicapper shall be void."

Law XII. is in two parts, the first part of which is old Law XI.; the second part fills the place of old Law XII., and reads: "Competitors in handicap competitions shall be required to send with their entries full and definite particulars of (1) the last four events in which they have competed; (2) their last performance at each of the distances entered for; and (3) the last heat or prize won by them at each of the distances entered for. No club shall be affiliated to the Association or registered as 'approved' unless it agrees to adopt the A.A.A. entry form."

Law XXI.—To the paragraph dealing with the broad jump add "The taking-off line shall be of wood."

Law XXV. is old Law XXVI.

Law XXVI. is old Law XXVII., with the addition of old Law XXV. as a N.B.

(II.) Recommendations.

The numbering of these recommendations has been altered as far as and including old 38; thus old 28 is now 27, old 29, 28, and so on to old 38, which is now 37. In new 34, which deals with the hammer, the following alterations occur: "The head . . . . of iron or lead or both. . . . and the handle. . . . of wood or metal or both." "The total length. . . . more than four feet, and no cross-piece, ring, or loop at the end of the handle shall be allowed."

Two new recommendations appear, Nos. 38 and 41; Nos. 39 and 40 remain as in the old rules.

Recommendation 38.—(1) No record can be made on any track that does not comply with the following conditions. (2) There shall be 10 flights of hurdles in each distance. (3) Each competitor shall keep his own flight of hurdles throughout. Hurdles to be 3 ft. out of the ground, with straight top-bars. (4) No competitor shall be allowed a record unless he break the worsted, so that a correct time can be taken. (5) Each track of hurdles must be measured the correct and full distance to the winning post. In 300 yard races—(6) the first hurdle shall be 45 yards from each competitor's scratch mark, and the remaining hurdles shall be as near as possible 25 yards apart. The distance from the last hurdle to the winning post shall be 30 yards. In 440 yard races—(7) The first hurdle shall be placed 50 yards from each competitor's scratch mark, and the remaining hurdles shall be as nearly as possible 40 yards apart, and the distance from the last hurdle to the winning post shall be 30 yards. (8) The last 75 yards, if possible, must be straight.

Recommendation 41.—That in any Inter-Club contest advertised "for first-claim men under A.A.A. Laws," where no other definition of first-claim men has been previously given, each competitor must have been a member of the club he represents at least three months immediately prior to the race; and in the event of his residing more than twenty miles from the head-quarters of his club, he must have been a member for one year immediately prior to the race. When a man is a member of two or more competing clubs, the club which can show the longest unbroken period of his present membership has first claim upon his services.

Extracts from the A.A.A. Rules of Importance to Athletes.

Rule XXVII.—In (*a*) substitute "six months" for "twelve, and "a month's notice" for "notice."

Record Rules.

Two new rules, numbered V. and VI., have been added.

Rule V.—Timekeepers must exhibit their watches to the judges if called upon immediately each race is completed.

Rule VI.—It is recommended that any claim for a record should be made within 14 days from the date of its performance.

Athletics.

Time Records—Walking.

Event.	*Record made by.*	*Time.*	*Date.*	*Club of which a Member.*
London to Brighton. 52½ miles.	E. Knott.	H. 8, M. 56, S. 44	April 10. 1897.	London.

Odd Events.

Event.	*Record made by.*	*Distance.*	*Date.*	*Club of which a Member.*
Long Jump.	W. J. M. Newburn.	FT. 24, IN. 0½	July 23, 1898.	Dublin A.C
Throwing the Hammer (16 lb.).	J. Flanagan.	147 0	April 6, 1896.	Gaelic A.A.A.

Best Amateur Records in America.

Event.	*Record.*	*Holder.*	*Club.*	*Games.*	*Date.*
120 Yards.	11⅖ secs.	B J. Wefers.	N.Y.A.C.	Worcester Mass.	Aug. 20, 1897.
Broad Jump.	23 ft. 8⅞ in.	M. Prinstein.	Syracuse Univ.	New York A.C	June 11, 1898.
Throwing Hammer, 16 lbs. (7 ft. circle.)	158 ft. 4 in.	J. Flanagan	N.Y.A.C.	Travers Island, N.Y.	June 11, 1898.

BADMINTON.

The Laws of Badminton.

The Courts.

1. The courts are laid out as in the succeeding diagram (A) and defined by white or black painted or chalk lines 1½ inches wide.

2. The net should be made of fine tanned cotton cord to a ¾ inch square mesh, 16 feet in length, 2 feet 6 inches in depth, 5 feet in height at the centre, and 5 feet 1 inch at the posts. The top of the net should be edged with a 3 inch white tape, doubled and supported by a cord run through the tape.

3. The posts should be sufficiently firm to keep the net strained as above, and should project at least 6 feet above the level of the net.

4. The shuttlecocks to weigh from 65 to 75 grains, to have 16 to 18 feathers fixed in a cork 1 inch in diameter, feathers to be 2½ inches long, to have 2¼ inches spread at the top, and to be tied in with thread one inch above the cork.

The Game.

5. The game is played by one or two players aside.

6. *The Choice of Courts.*—The choice of sides and the right of serving during the first game shall be decided by toss: provided that if the winner of the toss choose the right to serve, the other player shall have the choice of sides, and *vice versa*: and provided that the winner of the toss may, if he prefer it, require the other player to make the first choice; but the side winning a game is bound to begin the next. Either player on the winning side may begin the next game.

7. The game consists of 15 aces; at 13 all, the side which first reached 13 has the option of setting 5, at 14 all, of setting 3.

8. The rubber is the best of three games if the third game is played, the sides cross over when the leading score reaches eight.

Faults.

9. A fault made by a player whose side is "in" puts a hand out; if made by a player whose side is "out," it counts an ace to the "in" side.

10. It is a fault—

(*a*) If the service is overhand. (A service shall be deemed to be overhand within the meaning of this rule, if the shuttle at the instant of being struck be higher than the server's waist.)

(*b*) When the service falls into the wrong court (*i.e.*, not into the one diagonally opposite to the server), or falls short of the short service-line, or beyond the long service-line, or outside the boundary lines.

(*c*) Unless the server's feet are in his own court.

Note.—A foot on the line has been ruled to be out of court.

(*d*) If, either in service or play, the shuttlecock falls outside the bounds of the game, or does not pass between the posts, or the vertical lines above them, or passes through or under the net, or touches the roof or side walls, or the person or dress of any player.

Note.—A shuttlecock falling on any line is held to have fallen in the court of which such line is a boundary.

(*e*) If the shuttlecock be struck before it crosses the striker's side of the net, but the striker may follow the shuttle over the net with his racket.

(*f*) If, while the shuttle is in play, a player touches the net or its supports with racket or person.

DIAGRAM A.

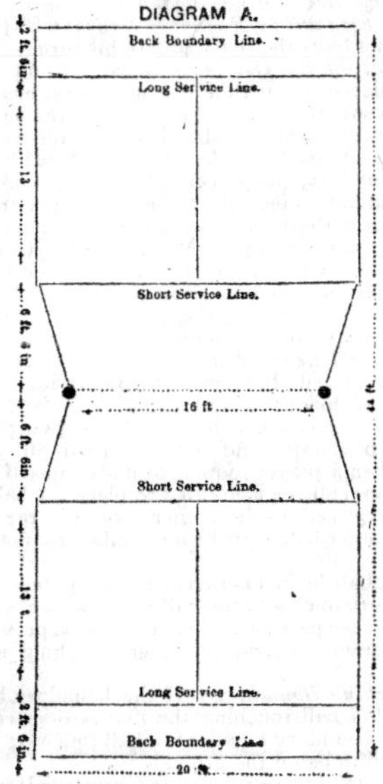

(*g*) If the shuttlecock be hit twice by the same player, or be hit by a player and his partner.

(*h*) If a player serves out of his proper turn, or from the wrong court provided that such fault be claimed and allowed before the next succeeding serve is returned.

The Play.

11. It having been decided which side is to have the first hand, the player in the right-hand court of that side commences the game by serving to the player in the adverse right-hand court. If that player return the shuttlecock before it touches the ground, it must be hit back by one of the "in" side, and then returned by the "out" side, till a fault is made or the shuttlecock touches the ground. If a fault is made by the "in" side, the server's hand is out, and the player in the right-hand adverse court now becomes the server; but if the service is not taken, or the fault is made by the "out" side, the "in" side score an ace. The "in" side then change courts, the server now being in the left court and serving to the adverse left court. The game is continued in this manner, serves being made alternately from each court into the one diagonally opposite, and courts being changed by the players on each side when, and only when, an ace is added to their respective scores. The first serve of a side in each innings shall be made from the right-hand court. The service-lines are disregarded after the service is taken.

General Rules.

12. The person served to may alone take the serve, and no player may take two consecutive serves.

13. The server may not serve till his opponent is ready, but if a return of the service be attempted the latter shall be deemed to be ready. If, in delivering the serve, the server makes preliminary feints, or otherwise baulks his opponent, the latter shall not be bound to take the service.

14. The side beginning a game has only one hand in its first innings.

15. The server may stand anywhere he likes in his own court, between the short and long-service lines.

16. If the shuttlecock touches the net or posts in service it is a let, but if in play it does not invalidate the stroke.

17. A "let" may be given by the umpire for any unforseen or accidental hindrance, on appeal from either player before the next service, when the ace will be replayed.

18. The decision of the umpire is final whether it is right or whether it is wrong.

Appendix.

In games of one player on each side, the above rules hold good, except that, notwithstanding Rules 11 and 12, both players change courts after each ace is scored, and consecutive serves are taken by the same player.

The game of Badminton may also be played by 3 or 4 players a side; in this case the game consists of 21 aces. At 19 all, the side which first reached that number has the option of setting 5; at 20 all, of setting 3.

The back boundary line of the court may become the long-service line, and the back player can take the service after it has passed the front player.

The side beginning a game has only two hands in its first innings. In every subsequent innings, each partner of a side has a hand, the first player of the "in" side after the second hand is out, changing places with the third player, and similarly the second player changing places with the fourth player after the third hand is out.

RULES OF BANDY.

Rule V.—The last two sentences have been replaced by "It is desirable to have it coloured red, and to be the present La-crosse ball."

Rule IX.—For "and," read "or."

Rule XIII.—In the last sentence read "first" for "just."

Rule XIV.—Read "On the occasion. . . . when the ball is hit off from a goal line or thrown from a side line. . . ."

RULES OF BOWLS.

Rule 40.—After the word playing add "neither must he point out to his partner how their opponents' bowls lie, but he may point out their own or request him to inspect their positions before playing."

THE LAWS OF CRICKET.

As Amended by the M.C.C., 1884, 1889, 1894, 1899, and 1900.

The most important alterations in the rules occur in Laws 10, 53, and 54.

Rule 10.—Read "the ball must be bowled; if thrown o jerked, *either* umpire shall call 'no ball.'"

Rule 13.—Substitute *six* for *five*.

Rule 33.—Has been subdivided into 33*a* and 33*b*: 33*a* st[illegible] exactly as the old 33; 33*b* reads "If the ball, whether struck [illegible] the bat or not, lodges in a batsman's clothing, the ball shall bec[illegible] 'dead.'"

Rule 46 has had appended to it the following: N.B.—

An appeal, "How's that?" covers all ways of being out (withi the jurisdiction of the Umpire appealed to), unless a specific way o getting out is stated by the person asking.

Rule 48*a* becomes 48, and now reads "If *either* umpire be not satisfied, . . . he shall call 'no ball."

Rule 48*b* is now numbered 48*a*.

Rules 53 and 54 have both had most important alterations made in them and now read:—

53.—The side which bats first and leads by 150 runs in a three days' match, or by 100 runs in a two days' match, shall have the option of requiring the other side to follow their innings.

54.—The In-side may declare their innings at an end in a three days' match, at or after the luncheon interval on the second day; in a two days' match on the second day, at any time; in a one day match at any time.

ONE DAY MATCHES.

Rule I. now reads:—"The side which bats first and leads by 75 runs shall have the option of requiring the other side to follow their innings."

Rule II. now contains both of the old rules 2 and 3, with the addition of this N.B.—A tie is included in the words "played out."

INSTRUCTIONS TO UMPIRES.

In the course of the season of 1899 the following additions to the Instructions to Umpires were approved by the M.C.C. Committee.

Law 54:—"Declaring."

(*A.*) If a side declare its innings during the luncheon interval, it must do so within fifteen minutes after the commencement of such interval, otherwise an extra ten minutes will be allowed for rolling.

(*B.*) If a side declare its innings closed in the morning before play commences, it must do so in sufficient time to enable the other side to choose the roller it prefers, otherwise an extra ten minutes will be allowed for rolling.

RULES OF COUNTY CRICKET.

The new rules came into force on Jan. 1st, 1900.

1. A cricketer born in one county and residing in another may not play for more than one county during the same season.

2. Qualification by birth.—A cricketer is always eligible to play for the county of his birth.

3. Qualification by Residence.—A cricketer is qualified to play for any county in which he has resided for the previous 24 months and is residing, but:—

(A) The mere acquirement or hiring of a tenement, unless used as a bona-fide home, does not constitute "residence."

(B) The occupation of a tenement during the cricket season only does not constitute "residence."

4. Where a cricketer uses as residences in the course of the year, tenements in more than one county, or where he leaves the country for the winter months, and in all other cases where his qualification is in any doubt, it is obligatory on the county for which he wishes to play to prove his qualification to the satisfaction of the M.C.C.

5. A cricketer who has played for a county for five successive years is qualified to play for that county for the rest of his cricket career, or until he plays for some other county.

6. A cricketer may play for his old county during the two years that he is qualifying for another.

7. TRANSFERS.—A cricketer, already qualified for a county but wishing to qualify by residence for another county, must give notice in writing to the Cricket Club Committee of the former county before he commences such residence; and a County Cricket Club wishing to engage, under a residential qualification, a cricketer, who is already qualified for another County Club, must inform the Committee of the latter before commencing negotiations with the cricketer.

8. APPEAL.—Should any question arise under these rules it shall be left to the decision of the committee of the Marylebone Club, which shall be final

THE COUNTY CHAMPIONSHIP.

At the meeting of County Secretaries on December 6th, 1898, it was moved and carried as a recommendation to the M.C.C. that the number of out and home matches qualifying for the championship should in 1899, in view of the Australian visit, be again reduced to six. This was subsequently agreed to by the M.C.C. Worcestershire having at the Secretaries' meeting secured six out and home matches with leading counties, made formal application to the M.C.C. to be promoted to a place among the first-class counties, and on December 12th their request was granted, subject to the usual regulations being complied with.

ENGLISH TEAMS IN AUSTRALIA.

1897–1898. A. E. Stoddart (Captain).

AUSTRALIAN TEAMS IN ENGLAND.

1898. J. Darling (Captain).

COUNTY CHAMPIONSHIP.

1897. Lancashire. 1898. Yorkshire.
1899. Surrey. 1900. Yorkshire.

THE LAWS OF CROQUET.

1. *Grounds.*—The dimensions of a full-sized Croquet Ground shall be 35yds. in length, by 28yds. in width, within a boundary line accurately defined. Smaller grounds should be made in the same proportion, *i.e.*, any multiple of 5 by 4.

2. *Mallets.*—Mallets may be of any size, weight, or material. The two ends of the heads must be parallel, and of equal size and similar shape. An indiarubber end may be used in taking croquet only. No point or roquet made by a stroke of an indiarubber end shall count. A player must not change his mallet during the game except in the case of bona-fide damage to it.

3. *Size, &c., of Balls.*—The Balls shall be 3⅝in. in diameter, of even weight. Each ball shall weigh not less than 14½oz. nor more than 15½oz.

4. *Choice of Lead and of Balls.*—It shall be decided by lot which side shall have choice of lead and balls. In a succession of games the choice of lead shall be alternate, the sides keeping the same balls.

5. *Commencement of Game.*—In commencing, each ball shall be placed on the starting spot (*vide* setting after Reg. 7). The striker's ball, when so placed and struck, is at once in play, and can roquet, or be roqueted by, any other ball in play, whether it has made the first hoop or not.

6. *The Stroke.*—The stroke shall be deemed to be taken if the ball be in any way moved by the mallet, or if the player strike at the ball with intent to move it. The mallet must be actuated by means of the handle only, and must not be kicked or struck. The ball must not be struck except with an end of the mallet head.

7. *Hoop, when run.*—A ball has run its hoop when, having passed through from the playing side and ceased to roll, it cannot be touched by a straight-edge placed against the wires on the playing side.

8. *Ball driven partly through Hoop.*—A ball driven partly through its hoop from the non-playing side cannot run the hoop at its next stroke, if it can be touched by a straight-edge placed against the wires on the non-playing side.

9. *Points scored to Non-Striker's Ball.*—A ball driven through its hoop, or against the turning peg, by any stroke (not foul) of its own side, or by any stroke of the adverse side, scores the point so made, provided that should the stroke of the adverse side be foul, or be made with an indiarubber end, the owner of the ball shall have the option of scoring the point or not, such option to be declared before the next stroke is taken.

10. *Points made for Adversary's Ball.*—If a point be made for an adversary's ball, the striker must inform his adversary of it. Should the striker neglect to do so, and the adversary make the point again, he may continue his turn as though he had played for his right point.

11. *The Turn.*—A player, when his turn comes round, may roquet each ball once, before making a point, and may do this again after each point made. The player continues his turn so long as he makes a point or a roquet, or takes croquet.

12. *Croquet imperative after Roquet.*—A player who roquets a ball must take croquet, and in so doing must move or shake perceptibly both balls. If the two balls do not touch before, and in the act of, taking croquet, the adversary may claim that the stroke be made over again. In taking croquet, the striker is not allowed to place his foot on the ball.

13. *Ball in Hand after Roquet.*—No point or roquet can be made by a ball which is in hand. If a ball in hand displace any other balls, they must remain where they are driven. Any point made in consequence of such displacement counts, notwithstanding that the ball displacing them is in hand.

14. *Balls Roqueted Simultaneously.*—When a player roquets two or more balls simultaneously, he may choose from which of them he will take croquet; another roquet will be required before he can take croquet from any other ball.

15. *Balls found Touching.*—If at the commencement of a turn the striker's ball be found touching another ball, a roquet is deemed to be made, and croquet must be taken at once; but if it be found touching two or more balls, the striker can take croquet off which ball he chooses. Another roquet will be required before he can take croquet from one of the other balls.

16. *Roquet and Hoop made by same Stroke.*—Should a ball, in making its hoop, roquet another that lies beyond the hoop and pass through, the hoop and the roquet both count. A ball is deemed to be beyond the hoop if it lies so that it cannot be touched by a straight-edge placed against the wires on the playing side. Should any part of the ball that is roqueted be lying on the playing side of the hoop, the roquet counts, but not the hoop.

17. *Pegging out.*—A rover can be pegged out by any stroke (not foul) of another rover, whether of the same or the adverse side. Should the stroke of the adverse side be foul, the owner of the ball shall have the option of scoring the point or not.

18. *Rover pegged out by Roquet.*—A rover who pegs out another rover by a roquet loses the remainder of his turn.*

19. *Balls sent off the Ground.*—A ball sent off the ground must at once be replaced 3ft. within the boundary, measured from the spot where it went off, and at right angles to the boundary. If this spot be already occupied, the ball last sent off is to be placed in contact with the other, but no ball is to be placed less or more than 3ft. from the boundary, the player merely having option whether he place the second ball going off at the same spot to right or left of the first ball; if a third ball goes off on the same spot it must be placed touching the first ball. When the player roquets or finds himself in contact with one of the balls, he is entitled to place the balls in any order, provided one remain 3ft. from the boundary, and the others touch it, or one of the other balls; but he must take croquet off the ball he has roqueted.

20. *Balls sent off near Corner.*—A ball sent off within 3ft. of a corner is to be replaced 3ft. from both boundaries. If more than one ball be sent off within 3ft. of any corner, the player shall place the ball last sent off in contact with the ball occupying the corner spot, 3ft. from one boundary, and not less than 3ft. from the other boundary. When a player roquets or finds himself in contact with one of the corner balls he is entitled to place the balls in any order, provided one be placed on the corner spot, and the others touch it or some other corner ball; but he must take croquet off the ball he has roqueted.

If a player's ball be in a corner with two or more other balls the player is at liberty to choose the ball off which he will take croquet, and he may alter the position of the other balls, provided one ball be placed on the corner spot, and the others touching it or some other corner ball.

21. *Ball touching Boundary.*—If the boundary be marked by a line on the turf, a ball touching the line is deemed to be off the ground. If the boundary be raised, a ball touching the boundary is similarly deemed to be off the ground.

22. *Ball sent off and returning to Ground.*—If a ball be sent off the ground, and return to it, the ball must be replaced, measuring from the point of first contact with the boundary.

23. *Ball sent within 3 feet of Boundary.*—A ball sent within 3 feet of the boundary, but not off the ground, is to be at once placed 3ft. from the boundary as though it had been sent off; except in the case of the striker's ball during a turn, in which case the striker has the option of so placing his ball, or of playing it from where it lies.

24. *Boundary interfering with Stroke.*—If it be found that the height of the boundary or any fixed obstacle outside it interferes with the stroke, the striker with the sanction of the umpire, or to the satisfaction of the adversary, may bring in the balls a longer distance than 3 feet, so as to allow a free swing of the mallet. Balls so brought in must be moved in the line of aim and placed at the same relative distance. Should the player not roquet the ball so brought in, it must at once be replaced.

25. *Dead Boundary.*—If, in taking croquet, the striker send his own ball, or the ball croqueted, off the ground, he loses the remainder of his turn, unless he make a roquet with the playing ball, the ball croqueted not passing the boundary.

26. *Balls touched by Adversary.*—Should a ball when rolling, even though it be in hand, be touched, diverted from its course, or stopped by an adversary, the striker may elect whether he will take the stroke again, or whether the ball shall remain where it stopped, or be placed where it would have rolled to in the judgment of the umpire, or of the striker if there be no umpire.

27. *Ball at rest accidentally moved.*—Should a ball at rest be accidentally moved by a player, except in striking or taking aim, it shall be replaced without penalty.

28. *Balls diverted or stopped by Umpire.*—Should a ball be diverted from its course or stopped by an umpire, he is to place it where he considers it would have rolled to, according to his own judgment.

29. *Foul Strokes.*—If a player make a foul stroke, he loses the remainder of his turn, and any point or roquet made by such stroke does not count. Balls moved by a foul stroke are to remain where they lie, or be replaced, at the option of the adversary If the foul stroke be made when taking croquet, and the adversary elect to

* A rover when pegged out is out of the game, therefore croquet cannot be taken from it.

have the balls replaced, they must be replaced in contact as they stood when the croquet was taken. The following are foul strokes:—

(*a*) To strike with the mallet another ball instead of or besides one's own, in making the stroke or taking aim.

(*b*) To spoon—*i.e.*, to push a ball without a distinct or audible knock.

(*c*) To strike a ball twice distinctly in the same stroke.

(*d*) To touch, divert from its course, or stop a ball when in play and rolling, whether this be done by the striker or his partner.

(*e*) To allow a ball to touch the mallet or any part of the player's person in rebounding from a peg, or wire, or from another ball, unless the player's ball be in hand.

(*f*) To move a ball which lies close to a peg or wire by striking the peg or wire without striking the ball.

(*g*) To press a ball round a peg or wire (crushing stroke).

(*h*) To play a stroke after roquet without taking croquet.

(*i*) To fail to move or shake both balls perceptibly in taking croquet.

(*k*) To take croquet from a ball without having first roqueted it.

(*l*) To knock a wire of the hoop out of the ground with the mallet when making, or attempting to make, a stroke.

(*m*) To hit a ball with any part of the mallet other than one of the ends of the head, or to kick or strike the mallet, or to make a stroke with the indiarubber end except in taking croquet.

(*n*) To handle improperly or touch a ball with foot or mallet.

30. *Playing out of Turn or with a Wrong Ball.*—If a player play out of turn, or with a wrong ball, the remainder of the turn, and any point or roquet made after the mistake, are lost. The balls remain where they lie when the penalty is claimed, or are replaced as they were before the last stroke was made, at the option of the adversary. If the adverse side play without claiming the penalty, the turn holds good. If the penalty be claimed, the adversary shall follow with that ball of his own side which would have been in order had no mistake occurred. If the penalty be not claimed, the adversary may follow with either ball of his own side.

31. *Marking Direction of Aim.*—No mark shall be made, or article placed upon the ground, to indicate a spot towards which it is desired to play a ball.

32. *Information as to Score.*—Every player is entitled to be informed which is the next ball to play, or the next point in order of any ball.

33. *State of Game, if in Doubt.*—When the state of the game is in doubt, it shall be decided by the position of the clips.

34. *Pegs or Hoops not upright.*—Any player may set upright a peg or hoop, except the one next in order; and that must not be altered except by the umpire or with the consent of the adversary.

35. *Ball lying in a Hole or on Bad Ground.*—A ball lying in a hole or on bad ground may only be moved with the sanction of the umpire or with the consent of the adversary. The ball must be put back, *i.e.*, away from the object aimed at, so as not to alter the line of aim.

36. *Umpires.*—The duties of an umpire are—

(*a*) To decide any questions that may arise during the game, if appealed to.

(*b*) To keep the score, and, if asked by a player, to disclose the state of the game.

(*c*) To move the clips, or to see that they are properly moved.

(*d*) To replace balls sent off the ground, or to see that they are properly replaced.

(*e*) To adjust hoops or pegs, or to see that they are properly adjusted.

An umpire shall not draw attention to, or give his opinion on any mistake made, unless appealed to by one of the players. The decision of an umpire on a question of fact shall be final, but on a question of law, if required by a player, he must appeal to the referee.

37. *Absence of Umpire.*—When there is no umpire present, permission to move a ball, or to set up a peg or hoop, or any other indulgence for which an umpire would be appealed to, must be asked of the other side.

Definitions.

(*a*) A Point is made when a hoop is run, or a peg is hit, in order.

(*b*) The hoop or peg in order is the point that has to be made next. (The order is shown by the arrows in the diagram of the setting.)

(*c*) A Roquet is made when the striker's ball, by a blow of the mallet, is made to hit another ball, which it has not already hit in the same turn or since making a point.

(*d*) Croquet is taken by the player placing his ball in contact with the ball roqueted, and then hitting it with the mallet. The ball which is in contact with the striker's ball must be moved or shaken perceptibly in the act of taking croquet, and is then called the croqueted ball. After taking croquet the player is entitled to another stroke.

(*e*) The striker's ball is in hand when it has roqueted another ball, and continues to be in hand until croquet is taken, when it is again in play.

(*f*) A Turn is the playing a ball in its proper order, and may consist of one or more strokes.

(*g*) A Break consists of making two or more points in the same turn.

(*h*) A Rover is a ball that has made all its points in order except the winning peg.

(*i*) Dead Boundary is a term used of the boundary in connection with taking croquet (*vide* Law 25).

(*j*) A Bisque is an extra turn which the player may take after completing his original turn. A Bisque may not be taken in continuation of the extra turn.

(*k*) A Boundary Ball is a ball which has been placed on a corner spot, or any other spot, three feet from the boundary of the ground (*vide* Laws 19, 20).

Diagram of the Setting.

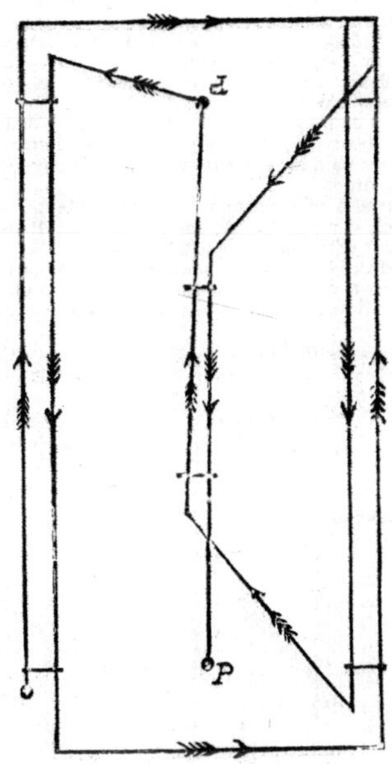

Starting point one foot from left-hand corner hoop, and opposite its centre.

Regulations for Prize Meetings.

1. In all public and club competitions the Laws of Croquet as issued by the Committee of the U.A.E.C.A. for the time being shall be in force.

2. Each ground shall, if possible, measure 35yds. in length by 28yds. in width; and the boundaries of each shall be accurately and distinctly marked by whitening, or by some other suitable means. A spot of whitening shall be placed accurately at each corner 3ft. from both boundaries, and on the starting point. Where four or more grounds are available, they should be numbered in plain figures. Flags shall be placed at the corners of each ground.

3. The hoops shall be made of ⅝in. round iron, and shall stand 12in. out of the ground. The crown shall be straight and at right angles to the uprights, which shall be 4in. apart, inside measurement.

4. The pegs shall be of wood of a uniform diameter above the ground of 1½in. They shall be 2ft. in height above the ground. Crossbars for the clips shall be added near the top. The winning peg shall be painted with rings in order, coloured Blue, Red, Black, Yellow. The turning peg shall be painted white.

5. The balls shall be made of boxwood or other suitable material, and each shall weigh not less than 14½oz., nor more than 15½oz., and be 3⅝in. in diameter. Each ball of a set shall be uniformly painted a separate colour, viz., Blue, Red, Black, Yellow.

6. Clips shall be painted the same colour as the balls.

7. The setting of the hoops and pegs shall be in accordance with the above diagram, and the order in which the points are to be made shall, unless otherwise specially provided for, be according to the arrows which appear thereon.

Measurements on a full-sized ground. Pegs in centre line of ground 7yds. from nearest boundary. Hoops up centre line of ground 7yds. from peg, and 7yds. apart. Corner hoops 7yds. from centre, and in a line with pegs.

8. A programme shall be issued which shall specify—

(*a*) The number and nature of the contests, whether each is single or double, and who may compete.

(*b*) The number and nature of the prizes.
(*c*) The time and place of meeting.
(*d*) The time and place of draw; and the date and hour of closing of entries.
(*e*) The time of commencement of play in each event.
(*f*) That every competitor shall wear tennis shoes if called upon, and provide his or her own mallet.
(*g*) The names of the Committee, the name and address of the Secretary, and the names of Handicappers and Referees.

9. The duties of a Referee shall be as follows:
(*a*) To handicap the competitors, if there be no Handicapper, and to be present at, and if necessary superintend the draw.
(*b*) To decide all questions concerning the interpretation of the Laws of Croquet which may be submitted to him.
(*c*) To appoint umpires, and to decide any matter submitted to him by them, or by umpires agreed upon by competitors.
(*d*) To decide, and if necessary enforce, any questions involving the disqualification of a competitor.
(*e*) To decide and declare any or all grounds to be unfit for play, and if necessary to postpone the meeting.
(*f*) To adjudicate upon any matter, other than one of fact, arising in a contest, which may be submitted to him.

10. No entry shall be valid the money for which has not been paid prior to the draw, or is not forthcoming on demand. Every competitor who has paid his entrance money shall have the right to be present at the draw.

11. For the purpose of determining how the players shall meet, the name of each competitor, or, in the case of foursomes, the names of each pair of competitors, shall be written on a separate slip of paper, and the slips shall be placed in a bowl or hat. They shall then be drawn out at random, one by one, and the names shall be written down, in the order drawn, on the competition card.

12. Byes shall be allotted in accordance with the following table:

Number of Competitors.		Number of Byes.	Number of Byes at top.	Matches.	Number of Byes at bottom.
5	3 short of 8	3	1	1	2
6	2 ,, 8	2	1	2	1
7	1 ,, 8	1	—	3	1
8	— ,, 8	—	—	4	—
9	7 ,, 16	7	3	1	4
10	6 ,, 16	6	3	2	3
11	5 ,, 16	5	2	3	3
12	4 ,, 16	4	2	4	2
13	3 ,, 16	3	1	5	2
14	2 ,, 16	2	1	6	1
15	1 ,, 16	1	—	7	1
16	— ,, 16	—	—	8	—
17	15 ,, 32	15	7	1	8
18	14 ,, 32	14	7	2	7
19	13 ,, 32	13	6	3	7
20	12 ,, 32	12	6	4	6
21	11 ,, 32	11	5	5	6
22	10 ,, 32	10	5	6	5
23	9 ,, 32	9	4	7	5
24	8 ,, 32	8	4	8	4
25	7 ,, 32	7	3	9	4
26	6 ,, 32	6	3	10	3
27	5 ,, 32	5	2	11	3
28	4 ,, 32	4	2	12	2
29	3 ,, 32	3	1	13	2
30	2 ,, 32	2	1	14	1
31	1 ,, 32	1	—	15	1
32	0 ,, 32	—	—	16	—
33	31 ,, 64	31	15	1	16
34	30 ,, 64	30	15	2	15
35	29 ,, 64	29	14	3	15
36	28 ,, 64	28	14	4	14
37	27 ,, 64	27	13	5	14
38	26 ,, 64	26	13	6	13
39	25 ,, 64	25	12	7	13
40	24 ,, 64	24	12	8	12
41	23 ,, 64	23	11	9	12
42	22 ,, 64	22	11	10	11
43	21 ,, 64	21	10	11	11
44	20 ,, 64	20	10	12	10
45	19 ,, 64	19	9	13	10
46	18 ,, 64	18	9	14	9
47	17 ,, 64	17	8	15	9
48	16 ,, 64	16	8	16	8

13. When the programme includes an open competition, and a competition confined to Ladies, no competitor shall be eligible for both.

14. If any competitor is absent, or is otherwise unable to play when called upon by the Referee, the name of such competitor may be scratched.

15. In handicap matches the players shall be handicapped, before the draw, in classes. Class 1 giving one bisque to Class 2 each game; two bisques to Class 3, and so on. In like manner, Class 2 gives one bisque to Class 3; two bisques to Class 4, and so on.

16. In foursomes the players shall be divided into Captains and Seconds; and no two players, each of whom receives less than five bisques from scratch, shall enter as partners in handicap foursomes.

17. In foursomes, the number of bisques to be given in each gam shall be half the differences of the classes. If the difference be a odd number, the half bisque shall entitle the receiving side to th option of commencing the game. Either partner, irrespective o the class to which he or she belongs, may take the bisques to whicl the side it entitled.

18. In handicaps, should the Referee consider that there is no sufficient time to allow of the whole game being played, he ma call upon any or all of the competitors to play a shorter game, start ing 1ft. in front of hoop No. 4. In singles two-thirds of the differ ence between the classes shall be allowed, and in the case of four somes the difference must first have been halved as usual (Reg. 17 In time handicaps no more than half the number of bisques shall b taken until 14 points have been made by the receiver of odds Should the number of bisques be uneven, the larger half may b taken before 14 points have been made.

19. A Silver Medal will be presented to any Associate reachin the semi-final stage in any open competition held in accordanc with the Laws and Bye-Laws of the Association where the entrie amount to sixteen. When the entries are fewer than sixteen Silve Medals will be presented to the first and second. No Associat can win more than one Silver Medal.

20. The Gold Medals of the Association will be played for annually by Associates.

CURLING.

The Rules of the Game of Curling.

Rule 4.—Read in sentence 2: "No stone, including handle and bolts, shall be of greater weight . . . ."

RUGBY FOOTBALL.*

Laws.

In the Glossary the definition of *touch* has been amended to the following: "Those portions of the ground immediately at the sides of the field-of-play and between the goal-lines, if produced, are called touch. The touch-lines and all posts and flags marking these lines, or the centre, or 25 yards lines, are in touch."

And to the definition of touch-in-goal the following has been added: "The corner posts and flags are in touch-in-goal."

In the section dealing with the referee most important alterations have been made, which compel him now to stop the game for breaches of the law without any appeal. The section now reads:—

In all matches a referee and two touch-judges must be appointed, the former being mutually agreed upon. The referee must carry a whistle, the blowing of which shall stop the game; he must whistle in the following cases:—

(*a*) When a player makes and claims a fair catch.
(*b*) When he notices rough or foul play or misconduct. For the first offence he shall either caution the player or order him off the ground, but for the second offence he must order him off. If ordered off, the player must be reported by him to this Union.
(*c*) When he considers that the continuation of play is dangerous.
(*d*) When he wishes to stop the game for any purpose.
(*e*) If the ball, or a player running with the ball, touch him.
(*f*) At half-time and no-side, he being the sole timekeeper, having sole power to allow extra time for delays; but he shall not whistl for half-time or no-side until the ball be held or out of play.
(*g*) When he notices any irregularity of play whereby the sid committing such gain an advantage.
(*h*) When he notices a breach of Laws 5 and 15.
(*i*) When he wishes to enforce any penalty under Law 11.

Duty of Touch-Judges.—Add: "and also to assist the referee, i requested by him, at kicks-at-goal."

There has been one general change of principle throughout th rules, to the expression of which it will be needless to refer in eacl case. Wherever there occur words implying the necessity of a appeal to the referee, those words have been removed. Alteration of this character will not be noted under each rule.

Rule 6.—The last sentence of this rule now reads: "If a playe . . . . be tackled . . . . he *must* at once put it fairly down betwee him and his opponents' goal-line."

Rule 8.—The second paragraph has been altered to: "An off-side player shall not . . . . tackle, or actively or passively obstruct, nor may he approach within ten yards."

Rule 9.—Read: "If . . . . a free kick, even though the whistle has been blown, for a knock-on, ..."

Rule 10.—In the sixth sentence, after the words "unless he has dropped the ball," delete the words "or touched it with his foot."

Rule 11, which deals with penalties, has been greatly altered and some new clauses added. Sections (*a*), (*b*), (*c*), and (*e*) are unaltered and the remainder are appended.

(*d*) Prevents an opponent getting up, or putting the ball down.
(*f*) Wilfully holds an opponent who has not got the ball.
(*g*) Wilfully hacks, hacks-over, or trips-up.
(*h*) Wilfully puts the ball unfairly into a scrummage, or, the ball having come out, wilfully shoves it forward with his hands again into the scrummage.
(*i*) Not himself running at the ball, charges or obstructs an opponent not holding the ball.
(*j*) Shouts "all on side," or words to that effect, when his players are not on side.
(*k*) Not in a scrummage wilfully obstructs his opponents' backs by standing on his oppenents' side of the ball when it is in a scrummage.
(*l*) Wilfully prevents the ball being fairly put into a scrummage.
(*m*) If any player or team wilfully and systematically break any law or laws for which the penalty is only a scrummage, wilfully and systematically cause unnecessary loss of time.

* See addenda at end of Appendix.

Rule 12, sect. (*a*), now reads: "Bounding it on the field-of-play at right-angles to the touch-line. After bounding it he may catch it, and then run with it, kick it, or pass it. When catching it he must have both feet in the field-of-play."

Rule 16.—A new clause has been added to the end of the first sentence: "or unless the opposite side gain an advantage."

Rule 17.—This law has been altered by the addition of the word "wilfully," so as to prevent accidental transgressions incurring any penalty. This leaves all such points to the discretion of the referee.

Rule 18 has been altogether changed, and now reads:—

Hacking, hacking-over, or tripping-up are illegal. The referee shall have full power to decide what part of a player's dress, including boots and projections thereon, buckles, rings, &c., are dangerous, and having once decided that any part is dangerous shall order such player to remove the same, and shall not allow him to take further part in the game until such be removed.

Rule 20, by which the annual close time is determined, now fixes that period as LASTING FROM APRIL 20TH TO SEPTEMBER 1ST.

Regulations for County Qualifications.

Rule I.—Three months has been substituted for six in section (*b*); section (*d*) has been deleted.

Rule II.—Delete "for three seasons."

Rule IV. has been entirely recast and now reads:—A man who has resided for three months previous to the time of playing in a county in which there is no County Club shall be qualified to play for any county adjoining the county in which he resides. Should, in the future, a County Club be formed and be admitted to the County Championship Competition, a player having a qualification under this regulation cannot retain it. Residence by members of the University at Oxford and Cambridge shall not afford a qualification under this regulation. This regulation shall not apply to the County of Monmouth.

Rules as to Professionalism.

Rule 5.—An additional offence has been added: "Knowingly playing or acting as referee or touch-judge on the ground of an expelled or suspended club."

Rule 6.—Add in the second sentence the word "such" before "written permission."

Rule 13 now reads:—This Union shall have power to deal with all acts which it may consider as acts of professionalism and which are not specifically provided for.

INTERNATIONAL MATCHES.

ENGLAND *v.* SCOTLAND.

England, 9; Scotland, 9; Drawn, 9.
1898—Edinburgh. 1 t—1 t | 1899—London. S, 1 g—nil
1900—Edinburgh. No score.

ENGLAND *v.* IRELAND.

England. 17; Ireland, 6; Drawn, 1.
1898—Richmond. I, 1 g, 2t—1 g, 1 t
1899—Dublin. I, 1 pen g, 1 t—nil
1900—Richmond. E, 2 g, 2 t—1 g

ENGLAND *v.* WALES.

England, 11; Wales, 5; Drawn, 1.
1898—Blackheath. E, 1 g, 3 t—1 g, 1 t
1899—Swansea. W, 4 g, 2 t—1 t
1900—Gloucester. W, 3 g, 1 t

SCOTLAND *v.* IRELAND.

Scotland, 17; Ireland, 3; Drawn, 3.
1898—Belfast. S, 2 g (1 pen)—nil
1899—Edinburgh. I, 3 t—1 pen g
1900—Dublin. No score.

SCOTLAND *v.* WALES.

Scotland, 10; Wales, 5; Drawn, 1.
1899—Edinburgh. S, 3 g, 3 t—2 g
1900—Swansea. W, 4 t—1 t

IRELAND *v.* WALES.

Ireland, 5; Wales, 8; Drawn, 1.
1898—Limerick. W, 2 g, 1 t—1 g | 1899—Cardiff. I, 1 t—nil
1900—Belfast. W, 1 t—nil

ASSOCIATION FOOTBALL.

LAWS OF THE GAME.

Rule I. has been altered somewhat. The chief alterations being (1) that the settled game should be played by eleven a side; (2), the maximum length is now 130 yards; (3). a half-way line is provided for, and the six yards line from the goal line is replaced by semi-circles drawn six yards from each goal-post. Further, the dimensions of the ground for international matches are fixed as maximum length, 120 yards, minimum length, 110; maximum breadth 80 yards, minimum, 70.

Rule II.—The duration of the game is now fixed at 90 minutes, unless otherwise mutually agreed upon.

Rule III.—*Add* "The interval at half-time shall not exceed five minutes, except by consent of the referee."

Rule V.—It is now provided that a goal shall not be scored from a throw in.

Rule VI.—A player offside is now prevented from "interfering in any way whatever" with an opponent.

Rule VIII. has been so altered that it is appended:—

A player shall not intentionally handle the ball under any pretence whatever, except in the case of the goal-keeper, who, within his own half of the field of play, shall be allowed to use his hands in defence of his goal, but not by carrying the ball. The goal-keeper may be changed during the game, but notice of such change must first be given to the referee.

Rule IX.—Substitute "Law 14" for "Law 13."

Rule X.—The last sentence now reads "The goal-keeper shall not be charged except when he is holding the ball or obstructing an opponent."

Rule XI.—Bars must now extend from side to side of the boot, and the additional proviso is made that the Referee shall, if required, examine the players' boots before the commencement of a match.

Rule XII.—Which deals with the powers of the Referee and of the linesmen, has been altogether recast; that portion dealing with the linesmen has been put into a separate rule numbered 13. Rule 12 now reads:—

A Referee shall be appointed, whose duties shall be to enforce the laws and decide all disputed points; and his decision on points of fact connected with the play shall be final. He shall also keep a record of the game and act as timekeeper. In the event of any ungentlemanly behaviour on the part of any of the players, the offender or offenders shall be cautioned, and if the offence is repeated, or in case of violent conduct without any previous caution, the Referee shall have power to order the offending player or players off the field of play, and shall transmit the name or names of such player or players to his or their (National) Association, who shall deal with the matter. The Referee shall have power to allow for time wasted, to suspend the game when he thinks fit, and to terminate the game whenever, by reason of darkness, interference by spectators, or other cause, he may deem necessary; but in all cases in which a game is so terminated he shall report the same to the Association under whose jurisdiction the game was played, who shall have full power to deal with the matter. The Referee shall have power to award a free kick in any case in which he thinks the conduct of a player dangerous, or likely to prove dangerous, but not sufficiently so as to justify him in putting in force the greater powers vested in him. The power of the Referee extends to offences committed when the play has been temporarily suspended, and when the ball is out of play.

Rule XIII. is a new one dealing with the duties of linesmen, which are unaltered save for the additional provision that they are to assist the Referee in carrying out the game in accordance with the Laws. The other alterations are merely verbal.

Rule XIV. is the old Rule 13, which deals with the penalty kick. The only alteration is that the word "intentionally" is substituted for "wilfully."

Rule XV. is the old Rule 14, and the old rule 15 disappears, its provisions having been incorporated in Rule 12.

Rule XVII.—For "forfeited to" read "awarded to."

DEFINITION OF TERMS.

Carrying is now defined as an offence confined to the goal-keeper, and is described as "taking more than two steps while holding the ball or bouncing it on the hand."

"*Touch*" is now that part of the ground on either side of the field of play.

Handling is "intentionally playing the ball with the hand or arm," and is now bracketed with *Tripping*.

For "the interpretations of the Council of the F.A. upon the Laws" section (*c*) has been excised; the present section (*c*) takes the place of (*d*), and section (*a*) that of (*f*). Section (*a*) has been amplified and now reads:—

"All reports by Referees to be made within three days after occurrence. The International Board has decided that in the event of any misconduct occurring in connection with the Cup ties of local Associations, or in other matches where the two clubs are not members of the Football Association, and in the jurisdiction of the same Local *affiliated* Association, the report of the referee may be made direct to the Local *affiliated* Association concerned."

The *Memorandum* issued by the F.A. has been considerably altered; section (*a*) remains. Sections (*b*), (*o*) and (*r*) disappear; sections (*c*), (*e*), (*f*), (*g*), (*h*), (*n*), (*k*), (*l*), (*m*) and (*n*) reappear as sections (*b*), (*d*), (*e*), (*f*), (*g*), (*h*), (*i*), (*k*), (*l*), and (*m*) respectively. Sections (*d*), (*p*), and (*q*) are altered and amplified and appear as sections (*c*), (*n*) and (*o*). The sections which are new and those which are recast are appended.

Section (*c*) Membership of any Club having a name similar to one already affiliated to the Association, shall not be recognized or accepted. The word "Association" or "Rugby" is not a sufficient distinction within the meaning of the Agreement between the Association and the Rugby Union to prevent a Club under one authority taking a name identical with that already held by a club under the other authority.

Section (*n*). Professional Registration forms signed on a Sunday are not valid. It is an offence for a Club to induce a player to sign on a Sunday, and the signing of a second registration form before the Council have declared the first form invalid, is also an offence. Clubs and players can be dealt with for these irregularities.

Section (*o*). A professional player may, with the consent of the Council, practise on the ground of a club other than the ground of the Club for which the player is registered.

Section (*p*). It is misconduct for any Association or Club, or any player, official, or member of any Association or Club to offer or attempt to offer, either directly or indirectly, any consideration whatever to another Club, player, or players of any other Club, with a view to influence the result of a match. It is misconduct for any Club, player, or players, to accept any such consideration.

Section (*q*). All claims by players against clubs for wages or expenses must be for not more than two months wages or expenses at a time, and must be made within two months of their becoming due, otherwise they will not be considered.

Section (*r*). The Council will require to be satisfied that the transfer of players is *bona fide*, and applications for the purpose of obtaining players for special matches will not be acceded to.

Section (*s*). Associations, Leagues, and Combinations to which consent is given under Rule 23 must not increase the number of their competing Clubs, or the area of their operations without the consent of the Council of the Football Association.

Section (*t*). A Club ought not to be compelled to play any match on Good Friday or Christmas Day.

Section (*u*). A Club may pay the doctor's fees for services rendered to an Amateur Player in consequence of injuries sustained in one of its matches.

Section (*v*). The Rules of the Football Association are sufficient to enable the Council, as the governing authority, to deal with all cases of misconduct, or failure to carry out the terms of professional players' engagements, and the Council are of opinion that legal proceedings should only be taken as a last resource, and then only with the previous consent of the Council.

Section (*w*). It is not permissible for a provisional agreement to be entered into between Clubs and their professional players.

INTERNATIONAL MATCHES.

ENGLAND *v.* SCOTLAND.

England, 9; Scotland, 14; Drawn, 6.

1898—Glasgow. E, 3—nil. | 1899—Birmingham. E, 2—1
1900—Glasgow. S, 4—1.

ENGLAND *v.* WALES.

England, 17; Wales, 2; Drawn 5.

1897-98—Wrexham. E, 3—0 | 1898-99—Bristol. E, 4—0
1899-00—Cardiff. 1—1

ENGLAND *v.* IRELAND.

England, 18; Ireland, 0; Drawn, 1.

1897-98—Belfast. E, 3—2 | 1898-99—Sunderland. E, 13—2
1899-1900—Dublin. E, 2-0

SCOTLAND *v.* WALES.

Scotland, 22; Wales, 0; Drawn, 2

1898—Motherwell. S, 5—2 | 1899—Wrexham. S, 6—0
1900—Aberdeen. S, 5—2

SCOTLAND *v.* IRELAND.

Scotland, 16; Ireland, 0; Drawn, 1.

1898—Belfast. S, 3—0 | 1899—Glasgow. S, 9—1
1900—Belfast. S, 3—0

IRELAND *v.* WALES.

Ireland, 6; Wales, 10; Drawn, 2.

1898—Llandudno. I, 1—0 | 1899—Belfast. I, 1—0
1900—Llandudno. W, 2—0.

RULES OF GOLF.

AS APPROVED BY THE ROYAL AND ANCIENT GOLF CLUB OF ST. ANDREWS.

1. ***Definitions*—(*a*)** The Game of Golf is played by sides, each playing its own ball. A side consists either of one or of two players. If one player play against another, the match is called "a single." If two play against two, it is called "a foursome." A single player may play against two, when the match is called "a threesome," or three players may play against each other, each playing his own ball, when the match is called "a three-ball match."

(*b*) The game consists in each side playing a ball from a teeing-ground into a hole by successive strokes, and the hole is won by the side which holes its ball in fewer strokes than the opposite side, except as otherwise provided for in the Rules. If the sides hole out in the same number of strokes, the hole is halved.

(*c*) The teeing-ground shall be indicated by two marks placed in a line, as nearly as possible at right angles to the course.

The hole shall be 4¼ inches in diameter, and at least 4 inches deep.

(*d*) The term "putting-green" shall mean all ground within 20 yards of the hole, except hazards.

(*e*) A "hazard" shall be any bunker, water (except casual water), sand, path, road, railway, whin, bush, rushes, rabbit scrape, fence, or ditch. Sand blown on to the grass, or sprinkled on the course for its preservation, bare patches, snow, and ice are not hazards. Permanent grass within a hazard shall not be considered part of the hazard.

(*f*) The term "through the green" shall mean all parts of the course except "hazards" and the putting-green which is being played to.

(*g*) The term "out of bounds" shall mean any place outside the defined or recognised boundaries of the course.

(*h*) "Casual water" shall mean any temporary accumulation of water (whether caused by rainfall or otherwise) which is not one of the ordinary and recognised hazards of the course.

(*i*) A ball shall be "in play" as soon as the player has made a stroke at the teeing-ground in each hole, and shall remain in play until holed out, except when lifted in accordance with the Rules.

(*j*) A ball shall be considered to have "moved" only if it leave its original position in the least degree, and stop in another; but if it merely oscillate, without finally leaving its original position, it shall not be considered to have "moved."

(*k*) A ball shall be considered "lost" if it be not found within five minutes after the search for it is begun.

(*l*) A "match" shall consist of one round of the Links, unless it be otherwise agreed.

A match is won by the side which is leading by a number of holes greater than the number of holes remaining to be played. If each side win the same number of holes, the match is halved.

(*m*) A "stroke" shall be any movement of the ball caused by the player, except as provided for in Rule 4, or any downward movement of the club made with the intention of striking the ball.

(*n*) A "penalty stroke" is a stroke added to the score of a side under certain rules, and shall not affect the rotation of play.

(*o*) The privilege of playing first from a teeing-ground is called "the honour."

(*p*) "Addressing the ball" shall mean that a player has taken up his position and grounded his club, or if in a hazard, that he has taken up his position preparatory to striking the ball.

(*q*) The reckoning of strokes is kept by the terms—"the odd," "two more," "three more," etc., and "one off three," "one off two," "the like." The reckoning of holes is kept by the terms—so many "holes up," or "all even," and so many "to play."

2. A match begins by each side playing a ball from the first teeing-ground.

The player who shall play first on each side shall be named by his own side.

The option of taking the honour at the first teeing-ground shall be decided, if necessary, by lot.

A ball played from in front of, or outside of, or more than two club lengths behind the two marks indicating the teeing-ground, or played by a player when his opponent should have had the honour, may be at once recalled by the opposite side, and may be re-teed.

The side which wins a hole shall have the honour at the next teeing-ground. If a hole has been halved the side which had the honour at the last teeing-ground shall again have the honour.

On beginning a new match the winner of the long match in the previous round shall have the honour, or if the previous match was halved the side which last won a hole shall have the honour.

3. A player shall not play while his ball is moving, under the penalty of the loss of the hole. But if the ball begin to move while the player is making his upward or downward swing, he shall incur no penalty, except as provided for in Rules 10, 18, and 27, and a stroke lost under Rule 27 shall not in these circumstances be counted as a stroke of the player.

4. If the ball fall or be knocked off the tee in addressing it, no penalty shall be incurred, and it may be replaced, and if struck when moving no penalty shall be incurred.

5. In a threesome or foursome the partners shall strike off alternately from the teeing-grounds, and shall strike alternately during the play of the hole.

If a player play when his partner should have done so, his side shall lose the hole.

6. When the balls are in play, the ball furthest from the hole which the players are approaching shall be played first, except as otherwise provided for in the Rules. If a player play when his opponent should have done so, the opponent may at once recall the stroke. A ball so recalled shall be dropped as near as possible to the place where it lay, without penalty.

7. The ball must be fairly struck at, not pushed, scraped, nor spooned, under penalty of the loss of the hole.

8. A ball must be played wherever it lies or the hole be given up, except as otherwise provided for in the Rules.

9. Unless with the opponent's consent, a ball in play shall not be moved, nor touched before the hole is played out, under penalty of one stroke, except as otherwise provided for in the Rules. But the player may touch his ball with his club in the act of addressing it, without penalty.

If the player's ball move the opponent's ball through the green, the opponent, if he choose, may drop a ball (without penalty) as near as possible to the place where it lay, but this must be done before another stroke is played.

10. Any loose impediment (not being in or touching a hazard) which is within a club length of the ball may be removed. If the player's ball move after any such loose impediment has been touched by the player, his partner, or either of their caddies, the penalty shall be one stroke. If any loose impediment (not being on the putting-green) which is more than a club length from the ball be removed, the penalty shall be the loss of the hole.

11. Any vessel, wheel-barrow, tool, roller, grass-cutter, box, or similar obstruction may be removed. If a ball be moved in so doing, it may be replaced without penalty. A ball lying on or touching such obstruction, or on clothes, nets, or ground under repair or covered up or opened for the purpose of the upkeep of the Links, may be lifted and dropped without penalty, as near as possible to the place where it lay, but not nearer the hole. A ball lifted in a hazard, under such circumstances, shall be dropped in the hazard.

A ball lying in a golf hole or flag hole, or in a hole made by the green keeper, may be lifted and dropped without penalty as near as possible to the place where it lay, but not nearer the hole.

12. Before striking at a ball in play, the player shall not move, bend, nor break anything fixed or growing near the ball, except in the act of placing his feet on the ground for the purpose of addressing the ball, in soling his club to address the ball, and in his upward or downward swing, under penalty of the loss of the hole, except as otherwise provided for in the Rules.

13. When a ball lies in or touches a hazard, nothing shall be done to improve its lie; the club shall not touch the ground, nor shall anything be touched or moved before the player strikes at the ball, subject to the following exceptions:—(1) The player may place his feet firmly on the ground for the purpose of addressing the ball; (2) In addressing the ball, or in the upward or downward swing, any grass, bent, whin, or other growing substance, or the side of a bunker, wall, paling, or other immovable obstacle may be touched; (3) Steps or planks placed in a hazard by the Green Committee for access to or egress from such hazard may be removed, and if a ball be moved in so doing, it may be replaced without penalty; (4) Any loose impediments may be removed from the putting-green; (5) The player shall be entitled to find his ball as provided for by Rule 30. The penalty for a breach of this Rule shall be the loss of the hole.

14. A player or caddie shall not press down nor remove any irregularities of surface near a ball in play. Dung, worm-casts, or mole-hills may be removed (but not pressed down) without penalty. The penalty for a breach of this Rule shall be the loss of the hole.

15. If a ball lie or be lost in water, the player may drop a ball, under the penalty of one stroke. But if a ball lie or be lost (1) in casual water through the green, a ball may be dropped without penalty; (2) in water in a hazard, or in casual water in a hazard, a ball may be dropped behind the hazard, under the penalty of one stroke; (3) in casual water on a putting-green, a ball may be placed by hand behind the water, without penalty.

16. When a ball has to be dropped the player himself shall drop it. He shall face the hole, stand erect behind the hazard or casual water, keep the spot from which the ball was lifted (or in the case of water or casual water, the spot at which it entered) in a line between himself and the hole, and drop the ball behind him from his head, standing as far behind the hazard or casual water as he may please. If it be impossible to drop the ball behind the hazard or casual water, it shall be dropped as near as possible to the place where it lay, but not nearer the hole. If the ball so dropped touch the player dropping it, there shall be no further penalty, and if the ball roll into a hazard, it may be re-dropped without further penalty.

17. When the balls lie within six inches of each other on a putting-green, or within a club length of each other through the green or in a hazard (the distance to be measured from their nearest points), the ball nearer the hole may, at the option of either the player or the opponent, be lifted until the other is played, and shall then be replaced as near as possible to the place where it lay. If the ball further from the hole be moved in so doing, or in measuring the distance, it shall be replaced without penalty. If the lie of the lifted ball be altered by the player in playing, the ball may be placed in a lie as nearly as possible similar to that from which it was lifted, but not nearer the hole.

18. Any loose impediments may be removed from the putting-green, irrespective of the position of the player's ball. The opponent's ball may not be moved except as provided for by the immediately preceding Rule. If the player's ball move after any loose impediment lying within six inches of it has been touched by the player, his partner, or either of their caddies, the penalty shall be one stroke.

19. When the ball is on the putting-green the player or his caddie may remove (but not press down) sand, earth, dung, worm-casts, mole-hills, snow, or ice lying round the hole or in the line of his putt. This shall be done by brushing lightly with the hand only across the putt and not along it. Dung may be removed by a club, but the club must not be laid with more than its own weight upon the ground. The line of the putt must not be touched, except with the club immediately in front of the ball, in the act of addressing it, or as above authorised. The penalty for a breach of this Rule is the loss of the hole.

20. When the ball is on the putting-green, no mark shall be placed, nor line drawn as a guide. The line of the putt may be pointed out by the player's caddy, his partner, or his partner's caddy, but the person doing so must not touch the ground.

The player's caddie, his partner, or his partner's caddie, may stand at the hole, but no player or caddie shall endeavour, by moving or otherwise, to influence the action of the wind upon the ball.

21. The penalty for a breach of this Rule is the loss of the hole.

When on the putting-green, a player shall not play until the opponent's ball is at rest, under the penalty of one stroke.

22. Either side is entitled to have the flag-stick removed when approaching the hole. If the ball rest against the flag-stick when in the hole, the player shall be entitled to remove the stick, and if the ball fall in, it shall be deemed as having been holed out at the last stroke. If the player's ball knock in the opponent's ball, the latter shall be deemed as having been holed out at the last stroke. If the player's ball move the opponent's ball, the opponent if he choose may replace it, but this must be done before another stroke is played. If the player's ball stop on the spot formerly occupied by the opponent's ball, and the opponent declare his intention to replace, the player shall first play another stroke, after which the opponent shall replace and play his ball. If the opponent's ball lie on the edge of the hole, the player, after holing out, may knock it away, claiming the hole if holing at the like, and the half if holing at the odd, provided that the player's ball does not strike the opponent's ball and set it in motion. If after the player's ball is in the hole, the player neglect to knock away the opponent's ball, and it fall in also, the opponent shall be deemed to have holed out at his last stroke.

23. If a ball *in motion* be stopped or deflected by any agency outside the match, or by the forecaddie, the ball must be played from where it lies, and the occurrence submitted to as a "rub of the green." If a ball lodge in anything moving, a ball shall be dropped as near as possible to the place where the object was when the ball lodged in it, without penalty. If a ball *at rest* be displaced by any agency outside the match, excepting wind, the player shall drop a ball as near as possible to the place where it lay, without penalty. On the putting-green the ball shall be replaced by hand, without penalty.

24. If the player's ball strike, or be moved by an opponent or an opponent's caddie or clubs, the opponent shall lose the hole.

25. If the player's ball strike, or be stopped by, himself or his partner, or either of their caddies or clubs, his side shall lose the hole.

26. If the player, when making a stroke, strike the ball twice, the penalty shall be one stroke.

27. If the player, when not intending to make a stroke, or his partner or either of their caddies, move his or their ball, or by touching anything cause it to move, when it is in play, the penalty shall be one stroke. If a ball in play move, after the player has grounded his club in the act of addressing it, or, when in a hazard, if he has taken up his stand to play it, he shall be deemed to have caused it to be moved, and shall lose a stroke, which shall be counted as a stroke of the player, except as provided in Rule 3.

28. If a player play the opponent's ball, his side shall lose the hole, unless (1) the opponent then play the player's ball, whereby the penalty is cancelled, and the hole must be played out with the balls thus exchanged, or (2) the mistake occur through wrong information given by the opponent or his caddie, in which case there shall be no penalty, but the mistake, if discovered before the opponent has played, must be rectified by placing a ball as near as possible to the place where the opponent's ball lay.

If it be discovered before either side has struck off from the next teeing-ground (or, after playing the last hole in the match, before any of the players have left the green) that one side has played out the hole with the ball of a party not engaged in the match, that side shall lose that hole.

29. If a ball be lost, except as otherwise provided for in the Rules, the player's side shall lose the hole; but if both balls be lost, the hole shall be considered halved.

30. If a ball be lost in fog, bent, whins, long grass, or the like, only so much thereof shall be touched as will enable the player to find his ball. The penalty for a breach of this rule shall be the loss of the hole.

31. If a ball be driven out of bounds, a ball shall be dropped at the spot from which the stroke was played, under penalty of loss of the distance.

32. In a three-ball match, if a player consider that an opponent's ball on the putting-green might interfere with his stroke, he may require the opponent either to lift or hole out his ball at the opponent's discretion.

If an opponent consider (1) that his own ball, if left, might be of assistance to the player, he is entitled to lift it, or hole out at his discretion; or (2) that the ball of the other opponent might be of such assistance, he may require that it be either lifted or holed out at the other opponent's discretion.

33. A player shall not ask for advice from any one except his own caddie, his partner, or his partner's caddie, nor shall he willingly be otherwise advised in any way whatever, under penalty of the loss of the hole.

34. If a ball split into separate pieces, another ball may be put down where the largest portion lies, or if two pieces are apparently of equal size, it may be put where either piece lies, at the option of the player. If a ball crack or become unfit for play, the player may change it, on intimating to his opponent his intention to do so. Mud adhering to a ball shall not be considered as making it unfit for play.

35. If a dispute arise on any point, the players have the right of determining the party or parties to whom it shall be referred, but should they not agree, either side may refer it to the Rules of Golf Committee, whose decision shall be final. If the point in dispute be not covered by the Rules of Golf, the arbiters must decide it by equity.

Special Rules for Stroke Competitions.

1. In stroke competitions, the competitor who holes the stipulated course in fewest strokes shall be the winner.

2. If the lowest scores be made by two or more competitors the tie, or ties, shall be decided by another round to be played on the same day. But if the Green Committee determine that to be inexpedient or impossible, they shall then appoint the following or some subsequent day whereon the tie, or ties, shall be decided.

3. New holes shall be made for Stroke Competitions, and thereafter no competitor, before starting, shall play any stroke on a putting-green, under penalty of disqualification.

4. The scores shall be kept by a special marker, or by the competitors noting each other's scores. The scores marked shall be checked after each hole. On completion of the round, the score of the competitor shall be signed by the marker, counter-signed by the competitor, and handed to the secretary or his deputy, after which, unless it be found that a card returned shows a score below that actually played (in which case the competitor shall be disqualified), no correction or alteration can be made.

5. If a competitor play from outside the limits of the teeing-ground, the penalty shall be disqualification.

6. If a ball be lost (except as otherwise provided for in the Rules of Golf), the competitor shall return as near as possible to the spot from which the lost ball was struck, tee a ball and lose a stroke. The lost ball shall continue in play, if it be found before the player has struck another ball.

7. If a competitor's ball strike himself, his clubs, or caddie, the penalty shall be one stroke.

8. If a competitor's ball strike another competitor, or his clubs or caddie, it is a "rub of the green," and the ball shall be played from where it lies. If a competitor's ball which is at rest be moved by another competitor or his caddie, or his club, or his ball, or by any outside agency excepting wind, it shall be replaced as near as possible to the place where it lay, without penalty.

9. A competitor shall hole out with his own ball every hole, under penalty of disqualification. But if it be discovered, before he has struck off from the next teeing-ground or, if the mistake occur at the last hole, before he has handed his card to the secretary or his deputy, that he has not holed out with his own ball, he shall be at liberty to return and hole out with his own ball, without penalty.

10. A ball may be lifted out of a difficulty of any description, and teed, if possible, behind it, under penalty of two strokes. If it be impossible to tee the ball behind the difficulty, it shall be teed as near as possible to the place where it lay, but not nearer the hole.

11. All balls shall be holed out, under penalty of disqualification. When a competitor's ball is within 20 yards of the hole, the competitor shall not play until the flag has been removed, under penalty of one stroke. If the ball nearer the hole might either interfere with the competitor's stroke, or in any way assist the competitor, such ball must be holed out or lifted, at the owner's option. Through the green a competitor may have any other competitor's ball lifted, if he find that it interferes with his stroke.

12. A competitor, unless specially authorised by the Green Committee, shall not play with a professional, and he may not willingly receive advice from any one but his caddie, in any way whatever, under penalty of disqualification.

A forecaddie may be employed.

13. Competitors shall not discontinue play on account of bad weather, under penalty of disqualification.

14. Where, in the "Rules of Golf," the penalty for the breach of any rule is the loss of the hole, in stroke competitions the penalty shall be the loss of two strokes, except where otherwise provided for in these Special Rules.

15. Any dispute regarding the play shall be determined by the Rules of Golf Committee.

16. The Rules of Golf, so far as they are not at variance with these Special Rules, shall apply to Stroke Competitions.

Etiquette of Golf.

1. A single player has no standing, and must always give way to a properly constituted match.

2. No player, caddie, or onlooker should move or talk during a stroke.

3. No player should play from the tee until the party in front have played their second strokes, and are out of range, nor play up to the putting-green till the party in front have holed out and moved away.

4. The player who has the honour should be allowed to play before his opponent tees his ball.

5. Players who have holed out should not try their putts over again when other players are following them.

6. Players looking for a lost ball must allow other matches coming up to pass them.

7. On request being made, a three ball match must allow a single, threesome, or foursome to pass. Any match playing a whole round may claim the right to pass a match playing a shorter round.

8. If a match fail to keep its place on the green, and lose in distance more than one clear hole on those in front, it may be passed, on request being made.

9. Turf cut or displaced by a stroke should be at once replaced.

10. A player should carefully fill up all holes made by himself in a bunker.

11. It is the duty of an umpire or referee to take cognisance of any breach of rule that he may observe, whether he be appealed to on the point or not.

HOCKEY.

The growing popularity of Hockey has caused the rules of the game to be considerably revised and amplified. In a few cases the wording has been altered simply to express the rule more plainly. The ground now may not be more than 60 nor less than 50 yards wide, the length having been unaltered. The rules which have been considerably altered are now given in their new form.

Rule 10. In all cases of a bully and penalty bully, the two players who are bullying shall stand facing the side lines. Every other player shall be between the ball and his own goal line, except in the case of a "penalty bully."

Rule 11. A goal is scored when the ball has passed entirely over the line between the goal posts under the bar, the ball having whilst within the striking circle been hit by or glanced off the stick of a player on the attacking side.

Rule 12. When a player hits the ball, any other player of the same side who is nearer his opponent's goal line at the moment when the ball is hit is off side, unless there be at least three of his opponents nearer their own goal line, and he may not touch the ball himself, nor approach, nor remain within five yards of it, nor in any way interfere with any other player until the ball has been touched, or hit by one of the other side.

Rule 13. The ball may be caught (but must at once be dropped on the ground) or stopped with any part of the body; but it must not be picked up, carried, kicked, knocked on or back, except with the stick. There shall be no play with the back of the stick, and no charging, kicking, collaring, shinning, or tripping shall be allowed. Fencing or hooking sticks is allowable only when one of the players is within striking distance of the ball. A player may hook the stick, but not the person of his opponent. A player shall not run in between his opponent and the ball so as to obstruct him, nor cross him from the left so as to foul him. In the event of a player crossing from the left and touching the ball before touching his opponent, it shall not be considered a foul. The goal keeper, who shall be named by his captain before the commencement of the game, shall, however, be allowed to kick the ball except in the case of a penalty bully, so long as it is within the striking circle.

Rule 16 has been slightly altered. The last sentence in the old rule now reads, "For any breach of Rules 12 and 15, can only claim a bully." But the following important addition has been made.

"For any breach of Rule 17 by the defending side, the attacking side may claim a penalty bully on the original spot, or where the breach occurred, such penalty bully to be taken by the same players, and, for any breach by the attacking side, the defending side shall, on appeal, be allowed a free hit. No claim for such a breach of rules by the defaulting side to be allowed.

Rule 17 disappears, and a new one takes its number, and reads:—

"For any breach of Rules 13 and 14 (except so far as Rule 14 applies to "sticks," for which a "bully" only to be allowed) committed by the defending side inside the striking circle, the attacking side may claim a 'penalty bully,' such 'penalty bully' (from which a goal may be scored direct) to be between the offender and one player selected by the other side, and to take place at the spot where the breach occurrs." At the time of the "penalty bully" both the defending and attacking sides to be outside the striking circle, and the ball shall not be in play for either side until driven outside the striking circle, when all the players shall be on side. The "penalty bully" to be in the discretion of the referee, if one, and if none, of the umpire in whose half the breach occurs, who shall have power to award a bully only.

Rule 18 has been removed and is now Rule 20; Rule 19 also is renumbered and has become the present Rule 21. The present Rule 18 is an adaptation of the old 17, and reads:—

When the ball passes over the "side line," it shall be rolled out along the ground from where it crossed the line by one of the opposite side to that of the player who last touched it in any direction except forward. No other player shall stand within 5yds. of the player rolling in the ball. The ball may be rolled out at once. The player who rolls it out must stand with both feet behind the side line, and must not touch the ball again until it has touched or been hit by another player.

Rule 19 is an altogether new Rule and reads:—

"When a breach of Rules 9, 10, or 18 occurs, the referee, or in his absence, an umpire, shall sound his whistle, without waiting for an appeal to be made, and direct that the bully or roll in from touch take place again."

Rule 20 is the old Rule 18 with the addition of "Provided that no goal can be scored from such free hit by the attacking side until the ball has been stopped dead by one of the attacking side, or has previously touched the person or stick of one of the defending side." "Stopped dead" has been ruled to mean "stopped dead on the ground."

Rule 21 is the old Rule 19 with the addition of "Where there are two umpires, but no referee, each umpire to take half the field and to give decisions in his half only, but to take the whole of one side line, the field to be divided across by a line, drawn at right angles to the side lines, through the centre of the ground. The two umpires shall not cross over at half time."

Two new rules have been added, Nos. 22 and 23.

Rule 22. On an appeal for rough play the umpire shall have a discretionary power to warn the offending player, and if the offence be repeated to suspend him from further participation in the game.

Rule 23. When a player (in the opinion of the referee, or, in his absence, of an umpire), is temporarily incapacitated, the umpire (if no referee) shall suspend the game immediately. When the game is resumed the ball shall be bullied off on the spot where, in the opinion of the umpire (if no referee) the ball was when the player was hurt.

LAWS OF LAWN-TENNIS.

The Single-handed Game.

Law 23.—The wording and scope of this law has been altered considerably, and now reads:—The players shall change sides at the end of the first, third, and every subsequent alternate game of each set, and at the end of each set, unless the number of games in such set be even. It shall, however, be open to the players by mutual consent and notification to the umpire before the opening of the second game of the match to change sides instead at the end of every set, until the odd and concluding set, in which they shall change sides at the end of the first, third, and every subsequent alternate game of such set.

PIGEON SHOOTING.

Rules of the National Gun Club.

Rules in Shooting.

1. A miss-fire with first barrel is no shot under any circumstances. If the shooter miss fire with the second barrel he shall have another shot, but with the ordinary charge of powder, and no shot in the first barrel.

2. If the gun be locked, or not cocked, or not loaded, and the bird flies away, it is a "lost bird"; if the stock or cock should break in the act of firing, it is "no bird."

3. If the trap is pulled without notice from the shooter, he has the option to take the bird or not.

4. The puller shall not pull the trap until the trapper and the dog are back in their places, even should the shooter call "pull."

5. If, on the trap being pulled, the bird does not rise, the shooter to take it or not at his option; but if not, he must declare it by saying "no bird," before it is on the wing. If, however, the bird rises and settles before the shooter fires, it shall be at his option to re use it or not.

6. If more than one bird be liberated, the shooter has the option of calling "no bird."

7. In shooting at a bird, should both barrels go off at once it shall score the same as if they had been let off "separately."

8. A bird to be scored good must be gathered by the dog or man without the aid of a ladder or any other instrument, and all birds not gathered in the ground, or gathered inside the pavilion enclosure, having flown over the railings, to be scored lost

9. If a bird which has been shot perches or settles on the top of

the fence, or on any of the buildings in the ground higher than the fence, it is to be scored a "lost bird."

10. If a bird once out of the ground return and fall dead within the boundary, it must be scored a "lost bird."

11. If the first barrel be fired whilst the bird is on the ground, should the bird be killed by either barrel it is "no bird"; if missed, it is lost. It may be shot on the ground with the second barrel if it has been fired at with the first barrel while on the wing.

12. The shooter is bound at once to gather his bird, or depute some person so to do when called upon; but in so doing he must not be assisted by any other person or use any description of implement. Should the shooter be in any way baffled by his opponent, or by any other person or dog, he can claim another bird with the sanction of the referee.

13. The shooter having once left the mark after shooting at the bird, cannot shoot at it again under any circumstances.

14. In matches or in sweepstakes any shooter found to have in his gun any more shot or powder than is allowed, to be at once disqualified.

15. Any shooter is compelled to unload his gun on being challenged; but if the charge is found not to exceed the allowance, the challenger shall pay £1 to the shooter; which must be paid before he (the challenger) shoots again.

16. Officers of the army and navy on full pay, provided they are *bonâ fide* guests of a member for the day, are allowed to shoot in any sweepstakes to which the club does not add prize or money. Members accredited from recognised foreign clubs shall only be allowed to shoot for four weeks during the season, after which they must be proposed and seconded as candidates if they desire to shoot.

17. Breech-loaders not to be loaded until the shooter is at the mark, and the trapper has returned to his place. On leaving the mark, should a cartridge not have been discharged, it is to be removed before the shooter turns his face from the traps.

18. No wire cartridges allowed; nor is any bone dust or other substance to be mixed with the shot.

19. Should any shooter shoot at a distance nearer than his proper distance, the bird, if killed, is "no bird," if missed, a "lost bird"; but should he, by direction of the referee or scorer, shoot at any wrong distance, the bird, if missed, shall be "no bird," and the shooter shall be allowed another, which, if killed, shall be scored.

20. $1\frac{1}{4}$ oz. of shot and 4 drachms of black powder, or its equivalent in any other description of gunpowder, is the maximum charge.

21. In shooting for the principal advertised events members can enter before the commencement of the third round, unless it shall be within the knowledge of the referee that any member proposing to enter has been on the ground during the first round, in which case he shall not be permitted to shoot after the commencement of the second round; for all other sweepstakes entries must be made before the commencement of the second round.

22. The sweepstakes preceding the chief event of the day, shall be divided in equal proportions by those shooters who may be in at the end of the round at or after three o'clock, as the referee may direct.

23. The baskets containing the birds for the whole day's shooting shall be numbered by paint at the back. The baskets, in the order they are to be brought out and trapped, shall be drawn for by the referee, and the baskets so marked shall be used in the order of rotation in which they are drawn.

Official Rules of The Inanimate Bird Shooting Association.

These rules have been completely revised and altered, chiefly however in the direction of re-arrangement. The corresponding numbers of the unaltered rules will first be given, then the absolutely new rules, and lastly those which have been altered as well as renumbered.

New Rule	3	corresponds to		6,	old rules.
,,	5	,,	,,	8	,,
,,	6	,,	,,	9	,,
,,	7	,,	,,	10	,,
,,	9	,,	,,	11	,,
,,	13	,,	,,	15	,,
,,	14	,,	,,	16	,,
,,	15	,,	,,	28	,,
,,	16	,,	,,	29	,,
,,	17	,,	,,	30	,,
,,	20	,,	,,	34	,,
,,	21	,,	,,	38	,,
,,	22	,,	,,	39	,,
,,	23	,,	,,	40	,,
,,	25	,,	,,	42	,,
,,	27	,,	,,	44	,,
,,	28	,,	,,	19	,,
,,	29	,,	,,	20	,,
,,	30	,,	,,	21	,,
,,	33	,,	,,	24	,,
,,	34	,,	,,	25	,,
,,	35	,,	,,	26	,,
,,	36	,,	,,	27	,,

The New Rules are:—

I. *Arrangement of Firing Marks.*—There shall be five firing marks, five yards apart, and shooters should stand at not less than 18 yards from the traps. The marks shall be numbered 1, 2, 3, 4, and 5, No. 1 being on the extreme left and No. 5 on the extreme right.

II. *Gun and Ammunition.*—No gun of a larger calibre than 12 gauge shall be used, and the charge of shot shall not exceed $1\frac{1}{8}$ ounce.

X. "*No-Birds" if Extra Ones Accidentally Thrown.*—In cases where a bird or birds are accidentally released so as to be flying in the air at the same time as the bird or birds at which the shooter is required to fire, it shall be counted a "no-bird."

XXVI. *Scoring double Rises.*—One point shall be given for each bird killed in a double-rise competition, and a shooter shall be entitled to fire both barrels at one bird.

The "Rose" System of Dividing Sweepstakes.

XXXVII. *Number of Divisions.*—The Club shall decide whether the shooters making the two top scores, or the three top scores (or any other suitable combination), shall participate in the division of the pool.

XXXVIII. *Proportions for each Order of Merit.*—Having decided what scores shall entitle the shooters to a share in the pool, the Club shall determine what number of shares shall be allotted to each order of merit, such as three shares for each shooter making the top score, two shares for the second score, and one share for the third score—or six shares, four shares, and one share respectively, as may be decided.

XXXIX. *Scratch and Handicap Events.*—This method of dividing pools shall be equally applicable to scratch and handicap events.

XL. *Method of Calculating Shares.*—In dividing the money the number of shooters making the top score shall be multiplied by the number of shares allotted to those making such score; in the same way the number of shooters making the second score shall be multiplied by the corresponding shares allotted to each, and the shares for the third score shall be similarly worked out. After deducting for birds used, &c., the amount remaining in the pool shall be divided by the total number of shares. The winners shall then be paid at the rate of three such shares to each of the shooters making the top score, and so on among the other shooters, according to the proportions decided upon by the Club.

The rules which have been altered as well as renumbered will have their old numbers in a bracket after the new number.

IV. (7). *Unauthorised Discharge of Gun.*—A shooter who, from any cause whatever, shall discharge his gun otherwise than in accordance with the regulations, shall be excluded from taking part in any further competitions during the day. All firing at passing birds, animals, or other unauthorised objects shall be strictly prohibited.

VIII. (18) *Precautions against Accidents.*—All guns must be kept open at the breech while the traps are being refilled, and until the trappers have returned to their places. Any person infringing this rule shall be fined one shilling. This rule does not apply to cases where there is a trench or other device, enabling the traps to be refilled while shooting is proceeding.

XI. (12). "*No Birds" from fault of Gun, &c.*—If the shooter's gun, being properly loaded and cocked, fails to fire at all from any cause whatever, excepting through the fault of the shooter, the bird shall be counted a no-bird. If the gun misses fire with the first barrel, and the shooter fires the second and "breaks," the shot shall be scored a "kill"; but if he fires the second and misses, it shall be scored a "miss"; and if he does not fire the second it shall be "no-bird." If the gun misses fire with the second barrel, the shooter shall be allowed another bird, using a cartridge primed and loaded with powder, but without a charge of shot, in the first barrel, and a loaded cartridge in the second barrel; and he shall pull the trigger of the first barrel after the trap has been released.

XIII. (13). "*Kills.*"—A bird to be scored a "kill" must have a piece visibly broken from it whilst in the air. The Referee shall be the sole judge as to whether a bird is broken, and any person impugning his decision shall be disqualified from the current competition. No bird shall under any circumstances be retrieved for examination.

XVIII. (32). *Unknown Angles.*—When the traps are set to throw at unknown angles, and there are two or more traps behind each screen, the puller should be informed by some suitable means which trap behind each screen he is to pull, so that the shooters shall be kept in ignorance of the angle at which his bird will be thrown.

XIX. (33). *Position of Shooter.*—The shooter shall stand at the centre mark and fire at five birds before leaving the line.

XXIV. (41).

XXXI. (22). *Penalty Points.*—A shooter shall be penalised one point for each and every prize or sweepstakes over the subscribed or declared value of 20s. he may win during the current month; this penalty, and any additional ones subsequently incurred, to continue in force until a new handicap is calculated. In the event of a division, the shooters dividing must arrange and declare which of them shall be penalised. This system of penalties shall equally apply to the winners of scratch events, but it shall not apply to the winning holdership of trophies, nor to the winner of rounds in the I.B.S.A. medal competitions.

XXXII. (23). *Limited Variation of Points.*—The points awarded to a shooter at the beginning of each month *shall not be varied by more than one point from the points he possessed*, as a result of averages and penalties, *at the end of the previous month.* This rule shall not apply to new members, whose points shall be allotted at the end of their first month, as laid down in Rule XXXI., provided in all cases that such handicap, as based on his scores, shall not be allotted until the new member has fired at not less than 100 birds since joining the Club.

POLO.

Rules and Regulations.

Rule 9.—This rule now reads:—"The bell shall be rung to signify to the players that the ten minutes has expired, and it shall be rung again when the ball next goes out of play, to show the time for changing ponies."

Rule 14.—From the second sentence this rule has been altogether recast and some additions been made It reads now beginning with the third sentence :—"If, however, the ball be hit behind the back line by one of the players whose line it is, they shall hit it off from behind the goal line between the posts, and all the defending side shall until the ball is hit off, remain behind their back line, and between two lines which shall be drawn at right angles to the goal line produced, from points ten yards distant from the centre of the goal on either side, the attacking side being free to place themselves where they choose, but not within twenty-five yards of the centre of the goal posts. The penalty shall not be exacted should the ball glance off a player or pony."

Rule 17.—After "behind," add "and his stick is neither over nor under his adversary's pony."

Rule 22.—Section (*b*); after "goal line," add "between the posts, none of the attacking side to be within twenty-five yards of the centre of the goal."

Rule 26.—For "the umpire must stop" read "the umpire shall, at his discretion, stop." The following N.B. is also added: "It is desirable that the game shall be stopped and the ball changed when the damaged ball is in such a position that neither side is favoured thereby."

Rule 32 is altogether new. It reads, "If two players are riding from opposite directions to hit the ball, one of these being a left-handed player, the latter must give way."

Rules 33 and 34 are the old 32 and 33 respectively.

Conditions for Cup Tournaments.

Champion Cup Conditions.

Rule 3 consists of two paragraphs, the latter of which is the old Rule 4.

Rule 4 deals with the question of substitutes as the old Rule 4 did, but sweeping alterations have been made. The rule now reads :—"In the contest for the Champion Cup of 1900, in case one or more of the players should be incapacitated from playing, one or more substitutes, and their ponies, may be brought in. This does not apply to Regiments who may play any ponies *bonâ fide* the property of Officers in that Regiment."

Rules 5 and 6 are the old 6 and 7 respectively.

Rules of Measurement.

Rule 3.—Read after "and shall pay" "to the Manager at Hurlingham and to the Official Measurer at other places, a fee of 10s. . . . ."

Rule 14.—In the second sentence read "one member" for "two members."

PUNT RACING RULES.

The only alteration is the addition of a rule numbered VIIA, which reads "When the course is specially marked out with buoys each punt shall keep its own water throughout the race. A punt departing from its own water will do so at the peril of disqualification if touched while out of it."

Amateur Championship.

1898 W. C. Romaine. 1899 N. M Cohen.
1900—C. R. Mullings.

Professional Championship.

1898 W. Haines. 1899 G. Haines.
1900 G. Haines.

RULES OF RACING.

Where a rule is given without any remark that rule takes the place completely of the rule bearing the same number in the Encyclopædia.

Racing Season.

Rule 4.—No race shall be run earlier than in the week which includes the 25th of March (unless that be the one next before Easter Sunday, in which case races may be run in the week preceding), nor later than in the week which includes the 22nd of November, but in the interval between the last and first-named weeks the Jockey Club will sanction weight-for-age races for four years old and upwards, over a distance of two miles and upwards, with a minimum weight of 9 st. 7 lb., and of not less value than £200, such races not to be selling races, and to be under the authority of the National Hunt Committee.

Rule 19.—Add : "No two offices, except those of Clerk of the Course and Stakeholder, shall be held by one person unless by special permission."

Rule 23.—Add: "*The Clerk of the Course shall see that at all Meetings where a charge is made for the admission of the public to the Paddock, all horses running at the Meeting shall be brought into the Paddock, and the attendants be provided with badges bearing numbers corresponding with those on the card. In the case of any horse not being brought into the Paddock, or a badge not being exhibited, the trainer shall be reported to the Stewards, unless special permission to saddle elsewhere has been obtained from the Stewards, and when such permission is given, a fee of 1 sov. must be paid.*"

Rule 26.—Add: "except that, by express permission of the Stewards, a weight may be affixed to a horse duly entered whose name or weight has been omitted from the handicap."

Rule 27.—No handicapper shall handicap at any other meeting held during the same week, except by express permission of the Stewards of the Jockey Club. He must attend the meeting either personally or by licensed deputy. The name of the handicapper attending the meeting shall appear in the Calendar containing the report.

The Starter.

Rule 35.—The starter shall give all orders necessary for securing a fair start. The horses must be started, as far as possible, in a line, but they may be started at such reasonable distance behind the starting post as the starter thinks necessary.

Rule 45.—Add : "and of this half not less than a moiety shall be for races of a mile and a quarter or upwards ; but where more than one Meeting is held at the same place during the current racing season the apportionment may be calculated over each Meeting, or over all the Meetings ; provided that in the case of Meetings where races are already closed, the Stewards of the Jockey Club shall have power to relax the above Rule as to the apportionment of the money. No two years old shall run in any race with more than 200 sov. added before the 1st of June."

Rule 46.—There shall be no race of less distance than five furlongs.

Rule 47.—The programme of each day shall be subject to the following regulations :—

(i) There shall be two races of a mile or upwards of the minimum aggregate distance of two miles and a half. These races must differ at least one furlong in distance, and they shall fill with five entries. Neither of these races shall be open to two years old ; and one of them shall be neither a handicap nor a race with selling conditions.

(ii) There shall not be more than two races, to which three years old or upwards are admitted, of less than seven furlongs, and of these two races only one may be less than six furlongs.

(iii) Of the races confined to two years old, there shall not be more than two races a day before September 1st, nor more than three a day at any time.

(iv) Matches and private sweepstakes may be sanctioned by the Stewards, independent of the above regulations.

47 (*a*) *Upon all Race-courses having four or more days' racing during the year (except those having only one fixture) there shall be at least one race confined to apprentices.*

Rule 53.—Add : "*In the advertisement of handicaps to close, the weight shall be stated below which no horse shall be handicapped.*"

Rule 56 commences with a new paragraph : "In no selling race shall the lowest selling price be less than 50 sov."

Rule 57.—Sect. (III.) Add after "scale," "but subject to the rules in cases of objection."

Rule 58.—Delete : "but subject to the rules in case of objection."

Rule 67.—Add after "a disqualified person" : "or to run in any race so long as any disqualified person has any interest in the horse's winnings in that race."

Rule 71.—The last sentence now reads : "No declaration of forfeit *affecting yearlings or two years old* shall be fixed to be made between the second Tuesday in October when they are yearlings, and the last Tuesday in March in the following year."

Rule 77.—From the second sentence delete : "before the time of weighing, or the horse shall not be qualified to start"

Rule 83.—Add : "Note.—The omission, under fine of horses from races for which they are not qualified, is now dealt with under Rule 108."

Rule 91.—When a horse is sold with his engagements, or any part of them, the seller cannot strike the horse out of any of such engagements, and, on default of the purchaser, remains liable for the amount of the forfeits in each ; but should the horse, or his owner, appear in the Forfeit List, the seller may, at any time before their names are removed from the list, strike the horse out of any engagement, if he can by this means reduce his liability. *An engagement in a Private Sweepstakes or Match cannot be transferred.*

Rule 92.—Sales, with engagements, by private treaty, must be registered, to entitle either seller or purchaser to avail himself of the conditions of the preceding rule ; but when the horse is sold by public auction or claimed out of a selling race the advertised conditions of either the race or sale are sufficient evidence. If certain engagements only be specified, those only are sold with the horse

Rule 94.—Delete : "and partnerships and leases republished annually as long as they continue," and "at once," and add : "within fourteen days," and "or a second fee will be incurred."

Rule 95.—Delete in Section I. : "under exceptional circumstances . . ." to end of sentence. In Sect. III. add : "annually."

Rule 101.—Add : "Every jockey sending in a charge for expenses at a meeting shall state at the same time what charge has been made to other owners for attending the same meeting."

Rule 118.—Delete : "from the commencement of the racing season."

Rule 123.—All penalties and allowances shall be calculated according to the amount of the value of each race as reported in the Racing Calendar. *And trainers will be required to declare by a time to be fixed the night before running, the weights for their horses in races where there are penalties for winning, or allowances other than selling ; also penalties incurred in handicaps. The trainer of a horse running in any such race where the weight is not so declared, or declared wrongly, shall be reported to the Stewards.*

Rule 126.—Substitute "United Kingdom" for "any country," and add : "but these allowances can only be claimed for horses bred in the United Kingdom."

Rule 140, Section I., now reads : "A horse which crosses another in any part of the race so as to interfere with that or any other horse's chance is liable to disqualification, unless it be proved that he was two clear lengths in front when he crossed."

Rule 145, Section I., now reads : "A dead heat for the first place shall be run off on the same day at a time to be appointed by the stewards, unless the owners agree to divide, *but if any one of the horses running a dead heat be two years old, the dead heat shall not be run off, and the owners shall divide.* The other horses shall be deemed to have been beaten, but they shall be entitled to their places (if any) as if the race had been finally determined the first time."

Rule 159.—In all races, should there be any surplus from entrance or subscription over the advertised value, it shall be paid to the *second, but if the surplus exceed* 50 *sov., two-thirds of the whole surplus shall go to the second, and one-third to the third.* A race may be declared void provided the number of entries required by advertisement be not obtained, but the value of a prize once advertised shall not be reduced.

Rule 180.—There shall also be payable the following maximum fees:—

For every entry, a Clerk's fee of 2*s.* 6*d.*

For weighing, a Clerk's fee of 2*s.* 6*d.*

The following fees are also payable—

Registration Fees:

Rule 181.—(i.) For registration of authority to act generally on behalf of an owner, five shillings.

(ii.) For every registration or change of an assumed name, £30.

(iii.) For every registration of partnership, and on every change thereof, 1 sovereign for each horse.

(iv.) For every annual registration of colours, five shillings.

(v.) For every registration of colours for life, five sovereigns.

(vi.) For registration of foreign and veterinary certificates, five shillings.

(vii.) For registration of an agreement with a jockey, five shillings.

(viii.) *For registration of a horse's name, 2s. 6d.*

(*b*) On fixtures being granted to a meeting, the following fees shall be paid (unless the Stewards of the Jockey Club shall see fit in any case to remit the same):—All meetings having four days consecutively, or six days at any time, 100 sov.: all others, 5 sov. a day.

MEMBERS OF THE JOCKEY CLUB.

To the list in the Encyclopædia add the following:—

Lord Brampton.	Arthur James, Esq.
L. Brassey, Esq.	Hon. Frederick W. Lambton.
Viscount Falmouth.	J. W. Larnach, Esq.
Sir R. Waldie Griffith, Bart.	Lord Wolverton.

And as honorary members, the Stewards of the Turf Club, Ireland.

RIFLE SHOOTING.

The only alteration here is that Sporting Rifles may be of *any* calibre.

ROWING.

RULES FOR REGATTAS.

Rule 9.—After the words "to compete" the rule now reads: "To which list the names of not more than *five* other members for an eight-oar, *three* for a four-oar carrying a coxswain, and two for a non-coxswain four-oar may be added as substitutes. Except in the last-mentioned case, one of such substitutes (if the full number be entered) shall be entered as a coxswain, and shall not be substituted except in that capacity."

Rules 13 *to* 20 correspond respectively to old Rules 14 to 21; old Rule 13 having been dropped, each succeeding rule is moved up one. Several additions have been made to two of the rules, to which attention is drawn in each case.

Rule 18.—To the definitions in old Rule 19 of a maiden oarsman and of a maiden sculler add respectively: "An oarsman who has won a maiden race at a regatta in which the construction of the boats was restricted may then row as a junior in restricted boats until the end of the year in which he wins a junior race, after which he must row as a junior in first-class boats and be subject to Rule 19."

"A sculler who has won a maiden sculling race at a regatta in which the construction of the boats was restricted may then scull as a junior in restricted boats until the end of the year in which he wins a junior race, after which he must scull as a junior in first-class boats and be subject to Rule 19."

Rule 19.—Delete in old Rule 20, after the definitions of a junior oarsman, the sentence commencing "No oarsman," and substitute "Save and except as permitted in Rule 18, no oarsman who has won a race at a regatta in which the construction of the boats was restricted, shall compete as a junior in any such race after the end of the current year."

And add to the definition of a junior sculler, "Save and except as permitted in Rule 18, no sculler who has won a sculling race at a regatta in which the construction of the boats was restricted shall compete as a junior in any such race after the end of the current year."

RESULTS OF INTER-UNIVERSITY BOAT RACE.

Year.	*Place of Rowing.*	*Winner.*	*M.*	*S.*	*Won by.*
1899.	Putney to Mortlake.	Cambridge.	21	4	3¼ lengths.
1900.	Putney to Mortlake.	Cambridge.	18	47	20 ,,

TESTS OF THE NATIONAL SKATING ASSOCIATION OF GREAT BRITAIN.

In the rules for the figure skating tests the word "turn" has been employed throughout instead of 3 to denote an "ordinary or 3 turn."

SECOND CLASS ICE FIGURE-SKATING TESTS.

Insert between paragraphs 1 and 2, "No candidate who has failed to pass a second class test is allowed to compete again within a week, except with the written permission of the judges on the occasion of the former failure.

Section (*e*) has lost its two last paragraphs, which together with a new condition make section (*f*).

Section (*f*). The judges shall call three "unseen" figures of quite simple character, in order to test the candidate's knowledge of calls and power of placing figures upon the ice (Add the last two paragraphs of old section (*e*).

FIRST CLASS ICE FIGURE-SKATING TEST.

Add to the conditions, "No candidate who has failed to pass a first-class test is allowed to compete again within a fortnight, except with the written permission of the judges on the occasion of the former failure."

Section A.

From the third, seventh and eighth sentences delete "in Part I."

Part II.

This part is entirely altered and simply reads:—"In addition to the above, the Judges shall call not more than five or less than three 'unseen' figures of moderately simple character in order to test the candidate's knowledge of calls and power of placing figures upon the ice."

Section B.

Group 15. Add "The curves before and after the turn must be 9 ft. long at least."

In the note "In groups 20–24," add, "A candidate shall not score for a figure in groups 21 or 22 if he has obtained marks for the corresponding figure in groups 15 or 18."

SPECIAL ICE FIGURE-SKATING TEST.

Part I.

Section A.

Division 6 has been dropped entirely and divisions 7 and 8 renumbered 6 and 7 respectively.

Section B.

The last sentence in the general condition has been changed from "each figure is to be skated on both feet" to "every movement must be skated on the right as well as on the left foot."

Part II.

Add after the last sentence of the general conditions, "subject to the above rules, latitude will be allowed as to the exact shape of the figures to be skated."

AMATEUR SWIMMING ASSOCIATION.

INTERNATIONAL RULES FOR WATER POLO.

Rule II.—The last sentence now reads "The goal-posts and goal-nets to be furnished by the home team." Delete the "Note."

Rule III.—Add:—"Both goal-keepers shall wear red caps."

Rule IV.—The last sentence now reads: "In baths the half-way line and also the four yards penalty lines shall be marked on both sides."

Rule VIII.—After the first sentence the rule runs, "He shall decide upon all goals, whether signified or not. The referee's decision is final." *Note.*—A referee may alter his decision provided such alteration be notified before the ball is again in play. A referee has power to stop play at any period of the game if in his opinion the behaviour of the players or spectators or other exceptional circumstances prevents the match from coming to a proper conclusion.

Rule XII.—Handled is here and in Rules XV. and XVIII. defined as "played with the hand below the wrist."

Rule XIV.—Section (*d*) now reads: "To interfere with an opponent or impede him in any way, unless he is holding the ball." Section (*e*). "To retain possession of the ball when ducked."

New sections (*f*), (*g*), (*h*), and (*i*) correspond respectively to old sections (*e*), (*f*), (*g*), and (*h*) and a fresh foul is introduced in section (*j*): "For the goal-keeper to go more than four yards from his own goal-line."

Rule 16 now reads:—"If in the opinion of the referee a player commits an ordinary foul wilfully, the referee shall at once order him out of the water until a goal has been scored. It shall be considered a wilful foul . . . . (to the end)."

Rule 17.—A new rule. "A player wilfully fouled when within four yards of his opponents' goal-line shall be awarded a penalty throw, and the player who commits the offence must be ordered out of the water until a goal has been scored. The penalty throw shall be taken four yards from any point on the goal-line. In the case of a penalty throw it shall not be necessary for the ball to be handled by any other player before a goal can be scored."

Rule 18 is old Rule 17 with the addition of:—"In the event of one or more players from each team committing a foul so nearly at the same moment as to make it impossible for the referee to distinguish who offended first, he shall have the ball out of the water and throw it in as nearly as possible at the place where the foul occurred, in such a manner that one member of each team may have equal chance of playing the ball. In such cases the ball must be allowed to touch the water before it is handled and must be handled by more than one player before a goal can be scored."

Rule 19 is old Rule 18 with the addition after the first sentence of "The goal-keeper must wear a red cap. He must keep within four yards of his own goal or concede a free throw from the four yard line to his nearest opponent," and, after the second sentence, to be allowed on arrival for differences in rating shall be according of "Except when injury or illness compels him to leave the water (when Rule 23 shall apply) the goal-keeper can only be changed at half-time."

Rule 20.—Old 19 with the addition after "to his opponents" of "and such free corner throw shall be taken by the player on the opposing side nearest the point where the ball leaves the field of play."

Rule 21.—Old 20 with the addition of a Note:—"The player nearest the point where the ball leaves the field of play must take the throw."

Rule 22.—Old 21 with the addition of "The time-keeper may notify half-time and time by whistle."

Rule 23.—Old 22.

Hints for the Guidance of Referees.

A. For the last sentence read, "See that the half-way line and the penalty line ...."

N.B. In International contests goal-nets are compulsory. They simplify the work of the Referee and should be used in all matches where practicable.

B. (*Rule* 3). For "distinctive coloured caps" read "Dark blue and white caps respectively." Add "The goal-keeper must always wear a red cap."

H.—In the first sentence of second paragraph now read, "Clauses D and F deal with the fouls most often committed." In the second sentence after "interfered with" add "or impeded in any way;" and to this paragraph add "swimming over or by the side of an opponent in such a manner as to prevent free use of the legs, or interfering with the arms in any way before the opponent is actually holding the ball, constitutes a foul."

I. (*Rule* 16). This rule has been introduced to check the fouling of an opponent when he has a reasonable certainty of scoring. Great power is left in the hands of the Referee, and it rests with him to stamp out at once the rough methods of tackling that are now practised. The penalty must in every case be inflicted if the attacking player is wilfully ducked or interfered with when within four yards of goal. Referees will note that the fact of allowing the penalty necessitates ordering the offender out of the water. The rule dealing with wilful has been altered to give the Referee the power to order a man out of the water at once for committing any ordinary foul wilfully.

Last paragraph is unaltered.

M. (*Rule* 1*a*).—After the first sentence add, "The goalkeeper may be treated as any other player when four or more yards from his own goal."

A memorandum headed "stopping a match" lays down that "By a ruling of the A.S.A. Committee on April 29, 1899, a Referee has power to stop play at any period of the game if in his opinion the behaviour of the players or spectators, or other exceptional circumstances prevents the match from coming to a proper conclusion."

Amateur Swimming Association

Amateur Records

Distance.	Time.	Made by	Club.	Date.	Venue.
YDS.	M. S.				
100	$60\frac{1}{5}$	J. H. Derbyshire.	Manchester Osborne.	Nov. 23, '98	Manchester.
150	1 $38\frac{4}{5}$	,,	,,	June 8, '99	Burslem.
220	2 $34\frac{4}{5}$	Lane and Derbyshire.	East Sydney. Manchester Osborne.	Sept. 18, 1900	Aston.
300	3 $47\frac{4}{5}$	F. C. V. Lane.	East Sydney.	Sept. 11, '99	Blackpool.
500	6 $42\frac{2}{5}$	J. A. Jarvis.	Leicester.	October 4, '99	Sunderland.
880	12 29	,,	,,	August 8, '99	Leicester.
1,000	14 10	,,	,,	July 15, '99	Walsall.
1 mile	25 $13\frac{2}{5}$	,,	,,	August 8, '99	Leicester.

Water Polo—Internationals.

England *v.* Scotland.

England, 7; Scotland, 3; Drawn, 0.

1898—Liverpool. E, 8–3 | 1899—Aberdeen. E, 5–1

England *v.* Ireland.

England, 3; Ireland, 0; Drawn, 0.

1898—Dublin. E, 7–0. | 1899—Westminster. E, 12–0

1900—Belfast

Scotland *v.* Wales.

Scotland, 2; Wales, 1; Drawn, 1.

1898—Aberdeen. 0–0 | 1899—Penarth. W, 6–4

1900—Edinburgh. S, 1–0

Scotland *v.* Ireland.

Scotland, 2; Ireland, 0; Drawn, 1.

1898—Glasgow. S, 9–3 | 1899—Belfast. S, 4–1

Ireland *v.* Wales.

Ireland, 0; Wales, 3; Drawn, 1.

1896—Westminster. W, 3–0 | 1897—Swansea. W, 3–2

1898—Belfast. 1–1 | 1899—Swansea. W, 6–3

England *v.* Wales.

England, ; Wales, ; Drawn, .

1898—Newport. E, 4–0 | 1899—Warrington, E, 8–0

1900—Penarth E, 7–3

UNIVERSITY CONTESTS

Results of Cricket Matches.

1899. Drawn.
1900. Drawn.

Results of Football Matches.

Rugby.

1898–1899. Cambridge, 1 goal, 2 tries to nil.
1899–1900. Cambridge, 2 goals, 4 tries to nil.

Association.

1898–1899. Cambridge, 3 to 1
1899–1900. Oxford, 2–0

Oxford and Cambridge Sports.

100 *Yards.*

		Won by	Official time.
1899.	C. R. Thomas (Ox.)	$1\frac{1}{2}$ yards.	$10\frac{2}{5}$
1900.	C. R. Thomas (Ox.) / A. M. Hollins (Ox.)	Dead Heat.	$10\frac{4}{5}$

Quarter Mile Flat.

1899.	A. M. Hollins (Ox.)	6 yards.	$51\frac{4}{5}$
1900.	A. M. Hollins (Ox.)	8 ,,	$50\frac{3}{5}$

Half Mile Flat.

*1899.	H. E. Graham	7 yards.	1 m. $59\frac{2}{5}$ sec
1900.	H. E. Graham	6 ,,	1 m. $58\frac{2}{5}$ sec.

* First year of race.

One Mile Flat.

1899.	A. Hunter (Cam.)	30 yards.	4 m. 35 sec.
1900.	F. C. Cockshott (Cam.)	16 ,,	4 m. $28\frac{2}{5}$ sec.

Three Miles Flat.

1899.	H. W. Workman (Cam.)	60 yards.	15 m. $45\frac{2}{5}$ sec.
1900.	H. W. Workman (Cam.)	100 ,,	15 m. $1\frac{2}{5}$ sec.

120 *Yards Hurdle Race.*

1899.	W. G. Paget-Tomlinson (Cam.)	2 yards.	16 sec.
1900.	W. G. Paget-Tomlinson (Cam.)	5 ,,	$16\frac{1}{5}$ sec.

Long Jump.

		Distance.
1899.	G. C. Vassall (Ox.)	23 ft. 3 in.
1900.	G. W. F. Kelly (Ox.)	21 ft. $5\frac{1}{8}$ in.

High Jump.

1899.	H. S. Adair (Ox.)	5 ft. $8\frac{1}{4}$ in.
1900.	E. B. Henderson (Ox.)	5 ft. $9\frac{1}{4}$ in.

Throwing the Hammer.

1899.	J. D. Greenshields (Ox.)	110 ft. 1 in.
1900.	J. D. Greenshields (Ox.)	115 ft. 2 in.

Putting the Weight.

1899.	G. W. Clark (Cam.)	34 ft.
1900.	E. R. May (Ox.)	36 ft. 8 in.

YACHTING.

Sailing Rules, 1900.

The Rules since 1898 have been so completely rearranged and recast that it has been absolutely impossible to indicate with any reasonable regard for simplicity and space the correspondence between the old and new rules. The course adopted therefore has been to print those new rules which involve any important alteration in the practical working of the old rules. The rating rules have been untouched, as the Y.R.A. are about to alter them again within the next four months.

1. *General Authority of Sailing Committee.*—All races, and yachts sailing therein, shall be under the direction of the Flag Officers, Sailing Committee, or Officers of the day of the Club under whose auspices the races are being sailed, hereinafter referred to, together or separately, as the Sailing Committee. All matters shall be subject to their approval and control; and all doubts, questions, and disputes which may arise shall be subject to their decision. Their decisions shall be based upon these rules so far as they will apply, but as no rules can be devised capable of meeting every incident and accident of sailing, the Sailing Committee should keep in view the ordinary customs of the sea, and discourage all attempts to win a race by other means than fair sailing and superior speed and skill.

2. *Recognised Yacht Clubs.*—The term, a recognised Yacht Club, shall include every British Yacht Club holding an Admiralty Warrant; and also such other Yacht and Sailing Clubs giving races under these rules as may be accepted as recognised yacht clubs by the Council.

The Council shall have the power of cancelling recognition of any Club should they deem it expedient to do so.

3. *Ownership of Yachts.*—Every yacht entered for a race must be the *bonâ fide* property of the person or persons in whose name or names she is entered, who must be a member or members of a recognised yacht club.

A yacht let on hire may be raced provided—

(*a*) That she is let for a period in excess of one month;

(*b*) That she is entered in the name of the owner, who is to be responsible in all contingencies, for all entries, racing expenses and damages;

(*c*) That the crew are to be considered the servants of the owner;

(*d*) That the hirer (who must be a member of a recognised yacht club) shall, as representative of the owner, comply with all the rules and regulations of the Y.R.A.

5. *Time Allowance.*—In all races under Y.R.A. rating the time

to the annexed scales, in proportion to the length of the course as notified on the programme or instructions.

6. *Entries.*—Entries shall be made with the secretary of the club in the following form at least forty-eight hours previous to noon of the day appointed for starting each race. In case of a Sunday intervening, twenty-four hours shall be added. Entries may be made by telegram, and it shall be deemed sufficient that the same shall have been despatched before noon of the day on which the entries close, subject to the provision as to Sundays, but such entries by telegram must be confirmed in the proper form, in course of post :

FORM OF ENTRY.

To be Signed by the Owner or his Representative.

Please enter the Yacht....................,owner.. ...., for the.............Race at......................, on the..........................
Her distinguishing flag is................ ....; her rig is .... ; and her Y.R.A. rating is...................*

And I agree to be bound by the Racing Rules of the Y.R.A.

Signed this........... .....day of.....................

* *The rating may be omitted for races not under Y.R.A. rating.*

In case the rating has from any reason been incorrectly stated in the Form of Entry, if the fact is notified to the Sailing Committee in writing before the entries close, the Sailing Committee shall regard only the yacht's correct rating at the time of starting ; but otherwise the yacht cannot sail at a lower rating than that entered.

9.—*Postponement of Races.* The Sailing Committee shall have power to postpone any Race, should unfavourable weather render such a course desirable. Letter N of the commercial code hoisted over the flag denoting the race shall be the signal that a race has been postponed.

No new entry shall be received under any circumstances whatever for a postponed Race.

12.—*Shortening Course.* The Sailing Committee may shorten the course during a Race, and the flag denoting the Race, hoisted under the White Peter, or in the case of fog or darkness two guns fired, shall be the signal that the Race is to finish with the round about to be completed, or at such mark as the Sailing Committee may appoint, and the time allowance shall be reduced in proportion.

17.—*Fittings and Ballast.* All Yachts exceeding 36 ft. rating must be fitted below deck with the ordinary fittings of a Yacht, including the following :—

In Yachts not Exceeding 42 ft. Rating.

Two complete transverse bulkheads of wood, of average thickness at least $\frac{5}{8}$ inch, the spaces between to be fitted to form a forecastle and also one or more cabins.

The cabin or cabins shall contain not less than two sofas upholstered, and two sideboards or sideboard lockers and a table.

Water-tanks of not less than 15 gallons' capacity.

In Yachts Exceeding 42 ft. and not Exceeding 52 ft. Rating.

Three complete transverse bulkheads of wood of average thickness at least $\frac{3}{4}$ inch, the spaces between to be fitted to form a forecastle and also one or more cabins.

The cabin or cabins shall contain not less than two sofas upholstered, or two standing cabin bunks fitted complete, two sideboards or sideboard lockers, one swing table, one fixed lavatory

Water-tanks of not less than 20 gallons' capacity.

One fixed under-water w.c. fitted complete with all pipes and connections.

In Yachts Exceeding 52 ft. and not Exceeding 65 ft. Rating.

Four bulkheads as described above, the spaces between to be fitted to form a forecastle, saloon and one or more other cabins.

The saloon to contain not less than two sofas upholstered, one swing table, two sideboards or sideboard lockers.

The cabins to contain not less than three standing cabin bunks fixed complete and two fixed lavatories.

Water-tanks of not less than 40 gallons' capacity.

Two w.c's as described above.

In Yachts Exceeding 65 ft. Rating.

Four bulkheads as described above, the spaces between as described for 65 ft. rating.

Saloon and cabins as described for 65 ft. rating, but cabins to contain not less than four standing cabin bunks.

Water-tanks of not less than 60 gallons' capacity.

Two w.c's as described above.

All Yachts exceeding 42 ft. rating shall have a fixed companion or ladder, and the forecastle furniture shall comprise cots or hammocks equal to the number of crew, and the usual lockers, seats, cooking apparatus, &c.

The following shall apply to all Yachts starting in a Race :—

During a Race, the platforms shall be kept down and bulkheads standing (and all the other fittings above specified retained on board except cots, cushions and bedding) ; no water may be started from or taken into the tanks ; no more than the usual anchors and chains may be carried ; (no bags of shot may be on board) ; all ballast must be properly stowed under platforms or in lockers ; and no ballast or other dead weights may be used as shifting ballast or for altering the trim of a Yacht.

No ballast shall be shipped, unshipped, or shifted, after 9 p.m. of the day previous to that on which the Race is sailed.

18.—*Boats and Lifebuoys.* Every Yacht exceeding a rating of 50 ft. and under a rating of 80 ft., shall carry a boat on deck not less than ten feet in length and four feet three inches beam, and every Yacht rated at 80 ft. and over, one of not less than twelve feet in length and four feet three inches beam, ready for immediate use, with oars lashed therein.

Every Yacht shall carry at least one lifebuoy on deck ready for use.

20. *Cruising Trim.*—When Yachts are ordered to sail in cruising trim, the following Rules are to be strictly observed throughout the Race :

1. No doors, tables, cabin skylights, or other cabin or deck fittings (davits excepted) shall be removed from their places before or during the Race.
2. No sails or other gear shall be put into the main cabin in Yachts exceeding a rating of 73 ft.
3. Anchors and chains suitable to the size of the Yacht shall be carried, and Yachts over 42 ft. shall carry one at least on deck, with chain rove and shackled on ready for use.
4. Every Yacht exceeding a rating of 50 ft., and under a rating of 80 ft., shall carry a boat on deck not less than ten feet in length and four feet three inches beam ; a Yacht rated at 80 ft. and over, her usual cutter and dinghy.
5. No extra paid hands, except a pilot, beyond the regular crew of the Yacht, shall be allowed.

27. *The Start.*—Fifteen minutes before the time of starting, one of the following Flags of the Commercial Code shall be hoisted as a preparatory Flag for the Yachts of each successive Race to approach the starting line, viz. :—

B of Commercial Code for the Yachts of the 1st Race.
C ——— ——————————— 2nd ,,
D ——— ——————————— 3rd ,,
F ——— ——————————— 4th ,,

and so on.

Five minutes before the start the preparatory Flag shall be lowered, a Blue Peter hoisted, and a gun fired ; after which, the Yachts in the Race shall be amenable to the Rules At the expiration of five minutes *exactly* the Blue Peter shall be hauled down and a second gun fired as a signal to start. Should a gun miss fire, the Blue Peter shall be the signal.

If any Yacht, or any part of her hull, spars, or other equipment be on or across the starting line when the signal to start is made, her recall number shall be displayed as soon as possible, and a suitable sound signal also given to call the attention of the competitors to the fact that a recall number is being displayed. The Yacht recalled must return and recross the line to the satisfaction of the Committee, and the number must be kept displayed until she has done so : and a Yacht so returning, or one working into position from the wrong side of the line after the signal to start has been made, must keep clear of all competing Yachts.

The numbers should be in white on a black ground, and the figures not less than 2ft. 6in. in height.

33. *Fouling or improperly rounding Marks.*—A Yacht must go fairly round the course, rounding the series of marks as specified in the instructions ; and, in order to round each mark, the Yacht's track from the preceding to the following mark must enclose it on the required side. A Yacht which, in rounding a mark, fouls it, or causes the mark vessel to shift her position to avoid a foul, shall be disqualified, unless on her protest it is established that she was wrongfully compelled to do so by another Yacht, in whch case such other Yacht shall be disqualified. The Yacht which fouled the mark must immediately either abandon the Race or hoist a protest flag.

39. *Man Overboard.*—In case of a man falling overboard from any Yacht, all other Yachts in a position to do so shall use their utmost endeavours to render assistance ; and if it should appear that any Yacht so assisting was thereby prevented from winning a prize, the Committee shall have power to order the race to be re-sailed between any Yacht or Yachts so prevented and the actual winners. A Yacht shall be disqualified from winning a prize in a Race or a re-sailed Race if, when in a position to render assistance, she shall have neglected to do so.

42. *Protests.*—A protest on the score of a breach of the Rules occurring during a Race, must be signified by showing a flag conspicuously in the main rigging of the protesting Yacht on first passing the Sailing Committee.

All protests must be made in writing and signed by the owner or his representative, and lodged with the Sailing Committee with such fee, if any, as may have been prescribed, within two hours of the arrival of the protesting Yacht, unless such arrival shall be after 9 o'clock p.m. and before 8 o'clock a.m. of the following day, in which case the time shall be extended to noon on that day.

A protest made in writing shall not be withdrawn.

43. *Sailing Committee's Decision.*—Before deciding a protest a Sailing Commtttee shall give notice to the party protested against, and shall hear such evidence and make such other inquiries as they may consider necessary.

44. *Appeals to Council.*—A protest which has been decided by a Sailing Committee shall be referred to the Council of the Y.R.A.

(*a*) If the Sailing Committee, at their own instance, should think proper to so refer it.

(*b*) If either of the parties interested make application for such reference, on a question of interpretation of these Rules, within one week of the Sailing Committee's decision.

In the latter case (*b*) such reference must be accompanied by a deposit of £5 in the case of Yachts exceeding 36-ft. rating, and of £3 for Yachts not exceeding 36-ft. rating, payable by the party appealing, to be forfeited to the funds of the Yacht Racing Association in the event of the appeal not being sustained.

45. *Particulars to be furnished by Sailing Committee.*—The

reference to the Council must be accompanied by the following particulars, as far as the same are applicable :—

1. A copy of the protest and all other written statements that may have been put in by the parties.

2. A plan showing—

(*a*) The course ;

(*b*) The direction and force of the wind ;

(*c*) The set of the tide ;

(*d*) The positions and tracks of the competing Yachts involved in the protest.

3. A copy of the advertised conditions of the race and the sailing instructions furnished to the Yachts.

4. The observations of the Sailing Committee thereon, with their decision.

45. *Expenses of re-measurement incurred by Protest.*—In the event of a protest involving the re-measurement of a Yacht, the fees and expenses of such remeasurement shall be paid by the unsuccessful party to the protest.

47. *Persons interested not to take part in Decisions.*—No Member of the Sailing Committee or Council shall take part in the discussion or decision upon any disputed question in which he is an interested party.

48. *Disqualification without Protest.*—Should it come to the knowledge of a Sailing Committee, or should they have reasonable grounds for supposing that a competitor in a race has in any way infringed these rules, they shall act on their own initiative as if a protest had been made.

49. Provides that neither steering nor sailing any yacht in races held under the Y.R.A. will be permitted to the owner of a yacht or his representative who flagrantly breaks any of these rules.

APPENDIX.

Further Recommendations to Sailing Committees.

Recommendations 4, 8, 9 and 13 are new ; the old recommendations 4, 5, 6, 7, 8, and 9 are now numbered respectively 5, 6, 7, 10, 11, and 12 ; and old 10 disappears.

4th. That if the start is to be made from anchors or moorings, lots shall be drawn for stations, and springs shall be allowed on the same bridle or anchor chain or warp as the bowfasts, but are not to be carried to a buoy, pier, other vessel, or fixed object. If any Yacht lets go or parts her bridle before the signal to start, or if she drags any moorings or anchor to which she is made fast for the purpose of starting, she shall be liable to be disqualified, unless such parting or dragging be explained to the satisfaction of the Committee, or unless she has returned, after the signal to start, within the line of starting buoys so as not to obtain any advantage by the accident.

In a race starting from moorings no paid hand may join or leave the Yacht after the first gun.

8th. That whenever practicable a clause should be inserted in the programme providing that there shall be no time allowance in races for the classes not exceeding 65 ft.

9th. Yachts which have been raced previously to 1896, and which are over the new classes of linear rating (corresponding with the classes they competed in under the old rating rule) shall be allowed to compete in such new classes by allowing time on the excess rating, providing no alteration has been made in their hulls and no increase made in their load water line length as defined by the Y.R.A. marks, and no increase made in their sail area since 1895.

13th. That when in the opinion of the Sailing Committee it is not desirable to observe the period of fifteen minutes provided for in Rule 27, the time may be shortened to ten or five minutes as may be desirable, but the time to elapse shall always be distinctly stated on the instructions for the Race.

List of recognised Yacht Clubs.

Add Alexandra Y.C. — Essex Y.C.
Gourock Y.C. — Hamble S.C.
Holy Loch S.C. — North of Ireland Y.C.

and delete Cultra Y.C.

Add N.B.—For definition of a recognised Yacht Club see Racing Rule 2.

The recognition of a Yacht Club does not necessarily, nor of itself, qualify a member of that Club as an amateur.

RUGBY FOOTBALL ADDENDA

Since going to press the Rugby Football Union has held their annual general meeting, and passed the subjoined alterations.

LAWS OF THE GAME.

Law 11, strike out (*j*). Alter *k* to *j*, *l* to *k*, and *m* to *l*.

Then commence a new paragraph :

"If a player shouts 'all on side,' or words to that effect, when his players are not all on side, the opposite side shall elect to have a free kick where the offence was committed, or a scrummage where the ball was last played."

Law 8 (*d*), line 8, after the words "nor may he approach," add "or wilfully remain."

Law 10, line 16, after the words "the ball for a place-kick," add "and it is the duty of the referees to see that the ball be kicked from the parallel line."

Law 13, in the first paragraph strike out "defending side," and in place thereof insert "referee."

In Law 20 the word "20th" is struck out, and "21st" inserted, and the following words are added to the Law :

"In the event in any year of the Tuesday in the Easter week falling later than April 21, for such year the close season shall commence from the Wednesday in the Easter week."

RULES AS TO PROFESSIONALISM.

After the introduction to the Rules as to Professionalism, *i.e.*, after the word "previously," add "and altered in conjunction with the Welsh Union in 1899-1900."

Rule 2 (1) B.—After Rule 6 at end to 4.

C.—Add, "unless such work was done before the receiver became a football player."

L.—Add, "but this shall not prevent this Union giving permission for a bona-fide charity match."

And a new subsection.

N.—Receiving money or other valuable consideration from any person or persons as an inducement towards playing football.

(2) L.—After the word "benefit," in second line, add "or charity," and "except permission to play which has previously been obtained from this Union."

N.—In first line strike out "one month," and substitute "any time ordered by this Union."

Read Rules 3, 4, and 5 as one rule, inserting the word "But" at commencement of old 5.

In Rule 3, first line, strike out and between L and M, and after M insert "and N."

After Rule 6 to 4, and add, "In case an English player wishes to join a Welsh club, or a Welsh player an English club, he may do so ; if requested by either Union, he shall produce a letter from his old club, stating they have no objection ; on receipt of this letter, the Union requesting such shall, if satisfied, give the necessary permission ; if not satisfied, they shall ask the other Union to hold a joint inquiry, such inquiry to be held by a joint committee of two representatives of each Union. The chair shall be taken alternately, but no chairman shall have a second or casting vote. In case of disagreement, a member of the Scottish Union shall be asked to arbitrate, or failing such, a member of the Irish Union. Any such joint committee or arbitrator shall have power to order the payment of expenses as they think fit, and all findings shall be final.

COUNTY CHAMPIONSHIP SCHEME.

The following alteration is made in the grouping :

South Eastern Group shall comprise : A—Eastern Counties, Hampshire, Sussex, and one of the Counties (Kent, Middlesex, and Surrey). B.—East Midlands, Midlands, and two of the Counties (Kent, Middlesex, and Surrey).

It shall be decided by drawing lots which County of the three (Kent, Middlesex, and Surrey) shall for the first year be in the A section ; in the second year the other two shall draw ; in the third year the County which has been in the B section for the two previous years shall be in the A section.

In regulation 5 the words "20th January" are struck out and 31st January inserted.